Quebec

STATE AND SOCIETY

Alain G. Gagnon

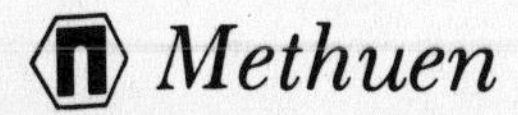

Toronto New York London Sydney Auckland

Quebec: State and Society

Canadian Cataloguing in Publication Data

Main entry under title:
Quebec : state and society

Bibliography: p.
ISBN 0-458-97460-9

1. Quebec (Province)—Politics and government—1960-1976—Addresses, essays, lectures.* 2. Quebec (Province)—Politics and government—1976-—Addresses, essays, lectures.* 3. Quebec (Province)—Social conditions—Addresses, essays, lectures.
I. Gagnon, Alain G.

FC2925.Q42 1984 971.4'04 C83-099308-8
F1053.2.Q42 1984

Printed and bound in Canada
1 2 3 4 84 88 87 86 85

Contents

Preface

Quebec: State and Society is intended for introductory courses that have Canadian or Quebec politics as a focal point. This book can also be used as a scholarly aid for courses given at both the undergraduate and graduate levels on Quebec or provincial politics. It should be particularly useful to the instructor who wishes to present a thematic approach to and alternative interpretations of the Quebec political milieu. This collection of essays should provide students with a better understanding of the environment and premises for state action.

Quebec: State and Society is composed of a collection of original or revised articles on the major topics in Quebec politics written by prominent and widely published specialists. The general aim of the book is to be comprehensive in its coverage of the main themes in the field. Also, the various contributions have been organized into six main sections: Quebec nationalism, the national question and social classes, the new middle class, the regional question, the state and groups, and language policies and educational reforms. An annotated bibliography on Quebec political economy between the years 1979 and 1982 is also included.

This volume not only offers a historical account of Quebec polictics, but an attempt has also been made to locate Quebec nationalism within a broader context while not ignoring the historical specificity of the Quebec experience. Also, the social, regional, and national questions are individually addressed: this way of proceeding has the advantage of giving needed attention to aspects of Quebec politics too often overlooked in existing textbooks. Moreover, this volume gives space to broader issues that have a major impact on Quebec: the fiscal crisis of the state and the problem of governability, the phenomenon of economic peripheralization within the continental economy, the constitutional debate, the polarization of political parties, the role of interest groups, the evolution of corporatism, and the development of language policies and educational reforms.

Several people have contributed to the completion of this volume. First, I wish to thank the contributors who have participated with great enthusiasm and diligence at all stages in the project. Second, I thank Pierre Alvarez, Claude Galipeau, Phil Resnick, and Roger Ryan for their well-appreciated work as translators. The superb work of Jan Carrick, Barbara Murphy, and Bernice Gallagher in typing this manuscript must be acknowledged. Also, for their comments and encouragement, I wish to express my gratitude to several of my colleagues at Carleton and Queen's universities: they are Jim Bickerton, Bill Irvine, Richard Simeon, and Hugh Thorburn. Finally, I would like to thank the Political Studies Department at Queen's University and Methuen Publications for their clerical and financial assistance at various stages of the research. Peter Milroy, Editorial Director at Methuen, has been supportive and encouraging throughout the preparation of the volume.

ALAIN G. GAGNON
Queen's University
August 31, 1983

Acknowledgements

Grateful acknowledgement is made for use of the following material:

All material from Canada Year Books, Statistics Canada, and The Report of the Royal Commission on Bilingualism and Biculturalism, Book III, *The Work World* (September 1969), reproduced by permission of the Minister of Supply and Services Canada.

Quotation reprinted from Robert Gilpin, "Integration and Disintegration on the North American Continent," *International Organization* 28: 4, by permission of The M.I.T. Press, Cambridge, Mass., and The World Peace Foundation.

Quotation from Anne Legaré, "Les classes sociales et le gouvernement du PQ," reprinted from *The Canadian Review of Sociology and Anthropology* 15: 2 by permission of the author and the publisher.

Quotations from Dale C. Thomson (ed.), *Quebec Society & Politics: Views from the Inside* (1973), pp. 152 and 210, and S.H. Milner and H. Milner, *The Decolonization of Quebec: An Analysis of Left-Wing Nationalism* (1973), pp. 71, 169, 191-92. Used by permission of The Canadian Publishers, McClelland and Stewart Limited, Toronto.

Excerpts from Wallace Clement, *The Canadian Corporate Elite: An Analysis of Economic Power* (Toronto: McClelland and Stewart Limited, 1975), pp. 233-34. Reprinted with permission of Carleton University Press Inc.

Excerpt from Dimitrios Roussopoulos (ed.), *Quebec and Radical Social Change* (1974), pp. 80-81, reprinted by permission of Black Rose Books, Montreal.

Quotation from Hubert Guindon, "Two Cultures: An Essay on Nationalism, Class and Ethnic Tensions," in R.H. Leach (ed.), *Contemporary Canada* (1968), p. 83. Copyright 1968 by Duke University Press.

Contributors

Clinton Archibald teaches political science at the Université d'Ottawa. He has written *Un Québec corporatiste?* and contributed articles to *Recherches sociographiques, Etudes canadiennes,* and *Perception.*

Elaine Carey-Bélanger is a member of the Department of Social Work at the Université Laval. She is currently working on the emergence of modern social welfare in the province of Québec.

Gilles Bourque teaches sociology at the Université du Québec à Montréal. He has written widely on Quebec Politics. His books include *L'Etat capitaliste et la question nationale* and *Classes sociales et la question nationale.* He is co-author of *Socialisme et indépendance* and *Le Québec, la question nationale.* He has also been active in *Parti Pris* and *Socialisme Québécois* and is on the editorial board of *Les Cahiers du socialisme.*

William D. Coleman is a member of the Department of Political Science at McMaster University. He has written extensively on language policies in Quebec and has contributed articles to *Studies in Political Economy* and the *Canadian Journal of Political Science.* He is currently taking part in an international research project on the role of business interest associations in advanced capitalist societies.

Pierre Fournier is chairman of the Department of Political Science at the Université du Québec à Montréal. A specialist in Canadian and Quebec political economy, his books include *The Quebec Establishment, Les sociétés d'Etat et les objectifs économiques du Québec, Le capitalisme au Québec,* and *Capitalisme et politique au Québec.*

Alain G. Gagnon teaches in the Department of Political Studies at Queen's University. He has published extensively on regional development and popular groups in Quebec, and has contributed articles to *Journal of Canadian Studies,* and *The American Review of Canadian Studies.* His books include *Les Opérations Dignité: Naissance d'un mouvement social* and *Le modèle centre-périphérie appliqué à l'Est du Québec.*

Francois-Pierre Gingras is a member of the Department of Political Science at the Université d'Ottawa. He has contributed to *Partis politiques au Québec* and is the author of several publications on Quebec society and politics, nationalism, and methodology.

Raymond Hudon, a specialist in the political economy of Quebec and Canada, teaches Political Science at the Université Laval. He has written several articles on Quebec politics and is co-author of *Patronage et politique au Québec.* He has contributed articles to *And No One Cheered* and *Crise économique, transformations politiques et changements idéologiques.*

Lizette Jalbert teaches Sociology at the Université du Québec à Montréal. She has written *Régionalisme et luttes politiques: une analyse des tiers partis au Canada et au Québec* and has contributed to *Espace régional et nation: Pour un nouveau débat sur le Québec.*

Anne Legaré, a leading Canadian and Quebec political economist, teaches in the Department of Political Science at the Université du Québec à Montréal. She has written *Les classes sociales au Québec* and is co-author of *Le Québec, la question nationale.* She has also contributed to *Le capitalisme au Québec* and *La chance au coureur* as well as to *Studies in Political Economy* and *Les Cahiers du socialisme.*

Carla Lipsig-Mummé teaches in the Faculty of Commerce and Administration at Concordia University. She has been a union organizer for the International Ladies' Garment Workers' Union and the United Farmworkers. She is completing a study of ethnic minorities in the Quebec labour movement.

Henry Milner teaches Political Science at the Collège Vanier. He has been an active member in the Parti Québécois' organization. He has published *Politics in the New Quebec* and co-authored *The Decolonization of Quebec.* Also, he has contributed to *The Canadian State* as well as to *Les Cahiers du socialisme* and *Canadian Dimension.* He is completing a study on the reform of Quebec's educational system.

Mary Beth Montcalm is a member of the Department of Political Studies at the University of Manitoba. A specialist in Comparative and Canadian Politics, she has written *Class in Ethnic Nationalism: Quebec Nationalism in Comparative Perspective* and has contributed to *Journal of Canadian Studies.*

Neil Nevitte teaches in the Department of Political Science at the University of Calgary. His publications include *The Future of North America, the United States, and Quebec Nationalism.* He specializes in comparative nationalist movements, public and elite attitudes, political parties, and electoral behaviour.

Jorge Niosi is a member of the Department of Sociology at the Université du Québec à Montréal. He is the author of *The Economy of Canada: A Study of Ownership and Control* and *Canadian Capitalism—A Study of Power in the Canadian Business Establishment.* He has also recently published *Les multinationales du Canada.*

Edmond Orban is a member of the Department of Political Science at the Université de Montréal. He has contributed to *Québec, un pays incertain, Fédéralisme et nations,* and was the editor of *La modernisation politique au Québec* and *Mécanismes pour une nouvelle constitution.* He is currently examining the process of centralization in four federal, industrial states.

Réjean Pelletier is a member of the Department of Political Science at the Université Laval. His publications include *Partis politiques au Québec, L'Etat du Québec en devenir,* and *Les militants du R.I.N.* He is currently working on the evolution of Canadian federalism, as well as on the transformation in the nature and role of political parties since the beginning of the Quiet Revolution.

Marc Renaud teaches in the Department of Sociology at the Université de Montréal. He has published several articles on the evolution of health and social welfare policies in Quebec. He is co-author of *Médecine et Société: les années '80.* He currently works on international comparisons of health policies in advanced capitalist countries and on the social impact of the recent Quebec occupational health legislation.

Stanley B. Ryerson is a member of the Department of History at the Université du Québec à Montréal. A marxist historian, he is one of the most praised intellectuals in Canada. His many publications include *French Canada: A Study in Canadian Democracy*; *Unequal Union: Confederation and the Roots of Conflict in the Canadas*; and *150 Ans de lutte: Histoire du mouvement ouvrier au Québec, 1825-1976.*

Brian Tanguay is a member of the Political Science Department at Carleton University. He is completing a study on the evolution of collective bargaining in Quebec and is pursuing further research on the relationships between the state and producer groups.

Jean-Guy Vaillancourt teaches in the Department of Sociology at the Université de Montréal. He has written *Mouvement écologiste, énergie et environnement* and contributed to *Studies in Political Economy* and *Sociologie et Sociétés.*

Reginald A. Whitaker teaches Canadian politics and political theory at the Department of Political Science at Carleton University. A leading theorist of Canadian political economy, he is the author of *The Government Party: Organizing and Financing the Liberal Party of Canada.* He has contributed to *The Canadian State* as well as to numerous learned journals.

Part I/Quebec Nationalism

In this section, a historical account of Quebec nationalism is provided, as well as various interpretations of its diverse origins and nature.

The Gingras-Nevitte chapter focuses both on the continuity of Quebec nationalism and on the forces that have contributed to its varying forms. The authors point out that the changes associated with the Quiet Revolution—which redirected the course of contemporary mainstream nationalism—are not as complete as many have supposed and that traditional and modern forms of nationalism continue to coexist. They argue that this dichotomy produces a tension that is reflected in the ideological and tactical differences within the contemporary nationalist movement.

The two following articles, by Gagnon and Montcalm and by Orban, elaborate an explanation of Quebec's unrest within the Canadian system. The first study demonstrates the influence of two postwar economic trends on the rivalry between Quebec and Ottawa: one is that the economic dynamism of the continental economy has shifted geographically to the south and west of the United States; the other is that Canadian economy has become increasingly integrated with the American one. In this process, the Canadian government's capacity for economic regulation, has been eroded and Quebec has been gradually "peripheralized" within the continental economy.

Orban's article develops the idea that the Québécois's feelings of alienation are rooted in the fact that francophones are part of an economic, political, social, and cultural minority in Canada. Consequently, the federal government has become the target of Quebec hostility, particularly as a result of the increasing public visibility of Ottawa's social and economic role that derives from the federal drive towards centralization.

In an attempt to place Quebec nationalism in a proper context, Montcalm draws a parallel between separatist movements in Belgium, France, Great Britain, and Spain with Quebec separatism. Her article examines the various contexts that have fostered these movements and concludes that the escalation in postwar separatist movements throughout the developed west is rooted in major changes in the postwar economy, in conjunction with the appearance and substantial expansion of a "new middle class" in these regions.

Professor Ryerson in his essay draws our attention to the 1982 Constitutional Act and indicates that current difficulties can only be understood if patriation is placed in its proper historical, cultural, socio-economic, and political contexts. The fundamental objective of the patriation, Ryerson proposes, is to preserve English ascendancy in the guise of a legalized, centralizing quasi federalism.

Chapter 1/The Evolution of Quebec Nationalism

François-Pierre Gingras
Neil Nevitte

Nationalism is widely regarded as one of the most influential ideologies of the 20th century, yet the precise meaning of the term remains controversial. There is no point in relating the debate here, but it is useful to start a discussion of the evolution of nationalism with a working definition of the central term. We will take nationalism to mean the making of claims in the name of or on behalf of the nation. Implications immediately relevant to the analysis of Quebec nationalism follow from adopting this sort of definition. First, it implies that the distinction between nation, a political-cultural idea, and the state, a legal-territorial concept, is significant not least of all because national claims may be made against the state. Second, the definition is versatile, in that it does not imply that all nationalists want independence, nor does it identify nationalism with any particular part of the ideological spectrum. National claims are not inherently right wing or left wing in their content or purpose; historically they have been both. Moreover, nationalism does not necessarily entail extremist or pathological behaviour. The third point to emphasize is that political parties are not the only vehicles capable of voicing national claims. It is true, of course, that nationalism became identified as a mass phenomenon after the expansion of the franchise and the development of broadly based political parties. Yet it is also the case that a wide variety of groups—such as literary associations, cultural societies, religious groups, and trade unions—have actively made claims aimed at protecting and advancing national cultures.

Historians, drawing on examples ranging from the *Patriotes* of the 1830s to the Alliance Laurentienne of the 1950s to the Parti Québécois in the 1970s and '80s, make the observation that nationalism has been an enduring feature of Quebec politics since pre-Confederation days. Like most generalizations, it suggests a perspective that is illuminating for some purposes, but it is also limiting in other important respects. It is illuminating because it highlights the importance of the idea of nationhood as a driving force in Quebec history, especially in the dialogue between Quebec and anglophone Canada. It is illuminating because it suggests, quite properly, that the electoral victory of the Parti Québécois in 1976 was perhaps not so much a radical departure from the past as a contemporary representation of forces deeply rooted in Quebec history. But to say that nationalism has always been a feature of Quebec politics implies a static uniformity where there is dynamic diversity; it deflects attention from the fact that, with the evolution of Quebec society, the style and form of Quebec nationalism has undergone substantial transformation.

It is not difficult to see, at least in abstract terms, why social change would be intimately connected with changes in the character of nationalism. Social change, reflected in shifts in the class structure and publicly held values, tends to be accompanied by the emergence of new groups contending for political power. New contenders carry competing views of the status quo, different visions of the future of the national society, and consequently alternative perspectives on the relationship between the national society and the state. Many commentators see Quebec's Quiet Revolution of the 1960s in these terms.[1] Regarded as Quebec's "coming of age," its belated emergence into the modern era, the Quiet Revolution is viewed as the important development in Quebec's recent history. After all, it was in the 1960s that a sizable and politically important middle class emerged and a whole range of traditional social, economic, cultural and political institutions, which had been the pillars of a traditional conservative style of nationalism, came under sustained attack. It is hardly surprising, then, that the electoral success of the Parti Québécois, the most widely supported vehicle of contemporary nationalism, is directly related to the changes implied by the Quiet Revolution.

The main purpose of this chapter is to illustrate both the continuity and the diversity of Quebec nationalism by broadly sketching the backdrop of its contemporary form. Not all nationalist groups have sought Quebec's complete political autonomy and there have been substantial ideological differences even among those who have called for independence; which is to say, the purposes of independence for these organizations have been very different. By way of conclusion we will suggest that, even though the Quiet Revolution marked a significant change that redirected the course of mainstream Quebec nationalism, it is unlikely that the changes of the 1960s were as complete or as sudden as many interpretations of the Quiet Revolution would have us believe.[2] We argue that a residue of traditional values remains lodged in a significant portion of Quebec society and that the coexistence of traditional and modern orientations provides a diverse context for the expression of contemporary Quebec nationalism.

Independence: The Recurrent Theme

The British conquest of New France dramatically focused the attention of New France's inhabitants on the question: how could they maintain their collective identity under British rule? Fears about the future of their culture, traditions, institutions, and laws were fed first by the knowledge that they were cut off from France (the historic source of immigration) and second, by the public declarations of various British governors about the desirability of assimilating the population.[3] The origins of the first organized attempt to achieve independence, however, can be traced directly to the parliamentary struggles in the Assembly of Lower Canada between 1791 and 1837. Disagreements over who should control the finances of Lower Canada culminated in an armed uprising and a *Patriote* declaration proclaiming Lower Canada an independent republic in 1838.[4]

For the British, colonization was primarily an economic rather than a military matter. British colonial interests wanted the province administered in a way that would favour the development of mercantile capitalism, whereas the francophone majority wanted sufficient autonomy to control and improve their economic situation within a traditional, essentially precapitalist, social structure. The ideological division within the Assembly was fairly clear. The so-called British party wanted economic liberalism but was politically conservative. It was opposed first by the Parti Canadien and later the Parti Patriote, who were economically conservative but politically reformist. The Westminster government's consistent backing of the governor's opposition to *Patriote* demands galvanized *Patriote* orientations into a nationalist stance. It was the radical element within the Patriotes who sought an independentist solution through armed uprising. The rebellion was crushed and a new, more centralized regime was installed.

The defeat of the *Patriotes* had significant consequences for the leadership of French Canada and the development of Quebec nationalism over the next century.[5] The *Patriote* leaders, drawn mostly from the professional service sectors and holding substantial support in the agricultural sector, proposed reforms that not only called for the recognition of French-Canadian national rights and the democratization of society but also for the declericalization of Lower Canada's institutions. They advocated a nonconfessional school system, the democratization of parish assemblies, and the more radical objected to the Church's meddling in politics. Louis Joseph Papineau, for instance, wanted a complete separation of Church and state. *Patriote* leadership, in other words, represented a direct threat to the authority of the Roman Catholic Church; the Church hierarchy, along with the rural clergy, therefore staunchly opposed *Patriote* reforms. The defeat of the *Patriote* leadership left the way clear for the entrenchment of clerical control; the fledgling republican, reformist, secular nationalism with an independentist thrust was superseded by an anti-reformist clerical nationalism that promised loyalty to the state.

It is not obvious, especially from a contemporary viewpoint, why the Church was able to have such a longlasting impact on the character of Quebec nationalism, but it must be recalled that the Church effectively penetrated most aspects of Quebec society. The Church's spiritual authority was unchallenged, its economic resources were considerable, and it provided many essential social services, such as education, health care, and welfare supports that today are provided by the state. In addition, the Church's institutional reach, hierarchically organized, extended throughout French Canada. In secular terms, the Church's ideological coherence and bureaucratic capacity easily translated into political power, particularly in the absence of an effectively organized French-Canadian counterelite. It was these complementary strands of power, which did not become unravelled until the 1950s, that fuelled the engine of traditional nationalism.

The ideological content of traditional nationalism revolved around the idea of *la survivance*. It was a staunchly anti-liberal nationalism that idealized an organic French-Canadian community life centred around the parish, the school, and the family, all operating in the larger context of a traditional rural economy.[6] A larger role for government was deemed unnecessary given the dominance of religious institutions in the province's infrastructure. That dominance not only helped to fuse French-Canadian religious and national identities to the point that religious rights became a surrogate for national rights, but it has also been held responsible for the retardation of Quebec's social, economic, and political development.[7] The ideology of *la survivance* resulted in a cultural isolationism that took refuge behind provincial autonomy. The stability and lifespan of traditional nonindependentist nationalism can be explained in large part as the result of an understanding between French Canada's traditional elites and the elites of anglophone Canada, reflected in exhortations to respect law and order, and the grip of French Canada's secular and nonsecular elites on a relatively passive population.

La survivance is premised on the idea that Quebec's national culture faces continual threats and the threats, historically, have been perceived as taking many forms. There have been infringements by federal and other provincial governments on the rights and privileges of French Canadians outside of Quebec. Canada's links to Britain meant the participation of French Canadians in imperial campaigns. Within Quebec, the forces of industrialization challenged traditional anti-materialism and the rural ideal. Although French Canadians established control over their political, social, cultural, and religious institutions, the economic penetration of Quebec—led by foreign interests attracted by low labour costs and government policies—resulted in the progressive exclusion of Québécois from increasingly powerful economic institutions.[8] In the larger context of the Canadian political system, demographic trends have operated to the disadvantage of francophones. For nationalists, their minority status in federal institutions offers insufficient protection for Quebec's interests, notwithstanding the significance of Quebec support for the electoral success of federal political parties.[9] The collective impact of these and other threats have given traditional nationalism its "culture under siege" quality.

It is difficult for any single explanation to adequately account for the modalities of nationalist movements—that is, the fluctuations in support for the movements, the alternating dominance of independentist vs. nonindependentist strategies, and the sometimes radical ideological shifts between right and left that movements seem to experience.[10] In the Quebec experience, however, political and economic crises have often been interpreted in the context of fundamental conflicts between the Quebec nation and the Canadian state. The constitutional arrangements of the state are seen to impose intolerable constraints on the Québécois. When important claims have been satisfied either through substantial policy changes or symbolic concessions or because of a general improvement in economic conditions, support for the radical independentist option tends to be replaced by the traditional defensive nationalism.

The Transition to Contemporary Independentism

By the 1950s the hold of traditional elites on Québécois began to loosen. The Asbestos Strike of 1949 set popular opinion against Duplessis's Union Nationale and the lower clergy against the hierarchy; the strike set in motion a realignment of traditional social allegiances. The origins of the contemporary independence movement are usually traced to the 1950s.[11] This transitional phase was characterized by the appearance of right-wing and left-wing nationalist movements.

The emergence of the right-wing Alliance Laurentienne, founded in 1957, may be seen as one of the last expressions of a dying reactionary separatist tradition. Support for the Alliance was never widespread; it was limited to a small segment of the traditional middle classes. The guiding principles of the movement echoed religionationalist sentiments popular in the 1920s and 1930s. The Alliance saw independence as the only way to protect the values of a French Catholic and humanistic civilization from the secular and materialistic intrusions of English speaking North America. "We are, on this land of old Quebec," they claimed, "the only Catholic nation which may oppose itself to American infiltration as an unassailable bulwark ... we are the only ones to resist the ascendancy of Matter over Mind."[12]

Since the Canadian federal system was an obstacle to the growth of French humanism and Catholic fundamentalism and since all nations had the right to self-determination, the Alliance Laurentienne proposed the creation of a new state that would include not only Quebec but also those predominantly French-speaking areas adjacent to Quebec. The new state would seek to reestablish a closely knit organic society by fostering corporatist institutions. Under a corporatist system, where the individual is attached to the state through a series of functionally defined interest groups, political parties would assume a less significant role. The anti-capitalist nationalism of the Alliance Laurentienne was basically nostalgic; its vision of Quebec was basically irrelevant to most Québécois and it faded into political oblivion in the 1960s.

Several leftist groups of varying sophistication and support emerged after 1959 and they too were opposed to capitalism. The first vocal one, which used *La Revue socialiste* as its mouthpiece, called for the "full independence of Quebec and the proletarian national liberation of French Canadians." This self-proclaimed vehicle of the "only authentic left in French Canada" denounced English-speaking Canadians as "colonialist ogres."[13] The themes drawn out in Pierre Vallières' *White Niggers of America*[14] show that the nationalists of the left moved gradually away from the grandiloquent rhetoric of misunderstood marxism towards a more sophisticated neo-marxist analysis of Quebec's "colonial situation" and exploitation.

For the most part, public support for the "hard left" of the independence movement has been limited. But this is a poor measure of the influence of the left in the 1960s because it provided a consistent critical ideological reference point that had programmatic and tactical consequences for mainstream nationalism. The neo-marxists viewed independence as one intermediary objective in the context of a larger revolutionary struggle. The terrorist activities of a small minority from 1963 through 1970, most notably the excesses of the Front de libération du Québec (FLQ), shocked most Québécois and attracted considerable international attention. The FLQ crisis had a significant impact on the independence movement: the democratic left dissociated itself from terrorist tactics; mainstream nationalist leaders such as Pierre Bourgault, André d'Allemagne, and Marcel Chaput realigned their strategy in order to maintain the respectability of the larger independentist movement.

The Realignment to Contemporary Quebec Independentism

The rise of such ideologically divergent independentist groups as the neo-fascists and the neo-marxists in the 1950s were signs that traditional mainstream nationalism was beginning to crumble. But it was not until the formation of the Rassemblement pour l'Indépendance Nationale (RIN) in 1960, a few months after Jean Lesage's Liberals had defeated the Union Nationale, that there were indications of a significant shift in mainstream nationalism itself. At the outset, the RIN was not identified with any particular ideological orientation or doctrine; it wanted to advance the cause of independence and its program included traditional nationalist claims such as French unilingualism and territorial claims to Labrador. The original ideological neutrality of the RIN gradually faded, however, as the party incorporated some of the social policies often identified with the programs of moderate European social-democratic parties. But the real importance of the RIN was that its brand of nationalism represented a fundamental rupture with the essence of traditional nationalism: the RIN's brand of nationalism was not simply a defensive reaction to unsatisfied demands, it was an assertive nationalism that could not be easily deflected by "concessions" from the federal government. At the heart of the matter was the RIN's dissatisfaction with the permanent minority status of the Québécois; the RIN wanted to be in a majority—and that implied independence.[15]

The RIN was the first independentist organization to try to spell out precisely how an independent Quebec might fit into the larger international political order. A significant part of its program addressed Quebec's potential role in the United Nations, its nonalignment, and the kinds of bilateral and multilateral agreements Quebec might sign with Canada, the United States, the European Economic Community, and the Third World.

The RIN's domestic-policy proposals departed from traditional concerns too. They emphasized such themes as a nonconfessional social democracy as well as a mixed economy where private companies, state corporations, and cooperatives could coexist, where public utility monopolies would be nationalized and worker participation developed. In other words, the RIN's nontraditional view of nationalism was complemented by nontraditional conceptions of the state and society; the party's program assigned an interventionist role to the state and urged a secularization of society.

Given the discrepancies between the RIN's policies and the historic concerns of traditional Quebec that had dominated for so long, it might seem farfetched for the RIN to have hoped for an audience receptive to these initiatives. Yet these initiatives did find a receptive audience, particularly among the anti-clerical intellectual nationalists, and the changes in society necessary for a more widespread acceptance of the RIN's program were under way in the form of the Quiet Revolution.[16] It is useful to recall the main themes of the Quiet Revolution in order to appreciate the significance of the RIN program more fully.

In general terms the Quiet Revolution represented a fundamental qualitative change in the orientation of Quebec society in at least two respects. First, the change involved an impetus towards greater participation by Québécois in a modern industrial economy; second, the change involved a reorientation of values, particularly the reaffirmation of the authenticity of Quebec culture. These two basic themes, the socioeconomic development of Quebec and Québécois as well as the value orientations leading to cultural affirmation, were viewed as complementary. Attitudes towards Quebec changed: *survivance*, which expressed the culturally defensive posture of old Quebec was replaced by *rattrapage*, which reflected a new confidence about Quebec's potential and the realization that precious time had been lost in Quebec's social and economic development. In all dimensions—political, economic, cultural, and social—the Quiet Revolution was a transition from an old order to a new order.[17]

The RIN program offered a concrete link for the two main themes of the Quiet Revolution. Independence and development were not discrete goals; they were interdependent. Economic and social development required political competence. Pierre Bourgault, leader of the RIN, remarked, "So far, we have never known where we were heading for because others were deciding. We now want to decide for ourselves and be responsible for our successes as well as our failures."[18] The RIN program outlined the connection between independence and development in the following terms:

> The R.I.N. has set its goal to establish the necessary prerequisites for the full development of the Québécois nation. Such a full development will be

> attainable only if and when the nation becomes responsible for its own destiny, particularly when it will have recuperated its entire initiative in the political realm and oriented the economy to the satisfaction of collective needs.[19]

Some of the RIN's specific proposals for Quebec's new socioeconomic system proceeded from a careful analysis of foreign systems, especially those of the U.S., France, Yugoslavia, the U.S.S.R., and most importantly Sweden. The goal was not just to blindly ape other systems; the program always referred to the uniqueness of Quebec's own traditions and institutions and it took into account the North American context. Actually, this type of syncretic approach is almost typical of ideologies found in developing countries: the design of new socioeconomic and political orders requires a balance of tradition and innovation, of tributes to the national heritage as well as adaptations from solutions found successful elsewhere. In this sense, the RIN differed from earlier separatist movements that emphasized the paramount importance of the past. The vistas of the RIN extended both beyond the boundaries of Quebec and into the future.

The RIN's systematic approach to the independence question was typical of the way they dealt with most problems. If independence was the key to development, then there must be social and economic planning—planning *for* Québécois *by* Québécois. They proposed that a central planning office be responsible for formulating short-term as well as long-term planning alternatives, taking into account regional, sectoral, and national priorities. The central planning office would be staffed exclusively by experts and would perform technical functions. The party's intellectual leadership believed that the plan's agenda—its objectives and priorities as well as the means for implementation—could be governed democratically. They envisaged a population democratically mobilized through a variety of interest groups such as trade unions, boards of trade, parent-teacher associations, and the like. The kind of democracy they advocated appeared to be a blend of two influences: the corporatist influence inherited from the nationalist movements of the 1920s and 1930s and the Alliance Laurentienne; and the socialist influence from the neo-marxist wing of the party. The RIN believed that it was a uniquely Québécois solution.

In retrospect there is little question that the RIN anticipated and gave direction to contemporary Quebec nationalism, but the party never reaped the electoral rewards for its keen appreciation of the new direction of Quebec politics and its scrupulously formulated program. Irresolvable differences between the revolutionary neo-marxist faction and Pierre Bourgault's moderates fatally split the RIN; the members voted to terminate the party during its annual convention in 1968. A considerable section of the membership had already joined the newly created Parti Québécois (PQ), which was an outgrowth of the Mouvement Souveraineté-Association (MSA) founded in 1967 by René Lévesque. Lévesque's experience as a key cabinet minister in the Lesage government and his popularity lent respectability to the movement when he quit the Liberals a year after their 1966 defeat. Most RIN members probably saw that the PQ's chances of advancing the cause of independence were better than those of a crippled RIN. The MSA, with its "working hypothesis" of a sovereign Québec, was a minor and temporary player. The mantle of mainstream nationalism passed almost immediately from the RIN to the Parti Québécois. While the electoral successes of the PQ first in 1976 and again in 1981 were victories for nationalism, they were not victories for the radical independentist solution. Actually, the deferral of the independence option was the price of the PQ's electoral successes.

Prospects for Independence

The character of the PQ, its ideological orientation, its links with unions and the new middle class, and its performance since 1976 are topics discussed elsewhere in this volume. It is more appropriate, therefore, for us to limit our concluding comments to an assessment of the prospects for independentist nationalism.

The PQ's electoral appeal in 1976 was partly a result of the way in which the party differentiated itself from its major rivals. Unlike the Liberals, the PQ proposed to be less concerned with Quebec's "business climate"; it openly courted alliances with the working classes and the unions, especially the public-sector unions. While the Liberals had a progressive legislative record on social policies, they were committed to a federalist solution to the national question. In contrast to the Union Nationale, the PQ promised to be an open democratic party encouraging participation from below and advocating a larger role for the state in promoting social democratic policies. Moreover, while the UN's nationalism was of the traditional nonindependentist variety, the PQ's nationalism was inherited from the RIN. In short, the PQ aimed at attracting those Québécois who embraced the nontraditional values and the nationalism associated with the Quiet Revolution.

Most of the evidence found in the scholarly literature shows that PQ support did come mainly from those sectors of Quebec society that endorsed the changes brought on by the Quiet Revolution.[20] The data in Table 1-1, drawn from a survey of Québécois conducted by the authors in November 1976, confirms these findings.[21] First, it shows that PQ support came disproportionately from the young: nearly two-thirds (64.5%) of those under 35 years of age supported the PQ. Further analysis of the same data shows that this segment of the population was well educated. It was this segment of the population which was directly affected by the educational reforms of the early 1960s, reforms that both secularized postsecondary educational institutions and expanded educational opportunities. Second, Table 1-1 also shows that the independence factor was significant in structuring the PQ vote. Nearly three-quarters (72.2%) of those who indicated that they favoured independence identified with the PQ.

Table 1-1 Age, Independence, and Party Support

	Parti Québécois	Liberal party	Union Nationale	Others*	None	All
*Age***						
Under 35	64.5	28.0	31.4	37.9	77.6	48.5
35-55	25.7	43.2	34.3	34.5	20.4	32.9
Over 55	9.8	28.8	34.3	27.6	2.0	18.6
	(100%)	(100%)	(100%)	(100%)	(100%)	(100%)
*Orientations to independence***						
In favour	72.2	7.3	2.5	0.0	30.9	36.6
Undecided	14.6	8.3	10.0	21.6	10.9	11.9
Opposed	13.2	84.3	87.5	78.4	58.2	51.5
	(100%)	(100%)	(100%)	(100%)	(100%)	(100%)
N =	343	313	40	37	55	787

*Includes 36 Créditistes and one supporter of the Parti National Populaire.
**The chi-square test shows that the probability of these distributions by chance is less than 0.001.
Source: N. Nevitte and F.-P. Gingras, Quebec survey (November 1976).

Taken together, these data tend to support the proposition suggested at the outset—namely, that social change has affected the form and substance of Quebec nationalism. However, it is also clear that the changed value orientations associated with the Quiet Revolution—secularization, for instance—have not percolated evenly throughout Quebec society. From

Table 1-2 Age, Party Support, and Traditional Religious Values

	The importance of religious values to Quebec's culture. Very important	Moderately important	Less important	Not important	All
*Age***					
Under 35	9.7	20.9	27.3	42.1	(100%)
35-55	27.9	27.8	23.7	20.5	(100%)
Over 55	44.5	26.0	14.5	13.0	(100%)
Means	(27.4)	(24.9)	(21.8)	(25.2)	
*Party Support***					
Parti Québécois	13.7	20.1	26.2	39.9	(100%)
Liberal	30.0	29.0	22.5	18.6	(100%)
Union Nationale	48.7	28.2	10.3	12.8	(100%)
Others*	48.6	17.1	20.0	14.3	(100%)
None	18.5	16.7	29.6	35.2	(100%)
Means	(23.7)	(23.6)	(23.9)	(28.8)	
Total N =	185	184	186	223	778

*Includes 36 Créditistes and one supporter of the Parti National Populaire.
**The chi-square test shows that the probability of these distributions by chance is less than 0.05.
Source: N. Nevitte and F.-P. Gingras, Quebec survey (November 1976).

Table 1-2 it is evident that the Quiet Revolution cohort, those under 35 years of age, is uniquely secular, but it is also clear that a substantial proportion of Québécois, about 47%, continue to hold to the traditional view that religious values are an important dimension of Quebec's national identity. Further analysis shows that these Québécois tend not to support the independentist option or the PQ, even though they strongly identify with the Quebec nation. Traditional and new nationalism continue to coexist.

One clear implication of these findings is that the prospect for an independentist nationalism depends on the extent to which Quiet Revolution independentist orientations will continue to displace traditional nationalist orientations. One school of thought argues that, because the institutions that produced the Quiet Revolution cohort are still in place, secular-independentist orientations will embrace progressively larger segments of Quebec's population. The expectation is that, as time passes, the chances for increased independentist support will improve. The alternative school of thought argues that, as the original Quiet Revolution cohort ages, as those under 35 in 1976 get older, they will gradually take on responsibilities that give them a greater stake in the status quo; they will therefore become progressively less inclined to support radical political solutions, like independence, which threaten the status quo. This perspective interprets the surge in support for independence as a passing phenomenon, as a part of the politics of a carefree youth. The points of difference between these two interpretations can be resolved only through a careful analysis of data gathered over time.

The prospects for independence are not uniquely determined by demographic trends alone. Other considerations—such as the shifting economic and political relationships between centres and peripheries, the dynamics of political alliances, inter- and intraparty changes—have all been important factors in the history of the movement. Experience teaches that it cannot be assumed that the PQ is the only vehicle available to the independentists or that the PQ will always be able to harness the independentist support it attracted in its early years. Independentists of the left and the right express dissatisfaction with the PQ's performance. The suspicion is that the PQ has compromised the independence issue for the sake of electoral success and that, in the process, it has become more like the traditional parties it sought to replace and that it has lost the drive, commitment, and openness it once had. Defections from within the PQ's left and the formation of the Mouvement Socialiste in 1982 point to the breakdown of the "open alliance" with the unions that the PQ promised to nourish in the 1970s. Whether the independentist left will continue to give electoral support to the PQ is in doubt. On the right, a reinvigorated Saint-Jean-Baptiste Society along with the Mouvement National des Québécois also criticize the PQ's independentist strategy. In short, mainstream Quebec nationalism continues to experience the pull of ideologically divergent forces.

In this chapter we have tried to show that the historical perspective is useful because it provides clues for understanding the modalities of contemporary nationalism. More specifically, we have emphasized the significance of the interplay of three major axes: first, the impact of social change on nationalism and the consequences of incomplete social change; second, the ideological range of nationalism; and, third, the importance of the strategic differences between independentist and nonindependentist nationalism. The lesson is that nationalism does not go away, it takes different forms, and the challenge is to understand what forces structure the form that nationalism takes.

Notes

1. For example, Marcel Rioux, *La Question du Québec* (Paris: Seghers, 1969), p. 106; Léon Dion, *Quebec: The Unfinished Revolution* (Montreal: McGill-Queen's University Press, 1976), ch. 1; and Fernand Dumont, *The Vigil of Quebec* (Toronto: University of Toronto Press, 1971), Part II.
2. Marcel Rioux, *Quebec in Question* (Toronto: Lorimer, 1978), pp. 73-111; Léon Dion, "Towards a Self-Determined Consciousness," in Dale Thomson (ed.), *Quebec Society and Politics* (Toronto: McClelland and Stewart, 1973), pp. 27-33.
3. At the time, assimilation was hardly a practical solution to Britain's strategic problem of consolidating its hold in North America because the inhabitants, of whom 99% were francophone, far outnumbered the colonists. But the strategic factor *was* significant because it forced the British to look for alliances within Lower Canada to stabilize and neutralize French Canadians during the struggle with the United States for control of North America.
4. Actually, the issues of which sectors should bear the tax burden and who should control expenditures were part of a larger conflict between the executive and the assembly. For a discussion of the larger context see D.G. Creighton, "The Struggle for Financial Control," *Canadian Historical Review* XII: 2 (June 1931).
5. For different perspectives see, Fernand Ouellet, "Les Fondements historiques de l'option séparatiste dans le Québec," *Canadian Historical Review* XLIII: 3 (Sept. 1962), pp. 185-203; and Denis Monière, *Idéologies in Quebec: The Historical Development* (Toronto: University of Toronto Press, 1981), pp. 107-20.
6. For a detailed description, see Jean-Claude Falardeau, "The Parish as an Institutional Type," *Canadian Journal of Economics and Political Science* 15 (August 1949).
7. Pierre Elliot Trudeau, "Some Obstacles to Democracy in Quebec," *The Canadian Journal of Economics and Political Science* 24 (August 1958).
8. This economic penetration is evident as far back as the 1830s. See A. de Tocqueville, *Journey to America*, J.P. Mayer (ed.) (New Haven: Yale University Press, 1959), pp. 184-94. For an analysis of the contemporary situation, see J.V. Veaudelle, *Les Sièges sociaux et l'environnement québécois* (1973); and P.E. Laporte, *L'usage des langues dans la vie économique au Québec: Situation actuelle et possibilités de changement* (1974), studies prepared for a Quebec government commission on the status of the French language and on linguistic rights.
9. See François-Pierre Gingras and Conrad Winn, "Bicultural Cleavage," in Winn and John McMenemy (eds.), *Political Parties in Canada* (Toronto: McGraw-Hill Ryerson, 1976), pp. 50-70.

10. For some recent attempts, see Edward A. Tiryakian and Ronald Rogowski (eds.), *New Nationalisms of the Developed West: Towards Explanation* (London and New York: Allen and Unwin, 1984), Part I.
11. François-Pierre Gingras, "L'idéologie indépendantiste au Québec: de la revendication nationale au projet social," *Cahiers internationaux de sociologie* LIX (1975), pp. 273-84.
12. Abbé Wilfrid Morin, *L'indépendance du Québec: le Québec aux Québécois* (Montréal: Editions de l'Alliance Laurentienne, 1960), p. 128.
13. *La Revue Socialiste* I (1959), passim; Raoul Roy, quoted by *Le Devoir* (June 15, 1961).
14. Originally published as *Nègres blancs d'Amérique* (Montreal: Parti Pris, 1968).
15. See *L'Indépendance* (May 16, 1967), p. 5.
16. There is some debate over whether the Quiet Revolution spanned the six-year period (1960-1966) when Lesage's Liberals were in office or the eight-year period (1960-1968), the end of which marked the formation of the Parti Québécois. Because the authors consider the Quiet Revolution to be unfinished business, the precise dates make little difference.
17. For a variety of interpretations, see Hubert Guindon, "Social Unrest, Social Class and Quebec's Bureaucratic Revolution," *Queen's Quarterly* 71 (summer 1964), pp. 150-62; Charles Taylor, "Nationalism and the Political Intelligentsia," *Queen's Quarterly* 72 (spring 1965); Marcel Rioux, *Quebec in Question* (Toronto: Lorimer, 1978), pp. 7-84; Fernand Dumont, *The Vigil of Quebec* (Toronto: University of Toronto Press, 1974), pp. 23-56.
18. Pierre Bourgault (personal communication).
19. Rassemblement pour l'Indépendance Nationale, *Programme politique du R.I.N. 1966-1967* (Montreal: Secrétariat du RIN, 1967), p. 3.
20. For example, see Maurice Pinard and Richard Hamilton, "The Bases of Parti Québécois Support in Recent Quebec Elections," *Canadian Journal of Political Science* 9 (March 1976); and Maurice Pinard and Richard Hamilton, "The Independence Issue and the Polarization of the Electorate: The 1973 Quebec Election," *Canadian Journal of Political Science* 10 (June 1977).
21. The methodology is reported in Gingras and Nevitte, "La Révolution en plan et le paradigme en cause," *Canadian Journal of Political Science* 16 (Dec. 1983).

Chapter 2/Economic Peripheralization and Quebec Unrest*

Alain G. Gagnon
Mary Beth Montcalm

The Canadian political scene has witnessed a substantial escalation in conflict between the province of Quebec and the federal government since the Second World War. In many aspects of Canadian intergovernmental relations, Quebec has taken noticeably firmer positions in opposition to Ottawa's initiatives than have other provinces. Disagreements at the postwar Reconstruction Conference and Quebec's subsequent opposition to both tax rentals and federal activities in social welfare were early manifestations of this conflictual pattern. Quebec's opting out of many shared-cost programs and the continuing dissension between Quebec and Ottawa over federal management of the Canadian economy are indicators of this conflict.

The strife between Quebec and Ottawa has received much journalistic and scholarly attention. Explanations, however, have more often than not tended to emphasize the cultural and political character of this friction. It is the contention in this chapter that attention to major economic shifts within the North American economy not only gives a useful corrective to what may well be an overemphasis on secondary factors, but also allows a more analytically satisfying explanation of Quebec's unrest within the Canadian federal system.

Since the Second World War, several macroeconomic trends have been evident. First, the Canadian economy has become increasingly integrated into the American economy. Second, the core of the continental economy has, particularly since the 1960s, shifted to the south and west of the United States. Finally, there has been increasing emphasis on resource-based industries, which has favoured the development of new types of economic activity in Canada's resource-rich western provinces. In fact, there has been an overall westward drift of economic activity throughout North America.

These changes have had a substantial impact on the relative economic importance of Quebec in the Canadian federation. One direct effect of these westward shifts has been the decline of Montreal as an economic centre relative to Toronto and the shift of economic momentum to provinces such as Alberta. While this development need not be devastating for the Quebec economy, the situation is further complicated by the manner in which economic policies are developed. These policies are devised to maximize overall economic growth; in the postwar environment, this means that federal economic policy disproportionately reflects the interests of Ontario, which is Canada's industrial heartland. Thus, the relative decline of the Quebec economy—or its "peripheralization" within the Canadian and

---

*This article first appeared in *Journal of Canadian Studies* 17:2 (1982).

North American economic market—is abetted by federal policies. When factors such as the rapid social changes within Quebec and the relative unattractiveness of westward migration to Québécois are added to these major economic changes, the pattern of conflict between Quebec and Ottawa is not surprising.

In this study we intend to illustrate how these major economic alterations have lent substantial credibility to claims made by Quebec governmental elites that the Canadian federation has not been economically beneficial to Québécois. In the first part, we offer a brief examination of major economic changes. In the second part, we illustrate the effects of these changes by examining two specific policy areas—namely, the question of the Auto Pact as well as federal and Quebec regional-development policies.

Conflictual Relations between Quebec and Ottawa

In explaining the intergovernmental conflict between Quebec and Ottawa, it is particularly useful to note that at present the Canadian economy can best be regarded as one element of an economy that is primarily capitalist and largely continental in scope. While Wallerstein, for example, argues that what exists today is one world economy,[1] it nevertheless remains true that in order to identify the major economic linkages of the Canadian economy one must begin by analyzing it within a continental perspective. The argument can be made that the Canadian economy is very little more than a minor element in the North American economy. To situate major trends within the Canadian setting, one has to broaden one's focus to include the entire North American economic dynamic as well as acknowledge that the Canadian economy, to the extent that one can identify such a distinct phenomenon, is essentially peripheral to the American economy.

Many scholars have argued that the Canadian economy is comprehensible only with reference to another major centre; it is generally accepted that the Canadian economy has always been a peripheral one. During approximately the first half-century of Canada's existence, the metropolis of the Canadian economy was the British economy. With the decline of Great Britain as a world economic power and the increasing economic strength of the United States, serious changes occurred in the Canadian economy.[2] These changes have been substantial; for example, by 1977 the United States was the principal importer of Canadian goods (close to 70%), while Great Britain accounted for less than 4.4% of Canadian exports. These facts are even more revealing if one recalls that in 1940 Canada exported more than 43% of its goods to Great Britain. (See Table 2-1.)

With the shift—particularly evident in the post-Second World War period—from British portfolio investment to American direct investment as the major impetus within the Canadian economy, came a move away from an economy based on an east-west axis and toward one based on a north-south axis. The penetration of the Canadian economy by American capital[3] has simultaneously increased the importance of Toronto as a financial and industrial centre and contributed to the erosion of Montreal's position as a major Canadian metropolis. It has also favoured economic developments in Canada's resource-rich provinces of Alberta and Saskatchewan. It has also contributed to a relative decline in the power of interests that benefit from east-west linkages and has facilitated the present ascendancy of interests that stand to gain the most from Quebec's increased autonomy and a growth in Quebec's state sector. The ramifications of this alteration to Quebec unrest have been substantial. The double peripheralization—Canada vis-à-vis the United States and Quebec within the continental economy—is a phenomenon that both underlies much of Quebec's discontent and has affected relations between Ottawa and Quebec. As Gilpin observes:

> What Canada is to the United States both economically and politically French Quebec is to English Canada. Just as the emergence of English-Canadian nationalism is one response to the economic and political forces integrating the periphery with the American core, so French-Canadian nationalism in Quebec is one response to similar forces within Canada itself which are believed to threaten French-Canadian culture and increasingly have made Quebec part of a Canadian periphery centred upon Toronto, the industrial and financial core of contemporary Canada.[4]

Thus, underlying any discussion of the political economy of Canada is the fundamental reality that the Canadian economy is peripheral to the American economy and, second, within this peripheral economy, Toronto is the industrial and financial centre of greatest importance.[5] Substantial changes in the continental economy have seriously exacerbated the economic position of Quebec.[6]

Table 2-1 Canadian Commercial Exchanges, percentages

	Exports to			Imports from		
	Britain	U.S.	Others	Britain	U.S.	Others
1870	38.1	51.4	10.5	56.1	32.4	11.5
1880	48.3	40.6	11.1	48.3	40.3	11.4
1890	48.7	42.5	8.8	38.8	46.0	15.2
1900	57.1	34.2	8.7	25.7	59.2	15.1
1910	50.0	37.3	12.7	25.8	58.9	15.3
1920	39.5	37.4	23.1	11.9	75.3	12.8
1930	25.1	46.0	28.9	15.2	67.9	16.9
1940	43.1	37.6	19.3	14.9	68.8	16.3
1950	15.1	64.8	20.1	12.7	67.1	20.2
1960	17.4	55.7	26.9	10.7	67.2	22.1
1970	8.9	64.7	26.4	5.3	71.1	23.5
1973	6.6	67.8	25.6	4.2	68.5	27.3
1974	5.9	66.3	27.8	3.5	67.3	29.2
1975	5.4	65.3	26.3	3.5	68.1	28.4
1976	4.9	67.6	27.5	3.1	68.7	28.2
1977	4.4	69.9	25.7	3.0	70.2	26.8

Source: Canada Year Books.

One illustration of this is the relocation of company headquarters from Montreal to Toronto. One study has revealed that in 1952 Montreal had 124 company headquarters for each 100 in Toronto, whereas in 1972 Montreal had only 62.[7] To the extent that Montreal and the overall Quebec economy participate significantly in north-south economic linkages, their ties are primarily with the northeastern United States. As the C.D. Howe Institute indicates, more than 80% of Quebec's exports to the United States are shipped to the Atlantic Centre, Northeast Centre, and New England states.[8] But, as noted earlier, the core of the American economy has meanwhile shifted markedly in the past 20 years to the south and the west,[9] thus eroding the strength of Montreal in relation to that of Toronto. Although this major economic transfer is also affecting Toronto's position relative to the west,[10] Montreal's economic decline does much to place Quebec unrest in an overall perspective. As Fernand Martin states:

> It should not be forgotten that Montreal is at the eastern end of the Quebec-Windsor corridor. Stagnation in U.S. regions near Montreal has therefore worked against Montreal's growth and to Toronto's advantage in that Toronto stands in an intermediary position in Montreal's relations with the new centres of U.S. economic activity, casting what geographers call an "urban shadow" on Montreal.[11]

In fact, despite the frequent observation that Quebec unrest has been a cause of the movement of capital and business headquarters out of Quebec, it is much more cogent to view this unrest as fuelled, at least in part, by the structural economic changes that have contributed to relative economic stagnation in Quebec and the fostering of new types of economic activity, particularly in Canada's west.[12]

Additionally, the "relative dependency" of the Canadian economy on that of the United States and the hold of capitalism leave Ottawa nearly powerless to alter this peripheralizing process. Canadian attempts at countering this trend by fiscal and monetary regulation have proved feeble. The Canadian economy is simply too minor within the continental economy and too subject to external decision making for the federal government to effectively control fiscal and economic policy.[13] It is therefore crucial not to exaggerate Ottawa's policy-making autonomy over major economic decisions. To the limited extent that Ottawa has been able to regulate the Canadian economy, its actions seem to have resulted in major stabilization policies that have favoured the interests of the Canadian industrial heartland of southern Ontario.[14] In its effort to maximize overall economic growth, the federal government has devised stabilization policies which are primarily responsive to major economic indicators that disproportionately reflect the influence of Ontario. Thus, the tendency of business cycles to be more severe in Quebec and the Maritimes than in Ontario has often been overlooked by the federal government as it imposed restrictive policies while these regional economies were still suffering from relatively high unemployment.[15] As the Quebec government described this situation in 1979:

It is not surprising that the effect of federal stabilization policies has varied regionally. These policies are developed on the basis of Canadian economic indicators that are especially influenced by the situation in Ontario. When the federal government adopts a restrictive policy to slow overly rapid growth, Ontario has attained full employment, whereas Quebec and the Maritime provinces still have high levels of unemployment. This has been the pattern repeated for the past 30 years.[16]

In the face of the powerful forces within the capitalist economy that favour resource extraction in Canada's west and that accord locational advantage[17] to the manufacture of durable goods in southern Ontario, federal policies have tended to leave Quebec's economy inherently dominated by the production of nondurable goods. As well, the greater competition by third-world countries in nondurables has had an increasingly deleterious effect on the Quebec economy.[18]

A serious problem is also posed by federal distributive policies, since they can be criticized for having effected little structural change in the Canadian economy. This is illustrated by the distribution of jobs in the primary, secondary, and tertiary sectors in Canada as a whole compared with the levels existing in Quebec during 1961-1974 (Table 2-2). In addition, one might look at the index of concentration of manufacturing industries in Canada (Table 2-3).

Not surprisingly, Quebec finds Ottawa's redistributive policies entirely inadequate. As Maxwell and Pestieau state:

> Some Quebecers would also argue that the interregional compensation system has been unfair, for two reasons: first, Quebec was not a significant net gainer from federal revenue and expenditure activities in the province until the 1970s; second, federal expenditures in Quebec have largely taken the form of transfer payments, such as unemployment insurance, that have tended to reinforce Quebec's economic dependency rather than build its self-reliance.[19]

Table 2-2 Percentage Distribution of Persons Working, by Sectors, Canada and Quebec, 1961-1974

	1961	1971	1974
Primary sector			
Canada	13.9	8.3	8.3
Quebec	11.4	5.6	5.9
Secondary sector			
Canada	29.6	26.0	28.8
Quebec	34.5	30.6	31.4
Tertiary sector			
Canada	54.0	57.7	62.7
Quebec	51.1	56.2	62.9

Sources: Statistics Canada, The Active Population. P. Allen, "Tendances des professions au Canada de 1891-1961," *L'Actualité Economique* (1965). Census of Canada (1971).

Since the Second World War, Quebec has been continually faced with what appears to be a multifaceted and cumulative problem. The increasing peripheralization of the Canadian economy by the American economy both favours Toronto and southern Ontario relative to Montreal and the Quebec economy and emphasizes economic growth in the western provinces. Also evident has been the federal government's relative impotence to counter macroeconomic forces that seem to be leading to Quebec's peripheralization. Instead, what is obvious is the multiplication of cases in which federal policies have been devised in response to conditions in the Canadian industrial heartland of Ontario and that have effectively worked against any sort of economic *rattrapage* for Quebec.[20] This peripheralization is not only taking place with regard to Quebec; it is even more obvious in the Maritime

Table 2-3 Index of Concentration of Manufacturing Industries,* Canada, 1880-1975

	Atlantic	Quebec	Ontario	Prairies	Pacific	Canada
1880	0.67	1.03	1.16	0.43	1.09	1.00
1910	0.58	1.03	1.45	0.34	1.14	1.00
1915	0.63	1.04	1.53	0.32	0.85	1.00
1926	0.40	1.11	1.52	0.32	1.14	1.00
1939	0.43	1.07	1.57	0.31	0.97	1.00
1949	0.37	1.07	1.56	0.34	0.93	1.00
1959	0.33	1.01	1.51	0.43	0.92	1.00
1969	0.36	1.00	1.50	0.40	0.85	1.00
1975**	—	1.00	1.41	—	—	1.00

*This index is simply a location quotient, the ratio of manufacturing value added per capita in a region to that in the country as a whole.
Source: H.M. Pinchin, *The Regional Impact of Canadian Tariff* (Ottawa: Economic Council of Canada, 1979), pp. 5, 110, 134-38.
**Roland Jouandet-Bernadat and Alfred Cossette, "Les structures," Annexe 10, *Prospective socio-économique du Québec, Sous-systèmes économiques (2), Collection: Etudes et Recherches* (Québec: Office de planification et de développement du Québec, 1977), p . 12.

provinces.[21] Significantly, however, the pattern of Quebec's peripheralization has coincided with deep social changes[22] and has placed increased political resources at the disposal of Quebec governmental leaders who are critical of Ottawa's apparent inactivity and impotence.[23]

The process of economic peripheralization of Quebec has coincided with substantial growth of Quebec's provincially initiated public sector. (See Table 2-4.) An excellent example of this type of intervention is provided by the expansion of *sociétés d'état* in Quebec. Through such mechanisms, Quebec has attempted to diminish the effects of economic concentration in Ontario.[24] In fact, if not for the tremendous degree of public-sector investment within Quebec (Table 2-5), Quebec's economic peripheralization might be far more evident.[25]

Table 2-4 Expenditures Made by Quebec Public Sector, in Terms of Gross Provincial Product, 1961-1975

	1961	1970	1974*	1975**
Goods and services	16.7	22.8	24.3	25.1
Transfers	11.6	14.1	18.1	20.3
Total	28.6	36.9	42.1	45.3

Excluding transfers between governments.
*Preliminary data
**Temporary data
Source: J. Vézina, "Les gouvernements," Annexe 11, *Prospective socio-économique du Québec, Première étape, Sous-systèmes économiques (2), Collection Etudes et Recherches* (Québec: Office de planification et de développement du Québec, 1977), p. 14.

In sum, the stimulus for economic growth has increasingly come from the Quebec provincial public sector. Also, as a consequence of the shifting continental economic heartland, Ottawa is less and less able to regulate the economy. The increasing fragility of the Canadian federal government in economic and, consequently, in political terms militates against finding a solution to the Quebec question. More and more, one witnesses situations in which the federal government is simply carried along, although this passivity is almost inevitable in the current context, where the shift of private capital encourages the peripheralization of Quebec. Yet it would be mistaken to consider Ottawa as able to do much else, since such an assumption requires that the federal government actually has the necessary political and economic power to do very much. However, within an overall acceptance of the current capitalist economy, such an assumption is debatable.

Case Studies

This second section illustrates the argument presented in the first by investigating two test cases, the Auto Pact and regional-development policies.

Regional Development

The Quebec government has of necessity taken an increasing role in the maintenance and expansion of its economy in recent years. Such actions have often involved jurisdictional disputes. The conflictual pattern between the

Table 2-5 Public Investment in Quebec, Ontario and Canada, 1963-79: percentage increases in nonresidential investment

	Quebec	Ontario	Canada
Public*	577	315	445
Private	309	425	462
Public and Private	427	379	455

*Public includes public enterprise, government departments, and institutions.
Source: Statistics Canada, *Public and Private Investment in Canada* (Ottawa, various years).

Quebec and federal governments is particularly evident in the context of the policies of regional development undertaken by these respective government levels. In this regard, a recent study reveals a pattern of federal intrusions in provincial jurisdiction.[26] These federal intrusions have had the effect of creating administrative problems and undercutting the effectiveness of programs undertaken by Quebec.[27] The stimulation of the pulp-and-paper industry in Quebec, of the salt mines of Iles-de-la-Madeleine, of the Mont Tremblant ski centre, of the Palais des congrès of Montreal, and the participation of Ottawa in the financing of Sidbec and Pétromont are just a few examples of serious disagreements between the two levels, which often result in a standstill in the undertaking of projects.

The Office de planification et de développement du Québec argues that the intrusion of federal bureaucrats in the planning, formulation, and administration of agreements runs the risk of reducing Quebec to a secondary role in the regional development context; it adds that the Department of Regional Economic Expansion (DREE) has become much more an instrument of intrusion into provincial jurisdiction than an instrument leading to the interprovincial redistribution of economic activity.[28]

While the cumulative expenditures of DREE during the period 1969-70 to 1972-73 indicate that 26.5% of total expenditures were in Quebec, it is noteworthy that the Quebec population represented 27.8% of the total Canadian population.[29] It is useful to situate these expenditures within the context of the degree of existing regional disparities. According to the Office de planification et de développement du Québec, a close correlation between DREE expenditures and regional disparities per se would lead to an expenditure of close to 50% of the DREE budget within Quebec. Considering that DREE's budget allocation represents only 1% of the total federal budget, it is difficult to argue that the federal government has a serious interest in reorienting the pattern of regional development in Canada.[30] This is also revealed when one scrutinizes the goals set out for DREE when it came into existence. DREE's main function, according to its enabling act, was "to ensure that economic growth was dispersed widely enough across Canada to bring employment and earnings opportunities in the slow-growth regions as close as possible to those in the other parts of the country"; significantly, it further specified "without interfering with a high overall rate of national growth."[31] Thus, one is entitled to question the real intentions of the federal government. The Quebec government, needless to say, finds such a situation almost incomprehensible:

> DREE programs have had no impact on the "pattern" of regional development in Canada. For example, of the 411,000 jobs created in manufacturing in Canada between 1961 and 1977, Quebec received 58,000 (or 14%) and Ontario 244,000 (or 60%).
>
> Since 1969, when DREE was created, Ontario has been the site of 66% of the new manufacturing jobs created in Canada (57,000 of 88,000), while

Quebec has lost almost 20,000 such positions. In sum, DREE's existence has not even marginally compensated for the negative effects of other federal policies.[32]

At another level, it is notable that from 1969 to 1975 the federal Ministry of Industry, Trade and Commerce (MITC) gave more grants to industry than did DREE ($437 million compared to $256 million). Quebec received an average of $7 per capita from MITC in this period, whereas Ontario obtained $9 per capita.[33] Moreover, per capita DREE expenditures in Quebec for the 1969-70 to 1976-77 period were less than the national average. Table 2-6 indicates the annual per capita DREE expenditures in Quebec and Canada as a whole. One notes a slight increase in expenditures in Quebec since 1977-78, curiously enough, following directly on the Parti Québécois's accession to power.

Analyzing the federal government's attempt to reduce regional disparities via DREE, the Economic Council of Canada (ECC) states that "The effects of such policies have been modest in reducing per capita income differences among regions."[34] The ECC goes on to say, "Empirical results demonstrate

Table 2-6 DREE Expenditures, in dollars per capita

	Quebec	Canada
1969-70 to 1975-76 (annual average)	17.27	16.90
1976-77	16.85	20.43
1977-78	26.12	22.53
1978-79	27.35	22.63

Source: Information taken from DREE annual reports (1975-76, 1976-77, 1977-78, and 1978-79).

that the Atlantic Region and Quebec are net beneficiaries from the DREE program to a much lesser extent than is commonly supposed. Quebec receives little or no net benefit. Quebec and the Atlantic region will be better off with increased equalization payments rather than the existing DREE program."[35] In addition, the ECC reports that DREE expenditures are only proportional to the percentage of tax paid in Quebec—that is, 24% of the total expenditures in 1969-75 and 25% of federal taxation.[36] Furthermore, as André Raynaud, former Chairman of the ECC has noted, regional-development policies have stimulated productivity in traditional sectors within each region without effectively modifying industrial structure.[37] Table 2-7 is highly indicative of such a tendency. In fact, the federal government, as indicated earlier (Table 2-3), has done little to relocate manufacturing activity in Canada.

Measures taken by the Quebec government in attempting to diminish existing regional disparities between Quebec and the rest of Canada have continually been counteracted by federal policies. For example, as it is noted in *L'Economie du Québec*:

> In the sphere of industrial assistance, the Quebec Ministry of Industry and Commerce put in place a series of incentives or measures of assistance of which the majority were rendered ineffective with the adoption of federal policies for regional development. The latter, in effect, required that all provincial aid be deducted from that given by Ottawa.[38]

One is therefore led to conclude that in the implementation of its regional-development policy, the federal government has contributed to the increasing peripheralization of Quebec in the Canadian economy. This explains how many of the efforts undertaken by the Société de développement du Québec, a corporation that aims at modifying Quebec's industrial structure, are being undercut by the federal level.[39]

Another serious problem is caused by the different approaches to regional development implemented by the two levels of government. On the one hand, the Quebec government favours the rapid development of key economic sectors, while on the other hand the federal government has adopted a somewhat indiscriminate and fragmented approach aimed primarily at maximizing employment in the short term.[40] This latter approach has been severely criticized by the Quebec government, since it does little to alter the peripheral character of the province's economy.

The Auto Pact

The Canada-U.S. Auto Pact that was signed in 1965 is one illustration of the pattern of what might be considered increasing peripheralization of Quebec's economy as a result of continental economic integration. While the pact was essentially an effort at rationalizing the auto industry,[41] it was also a significant step in North American continental integration. There is much legitimate controversy over the continuing Canadian deficit as a result of this

Table 2-7 Subsidies provided by DREE to Quebec, 1969-1975

	Subsidies to Quebec (%)		Subsidies to Quebec (%)
Wood, furniture	20.27	Chemical industries	2.95
Metallic products	17.67	Clothing	2.61
Paper	10.87	Hosiery	1.81
Machinery, transportation material	8.28	Various industries	1.81
Electrical products	7.29	Printing	1.70
Textiles	7.15	Leather	1.54
Food, beverages	6.55	Petroleum, coal	0.04
Nonmetallic mineral	5.41	*Total*	100.00
Rubber	4.05		

Source: Roland Jouandet-Bernadat and Alfred Cossette, "Les structures," Annexe 10, *Prospective socio-économique du Québec, Première étape, Sous-systèmes économiques (2), Collection: Etudes et Recherches* (Québec: Office de Planification et de Développement du Québec, 1977), p. 16.

pact. Yet, while the Auto Pact has resulted in serious problems for the Canadian economy as a whole, a general discussion of this problem is somewhat beyond the scope of this study. However, two aspects of the Auto Pact are salient: first, the Auto Pact is a major example of continental economic integration, of integration of the Canadian economic periphery into the American economic core; second, the Auto Pact has been a major sore point between the federal and the Quebec governments, for Quebec feels strongly that the Canadian benefits derived from the Auto Pact have not been fairly distributed; rather, the Canadian industrial heartland of southern Ontario has benefited disproportionately from its implementation. As the Quebec government has observed:

> The Canada-U.S. Auto Pact, which might be described as a shift away from Canadian protectionist policies, has been to the almost exclusive benefit of Ontario. The safety clauses provided that the companies in question increase their production and investment in Canada, but the regional distribution was not specified in the agreement. As well, again because of its overall advantage, Ontario has been the principal—indeed, the sole—beneficiary. The recent location of a Ford motor-manufacturing plant in Ontario, thanks to generous subsidies from the federal government, is an example of this policy.[42]

The federal adoption of the Auto Pact has contributed significantly to increasing intergovernmental conflict in Canada. In fact, it has been claimed that the adoption of such policies as the Auto Pact by the federal government has tended to counterbalance the effects of the much vaunted federal interregional transfers.[43] Under the Auto Pact, the overwhelming benefits have flown to the Ontario economic core[44]; the Quebec government, for one, knows of this disproportion and points out the discrepancy between benefits to Ontario and the relatively minimal benefits trickling down to Quebec.[45]

It is essential, however, to note that the federal government's actions are not being considered here as somehow deliberately harmful to Quebec (or for that matter to other provinces outside the industrial core). In its negotiations, the federal government has obviously wanted to maximize the net benefits to the Canadian economy as a whole. However, since southern Ontario represents the industrial core of the peripheral Canadian economy, the federal policies disproportionately represent Ontario's economic interests. Again, as the C.D. Howe Institute states, the Auto Pact is one example of the way in which the federal government makes policies that tend to "strengthen the strong,"[46] while they are attempting to maximize net overall economic benefits. As Carl Beigie mentioned in his research on the Auto Pact, negotiators on both sides admitted that they never assessed the regional consequences of the pact during the negotiation period.[47]

The Auto Pact exemplifies the degree to which a peripheral economy, whose orientation is dictated by a politically exterior economic core, has uneven economic development and continuing internal peripheralization. It can be argued that both of these phenomena underlie at least one major conflictual element of relations between Quebec and Ottawa.

Summary

Overall, then, in our examination of the Auto Pact and regional-development policies, two dimensions of the conflictual relationship existing between the federal government and the government of Quebec have been highlighted. The discussion of regional development policies exemplifies one aspect of the conflicting policy approaches of the federal and provincial governments. On the other hand, conflict over the Auto Pact touches closely on the phenomenon of continentalization and illustrates the almost inevitable political conflicts from the tradeoff entailed in continentalization.

It is important to stress that the peripheralization of the Quebec economy has not been diminished by the federal level. In fact, we have argued that distributive and stabilization policies have favoured the industrial heartland of Ontario and that fiscal and monetary regulation, which depend on external factors and are primarily responsive to economic conditions in Ontario, have often proven deleterious for Quebec. This reality is widely alluded to by governmental elites in Quebec and undoubtedly provides ammunition for those who see the Canadian federation as detrimental to the Quebec economy. In addition, while Quebec government intervention in the provincial economy has in part compensated for economic peripheralization, it has probably also contributed to the strengthening of anti-federalist elements. A major byproduct of the increasing scope of Quebec's public sector is the expansion and increasing ascendancy of a bureaucratic and technocratic middle class whose interests are maximized by every step toward decentralization.

Conclusion

The preceding considerations demonstrate that the relationship of Quebec to the Canadian and continental economies is characterized by increasing peripheralization. As Gourevitch observes, "Change in the geographic distribution of economic activity not only encourages separatism in Quebec, but also increases limits on the federal government's ability to deal with it."[48] Moreover, the federal government's inability to regulate the economy for the economic development of Quebec (as in the cases of the Auto Pact and regional-development policies) provides an excellent political resource for the current governmental elite in Quebec.

The impact of this peripheralization poses a serious challenge for national integration in Canada. Gilpin, for one, sees this problem:

> Economic growth tends toward the creation of core-periphery relationship, and where core and periphery represent different cultural, ethnic, and political groupings, the consequence is the intensification of economic nationalism and the emergence of powerful movements toward economic and political disintegration.[49]

This study has shown that Quebec discontent is contributed to by the shift of the continental economy to the south and west as well as by the incapacity of the federal government to alter this trend. Furthermore, it has been underlined that the scope of federal economic activity is severely restricted by macroeconomic trends beyond its control. The likelihood of the federal government's actively countering a major economic shift is remote; the chance of success if it were to undertake such measures is even more distant. Instead, the federal government is largely restricted to piecemeal efforts aimed at maximizing the possibilities of overall economic growth within the Canadian economy. In the postwar environment, this has effectively meant that federal economic policy has disproportionately aided the interests of Ontario's industrial heartland.

This state of affairs provides an excellent opportunity for representatives of the Quebec government to use the federal government as something of a scapegoat. Even so, pointing fingers will not alter the evolution of the North American economy, as economist Philippe Garigue warns:

> Le déclin des activités économiques, les difficultés d'un développement socio-économique équilibré, etc., relèvent de l'ensemble de l'évolution de l'Amérique du Nord. Il s'ensuit que l'intention du Parti Québécois ... pour transformer les conditions des francophones, ne saurait résoudre fondamentalement les causes des difficultés actuelles.[50]

Nevertheless, it is important to note that the pattern of economic growth in Canada does not meet Quebec's aspirations and that, on the contrary, it constitutes a threat to its very existence as a distinct collectivity on the North American continent. Additionally, the relative unwillingness—not to say impossibility—of the Quebec populace to migrate westward further complicates an already difficult situation in the light of the westward drift of the Canadian economy.

It is evident that the altered distribution of economic activity has provided ample ammunition for interests that stand to gain from Quebec's autonomy. And, while the linkage between economic trends and the mobilization of discontent is somewhat problematic, it would appear that the behaviour of elites or classes whose interests are closely allied with increased provincial scope and autonomy provides precisely such a link. In fact, it appears that broad macroeconomic trends within the continental economy have led to a relative stagnation in the Quebec economy and, as well, have provided Quebec elites interested in selling the idea of independence to Québécois with an invaluable political resource.

Notes

1. I. Wallerstein, "The Rise and Future Demise of the World Capitalist System: Concepts for Comparative Analysis," *Comparative Studies in Society and History* 16 (1974), pp. 387-414.
2. Harold A. Innis, *Essays in Canadian Economic History* (Toronto: University of Toronto Press, 1956); Kari Levitt, *Silent Surrender* (Toronto: Macmillan, 1970);

Ian Lumsden (ed.), *Close the 49th Parallel etc.* (Toronto: University of Toronto Press, 1970).

3. Wallace Clement, *Continental Corporate Power* (Toronto: McClelland and Stewart, 1977); "Uneven Development: Some Implications of Continental Capitalism for Canada," in J.A. Fry (ed.), *Economy, Class and Social Reality* (Toronto: Butterworth, 1979), pp. 78-96; see also Garth Stevenson, "Canadian Regionalism in Continental Perspective," *Journal of Canadian Studies* 15: 2 (1980), p. 23.
4. Robert Gilpin, "Integration and Disintegration on the North American Continent," *International Organization* 28: 4 (1974), p. 867.
5. P. Fréchette et al., *L'Economie du Québec* (Montréal: Les Editions HRW, 1975), pp. 90-91; Maurice Saint-Germain, *Une économie à libérer* (Montréal: Les presses de l'Université de Montréal, 1973), pp. 59-65; R. Gilpin, op. cit., p. 867.
6. Office de planification et de développement du Québec, *Politiques fédérales et économie du Québec*, 2nd ed. (Québec, 1979), pp. 31-32, 49, 54-55, 61; André Bernard, "Une analyse prospective de la situation canadienne," in *La vie politique au Canada*, Actes du colloque de Mons (April 24-26, 1978), p. 144; F. Poulin and Y. Dion, *Les Disparités régionales au Canada et au Québec: les politiques et les programmes, 1960-1973*, CRDE (Montreal: Université de Montréal, 1973), p. 93; Daniel Latouche (ed.), *Premier Mandat*, vol. 1 (Montreal; Les Editions de l'Aurore, 1977), pp. 52-53; Gouvernement du Québec, *Bâtir le Québec* (1979), pp. 23-27.
7. J.H. Chung. "La nature du déclin économique de la région de Montréal," *L'Actualité économique* (summer 1974), pp. 326-41.
8. Judith Maxwell and Caroline Pestieau, *Economic Realities of Contemporary Confederation* (Montreal: C.D. Howe Research Institute, 1980), p. 97.
9. Benjamin Higgins, "Regional Interactions, the Frontier and Economic Growth," in A.R. Kuklinskis (ed.), *Growth Poles and Regional Policies* (The Hague: Mouton, 1972).
10. "Croissance nulle au Québec et négative en 80," *Le Devoir* (April 25, 1980), p. 21.
11. Fernand Martin, *Montreal: An Economic Perspective* (Montreal: C.D. Howe Research Institute, 1979), p.14.
12. Peter Gourevitch, "Quebec Separatism in Comparative Perspective," in E. Feldman and N. Nevitte (eds.), *The Future of North America: Canada, the United States, and Quebec Nationalism* (Cambridge, Mass.: Harvard University Press, 1979), p.242.
13. J. Maxwell and C. Pestieau, op.cit., pp.43-44; "L'industrie automobile: La politique fédérale du transport empêche toute expansion au Québec," *Le Devoir* (March 25, 1980), p.13.
14. Yves Rabeau and Robert Lacroix, "La stabilisation économique et les régions: le dilemme canadien" (Ottawa: Economic Council of Canada, 1978); *Bâtir le Québec*, op. cit., pp. 24-25; *Politiques fédérales et économie du Québec*, op. cit., p. 33. Ottawa's pursuit of an industrial policy based on resource projects similarly disadvantages Quebec. See, for instance, G. Bruce Doern (ed.), *How Ottawa Spends Your Tax Dollars: National Policy and Economic Development 1982* (Toronto: Lorimer, 1982), p. 13.
15. J. Maxwell, C. Pestieau, op. cit., p. 19.
16. *Bâtir le Québec*, op. cit., p. 24, our translation.
17. For an extensive discussion of locational theory with reference to comparative

advantage in manufacturing, see D.C. North, "Location theory and Regional Economic Growth," in *Journal of Political Economy* 63 (1955), pp. 243-58; J.N.H. Britton, "Location Perspective on Free Trade for Canada," *Canadian Public Policy* 4: 1 (1978), pp. 4-19; and J.M. Gilmour, "Structural Divergence in Canada's Manufacturing Belt," *Canadian Geographer* 17: 1 (1973), pp. 1-18.

18. *Politiques fédérales et économie du Québec,* op. cit., p. 34.
19. Maxwell and Pestieau, op. cit., p. 23.
20. *Bâtir le Québec,* op. cit., pp. 24ff.
21. Bruce Archibald, "Atlantic Regional Underdevelopment and Socialism," in L. Lapierre et al., *Essays on the Left* (Toronto: McClelland and Stewart, 1971), pp. 102-20; Robert J. Brym and R. James Sacouman (eds.), *Underdevelopment and Social Movements in Atlantic Canada* (Toronto: New Hogtown Press, 1979).
22. Hubert Guindon, "The Social Evolution of Quebec Reconsidered," *Canadian Journal of Economics and Political Science* 26: 4 (1960), pp. 533-51; "Social Unrest, Social Class and Quebec's Bureaucratic Revolution," *Queen's Quarterly* 71 (summer 1964), pp. 150-62; "The Modernization of Quebec and the Legitimacy of the Canadian State," in D. Glenday et al., *Modernization and the Canadian State* (Toronto: Macmillan, 1978), pp. 212-46.
23. *Politiques fédérales et économie du Québec,* op.cit., p. 32.
24. Pierre Fournier, *Les Sociétés d' État et les objectifs économiques du Québec: une évaluation préliminaire* (Québec: Editeur officiel du Québec, 1978), pp. 13-17; L.O. Gerther, *Regional Planning in Canada* (Montréal: Harvest House, 1972), pp. 57-60.
25. Maxwell and Pestieau, op. cit., p. 99.
26. Lucien Metras, "Quelques aspects de la mise en oeuvre de programmes conjoints de développement régional," communication présentée à l'Association de science régionale de la langue française (Quebec, September 28, 1976).
27. Bernard Descoteaux, "Le budget du MEER au Québec devrait être administré par l'OPDQ (Léonard)", *Le Devoir* (Nov. 23, 1979), p.17; see also Paul Morisset, "Le transfert du MEER à l'OPDQ: j'y penserai, dit McKay à Léonard," *Le Devoir* (Nov. 27, 1979), p. 17.
28. *Politiques fédérales et économie du Québec,* op. cit., p. 84; Germain Julien and Marcel Proulx, *Le chevauchement des programmes fédéraux et québécois.* (Québec: L'École nationale d'administration publique, 1978), pp. A-80, A-81, and A-82.
29. R.W. Phidd, "Regional Development Policy," in G. Bruce Doern and V.S. Wilson (eds.), *Canadian Public Policy* (Toronto: Macmillan, 1974), p. 187.
30. *Politiques fédérales et économie du Québec,* op. cit., pp. 43-44.
31. A full outline of the act that created DREE can be found in any Canada Year Book from 1969 onward. This quote came from the 1969 one, p. 1133.
32. *Politiques fédérales et économie du Québec.,* op. cit., pp. x, 40, our translation.
33. Ibid., p. 43.
34. W. Irwin Gillespie and Richard Kerr, *The Impact of Federal Regional Economic Expansion Policies on the Distribution of Income in Canada,* Discussion Paper no. 85 (Ottawa: Economic Council of Canada, 1977), p. 99. The point has also been documented in a DREE publication, *Climate for Regional Development* (Ottawa, 1975), p. 34.
35. Ibid., p. 100.
36. Ibid., p. 77.

37. According to a presentation made at Fredericton by André Raynauld while Chairman of the Economic Council of Canada. In this context, see Claude Tessier, "Echec de la politique de développement régional," *Le Soleil* (Oct. 9, 1975).
38. P. Fréchette et al., op. cit., pp. 374-75, our translation.
39. Ibid.
40. Ibid., p. 375; see also Pierre Fréchette, "Y a-t-il un avenir pour les régions," in D. Latouche (ed.), op. cit., p. 82. This policy of *saupoudrage* has replaced the "growth pole" approach on which DREE was originally established in 1969; see B. Higgins, F. Martin, and A. Raynauld, *Les orientations du développement économique régional de la province du Québec* (Ottawa: DREE, 1970).
41. Jim Laxer, "Canadian Manufacturing and U.S. Trade Policy," in Robert M. Laxer (ed.), *Canada Ltd.* (Toronto: McClelland and Stewart, 1973), p. 134.
42. *Bâtir le Québec*, op. cit., p. 24, our translation.
43. Maxwell and Pestieau, op. cit., p. 19.
44. Fernand Martin, "Regional Impact of Selected Non-Expenditure Decisions of the Federal Government," in *Proceedings of the Workshop on the Political Economy of Confederation* (Kingston: November 8-10, 1978), pp. 331-56.
45. *Politiques fédérales et économie du Québec*, op. cit., p. 39.
46. Maxwell and Pestieau, op. cit., p. 100.
47. As cited in J. Maxwell, C. Pestieau, op. cit., p. 83, n11.
48. P. Gourevitch, op. cit., p. 243.
49. R. Gilpin, op. cit., p. 874.
50. Philippe Garigue, "Le fédéralisme, solution supérieure," *Le Devoir* (May 6, 1980), p. 7.

Chapter 3/Quebec Alienation and the Trend toward Centralization

Edmond Orban

The Relative Alienation of Quebec

The modern concept of alienation finds its root in the Latin word *alienus*, which means "belonging to someone else." Today, alienation is considered to be a process or the result of a process where the individual does not control his or her own life and is treated like an object because of external economic and/or political conditions. By extension, alienation also means that a group of people loses its rights, or at least what it considers to be its rights. However, our evaluation of the nature and degree of alienation suffered by a group often depends on our own perceptions and is not always based on objective or clear criteria.

Thus, a person completely unaware of the political situation in Canada and, more specifically, in Quebec might decide that, according to his own criteria and experiences, there is no real alienation in that province. As he evaluates the situation, several more or less subjective variables come into play, including his personal past and present. For this reason, a foreign visitor or an immigrant coming from a totalitarian state may be inclined to underestimate the degree of alienation affecting the francophones with regard to the federal government and the anglophone majority since he has in mind a very different schema of reference. On the other hand, if the observer has lived in a small, democratic, industrial country that has minorities, his perception of the same situation would probably be substantially different. He also compares Canada to his own country, but he tends to use criteria more appropriate to the situation and his sensitivity is far more accurate. To be objective, therefore, we must compare structures, systems, and regimes between which the differences are neither too large nor too deep to avoid oversimplifying or obscuring of the many facets of the phenomenon to be analyzed.

The perception of alienation is different for someone born or living in Quebec, because he views his situation from inside the system in which he lives. He feels more or less alienated in relation to what he believes the system (political or economic) ought to provide for him in terms of goods, services, and other gratifications. He does consider countries and regimes outside of his own environment. To become politically mobilized, the individual must be aware that he and his group are suffering more deprivation than other groups in the same society. For this reason, the "lumpen proletariat" mentioned by Marx are condemned to inaction for lack of consciousness. At the top of the social scale, those people enjoying the benefits created by the regime are not overly sensitive to deprivation. Their natural tendency is to avoid or deny its very existence, except when confronted by a sudden, dramatic event resulting from the real alienation of the masses. Thus, the two extremes of the social scale are not well prepared to work out solutions.

To sum up, to be translated into a strong political movement, alienation—whether real or perceived—needs the support of influential and dedicated people, aware of belonging to an alienated group. In Quebec this consciousness has grown with the development of the mass media and the educational system. During the last three decades, we have observed the accelerated construction of many new public colleges and universities and a spectacular increase in the number of students in new fields of knowledge. This phenomenon is of itself a determinant, in the sense that it has helped the francophone groups to become better equipped to use their own human and material resources, while at the same time they have become more inclined to criticize the Canadian political system when it did not respond to their new expectations.

According to some people, the mass media are manipulated by strong economic pressure groups, who tend to downplay the so-called alienation of the francophones in Quebec, but even the most conservative newspaper cannot avoid speaking in terms of the competition and confrontation between the two main cultures in the province. Without referring explicitly to alienation, they often hint that there is at least some degree of hostility. The media approach is generally informal compared to the emotional approach of artists (often at the vanguard of nationalism) and the more systematic analysis of academics. But even social scientists treat the alienation of Quebec in various ways, according to the disciplines and schools to which they belong and the type of evidence they use. Nevertheless, throughout Quebec we find a broad consensus that feelings of alienation do exist and appear to be sufficiently widespread and strong in the younger generation to encourage resentment towards the current regime and to seek fundamental reforms not only in the political system but also in the economic structures. Of course, this feeling and its subsequent demands are integrated into the programs of nationalist parties like the former RIN (Rassemblement pour l'indépendance nationale) or the PQ (Parti Québécois). But even in the provincial Liberal party we find some elements of this feeling, particularly when confronted with the strongly centralist view of a charismatic leader like Pierre Trudeau.

But why does this feeling of alienation seem to be more keen in Quebec than elsewhere in Canada, even in the western provinces? Why is the process of centralization not perceived in the same way and with the same intensity as in Quebec? In other words, why is this process perceived by many Québécois as a threat, not only to their provincial institutions but also to their survival as a distinct cultural entity? It is sometimes difficult for the members of a majority (for example, anglophones in North America) to understand what it means to be severed from one's own culture and finally assimilated against one's will. It is difficult even when a significant French-speaking minority exists in their own province, as we can see in Ontario or in the New England states. The situation is still worse in most foreign countries, which do not even pretend to be the home for two cultures.

The Development of Alienation

The Early Stages

Since its very beginning, Canadian history has been marked by examples of dissent and conflict. Some historians do not stress these aspects, while others concentrate on the conflicts between francophones and the federal government and its supporters. In this context, it is believed that a cursory review of the formative stages of Quebec political culture should better situate the present study.

Since the British conquest, anglophones have dominated the federal government, despite the fact that they did not always comprise the majority of the population. In this way they have been able to impose their views and protect their interests throughout Canada. Today, this domination is guaranteed by the rule of a democratic majority in a country where the percentage of the francophone population has steadily declined. The result has been a permanent feeling of insecurity among francophones in Quebec and even more so outside that province. The intensity of this feeling has fluctuated over time, but expresses itself most strongly in times of crisis that constitute clearly visible signs or landmarks in the political life of the people.

During the Nouvelle France regime, the two "founding peoples" had few occasions to collaborate peacefully. They were the fragments of two great European states competing against each other to control large areas throughout the world. After the British conquest in 1763, the anglophone establishment, faced with a francophone majority, was naturally tempted to try and assimilate this group in the name of unity. This experiment failed, but we cannot avoid speaking of the conquered complex caused by the deep changes involved with a total defeat. From that time onwards, political and economic power slipped out of the hands of the "Canadiens" to their new masters. But certain cultural traits endured and for a long time they remained obstacles to the harmonious integration of the francophone community.

There are many examples of cooperation between individuals of the two groups, but too often we see only the conflicts of interest and values that explode during crises of different causes and nature. The evaluation of these events varies according to the different approaches and interpretations of the past, but if we examine books on the history of Canada written by French-speaking Québécois, we discover a tendency to emphasize only the conflicts. Indeed, having learned about the founding and development of "La Nouvelle France," the reader is struck by the dramatic collapse of this new country, when at the same time New England was preparing for its independence. We are told of the terrible consequences of a military occupation, spoliation, alienation, and the end of a great adventure for the first Canadiens, now subjects of a foreign and sometimes hostile country.

Thus, many authors speak of *la survivance,* a concept implying a permanent threat.

From this perspective, the rebellion of 1837 was a turning point, as even today the uprising and the "Parti des Patriotes" are symbolically important for some nationalist Québécois. For many others the rebellion is an indication of the profound dissent between the two main groups of the country, even though the rebellion was not limited to Lower Canada. The suppression of the *Patriotes* by the English army left Lower Canada internally divided, humiliated, and once again alienated. This new defeat was followed by a new attempt to assimilate the francophones, and the Durham Report remains to this day a target for their resentment and the best official proof that the threat to their survival was real and permanent, hanging above their heads like the "sword of Damocles." The union of the two Canadas was generally denounced as a manoeuvre designed to put an end to the resistance of the francophones and to their aspirations for greater autonomy. Regardless, it was an absolute failure and was replaced by Confederation in 1867. Some serious doubts have been expressed about the nature and the importance of the consensus involved in the drafting of the British North America Act. Many historians insist on the opposition of the Quebec Liberals, led by A.A. Dorion, who saw in the new federal state a tool for the centralization of power into the union hands of the anglophones and "their" leader, John A. Macdonald.

Since then, many occasions have exemplified the clashes involving the federal government and francophones, some of which took place outside of Quebec. The abolition of the French education system in Manitoba and Ontario are notable examples. After another bloody rebellion, this time in the west and centred around a land problem, Louis Riel, the French-speaking leader of the Métis, was condemned to death by judges selected by the Canadian government in Ottawa. In sharp reaction to this decision, the nationalist Honoré Mercier was elected as the head of the provincial government of Quebec. The relations between the two levels of government were marked by a deep division, and the death of Riel was considered a further defeat for non-Quebec francophones.

Of course, there were long periods of peaceful relations as well, but people mainly tend to remember the most dramatic events, which take on the significance and importance of symbols. Two external conflicts indicate once again the dissent between the two groups—as, during the two world wars, the majority of anglophones voted in favour of conscription, while the majority of francophones was strongly opposed. In the other Allied countries, these wars (at least in their beginning) were generally an opportunity to "rally round the flag" in face of a common enemy. But in Canada the federal government, which is responsible for defense and the use of the Armed Forces, was opposed by the majority of the francophones.

It has become clear that there has been a tendency to use the federal government as a scapegoat, even when its culpability is not well established. Two further examples are Ottawa's failure to solve economic crises, as outlined in Chapter 2, and the awarding of the Labrador territory to Newfoundland by Britain's Judicial Committee of the Privy Council. In each case Ottawa was blamed by Quebec francophones, even though it was not entirely responsible for the outcome.

The Link of Culture, Alienation, and Centralization

The more the federal government intervenes in society, even within the fields of its own jurisdiction, the more there are occasions for conflict with the provincial government of Quebec. Using an approach based on the competition between the two centres of power, one finds a national centre controlled by an anglophone majority and sees a provincial government with much less power in the hands of a francophone minority in the country as a whole. Such an approach is rejected by people who choose to stress the many fields of cooperation between the two levels of government, despite occasional and "functional" conflicts. Thus, it is also a matter of emphasis.

Marxists and neo-marxists tend to see the relations between the two groups and the relation between centralization and alienation on a very different plane, where the struggle between social classes dominates the national question.[1] Nevertheless, the federal government is a key element in the debate, for it is considered to be a tool in the hands of a Canadian bourgeoisie, more or less subordinate to foreign, especially American, interests. As the dominant class is anglophone, it would be logical, according to these views, to link together centralization and the alienation of the francophones as a group.

The other provinces and regions in Canada also have numerous reasons to criticize the federal government, and too many Québécois seem to underestimate the protest movement of the western provinces. But these claims do not have the same background nor as long a tradition as in Quebec and, above all, they do not question so deeply the very distribution of powers. The cultural factor (many Québécois maintain that they form a nation) seems to override the social, economic, and political cleavages and reinforces them by identifying a visible and distinct group. The same function of identification does not occur in such a way in the relations between the other provinces and the federal government. Even if some writers speak of distinct Prairie or Maritime regional cultures, in the eyes of most of Québécois, these do not have the same deep roots on the North American continent. In any case, they do not have a language and a culture distinct from the rest of anglophone Canada. If we want to complicate the debate, let us add that the francophones in Canada are North Americans in many ways and do not consider themselves as the "French of Canada" of Charles de Gaulle. Historically, the feeling of alienation from the former "fatherland" has also been part of the collective French-Canadian psyche, but much less so today.

The Québécois are an easily identifiable group in Canada; if they had all been assimilated there would not be the same dramatization of many problems, nor the same feelings of frustrations of their general expectations. The process of centralization would be severed from several of its basic elements and reduced to more acceptable proportions. We would perhaps have a kind of federal state similar to West Germany where there is strong decentralization in the administration of federal law. In this system, the centralization of the main decision-making powers is granted to the Länder—the equivalent of a province—because there is sufficient consensus in this more homogeneous society despite some remaining regional disparities.

In Canada we have a very different pattern and it looks now as if Ottawa and Quebec are playing a zero-sum game where there can be only one winner and one loser. In that case, the antagonism between the two levels of government will probably increase: first because of the many questions where there is not a clear-cut separation of powers; and second because the federal government seems to judge that it has gone too far toward decentralization and wants to reestablish its authority, primarily in the economic field. At the forefront stands a provincial government demanding a new distribution of powers in its favour and a transformation of the entire political system in Ottawa. Past Quebec governments, Union Nationale and Libéral alike, have stood for greater provincial autonomy that would allow them to be "*Maîtres chez nous.*"[2] Between the two levels of government exists a widening gap resulting from two fundamentally different conceptions of the political system.

If a solution is not rapidly found, a point of rupture will eventually be reached, for not since 1837 has the whole system been under such stress. The defeat of the PQ in the referendum on sovereignty-association and the current constitutional arrangements do not diminish that possibility; rather, they accomplish just the opposite. The patriation of the constitution was another example of disunity, leaving Quebec alone against the federal government and nine other provinces. The majority of Québécois (pro- and anti-PQ alike) did not accept the unilateral initiative of the federal government. It is outside the realm of this article to assign the responsibility for this crisis; it is only noted here that once again the federal government is considered as asserting itself at the expense of Quebec.

Stronger Linkages between Alienation and the Process of Centralization

The preceding section mentioned examples around which the feeling of Quebec alienation had crystallized and are still symbolically important. In every case (military, political, economic, or cultural), the federal government tended to be the focal point. To many people it does not matter greatly whether that government is in fact responsible or not for the conflict or which forces (internal or external) are being exerted.

During the last century, the federal government could not use the same powers and tools as it does today, particularly in the economic field. But, because it is now much better equipped to intervene, some people are inclined to criticize the federal government's past behaviour and performance still more severely than their ancestors were. They do so by using modern schemes of reference. For example, consider the massive emigration of more than half a million Québécois to the United States between 1850 and 1910. This exodus had the same demographic consequences as the bloodiest military defeat we could imagine for such a small population. We know that it was generally due to the unemployment rate in Quebec, but what is important to recognize is that it occurred in an economic system dominated almost exclusively by an anglophone establishment. Some go one step further and say that the federal state itself was in the hands of the same elite, with only a few token francophones.

From here we can reach some plausible conclusions. On the one hand, the federal government has tolerated and perhaps encouraged the francophone emigration out of the country, while on the other it has pursued the immigration of anglophones or easily assimilable people. Both aspects of this one policy were aimed at reducing the relative number of francophones, thus facilitating their assimilation into the English-Canadian melting pot. At first glance, this scenario seems machiavellian, but it is the kind of conclusion people may draw when starting from limited premises on the role of the federal government. Too many facets of its policy in matters of immigration have contributed to give credence to this thesis.

Further, consider how the natural tendency to link centralization and alienation may grow if intensive and original reforms are not implemented to limit the dangerous polarization of views. Centralization is not necessarily the main cause of alienation, but, in the eyes of many, these two elements appear to be linked because of the structural arrangements. The two form a vicious circle where centralization causes alienation, which in turn breeds mistrust of centralization as the alienated groups feel that they can never control the process. And this is precisely the definition of an alienated individual, a stranger in his own country and even in his own province, where even today great imbalances of socioeconomic status exist between the francophone majority and the anglophone minority. Of course, the English-speaking people all across Canada present many different social classes, cultures and regional interests, but they belong, in the eyes of the Québécois, to a distinct majority. And even if there is an increasing number of exchanges and communications between the individuals of the two main groups at different levels, they cannot avoid speaking in terms of us and them, as suggested by the theme of the two solitudes. Neither can we avoid reference to a majority-minority relationship, at least during crises.

To be alienated, a minority must feel that it always loses. Perhaps this is why the francophone minority in the western part of Switzerland does not appear to be alienated, for, while they cannot control the national government, they do play a political role disproportionate to their small number. Sometimes frustrated by some central decisions, they can compensate to some degree by enjoying a high standard of living (one of the highest in the world in the *canton* of Geneva, for example), and they do not have the feeling of being culturally threatened by the European environment, because the French culture next door remains strong.

The situation of the Québécois is different in Canada and in the northeastern United States, where different economic, political, and cultural factors have had a negative cumulative effect. Therefore, if we generally accept these premises, it is easier to understand why, despite their traditional distrust towards the state, Québécois are attempting to build a modern state to partly compensate for the economic, political, and cultural inequality from which they think they have suffered for so long. For this very reason they are driven to ask for more resources and powers to implement their own policy, with the increasing and inevitable risk of conflicting with the federal government.

We must also add that the feeling of being alienated is sometimes contradictory as people tend to ask for more once they are less dominated. The more they obtain, the more they seek, because of their rising expectations. Some American authors[3] have formulated interesting theories about the "J-curve" in relation to the increase in economic and political resources. There is a dilemma, however: if the political expectations are too high, the federal government must choose between giving up more powers and blocking the provincial demands to increase its own grip on the whole system. Inbetween are many other possible combinations and compromises. But people starting from the hypothesis that alienation is widely felt among the francophones in Quebec may choose a conflictual approach of the zero-sum-game type. In this case, the main target will be the process of centralization competing with Quebec's struggle for autonomy. At least for the moment we have chosen this latter approach to better understand the feeling of alienation in relation to the process of centralization.

Economic Stabilization, Centralization, and Decentralization

The "Bible of the Centralization" and Some Quebec Reactions

The Rowell-Sirois Report was submitted in 1940, almost five years after the publication of Keynes's *General Theory of Employment, Interest and Money*, and was greatly influenced by its theories. The report, in concert with new economic problems caused by the Second World War and the fear of an impending recession, forecast the end of laissez-faire liberalism as the federal government adopted the goals of price stability and full employment. The report strongly recommended that the poorer provinces improve their public services to levels at least comparable to those of the wealthier provinces. It also suggested that the federal government assume the responsibility for unemployment insurance and a national old-age pension plan. Provinces were invited to give up their control over income taxes to the federal government in exchange for subsidies in order to assure that all public services would meet national standards. These subsidies would raise the minimum level of social services and education, although it was recognized that those fields were linked to the culture and thus overlapped provincial jurisdiction.

In Quebec, several Liberals, such as Professor Lamontagne,[4] although in favour of the general approach of the report, pointed out that it might be dangerous to try and resolve economic problems (like unemployment) as if they had the same causes and intensity all over the country and as if they could be dealt with by universal economic, industrial, and regional policies.

In response to these recommendations, which some called the "Bible of centralization," a strong reaction developed in the province of Quebec. The Tremblay Report may be considered as a counteroffensive against centralization: it called for a transformation of the income-tax system in order to maintain provincial autonomy in cultural and social matters. It was argued, therefore, that the provinces needed to retain a substantial part of the direct taxes and revenues drawn from the exploitation of natural resources. But, at the same time, the philosophy of Rowell-Sirois was under attack, as it was accused of recommending a unitary and centralized state by emphasizing the federal government's powers in economic and social matters. It was underlined by francophones that the Protestant anglophones controlled the nine other provinces as well as the federal government itself. The conclusion was that, because the French-Canadian culture had its only true base in Quebec, it was the responsibility of that province to make decisions in social and cultural matters, for it was becoming more and more difficult to separate them from economic policy. For this reason, the provincial government assumed that it had the right to intervene in these policy areas.

The Tremblay Report stated that each level of government must stay within the fields prescribed by the Constitution and took the opportunity to sharply criticize the encroachments of the federal government into areas of provincial jurisdictions. Despite some contradictions and weaknesses, the Tremblay Report had a considerable impact, because it offered to French Canadians a model favouring financial decentralization. But, above all, by its systematic affirmation of the Canadian duality, it contributed to the reinforcement of the "concept of the two nations."

Later, the RIN and the Parti Québécois carried on the tradition more systematically by putting this concept at the centre of their "problématique." But the Parti Québécois now speaks of a Quebec nation having dropped the "French Canadian" concept because, according to this interpretation, Quebec is the only homeland for the French-speaking population in Canada, due to the declining use of French outside of that province.

Of course, there is some continuity and progression in the claims for greater autonomy, between the Tremblay Report and the white paper of the

PQ.[5] The main difference, however, lies in the fact that the Tremblay Report, like the *Maîtres chez nous* program of Jean Lesage, still believed that it was possible to find solutions within the federal framework, despite the fact that it speaks of an association of states sharing powers. On the other hand, the white paper believes that such an association could be successful only after the patriation of power from Ottawa to Quebec. All these reactions, plus the *Egalité ou l'indépendance* of Daniel Johnson, have a common target, the overcentralization of powers in Ottawa. More and more it was stated that, after all, Quebec has at its disposal human and material resources comparable to those of many independent states in the world. But the Quebec government cannot control its monetary policy nor its rate of exchange and has little influence in the areas of immigration and trade policies.

Returning to the Union Nationale of the 1950s, we see that, for this party, personal and corporate income taxes were important tools for the economic stabilization of the province. Thus, Quebec and many other provinces followed the way indicated by Keynes. But Quebec followed like a cripple, since it remained and is still isolated from the main economic powers concentrated in the hands of the federal government. Meanwhile, the provincial government tended to compete more and more frequently and directly with Ottawa over economic policy making.

From 1960 until now, the public service in Quebec has developed and modernized, attempting not only to fully occupy its own field of jurisdiction, but also at least part of the no man's land where the two levels of government have the most opportunities to cooperate or to clash together. Paradoxically, this reaction against the centralization process has occurred when many people were expecting the contrary, for the "French power" in Ottawa was supposed to be a great advantage for the Québécois. There are several explanations for this, one of which is the behaviour of the Prime Minister himself. But mainly it is due to the process of centralization.

A More Centralist View and the Quebec Counteroffensive

The federal white paper of 1968[6] set up a clear-cut model adopted and followed by Prime Minister Trudeau until now with few alterations. Contrary to the "two nations" concept, it stated that the interest of the provinces and ethnic groups could not be defended by transferring powers from Ottawa to the provinces. These interests were to find their expression through constitutional guarantees and central institutions. The sharing of powers was to be dictated by functional rules rather than by ethnic considerations.

Remaining faithful to Keynesian theory and the philosophy of the Rowell-Sirois Report, the white paper asserted that Parliament had to be responsible for the main economic levers to stimulate employment and control inflation. It needed to have control over monetary, fiscal, credit, and tariff policy to stabilize the economy. The white paper reasserted the responsibilities of the federal government in the areas of international and interprovincial trade. But, above all, it stated that the federal government had to stimulate the economy, a policy that, directly in some cases and unintentionally in others, had a direct impact on the economic development of the regions. This impact resulted largely from the responsibility of the federal government to reduce the disparity between regions and between individuals all over the country. This responsibility implies the right to allocate money in favour of individuals, to maintain the level of revenues, old-age pension, unemployment insurance, and family allowances.

The white paper, starting from the fact that the federal government is dominant in foreign and international affairs, concluded that at this level Ottawa must also play an active role in the development of technology and culture. It underlined the importance of the provinces in their traditional jurisdictions of education, health, and welfare but added that the federal government could also intervene in these areas through transfers of money in order to assure a minimum of services, as mentioned before. Noticing that, due to their spending power and their right to borrow, the provinces can also influence the economic policies, the white paper recommended increased cooperation between the two levels of government through the framework of federal-provincial conferences.

To fulfill all of these principles, the federal government needed to extend its own fields of jurisdiction. In fact, if it was to be considered as the leader of the fight against inflation and unemployment and if it wanted to reduce the regional disparities, it would have been almost impossible not to intervene, at least partly and indirectly, in the provincial domains of social affairs and education, for example.

The white paper, like Prime Minister Trudeau himself, avoided speaking of exclusive powers and put the stress on the need for cooperation. At the same time, the white paper clearly confirmed Ottawa as the main centre of decision making. Thus, there was no question of giving up certain powers to the provinces and it rejected all proposals for institutionalized bilateral relation between the federal government and individual provinces.

If these principles were fully applied, Canada would be transformed, at best, into a federal state where, as in West Germany, the important political decisions are made in Bonn with the cooperation of the Länder in the Bundesrat and then applied by the Länder. In this way, we would have a model based on two principles: political centralization and administrative decentralization. In that kind of model we might also see a federal government refusing to be overloaded with certain functions and reserving the application of its decisions to the provinces in certain matters no longer interesting from an electoral point of view, such as preuniversitary education. Free from these secondary tasks, it could concentrate on essential issues.

To reinforce its legitimacy, the federal government has been emphasizing the need of preserving the Canadian "common market," implying free movements of goods, persons, and services. This aim precludes all forms of provincial protectionism and allows the federal government to intervene in many domains, such as energy policy, interprovincial trade, and investment policy. Facing such an approach, the reactions of Quebec seem to be diversified and even contradictory if we analyze the differences between the provincial Liberals' beige paper (1980) and the PQ white paper (1979).[7]

At first glance, the PQ position is very clear because it seeks to use within its boundaries almost all powers belonging to the federal government. The provincial Liberal position is much more difficult because it is caught between two extremes. On one side, the federal government claims that decisions should be made by the federal institutions (including perhaps a new upper house for the provinces), while on the other the PQ fights to gain provincial sovereignty. Therefore, the criticism of the process of centralization will vary considerably among the Quebec political actors themselves. In the group favouring centralization are representatives of Liberal party of Canada in Ottawa, while in Quebec the National Assembly is yet again divided between the PQ and the Liberals.

Despite many differences of opinion on the rise, nature, and consequences of centralization, the great majority of Québécois seem to have at least a strong common sense of belonging to a Quebec nation, deeply rooted in the past and the present. One cannot understand the feeling of the Québécois when confronted with the issue of centralization without having in mind that fact and its relationship to the alienation question.

The Bipolarization of Conflicts

In *Conflict of Taste and Conflict of Claim*, Richard Simeon and Jack Mintz tell us that, when the overall responsibility is centralized, the government should respect at least two conditions: first, that each region feels it has a voice in the decision-making process through representation in the council of the federal government and, second, that the same government does not automatically use the rule of the majority.[8] The advice is judicious, but this behaviour depends too much on the good, or the bad, will of the federal government in a system where there are no mechanisms or institutions enforcing such arrangements.

When there is a "consensus" between the two levels of government, negotiation and cooperation on problems and policies are much easier. But, if instead of putting the stress on the concept of interdependence, the federal government wants to increase its powers while a province is asking for more autonomy and powers, they become involved in a zero-sum game. In that case, a conflictual model seems more appropriate to understand their relationship, even if conflict and cooperation are not always mutually exclusive. The conflicts may concern the exclusive powers of one of the two governments, but also domains inbetween the two, constituting a no man's land where neither government has clearly defined authority. Thus, instead of having a large degree of cooperation, we may have a battleground, as is the case with the Quebec government's complaints about overlapping programs. Here we have two governments and two bureaucracies, which in practice are forced to cooperate, but are often inclined to compete or to flight when a question of powers or influence is involved.

Seen from Quebec, the fight seems to be unequal, for Ottawa can use the tools of a "full state," while Quebec has only those of a half or embryonic state at its disposal. Québécois cannot avoid being frustrated in remembering the sum of defeats suffered since the conquest. With this in mind, almost any question might be an occasion for acrimonious debate, because one of the principal actors constantly feels threatened and its aspirations blocked.

If we consider a more visible reality, the territory of Quebec itself, the value of this kind of conflictual approach becomes particularly clear. Indeed, since the "amputation" of the Labrador area in 1927, there has been a succession of minor "operations," deriving from the normal application of the federal government's powers. But these operations are interpreted as a loss for Quebec when Ottawa, already the owner of an immense territory (including some oceanic areas), imposes its jurisdiction on new areas in the heart of the Quebec territory. These operations include, among other things, the creation or expansion of national harbours and airports with expropriated land, often against the wishes of the local population and the provincial government, as was the case of Mirabel Airport, the creation of national parks (Forillon, for example), the building of prisons, military bases, trans-Canadian railways and highways, and the expansion of the national capital in the Ottawa-Hull area.

Psychological aspects are also derived from the way these operations are conducted, as many Québécois are inclined to view such actions with at least feelings of suspicion—even alienation—depending on the case (Labrador, for example). Recently, the federal threat to create a corridor for the transportation of the electric power from Newfoundland to the United States across Quebec territory has exacerbated these feelings. Even if there is a network of complex forces acting on the federal government behind the scenes, this government is the most visible part of the iceberg, so it tends to be the main target for those people who see their cultural survival threatened.

Conclusion

Even with a change of personnel in the governments in Ottawa and Quebec City, the profound differences and the conflict between two levels of government, between a state and a semi-state, will persist. The state speaks English, while the semi-state speaks French. From a Québécois point of view, the situation is aggravated by feelings of frustrated aspirations and threats from a government with a unilingual bureaucracy, despite Trudeau's bilingual policies. The Parliament itself, with its symbols and its system of majority rule, does not help to make Québécois feel at home in Ottawa.

Federal political decisions, even when responding to Quebec interests, risk misinterpretation because they are made in a system where the Québécois always have been and always will be a minority. Under these conditions, the inevitable process of centralization will increasingly conflict with the claims of a Quebec demanding more powers and full jurisdiction over its own territory. Thus, the gap between Quebec's aspirations and the confusing output of the larger system will deepen. Of course, there are other facets in the relationship between these two levels of government; only two variables—alienation and centralization—have been examined here. A conflict approach emphasizes the linkage between these two elements.

The current system will not be workable in the long term, then, because its structures, rather than reducing the phenomenon of polarization of conflicts between a majority and a region calling itself a nation, tend to accentuate conflicts. In a modern society, we should be able to develop new political arrangements whereby the needs of autonomy and interdependence can be better conciliated. But this is another question that too many people in Canada prefer to ignore.

Notes

1. For example, Stanley B. Ryerson, "Mutations potentielles des rapports de force Canada/Québec," in E. Orban (ed.), *La modernisation politique du Québec* (Sillery, Que.: Boréal Express, 1976), pp. 55-78. Also, in this volume, one may refer to the various articles dealing with the national question and social classes.
2. Daniel Johnson, *Egalité ou indépendance* (Montréal: Editions Renaissance, 1965).
3. James Davies (ed.), *When Men Revolt and Why* (New York: The Free Press, 1971).
4. Maurice Lamontagne, *Le fédéralisme canadien: évolution et problèmes* (Québec: Les Presses de l'Université Laval, 1954).
5. Gouvernement du Québec, *La nouvelle entente Québec-Canada*, white paper (Québec: 1979).
6. Gouvernement du Canada, *Le fédéralisme et l'avenir* (Ottawa: Queen's Printer, 1968).
7. For a comprehensive study, refer to K. Banting and R. Simeon (eds.), *And No One Cheered: Federalism, Democracy and the Constitution Act* (Toronto: Methuen, 1983).
8. J. Mintz and R. Simeon, *Conflict of Taste and Conflict of Claim* (Kingston: Institute of Intergovernmental Relations, Queen's University, 1982), p. 38.

Chapter 4/Quebec Separatism in a Comparative Perspective

Mary Beth Montcalm

Today, western countries face challenges to their capacity as states. One of the most potent of these is from separatist movements, which have dramatically escalated since the Second World War and especially since the 1960s. While other trends in developed western systems, such as the neo-conservative movement, threaten state activity because they disagree with its *orientation* or because they question its *degree* and *scope*, separatism challenges a state's very legitimacy. Since separatists claim an existent state is unrepresentative of a given nation, all state activities as they affect that nation are regarded as illegitimate. It is a clash between the political authority over a geographic area and a culturally based collectivity.

In recent years, Canadians have been keenly aware of controversy surrounding the role of Quebec within the Canadian state. Although nationalist sentiment has a long history in Quebec, it took on remarkable new momentum with the election of the Lesage government in 1960. As well, the increasingly separatist orientation of Quebec nationalism became unmistakable with the election of the Parti Québécois in 1976.

Despite relative consensus about the existence and strength of Quebec separatism, there is limited agreement on the conditions fostering its postwar escalation. Indeed, a wide variety of factors (some appearing incompatible if not contradictory) are suggested as fuelling this trend. Such factors include modernization among the traditionally backward Québécois, which fostered rising material aspirations; blockage of the Québécois's upward social mobility by anglophone domination of the Quebec economy; persistent discrimination against French Canadians by Ottawa; centralist trends through which the federal government encroached on policy spheres of Quebec's provincial government; economic exploitation of Quebec by English Canada; and denial of the bilingual and bicultural character of Canada in Ottawa and the other nine provinces.

A comparative context provides an invaluable resource for the evaluation of such factors. Although discussions of Quebec separatism frequently assume it to be a unique phenomenon, this is clearly a misperception. In fact, several western states—such as Great Britain, France, Spain, and Belgium—contain separatist movements which have dramatically escalated since the Second World War and, as in Quebec, particularly since 1960. Moreover, the simultaneous mobilization of separatism in western states suggests that their resurgence is a generalized phenomenon and that the conditions hypothesized to be facilitating separatism in Quebec can reasonably be anticipated in these comparable settings.

The type of movement which includes Quebec separatism has been variously identified and defined. In some cases, it is referred to as ethnic separatism;[1] in others, it is called a secessionist[2] or nationalist movement.[3] This article examines movements in western states that, on the basis of representing a distinct nation, demand devolution of state power to the national group. Separatist movements differ mainly in the degree of violence they use; they tend to share the same rhetoric, tactics, and philosophical evolution—from demands for limited autonomy to outright separation.

The course of Quebec separatism is relatively well known to most observers of the Quebec scene. A French-Canadian nationalism has existed throughout Canadian history. Almost from the beginning, however, it has contained two divergent strains. One view of the French-Canadian nation saw it as integrally linked to a Canada that was bilingual and bicultural. A second strain was largely separatist, holding that the French-Canadian nation could be adequately protected only with its own political structures and within a distinct state. Although coexistence of these two divergent views was always uneasy, by the 1930s, 1940s, and 1950s, prominent thinkers within the French-Canadian nation grew pessimistic about the possibility of a bilingual and bicultural Canada. In effect, a shift took place to the more separatist view.[4]

While this shift was a relative one, an unmistakable change occurred in the thinking on the relationship of Quebec to the Canadian state. The change was increasingly to the attitude that only Quebec political structures could serve the French-Canadian nation. This transition was obvious by the 1950s, but it took firm political form with the 1960 election of the provincial Liberal party led by Jean Lesage. With this election, the Quiet Revolution was begun.

Far too much has been written about the Quiet Revolution for it to be adequately dealt with in a brief article, especially one devoted to a comparative look at Quebec separatism. Essential to note about this period, however, is the degree to which it epitomized the change to viewing the province of Quebec—and the political and economic resources at its disposal—as the major vehicle for realizing the aspirations of the people of Quebec. As the Quebec Premier, Jean Lesage, said in 1963, "The Québécois have only one powerful institution: their government. And now they want to use this institution to build a new era to which they could not formerly aspire."[5]

Although it is frequently assumed that separatism within Quebec can be identified with the electoral fortunes of the Parti Québécois, this assumption misconstrues the degree of change in Quebec thought. Today, no political party that does not emphasize a "Quebec first" approach can realistically aspire to form the government of that province. After 1960, the framework of political dialogue within Quebec changed fundamentally. Since then, separatist thought has been a far more vital force within Quebec society.

Movements among the Flemish and Walloons in Belgium, the Basques in Spain, the Scots and Welsh in Great Britain, and the Bretons in France parallel Quebec separatism to such a degree that they cannot be ignored in any systematic effort to understand conditions fostering Quebec separatism. The unmistakably coincident escalation in these movements suggests that factors hypothesized as fuelling Quebec separatism should be evident in most of these comparable settings.

Tension between the Flemish and the Walloons in Belgium is a longstanding problem. Historically, the Walloon (French-speaking) part of the country has been more modern and industrial. The Flemish culture and language (Germanic) were regarded as inferior by both the Walloons and the Flemish, and the French-speaking Walloons held the bulk of political power within the Belgian state.

Although tension grew in the early part of the twentieth century, the level of conflict between these roughly equal groups markedly escalated after the Second World War and especially after 1960. By 1978, the level of conflict was so severe that all major political parties were organized along ethnic lines[6] and the conflictual pattern between the Flemish and Walloons is generally considered "the fundamental problem of the Belgian state."[7] The wrangling even includes seemingly irresolvable disputes about the status of Brussels, the national capital.

One of the strategies aimed at eliminating separatist demands in Belgium has involved considerable decentralization of political and economic power to the two major regions. Although the process of federalization has progressed with relative rapidity, it seems to have fuelled rather than assuaged separatist sentiment. The process of decentralization has been marked by continuous charges of federal government's favouritism of the other region; dissension over decentralization plans has brought the downfall of several Belgian governments.

Despite attempts to overcome separatist appeal by increasing regional decentralization, the Belgian state remains weakly legitimated in both Wallonia and Flanders. Opinion polls taken in 1979 and 1980, for example, revealed that attachment to the linguistic regions in Belgium is greater than attachment to the Belgian state; separatist sentiment is reported to be even greater among those located in the capital area of Brussels.[8]

Mobilization of separatism has similarly escalated in Spain in recent years. And, although it is evident in several Spanish regions, the case of the Basques is probably the most noteworthy. Despite strong centralist trends in the Franco era, the Basque provinces (four in northern Spain, three in southwestern France) are accustomed to considerable political autonomy within the Spanish state. In fact, the Basques have a tradition of *fueros* dating back to the Middle Ages whereby they traded tithes and military service for political autonomy within Spain.[9]

There is little evidence that sentiment in support of marked decentralization to the Basque region ever waned despite repression of virtually all such sentiment under Franco. With democratizing trends in the 1960s and '70s, however, Basque separatism resurfaced as a potent threat to the integrity of the Spanish state. Support for Basque separatism is expressed in several ways, including electoral support of the Basque nationalist party (the PNV) and the violence of ETA, a marxist-oriented separatist group.

The continuing threat of ETA violence and effective pressure from the democratically oriented PNV have been instrumental in bringing about decentralization of several powers to the Basque region, as well as other areas within Spain. In 1979 referenda, constitutional statutes were approved that gave the Basque territory its own parliament; control of taxation; and its own police, education, and broadcasting.[10] In 1980, further home-rule powers were granted within the Spanish state system.

Despite the degree of decentralization granted by central Spanish authorities, separatist sentiment in the Basque area remains strong. In 1979, the *Wall Street Journal* spoke of Basque separatism as "the biggest problem facing Spain and the greatest threat to its delicate democracy."[11] Subsequent events in Spain, such as the abortive coup in February 1981, corroborate this assessment.

Separatism exists among both Scots and Welsh in Great Britain. And, while separatism does not pose as significant a threat to the British state as it does in Belgium, Canada, and Spain, it has clearly escalated since the Second World War.

As in Quebec, Spain, and Belgium, the Scots and Welsh have home-rule traditions dating back to the 19th century. Scotland also has a tradition of decentralized legal, educational, and religious institutions within Britain. In fact, observers of Scottish and Welsh nationalism usually attribute the greater strength of Scottish nationalism to this traditionally wider independence. Nevertheless, there has been a clear upsurge in both movements in recent years.

Especially in the past 25 years, separatist sentiment in Scotland has received consistent support from a minority of Scots. Despite fluctation in electoral support for the Scottish National Party, the issue of separatism has remained on the political scene.[12] Moreover, observers of Scottish nationalism, such as Jack Brand, assert that since 1970 a core of about 20% of the Scottish populace would choose complete independence.[13]

Unlike Scotland, Wales has traditionally been highly integrated with England. In fact, as late as 1974, Wales was administered in the same way as England; at that time some administrative devolution of public services was undertaken in response to pressure from Welsh separatists.[14] Nevertheless, the Welsh nationalist party, Plaid Cymru, has never received more than 11.5% of the Welsh popular vote[15]; in the 1979 referendum on devolution, the proposal was overwhelmingly defeated in Wales—80% of the voters opposed it. Notwithstanding its relative weakness, separatism has become more politically mobilized since the Second World War and is much more evident among the most modernized sectors of Welsh society.[16] Consequently, the

Welsh case should be included in any consideration of separatist resurgence as a generalized phenomenon.

Breton separatism is, like Welsh separatism, usually regarded as weak. Krejci goes so far as to suggest that in Wales and Brittany communal consciousness may very well have been superseded by attachment to Great Britain and France, respectively.[17] Yet, like other current separatist movements, the modern Breton movement can trace its roots to the 19th century and it has shown recent resurgence.

Throughout the 20th century, Breton mobilization against the French state has been alternately nationalist and purely regional in orientation. While the demands are similar, nationalists' arguments are founded on the existence of a distinct nation. Political mobilization within Britanny has, moreover, been somewhat sporadic. Nevertheless, the area displays both a distinctive culture and recurrent separatism. In the 1960s and '70s, separatist sentiment was clearly in evidence. One nationalist organization, the Front de Libération de la Bretagne (FLB), while far less extreme in its violence than the Basque ETA, did much to keep Breton nationalism in the public eye. And, although Breton separatism does not pose an effective threat to the integrity of the French state, Brittany has been a leader in demands for regional devolution within France.

While cases in Great Britain, France, Spain, and Belgium by no means exhaust the possible choices for comparison with Quebec nationalism, they serve to cast theoretical speculation about presentday separatism in a broad context and, since they vary on so many points of detail, provide a more useful test of theorizing about the generalized resurgence of separatism than that afforded by the Quebec case alone. On many issues the cases observed here range widely. Included among them are strong movements (Flanders) and weak movements (Wales, Britanny), peaceful movements (Scotland), and violent movements (the Basque ETA).

Structural factors have been proposed as facilitating separatist movements. Among the most prominent are modernization,[18] economic trends such as that toward an increasingly international economy,[19] the incidence of uneven economic development or internal colonialism,[20] centralization of policy making in modern states,[21] a tradition of decentralized political institutions,[22] and discrimination within the state against the national group with a mobilized separatism.[23] Although scholars of various perspectives have suggested a broad range of conditions as stimulants of separatism, these six factors are undoubtedly among the most commonly proposed.

One striking fact about the cases of separatist escalation in Belgium, Spain, Great Britain, and Canada is the difficulty of establishing an unambiguous link for these six hypothetically facilitating factors and the actual incidence and strength of separatist movements. Thus, while they are regularly proposed, none of them provides an uncomplicated pattern to explain completely the current strength of separatist resurgence.

Uneven economic development or internal colonialism, which posits a link between separatist resurgence and longstanding conditions of economic backwardness due to exploitation by the dominant group within the state, is probably most frequently cited as a facilitator of separatist mobilization. When closely scrutinized, however, it leaves as much unexplained as it explains. The strength of Basque separatism in the postwar era is impossible to fit into an explanatory framework that stresses the role of uneven economic development. The Basque area has long been one of the most prosperous in Spain; in 1979, *The Economist* claimed Basque per capita income was still 25% higher than in Spain as a whole.[24] Whereas in the traditionally affluent Basque area there is a relatively strong separatist movement, in Brittany, one of the most improverished areas in France, there is only weak separatist mobilization. Separatism in Belgium is similarly difficult to explain when the traditionally backward Flemish area has experienced economic growth, the traditionally industrialized Walloon area has experienced economic decline, and both have separatist mobilization.

The condition of discrimination within a state system is also insufficiently explanatory. Most of the groups currently with strong separatist mobilization can make at least plausible claims about systematic discrimination within the state system. A major problem with this factor, however, is that it explains neither the timing of separatist escalation nor its varying strength. In most of the areas where separatist mobilization is evident, discrimination has, if anything, lessened in the period during which escalation has occurred. Thus, just as the lot of the Flemish has improved within the Belgian state system, separatist agitation among them has increased. A comparable assessment of the Québécois dynamic could probably be offered. Furthermore, the Breton movement once again seems inexplicably weak if discrimination within the state system is considered an important facilitator of separatism. Even in Brittany itself, let alone the French state, high-status positions are "monopolized by metropolitan Frenchmen or thoroughly Gallicized indigenes."[25]

Both centralization of policy making at the state level and the existence of decentralized political structures have been claimed to foster separatist agitation. Both of them, however, leave certain dynamics unexplained. Even at face value, centralization of policy making has limited explanatory value. France, which is highly centralized, has weak separatist movements, whereas countries with far less centralization have considerably stronger ones. The argument in support of the role played by decentralized political institutions is supported in several cases. Quebec and the Basque area both have long traditions of political autonomy. Scotland, which has a stronger tradition of decentralization than does Wales, similarly reveals greater separatism. Far more difficult to explain by reliance on this factor, however, is postwar separatist mobilization in Belgium, which has traditionally been a unified state and has only recently adopted decentralized structures. The timing of separatist escalation is also difficult to explain with reference to this condition since many of the cases included here have traditions of decentralization that long predate the recent upsurge in separatism.

Of the six factors, modernization and growing international economic interdependence would appear to be the explanations. In a sense, though, their impact is most fully comprehended when interaction between them is noted and when attention is paid to the major changes they have implied in the fabric of western societies.

Since the Second World War, revolutionary changes have occurred in the world economy. Today, major companies are international and they transcend state boundaries to an unprecedented degree. Numerous observers of the economic scene have suggested that, since economic markets no longer coincide with existent state boundaries, state structures as we have come to know them are ineffective and even obsolete.[26] As well, students of separatism have observed that the weakness of states has facilitated challenges to their authority by groups within them who claim to represent distinct nationalities. Examination of the comparative context suggests that major postwar economic changes and their impact on western systems (for example, the degree to which social modernization has been stimulated) underlie the current resurgence of separatism in western states.

As western economies have undergone significant metamorphosis in the postwar era, changes have also been implied for basic societal patterns. The increasing external influence on state economies has led to altered industrial patterns, trade patterns, and even regional prosperity. (Chapter 2 provides a Canadian illustration.) With postwar revolutions in communication and transportation, dramatic consequences have ensued in, for example, the structure of the workforce. One such change has been in the massive expansion of the tertiary sector in general and the public sector in particular. Macroeconomic changes since the Second World War have not only required greater social modernization[27] to meet the needs of economic development (as measured by increasing industrialization and technological innovation) but also, in altering the nature of the workforce, modified the class structure that maintained social stability. More specifically, the expansion of the tertiary sector in countries like Great Britain, France, Belgium, Canada, and Spain has swelled the ranks of a "new middle class" which stands to benefit from separatism. It is in this interaction of macroeconomic trends, the social modernization which they required, and the creation of a "new middle class" in western states, that the major stimulant of separatist resurgence can be located.

One of the most obvious postwar transformations in western countries has been extensive growth in the tertiary sector. In this expansion, a sizable new middle class with considerable political power and distinct class interests has been created. Advanced capitalist economies have expanded the role played by this class of, for example, bureaucrats, administrators, educators, artists, writers, journalists, engineers, and members of the liberal professions (such as lawyers)—"wage earners and independent producers who live by the word."[28] Moreover, this new middle class—which is characterized by high levels of education, professional occupational status, relative youth, and relatively high incomes[29]—has class interests that differ from those of the bourgeoisie (which owns and controls private capital) and those of the proletariat (which is engaged primarily in material production).

Like other classes, the new middle class seeks societal changes in harmony with its own class interests. And one change preeminently in its interest is expansion of the public sector. Since the bureaucratic sector emphasizes the technocratic skills and talents characteristic of the new middle class, any expansion of this sector enhances opportunities for its upward social mobility and expanded scope. It also fosters the independence of this class from the bourgeoisie to a greater degree than employment in the private sector could. Expansion of the state sector services the general interests of the new middle class in western systems as a whole.[30] Where this new middle class is part of a regionally concentrated minority within a state system, however, its class interests are even better served by devolution of state power to the regional level or, ideally, creation of entirely distinct state structures.

If one examines the class interests of the new middle class in settings such as Quebec, Scotland, Wales, Flanders and Wallonia, Brittany, and the Basque territory, gravitation to separatist movements is entirely understandable. While expansion of the state sector in most western states coincides with the interests of the new middle class, devolved political structures more closely coincide with the interests of this class where it forms part of a national minority within a state. Federal structures, devolved political institutions, or creation of a new state structure, by expanding the state sector, multiply the career opportunities available to this class. Where ethnic differentiation and linguistic differences have proven obstacles to the upward mobility of a regionally concentrated new middle class, demands for political devolution are to be anticipated, since they simultaneously expand employment opportunities for this class and turn the tables on systematic discrimination. Political decentralization, then, can remove institutional obstacles to the aspirations of a regionally concentrated and ethnically distinct new middle class.

Among the most striking patterns evident in the movements examined here is the degree to which separatist sentiment is both preeminently located in areas where tertiarization is most in evidence and in the new middle class created by social modernization. As well, where there has been a substantial expansion in this class, separatist sentiment is stronger than where this class is not much in evidence. The argument can be put, in fact, that the coincidence of separatist mobilization with the strength of this new middle class is more consistently explanatory than any other structural condition currently being proposed.

There is considerable evidence of the central role played by the new technocratic middle class in the change in Quebec politics since 1960. One of the most dramatic features of the Quiet Revolution was expansion of the public sector in the disproportionate interest of Quebec's new middle class.[31] As Gow has calculated, between 1959-60 and 1969-70 the number of provincial bureaucrats and employees in ministries and related organizations went from 32,000 to 70,000.[32] By 1970, the public sector contained 40% of the unionized workers of Quebec.[33] A 1973 survey found that 53.8% of francophone university graduates worked for the Quebec state; among younger university graduates the rate was even higher—fully 65.3% were employed by the Quebec state. (See Chapter 10.) By 1982, it was possible for the Quebec Minister of Finance to observe that in Quebec the ratio of employees per student in its schools, per patient in its hospitals, and per citizen was higher than anywhere else in North America.[34] Not only did the Quebec public sector become the major employer of the new middle class in Quebec, but also it has governed in such a way as to disproportionately benefit this class.[35]

Ever-escalating demands by Quebec governments for greater jurisdictional scope and increasing restrictions on the use of the English language, particularly as it pertains to the work world, are best understood as attempts by Quebec's new middle class to expand its base of power. This is particularly so since, by the late 1970s, the growth of the provincial public sector had neared its limits. (See Chapter 18.) In order to provide for the rising expectations of Quebec's new middle class, Quebec governments require wider jurisdictional spheres and commensurately expanded powers of taxation. It comes as no surprise that this new middle class has largely constituted both the leadership and the supporters of nationalist parties, including the Parti Québécois.[36] Moreover, in a 1976 article on the bases of Parti Québécois support, Maurice Pinard and Richard Hamilton have documented the disproportionate role played by Quebec's state-related (as opposed to private sector) new middle class in the PQ's support.[37] McRoberts and Posgate similarly observe that, while the Parti Québécois and its adherents are not confined to the new middle class and its preoccupations, its support is preeminently in "the various elites lodged in the structures of the Quebec state or closely linked to it, as with perhaps the cooperative movement."[38]

Although Quebec separatist mobilization is often identified with the interests of the new middle class in the Quebec setting, the degree to which this pattern is replicated elsewhere is generally overlooked. Yet, as Jack Brand has observed of Scottish separatism, "It is possible to see parallels between the growth of nationalism in the modernized parts of the Scottish economy and the growth of nationalism after the 'Quiet Revolution' in Quebec."[39] The degree to which social modernization has altered class structure in Scotland is obviously related to the growth in separatist sentiment. Until 1960, Scotland had a weak middle class. Since that time it has rapidly modernized. Moreover, nationalist sentiment is predominantly found in precisely the new middle class created by the impact of modernization.[40] In Wales, where the impact of social modernization has not been as great as elsewhere in Britain, nationalism is not as strong as in Scotland. Nevertheless, Welsh separatism is closely correlated with growth in modernization. Charles Ragin, for example, has documented that it is strongest in the most modernized sectors of the Welsh populace and in areas where there has been considerable growth in the tertiary sector.[41] Thus, while Welsh separatism is weaker than most of the movements included in this study, it is reasonable to infer that this is largely due to the relative weakness of its new middle class.

Brittany, which like Wales has not been markedly affected by modernization, similarly displays a weak separatist movement. Despite the weakness of the Breton movement, however, the limited evidence available supports a link between creation of a new middle class and nationalist attitudes. William R. Beer has illustrated the degree to which a professional middle class is the strength of the nationalist movement in Brittany and elsewhere in France where these movements are evident.[42] From his survey, Beer concluded that the leaders of nationalist movements in France were predominantly white-collar and professional workers, especially teachers, and that these leaders are much more upwardly mobile than the population at large. Thus, while Brittany remains a relatively traditional society, nationalist leaders are part of Brittany's limited new middle class.

In many ways, Belgium is fraught with "communal" or separatist tensions. Nevertheless, certain patterns regarding the concentration of nationalist sentiment are evident. While separatism is apparent in both the more recently modernized Flemish region and the long-modern, but now economically declining Walloon area, it is obviously stronger in Flanders where modernization has most recently had a substantial impact.[43] Equally noteworthy is that nationalist sentiment once again appears to be concentrated in the new middle class in the country. Both Anthony Mughan and François Nielsen document significant correspondence between the growth of the tertiary sector in Flanders and support for the *Volksunie*, the Flemish nationalist party.[44] Other research similarly documents the disproportionate participation in the Flemish separatist movement by the modernized Flemish middle class. In a 1978 article, Ter Hoeven reported the findings of a series of interviews with *Volksunie* members. In reporting that *Volksunie* voters "tend to be young, male, urban middle class and better educated," he observes that it is the "by now familiar picture."[45]

In Wallonia where the postwar impact of the dramatic social change brought on by modernization has been less evident, the nationalist movement is weaker than in Flanders. Yet, while Walloon separatism is weaker—indeed, it is frequently overlooked in discussions of current separatism—it displays characteristics common to the other movements assessed here. For one, participation by the new middle class in this movement appears substantial;[46] from the mid-1970s, Walloon nationalism has also been increasingly correlated, apparently, with growth in the regional tertiary sector.[47]

The Belgian case offers further corroboration of the assertion that nationalist sentiment is most concentrated in the upwardly mobile professional strata. In the Brussels area, where there is a concentration of the technocratic middle class, ethnic tension is consistently high and the communal or nationalist party there, the *Front démocratique des Francophones* (FDF), receives proportionally more electoral support than does the *Volksunie* or the *Rassemblement Wallon*.[48] Thus, in Belgium not only is separatist sentiment strongest in the region that has recently experienced modernization and a substantial alteration in its class structure, but also, throughout the country, nationalist sentiment is strongest in the professional middle class, which has largely been created by the impact of modernization.

Support of links between the effect of modernization, the strength of a new middle class, and Basque separatism is problematic because data on Spanish politics and society are considerably less available than those about other western societies. The limited information available suggests that the pattern clearly evident in Quebec, Scotland, Wales, Brittany, and Belgium may well exist in the Basque area. PNV support has historically come from the Basque middle class[49]; there is every reason to suspect that the democratic nationalists in the Basque area (who are numerically far greater than the ETA) resemble separatists in, for example, Quebec, Flanders, and Scotland, in being disproportionately middle-class professionals. Moreover, the Basque provinces that have been the hotbeds of separatist agitation, Guipuzcoa and Vizcaya, have long been the most modernized provinces within the Basque region and those within which tertiarization is most likely to have had the greatest impact.

The findings noted here about the coincident postwar growth in a new middle class in Quebec, Scotland and Wales, Brittany, Flanders and Wallonia, and the Basque area as well as escalation in separatist demands suggest that commonly experienced conditions in developed western states underlie this escalation. Furthermore, the findings suggest that, despite the explanatory appeal of many of the structural conditions regularly cited as fostering separatism (for example, the existence of systematic discrimination within the existent state), these conditions alone explain neither the timing nor the varying strength of separatist mobilization in the postwar period. Thus, while conditions of systematic discrimination or longstanding patterns of decentralization undoubtedly play a role in escalating separatist demands, their full contribution to the escalating pattern is only comprehended when their role is juxtaposed with their strategic impact on the size and relative strength of the new middle class. In other words, these conditions undoubtedly play a role in separatist mobilization, but this role can be grasped only when the role of a new middle class is regarded as primarily important in the constellation of forces involved in this mobilization. Of course, the expansion of this new middle class throughout the western world is not somehow ahistorical but is fundamentally rooted in macroeconomic changes in western capitalism.

Identification and evaluation of the role of a new middle class in postwar politics are at a relatively undeveloped stage. The impact of this class on western societies needs considerable further investigation. As well, the role of this class in current separatist movements requires greater exploration and documentation. Yet, while the positing of a link between a new middle class and the generalized escalation of separatist movements in Quebec and elsewhere in developed western societies may seem novel, it is, in fact, tapping something very old. One of the most recurring themes in the literature on nationalist movements is the degree to which they have usually been led by and based on an urban middle class.[50] Since macroeconomic trends are serving to vastly expand this class in the postwar west, separatist resurgence should not be overly surprising. Moreover, those who wish to prognosticate about the likely course of separatism in Quebec and elsewhere should pay particular attention to macroeconomic change as it affects western societies in general and Canada in particular as well as to the alterations this change will make in class structure.

Notes

1. Anthony D. Smith, "Towards a theory of ethnic separatism," *Ethnic and Racial Studies* 2: 1 (1979).
2. Donald L. Horowitz, "Patterns of Ethnic Separatism," *Comparative Studies in Society and History* 23: 2 (1981).
3. A.H. Birch, "Minority Nationalist Movements and Theories of Political Integration," *World Politics* 30: 3 (1975), e.g. p. 332; Peter Gourevitch, "The Resurgence of Peripheral Nationalisms," *Comparative Studies in Society and History* 21: 3 (1979).
4. For a tracing of this shift and the dichotomies within French-Canadian nationalism, see Ramsay Cook (ed.), *French-Canadian Nationalism* (Toronto: Macmillan, 1969), passim.
5. As quoted in Louis Balthazar, "La dynamique du nationalisme québécois," in Gérard Bergeron and Réjean Pelletier (ed.), *L'Etat du Québec en devenir* (Montreal: Boréal Express, 1980), p. 46. This passage has been translated from the original French.
6. *Facts on File* (Dec. 15, 1978), p. 968.
7. Lode Claes, "The Process of Federalization in Belgium," *Delta* 6: 4 (1963-64), p. 52.
8. "L'opinion publique et les problèmes communautaires," *Courrier Hebdomadaire du C.R.I.S.P.* no. 927-928 (July 3, 1981), p. 23, Table 1.
9. *U.S. News and World Report* (March 17, 1980), p. 59.
10. *Facts on File* (Feb. 8, 1980), p. 101.
11. "Spain's Basque Problem," *Wall Street Journal* (Aug. 3 1979), p. 8.
12. The relationship between nationalist attitudes and support for nationalist parties is not unilinear. See, for example, Jack Brand, *The National Movement in Scotland* (London: Routledge and Kegan Paul, 1978), pp. 155-56; H.M. Drucker and Gordon Brown, *The Politics of Nationalism and Devolution* (London: Longman Group, 1980), p. 50.
13. Brand, op. cit., p. 161.

14. A.H. Birch, *Political Integration and Disintegration in the British Isles* (London: George Allen and Unwin, 1977), p. 26.
15. F.W.S. Craig (ed.), *British Electoral Facts 1885-1975* (London: Macmillan Press, 1976), Table 7.08, p. 89; *Europa Year Book 1980* vol. 1, p. 1354.
16. Drucker and Brown, op. cit., p. 38; Charles Ragin, "Ethnic Political Mobilization: The Welsh Case," *American Sociological Review* 44: 3 (1979), p. 633.
17. Jaroslav Krejci, "Ethnic Problems in Europe," in Salvador Giner and Margaret S. Archer (eds.), *Contemporary Europe: Social Structures and Cultural Patterns* (London: Routledge and Kegan Paul, 1978), p. 128.
18. Smith, "Towards a theory," op. cit., p. 31.
19. Andrew Martin, "Is Democratic Control of Capitalist Economies Possible?" in Leon N. Lindberg et al. (ed.), *Stress and Contradiction in Modern Capitalism* (Toronto: Heath, 1975), p. 52; Eric Hobsbawm, "Some Reflections on the Break-Up of Britain," *New Left Review* #105 (Sept.-Oct. 1977), p. 7; Phillip M. Rawkins, "Outsiders as Insiders: The Implications of Minority Nationalism in Scotland and Wales," *Comparative Politics*, 10: 4 (1979), p. 522.
20. Anthony D. Smith, *Nationalism in the Twentieth Century* (Oxford: Martin Robertson, 1979), p. 21.
21. Davydd J. Greenwood, "Continuity in Change," in Milton Esman (ed.), *Ethnic Conflict in the Western World* (Ithaca, N.Y.: Cornell University Press, 1977), p. 101; S. Berger, "Bretons, Basques, Scots and Other European Nations," *Journal of Interdisciplinary History* 3: 1 (1972-73), p. 175.
22. Rawkins, op. cit., p. 524; Michael Hechter and Margaret Levi, "The Comparative Analysis of Ethnoregional Movements," *Ethnic and Racial Studies* 2: 3 (1979), pp. 265ff.
23. Michael Hechter, *Internal Colonialism* (London: Routledge and Kegan Paul, 1975), passim; Donald Horowitz, "Three Dimensions of Ethnic Politics," *World Politics* 23: 2 (1971); and Nathan Glazer and Daniel P. Moynihan (eds.), *Ethnicity: Theory and Experience* (Cambridge, Mass.: Harvard University Press, 1979), e.g. p. 7.
24. *The Economist* (Nov. 3, 1979), Survey, p. 7.
25. Jack E. Reece, "Internal Colonialism: the case of Brittany," *Ethnic and Racial Studies* 2: 3 (1979), p. 283. Also, in Chapter 3 Edmond Orban points out the effect of rising expectations on the extent of alienation from the state.
26. Charles Kindleberger, "Size of Firm and Size of Nation," in John H. Dunning (ed.), *Economic Analysis and the Multinational Enterprise* (New York: Praeger, 1974); Assar Lindbeck, "The Changing Role of the National State," *Kyklos* 28: 1 (1975).
27. Characteristic features of modernization are secularization, urbanization, the spread of education, the growing influence of the mass media, and shifts away from traditional and ascriptive norms to those of bureaucracy and achievement.
28. Jorge Niosi, *Canadian Capitalism: A Study of Power in the Canadian Business Establishment* (Toronto: Lorimer, 1981), p. 67.
29. B. Bruce-Briggs (ed.), *The New Class?* (Toronto: McGraw-Hill Ryerson, 1979), p. 5.
30. For a discussion of the general impact of growth of this new middle class in various western systems, see Ronald Inglehart, "The Silent Revolution in Europe," *American Political Science Review* 65: 4 (1971) , pp. 991-1017; "Post-Materialism in an Environment of Security," *American Political Science*

Review 75: 4 (1981); and *The Silent Revolution* (Princeton, N.J.: Princeton University Press, 1977); Alvin Gouldner, *The Future of Intellectuals and the Rise of the New Class* (New York: Seabury Press, 1979).

31. Kenneth McRoberts and Dale Posgate, *Quebec: Social Change and Political Crisis*, rev. ed. (Toronto: McClelland and Stewart, 1980), p. 109.
32. James Ian Gow, "La Modernisation et l'administration publique," in Edmond Orban (ed.), *La modernisation politique du Québec* (Sillery, Que.: Boréal Express, 1976), p. 167.
33. McRoberts and Posgate, op. cit., p. 139.
34. *Globe and Mail* Report on Business (April 7, 1982), p. B3.
35. Albert Breton, "The Economics of Nationalism," *Journal of Political Economy* 72 (1964), p. 385; McRoberts and Posgate, op. cit., p. 138.
36. William Hagy, "Quebec Separatists: The First Twelve years," *Queen's Quarterly* 76: 2 (1969), pp. 234-35; *Globe and Mail* (Oct. 18, 1969), p. 1.
37. Richard Hamilton and Maurice Pinard, "The Bases of Parti Québécois Support in Recent Elections," *Canadian Journal of Political Science* 9: 1 (1976), pp. 3-26; see also McRoberts and Posgate, op. cit., p. 187.
38. McRoberts and Posgate, op. cit., p. 189.
39. Brand, p. 86.
40. Drucker and Brown, p. 33.
41. Drucker and Brown, p. 38; Ragin, p. 633.
42. William R. Beer, "Ethnic Activities in Contemporary France: Social Class and Social Mobility," *Europa Ethnica* 32: 2 (1978), pp. 50-58.
43. George Armstrong Kelly, "Belgium: New Nationalism in an Old World," *Comparative Politics* 1: 3 (1969), p. 358.
44. Anthony Mughan, "Modernization and Ethnic Conflict in Belgium," *Political Studies* 27: 1 (1979), p. 34; François Nielsen, "The Flemish Movement in Belgium after World War II," *American Sociological Review* 45: 1 (1980), p. 89.
45. P.J. Augustinus Ter Hoeven, "The Social Bases of Flemish Nationalism," *International Journal of the Sociology of Language* 15 (1978), p. 23.
46. Ronald Inglehart, "The Silent Revolution," p. 1011.
47. Mughan, p. 37.
48. Xavier Mabille, "Les élections législative du 8 novembre, 1981," Parts 1 and 2, *Courrier Hebdomadaire du C.R.I.S.P.*, 943-944 (Dec. 1981).
49. Robert P. Clark, *The Basques: The Franco Years and Beyond* (Reno: University of Nevada Press, 1979), pp. 246-47.
50. Smith, *Nationalism in the Twentieth Century*, p. 25.

Chapter 5/Disputed Claims: Quebec/Canada

Stanley B. Ryerson

The transfer to Canada on April 17, 1982, of a modified version of the 1867 British North America Act, with the sanction and in the presence of the Queen, has been hailed as ending "the last vestiges of the colonial relationship between Canada and Britain."[1] For some, it constituted the resolution at long last of our "crisis of Confederation." A trifle hasty, this, for on June 23, 1982, the Québec National Assembly enacted Bill 62, removing from the purview of the new Canadian Constitution (1982) those areas of Quebec law on which it encroached. Put plainly, this was a gesture of defiance of a Constitution held by the Government of Quebec to be illegitimate—and unconstitutional. True, it was mitigated defiance: Quebec's rejection of the jurisdiction of the Constitution Act of 1982 took the form of invoking Section 33, the "notwithstanding" or opting-out clause of that very act. This sort of ambiguity remains characteristic of the whole constitutional hassle.

In the twelvemonth since, signs multiplied, foreshadowing a determined push by Ottawa for enhancement of the central power, with corresponding shrinkage of that of provinces and regions. A centripetal shift, enlarging the scope of federal jurisdiction: such is the sense of Ottawa's vision of "renovated federalism." "Reprise du débat constitutionnel" ran a heading in *La Presse,* July 23, 1983: editorialist Marcel Adam enumerated areas of contention over the distribution of powers, the Commission on Economic Union, the joint committee on Senate reform. To the foregoing one might add the straws in the wind from Ottawa pointing towards enlarged assertion of federal jurisdictional claims relating to such diverse areas as offshore mineral rights, energy-sources control, microcomputers, cable TV. Such was indeed to be expected, following on the nationalist defeat in the 1980 Quebec referendum on sovereignty-association. Indeed, the Constitution Act of 1982 was the first major step in the aftermath of the federalist success. Its tenor and implications cannot be fully grasped unless one puts this constitutional "patriation" in context—historical, cultural, socioeconomic, political—with particular emphasis on what, of the past, has persisting relevance for our puzzles of the present.

> The question of federalism lies today at the very heart of the conflict which places Ottawa and Quebec in opposition. If Canada had been a state of unitary form or, if Quebec had wittingly agreed to disappear as an autonomous political body, no such conflict would have been possible.[2]

Federalism, as the *Tremblay Report* makes clear, "means a regime of association as opposed to a unitary regime." In the case of British North America, there were associated, in forms that varied, entities that were both ethnic and regional in character. And the state framework within which they had their being was that of Empire. Following the Conquest of 1763, issues of contention arose in the following spheres:

- Autonomy of the colonies vs. imperial authority; self-government
- Democracy vs. oligarchic rule
- Equal rights of nationalities
- Property, land, trade, industry.

Chronologically or schematically, the path of development was roughly this:

- 1774: the Quebec Act accords to the Catholic French Canadians the right to retain their identity (language, religion, land tenure, laws) in exchange for allegiance to Britain, threatened with revolt from the colonies to the south. A clerical-seigneurial class bloc with British colonial elite sets the sociopolitical pattern for over a century.
- 1791: Constitutional Act creates representative elective Assemblies; with Loyalist immigration, Upper Canada and Lower Canada form colonial provinces, one English-speaking, the other predominantly French.
- 1837-39: a quarter-century of struggle in the Canadas for control of executive powers by the assemblies, against land monopolies, imperial coercion by Downing Street, for equal rights and ultimately independence culminates in armed uprisings in both provinces; suppression by British troops; constitution of Lower Canada suspended.
- 1841: Act of Union merges Upper Canada and Lower Canada into the "Province of Canada," with Anglo majority, attempt to proscribe French in the new Assembly. London-based finance operation to underwrite canal building and promote imperial commerce.
- 1848: granting of "responsible government," restoring equal language rights of French, result of democratic popular pressure and turn to free-trade liberalism in Britain. Baldwin-LaFontaine ministry heads "double majority," from areas of former Upper and Lower Canada.
- 1867: federal union of provinces of Canada, New Brunswick, and Nova Scotia; British North America Act of the imperial Parliament. Division anew of "Province of Canada" into Ontario and Quebec.

From 1763 to 1867, the association of the scattered British North American colonies resided in their common allegiance to the crown, with the Governor General embodying its imperial authority. The nature and substance of this association were to evolve with the changing relationships of merchant empire, colonial commerce, emergent industrialism. Politically, the crucial areas of change—democracy, self-government, national equality—found expression in constitutional laws and customary practices. Thus, from 1791 on, representative parliamentary institutions are in being: rudimentary, limited, but with potentialities for enlargement.

The existence of the assemblies allows a measure of representation of popular opinion, while keeping well out of reach of the electors and their deputies the closely guarded preserve of executive power. The crown and its representative, with the aid of appointed councillors, embody the state function of class and colonial rule. In this colonial, class society, it has taken mass popular pressure (reinforced by the weight of democratic tradition born of earlier struggles in Britain and America) to win the right to vote.

It was to take further decades of struggle, including unsuccessful rebellions in each of the two Canadas, to establish some limited measure of majority control over the executive: "responsible government." This was the requirement (established in 1848) that the ministry be answerable to a majority of the assembly and hold office only so long as it enjoyed majority support. A cornerstone of parliamentary democracy, this element of "majority rule" has never been inscribed in the law of the Canadian (or the British) constitution. It is a "convention." But, as our Supreme Court recently recalled (we shall return to this point in a related connection), "It should be borne in mind . . . that while they are not laws, some conventions may be more important than some laws."[3] Cited as the pivotal constitutional value in the convention "relating to responsible government, is the democratic principle: the powers of the state must be exercised in accordance with the wishes of the electorate."[4]

Early colonial democracy had to contend with the entrenched class powers of property of the merchant magnates and large landowners backed by the imperial authorities overseas. Interwoven with class was nationality. First, by reason of colonialism itself, as more and more English-speaking settlers experienced the conflict of interest between the development of their own community and the burden of imperial interests and constraints, they came to demand with growing insistence—after the War of 1812 particularly—autonomy, self-government, even independence. They saw themselves, in opposition to Downing Street, as *Canadians*. (This dimension of national identity versus an external, "baneful domination" was to reappear a century or so later in Canadian resistance to the encroachments of the new world-dominant military-industrial empire of the United States.)

A more intense and pervasive national consciousness was that of the French Canadian. Theirs from the outset was the experience of an imperial/colonial relationship of domination through conquest; it was subsequently to be paralleled, in part at least, by the English-Canadian dependency and pressure for colonial self-government. As the following passages from Alexis de Tocqueville's journal indicate, the asymmetric pattern that emerged included both an element of solidarity (versus external dominance) and a profound cleavage and tension born of inequality as between the two nation communities whose identity and duality were recognized by the dividing line of 1791[5]:

> The basic population and the vast majority everywhere are French. But it is easy to see that the French are the conquered people. The wealthy classes belong for the most part to the English race. Although French is the language spoken almost universally, most newspapers, posters, even the signboards of French merchants, are in English. To them belong almost all the commercial enterprises. They are truly the ruling class in Canada.
>
> —August 25, 1831
>
> Lower Canada (happily for the French . . .) forms a state apart. Now, in Lower Canada the French population is to the English proportionately ten to one. It has its government, its own Parliament. It veritably forms the body of a distinct nation.
>
> In the towns, English and Canadians form two societies. The English display considerable wealth: among the *Canadiens* there are but very limited fortunes . . . The English control the whole of foreign trade and manage all the domestic commerce . . .
>
> —September 1, 1831
>
> The *Canadiens* form a people apart in America, a people in possession of a distinct and lively nationality, a young, healthy people, with military origins, having its own language, religion, laws and customs, which is more cohesive than any other population of the New World, which can be vanquished but not forcibly fused with the Anglo-American race. Time alone might bring about that result, but not legislation nor the sword.
>
> —January 3, 1838

In different ways, the 1774 Quebec Act and the 1791 creation of Lower Canada as a province with a francophone majority had each constituted recognition of a community of distinct nationality within the structure of colonial power. Efforts to blunt or annul that recognition, or somehow cancel the conditions that had made it necessary, were many and varied.

The rationale for a union that promised the swamping of the French in an English-dominated Canada—such is the burden of Lord Durham's Report of 1839[6]:

> If the British Government intends to maintain its hold of the Canadas, it can rely on the English population alone . . . The French Canadians . . . are but the remains of an ancient colonization, and are and ever must be isolated in the midst of an Anglo-Saxon world. Whatever may happen, whatever government shall be established over them, British or American, they can see no hope for their nationality . . . it is but a question of time and mode; it is but to determine whether the small number of French who now inhabit Lower Canada shall be made English, under a Government which can protect them, or whether the process shall be delayed until a much larger number shall have to undergo, at the rude hands of its uncontrolled rivals, the extinction of a nationality strengthened and embittered by continuance.
>
> And is this French Canadian nationality one which, for the good merely of that people, we ought to strive to perpetuate, even if it were

> possible? I know of no national distinctions marking and continuing a more hopeless inferiority . . . it is to elevate them from that inferiority that I desire to give to the Canadians our English character.
>
> —Lord Durham on the Canadas, 1839

Extinction of the French-Canadian identity appears as the indispensable precondition for colonial self-government. Whether peaceably or forcibly, assimilation must occur. Should the Canadians persist in resisting anglicization (linguistic and religious alike), then a highly explosive prospect lies ahead. As though His Lordship, being endowed with second sight, had a clear presentiment of something like the October Crisis of 1970, he left us this admonition concerning the *Canadiens*:

> If they attempt to better their condition by extending themselves over the neighbouring country, they will necessarily get more and more mingled with an English population: if they prefer remaining stationary, the greater part of them must be labourers in the employ of English capitalists. In either case it would appear, that the great mass of the French Canadians are doomed, in some measure, to occupy an inferior position, and to be dependent on the English for employment. The evils of poverty and dependence would merely be aggravated in a ten-fold degree, by a spirit of jealous and resentful nationality, which should separate the working-class of the community from the possessors of wealth and employers of labour.[7]

What will become of a community, Durham seems to be asking, in which "the evils of poverty and dependence" of workers in the employ of capital are compounded by national inferiority and oppression, with class cleavage coinciding with that of nationality? He continues, "Complaints of distress are constant, and the deterioration of the condition of a great part of the population admitted on all hands. A people so circumstanced must alter their mode of life."

The meshing of tensions of nationality and class remarked on by Tocqueville as well as Durham was central to the sociopolitical crisis of that time. It is no stranger to our own.

The Dominion of Canada took form as an imperial project, worked out in conjunction with the political and business elites of the colonial provinces. Trade routes of Empire, traversing British North America by telegraph and rail would serve to link London with Hong Kong and Shanghai. A union *a mari usque ad mare* entailed railways: the agreements on federation were to include building the Intercolonial Railway to the Atlantic, the CPR to the Pacific. Capitalist development in Canada required political unification. "Railways are my politics" was Sir Allan MacNab's motto in the 1850s, Sir John A. Macdonald's practice in the 1870s, with the "Pacific Scandal." Capitalist industrialization was underway, and the "last spike" driven on the CPR in 1885 marked the completion of its infrastructure. That year also saw the execution of Louis Riel: the first major crisis of Confederation.

What, actually was the nature of the agreement of 1867? Posed afresh a century later, with the rise of a strong Quebec nationalist movement calling for a restructuring (at the very least) of the Canadian state, the question of its origins and legitimacy is once more relevant. The old controversy has revived over whether Confederation was a kind of treaty or "compact" among its historical constituents, or else solely a statute law of the Parliament at Westminster. The answer to this question becomes crucial when constitutional amendment is at stake: is prior agreement of the provinces a requisite of change to the BNA Act?

Thus, in the Supreme Court proceedings of September 1981, it was argued that no such prior consent is called for, since the BNA Act was no "treaty," but an imperial statute. Moreover, the provinces were themselves not sovereign entities, but mere colonial dependencies. In terms of law, the argument holds. But the Constitution is broader than the law; "summarized in an equation: constitutional conventions plus constitutional law equal the total Constitution of the country." So runs the majority decision of the court on "Constitutional Convention."[8]

Could it then be that the legal enactment of 1867 was in fact the product of long-drawn-out negotiations and tractates involving representatives of provinces, regions, and even nationalities? That the choice of the federal rather than the unitary principle expressed agreement on a compromise? Despite complexity of issues, agreement was indeed arrived at. There took place a union of provinces and regions. Legislative union or federation? Maritimes regional particularism weighed in favour of the latter. There was to be an association of nationalities or "nation communities" of "French" and "English." The former would insist on federation (if not on the looser form of a confederacy, favoured by A.A. Dorion and the left-liberal *rouges*). Macdonald and the leading Montreal business interests shared a preference for legislative union, the unitary state. But in Macdonald's words, "We found that such a system was impracticable. In the first place it would not meet the assent of the people of Lower Canada . . . being a minority with a different language, nationality and religion from the majority . . . it was found that any proposition which involved the absorption of the individuality of Lower Canada . . . would not be received with favour by her people."[9]

In *The Road to Confederation*, Donald Creighton quotes Macdonald as urging that "the Conservatives must learn to recognize and respect not only the multiple religious divisions of Canada West, but also the single basic cultural division between English-speaking and French-speaking Canada . . . [Macdonald] was prepared to accept the cultural duality of Canadian life, to recognize that what was in form a unitary province was in fact a half-acknowledged federal state. The union could only be preserved by series of compromises and conventions which sanctioned this cultural duality."[10]

The time was in the 1850s; the place, the Province of Canada. Shortly before, the constitutional convention of ministerial responsibility—"responsible government"—had been achieved by the combined Reform forces under LaFontaine and Baldwin, spokesmen of the mass democratic demand for change in both sections of the province, francophone and anglophone. Recognition of duality on a footing of national equality might likewise acquire the status of an established constitutional convention. A step in that direction was restoration of the French-majority province that Lower Canada had been till its effacement in 1841. Its reemergence as the province of Quebec was a manifestation of the "compact" in action as historical reality.

> For French Canada, the real benefit of Confederation was the provision of a range of powers, limited but sacrosanct, over its own affairs. It meant that the Province of Quebec could serve as a concrete political unit, protected by the Constitution, in which the French-Canadian community could be clearly dominant and thus have a chance to survive on its own terms. Confederation also entailed a risk, since, at the federal level, French Canadians were relegated to the position of a permanent minority, where their rights and powers were subject to the actions of the Anglo-Canadian majority.[11]

The benefit—and the risk. Precarious "compact," never spelled out, never adopted wholly. In light of the experience of two world wars and two world economic crises, the meaning of dominance of the central power has been made apparent. The Anglo-Canadian version of its "national unity" prevails. J.R. Mallory has suggested that Canada might be more accurately described as "two federal systems": one, juridically speaking, a federation of provinces that could in time develop into a unitary state "as the geographical barriers to efficient large scale administration were overcome, and the 'nationalizing' effects of education, the communications media and increasing mobility of the population eroded regional sentiments." In another sense, the union is not a federation of provinces at all, but a union of the two "founding peoples." A view "widely accepted by French Canadians in Quebec, is that Canada is a binational state in which the federal government epitomizes the 'national state' for English-speaking Canadians, but that the only acceptable 'national state' for French Canadians is the province of Quebec."[12]

Between these two approaches there is political deadlock. Hegemony of the Anglo-Canadian corporate business bloc, after 1970, 1980, and 1982, appears to stand unshaken, capable now of taking the offensive. Yet the mass movement voicing "French-Canadian aspirations for ethnic, cultural, and political self-determination"[13] has made a vital difference. The fact of a new affirmation of francophone democratic will to achieve a changed sociopolitical relationship with anglophone Canada; the establishment in Quebec of a government whose object, sovereignty-association, goes historically in the sense of the "*Maîtres chez nous*" and "*Egalité ou indépendance*" of the Quiet Revolution; the posing for the first time ever, in the Referendum, of the issue of a change in the status of Quebec (with one francophone elector out of every two voting in the affirmative)—all this has altered the climate. In English-speaking Canada, there have been intimations of a readiness to rethink some ancient fears and prejudices. In the Quebec labour movement, present only to a limited degree on the national equality issue, the urgent need for a labour/national-democratic bloc, hinted at but never achieved, calls for a radical rethinking of the dogmatic anti-nationalism that has been zealously spread by neo-marxists, to the visible satisfaction of the big-business federalist right.

It is rather as though history had caught us, in this time of systems in crisis, revolution of technologies, and menace of thermonuclear extermination, with two particularly acute problems (among several!). Both derive, in the case of Canada/Quebec, from what could well be termed underdeveloped democratization:

- "Responsible government," as the answerability of those holding power to the elected representatives of the people, is a principle that is supposed to pervade democratic society, but its operation stops at the plant gate. The idea of extending it to the point where the existing irresponsible autocracy of great property, of profiteering corporate business enterprise works its will on society—that would be a considerable development of societal democracy.
- A "compact of association as equals": this sense of a historic "convention of the Constitution" has surfaced uncertainly, intermittently; it was hinted at in Lester Pearson's statement that "Quebec is in a sense the homeland of a people"[14]; in the Bilingualism and Biculturalism Commission's reference to the right of self-determination as an issue of political equality; it is clearly involved in the Supreme Court's majority decision on prior provincial consultation on Constitutional amendment as being indeed a "convention," its omission entailing illegitimacy and unconstitutionality (even though technically "legal"). It will be interesting to see what their stand will be on Quebec's claim in its own right, as against that of "provinces in general," since this is crucial to the "compact as between nationalities" case.

  What has happened, of course, is that the ambiguous structure of the 1867 Constitution has provided the mechanism for preserving Anglo dominance in the guise of a legalized centralizing quasi federalism. The power of big capital, Canadian satellite of the American military-industrial elite, "manages" the cycle of boom and bust, the dependent operation of the new technologies, the commercialization of popular culture. Against this overweening power, only a democratic alignment of the forces of labour and culture, in all areas of our collective being, could possibly prevail.

  The issues of women's rights and full equality weigh in the scales of history on the side of democratization. So do those of environment, the saving of our surroundings that are our means to life. And the averting of the final war.

In the "new Constitution," if the rights of native peoples—Indian, Inuit, and Métis—for the first time find recognition (however verbal), it is because of mass struggles from Labrador and James Bay to the Mackenzie Valley and the Pacific.[15] When American transnational petroleum operations trample a promise to obtain "prior consent" of the Dene people, is the natives' resistance to be understood as national struggle or struggle of social class or of community? Of course it is all of these; and only in such a spirit will we advance toward democratization on the scale of society itself.

Notes

1. *The Supreme Court Decisions on the Constitution* (Toronto: Lorimer, 1981), p. vii.
2. D. Kwavnick (ed.), *The Tremblay Report* (Toronto: McClelland and Stewart, 1977), p. 80.
3. *The Supreme Court*, op. cit., p. 93.
4. Alexis De Tocqueville, *Voyage aux Etats-Unis et en Sicile*, 1831.
5. Ibid., p. 90.
6. G.M. Craig (ed.), *Lord Durham's Report* (Toronto: McClelland and Stewart, 1969), pp. 148-49.
7. Ibid., p. 150.
8. *The Supreme Court*, p. 94.
9. P.B. Waite (ed.), *The Confederation Debates in the Province of Canada, 1865* (Toronto: McClelland and Stewart, 1963), p. 29.
10. Donald Creighton, *The Road to Confederation: The Emergence of Canada, 1863-1867* (Toronto: Macmillan, 1964), p. 145.
11. K. McRoberts and D. Posgate, *Quebec, Social Change and Political Crisis* (Toronto: McClelland and Stewart, 1981), p. 32.
12. J.R. Mallory, *The Structure of Canadian Government* (Toronto: Macmillan, 1971), pp. 393-94.
13. E. McWhinney, *Quebec and the Constitution, 1960-1978* (Toronto: University of Toronto Press, 1979), p. vii.
14. Speech of January 5, 1964; cf. Peter Stursberg, *Lester Pearson and the Dream of Unity* (Toronto: Doubleday, 1978), p. 198.
15. Jean Morisset, *Les chiens s'entre-dévorent . . . indiens, blancs et métis dans le grand nord canadien* (Montreal: Nouvelle Optique, 1977), pp. 220-24.

Part II/The National Question and Social Classes

The focus shifts to the relationships between the national question and social classes.

Whitaker presents a survey of political development in Quebec, with special emphasis on the forms of Quebec nationalism and their relation to class structure and the Quebec economy. The emergence of the Parti Québécois and the rise and fall of the idea of sovereignty-association is given special consideration. Also, the challenges posed to the PQ by the new constitution and the strains of economic recession are assessed.

In her first article, Legaré offers an overview of the contributions made by leftist intellectuals regarding the role of social classes in Quebec since the beginning of the Quiet Revolution. Her second essay addresses the claim that the struggles of classes and social movements have been united through the PQ, which represents, in effect, a historical agent capable of introducing a new matrix of social relations. She believes in the recently acquired importance of the noninstitutionalized cultural voices in search of a collective identity.

Finally, Bourque argues that any understanding of Quebec society needs to be situated in its Canadian context. The author also shows that a narrow single-class analysis cannot fully account for Quebec political reality. He asserts that the PQ will not lead Quebec to independence, although the national queston will continue to have a high profile as one of Canada's regional questions.

Chapter 6/The Quebec Cauldron: A Recent Account*

Reginald A. Whitaker

The Quiet Revolution, the FLQ, "bilingualism and biculturalism," "special status," "égalité ou indépendance," the 1970 October Crisis and the War Measures Act, the Parti Québécois and "sovereignty-association," the May 1980 referendum—for 20 years Quebec has been constantly in the headlines, a bomb always seemingly about to explode, an enigma and a question mark always hovering on the Canadian horizon. "What does Quebec want?" has become a cliché of English-Canadian political discourse in the 1960s and 1970s, and no doubt will continue through the 1980s. It is surely impossible, if not absurd, to try to understand the dynamic and the rhythm of Canadian political development without understanding the forces which have gone into the Quebec upheaval.

The first problem is inherent in the question, what does Quebec want? With remarkable consistency, while working at complete cross-purposes, both the Quebec nationalists and their English-Canadian opponents have operated on the assumption that there is something called "Quebec"—a monolithic, collective leviathan that speaks with the united voice of six million Québécois. Whether as a mythical construct of nationalist yearnings or the equally mythical nightmare of anglophone bigotry, "Quebec" does not in reality have a concrete, material existence any more than does "Canada." This is not to say that one cannot speak of a Quebec nation, which we surely can; nor does it mean that we cannot speak of Quebec nationalism as a force and a passion that far surpasses Canadian nationalism, for it certainly does. It is to say that the dynamic of events in Quebec, the explanation of the vast changes during the past two decades, can only be understood when "Quebec" is viewed as a forum or framework within which conflict and struggle between contending forces, class, linguistic, and ethnic, have taken place and continue to take place. Far from being a monolith, Quebec's extraordinary dynamic in recent years derives from its status as a battleground for conflicts perhaps more bitter and more profound than the contentions that have riven English Canada.

Any analysis of Quebec that locates events solely within the framework of nationalism tends to be tautological and ultimately void of explanatory power. Nationalism, in the sense of a strong feeling of national identity and, at least since 1960, a tendency to formulate demands on the political system grounded in concepts of the national interest, is a force that permeates almost

---

*This paper is an updated version of an article published in M.S. Whittington and G. Williams (eds.), *Canadian Politics in the 1980s* (Toronto: Methuen, 1981).

all areas of Quebec life and cuts across class and other social divisions. But to explain why Quebec has become such a disruptive and contentious force within the Canadian Confederation since 1960, "nationalism" tells us very little. After all, Quebec nationalism can be truthfully called a constant of Quebec history. The real question is why nationalism has taken the particular forms it has assumed since 1960. And to answer that question, one must examine the conflicting forces at work within Quebec and how various formulations of nationalism have expressed the class and other interests of these conflicting forces. Thus, when one analyst of Quebec politics writes that the Parti Québécois is not merely a party but "the embodiment of the national identity and the collective will,"[1] he is writing nonsense. And those who assumed that the evolution of Quebec was an inevitable, irresistible flowering of the Quebec nation into the status of sovereignty failed to remember that history is innocent of "inevitabilities" imposed on it by ideologists. At the same time, it would be equally fallacious (and equally tempting to those seeking simple answers) to assume that the 60% "no" vote in the 1980 referendum means that "Quebec" has singlemindedly rejected sovereignty-association and the independence option. The forces continue to contend and the options remain open.

Let us begin where Quebec itself begins as a nation—with the Conquest of New France by the British in 1763. A possible fate of the French-speaking Catholic inhabitants was assimilation or worse by their English-speaking Protestant conquerors. After all, such has indeed been the fate of numerous other people unlucky enough to have fallen under foreign military domination. In the event, the French language and certain French customs, such as the civil code, were preserved, along with the Catholic Church and the educational system, which went along with the Church's domination of Quebec cultural life. As a result, what had begun as a tiny colony four centuries ago is today a modern, wealthy, and confident nation poised, many would say, at the brink of national sovereignty. This long odyssey from conquered colony to a nation within the Canadian Confederation might seem to speak well of the tolerance and generosity of the conquerors. In fact it rather speaks more strongly of the courage and tenacity of this small people who would not give up what has made them distinctive in North America. For the survival of Quebec, and of French Canada, has been above all a story of *resistance* to pressures for assimilation or repression, resistance that has forced the English and then the English-speaking Canadians to make compromises and concessions over time that have taken form in various shifting accommodations. The simple reality of New France at the time of the Conquest was, as Pierre Trudeau once wrote, that the French were too weak to become themselves an independent nation, yet too strong to be crushed by the conquerors. There is a sense in which this basic paradox has remained true down to the present day.

By examining the bases of the various accommodations that have been arrived at over time, one can begin to understand the logic of Quebec's relation to Canada. And these accommodations have been above all economic accommodations of class alliances cutting across the two ethnic and linguistic communities. Following the Conquest, a tacit alliance was struck between the English military and the English-speaking merchants who had come in the wake of the Conquest, on the one hand, and the Catholic clergy and the seigneurial landlords who benefited from the feudal land-tenure system of New France. The core of this alliance was to be founded on a fateful tradeoff of mutual elite interests: the English were to be left formal political control and major economic activity—that is, the "dream" of opening up a transcontinental economy along the "empire of the St. Lawrence"—the clergy would be left with "cultural" matters, such as religion and education. This arrangement guaranteed that the two dominant elites of New France would retain their privileges, but at the expense of economic development. At the same time, the English bought economic superiority at the expense of leaving the major institutions of the conquered people intact. Under these circumstances, Quebec would find it difficult to develop the indigenous bourgeoisie so necessary for autonomous capitalist development and would be saddled with elites who depended on the English and who had a vested interest in fostering economic backwardness and political subservience among the mass of the population.

The first and greatest manifestation of discontent spilling over into revolution against the English came with the rebellions of 1837-38, which were much more serious and sustained than the rebellion in Upper Canada, where discontent lacked the reinforcement of ethnic division. But the rebellions themselves were the desperate product of a growing resistance symbolized by the deadlock in the government of the colony between the ruling anglophone clique and the assembly dominated by francophones. The latter group were led by a class element generated by the anomalies of the accommodation referred to above: professionals such as lawyers and doctors who had been educated above their largely peasant origins but who could find no place in the state administration controlled by anglophone patronage. Forced to return to their places of origin, these "new middle class" elements remained close to the people but had the voice and education to agitate on behalf of French grievances in the assembly.

When worsening economic conditions and growing reaction among the English and the ruling clique finally forced matters to open rebellion, left and right were further polarized within the rebellious *Patriote* movement itself. Just as in the American Revolution over a half-century earlier, events drove many rebels toward more radical liberal and democratic views—although in this case always within the context of a strong sense of nationalism, which reinforced in some *Patriotes* a radical drive to overthrow the internal elites who were perpetuating their national subservience.

The movement failed, however, to develop the kind of mass base that could eventually drive out the English. The final defeat of the rebellion in 1838 had fateful consequences: not only did it confirm English hegemony in

Quebec, but it also confirmed the dominance of the Church over Quebec life, a dominance that was to last for well over a century. For this period, French-Canadian nationalism was largely stripped of the liberal-democratic promise of 1837 and was instead characterized by social and political conservatism, under the close tutelage of the Church, which had become perforce the only institutionalized defender of the French language and culture. The general aversion of clerical nationalism to anything smacking of economic "radicalism" left the English-speaking capitalists more or less free reign. And the latter were only too happy to leave the Church in charge of educating a population that was more and more to provide a cheap and docile labour force for English, American, and English-Canadian capital.

At the same time, French Canadians were showing considerable skill in using English parliamentary institutions to ensure national survival. The legislative union of Upper and Lower Canada in 1840 was designed to sink the francophone majority in Lower Canada into an overall minority, but this scheme immediately foundered on the capacity of the French members to act as a cohesive ethnic bloc which had to be accommodated by the warring partisan factions among the anglophone members, if they wished to form a government. It was partially out of a desire to break this stranglehold that anglophone politicians finally agreed to set out on the road to the Confederation agreement of 1867, but along the way they were forced to concede provincial status to Quebec, along with considerable powers over education and culture, and recognition of the French language in Quebec at least.

Moreover, it was soon apparent that in practice a French-Canadian presence would have to be granted in the makeup of the federal cabinet and other federal institutions, since any national government without Quebec support would prove precarious. Yet the old economics-culture tradeoff, implicit in the tacit bargain struck after the Conquest and made explicit in the provisions of the BNA Act—which granted almost all important economic responsibilities and all important revenue sources to the national government—was itself reinforced in the elite accommodation of the cabinet: until the 1960s no important economic portfolio was given to a French-Canadian minister. Indeed, it was well over a century until a francophone was appointed minister of finance, in the late 1970s. In addition, the two greatest crises of English-French relations in Canada's first half-century—the hanging of Louis Riel and the imposition of conscription on an unwilling Quebec population during the First World War—demonstrated that the west would be an exclusively anglophone preserve (thus clearly tilting the balance of Confederation) and that, when an issue sharply divided the two communities, the English majority would always win. These events also sealed the fate of the Conservative party as a vehicle of accommodation of francophone political elites, thus ultimately ensuring that only one party, the Liberals, could effectively play this role.

By the early 20th century, two main variants of nationalist ideology had emerged. One was symbolized by Henri Bourassa, politician, journalist and founder of *Le Devoir*; the other by the historian, Canon Lionel Groulx. The former was founded on the vision of *French Canada* and saw the best protection for the French-Canadian nation in equal partnership with English Canada along bilingual and bicultural lines. The latter variant increasingly saw *Quebec* as the only viable basis of French-Canadian nationhood and often looked to right-wing corporatist and authoritarian movements as the way to success—as opposed to the more liberal politics of Bourassa. Yet both variants finally failed to address themselves to the real core of the problem of French-Canadian inferiority: their economic subservience. And it must be said that Bourassa's pan-Canadian liberalism, just as much as Groulx's more inward-looking nationalism, drove English Canadians to near violent opposition—as during the First World War conscription crisis.

Consequently, by the 1940s and 1950s Quebec was increasingly the scene of insupportable contradictions. The francophone majority was manifestly worse off than the anglophone minority by virtually any measure one wished to use. At the same time they were mired in an ideology that had little or no connection with reality, a backward-looking rural vision of Catholic and anti-materialist values. The irony was that Quebec had early in the century become the most heavily urbanized of all the Canadian provinces. Yet in this case urbanization did not mean modernization; instead, it meant the aggregation of a cheap labour force for English-Canadian and American capital.

There was a saying that in Quebec capital speaks English and labour speaks French. This not only caught the essence of the situation, but also indicated exactly how, in the long run, class and nationality would become mutually reinforcing characteristics. But so long as the traditional elites—the clergy, the politicians, and the local notables and petty bourgeoisie—kept up their tacit alliance with English-Canadian capital and the Canadian state, the situation remained frozen. Thus, under Maurice Duplessis' Union Nationale government (1936-1939, 1944-1960), political corruption, patronage, and intimidation helped maintain a regime that in fact challenged capital and the Canadian state only at the rhetorical level. Rural votes were mobilized to maintain a regime that was turning its energies to selling out Quebec's natural resources and encouraging industry seeking low labour costs.

Yet enormous changes were in the making. The 1949 asbestos strike drew 5,000 miners out in defiance not only of the American company but also of the Duplessis government in a four-month confrontation widely viewed at the time as quasi revolutionary, and which drew the support of a number of journalists, labour leaders, and academics—presaging in a small but dramatic way the coming cataclysm of the 1960s.

This was on the surface. Underneath were far-reaching changes in the very structure of Quebec society. As industrialization and urbanization proceeded, it was inevitable that the political and ideological superstructure would suffer increasing tension and pressure from new forces with no place in the antiquated world of politics. Corporate capital requires a certain kind of labour force; it also requires a growing middle stratum of technical and professional white-collar workers. Slowly, inefficiently, the Quebec educational system was beginning to respond to the demand for more technical, professional, and commercial skills.

Yet the emergent new middle class found precious little scope for their ambitions and talents. The corporate world was strongly anglophone and largely impervious to the advancement of francophones past the middle range, at best. The Canadian state presented an equally hostile face. And the Quebec provincial state under Duplessis presented little scope to any technical-professional middle class, whether francophone or anglophone, since it avoided economic intervention of the Keynesian variety and left social programs to the Church and the private sector. In fact, it was very much in this latter location that the new middle class was taking shape. The Church-controlled educational and health sectors required the services of a growing number of lay persons with technical qualifications to staff the schools, hospitals, and other social institutions which in English Canada were under public jurisdiction. These persons were generally underpaid and had very little say in running the institutions they staffed. During the 1950s there was a notable increase in the number of Catholic lay organizations seeking a voice in the direction of their society. Much of this activity remained largely apolitical and well within the bounds of Catholic orthodoxy. Yet even in the 1950s—the era later became known as *la grande noirceur* (the dark ages)—there were those who began to question more deeply. The revue *Cité libre* carried on a long war with clerical and political reaction, featuring a roster of future "stars" of Quebec life in the 1960s and 1970s from Pierre Elliott Trudeau to future *indépendantiste* intellectuals. And the Quebec Liberal party, shut out by Duplessis as well as by the federal Liberal party in Ottawa, began a democratization of the party structures in the late 1950s, which had the effect of opening up the party to the new forces brewing beneath the surface.

The death of Maurice Duplessis in 1959 was like the breaking of a spell. First, the Union Nationale under Duplessis's successor, Paul Sauvé, appeared to be about to undergo changes itself, but Sauvé's untimely death left the UN without new direction, and in 1960 the Liberals under Jean Lesage returned to power after 16 years of opposition. For once, a change in government was much more than a mere change in faces at the top and patronage to supporters below. The Liberal victory signalled the Quiet Revolution, a massive *déblocage* that opened up Quebec's great springtime. The Lesage government drastically revised the role of the provincial government in Quebec life, from the nationalization of private hydroelectricity (under then-Liberal minister René Lévesque) to the secularization of the educational system, to the reform of the civil service, to the setting of a whole new host of demands on Confederation which shook Canadian federalism to its roots. But this was by no means a period of change from the top down. Political events moved to a new rhythm: the seething demands and desires of a population suddenly liberated from generations of constraint and backwardness. For a while it seemed as if everything was in question and that everything was possible. All the promise of modernity which had lain before English Canadians for so long appeared as a kind of revelation to this people so long repressed. Young people, intellectuals, and artists in particular responded: the early 1960s became a festival of innovation in culture and ideas. It also became a time of violence, when radical demands for independence took the form of demonstrations and even terrorist groups like the FLQ, which took to bombs.

Revolutions, quiet or otherwise, are in the nature of things more or less civil wars. Not everyone in Quebec was swept away by enthusiasm for what was happening. Many elements—particularly from the older, rural, and more traditional Quebec—were increasingly worried by the onrush of change and by their place in the new Quebec. In part this was masked by the fact that the new regime clothed its policies in the garb of nationalism, now given a brighter and more modern hue by a willingness to dispense with the age-old tacit bargain that had traded off economics for culture, and to make demands that struck at the very heart of the "unequal union," in Stanley Ryerson's phrase, of English and French in Canada. To this extent the Lesage Liberals were the most potent champions of the fundamental desire for national survival who had yet appeared on the scene; they were thus able to mobilize widespread support behind policies that might otherwise have proven highly divisive. In retrospect, however, it is apparent that the nationalism of the Quiet Revolution was above all a nationalism of the new middle class, who expressed their demands for a place in the sun in a language that was no doubt sincerely nationalist in its cultural identification but at the same time an expression of their self-interest as a class or, more precisely, a class fraction.

In fact, the entire logic of the modernization of the Quebec state and its transformation from a *laissez faire* operation of local notables to Keynesian interventionism was predicated on the ascent of the new middle class. Locked out from both the corporate world and the national state, the francophone middle class would build a state in Quebec that would be open to its talents. The nationalization of hydro, for example, created Hydro-Québec, a vast state enterprise staffed from top to bottom by a francophone technical and professional middle class. The reform of the civil service, the attack on the old patronage system of appointment, and the expansion of technical tasks on the state's agenda all served to transform the provincial state apparatus into a pole of attraction for ambitious young francophone university graduates. The demands of the Lesage Liberals for control of the pension plan and medicare legislation being introduced by the federal Liberal government in the 1960s arose not so much from a traditional Quebec aversion to state social services but from a desire to control the vast investment funds that come with such schemes so as to strategically influence the economic development of the province.

This *étatist* orientation not only effectively renegotiated the terms of accommodation between the elites of English and French Canada, but it also tended to redefine the very subject of nationalism itself. "French Canada" increasingly began to give way to "Quebec" in nationalist discourse. In part this reflected a realization that the future of francophone communities outside Quebec was dim and that efforts would be best concentrated on the one jurisdiction where francophones formed an indisputable majority and could control the machinery of government. But in a deeper sense it was a reflection on the ideological level of the fact of the Quebec state's emergence as a powerful bureaucratic actor on the Canadian stage. That nationalism would increasingly be seen as Quebec rather than French-Canadian nationalism symbolized the drawing together of nationalist ideology with the interests of the new middle class and other elements who saw their interests closely identified with the Quebec state. The interpretation of nationalism in generalized cultural or ethnic terms fails to grasp the specific class interests that had appropriated nationalist discourse for statist purposes.

If we accept this nationalist-statist discourse on its own terms, we simply see a kind of collective self-fulfillment, and *épanouissement* or flowering and the popular slogan *maîtres chez nous* (masters in our own house). In reality we find class conflict and the heightening of contradictions. Just who were to be the new *maîtres*? The 1960s saw the growth of working-class consciousness and increasing labour militancy, as the previously excluded workers sought their own share. Ironically, given the statist orientation of Quebec development, this increasing labour militancy bore most heavily on the swollen state sector, so that by the 1970s the political leadership in Quebec, including the PQ after 1976, found themselves in an adversarial position with the teachers and other organized state employees. It is impossible to disentangle the developing class consciousness of Quebec workers from their developing national consciousness; in many ways the two were mutually reinforcing phenomena. Yet it would also be a mistake to simply subsume working-class consciousness under the rubric of nationalism: first, because nationalist demands articulated by the working class always differ in significant ways from nationalist demands articulated by the new middle class; second, because the confrontation with the Quebec state as employer pitted working class francophones against a francophone elite, with both sides appealing to public opinion. This is a familiar enough scenario elsewhere in the western world, but it fits rather uneasily into a simplistic nationalist schema.

In fact, the Quebec union movement has displayed an even more adversarial attitude toward the Quebec state than many English-Canadian unions have displayed toward the federal or provincial states. This has remained true even when the PQ, closer to a social-democratic party than any previous provincial party, came to power. Why this should be so may become clearer when we examine the deepest failing of the Quiet Revolution and its successors, the inability to actually confront the structures of English-Canadian and American capital in any significant way. Apart from the nationalization of hydro, which indeed only followed the example of the Conservative government of Ontario that had created Ontario Hydro a half-century earlier, the Lesage Liberals did not make any real inroads into the power of capital. Like moderate reform governments everywhere, they were cowed by the necessity to maintain business confidence, to retain their credit rating in the bond markets, to encourage investment, and to prevent flights of capital and consequent disappearance of jobs.

The Quebec Liberal party was in no way a vehicle for the mobilization of a mass working-class movement that might have formed an alternative centre of pressure and direction. The long-term result was that *maîtres chez nous* became an empty slogan when matched against the commanding power of "foreign" capital in making the really crucial decisions about the shape of Quebec development. To be sure, the Quebec state gained a greater leverage than before in setting guidelines, regulating, and in exercising its own voice in deploying the investment funds it now controlled. But this was a long way from mastering the Quebec economy in the name of the people who elected the provincial government. It also meant that the Quiet Revolution ultimately satisfied neither the new-middle-class elite of strongly nationalist persuasion nor the working class who began more and more to see the Quebec state as an ally of their enemies, or in some cases as the enemy itself.

In any event the Lesage Liberals were themselves driven out of office in 1966 by a revivified Union Nationale under Daniel Johnson, who had quietly built up an alliance of all the elements in Quebec society that had reason to fear and mistrust the Liberal thrust toward modernization, especially in the rural areas and small towns. Johnson's problem, and that of his successor following his death, Jean-Jacques Bertrand, was an inability to construct a viable modern version of the old UN nationalism. With a social base in the old Quebec and no means of building a new base on the forces unleashed by the Quiet Revolution, the UN remained suspended uneasily between rhetorical nationalism and aggressive demands for equal partnership in Confederation. (*Egalité ou l'indépendance* was the name of a book that Johnson authored.) This came out most acutely in the crisis set off by the UN's attempt to enact language legislation with the ostensible purpose of strengthening the position of French: in fact, they ended by antagonizing both francophone and anglophone without meeting either set of demands.

Meanwhile, another event of historic significance had taken place in 1965 when Pierre Elliott Trudeau, Jean Marchand of the CSN union federation, and the journalist Gérard Pelletier announced their adherence to the federal Liberal party and were elected to Parliament in the federal election of that year. This act indicated in a dramatic way that the new middle class was by no means united in its nationalist ideology. Some elements of the provincial Liberals, such as René Lévesque, were clearly moving in the inexorable direction of *indépendantisme*, the logical result of the philosophy of *maîtres chez nous*. Trudeau, Marchand, and Pelletier went to Ottawa to create a federalist counterpole of attraction.

When Trudeau won the leadership of the Liberal party three years later and a landslide victory in the general election that followed, this became in effect the official policy of the national government. The passage of the Official Languages Act and the promotion of bilingualism in the federal civil service were two prongs of a policy of attempting to renegotiate a new basis of elite accommodation between English and French Canada. Another was the concerted attempt to revitalize the federal Liberal party in Quebec, to appoint francophones to economic portfolios in the cabinet hitherto reserved to anglophones, and to promote a francophone presence at the highest levels of the federal public service. Underlying all this was an ideological appeal to *French-Canadian* nationalism, as opposed to *Quebec* nationalism, and an appeal to the pride of francophones to seek their fulfillment within the wider sphere of a federal system in which the rights of the French language and French-Canadian culture would be guaranteed. The figure of Pierre Trudeau himself, the francophone who became one of Canada's most electorally successful prime ministers and a statesman of world status, was assiduously cultivated to symbolize the potential for French Canadians within the federal system. And, indeed, opinion polls over the last decade have consistently shown Trudeau to be the most respected public figure among francophone Québécois.

The new-found confidence in Ottawa was parlayed into a new toughness on behalf of federal interests in negotiation with Quebec governments, putting an end to the apparent slide of the Pearson Liberals toward giving Quebec *de facto* special status. In some ways, the Trudeau style rather belied the reality that Quebec did continue to be treated somewhat differently from other provinces, in recognition that it is, after all, in Trudeau's own phrase, the "homeland and centre of gravity of the French-Canadian nation." But there would be no *formal* recognition of special constitutional status: Trudeau has always been adamant on the fundamental philosophical point that the best guarantees of the French-Canadian language and culture are through *individual* rights, unlike recognition of *collective* rights, which would be discriminatory and illiberal.

When René Lévesque left the provincial Liberal party in 1967 to form a new group that ultimately became the Parti Québécois, he tended to take away with him not only the more nationalist elements of the Liberal party but also the more socially progressive as well. This left the Liberals as a much more right-wing group than before, as most of the dynamic thrust of the Quiet Revolution left with Lévesque. But it also served to realign Quebec politics. Lévesque incorporated two fringe groupings, the RIN, a left-wing separatist force that had contested the 1966 election, and the small right-wing RN. As well, some of the more nationalist elements of the UN joined in. Yet, even in its initial formulations, the PQ was notably moderate in its version of independence: the idea of linking political independence with economic association was not a later adjustment to political reality but a founding idea.

Shortly after the PQ had contested its first election in 1970—the same election that saw the Liberals under Robert Bourassa come back to power in a landslide—a series of events unfolded that dramatically highlighted the forces at play in the Quebec cauldron and indicated the direction of the 1970s. What has been called the October Crisis began when the terrorist FLQ kidnapped a British diplomat and later kidnapped and murdered the Quebec minister of labour, Pierre Laporte. The response of the federal government in invoking the War Measures Act against an "apprehended insurrection" and the subsequent arrests and incarceration of numerous persons, few of whom had anything to do with the FLQ, remains a hotly debated question of public policy. What is relevant here is that the entire affair was in fact played out among different factions of Québécois: the federal Liberals, the Bourassa regime, and the Montreal government of Mayor Jean Drapeau on the one side; and, on the other, the FLQ and their public sympathizers, such as the labour leader Michel Chartrand and the revolutionary theorist Pierre Vallières. In the event, the clear superiority of the federal government over the provincial state was demonstrated. Moreover, the might the federal government could thus array in effect broke the back of the tiny terrorist organization, which failed to mobilize popular resistance or even much public support. By the end of the crisis the field had at least been cleared. The PQ, with its moderate, constitutionalist approach of respecting the democratic electorate and observing due process, would be henceforth the only voice of *indépendantisme*.

The Bourassa regime turned to an economic-development strategy that emphasized above all the attraction of private investment and the promotion of large public-works projects—one of which, the James Bay Hydro development, was an immense success that gives Quebec a solid renewable energy resource base for the future and another of which, the Olympic Games project, turned out to be a financial disaster and an administrative fiasco. In a sense, the Bourassa regime represented a reversion to the Duplessis era, inasmuch as everything was subordinated to the encouragement of private investment and business was given a distinctly privileged place in dealings with the provincial government; at the same time, union bashing became more or less official policy. Another aspect of Duplessism came to the fore as well: political patronage and corruption. Moreover, the apparent servility of Bourassa to his "big brothers" in Ottawa began to grate on the nerves of nationalists, even those who were far from being separatists. This was particularly true when an anti-bilingual backlash developed in English

Canada, calling the viability of Trudeau's national bilingualism into question, a dilemma symbolized by the strike of airline pilots over the use of French in air traffic control in Quebec and by the apparent capitulation of the federal government in the face of an anti-French backlash.

When the Quebec Liberals were still able to paint the PQ as a dangerous party that threatened the economic stability of Quebec by their "separatist" designs, they were able to mobilize public support, winning a huge landslide in 1973. But when the PQ hit on the strategy of promising a referendum on sovereignty-association and ran on the platform of competence and honesty in government, as well as on a mildly social-democratic program, an electorate sick of scandals and sellouts turned the Liberals out of office. The coming of the PQ signalled the gravest crisis yet of Canadian federalism.

The PQ government that took office in 1976 appeared on the surface to be the true heirs of the Quiet Revolution; the cabinet was a who's who of the Quebec political, administrative, academic, and media elites. It must be said that the PQ has in its terms of office largely delivered on its promise of good government, in the sense of administrative competence and efficiency, along with a reasonable degree of public honesty. A pursuit of the policy of *maîtres chez nous* was now given a much more hardnosed economic and political thrust than it had in the days of Lesage. Attempting to pursue the goal of sovereignty while operating a provincial government within the context of the existing Canadian federation is not, however, without its ironies.

One of the greatest ironies of all is that what may be the PQ's most enduring achievement probably undermined its own independence option. The PQ language legislation succeeded where the Liberals and the UN had failed before them: to secure the position of the French language in Quebec life. By contrast with its predecessors, Camille Laurin's language act was clear in intention and followed through its aims with rigorous consistency, avoiding the anxiety-producing uncertainties of earlier acts. A wild uproar in the anglophone community led to streams of affluent refugees fleeing to Toronto and parts west. Among those who stayed there is now a much greater acceptance of the predominantly French character of Quebec. The immigrants, despite long simmering conflicts with Montreal working-class francophones with whom they were competing, have adjusted for the most part with surprisingly good grace. Once the situation was made clear, those who had already made a decision to live their lives in a new language showed that they could adapt as well to French as to English. And since it was above all the immigrants overwhelmingly adopting English who had been the real threat to the linguistic balance, the PQ thus neatly defused what had been an explosive situation of ethnic conflict.

Now the francophones of Quebec feel a new security: Quebec is to remain unmistakably French in character. Hence, the mere existence of an anglophone minority tied to an anglophone majority outside Quebec began to lose the threatening quality it once posed to the integrity of Québécois culture and identity. In short, the PQ reversed what had been one of the most significant weaknesses of Trudeau's official languages policy: a cultural and linguistic insecurity it had actually encouraged in Quebec. The profound irony for the PQ is that this achievement may well be seen as a necessary condition for Quebec's continued place within Confederation. Without it, the case for independence would certainly have been much stronger. With the substantive and psychological victory of the language law, Quebec may well feel more confident about playing a continued role in Confederation.

In economic policy, the PQ's approach has been severely restrained, even to the extent of mitigating in office its moderate social-democratic philosophy. In part this reflects a general disillusion with the statist ventures of the Lesage period, many of which (Hydro-Québec aside) have proven to be particularly ineffective. Partly it reflects the unpleasant economic realities of the 1970s and 1980s when inflation and unemployment have combined to discredit much of the earlier Keynesian interventionism. But above all it represents the conundrum of a party dedicated to seeking a major structural change in the national and constitutional status of Quebec. Since business fears uncertainty more than anything else and since the PQ project was premised on the maintenance of existing living standards and investment levels in Quebec, the PQ government was forced to go to greater lengths to reassure business than less "dangerous" governments have to. The PQ's fiscal and monetary policies have thus turned out to be cautious and conservative.

In the case of its economic-development strategy, the PQ represents, if anything, a step back from the Quiet Revolution. Apart from the more or less symbolic nationalization of the asbestos corporation (a ritual bow to the memory of the strike of 1949?), which was in any event a declining industry, the PQ has been notably loath to engage in direct state intervention. In fact, its development strategy has been largely along the lines inscribed by Bourassa's Liberals: a heavy reliance on private investment by multinationals based on the availability of natural resources and energy (James Bay), state agencies as facilitators of private enterprise, and a reduction of regulatory and control devices over business. The one area where they have differed from the Liberals is in the vast program of assistance and encouragement of small and medium enterprises (which of course are those most strongly francophone in ownership). Even this emphasis, strong in their first term, has begun to weaken in their second, with the realization that small and medium enterprises make only a small dent in the unemployment picture. As well, they have begun emphasizing that the rationalization and consolidation of certain aging sectors of the economy will also be necessary, even at the cost of short-term dislocations. In short, they seem to be moving more and more into the kind of development strategy, heavily dependent on large multinational capital and tied to resource sectors, that is characteristic of other provincial governments in Canada.

This raises another crucially important point about the nature of the PQ project for sovereignty: its economic base. Some have viewed the PQ as *merely* a vehicle for new-middle-class nationalism, rooted in the state elite. Yet the PQ has not behaved as if it were a mere reflection of a bureaucratic class fraction. Is this just a failure of will in the face of the power of "foreign" capital? It was, in fact, no longer true in the 1970s that francophones were shut out of the corporate sector. The emergence of a francophone bourgeoisie—not located in the small-business sector alone—is obviously of critical importance for evaluating the relationship of Quebec to its Canadian, and North American, environment. That elements of a francophone bourgeoisie do exist is no longer a matter of much dispute; the hotly debated question has to do with its relationship to North American capitalism. Is it a "French-Canadian" bourgeoisie linked to a pan-Canadian economy, a regional Quebec bourgeoisie offering a potential base for sovereignty-association, or is it itself divided into different fractions, with fragmented political plans?[2] These and other questions (such as the relationship between this bourgeoisie and the state elite located in such crucial positions as Hydro-Québec and the various investment funds) await definitive answers. Suffice to say for now that the PQ plan for a sovereign Quebec seems to have been predicated on some concept of a francophone bourgeoisie, assisted by the state, developing its place in the sun through a renegotiated settlement with English Canada and even, perhaps, through an eventual common market with the United States. A sovereign Quebec was not seen as a socialist Quebec—although there have always been minority elements in the PQ who have retained more radical perspectives than the conservative and technocratic leadership. In any event, the support of business, including francophone business, for the "no" side of the referendum was not a sign that this emergent bourgeoisie saw itself as having *indépendantiste* aspirations, at least at this time.

If the PQ has not seen its role as that of a socialist party mobilizing the working class against foreign capitalist domination, it did see its role in relation to the organized working class as distinct from that of the Liberals. The PQ began with a more conciliatory line in labour relations, including the passage of an anti-scab law more progressive than anything existing in any other North American jurisdiction. While it has generally shown more adroitness and finesse in handling labour relations than its predecessors, it has not gained the formal allegiance of the unions, who have no official affiliation with the party—although the majority of working-class voters appear to vote PQ. The fiscal crisis of the Quebec state, in part exacerbated by the PQ's studied largesse in encouraging its state-sector supporters in the years leading up to the referendum on sovereignty-association, came home to roost in 1982-83 when the PQ was forced into confrontation with its own employees, which has done severe damage to its image as progressive in labour relations. While the federal and other provincial governments have frozen or limited salaries of public employees, the Quebec government actually rolled back wages, under the authority of special legislation. The refusal of teachers to accept the government's terms brought down on their heads one of the most draconian pieces of special anti-labour legislation passed in recent years in any Canadian legislature, including the specific exemption of the legislation from the provisions of both the federal and Quebec charters of rights. It now seems doubtful whether the PQ can repair its relations with organized labour in time for the next election.

The PQ has attempted to reconcile the contradictions of its labour policy by pushing for a series of quasi corporatist-style government-business-labour advisory bodies. Although they hoped that common nationalist aspirations might overcome class divisions, not much has in fact come of these initiatives, nor is much likely to come. Nationalism does not in fact override the structural division of a capitalist economy, when bread and butter issues, as opposed to nationalist symbolism, are in question. On the other hand, the reaction from the labour leaders and from the political left in the wake of the PQ's cutbacks and special anti-labour legislation has gone to such extremes as to label the party as a reactionary betrayer of the working class. Since the PQ did not claim to be a workers' party in the first place, the degree of disillusion seems exaggerated.

Indeed, in continuity with its past, the PQ today seems to be pursuing a populist line, in which it portrays itself as the defender of the "little guys" against the special interests, even where these interests include the unions, especially when they include the "privileged" ranks of the state employees. Of course, this may damage its support among the new middle class, particularly the participation of new middle class activists in the party organization. On the other hand, the party may become a different kind of organization, eschewing its former role as a mass party, instead coming to resemble a kind of modernized version of the old Duplessis Union Nationale: nationalist, populist, firmly rooted in a network of local supporters tied together by patronage and shared partisan identity, and solidly under the control of *le chef*. Of course, there are many differences with the old UN, but so too are there some striking similarities. That the PQ began as a reformist party is no surprise; so did the UN. (Duplessis was allied with young left-wing nationalists and promised the nationalization of hydroelectric power.) In both cases, nationalism was the predominant thrust; in both cases, social reformism was always secondary. It might be added that, in the case of the UN, the combination of populism and nationalism was sustained by substantial working-class support at the polls, even in the face of repressive anti-labour activities by the state.

If the PQ has a blurred conservative image in its economic and social policies, its constitutional formulation of its nationalist position has been even more riven with hesitation and contradiction. Despite hysterical anglophone allegations that the PQ is "racist" and that its independence project resembled some variant of "fascism," the truth is far different. Faced with the thorny problem of expressing a francophone nationalist vision in a society where about one in five does not share in this cultural and linguistic identity, the PQ (not without some hesitations and self-deceptions) has not officially supported an *exclusionary* definition of nationality, but instead generally has chosen a *liberal* interpretation, which left membership open to all those willing to participate voluntarily in the national culture, along with guarantees for minorities. Indeed, the entire ethos of the PQ has been so permeated with a full acceptance of liberal-democratic principles as to make any allegations of totalitarianism laughable—as well as to sharply differentiate the PQ from older reactionary and authoritarian expressions of Quebec nationalism. A close reading of the official documents produced by the PQ in power—from the constitution to culture to economics—indicates a liberal-democratic discourse to which various nationalist themes are rhetorically wedded in an uneasy and contradictory manner. In some cases, as in the official economic-development strategy (*Bâtir le Québec*), nationalist themes virtually disappear. In others, like the white paper on sovereignty-association, the tension is reflected in glaring inconsistencies.

Partly out of its basic inability to clearly define its own nationalist direction, partly out of the constraints of trying to reassure business and voters, the PQ's constitutional option was blurred. Since it has insisted on linking political sovereignty with economic association—that is, to argue that national independence was a constitutional superstructure unrelated to the economic base—it has in effect put a double proposition to the voters: first, that there was a will to seek political sovereignty; second, that this will to independence was linked to the continuance of existing economic relations with English Canada, in some cases on a new basis, in some cases on a basis suspiciously like the present. The problem with this duality was that the first part could be a unilateral expression, with which English Canada would have to deal; the second was a matter for negotiation, which cannot be unilateral. Yet the first was linked to the second. The paradox for the PQ was that Quebec opinion, as revealed in the government's own polls, was contingent on English Canada's reaction; this was summed up neatly in a cartoon in *Le Devoir* showing Quebec as a boxer in the corner saying, "We're ready to come out and fight, if English Canada allows us to win." Trudeau paraphrased the referendum question as: "Do you want to have your cake and eat it too?" Even worse was the PQ's promise that the economic association would be based on the principle of equality (*égal à égal*). Why English Canada, representing 70% of the population should agree to a 50-50 relationship with 30% of the population in Quebec was never obvious. Presumably the *formal* equality involved in bilateral relations between sovereign nations would be in effect, but formal equality between materially unequal nations is an empty equality.

The referendum result revealed an underlying reality of Quebec's relationship to Canada, which appears to have escaped the attention of the most militant *indépendantistes*. Quebeckers have a long history—and, doubtless, a long future—of demanding more power and autonomy for the province. *Péquistes* made the mistake of assuming that this was a cumulative process which would inevitably lead to sovereignty. But demands made *in the provincial sphere* for provincial goals are not the same as demands made *in the federal sphere*. Hence, the sometimes bizarre contrasts between provincial and federal voting in Quebec (*Péquistes* to Quebec City and Liberals to Ottawa). In pursuing apparently divergent ideological and constitutional paths in federal and provincial politics, Quebeckers are not necessarily being irrational. Quite the contrary. A strong voice for the province of Quebec in federal-provincial negotiations need not be a contradiction of a strong Quebec presence in Ottawa—the irrationality may perhaps be discerned in the *structures* of federalism, which set one political elite from Quebec against another elite in an adversarial bargaining confrontation, but that is another story. Pierre Trudeau *and* René Lévesque were both perceived by the bulk of voters in Quebec as champions of Quebec interests. And so they were.

The PQ's fatal error was to demand in effect that the people of Quebec be forced to choose, definitively, between two levels of government to which they were still by and large attached. If the federalist option had been successfully portrayed as a unitary centralism, within which the Quebec provincial state would inevitably disappear, the PQ's option could have won considerably greater support. A small number of *Péquiste* zealots aside, such a scenario could gain little credibility. Anyone with much of a memory could see tangible evidence that the Quebec state, under federalism, had gained enormously in fiscal power and responsibility over the 20 years since 1960. The real choice was between federalism, with its two levels of government, and sovereignty, with its one level. Of course, the PQ hastened to muddy this with its arguments about sovereignty-association and its curious recreation under different names of federalist structures (although as decided *bureaucratic* structures without the legitimation of direct popular election). But, in order to mobilize support for the "yes" vote, it was necessary to rhetorically identify loyalty to Quebec exclusively with a sovereign Quebec, thus excluding the notion of attachment to the federal dimension.

When the "no" strategists devised the slogan "*Je suis fier d'être québécois et canadien*," they quite brilliantly distilled the quintessence of the reluctance of the mass of the population to make the choice demanded by the PQ. Although a vast majority unsurprisingly agreed with a mid-referendum questionnaire statement that "I am profoundly attached to Quebec," it was perhaps less expected that 76% of the same sample agreed with the statement "I am profoundly attached to Canada"—including an extraordinary 47% of those who intended to vote "yes."[3]

As the "no" campaign gained in confidence, an interesting phenomenon came to the fore. The display of Canadian flags and the singing of "O Canada" became features not only in predominantly anglophone gatherings but in francophone ones as well. The point to be made here is not that Quebec francophones are really Canadians first; rather, it is that the steady growth over recent years of popular identification as "Québécois" has not necessarily meant that "Canadien" has suffered an equivalent elimination. Obviously, for a body of *indépendantiste* activists and perhaps for certain occupational categories such as intellectuals and artists, Quebec and Canada have tended to become mutually exclusive categories. But, for a sizable section of the population, the intensification of emotional, nationalistic attachment to Quebec that began with the Quiet Revolution did not in itself subvert an attachment to federalism and a Canadian identification which no doubt lacks the warmth and sentimentality of loyalty to Quebec, but maintains tenacious roots. Perhaps Pierre Trudeau's notion that passionate national loyalties to French Canada are matched by a cooler, more "rationalist" or functionalist base of loyalty to Canada as a whole may have some relevance here.

This raises another question. It has been argued, especially by left-wing independence supporters, that the "no" campaign was largely one of fear, in which pro-federalist forces combined with the big corporations to intimidate working-class and vulnerable middle-class voters into backing away from sovereignty-association under the threat, implied or direct, of a flight of capital. This charge has an element of truth, but it can be exaggerated. The PQ hardly posed a radical alternative to capitalism in its referendum question. Moreover, it suggests a deep contempt of the Quebec people themselves to argue that federal anti-alcohol ads with the theme "*non merci*" somehow stampeded impressionable voters into the "no" side. In any event, the PQ had four years of control over government advertising in the media to drive *its* point home.

Despite some rather tortured attempts to argue that the majority of francophone voters had actually voted *yes* (it being necessary to assume a sharply higher turnout among anglophones than among francophones *and* an extraordinarily high *no* percentage among all nonfrancophones), it seems likely that in fact more francophones voted *no* than voted *yes*. It should also be obvious that the percentage of francophones who did vote *yes* was quite high, even if not a clear majority. Although the referendum was run on a simple majority basis, with no distinctions formally being made between francophones and anglophone voters, the political reality was, of course, quite different. An overall "no" majority of, say, 51% would clearly have lacked any legitimacy, since under such circumstances it would have been obvious that the francophones had voted decisively "yes." The resulting crisis would have been extremely volatile and dangerous for relations between the two communities in Quebec and would have left matters hanging intolerably for the rest of Canada. A clear result, one way or another, was obviously preferable and was in fact produced.

The question remains whether the result of the referendum can be seen as *definitive*. Predictions about the long run are best left to astrologers, but there has been a growing sense in the years since the referendum that in the short run—say, the next decade or so—the result will be determining. Despite the increasingly ritualistic reiterations by government leaders that sovereignty remains just around the corner and despite repeated promises to run the next general election as a referendum on sovereignty, there is a pervasive feeling in Quebec that *indépendantisme* is yesterday's issue. There are a number of reasons for the waning of this question that so dominated Quebec politics for so many years.

The referendum was, in some ways, a moving example of a people undertaking a collective decision that would determine their destiny for the future. The debate penetrated into levels of society normally left untouched by party politics, and in some senses represented a moment of true democracy rarely witnessed in Quebec or elsewhere. The other side of this coin is that it was a traumatic event for many, to those whose families and personal relations were rent by political divisions, and above all to those who threw themselves body and soul into the "yes" campaign, then saw their dream rejected by 60 per cent of their fellow citizens. The historic moment arrived and the vision suddenly shattered. It may be difficult for this generation of *indépendantiste* activists to put themselves again through that kind of traumatic public vulnerability for some time.

Apart from psychological suppositions, there are deeper reasons to suspect that the referendum has settled matters for a good while. For instance, growing evidence suggests that the ancient complaint of francophones that they have no future in the corporate sector is becoming less credible as capitalism adjusts to making profits in French as well as in English. Moreover, there is a marked shift among francophone students towards commerce and business administration, which is eliminating the differences in career orientation that until recently had separated anglophone from francophone. A study published in 1981 under the sponsorship of the *Conseil de la langue française* revealed that, when age is taken into account, there is little if any evidence of higher income among anglophones than among francophones in their 40s and younger in similar occupations in Quebec; indeed, there is marginal evidence that some francophones now make more than their anglophone counterparts.[4] In short, the generation who came of age at the time of the Quiet Revolution has moved through a historic alteration of the old pattern of unequal accommodation between the two language groups. The generation coming of age in the 1980s faces fewer of the blatant aggravations that galvanized an earlier generation into militant *indépendantiste* politics. Lévesque claimed on referendum night that his sovereignty-association option had been defeated by "*le vieux Québec*." The assertion that the younger voters are naturally *indépendantistes* and that opposition to the PQ option will pass away with time—an assertion repeated once again for the benefit of the French media on Lévesque's 1983 visit to France—appears to be another comforting, but insubstantial, PQ myth. PQ support is in fact weakening among the very youngest voters; 18- to 21-year-old voters appear to have divided pretty much in the same proportions as their elders on the referendum's question.

The problematic character of Quebec youth's attachment to independence was dramatically highlighted in August of 1983 when a summit meeting of youth organizations voted against a resolution expressing support for an independent Quebec. As some of the delegates made clear, this result arose perhaps not so much out of positive support for Canadian federalism as from disillusion with an *indépendantiste* government that, instead of solving problems whose solution already lay within provincial jurisdiction, persisted in trying to use these problems as a means of mobilizing support for sovereignty as a panacea.

The backdrop to the referendum and to the subsequent confrontation between the PQ government and Ottawa over the new constitution has, of course, been the continued economic recession that has cut even more deeply into Quebec than into some other parts of Canada, given the historically limited nature of Quebec's industrialization. The PQ has attempted to fix the blame for this squarely on the federal government's policies and to argue that salvation can come only through independence. Yet, far from intensifying popular support for sovereignty, hard economic times seem to have deepened uninterest in nationalist adventures. In part this lack of interest derives from fear of more political uncertainty driving out investment and jobs; in part it derives from a desire to see both levels of government stop their petty conflicts over place and prestige and get down to the job of cooperating for economic recovery.

The PQ's role in the constitutional negotiations following the referendum must also be critically scrutinized to understand their waning prestige within Quebec as the defenders of the Quebec nation. Having misfired their own constitutional option, the PQ proved singularly inept at negotiating a new constitutional arrangement within Canada. Lévesque actually signed an accord with the premiers in opposition to Trudeau's unilateral initiative, which failed to recognize a special veto for Quebec on amendments (the federal government's proposals did include a Quebec veto), then bitterly denounced Ottawa for denying Quebec's "historic" right to a veto when the accord to which he had agreed was accepted. At a premiers' conference in the 1970s, Lévesque had offered a reciprocal exchange of minority-language rights in education with the English-Canadian premiers—then vehemently denounced the exact same agreement, when written into the new constitution, as an attack on Quebec's linguistic rights.

Lévesque's negotiating tactics make sense only if they are seen as resulting from *une politique du pire*—that is to say, a policy of ensuring defeat in order to demonstrate that things are so bad under federalism that sovereignty is the only salvation. If that were indeed the plan, the effect on public opinion may have been badly misjudged. Quebec voters have always wanted their provincial government to stand up for Quebec in federal-provincial relations. While some may interpret the Constitution Act of 1982 as a sign that there is no future for Quebec within Canada, a great many more may well conclude that the PQ is simply a poor negotiator on behalf of Quebec interests. Moreover, while the absence of a Quebec veto is dangerous in a binational state, things are not so dark as the PQ would have people believe. Provinces can, after all, opt out of constitutional amendments of which they disapprove and, where such amendments have to do with educational or cultural matters, they can receive fiscal compensation—a clear indication of a special status for Quebec. The main lines of the Quebec language law (French as the language of work, French for signs and advertising, and the assimilation of the nonanglophone immigrants into French-language education) are now preserved by the Consitution, with only such marginal matters as bilingual statutes and debate in the National Assembly, and the right of anglophones coming from other provinces to send their children to English schools open to change by constitutional interpretation. In exchange, there has been a major concession to French language rights in education in English-Canadian provinces, and the extension of official bilingualism to New Brunswick, with its large Acadian minority.

In fact, the new Constitution does clearly recognize the linguistic and cultural duality of Canada—that is, the duality of English and French Canada. But it does not recognize duality of the Quebec and Canadian *states*, as states. In short, the constitutional resolution of 1982 was a victory for Pierre Trudeau's longstanding belief that the question was one of individual rights of English and French Canadians, and a defeat for the *Péquiste* position that linguistic and cultural survival demands a sovereign state as its only sure guarantee. Time alone will tell if the Trudeau solution will actually work; just as obviously, it is requisite to the PQ's survival as a force that it *not* work. The conundrum for the PQ is whether *la politique du pire* is defensible strategy to sell to the people. For instance, the PQ, alone among the provincial governments, has decided to invoke the "notwithstanding" clause on each and every piece of legislation it introduces into the National Assembly, thus exempting Quebec from the Charter of Rights. Can it, in the long run, justify to its own citizens the denial of the protection of individual rights, in the name of a (negative) defence of the rights of the Quebec state?

The difficulties encountered by a government attempting this kind of strategy were painfully highlighted in the immediate aftermath of the constitutional accord, at a PQ congress. After escalating the rhetorical level to suggest that Quebec was being virtually raped by the federal government and the English-Canadian provinces, Lévesque in effect incited the extreme nationalist wing of the party to push for an out-and-out sovereignty position. Aware at the same time that this extreme reaction would be rejected by the voters, Lévesque refused to accept the majority decisions of the congress, and subjected the party to the humiliating exercise of a mailed ballot (the so-called "*Renérendum*"), in which party members were asked to recant their views or to force *le chef* to resign. Obedience to *le chef* won over party democracy. The confusion in all this is profound and the contradictions may well be insupportable. Certainly doubts must remain that the PQ will actually fulfill its stated determination to fight the next provincial election on the sovereignty issue. Or, if it does, that it can be anything other than a suicidal decision. In 1970, 1973, and 1980 the PQ was the party of sovereignty, and was rejected by the voters. In 1976 and 1981, it was the party of good government, and was endorsed.

An interesting feature of the 1981 election was the decline in ethnic polarization. More anglophones and especially other ethnics voted PQ than before, and two anglophones were elected as PQ members in predominantly francophone seats. In the Montreal civic elections of 1982, ethnic and linguistic polarization seems to have broken down entirely under the counterpressure of a struggle between the old Jean Drapeau machine and a francophone-anglophone reformist party. It is possible that Quebec politics will become more oriented toward economic and social issues and less dominated by an overarching concern for nationalism without social content. Ironically, the PQ will have helped bring this about, both through creating a legislative framework conducive to the enhanced position of francophone identity in Quebec and by finally stretching the nationalist issue nearly to the breaking point. How well the PQ can itself survive its ironic success is another matter.

Beyond party politics, there remains the deeper and more significant question of the relationship of Quebec society to Canada and to North America. The problem to be addressed in the 1980s is that of the integration of Quebec into the economic structures of North American capitalism. To what extent this process will continue, to what effect on the class structure of Quebec, and to what effect on Quebec culture and identity—these questions will ultimately determine whether the referendum of 1980 was the last gasp of the kind of nationalism unleashed by the 1960s or merely another shot in a gathering campaign. Of course, English Canada's *political* responses to Quebec will play a role in this, but not so important a role as the structural changes in Quebec itself. To return to where this essay began: one thing alone is certain, that Quebec nationalism will continue; what specific form and expression that nationalism will take will ultimately be a product of forces deeper than politics alone.

Notes

1. H. Milner *Politics in the New Quebec* (Toronto: McClelland and Stewart, 1978), p. 148.
2. Some of this debate has been translated into English in *Studies in Political Economy*. See Jorge Niosi, "The New French-Canada Bourgeoisie," I (spring 1979); Gilles Bourque, "Class, nation, and the Parti québécois," II (fall 1979); Pierre Fournier, "Parameters of the new Quebec bourgeoisie," III (spring 1980). As well, see Part III of this volume.
3. Maurice Pinard and Richard Hamilton, poll reported in *Le Devoir* (May 17, 1979), p. 9.
4. Robert Lacroix and François Vaillancourt, *Les revenus et la langue au Québec (1970-1978)* (Quebec, 1981).

Chapter 7/The Times and Promises of a Debate: Class Analyses in Quebec (1960-1980)*

Anne Legaré

The time is ripe to assess the evolution of the contribution made in the past 15 years by leftist intellectuals to the study of social classes in Quebec. The assessment I intend to make comprises two main parts. The first will try to situate in their historical contexts the work that emerged from the Quiet Revolution until the election victory of the Parti Québécois in 1976; this section recalls, across this chronology, the development of these analyses. The second part synthesizes the debate over the nature of the bourgeoisie (which has dominated the period of the PQ regime) and attempts to summarize the ideological and political propositions linked to it.

The debate on social classes since the beginning of the Quiet Revolution has been demarcated, in my opinion, by four major questions, each one revealing the major preoccupations of intellectuals according to their links with components of the labour movement. Dofny and Rioux, in 1962, stated the first question: what separates and what unites the social classes in Quebec? Their answer was that Quebec had only one class, united by ethnicity.[1] In 1970, Bourque and Laurin-Frenette posed two other questions: the first concerned the social composition of Quebec's petty bourgeoisie; the second, in essence, concerned the existence of a Quebec bourgeoisie.[2] This second question was taken up again from 1976 onwards. Finally, mostly since 1974, the question of the location of the social division between the working class and the petty bourgeoisie has emerged.

In my opinion, three related factors have governed the orientation of the debate:

1. The relationship of these questions to the historical conjuncture, namely:
   - (a) first, the split in the Quebec NDP and the formation of the Parti socialiste du Québec (PSQ);
   - (b) the creation of the Mouvement souveraineté-association (MSA) and then of the PQ;
   - (c) the period preceding the election of the PQ, characterized by electoralism and the development of the extreme left;
   - (d) the accession to power of the Parti Québécois.
2. The specificity of the themes evoked, concerning the theory and the politics of the analysis of social relations.

---

*This chapter is a slightly modified version of "Heures et promesses d'un débat: les analyses des classes au Québec (1960-1980)," *Cahiers du socialisme* 5 (spring 1980), and was translated by Claude Galipeau, Political Studies Department, Queen's University.

3. Finally, the relevance of these analyses and their political resonance since the accession to power of the PQ.

The General Historical Context

In the past 15 years, the approaches and themes have evolved a great deal. Nonetheless, the national question has remained at the centre of all these analyses. Nationalist oppression has at times been considered as the only important aspect of the social dimension, yet occasionally it has been seen as second to the class division. Oppression of French Canadians has been studied most recently as the essence of the class structure itself. The evolution of viewpoints on the relationship between classes and nationhood indicate a remarkable progression in socialist and marxist thinking in Quebec; this progression has been shaped by the development of the sociopolitical context.

This evolution was consolidated by the growing irrefutable demonstration of the PQ's fundamental political conservatism. Around this slow and progressive updating, as it was carried through the exercise of political power until now, the interests of concerned classes and class fractions were progressively clarified and are continuing to be clarified.

The debate has evolved with the transformations in class relations. Actually, the researchers who analyzed social class initially had as their principal concern, and with just cause, the necessity to relate their findings to their perceptions of the most important strategic questions for the labour movement in Quebec. Sometimes their results were apt, while on other occasions they proceeded in the wrong direction. In addition, these findings were often marginalized by the contingencies of the movement itself. For we cannot yet justly speak of a full recognition by the movement of this work. The blame for this cannot be ascribed to the researchers, or to the workers' organizations. Intellectuals are neither on the sideline or above historical events; they are in history and, as such, suffer its specific conditions. The last 15 years have been a test for Quebec workers. The nationalist question, made into an ornament by the PQ, has confused the game. The organization of the labour movement has been checked and the work of the intellectuals on the left has suffered from this difficult birth.

The intellectual debate therefore depended on class relations in a way that, as will be seen, the studies on social classes were joined to the specificity of the organizational problems of the labour movement and tried through this diversity to answer one main question: which party would, through the various movements, satisfy the general interests of the dominated social classes? This question was not answered by the labour movement itself. Next, this process of reflection and research depended on the successive phases of the labour movement as far as these works remained isolated and were not directly inscribed into the prevailing struggles.

Thus, during this period, the study of class relations was dominated by an enormous effort to clarify each party's interests, a clarification made first with reference to the negative experience of power under the PQ government. Mixed with this historical process were the efforts of specific intellectuals to give a differentiated understanding of the various phases which the nationalist movement was undergoing. Dofny and Rioux dealt with these ideological preoccupations.[3] Their article—taken up by Jean-Marc Piotte in 1966,[4] who was in turn criticized by Michel Van Schendel in 1969[5] and by Gilles Bourque and Nicole Laurin-Frenette in 1970[6]—shows the dominant questions of that time: their proposals for analyses were coloured by nationalism.

One merely has to remember the numerous accompanying events. Social movements in Quebec resulted in the founding of the Rassemblement pour l'indépendance nationale (RIN) in 1960 and its transformations into a party in 1963, the forming of the Confédération des syndicats nationaux (1960), the founding of the NDP (1961), the Parent Report, the emergence of the Front de libération du Québec (FLQ), the schism in the Quebec NDP and the formation of the Parti socialiste du Québec, then the launching of the periodical *Parti Pris* in 1963; as well, there was the creation of the Ministry of Education, the acquisition of the right to strike in the public sector, and the creation of the Union générale des étudiants du Québec in 1964; finally, the numerous strikes of 1965-66 and, at last, the founding of the MSA in 1967. The year of *Parti Pris*'s launching marked a particular effort to recognize the social and political differences confronting each other through the national question and to bring out some corresponding interests, whether this be in the Ralliement national (RN), the RIN, or the MSA (and then in the PQ).

In 1968, after the founding of the MSA, the positions of intellectuals became divided by the analysis of the link of the MSA to social class. On one side, Jean-Marc Piotte encouraged support for the MSA, since "a large fraction of the most conscious and politicized of the masses were following Lévesque. . . . To be situated outside of the MSA was to shut oneself off from the most progressive fraction of the masses."[7] Piotte returned to this issue when, in 1975, he criticized the PQ's alliance with imperialism and stated, "Actually, faced with the PQ and taking into account the weakness and division among socialist organizations, we must clearly disassociate ourselves from the independentist project and defend the only solution to the fundamental problems of the workers: socialism."[8]

On the other side, after the fashion of Piotte as well as, in the summer of 1968, Gilles Bourque, Luc Racine, and Gilles Dostaler founded the Comité Indépendance-Socialisme and formulated a severe critique of the interests represented by Lévesque, which they said were those of a "class antagonistic to the workers."[9] Already, the most distressing as well as the most decisive question was at the centre of the debate: in supporting the MSA, or later the PQ, would the workers be progressing towards their own defeat as a class? All further research was to be haunted by this persistent question.

Some Historical Analyses

Before considering the studies that aimed to meticulously relate the political scene to the classes in struggle, the following is an overview of works of a more general historical perspective. These studies furnish a general framework indispensable to an understanding of the following articles. They also show the changes in this general perspective and what impact they made on the political scene. (I have attempted throughout this chapter to scrupulously respect the chronology of these works, as well as selecting all the principal ones.)

In 1967, Alfred Dubuc described the process of the formation of the Canadian state as a means used to aid the centralization of the financial capital necessary for the development of the bourgeoisie.[10] According to this thesis, the Canadian state is more the instrument of commercial and financial capital than the product of specific class relations. In 1970, there followed the first work by Gilles Bourque, entitled *Classes sociales et question nationale au Québec*.[11] This book contains the thesis of the double structure of classes, superimposed and each referring to one of the two nations. Bourque would later critique his own thesis in the first issue of *Les Cahiers du socialisme*, stating, "We cannot state a 'classical' definition of a nation without falling into reductionism and, curiously, into nationalism itself. In the last case, we risk the effect of coming close to claiming the existence of nationally heterogeneous class structures."[12] Under the same rubric of preoccupations, a reworked, corrected, and elaborated version of themes in *Unequal Union* by Stanley Ryerson appeared in English in 1968 and was translated into French in 1972.[13] A central theme of this work is that the nationalist movement of the *Patriotes* of 1837 had a basically "democratic and anti-imperialistic character." Ryerson emphasizes the emergence "of domestic manufacturing, of local and indigenous industry" and the formation of a "colonial class."

In a 1975 article, Hélène David relates the political scene to the labour movement and dismisses the conventional period assigned to the Quiet Revolution in an attempt to expose the conditions for the different "five moments of crisis" that typified this period.[14]

Dorval Brunelle provides, in *La désillusion tranquille* (1978), some new and original elements in the analysis of both interprovincial and federal-provincial relations: his principal thesis attempts to bring out that "Canada is mainly the sum of [provincial] governments" characterized "by the total lack of integration in economic relations."[15] Further, through an analysis of political history, and especially that of the Conseil d'orientation économique, the study exposes the evolution of the political conditions for the development of the Quebec bourgeoisie during the 1960s.

Nicole Laurin-Frenette elaborated in 1978 a new conceptual scheme for the analysis of the nation. She claims the process that creates the state assigns to its agents and to the nation their place as well as that of the structures that reproduce them.[16] The role of nationalism is to "guarantee the reproduction of a place for the [national] state." Laurin-Frenette applies her theoretical postulate in an analysis of six crises and renounces the thesis she professed with Gilles Bourque in 1970 which related the sovereignty-association drive to the interests of a technocratic petty bourgeoisie.

May 1979 saw the release of a work by Roch Denis,[17] which emphasizes the links between the labour movement and the national question, and concludes with the difficulties facing the formation of a party that does not seek a transitional integration with union organizations. The work ends with this conclusion after a long analysis of the different stages followed by the labour movement and its organizations, as well as the role played therein by intellectuals since 1948.

Finally, Gilles Bourque and I[18] tried in our book *Le Québec, la question nationale* to link the political events since the Conquest to the social relations and transformations of the modes and forms of production. The principal theses developed concerned the peasants' resistance to the development of the capitalist mode of production; the formation of the Canadian state, whose structure tends towards rupture; the privileged position the UN and Duplessis had with the local bourgeoisie; the links the provincial Liberals and the Quiet Revolution had with the Canadian bourgeoisie; the connections the drive for sovereignty-association and the *Péquiste* government had with the nonmonopolistic bourgeoisie of Quebec; and, finally, the outcome of the actual referendum battle.

From the Quiet Revolution to the Formation of the PQ in 1968: The Awakening of Leftist Nationalism

To tackle the works dealing mainly with the relationship of classes to the political scene, this first segment of the periodization in our analysis is required, for it brings forth the questions which were later raised with the formation of the Parti Québécois.

This is no doubt the reason why the 1962 article by Dofny and Rioux caused such reverberations, as if some spark had ignited the smouldering and latent thoughts of the time. Its principal thesis consists of describing the people of Quebec as an "ethnic" class, unified by its own original social stratification and opposed to the dominant anglophone group.

One year later, Mario Dumais, like Jacques Dofny and Marcel Rioux, wanted to "open the road for a coherent political strategy." His article opens with a long theoretical elaboration on the fact that social classes exist, then proposes the proper marxist method to understand this fact.[19] This work makes no distinction between the bourgeoisie and the traditional petty bourgeoisie; the working class is composed of "rural, manual, and non-manual" labourers, comprising "office employees, technicians, and intellectuals" as well; the social strata also exhibit a division between the sexes. The article represents, then, the first example of concrete research on the social division of labour in Quebec. However, some weaknesses precluded a more diversified use of its conceptual scheme.

Jean-Marc Piotte's 1966 article tries to synthesize the principal claims of Dofny-Rioux and Dumais. He recounts the "values, institutions, and behaviour of Quebeckers" (as Dofny and Rioux did) to show how they are often "North Americans before being Canadians or French Canadians"; he develops his own thesis that Quebec is an ethnic class within Canadian society as a whole. This brought Piotte to affirm that the "RIN has an essential, though transitory, historical role as a vanguard in the process of liberation led by 'white collar' workers." We see here that for Piotte, as well as for others, the concept of the petty bourgeoisie covers only the owners of small and medium-sized enterprises, professionals, and artisans. White-collar workers represent a segment of the vaster "working class."

Musing on the spirit that compelled the group at *Parti Pris* in the 1960s, Piotte has since written about that period, "Living the rupture as if it were an intellectual liberation, we were in no hurry to find for ourselves some historical roots. We took ourselves for the intellectual vanguard of the revolution. . . . Rereading my work, I was astonished: I thought myself a marxist when in fact my fundamental analytical category—with the exception of *Notes sur le milieu rural,* the only research done in the field—was basically the nation."[20] And, commenting on his 1966 article, Piotte writes, "My study of Quebec was not based on the class struggle through which I could articulate the national liberation movements; rather, it was based on seeking the nation and then illuminating it with a description of the social classes."[21] The six works in the period from 1968 to 1976, which are described below, marked a notable progress on this last tendency.

The first work of the next period, "Pour un mouvement socialiste et indépendantiste" by Bourque, Racine, and Dostaler, contains, first, a radical critique of the MSA, which was inspired by Bourque's article published a few months earlier in *Parti Pris.*[22] Bourque, at that time, was already at work on his *Classes sociales et question nationale au Québec, 1760-1840.* With this article, the three authors point out as central the persistence and dominance of bourgeois interests in the MSA due to the presence of Lévesque and his colleagues. The authors recognize the presence of certain "disorganized" leftist elements in the movement, but they claim these are used to obfuscate the real conservative aspect of the movement.

After this followed the first critique, "Pour une théorie du socialisme au Québec" by Michel Van Schendel, of the thesis published by Dofny and Rioux in 1962. Van Schendel tries to discern what he "structurally" defines as the working class in Quebec. This article also contains a cogent critique of the concepts of class and ethnic consciousness used by Dofny and Rioux, as opposed to historical materialism. Van Schendel thus played an important role for the group of editors of the review *Socialisme québécois.*

One year later, in 1970, there appeared the article by Luc Racine and Roch Denis, which is (with the editorial in this issue prepared by Van Schendel and E. de Ipola) the first work of this period to recognize the existence of a "middle, French-Canadian bourgeoisie."[23] More than a simple metaphorical allusion, this article, although prudently, specifies this bourgeoisie as a subcontracting one and that the PQ is the representative of its nationalist fraction. This article also makes pertinent distinctions between a bourgeoisie and a petty bourgeoisie. However, if the latter indicates a process of "gradual proletarianization," the concept of "working class" indistinctively covers all manual workers and intellectuals, factory workers and employees. Because it is more clearly pro-imperialist than the RIN was, the PQ is seen as a step backwards from the position of the MSA.

After the text published in 1962 by Jacques Dofny and Marcel Rioux, the article by Bourque and Laurin-Frenette, though following an ostensible marxist perspective, represents the second major tendency of leftist nationalism in Quebec sociology. Even though this article aims "to indicate at least the basic elements of a marxist theory of the nation, of nationalism, and of the relations among social classes, nations, and ideologies of nationalism" and "is inspired by the practice of the revolutionary movement in Quebec of the past ten years,"[24] it contains some extrapolations still of use in arguments for nationalist theses. Gilles Bourque has since then criticized most of this article's positions on the grounds that the PQ is a representative of the petty bourgeoisie: "I cannot follow Niosi when he deduces ... the exclusively petty-bourgeois nature of the Parti Québécois. Beyond specific theoretical differences ... it seems to me of the utmost urgency to rethink the implicit problematic dealt with in most analyses until now."[25]

Nicole Laurin-Frenette has also rejected this article's positions: "We were seeking the objective bases of the nation and, like many others, we were finding on all sides mirages through which we attempted to distinguish the object, the nation, from its reflection in the mirror of nationalism."[26] Ignoring the authors' self-critiques, many writers (like Sales, Niosi, and Monière) still cite the article.

One year after the publication of the article by Bourque and Laurin-Frenette, Michel Van Schendel pointed out their confusion on the subject of the bourgeoisie.[27] He claims that in fact a Quebec bourgeoisie accumulates and tends through its *Péquiste* representatives, who are of petty-bourgeois origins, to "take on the appearance of a state-patron bourgeoisie." Van Schendel emphasizes that this "disarming consequence" of Bourque-Frenette's analysis was, as he states, "decidedly contrary to their theoretical premises." Finally, Van Schendel defines the Quebec working class as "typical of centre-dominant capitalism." From this article, a debate was launched and two major problems were thus imposed on future research: the existence of a Quebec bourgeoisie and the composition of the working class.

In the fall of 1971, a research group in the Centre de formation populaire (CFP) was founded. The membership of the group consisted of three militants of popular organizations; Jean Roy of the Centre de recherche et d'information du Québec (CRIQ), Charles Gagnon of the Central Council of the Confédération des syndicats nationaux in Montreal, and Bernard Normand of the CFP, as well as three intellectuals: Céline St-Pierre, Gilles Bourque, and myself. During eight months of meetings, the criteria applied to the social division of labour were elaborated. In this way, the group brought out the distinction between directly or indirectly productive labour, which was later to become the basis of future theoretical elaboration by Céline St-Pierre.[28] Some of the aspects of the position arrived at by St-Pierre did not produce a consensus, so she finished on her own what had been until then a collective project.

This article was important in many respects. First, St-Pierre states that the working class consists of *directly* productive workers and a labouring class, which comprises workers who are *indirectly* productive as well as all the manual workers who are nonproductive. Thus, the proletariat encompasses all these areas—that is, both the working class and the labouring class. The new petty bourgeoisie consists of those intellectual workers who help to reproduce the work force. The political function of this approach is thus to extend the working class to include the largest possible segment of salaried workers. This elaboration still has a large following among Quebec intellectuals. Jean-Marc Piotte has added a few more details. "I thus differ from Céline St-Pierre on the following points. The use of the Gramscian distinction between intellectual and manual workers enables me to separate more clearly the new petty bourgeoisie from nonproductive workers who are, themselves, members of the labouring class, and who also work to reproduce the social relations essential for the production of surplus-value. ... I designated as labouring class what Céline St-Pierre calls 'the labouring classes other than the working class'."[29]

My own book, *Les classes sociales au Québec,* was published in the autumn of 1977. This work is characterized principally by the fact that the classes and their fractions simultaneously condense economic distinctions as well as criteria of domination/subordination, of sexes, of salaries, of authority/execution, among others. The petty bourgeoisie is a fragmented class. The ideological contribution of this work consists, in my opinion, in having established throughout the analysis of the social divisions in Quebec a cross-checking to include the position of women. To distinguish between females and males of the working class, between housewives and productive workers, between the female level of nonproductive manual work and the male level is as important and contentious as the separation of the petty bourgeoisie from the working class. It is not that women form a class, but that their existence in classes doubly reproduces power relations. My study emphasizes this point. In my representation of the class structure, the dividing up of the whole took into account housewives, which disturbed the usual statistical distributions. In addition, I included in that fraction of the proletarized petty bourgeoisie the nonproductive salaried and salaried manual workers, which in effect corresponds to 7% of the population.[30]

Finally, I must make one last point about the future of class analyses. It seems to me more and more essential to take into account the concrete modes through which social wholes live their relationship to society, like the difference between the sexes in social identification. (In theory, the working class has no sexual dimension.) Also, to forget the nature of classes as subjects seems to me to be a political and theoretical error: the historical dimension must also be included in any analysis.

For the large alliance sought by the defenders of the large concept of the proletariat or of the working class encompassing all oppressed salaried workers should testify to multiple social differences. In reality, there is no monolithic working class, or class without sex, without age, without ethnicity, without real physical space. What exists is the union of multiple determinations with specific social formations.

It is when confronted with a change and political action that the traditional leftist parties stumble over these differences. This is why our research must become more and more specific and recognize the plurality of the social system.

The Reign of the Parti Québécois before the Referendum: Fundamental Theoretical Differences

In contrast with preceding periods, an exceptional profusion of articles was produced from 1976 to 1980. This period has been marked by analyses of the composition of classes and of the alliance maintained by the *Péquiste* government. The reflection on the class nature of this alliance evidently presupposes an appropriate understanding of the sociopolitical wholes making up this social structure and which come to interact in concrete political struggles. On this last point, the various stages taken by this debate have revealed some fundamental theoretical differences.

The following section of this essay will thus proceed from an examination of internal events that occurred in the movement of the intellectual left. Indeed, in contrast to the two preceding periods in which articles followed contemporary events and were mainly the product of closed collectives (*Parti Pris, Socialisme québécoise,* and the research group at CFP), the works published since November 1976 show more and more complex preoccupations, with a larger audience and coming out of public meetings and debates. Two colloquia held in November 1977 first indicated the formulation of tendencies that were to principally rival each other in the analysis of the PQ. These tendencies gave rise to numerous articles on the Quebec bourgeoisie and the national question. To illustrate this phenomenon, here are a few examples of the titles of articles to be studied below: "La nouvelle bourgeoisie canadienne-francaise" (Niosi), "Les nouveaux paramètres de la bourgeoisie québécoise" (Fournier), and "Petite bourgeoisie envahissante et bourgeoisie ténébreuse" (Bourque). I will make a more systematic study of the main articles directly linked to these colloquia, considering that their polemical aspect and evolution gives them, apart from this dynamic character, a major ideological importance.

On November 10 and 11, 1977, the Canadian Political Science Association and the Association canadienne des sociologues et des anthropologues de langue française organized a colloquium (convened by Jean-François Léonard) with the proposed theme to be a "survey of the Parti Québécois government" entitled "One Year After." During the colloquium, of the general analyses concerning the PQ, the papers given by Pierre Fournier, Arnaud Sales, and Gilles Bourque dealt more exclusively with the PQ's link to social classes. These three papers were published in *La chance au coureur*[31] and marked the starting point of a long search towards a consensus. One week later, in Toronto, on November 18 and 19, 1977, a colloquium was held on "The American Empire and Dependent States: Canada and the Third World." One session in particular was devoted to Quebec and had for its theme "The Parti Québécois government, social classes and the state." Jorge Niosi and I presented papers whose commentators were Pierre Fournier and Jean-Guy Vaillancourt. Many Quebec researchers attended and participated in the discussions of this colloquium; among them were Arnaud Sales, Carol Levasseur, Paul Bélanger, and Gilles Bourque. Jorge Niosi's contribution was very much in line with what he published six months later in the first issue of *Les Cahiers du socialisme*.[32] My paper was published by the *Canadian Review of Sociology and Anthropology* in its May 1978 issue.[33]

Following this, various propositions for the study of the Parti Québécois were analyzed, criticized, and qualified in the first three issues of *Les Cahiers du socialisme* (1978-79) and a special issue of *Politique Aujourd'hui* was published in the spring of 1978 as well as in a reader edited by Pierre Fournier published the following December. Since the ideological and political factors analyzed in this colloquium and published in some articles have direct implications for understanding the times to come, they merit attention.

Yet, before engaging in this analysis, I want to mention some other works no less important on that matter. I am thinking in particular of works like Dorval Brunelle's *La désillusion tranquille*, which was the first to show precisely how the Quebec bourgeoisie has put into place measures to assure the development of its own economic resources. I am also thinking of the works by Jorge Niosi on Canadian capitalism and by Arnaud Sales on the English- and French-Canadian industrial bourgeoisie in Quebec[34] as well as the essay by Jacques Mascotto and Pierre-Yves Soucy.[35] Finally, I would single out, among others, the excellent article by Carol Levasseur and Jean-Guy Lacroix, which appeared in the autumn of 1978 in the second issue of *Les Cahiers du socialisme*.[36] Even though I do not share all the views expressed in all of these works, I would have liked to dedicate a detailed study of them in light of the more recent debates on the Quebec bourgeoisie. Within the limits of this chapter, however, it is impossible for me to do so.

A Problematic

Five points comprise the essence of my analysis of the bourgeoisie and the Parti Québécois:

1. The PQ is the representative of the interests of the nonmonopolistic bourgeoisie in Quebec.
2. The superstructural aspects that determine the place of the nonmonopolistic Quebec bourgeoisie effectively dominate its constitution. With only its economic determination (in spite of its own structural weakness, which is itself overdetermined) and clinging tenaciously to vague desires for autonomy under many banners, the Quebec bourgeoisie would not have lasted very long.
3. From its structural composition into distinct practical, economic, judicial, political, and ideological interests, this capital becomes a socially organized force, producing effects on all classes and parties in Quebec and even in all of Canada. It is the constitution of the nonmonopolistic Quebec bourgeoisie into an *autonomous* class fraction by its expression as a party.
4. Those French-Canadian elements who participate in relations with monopolistic interests amalgamate themselves with these interests in such a way that their "ethnic" character *does not yet support any division.*
5. We can well see that the analysis of a political party does not consist only of identifying the character of its members, but mostly of its relation to the places classes have in the social structure. Thus, the analyses that explain the PQ by its "technocratic" composition lead to an oversimplification and obscure the problem of struggles within the state and, indirectly, within Canadian federalism. The PQ is an organization of the nonmonopolistic bourgeoisie with working-class and petty-bourgeois supporters.[37]

To isolate these elements enables one to grasp the course of the debates on classes. As will be seen later, oppositions and agreements successively came forth around these elements.

Denis Monière wrote in October 1979:

> Is it possible to speak of a bourgeoisie 'Québécoise' in the full sense of the term, when the latter's ties prevent it from autonomously determining the economic development of Quebec? This manacled and dependent bourgeoisie can be called Québécoise only in the minimal sense that it resides in a specific geographic area, Quebec. Can this bourgeoisie which lives in Quebec really identify itself with a nationalist policy and thus risk compromising its position vis-à-vis capital and a Canadian bourgeoisie for which it is only the representative of an ethnic but dependent fraction? This answer can only be a negative one. [As a consequence of this first position,] sovereignty-association . . . implies that a larger part of political power will be controlled by a new petty bourgeoisie which could in turn accede to power in the economic elite.[38]

Although the political tendencies resisting these positions are clear, their theoretical premises are more complex, but unfortunately I can give only a brief overview of them here. The foundations of the theoretical and methodological differences are, of course, ideological. Nevertheless, these differences can sometimes show the prevalent influence of a particular approach at a specific time within the social-science community, and this does not necessarily mean that the positions of these authors did not evolve or that they accepted definite or full responsibility each time for all the consequences. This is why I will cautiously treat these divergences without any predictions for their future. However, before unravelling this evolution, it would seem to me to be useful to state in general the main presuppositions for those interpretations.

Some Theoretical Differences

Of course, a consensus on the structure of social relations in Quebec would have led to a greater unity in the analysis of the Parti Québécois and, as a result, in the strategy and tactics which had to be put into effect by the left in Quebec.

But this, in fact, did not materialize. Those whom I call here "university researchers of the left" (without implying a slight to other marxist researchers whose works are not studied here) for the simple convenience of the sociological expression, and who thus have a strong adherence to historical materialism, were divided on the definition of the social division of labour in Quebec—that is, what classes existed, their internal composition, and which of them were more important than others.

The disagreements concerning the bourgeoisie were without a doubt the basis of most debates. For some, there is no real Quebec bourgeoisie; for others, the distinction between a French-Canadian and a Quebec bourgeoisie is an object of contention. For still others, the recognition of a nationalist bourgeoisie and/or a compradore bourgeoisie is obvious, yet, for others, this is not so important. Finally, some find it essential to make distinctions between monopoly capital and nonmonopolistic capital, between petty bourgeoisie and small and medium-sized enterprises, while others consider these distinctions as superfluous. The incorporation or exclusion of one or another of these criteria affects the particular perception of the PQ as well as the political positions taken therefrom.

Just as the schools of thought on the bourgeoisie diverge, so do schools of thought on the petty bourgeoisie. In effect, because of its intermediate position between the bourgeoisie and the working class, the criteria used to define this class, as much towards an ascending or descending tendency, cause numerous disagreements. Many definitions diverge concerning the boundary between the bourgeoisie and the petty bourgeoisie.[39] Some, for example, include all professionals, embracing those who accumulate and concentrate their resources while rendering the organization of labour into a manifold of more complex levels and services; when researchers classify them in such cases as petty bourgeois (no matter their concentrated revenues), they claim more emphasis on the abstract nature of their work as professionals, independent of the transformation of social relations. The same works tend to deny the existence of a Quebec bourgeoisie, since the nationalist petty bourgeoisie holds a dominant class position in Quebec opposed to the Canadian bourgeoisie. Administrators of equity capital and high levels of the state, and often the small and medium-sized businesses, thus fall into the petty-bourgeoisie category. For this tendency, the petty bourgeoisie is a class with a strong upward polarization. Further, many levels of salaried intellectual workers (white collar) and all salaried employees and production workers compose the working class. More often than not, this model ends with two particularly Quebec classes: (1) a petty bourgeoisie of artisans, bureaucrats, professionals, high-level state bureaucrats, and intellectuals who aid social reproduction and (2) a working class covering all the rest of salaried employees. At the level of analysis of contemporary events, this conceptual model supports the analysis of the PQ as a party of the petty bourgeoisie in a popular alliance with the working class or, to say the same thing, the rest of the Quebec population. These same writers will thus deny, on one hand, the existence of a Quebec bourgeoisie and will present the PQ, on the other, as a party with social-democratic leanings under the leadership of petty-bourgeois interests.

In a completely different vein, other writers recognize the existence of a Quebec bourgeoisie with its own political position and a petty bourgeoisie that is less the amalgamation of the economic interests of an elite than a profoundly contradictory class, comprised of a vast network of salaried employees socially distinct from the working class, yet polarized towards it and the bourgeoisie. Consequently, for this second trend, the Parti Québécois appears as a more complex entity, with its relationship to the Quebec bourgeoisie as a central and dominant factor and with a more contradictory alliance with the socially dominated levels, or those of the petty bourgeoisie and the working class. This last trend does not see the PQ as a social-democratic party, since its political and ideological relationship with the dominated classes is one of legitimation of the underlying interests of a Quebec nationalist bourgeoisie that directs its designs.

Finally, the working class is the great loser in the analyses of this period. Seen as an electoral client of and support for the large parties, the working class is used by nationalists to increase the standing of the support given to the Parti Québécois; the critics who see the PQ as giving short shrift to the interests of workers must seek the development of a truly independentist socialist movement with all the necessary formations therefrom. From the viewpoint of the different theoretical approaches, the working class had not been before the referendum a privileged object of study.

In Search of a Consensus

The method I will use to depict the successive stages of thought on the Quebec bourgeoisie in the years 1976-1980 will consist of ascertaining the main points through a chronological reading of the works whose evolution profited much from polemics. These points do not represent a summary of those attributes that would set themselves down like so many superimposed levels on our former vacuous understanding! Rather, they came more from a slow maturation and appear, it seems to me, in the form of a rupture, at least at the level of the works under study here. In effect, the strong colouring of the methodological oppositions incontestably led to the deepening of a political approach, to the detriment of an economism that was too reductionist. In fact, this qualitative turn in thought did occur, but it consolidated itself under pressure from opposed perspectives. The analysis by Gilles Bourque (cited in note 25) is revealing in this respect, since it is a synthesis of the postulates underlying the work since the autumn of 1977 and it enriches the debate with more subtle conceptual tools, which correspond better to the complexity of the real.

In leftist literature, the question of the Quebec bourgeoisie has always been problematic. It is not necessary, I believe, to come back to this point, since many authors have abundantly dealt with it. We essentially need to remember the texts by Roch Denis and Luc Racine, by Michel Van Schendel, as well as the editorial in the 20-21 issue of *Socialisme* of 1970, then of the works of Dorval Brunelle and the article by Alfred Dubuc in *Politique Aujourd'hui*: all these authors claim the existence of a Quebec bourgeoisie, whether it be called middle class, compradore, or something else. The only important paper that denies the existence of a bourgeoisie is the aforementioned famous article of 1970 by Bourque and Laurin-Frenette, which the authors themselves have largely recanted. It is nevertheless without scruples that certain analyses make a short nationalist trip into marxism to use it as an exhibit in the file on the PQ—petty-bourgeois social-democratic party.

It was at a colloquium during the Congress of Socialist Studies held under the auspices of the Association canadienne-française pour l'avancement des sciences at Laval University in June 1976 that Pierre Fournier raised anew the question so often repeated in the past 20 years: "Vers une grande bourgeoisie canadienne-française?" Taken up in November following the occasion of the survey "One year later," he tried to respond more positively by stating that "the policy of sovereignty-association is the logical extention of the economic and political ambitions of the local bourgeoisie."[40] Pierre Fournier was still speaking at the time "of francophone capital, of a local bourgeoisie." He added, "There is little to be hoped for from the small and medium-sized enterprises in Quebec."[41] At the same colloquium, Arnaud Sales stated his point by strongly emphasizing the "weak representation of French Canadians in the ownership of capital"[42]; consequently, since the theoretical space for a distinction among "the Quebec bourgeoisie, the French-Canadian bourgeoisie, and the Canadian bourgeoisie" had not yet been elaborated, the PQ's policy was, according to Sales, that of a "statist technobureaucracy."[43] During the same colloquium, Gilles Bourque returned to the themes presented in my book, *Les classes sociales au Québec*, and stated that "the policies of the PQ favour, *in the last analysis,* the goals of a Quebec bourgeoisie whose principal elements are actually *nonmonopolistic,*"[44] "that the specificity produced in Quebec by the double reality of the nationalist question and of the existence of regional political power permits us to constitute the Quebec bourgeoisie into a *social force* capable of provoking the dismemberment of the Canadian State,"[45] and, finally, that "when we speak of the PQ," we must distinguish "between the interests that prevail in the last analysis and the social *origins* of its political cadres, of its political representatives and of its preferred supporters."[46]

The two positions with which Jorge Niosi and I confronted each other for the first time a week later at the Toronto colloquium further pointed up the differences in perspectives. Niosi mainly developed the view that there exists "a new French-Canadian bourgeoisie which has come of age in the post-Second World War period"[47]; however, "it is nothing but the French-Canadian section of the Canadian capitalist class ... not in the least interested in the separation of Quebec" and "therefore Bourque and Laurin-Frenette have minimized the possibilities of connections." This, consequently, made Niosi state (in a thesis similar to one by Arnaud Sales) that "the PQ represents a part of the traditional petty bourgeoisie, the liberal professions, as well as a majority of teachers and bureaucrats" while "the petty bourgeoisie, joined together in the cooperative movement [Niosi means here the administrators and users of the Caisses populaires Desjardins (CPD)], can find in the program and practice of the *Péquiste* government something to fuel its dreams of self-defense against the aggressions of big capital." The criteria used by Niosi in his argument against the existence of a bourgeoisie rested on the fact that "the market, the investments, and designs" of this capital are pan-Canadian. In addition, the administrators of the Desjardins movement cannot be part of the bourgeoisie according to Niosi because they "come from the petty bourgeoisie ..., that they are not the private owners of the movement, and that they cannot either benefit in a personal way from the assets of these institutions or finance a political party of their own choice." All this enabled Niosi to conclude that "if the working class wants one day to become the hegemonic class of Quebec or Canadian society, it will have to—in a strategy of class alliance—take back for its own at least a part of the demands of the nationalist petty bourgeoisie in Quebec."[48]

At the same colloquium, I maintained that:

> Weak as it is economically, the Quebec nonmonopolistic capital finds in the superstructure, the nationalist question, and the formal rupture of the power of the Canadian state those elements that constitute it as an autonomous fraction of a class ... which is saying that it operates as a social force, producing its own effects in the political struggle, on the other fractions and classes. ... The Quebec nonmonopolistic capital represents an *autonomous* fraction of the bourgeoisie; that is, it functions with its own unity and this is, in my opinion, what the PQ has just demonstrated."[49]

I indicated, in the same article, what seemed to me to be the basis of the relationship of a party to classes and, as an example, described the most recent modifications in Quebec's social structure which had brought the "internal transformation of Quebec nonmonopolistic capital which, through its adoption of a diversified facade, had acquired a new social composition." I reiterated that "the class membership of the PQ is not defined by its supporters, nor by the social origin of its members."[50]

The two colloquia of November 1977 showed that there were still some ambiguities:

1. The Quebec bourgeoisie and French-Canadian bourgeoisie were still not distinct.
2. The economic foundations of the Quebec bourgeoisie were not yet sufficiently elucidated;
3. The weight of political factors in its constitution were not agreed on.
4. The sector of the small and medium-sized enterprises was either understated or reduced to the petty bourgeoisie.

The spring issue of the French periodical *Politique Aujourd'hui* gave Bourque and Fournier the opportunity to elaborate on some of their earlier claims. Bourque again took up positions that we had stated together and he added some further useful distinctions. He defined the Quebec bourgeoisie as "a class with a base of accumulation initially in Quebec and which principally pressures the provincial state to defend its interests." Thus, a regional bourgeoisie like the Quebec bourgeoisie which, in a "normal" situation, should play but a marginal political role can, with the grace of a fusion of the double phenomena of regional powers and a nationalist question, put into danger the very existence of the Canadian state.[51]

Returning to the centre of the debate, Bourque writes again of the "lack of cohesion, of the dispersion and the extreme economic weakness" of this bourgeoisie, which, he said, "with the grace of the development of the state can develop into a socially autonomous force." Finally, Bourque again considers the difference between "the interests defended by a party in the last analysis and the class situation of its middle-level political cadres, of its political representatives and of its preferred supporters." He insists in the end that the PQ is not "a socially monolithic party."[52]

Pierre Fournier also announced what would become the principal asset of his contributions: he designates "the three levels of the francophone bourgeoisie as the private sector, the state, and the cooperative movement"; in addition, he distinguishes different fractions within the bourgeoisie, which he calls "québécoise": a federalist fraction . . . and a nationalist fraction."[53]

Six months later, Jorge Niosi crystallized the axes in the "Fournier-Bourque-Niosi" debate. Adhering anew to the thesis that the PQ is a (technocratic) petty-bourgeois party, he collects in his stride the works of Denis Monière, Vera Murray, Henry Milner, and Marcel Fournier.[54] Since his argument was criticized by Bourque in the following issue of *Les Cahiers du socialisme,* I will avoid a critical treatment here. For the main, I will underline that besides the severe criticism he makes of the PQ's ostensible social-democratic aspect, which he considers as "an illusion" and with the fact that perhaps "some leaders of the PQ consider themselves as true representatives of Quebec's national interests, as well as those of its bourgeoisie,"[55] Niosi again affirms that what is meant here is the "representative of the technocratic petty bourgeoisie." Hard on the theses of Fournier and Bourque, he brings forth the juridicoeconomic criteria he most favours.

If, and there is no reason to doubt it, Niosi's position cannot be reduced to the points cited in this analysis, then there remains the fact that the themes of this debate condensed in these articles contributed, no matter what their nuances, to the strengthening of distinct ideological poles. This is why I spoke above of a rupture and a "qualitative turn": the following two articles mark an important phase in the response to the position that claims the PQ is a petty-bourgeois party.

Pierre Fournier, in January 1979, gave us the last in the stream of this polemic. Strengthened by previous confrontations, Fournier separated these results:

1. The rejection of the concept "French-Canadian bourgeoisie" and affirmation of a distinction between a Quebec bourgeoisie and a Canadian one in which we find some Quebec elements;
2. Recognition of the "important superstructural factor to help find class fractions."
3. Recognition that "the Quebec bourgeoisie has its own bases of accumulation."
4. Recognition "of the economic weight and potential of the small and medium-sized enterprises."[56]

As well, Fournier expresses reservations about the pertinence of the distinction between monopolistic and nonmonopolistic capital, and puts forth the hypothesis that the Quebec bourgeoisie is monopolistic.[57]

The spring 1979 article by Gilles Bourque disentangled anew, in an even more subtle form, the essential theses. Again, he reminds us of the superstructural factors in the constitution of the regional Quebec bourgeoisie: "the nationalist question, the specificity of the Keynesian state in the Canadian political division, the particularity of nonmonopolistic regional capital" does not give it "the degree of economic cohesiveness characteristic of a truly national bourgeoisie which is capable of sustaining an autonomous policy orientation separating itself, at least in a minimal sense, from imperialist interests." Bourque adds, "If the *Péquiste* policy shows the potential for an eventual affirmation of a Quebec monopolistic capital, based on a few industries which tend towards monopoly (Hydro-Québec, Sidbec, Provigo), then the contradictions between monopoly capital and nonmonopolistic capital still principally oppose Canadian capital against

Quebec capital."[58] I had myself previously put forward this claim by stating in 1977, "The analysis of the concrete base of the social division of labour in Quebec permits one to see that the nationalist question is ultimately tied to the conditions in Quebec for the struggle between nonmonopolistic and monopoly capital."[59]

The scope of these debates, which cannot of course be reduced to just the articles considered here, has nonetheless produced a limbering up of the tools for analysis. This is what made Bourque want to insist, in the third issue of *Les Cahiers du socialisme,* on the danger of reducing "the PQ to the restrained and short-term interests of one single class." This is why the concept of "hegemonic fraction of the party" becomes pertinent to designate in the last analysis the dominant social force. Thus, the PQ comes out as a "political formation which enabled the hegemonization of the nationalist movement principally initiated by the new petty bourgeoisie (and, secondly, by the traditional petty bourgeoisie) for the profit of the regional Quebec bourgeoisie."[60]

The debate was not yet closed. In November 1979, Monière stated once more the theses of the technocratic petty bourgeoisie and of the nonexistence of a Quebec bourgeoisie in order to, in what would be one of the privileged intellectual summersaults of leftist nationalism, "present the indispensable facts for clear decision making"[61] on the referendum.

Conclusion

The first and, what seems to me, the most blinding position consists of recognizing the precariousness of the questioning. These writings, in their evolution, progress, and hesitations, well reflect the difficult stage we have been going through. As much as certain analyses sometimes diverged, at just as many times did the conditions of the struggles and the progress of the labour movement bring them closer, above and beyond the differences. Such occurrences are essential. I will conclude by emphasizing that in these debates—deeply linked together by their content, their preoccupations, and their conclusions for the Quebec labour movement—a new tendency seems to have broken with the economistic reductions that characterized and confined the articles of the past 15 years to a narrow nationalist vision. In the name of marxism, at the time a certain economism filled an important occluding function in the political battles that followed. It is necessary to add that criticizing petty-bourgeois nationalism does not signify a rejection of a true independence plan. Thus, let it be permitted to hope that the differences will still generously confront and that the larger forces of Quebec's social movements will not escape from that principle of diversity that has made its history and will continue to make it change.

Notes

1. Jacques Dofny and Marcel Rioux, "Les classes sociales au Canada français," *Revue française de Sociologie* 3: 3 (summer 1962).

2. Gilles Bourque and Nicole Laurin-Frenette, "Classes sociales et idéologies nationalistes au Québec (1760-1970)," *Socialisme* 20 (1970), pp. 13-55, and "La structure nationale québécoise," *Socialisme* 21-22, pp. 109-55.
3. Dofny and Rioux, op. cit.
4. Jean-Marc Piotte, "Sens et limites du néo-nationalisme," *Parti Pris* 4: 1 (Sept.-Oct. 1966), pp. 24-39.
5. Michel Van Schendel, "Pour une théorie du socialisme au Québec," *Socialisme* 17 (1969), pp. 7-20.
6. Bourque and Laurin-Frenette, op. cit.
7. Jean-Marc Piotte, *Un parti pris politique* (Montreal: VLB Editions, 1979), p. 132.
8. Ibid., p. 170.
9. Gilles Bourque, Luc Racine, and Gilles Dostaler, "Pour un mouvement socialiste et indépendantiste," *Parti Pris* 5: 8 (summer 1968), p. 30.
10. Alfred Dubuc, "Les classes sociales au Canada de 1760 à 1840," *Annales ESC* (Université de Montréal) 22: 4 (1967), pp. 829-44.
11. Gilles Bourque, *Classes sociales et question nationale au Québec—1760-1840* (Montreal: Editions Parti Pris, 1970).
12. Gilles Bourque, "La nation," *Les Cahiers du socialisme* 1 (spring 1978), p. 195.
13. Stanley B. Ryerson, *Le capitalisme et la confédération, aux sources du conflit Canada-Québec (1760-1873)* (Montreal: Editions Parti Pris, 1972).
14. Hélène David, "L'état des rapports de classes au Québec—1945-1967," *Sociologie et Société* VII: 2 (1975), pp. 33-67.
15. Dorval Brunelle, *La désillusion tranquille* (Montreal: Hurtubise/HMH, Cahiers du Québec, Collection Sociologie, 1978).
16. Nicole Laurin-Frenette, *Production de l'état et formes de la nation* (Montreal: Nouvelle-Optique, 1978).
17. Roch Denis, *Luttes de classes et question nationale au Québec, 1948-1968* (Montreal: Paris, 1979).
18. Gilles Bourque and Anne Legaré, *Le Québec—La question nationale* (Paris: Maspero, 1979).
19. Mario Dumais, "Les classes sociales au Québec," *Parti Pris* 3: 1-2 (1966), pp. 42-63.
20. Jean-Marc Piotte, *Un parti pris politique* (Montreal: VLB Editions, 1979), pp. 14-15.
21. Ibid., p. 16.
22. Gilles Bourque, "On n'est pas le Congo," *Parti Pris* 5: 5 (Feb. 1968).
23. Luc Racine and Roch Denis, "La conjoncture politique québécoise depuis 1960," *Socialisme québécois* 21-22 (1970), pp. 17-78.
24. Bourque and Laurin-Frenette, op. cit., p. 13.
25. Gilles Bourque, "Petite bourgeoisie envahissante et bourgeoisie ténébreuse," *Les Cahiers du socialisme* 3 (spring 1979), p. 122. Chapter 9 in this book is a translation of this article.
26. Laurin-Frenette, op. cit., p. 55.
27. Michel Van Schendel, "Impérialisme et classe ouvrière au Québec," *Revue Socialisme québécois* 21-22 (1971), pp. 156-209.
28. Céline St-Pierre, "De l'analyse marxiste des classes dans le mode de production capitaliste," *Socialisme québécois* 24 (1974).
29. Piotte, *Un parti pris politique*, op. cit., p. 212.

30. Anne Legaré, *Les classes sociales au Québec* (Montreal: Presses de l'Université du Quebec, 1977).
31. Arnaud Sales, "Vers une techno-bureaucratie de l'état," Pierre Fournier, "Projet national et affrontement des bourgeiosies québécoise et canadienne," and Gilles Bourque, "Question nationale et réforme constitutionnelle," all in *La Chance au coureur* (Montreal: Nouvelle-Optique, 1978).
32. Jorge Niosi, "La nouvelle bourgeoisie canadienne-française," *Les Cahiers du socialisme* 1 (spring 1978), pp. 5-51.
33. Anne Legaré, "Les classes sociales et le gouvernement du PQ," *Canadian Review of Sociology and Anthropology* 15: 2 (1978), pp. 218-27.
34. Arnaud Sales, *La bourgeoisie industrielle au Québec* (Montreal: Les Presses de l'Université de Montréal, 1979).
35. Jacques Mascotto and Pierre-Yves Soucy, *Sociologie politique de la question nationale* (Montreal: Albert St-Martin, 1979).
36. Carol Levasseur and Jean-Guy Lacroix, "Rapports des classes et obstacles économiques à l'association," *Les Cahiers du socialisme* 2 (fall 1978), pp. 87-122.
37. Legaré, *Les classes sociales au Québec*, op. cit., pp. 189-94.
38. Denis Monière, *Les enjeux du référendum* (Montreal: Editions Québec-Amérique, 1979), p. 157.
39. As Alfred Dubuc has stated, "The analysis that indifferently imputes to the petty bourgeoisie all the smalltime manufacturers as well as bureaucrats of all levels lacks refinement and subtlety." See Dubuc, *Le capitalisme au Quebec* (Montreal: Albert St-Martin, 1978), pp. 40-47, 62-63.
40. Fournier, "Projet national et affrontement des bourgeoisies québécoise et canadienne," op. cit., p. 56.
41. Ibid., p. 52.
42. Sales, "Vers une techno-bureaucratie d'état," op. cit., p. 28.
43. Ibid., p. 39.
44. Bourque, "Question nationale," op. cit., p. 196.
45. Ibid., p. 197.
46. Ibid., p. 196.
47. Niosi, "La nouvelle bourgeoisie canadienne-française," op. cit., p. 14.
48. Ibid., pp. 30, 35, 37.
49. Legaré, "Les classes sociales et le gouvernement du PQ," p. 224.
50. Ibid., pp. 219-23.
51. Gilles Bourque, "Le Parti Québécois dans les rapports de classes," *Politiques Aujourd'hui* 7-8 (1978), pp. 87, 89.
52. Ibid., pp. 89-90.
53. Pierre Fournier, "Le Parti Québécois et la conjoncture économique au Québec," *Politique Aujourd'hui* 7-8 (1978), p. 75.
54. For Marcel Fournier particularly, "the political nationalism" of the PQ corresponds to the "social conversions" of the traditional petty bourgeoisie as well as some elements of the francophone bourgeoisie, he says, "which leads them to be transformed into a new petty bourgeoisie and a new bourgeoisie, respectively." See *La chance au coureur* (Montreal: Nouvelle-Optique, 1978), p. 180.
55. Jorge Niosi, "Le gouvernement du PQ deux ans après," *Les Cahiers du*

socialisme 2 (fall 1978), p. 45.

56. Pierre Fournier, "Les nouveaux paramètres de la bourgeoisie québécoise," *Le capitalisme au Québec* (Montreal: Albert St-Martin, 1978), pp. 138, 140. A revised and updated version of this article appears in English as Chapter 12 of this book.
57. Ibid., p. 142.
58. Bourque, "Petite bourgeoisie," op. cit., pp. 141, 139, 144.
59. Legaré, *Les classes sociales au Québec*, op. cit., p. 122.
60. Bourque, "Petite bourgeoisie," op. cit., pp. 122, 150.
61. Monière, op. cit.

Chapter 8/Quebec: One or Many Roads toward Change?*

Anne Legaré

In any serious study of the transformations within Quebec society, the national question is at the forefront of most perspectives. Can we claim that the multiple struggles of classes and social movements have been united through the Parti Québécois to form a common denominator leading to the ascension of a historical agent capable of carrying on new social relations? In short, from a class analysis doomed to failure due to simplistic and pretentious reductions, can the national movement in Quebec be in good position to articulate a policy of change sufficiently wideranging to transcend the pitfalls of those simplistic perspectives that have so often hindered the socialist movement?

Certainly we are quite far from such a perspective, but it is not pointless to ask these questions when the labour movement is slowly disintegrating because it has lost its direction. Today we can admit that the socialist question can no longer be schematized and it is never too soon to show a strong hand in the face of pressing situations and develop multidimensional projects, irreducible to either orthodox class analyses of democratic practices perverted by institutionalism. How and at what cost should we modify our thinking to give due respect to history which has, as many have said before, shown us numerous examples for critical hindsight? This is not a step backwards, but merely the posing of a legitimate question: what collective subject will emerge from the variegated identities in the Quebec nation to carry it towards a better future? This article cannot conjure one up; rather, it will try to escape an excessively mechanical analysis in order to remind the reader of some of the ponderous diversities that elicit debate in contemporary Quebec.

Should we then ask what would be desirable for Quebec or Canada and how we might obtain it? Or should we not look instead to the sociocultural and political transformations that are occurring already and constitute the underpinning for change? I find this second question more interesting and will try to concentrate on noninstitutional developments now going on, rather than on the political fortunes of the left within the political parties or trade-union movement.

I do not underestimate the importance of trade-union organization or working-class mobilization in any evolution towards socialism in Quebec. But socialists must also examine the superstructure, which is itself an object of transformation. I am thinking of noninstitutional and collective processes of creation in which the democratic experience is an internal objective. Such

---

*Translated by Philip Resnick, Department of Political Science, University of British Columbia.

experiences seek to overcome the domination-subordination relation of class society and to avoid the pitfalls of authoritarianism, sexual division, and elitism that so profoundly mark working-class organizations today.

My decision to focus on the quest for cultural identity and democratization does not mean I would make light of the diverse groups on the left and far left in Quebec. Whether they seek grand political alliances or define themselves as formations with fixed and rival ideologies, their attempts at developing the subjective consciousness of the working class make them important elements. However, in the absence of a mass movement, there would be little point in my weighing their relative importance, especially since each group, in seeking hegemony over the others, twists the facts to suit its purpose.

Some might also have hoped that I would address the conditions for the formation of a vast organization of the Quebec working class, quite independent of the PQ or, for that matter, the NDP. While I will not discuss party politics directly, it does indirectly enter into my concerns in this chapter. I maintain that the socialist option must emerge out of conditions qualitatively different from those of a class society; hence, the *internal democratic capacity* of the organization or movements, large or small, counts as much as membership, persuasive power, ideology, or strategy. I am in fact opting for Gramsci's conception, whereby the conditions for the formation of a new hegemony entail a slow process of penetrating the existing social institutions *before* the reversal of bourgeois power.

For the outside observer, there would be no difficulty in recognizing that Quebec is passing through an important phase in its history and that the future of Canada is still closely tied to it. Some would even claim that the national question in Quebec is the direct road to socialism. Let us try to evaluate the complexity and richness of the political and cultural stakes in Quebec today.

As my point of departure I would argue that the cultural space—that is, the customs, behavioural patterns, relations to the world (including artistic expression and creation of a people or nation)—constitutes a privileged place of encounter between the national and the social questions: it can also transform into a sociocultural movement; we cannot reduce the study of Quebec to analyzing only the path of its political parties. The history of New France, of Canada, and of contemporary Quebec has been such that partisan politics only narrowly comes to terms with the social movement that shapes Quebec's condition. The provincial political system is now bipartisan: the passage of time has eliminated would-be third parties. The traditional left has had no direct access to the political stage. Since the rise of nationalism in the 1970s, there have been two electoral interlocutors, the pro-federalist Liberal party of Quebec and the Parti Québécois, promoter of sovereignty-association.

Alongside these political parties, the double power of the federal and provincial governments controls all state institutions and penetrates the cultural sphere. Here we note a particular Quebec characteristic. As a response to national oppression within the juridicopolitical framework of the federal regime, the traditional ideological apparatuses and the civil society as a whole become obsessed with the search for a national identity and a sovereign culture. The government of Quebec and diverse social groupings promote this search.

What follows is a profound overdetermination of the cultural domain by the national question and, as a result, the appropriation of these foci of power by social classes that articulate a national project. These can be either an autonomous bourgeoisie playing for the maximum political stakes or the petty bourgeoisie carrying on with its functions of social reproduction.

These autonomous tendencies of the Quebec bourgeoisie and petty bourgeoisie run smack into numerous obstacles: foreign (English Canadian or American) control of the "cultural industries,"[1] English-Canadian political culture, and a polarization towards the federal nation-state that the French-Canadian federalist elite promotes. In the last two decades, especially since the founding of the Parti Québécois in 1968, we have seen a hardening of positions on both sides.

Because of the strategic difficulties inherent in its position and its own political astigmatism, the PQ has had to significantly water down its social program as well as its commitment to independence. In the absence of any alternative derived from a more advanced social policy, supporters of independence were reduced to repeating the same old slogans. The PQ's social commitments went by the board, as nationalist demands gave way to constitutional ones, adapted to association with the rest of Canada.

More fervent spirits, while not completely spurning the PQ, began to look for alternative paths. Instead of carrying on the struggle in the same partisan way as before, they came to adopt a position of critical support for the PQ on the one hand and the development of autonomous and extra-institutional forms of activity on the other. Their preferred venue was cultural. Thus, supporters of independence directed their energy into a series of plans and projects trying to escape to the sphere of the state and the PQ, but aiming at the Quebec society of tomorrow.

Was this prodigious displacement the direct consequence of the crisis of the party system common to advanced industrial societies? Was it a consequence of the individualistic instincts of these actors? Was it a natural reaction to the PQ's attempt to shore up its support among a more conservative base? What I would suggest, rather, is that we need to open our conceptual horizons to cultural concerns, no less than to sociopolitical factors of the traditional sort. Perhaps the impertinence of this frantic search heralded explosive paradoxes rather than political consistency. This, I believe, is where we must begin to explore cultural production and, through it, the transformations going on in Quebec.

In any case, my methodological bias lies here. And I might add that I am highly critical of the type of centralization of thought in the social sciences that would restrict the study of change almost exclusively to parties and trade unions. If such analyses were adequate for liberal societies at the competitive stage, if they are still highly useful in analyzing the relationship between ruling classes and the state, they do not allow us to map the undercurrents that agitate the rest of society and constantly undermine hegemonic institutions. The central position we give to political parties in analyzing the politics of capitalist states masks what is really happening and leads to a reductive, rather than a qualitative, conception of social change. That is why this chapter criticizes what I call a "partyist" bias that implies no salvation outside of parties.

This is not the place to get into a long discussion of this question. Suffice it to say that the particularities of new movements in Quebec lie at least as much in the noninstitutional and cultural domains as in parties, trade unions, and institutions that I myself have worked on before. I shall return to this theme shortly. First, however, some remarks about the principal tendencies in the structure of social relations in Quebec and about the situation the PQ finds itself in.

Changes in the Social Structure

During the 1960s, Quebec underwent radical and sudden changes. The Liberal government of Jean Lesage called this period the Quiet Revolution, but a Quebec sociologist has realistically changed this to the "Quiet Disillusionment." What was happening was not a real social renewal but an adaptation to the imperatives of a modernized mode of production and a catching up with Ontario. Table 8-1 shows how Dorval Brunelle traces the evolution of the work force between 1951 and 1971.

These figures show the increased importance of "intellectual" labour. In conjunction with the growth of office work, the total increase was about 15% in 20 years. Manual employment, by comparison, declined by a similar percentage, though absolute numbers may have increased. We can therefore speak of a striking tendency to the bureaucratization of salaried labour.

In the same vein, we should note the evolution of the primary, secondary, and tertiary sectors during the 1961-1971 period. (See Table 8-2.) The growth of the tertiary sector, which encompasses many of the functions of social reproduction as well as of office work, backs up the preceding data.

According to my own study of social classes using 1961 statistics, productive manual labourers constituted 22%, manual labourers separated from direct production and salaried intellectual and clerical workers 22%, the traditional petty bourgeoisie 5.4%, housewives outside the sphere of social production 44%, and capital 5% of the total.[2]

For its part, the new petty bourgeoisie, because of its close links to the social division of labour and to the national question, is a qualitatively important class in Quebec. Three fractions of this class can be isolated, for they represent particular ideological and political tendencies:

1. A proletarianized and highly feminized fraction, whose relationship to the national question is, at best, subordinated to its trade-union affiliation.
2. A bipolarized intellectual fraction, strongly influenced by sociocultural transformations and finding ideological and political expression through cultural outlets.
3. A fraction that exercises functions of domination and authority in the work process (foremen, technicians, teachers, artists) and that tends towards unconditional support for the PQ.

The first two groups suffer from instability of employment and often choose to escape from their condition through marginal activities or planned seasonal unemployment. It is from its ranks that we see the recruitment of a young, floating population, socially marginal, politicized, and fervently nationalist.

Sociological analysis neglected an ethnically diverse working class for a long time because of those workers' organizational weakness and corporatist tradition. The main trade-union organizations in Quebec adopted three different strategies during the 1980 referendum on sovereignty-association. The labour aristocracy (in part in the metal trades) opted, along with the salaried members of the Quebec Federation of Labour, for the PQ. The Confederation of National Trade Unions and the Quebec Teachers Federation, with their base in the public sector—education and social services, for

Table 8-1 Salaried Workers Divided into Four Professional Categories, Quebec percentages

	1951	1961	1971
Manual workers	87.4	84	79.3
Blue collar	54.5	48.6	39
White collar	32.9	35.4	40.3
Intellectual workers	8.1	10.1	13
Administrators and Directors	3.7	4.7	5.5
Professionals	0.8	1.2	2.2

Source: Dorval Brunelle, *La désillusion tranquille*, Cahiers du Québec, (Montréal: Hurtubise/HMH, 1978), p. 55.

Table 8-2 Number of Employees by Sector of Production, Quebec percentages

Sectors	1961	1971
Primary	3.5	2.5
Secondary	51.1	44.2
Tertiary	45.4	53.2

Source: Same as Table 8-1, p. 60.

example—opted for critical support of the "yes." Finally, the Confederation of Democratic Unions, with its base in the traditional industries, refused to take sides.

As discussed in Chapter 7 of this book, in recent years the nature of the bourgeoisie has been heatedly debated; one position in Quebec argues that we must distinguish between the French-Canadian and the Quebec bourgeoisie.[3] The French-Canadian bourgeoisie is politically and economically part of the Canadian bourgeoisie of which it is a subgroup, though not an autonomous fraction. The Quebec bourgeoisie, for its part, has been closely involved in the formation of the Parti Québécois. This class can be broken down into four sectors[4]:

1. A nonmonopolistic sector (in commerce, financial institutions, construction, and subcontracting for industries).
2. A developing monopolistic sector, linked to state enterprises.
3. The state sector, which has continually grown for the last 10 years, with a base in natural resources such as hydro, steel, mining, and forestry, as well as in industrial research and investment.
4. Finally, the cooperative sector, with its important financial outlets (the *caisses populaires*) which compete with the banks and attract a good deal of Quebec's savings.

These four sectors of Quebec-based capital achieve a fair degree of political unity on the national and regional questions. Their interdependence with the provincial level of state power leads some of its members to support sovereignty. Superstructural elements thus turn a fraction of the Quebec bourgeoisie into a *social force* with a *regional and nationalist* character.

The nationalist question is therefore a factor of ideological cohesion which acts on diverse fractions of the Quebec regional bourgeoisie and petty bourgeoisie. As such, it tends to overdetermine the place of certain agents within the structure according to their social-class basis, while tending to absorb these differences through common electoral objectives.

Let us make no bones about it. This celebrated Quebec nation disturbs social relations and the political map of the whole of Canada. Not only has it helped all provincial parties across Canada to question their own allegiance to the centralizing tendency within the Canadian state, but it has also helped shatter the complacent harmony that reigned *within the Canadian power bloc*. Take, for example, the dispute between Ottawa and Alberta over energy pricing. True, Alberta's oil resources and the power the provinces have over natural resources under the Constitution contributed directly to this crisis in federalism. But the decentralizing movement sparked by Quebec was also a factor in moving regional bourgeoisies in this direction. In our book, *Le Québec—la Question Nationale*, Gilles Bourque and I spoke of "a structural tendency to fly apart" as characterizing the Canadian state.[5] Until the events of autumn 1981, this was very much the case.

The Parti Québécois

One can understand the ideological nature of this party when it was formed in 1968, and its subsequent growth in popularity, only by reference to the preceding 10 years. Under Maurice Duplessis, Quebec had known what several have called "the dark ages" (or *la grande noirceur*) to describe the ideological and political isolation that the government, in alliance with the Church, had imposed for 20 years. Duplessis turned his support among the farmers into a conservative force: "The farmer is an element of economic stability and *social order*. We must maintain and protect *our rural base*."[6] On leaving this long night, Quebec found itself hustled into a process of modernization that awakened many hopes and dreams.

The Rassemblement pour l'Indépendance Nationale (RIN), an independence party, was formed in 1963. Its radicalism inspires the social-democratic fringe of the PQ today. The nationalist bourgeoisie may have won hegemony within the party,[7] but a radical independentist sentiment remains very much alive at the ideological level, especially among those whom the sociologist Marcel Fournier has called "language workers."[8]

The RIN was forced to dissolve itself in 1968 and most of its members joined the PQ, "the party of the rising generation, those under 40, highly educated, who had believed in education as a source of social mobility."[9] The PQ abandoned the platform of independence for an arsenal of electoral planks, including linguistic and cultural reforms at the internal level and a political and economic association with Canada. As Monière puts it, its program "meant the consolidation and expansion of Quebec capitalism." In a period of economic crisis, of crisis in federalism and of weakening American hegemony, the repressive and at times centralizing interventions of the provincial government made PQ supporters bitterly unhappy with the leadership's intentions "to bring humanity into the capitalist system."[10]

The Following Period

On May 20, 1980, 60% of the Quebec electorate turned down the PQ's soft-option proposal of sovereignty-association. According to Maurice Pinard, 48% of francophones voted "yes" in the referendum. More than one Quebec francophone out of two voted against sovereignty-association.[11]

The PQ, however, is the official heir to Quebec nationalism. It has occupied the whole stage since 1968; few Quebec nationalists, however disappointed they might have been with the PQ, would have refused to vote "yes" in the referendum. Statistics aside, however, we must begin to talk about the stagnation of the sovereignty option, of the disavowal of the PQ by supporters of independence, of profound internal splits. Pierre Bourgault, the founder of the RIN demanded René Lévesque's resignation as premier on August 15, 1980, declaring, "We must go back to the fundamental objective of the PQ, independence."[12] Jacques Parizeau, followed by the party executive, declared that same month, "It is clear that any action by which we would try once again to win majority support for Quebec independence is not for tomorrow. . . . The PQ must put sovereignty-association on ice for the coming elections."[13]

What had happened? The PQ had received 40% of the vote in the referendum for at least two reasons. First, the PQ had the monopoly on the national question and had succeeded, through its strong support in the petty bourgeoisie, in blocking the formation of any other independentist party on its left. Second, the PQ held onto the support of this clientele, by moving to the centre against the right-wing option of the Liberals and Conservatives in the federalist camp.

If these calculations had worked out, it was also clear that the PQ government was incapable of using the national question to develop the mass movement that had supported it. There were two structural obstacles in the way, which the bourgeois leadership of the party could not, for good class reasons, overcome. The first had to do with the hegemonic place of monopoly capital at the heart of the Canadian state. The regional bourgeoisie's hold on the provincial political scene had to be weakened by the federal level of the state closer to this class. The second lay in the Canadian power bloc's need for at least a modicum of unity among the different regional interests and, hence, for a minimum of rapport between provincial parties and the federal government.

Given the nature of its policy, the PQ could not hope to demonstrate relevance without the support of a vast social movement. Instead of fostering such a movement, it held it back. If there is to be any cultural and social revitalization in Quebec, its occurrence has to be outside of the party system, and more particularly through the development of relationships and movements that tend to be *external* to the state.

The Cultural as a Means of Bypassing Institutional Politics

The limits of a leftist *institutional* politics are evident in Quebec. The mass movement lacks cohesion and ideological direction. Leftist intellectuals are mainly isolated from it and many blindly subscribe to technocratic domination and to the institutions of liberal democracy. All attempts at renewal become entangled in American influence, Anglo-Saxon toleration, a nostalgia for the mother country, an acute search for identity, and so on. These are the contours of a culture without faith and without laws.

A nationalist playwright, Jean-Claude Germain, addresses the problem: "The PQ is in contradiction with its own coming to power because, given the choice between life and death, it has chosen death, i.e. the traditional agony."[14] If the PQ has chosen to agonize, Germain adds, "There is no point for Quebec to go through the trouble of becoming a country to end up as a facsimile instead."[15]

Germain opens the door to a noninstitutional approach. All forms of creation, be they by a single artist or by a group, express an authentic search for cultural identity *set off from state legitimacy, whether that of Quebec or any other.* Creation becomes institutionalized when it must submit to the norms of social reproduction—for example, the legitimacy of relations of domination, of inequality, of cultural domination. True, there is no hard and fast frontier between the state and movements that escape reproduction. Several activities occupy an intermediary space.

My argument is that all processes of creation that have tended since the 1960s to the affirmation of a Quebec cultural identity that is *autonomous from the state*—that is, towards either federal or provincial centres of power—can be seen as *an institutional break.* The Quebec cultural domain therefore spawns new conditions for challenging hegemony. The contradictions described here help expose the causes of the impasse in the political situation in Quebec.

As I indicated above, Quebec's proximity to the North American cultural market, its close links to English Canada, its nostalgia for its French origin, the disenchantment with traditional politics—all make unity around a national policy difficult. That makes it especially important for anyone interested in the future of Quebec society to study the cultural fields. The development of a *nonstatist culture,* autonomous from all legitimacies, is itself a terrain of change. Noninstitutional forms of creating a national identity characterize the present historical moment. The social structure and relations between Quebec and Canada shape these forms and the identities the forms express. In the search for greater autonomy, these collective policies may outline the profile of a new society.

If the national question has still not succeeded, because of the blindness of the PQ's social project, in being transformed into a social question, if working-class and petty-bourgeois nationalism have stagnated under the leadership of the nationalist Quebec bourgeoisie, the live forces of change find expression through other forms. For, with these two dimensions, the structural face of the shattered Canadian state and for the movement of resistance and transformation confronting the actual pan-Canadian hegemony, we still must derive one last connotation—because neither of these dimensions, seen as sleek and qualitatively irreducible in a classical symmetry of contraries, can exhibit the extraordinary diversity they produce. The regional dimension is at the same time both a reductionist and a multiplicating factor. As soon as a consensus on the national question arises, a variety of positions on this common denominator arises. It is as if the new pole of identity produces by itself these distortions. There is a national and regional Québécois identity made up of as many viewpoints and modes of life as there are classes, sexes, subregions, institutions, movements, and so on. The homogeneity is made from its own breakdown, ceaselessly made anew, without the realization of the goal, as if it were cloth defined only by its colourful hues.

This is the course of the current unfolding project, whose maturation is slow and often reversed by the hard face of the state or absorbed in the rehash of a common life in search of a placid security without versatility or differences.

But this cannot be. The social and the national can from now on be nothing else but diversified. And it is thus that they emerge. The deepening of the relative autonomy of the state, followed by the play of regional forces, has a double effect. On the one side is the development of a possible course free from the old hegemony; on the other is secreted within it a new statist legitimation. From this point on, Quebec as a region will try to transform itself into a new referential polarity: the region passes the reduction process of a historical subject into a class subject onto a new universal, the nation.

Already in Quebec this last movement has run its course. Out of the failure to be reduced to one single national subject has arisen a multitude of cultural identities unrepresented by the new power holders. The creation of democracy is always the product of attempts to remain independent from the state. Independence—the backbone of variegated political bodies and of rights to subjectivity, difference, and identity within collective projects for equality—is forged by severing all the legitimate cultural processes of statist legitimation.

In the Canadian-Québécois context, with a state tending to structurally fly apart and a region overdetermined by the national question, the emergence of noninstitutionalized cultural voices without partisan affiliations has a strong political meaning. Everywhere the voices, obstinate in their differences, promise a democracy that can only be continually a search and a creature of the complexities derived from the collective denominator. It is only when struggles against the exploitation of labour will be linked to the struggle against all legitimacy, against organizational centralism, against sexual domination, that the traditional institutions in the struggle for socialism, having themselves been transformed, will become the carriers of change.

Notes

1. Regarding the concept of "cultural industries," see, for example, A. Mattelart and J.P. Piemme, *Télévision: enjeux sans frontières* (Paris: PUF, 1980, pp. 11-30.
2. Anne Légaré, *Les classes sociales au Québec* (Montreal; PUQ, 1977), pp. 116-17.
3. See the article by Pierre Fournier, "Les nouveaux paramètres de la bourgeoisie québécoise," in *Le capitalisme au Québec* (Montreal: Editions Albert St. Martin, 1978), pp. 135-83. Chapter 12 of this book is an updated version of this article.
4. Ibid.
5. G. Bourque and A. Legaré, *Le Québec, la question nationale* (Paris: Maspero, 1979), pp. 217-25.
6. Ibid., p. 141.
7. See Gilles Bourque, "Class, Nation and the Parti Québécois," *Studies in Political Economy* 2 (fall 1979), pp. 129-59, and Chapter 9 of this book.

8. Marcel Fournier in *La chance au coureur,* (Montreal: Nouvelle-Optique, 1978), p. 17.
9. Denis Monière, *Ideologies in Quebec: The Historical Development* (Toronto: University of Toronto Press, 1981), p. 264.
10. Ibid., p. 266.
11. *Le Devoir* (July 25, 1980), p. 9.
12. *Le Devoir* (Aug. 16, 1980), p. 1.
13. *Le Devoir* (Aug. 14, 1980), p. 1. This programmatic retreat bore electoral fruits: witness the important PQ victory on April 13, 1981.
14. J.C. Germain, *Jeu* 12 (fall 1979), pp. 38-40.
15. Ibid., p. 70.

Chapter 9/Class, Nation, and the Parti Québécois*

Gilles Bourque

The election of a Parti Québécois government has revived debate on the relationship among class structure, political parties, and the national question. In an attempt to elucidate the complexity of the social and national dynamics, several studies have isolated one of the above realities—particularly the class basis of the PQ—and the permanence of the Quebec national question vis-à-vis the Canadian state. These are fundamental concerns for the labour movement and affect both the form of organizations and the effectiveness of nationalist discourse among the masses. Although the two problems cannot be separated entirely, this chapter will attempt to bring some thoughts to bear on the analysis of the Parti Québécois.[1]

Whose Party?

In the first two issues of *Les Cahiers du socialisme,* Jorge Niosi questions once more the thesis that the PQ is a bourgeois party.[2] He bases his critique on my arguments in the French periodical *Politique Aujourd'hui* and on those of Pierre Fournier in *La chance au coureur.*[3] Niosi maintains that the interests of the Quebec francophone bourgeoisie are pan-Canadian and that the PQ is therefore a petty-bourgeois party. He further disputes the fact that the upper state echelons (high-ranking civil servants, ministers, directors of corporations and "institutions") and the managerial ranks of the cooperative movements (Mouvement Desjardins, Coopérative Fédérée, Caisses d'Entraide) belong to the bourgeoisie.

Niosi's article has the merit of demonstrating the impossibility of identifying, one to one, the PQ and the bourgeoisie (a thesis, moreover, that I have never put forward). "PQ—parti bourgeois" may be a catchy slogan, but it is no substitute for an analysis of the much more complex social reality. It is a gross simplification to identify the PQ as a mere object of a francophone bourgeoisie. I cannot, however, subscribe to Niosi's conclusion that the PQ is exclusively petty bourgeois. Apart from my specific disagreements on theory, which I shall outline below, I believe that the implicit problematic of most analyses to date has to be reexamined.

Lengthy demonstrations of the link between the PQ and the limited short-term interests of one social class fall prey to reductionism. A political party poses the question of power amid the whole process of the class struggle. Its aim is at least relative control over a continuous process of disorganization and reorganization of social relations. By definition it cannot

*This chapter is an expanded version of an article that appeared in English in *Studies in Political Economy* 2 (fall 1979).

assert itself as the unilateral, unequivocal instrument of one class or class fragment. The struggle between parties in liberal democracies is not a tournament with as many teams as there are classes or fragments.

While, first of all, it is inside a party that the hegemony of one class (or fragment) is imposed on other classes (or fragments), at another level a party constitutes an apparatus allowing for the exertion of maximum pressure on the process of social relations, in the direction of the specific interests it defends. A party appears, then, as one of the important points of internalization of the relations of forces found in a social formation. We may be able to identify the hegemonic fragment of class with a party, but we should not conclude that we have therefore determined the only social force constituting that formation in its specificity.

It is important to relate the analysis of a political party to the totality of the process of transformation of the class struggle. As will be seen, we can thereby avoid certain vicious circles inherent in the present debate, which sees every sociologist, every political scientist, linking the PQ to a different class fragment.

The Process of Transformation of the Class Struggle

In many recent analyses, a political party is implicitly treated as a corporate organization. But a party is not a trade union, not an employers' association, much less a professional association. A party's existence implies a transition from the defence of corporate interests to the promotion of a specific project for society: it must be analyzed in its direct relation to the question of power.

Involved in a party is social space in its totality. A party undertakes not only the promotion of specific, multiple, and heterogeneous interests, but also the reproduction of the totality of the social formation. In it unfolds the whole domain of hegemony, alliances, and compromises. A party seeks to create those political and ideological conditions most favourable to the promotion of the economic interests it defends, whether or not these interests are dominant within the social formation. While it is true that a party does not enjoy the same autonomy vis-à-vis its hegemonic class—or even subordinate classes and fragments in its midst—as the state vis-à-vis the totality of classes, a party is less directly controlled than is a corporate organization by the short-term economic interests of its members. The platform of a party, much less the policy of a government, cannot be unequivocally identified with the specific interests of its hegemonic class. While the legislation of a government may be used as an indication of the class interests defended by a party in power, this is not a demonstration of the operating social forces.

Conversely, a party is not the only instrument for political intervention by a class. Political scientists long ago demonstrated how a class, a fragment, a category, or a social stratum can control certain branches of the state apparatus or certain ideological apparatuses. Corporate organizations can be used for political intervention—for example, the numerous statements emanating from the Chamber of Commerce. This is an important fact to remember, for there is a tendency to take certain corporate stances literally and to deduce from them relations between a class and a party. Thus, some would claim to have proved that the top executives of the cooperative movement do not support the PQ, since they do not openly declare themselves independentist. This spontaneous sociology can be as misleading as the simple addition of legislation, for once more it involves making a one-to-one political relation. An organization may well make lukewarm or conditional comments on the policy of the very party that defends the class interests associated with the organization. Since a political party is a point of internalization of power relations, corporate organizations or even certain branches or apparatuses of the state can provide useful outlets for a class in its relations with its own party.

In conclusion, it is important to consider a political party as internalizing the whole complexity of class relations. Thus, it can be explained why a party in power may be identified with a class that is not hegemonic within the social formation. Until the 1960s, for instance, the Union Nationale controlled the process of the transformation of the class struggle: the reproduction of monopolistic (and Canadian state) capital had to go through the Quebec elite's state. But this control ensured a dominant place for neither the regional bourgeoisie nor the traditional petty bourgeoisie. It did, however, open up for them the greatest possible space in the process of enlarged reproduction of monopoly capitalism and in the dissolution of precapitalist production relations. The various indicators used in studying a party become pertinent, then, only in light of the place of a party in the transformation process that it seeks to inflect.

Important consideration must be given, beyond superficial formulas, to the historical constitution of this process. A party intervenes in order to inflect a process in the direction of specific transformations. While this process is basically determined in the class struggle, it implies a disorganization and reorganization of the totality of social relations, affecting not only classes but also categories and social strata (bureaucracy, clergy, labour aristocracy). Let us see what this problematic can contribute to present debate.

I shall first touch on the history of the formation of the PQ, emphasizing the principal indicators used to determine the class character of the parties (RIN and RN) and the movement (MSA) from which it was formed.

The Prelude to the PQ

The PQ was formed in a regional space of class alliances materializing in the specificity of certain political apparatuses and accompanied by a double process of disorganization and reorganization of class relations:

1. The transition of Quebec to monopoly capitalism and the Keynesian state.
2. The world economic crisis.

The nationalist movement was formed and grew stronger during the transition from a noninterventionist state to the Keynesian state. In an article in *Le Devoir*,[4] I attempted to show how Duplessism, during and following the Depression, was able to come to the fore thanks to the constitution of a rural social bloc. Relying on the support of the peasantry, the Quebec elite (bourgeois with interests centred on the local market and traditional petty bourgeois) imposed on Quebec the maintenance of a pre-Keynesian state, at the very time when the federal state was becoming interventionist. Federal-provincial contradictions under Duplessis stemmed from the question of the articulation of the means of production and the differential (and unequal) development of capitalism.

Strangely enough, the history of the PQ resembles, in certain aspects, that of the Union Nationale. Just as the ALN (Action libérale nationale) initiated the movement leading to the creation of the UN, the nationalist movement of the 1960s was organized first around the RIN and the RN, parties identifiable with the new and the traditional petty bourgeoisie, a class severely affected by the transformations in the social fabric in the 1930s and the 1960s. This class was the first to sound the charge, for both its narrowly economic interests and its place (to be redefined) in the reproduction of social relations were in question.

The labelling of these parties as petty bourgeois is due to two factors: the class position of party agents and the political discourse (their program and propaganda). The political personnel of the RIN, identifiable with the new petty bourgeoisie, practised a discourse reflecting this class's interest. Discriminated against nationally in the private sector and called on to play a new role in the reproduction of social relations, it was led to redefine clerical nationalism. Likewise, the RN is labelled petty bourgeois because its membership (the traditional petty bourgeoisie) carried on a neo-Créditiste discourse typical of those social strata threatened by proletarianization.

Certain analyses seek to relate the agents' place, the party discourse, and the presumed direction of the transformation of social relations. Thus, a party will be called petty bourgeois when the proposed intervention is out of tune with the process, either because of the elaboration of hybrid reformism (the dreams of the RIN: at once étatiste, neo-socialist, and neo-capitalist) or inoperative (the Créditiste money machine).

In the analyses of the RN, the RIN, and the ALN, the identification of the party as petty bourgeois seems a self-evident choice as all indicators agree: the class membership of most of the party workers, their discourse, and the process of transformation of the class struggle. It is not always so simple, however. How can we characterize the Bloc Populaire, in view of our rudimentary knowledge in these areas? We do know it was composed of petty bourgeois, such as André Laurendeau, but a few well-known francophone bourgeois, such as Maxime Raymond, were closely linked to its formation. Certain aspects of its program were clearly petty bourgeois. What more can we say, without delving very deeply into matters, except that the mere consideration of the social actors and of the discourse cannot fundamentally inform us about the nature of the class defended by a political party? The case of the PQ is an even more striking demonstration of this fact.

The evidence given above, for the RN and the RIN, results from the obvious confluence of three indicators: the agents' place of class, the political discourse, and the direction in the transformation of social relations. In the study of the PQ, however, the third criterion seems to have been forgotten, while the first two are widely used and provoke vigorous debate. Could it be that the analysis, in the case of the RN and the RIN, worked almost automatically and that the writers were unaware of this?

The Sovereignty-Association Party

After the formation of the MSA and its fusion with the RN, the Parti Québécois was founded. Most members of the RIN joined the PQ following the dissolution of their party. Using, more or less systematically, the two indicators mentioned above (agents and discourse), a great many analysts have tried to show that there was indeed a social difference between the former members of the RIN and the RN, and those of the MSA, who took over the nationalist movement in the PQ.

Various theses have presented the ex-Liberals of the MSA as the representatives of a technocratic fragment of the petty bourgeoisie (from the upper echelons of the state and, by extension, the cooperative movement) or more recently as the promoters and defenders of a state bourgeoisie. The formation of the MSA demonstrates in fact—at least at the level of the actors—the appearance of a group of individuals whose itinerary is identifiable with that of a bourgeoisie of the Quebec state. Their presence is obvious in the party and poses the question of the places of capital in the bourgeois state. At this level, I continue to disagree totally with Niosi, who restricts these places to merely directors of state corporations. There exist in the state, apart from individuals making their careers and the legal character of property, a set of places whose characteristic is participation in the possession (control) of the means of production and, by extension, the exploitation of the labour force and the accumulation of capital: directors of economic enterprises (state corporations), directors of institutions (hospitals), upper echelons of the state (cabinet ministers and high-ranking civil servants) who intervene in the management and reproduction of social capital. Similarly, the top executives of the cooperative movement may be considered as individuals objectively occupying places of capital. While these individuals do not accumulate as do members of the private-sector bourgeoisie, the careers of the grand clerks of the state are quite comfortable and generally in symbiosis with private capital; they offer as much, or more, security as those of local small businesses. Our concern is mainly places of capital and the reproduction of these private or public places in relation to a political party.

It has been shown that the PQ brought new groups into the nationalist movement. However, a study of its agents is not sufficiently informative about the relation of the party to the whole of the bourgeoisie. After a partly theoretical consideration of the class place of the agents of capital in the state and in the cooperative movement, the analysis may come to an abrupt end. At this point, some observers believe they are able to assert rather peremptorily that the PQ is petty bourgeois, while others proceed to examine the political discourse of these latter-day nationalists.

Evidence abounds, so I have no intention of repeating an analysis of the party program and the economic discourse of the chorus in the National Assembly. Simply put, the goal of the *Péquiste* economic policy is the development of Quebec capitalism through the coordination of intervention and state enterprise, the cooperative movement, and regional private enterprise. To quote René Lévesque, "*We* [Québécois] will decide whether an enterprise will be private, public, or mixed. But it must be Québécois."[5]

Is the PQ a petty-bourgeois party calling for the development of capitalism? Or is it purely bourgeois? At this stage of analysis, statements linking a party to one class are already problematic. They do not allow for a study of the question of the relations of forces within the party, apart from trivial comments on the origins of the actors. In fact, there exists a set of shifts in discourse, of differential practices, which must be explained.

With the two indicators we have used above (discourse and the class membership of agents), we can evoke two series of major events in the history of the PQ: first, the ousting of the leadership of the RIN and the RN (Bourgault, Ferretti, Grégoire). Even if a few rare individuals such as Pierre Renaud maintain a certain influence in the backstage that is now the party itself, the organization of the original forces in the nationalist movement was broken up. Within the nationalist movement, former members of the MSA wrested control of the PQ.

This successful struggle for hegemony is confirmed at the level of the discourse, which breaks with all the socialist leanings of RIN propaganda as well as the shades of Créditisme of the old RN. The RIN's remote evocation of socialism is replaced by that, almost as remote, of social democracy, while independence is replaced by sovereignty-association. This is a very clear shift.

In fact, the sovereignty-association project constitutes a major limitation of independentism. The domain of independence is explicitly limited to the exercise of jurisdictional power: "Quebec will be sovereign when its National Assembly will be the only parliament able to legislate over its territory, and when the people of Quebec will have to pay only those taxes that they decide to impose on themselves."[6] And as if this might still be unclear, the word "association" had to be added: politically sovereign, but economically associated. The plot thickens. How can formal sovereignty and economic association be reconciled, since the latter, in this day of the Keynesian state, demands a centralized management of the numerous mechanisms for economic intervention? Without the delegation of power to an authority common to both associate states, there can be no association. But, given such a delegation, there can be no sovereignty—even formal. René

Lévesque evokes "a kind of delegated parliament,"[7] which is likely to be the solution to be put forward by the PQ. The sovereignist honour is safe. The legal formalism of PQ sovereignism leads to a strengthening of the anti-democratic character of the bourgeois state.

The capitalist state, at the monopolistic stage, is characterized by a strengthening of the executive at the expense of the legislature. The PQ project implies the intensification of this tendency. In the *Péquiste* state, the great economic decisions will be made by a specialized, indirectly elected body. These superministers and supertechnocrats could (is this an alarmist thought?) get almost anything passed by the common elected members of the associate states.

The PQ project of sovereignty seems highly undemocratic. What a sacrifice to pay for right-thinking nationalism! Politically sovereign (or autonomous), economically associated, and internationally subjugated (NATO and NORAD, for instance): that is what remains of the "decolonization" of the 1960s.

The emergence of the MSA in the nationalist movement distorted the discourse. In effect it started a process whereby a political party (the PQ) identifiable with individuals occupying places of capital in the Quebec state was put into power. This analysis does not go far enough, however, for we have not examined the party's relation to the whole process of the class struggle in this country.

A Double Process

Above, the necessity of considering a double process was evoked: the world economic crisis and the transition to a Keynesian state. The crisis, like all crises, implies a disorganization and reorganization of the relations of forces between classes. At a superficial level, this can be seen in corporate takeovers like the Hudson's Bay Company, Crédit Foncier, Nordair, MacMillan Bloedel. An analysis of these takeovers points to much larger changes linked to the restructuring of relations of forces on a world scale.[8] These struggles have repercussions and take place on a Canadian scale as well. Just as the Duplessis regime cannot be analyzed without reference to the Depression, the current crisis cannot be ignored when the PQ is examined. The PQ is part of and attempts to control—at least partially—a process of reorganization of the relations of forces among the dominant classes as well as between the dominant and dominated classes. Let this one statement suffice for now, for it concerns the relations between the Canadian bourgeoisie and the regional bourgeoisie in Canada.

The Canadian State

The PQ poses the question of Canada, at least apparently. It takes on its true dimensions only in reference to the history of the Canadian social formation.

Since Confederation, the Canadian state has had to cope with the onerous reality of regionalism and national questions. The federal-provincial structure results from a compromise. Caught between British imperialism and the formidable development of American capitalism, the Canadian colonial bourgeoisie, with predominantly commercial and banking interests, was driven to create a national state. The need for a national market meant that intranational trade had to be developed and that a labour force attracted by American industry had to be domesticated and reproduced. The Canadian state was created from the colonies of British North America. Political unity had to be realized with such celerity that Canadian capitalism was not able to rely on truly structured centralist forces.

This had economic as well as political and ideological consequences. On the economic level, the Canadian bourgeoisie was never able to satisfactorily realize the integration of banking capital and industrial capital; hence, it was unable to form the centre of attraction for a truly national bourgeoisie. There is no doubt that numerous attempts at integration have been made (during the first 30 years of this century, beginning with the forest industry, for example) and there is no doubt that a Canadian industrial bourgeoisie has developed, but it has never been able to resist imperialist domination. This can be largely explained by the specificity of the Canadian political structure. While the Fathers of Confederation may have had divergent aims, this political structure created and reproduced a division of political apparatuses favouring balkanization. On the economic level, the provincial states were able to support regional capitalist interests much more than is the case in most dominant capitalist states. On the political and ideological level, the Canadian political structure disperses the hegemonic instrument of legitimation, hindering the production and the diffusion of a truly national ideology shared by all Canadians.

Political provincialism can thus only reinforce the historical weight of class alliances and regional social movements. Regionalism plays a much more important role in Canada than in most dominant states.[9] Around provincial states are organized social movements grouping bourgeois interests centred on the regional market and important fragments of the petty bourgeoisie maintaining privileged relations with a provincial state having full jurisdiction over education, culture, and social welfare.

The tendency towards balkanization peculiar to the Canadian Confederation is not limited to technical questions of the distribution of powers, but also results from a whole set of historical conditions that favoured the reproduction of relatively strong regional and national movements centred on provincial states.

The Transition to the Keynesian State

The current economic crisis is not, it should be emphasized, an absolute cause imposed from without. It produces its effects only through the specific political struggles and balkanizing tendency outlined above. The transformations generated by the crisis—the latter setting in as early as 1965, according to some economists—fit into a process of transition that eliminated the last vestiges of Quebec's precapitalist merchant (agricultural) society. This transition provoked the disorganization of the predominantly rural social bloc, characteristic of Duplessism and the pre-Keynesian provincial state; at the same time it provoked the reorganization of a predominantly urban social bloc pressing for the structuring of a Keynesian, interventionist state in Quebec.

These upheavals, at a time of monopoly capitalism, began to provoke important contradictions. The first concerns the nature of the Canadian state in its relation to the Keynesian state. It was shown above how the existence of provincial states made for the strengthening of regional capital at the expense of the Canadian bourgeoisie. It is in the nature of the interventionist state to create a multiplicity of places of capital in the state; we can already presume that the provincial states would further strengthen regional capital. But this must be seen in a broader framework.

An Accumulation Base

When studying the state, or a particular state, one must examine the constitution of a specific accumulation base through the process of an equally specific class struggle. The city, the feudal seigneury, and the national state indicate areas of exploitation permitting the extortion (and potential accumulation) of the fruits of surplus labour. These are very general, but pertinent, remarks for this analysis.

It is too easily forgotten, in fact, that the Canadian state is divided, that this strengthens a multiplicity of regional accumulation bases (the provinces), and this division retards a deepening and broadening of a pan-Canadian capitalist accumulation.[10] When, for example, British Columbia prevents MacMillan Bloedel from being swallowed up by Canadian Pacific, under the pretext that this is foreign capital (!), the question of the accumulation base is raised. B.C. vs. Canada: at stake is the reproduction of regional capital and the objective weakening of larger Canadian capital. While the Canadian bourgeoisie must be more cohesive to remain competitive on a world scale, it is hampered in its moves for concentration by the very Keynesian state itself (which developed through the need for monopolization) because of the particular political structures of this country.

The Quebec state reproduces a sizable, though still marginal, capitalist accumulation base. But we shall not deal with this in a narrowly economistic problematic. This base is constituted only through and in the historical process of class alliances and struggle. It goes beyond strictly economic reality and embraces the totality of social relations. It implies the production, reproduction, and at times the strengthening of a set of apparatuses (economic, political, and ideological) that allow for the composition, maintenance, and possibly reorganization of these alliances and the reproduction of these struggles.

In this sense, the Quebec state is not simply the functional relay of the Canadian state, in which a few petty bourgeois (or a few members of an evanescent and poorly defined dominant class) contribute to solving regional-national problems of pan-Canadian reproduction. The Quebec state is the historical product of a specific area of capitalist accumulation and allows at the same time for its reproduction and even enlargement.

An accumulation base constitutes a given area within which is created a specific capital through the maintenance and reproduction of a specialized hegemonic instrument (from the Chamber of Commerce to the Montreal Canadiens to the Quebec state).[11]

The economic space opened up by the constitution of an accumulation base is obviously not watertight. Thus, the Quebec regional space and the Canadian space are at once complementary and antagonistic. The Quebec regional space is occupied by a largely nonmonopolistic bourgeoisie whose capital lacks centralization and concentration and is hence regularly "visited" by Canadian capital. Regional capital often plays on both sides, profiting from Quebec state contracts while accepting, for example, federal subsidies.

It follows that a geographical area can contain and demarcate the clash of several spaces: hence the multiple symbioses, interactions, and contradictions among American, Canadian, and Quebec capital. The differential reality of these three spaces is in no way denied if several individual capitals are active on several levels. And, contrary to a widespread misconception, there is no absolute equivalence between these spaces and the national character of capital. Imperialist capital speaks American above all, but also German and Japanese at times. Canadian capital speaks English, but sometimes French; Quebec capital speaks French, but at times English. We must not confuse the concept and reality of a Quebec regional bourgeoisie with that of a francophone bourgeoisie: there are francophone Canadian bourgeois and anglophone Quebec bourgeois.

We must also not confuse the economic space opened up by an accumulation base with the expansion of capital. The notion of space used here does not refer to a circumscribed universe. All capital tends to conquer new markets. Quebec nonmonopolistic capital is therefore encouraged by the state to export to the periphery and to "conquer" the North American market. The accumulation base creates a space to be developed and enlarged. It does not imprison capital in a closed space. While the notion of accumulation base involves, by definition, a historical place more or less well defined, that of economic space permits us to take account of the possible internal and external extension of capital operating from the base.

The Quebec Bourgeoisie

The existence of a specific bourgeoisie is founded, of course, on an accumulation base—even if there is more than one economic space—and implies, as Pierre Fournier remarks, a more or less structured economic network.[12]

Elsewhere, I have called the Quebec bourgeoisie timid and splintered.[13] By that I mean that this bourgeoisie lacks the necessary degree of economic coherence characteristic of a true national bourgeoisie that is capable of sustaining a minimally autonomous policy outside imperialism. Regional Quebec capital, predominantly nonmonopolistic, is divided among the public, cooperative, and private sectors; it occupies the interstices of large capital when it is not simply integrated in its development. Despite Hydro-Québec, the Caisses d'Entraide, and the construction industry, most Quebec capital is in the backwaters of large American and Canadian monopoly capital. This hinders the establishment and affirmation of self-centred economic policies permitting the formation of a full-fledged national bourgeoisie.

The Canadian regional bourgeoisies are a distinctive reality among dominant capitalist states. While they are much stronger than regional capital in most of these countries, they remain in a vulnerable position vis-à-vis the forces of imperialism and of the Canadian bourgeoisie, which more often than not they simply play off against each other. Quebec is an exception, however, among exceptions. In my opinion, the paradox to explain is the following: how can such a weak bourgeoisie support such a radical plan for constitutional reform? Historiography and sociography are baffled by this paradox and tend to solve the difficulty by denying the existence of a Quebec regional bourgeoisie with relatively specific interests.

Much has been written on the development of a Quebec state bourgeoisie, with the PQ as a political prop for the constitution of a state capitalism with a hegemonic vocation. This thesis rests on a unilateral vision of recent history, but indicates nonetheless the location of a problem involving the effects of the development of the Keynesian state in the process of the class struggle in Quebec. The transition from the elite's to the technocrats' state in effect provoked the proliferation of a set of agents of capital in the state (the numerous state corporations) and the state control of certain objective places of capital formerly exercised in the private sector (management of hospitals, for example). This very important point is often underestimated.[14] The nationalization of education and of health and welfare brought under the control of the Quebec state a set of places previously divided between the private (the clergy) and the public sectors.

This operation strengthened the bourgeoisie by enlarging its base, giving it greater cohesion than ever before, and reducing the role of the clergy. In one process, we see the development of the bourgeoisie, the affirmation of the social category of the regional bourgeoisie, and the weakening of the clergy.

The radicalization of the autonomist ideology supported by the pre-1960 clergy and regional bourgeoisie can thereby be explained in part. Involved are alliances of classes and of the social forces that can be developed from those alliances. The nationalization of certain objective places of capital and the bureaucratization of the Quebec state necessarily aggravate constitutional struggles, as this capital and this bourgeoisie tend to favour the Quebec state over the federal state.

But can we speak of a state bourgeoisie or even of a state fragment in the Quebec bourgeoisie? To do so would be to overestimate the consistency of those agents' practice and to attribute to it an innovative role it has never held. In the bourgeoisie of the Quebec state are the contradictions between the various fragments of the bourgeoisie.[15] The places of capital in the Quebec state are subject to all the contradictions of triple space outlined above. Thus, just as all agents of capital are not *Péquistes* by definition, so the economic apparatuses that most favour the Quebec bourgeoisie (Caisse de dépôt, Société générale de financement) are not impenetrable barricades which escape an internalization of the contradictions among the fragments of the bourgeoisie.

We must, however, explain why the agents of capital in the Quebec state are led to exercise real leadership in the promotion of the interests of the regional bourgeoisie. I have indicated elsewhere[16] that the explanation can be found in the national question, the specificity of the Keynesian state in the Canadian political division, and the nonmonopolistic character of regional capital. The usual role of agents of capital in the Keynesian state is to initiate the relations between banking capital and nonmonopolistic industrial capital. In a politically divided Canada and in a region marked by persistent national contradictions, this role is transformed into that of the true political leadership of a set of agents placed at the focal point (the provincial state) of the reorganization of nonmonopolistic regional capital and of the potential and desired transformation of part of this capital into monopoly capital. It is true now that the bourgeois of the state exercises political and economic leadership amid the Quebec bourgeoisie, as the strengthening of the latter depends on an intensification, for the time being at least, of state intervention. But I do not see how this is evidence for an exclusivist state bourgeoisie. We must not confuse a point in a process with its fundamental determinations.

The bourgeoisie of the state is in fact far from alone in the Quebec regional bourgeoisie. The upper echelons of the cooperative movement (Coop Fédérée, Mouvement Desjardins, Caisse d'entraide économique) demarcate a set of places of capital that also contribute to the broadening of the Quebec accumulation base. The economic importance of the cooperative movement is acknowledged by all. However, some writers have been led by a different problematic to consider its leaders as petty bourgeois. Ideologically, the bourgeoisie of the cooperative movement appears to be best prepared to collaborate with state capital, in view of the collectivist illusion conveyed by both these forms of accumulation.

Let us not forget private capital in Quebec. It exists, even if it is not always quoted on the stock market. It is mainly francophone, nonmonopolistic, and centred on the region. It is in ever-greater need of the state in order to resist the monopolistic onslaught for its financing, its markets, and its access to technological innovation. It must modernize in order to retain its position under monopoly capital. Since the publication of Dorval Brunelle's *La désillusion tranquille*,[17] we know that this regional bourgeoisie is capable of sustaining specific economic policy. Brunelle showed that this capital itself, in the 1950s, called for the intervention of the state and the creation of the Conseil d'orientation économique du Québec. The establishment of state corporations for the strengthening of Quebec capital originated in this very body. Thus, the defence of the specificity of regional capital was not invented by technocrats. Quebec regional capital exists and knows it exists. It even seeks to defend its room to manoeuvre. While it remains timid because of its nonmonopolist weakness, it can sustain a moderate political project that permits it to develop its accumulation base while not shutting itself off completely from the Canadian space.

We should not, however, expect local capitalists to make explosive statements: their relative weakness prevents this. But, to take one example, when Pierre Péladeau appoints Jacques Gagnon of the Caisse d'entraide économique to his board of directors, and when Jean-Guy Cardinal attends meetings of the board, we can hardly say he is ignoring his Quebec space.[18] Private regional capital is divided between support for the Union Nationale and for the PQ, but it will not openly champion total independence. Yet it is certainly neither opposed nor absolutely indifferent to a project for enlarging the Quebec economic space. While small enterprise has remained attached to the Union Nationale, medium-scale capital—which is the most subject to the transformations generated by monopolistic capital, by whose growth it may be swallowed up—seems more open to state intervention and an increase in provincial powers. But what is the orientation of the PQ?

Forms and Contradictions of Quebec Capital

Quebec capital has three different forms of accumulation: state, cooperative, and private. And it is represented by three corresponding ideologies: technocratic, collectivist (or populist), and liberal.

In addition to these specific contradictions due to different forms of accumulation, there are those between banking capital and industrial capital, typical of nonmonopolistic capital. Quebec capital is not yet dominated by a division between monopolistic and nonmonopolistic capital. While the *Péquiste* project outlines a potential affirmation of Quebec monopoly capital, beginning with enterprises already monopolistic or on the way to becoming so (Hydro-Québec, Sidbec, Provigo), the contradictions between monopolistic and nonmonopolistic capital still involve mainly the opposition of Canadian to Quebec capital. It is in the latter that we should look for contradictions in the scale of accumulation, between small, local, family-run capital and medium-scale enterprise now modernizing with the help of state intervention.

The PQ is therefore not the unequivocal vehicle of a developing state bourgeoisie. As shown by Dorval Brunelle, the Quebec private-sector regional bourgeoisie itself has appealed to the state. In the process of the reorganization of nonmonopolistic capital, the bourgeoisie of the Quebec state has exercised an obvious political leadership. Its economic base is relatively more secure than small and medium-sized private capital and is ideologically better placed to appeal to the nation—hence, since the mid-1960s it has had a real vocation for leadership. But neither the whole process of the development of capitalism nor even the practice of the PQ government shows a tendency to crush private regional capital. As is true everywhere else, the bourgeoisie of the state has grown in strength with the development of Keynesianism; contradictions have developed between private and state forms of accumulation. As in the other regions of Canada, the bourgeois of the Keynesian provincial state has held an important place in the promotion of regional capital. In the present phase of the class struggle, in spite of the double reality of economic crisis and state interventionism, there is no evidence for state capital's tendency to swallow up or even to dominate Quebec capital. René Lévesque has declared, for example, "We are anxious for our main iron and steel enterprise to remain a collective Quebec property, until the day when we can, perhaps, make it mixed, when it will be sufficiently strong."[19] The liberal state directly subsidizes private capital (the "adventure" of the Canadian railways); the Keynesian state buys, consolidates, then "merges" with private capital.

The reorganization and enlarged reproduction of regional capital requires the strengthening (for now, at least) of the places of capital in the state bourgeoisie, but an enlargement of the Quebec accumulation base benefits capital that remains largely outside the economic apparatuses of the Quebec state.

The PQ Alliance

We have so far touched on the forces inside the PQ as more or less fixed realities. We must now look more closely at the alliances and support that make possible an objective attempt to control (relatively) the process of the transformation of the class struggle.

Potential Alliances

So far, we have linked the PQ with the regional bourgeoisie, the new petty bourgeoisie, and with certain fringes of the traditional petty bourgeoisie. We have also referred to the social category constituted by the Quebec bureaucracy. These groups are led by the process of the development of monopolistic capital and the Keynesian state to combine their efforts to deepen the Quebec accumulation base, to enlarge the places of capital and the directly or indirectly delegated functions of capital in the public, parapublic, cooperative, and private sectors.

The Keynesian provincial state and its bureaucracy will be, for the new petty bourgeoisie, a favourite area for reproduction, promotion, and formulation of ideology, just as the clergy was for the traditional petty bourgeoisie. In the transition from the state of elites to the interventionist state, the largest share of the exercise of places by the new petty bourgeoisie is linked to the reinforcement of the Quebec state and the specificity of its national character. Access to positions, the defence of the language, and the extension of the powers of the Quebec state are intimately related.

The Limits of the Alliance

The very nature of this alliance imposes severe limits. In official discourse it is simply realism. In radical independentist reasoning it is a matter of tactics. But the agents, the discourse, and the whole process of the class struggle combine to make sovereignty-association the maximum extension of the *Péquiste* project.

The project of sovereignty fits into the context of the relations of forces on a North American scale and ultimately that of geopolitics dominated by the United States. The PQ's policy aims at the reproduction of the whole complex of the relations of capitalist forces in Quebec. It implies the relative control of a process of reproduction of American and Canadian capital, inside which Quebec would have the largest possible space. The Quebec accumulation base is to be increased without questioning imperialism, without attacking the structure of the Canadian space. The national question is at the service of the reproduction of the Canadian state.

The Foundations of the Alliance

It is only through the relation of the dominant classes to the popular classes that it is possible to fully explain the particularity of the class struggle in Quebec. Here converge the Canadian constitutional division, the national question, and the question of class alliances.

The Duplessist struggles were based on an alliance with the peasantry through a rural social bloc. At a time when the interventionist state was being organized at the federal level, the particular social composition of Quebec (partly explicable by unequal development) prevented federalist forces from finding the allies necessary for the establishment of Keynesian policies in Quebec and favoured—while not absolutely predetermining it—the Duplessist rural bloc. This means, in other words, that the Duplessist state of notables (local and regional bourgeoisie, traditional petty bourgeoisie) was constituted on the sole basis of a peasantry that was still politically significant.[20] A double contradiction hindered the Canadian capitalist state in its reforms through resistance stemming partly from the unequal development it had itself created and partly from the political division among the masses that it had increased through the maintenance of 11 separate states.

This is not to say that the development of a broad and organized working-class base solved these problems. The import of Keynesian reformism into the Quebec state posed, on the contrary, in a new, even more explosive form the question of the relation with the masses. Recently, it has been shown that the Keynesian state is characterized by an attempt to integrate the working class politically and ideologically.[21] Analyses of the Quebec situation have shown how certain reforms of the Quiet Revolution were realized thanks to the support of the working class (education, health and welfare, labour).[22] This support helped to dislodge the old clerical leadership and generally to dismantle the apparatuses of the state of notables. But observers have virtually forgotten to broaden the perspective by situating this reality in the context of the contradictions of the Canadian state.

Keynesianism reinforced the nationalization (or the counternationalization) of the Quebec masses. By posing the question of the integration of the working class, the development in Canada of the interventionism particular to the monopolistic state posed acutely the problem of political division. Given this base of support from at least the most advantaged strata of the working class, Canadian political provincialism could only provoke a tendency towards the strengthening of class alliances sustaining relatively strong regional social movements.

This analysis would require a more elaborate study of the relations among the national question, class alliances, and the forms of the capitalist state. Let me simply point out the potential importance of class alliances in Quebec as they relate to a regional accumulation base. As stated above, an accumulation base does not refer to a narrowly economic space, but to the broader reality of the totality of social relations. The constitution of a specific accumulation base, whatever its size, rests on the potential of class alliances.

The struggles between the Canadian and the Quebec regional bourgeoisies can be better clarified in this context. With the advent of the Keynesian state and because of the national question, the capacity of the Quebec regional bourgeoisie to constitute for itself a sphere of alliances and support was increased. It was indeed through the potential growth of these alliances and this support that the Quebec regional bourgeoisie could appreciably enlarge its accumulation base at the expense of the Canadian bourgeoisie. After the unanimity and the conviviality of the Quiet Revolution, which objectively accentuated the Quebec character of the labour movement—development of the Confédération des syndicats nationaux, of the Corporation des enseignants du Québec, the autonomization of the Fédération des travailleurs du Québec vis-à-vis the Canadian Labour Congress—the Liberal party, under the hegemony of the Canadian bourgeoisie, ceased its flirtation with the working class and emphasized state authoritarianism. Conversely, with its favourable attitude towards the working class, the Parti Québécois has tried to continue the Quiet Revolution, attempting to profit from this class's integration to enlarge the Quebec accumulation base. From the labour laws of the Quiet Revolution (the right to strike in the public sector, for instance), the practice of economic summits, to the project of sovereignty, there is only a small step—and that step is the development of the contradictions peculiar to the Canadian state in the Keynesian era, with their principal coordinates as the struggles between the Canadian and Quebec bourgeoisies and the integration of the working class.

The Four Poles on the PQ Horizon

This analysis has led from the agents and discourse of the PQ to the process of the transformation of the class struggle. The PQ may be characterized as the political formation that has permitted the nationalist movement's hegemony initiated mainly by the new petty bourgeoisie (and secondarily by the traditional petty bourgeoisie) to the advantage of the Quebec regional bourgeoisie. The PQ must be considered a multiclass party, because it results from an alliance between socially identifiable parties and a movement (RIN-RN-MSA), in a framework of the nationalist movement.

This problematic permits us to glimpse the possibility of a freer reading of the gradualist traps set by the very object of analysis. Most discussions of the PQ project focus on the potential for realization of an objective, independence, that it does not set for itself, but merely evokes. This is an independentist reading, which occupies one of the four poles of the PQ. But how in fact is this discourse organized?

At the centre is sovereignty, a shifting project if ever there was one, which will get off the ground only in its unsteady relation to four socially identifiable coordinates. The first point of convergence: independentism, which posits sovereignty as a stage leading to possible independence. The pairing of sovereignty and independence appeals principally to petty-bourgeois radicalism. The second point: association, which seeks to reassure the Canadian bourgeoisie and no doubt the regional bourgeoisie itself about the risks of a "leftist" swing in its constitutional adventure and which also wants to guarantee access to a reasonably extensive market. The pairing of sovereignty and association addresses the various fractions of the bourgeoisie. The third point: a favourable attitude towards the working class, seeking to link the PQ project to a popular base. The fourth point: the friendliness of the PQ to the United States, which, through sanctimonious proclamations on the quality of the PQ government, is aimed at the imperialist forces: sovereignty within the normal capitalist order—what could be more reassuring?

Placed at the centre of these specialized discourses, the project of sovereignty can only be vague and indefinite. *Péquism* operates on vagueness; it relies on permanent gradualism.

The *Péquiste* Diversion

The gradualist strategy goes far beyond the realm of election tactics. It is found throughout the discourse on sovereignism. It involves not only the question of sovereignty-association but also that of social democracy. In *La Passion du Québec,* René Lévesque defines a social democracy that is just as weak as *Péquiste* independence. It is limited to ensuring equality of opportunity, reducing income disparities, and increasing participation in political life and in enterprise. But these objectives appear so revolutionary that they can be achieved only in stages. In Lévesque's own words, "That is where gradualism comes in."[23]

There is no need to dwell on the close parallel between the gradualism in the achievement of a meagre social democracy and the relentless gradualism in the negotiation of sovereignty in association. It is important to understand the very necessity of this gradualism to the political project of the PQ.

The PQ seeks to achieve the maximum possible autonomy within the framework of the relations of capitalist production. It therefore seeks to bring about a diversion of this process by enlarging as much as possible the space of Quebec capital. It seeks to achieve an even broader accumulation base, then, but in an orderly fashion, without fundamentally disturbing the relations of forces. The Canadian association is to be imposed, with Quebec's integration as a subordinate into the imperialist chain. The PQ proposes the reproduction of the totality of fractions of capital. It seeks to divert the process of the transformation of social relations into the central perspective of a strengthening of Quebec capital. Thus, the PQ project implies the internalization of the interests of Canadian capital in the sovereignist state itself, even supposing that it would be absolutely sovereign.

It should be clearly stated that the sovereignty-association thesis implies the reproduction, on a new basis, of the Canadian state itself. Association and the delegated parliament are not concessions to political realism. They aim at opening up a market to Quebec capitalist interests. We can now better understand the permanent gradualist vocation of the discourse. Essentially, it is a matter of winning the greatest possible space without going over to the other side, to the working class and the masses. To gain the support of the masses without granting important concessions, to win over the petty bourgeoisie by making its independentist project less dangerous for the capitalist social order, to carve out the greatest possible economic space at the expense of Canadian capital while seeking to remain or become its partner, to convince the imperialist forces that the party ultimately presents the only possible alternative to the Canadian problem—that is the program of the PQ. René Lévesque has declared in the National Assembly, "We do not want to break up, but rather radically transform, our union with the rest of Canada, so that henceforth our relations will be pursued on the basis of full and complete equality."[24] Quebec is seeking only to extend an already partly acquired sovereignty, "Having achieved, in the last century, the partial sovereignty of a province, we have never stopped demanding its extension."[25] The radical nature of the transformation referred to by Lévesque consists of a reform of the Canadian state through an increase in the sovereignty-autonomy of Quebec.

The reality of national oppression permits the regional bourgeoisie to create a crisis for the Canadian state by relying on the support of the petty bourgeoisie (and, from afar, of the masses). Canadian political division permits this bourgeoisie, in the era of the Keynesian state, to integrate partially the working class at the expense of the monopolistic pan-Canadian bourgeoisie. But the regional bourgeoisie, because of its relative weakness and its economic interests (integration into monopolistic capital and access to the Canadian market), promotes an ambiguous project that can lead only to the reproduction of the Canadian state.

The gradualism of the PQ project relies on current conditions. Underlying the temporality of the PQ is a curious paradox: there is a continual stalling for time in the realization of a forever-postponed project. Forever towards independence, forever towards social democracy, from state to stage, until the final nonevent. While independence and social democracy are merely profiled, the *Péquiste* state is being built. And this is the real function of the constant temporization. Time is not really lost. There is the favourable attitude towards the working class to have it accept the same economic policies as elsewhere in Canada and in most capitalist states. There is independence to be "ultimately achieved," while elaborating the initial MSA project of more or less associate states and more or less confederated sovereignty.

Just as Duplessism attained a maximum autonomy through the pre-Keynesian state of notables, so *Péquism* will push to the limit the potential for autonomy of the Quebec Keynesian state inside the Canadian state. From victory to victory until the final surprise!

In Practice

Jorge Niosi maintains that the practices of the PQ during the first two years of its mandate invalidate the thesis that the PQ represents the interests of the Quebec bourgeoisie.[26] He is not entirely convincing. He underestimates the fact that the first year of power simply consisted of good management of the legacy of the preceding government. He ignores the obvious tendency towards the strengthening of state corporations. The PQ government has an unprecedented desire to rationalize and control. Niosi does not sufficiently insist on the policy of creating and developing "leading" enterprises that promote indigenous capital. There has been the purchase of Asbestos Corporation to create asbestos processing in Quebec, support for the internationalization of the engineering companies operating in the sphere of Hydro-Québec, the strengthening of Sidbec-Dosco following the collapse of Questeel (which resulted from the refusal of government support). At the time Niosi wrote his article, the growing tendency to promote Quebec capital through state corporations was not as clear as it is today. Tremblay's plan for two new corporations, Investissement-Québec and Exportation-Québec, is a convincing illustration.[27] There are plans for a business bank to facilitate the concentration of nonmonopolistic capital, which is now too dispersed and is unable to tap private sources of financing. There is a desire to promote dynamic Quebec enterprise by opening up export markets (mainly in developing countries). While the specific plan for two new corporations may not be unanimously supported in the cabinet, this is not true of the underlying objectives.

To illustrate the close relationship between the Quebec bourgeois of the provincial state and those of the cooperative movement, we can point to the appointment of Alfred Rouleau, the President of the Caisses populaires Desjardins, as president of the Institut national de la productivité.[28]

There is no doubt that the PQ supports regional capital. But its policy must internalize American and, to a certain extent, Canadian monopolistic interests. Neither its program nor the practice of state corporations is unilaterally devoted to supporting Quebec capital. But, through the daily observable contradictions, a double tendency to support Quebec capital can be seen in the reorganization, leading towards concentration and technological innovation, of Quebec nonmonopolistic capital in terms of its insertion into monopolistic capital. This latter development is achieved in three ways: through enterprises or sectors that have been "given over" to the state by large capital (Hydro-Québec) or that the latter has deemed less profitable (Asbestos Corporation), through a few enterprises termed "leaders"[29] (Bombardier, Sidbec-Dosco), and through certain sectors without complete large capital investment (food production, culture). This operation relies on the concentration of Quebec banking capital (the cooperative movement and Quebec banks) in conjunction with the Régime des rentes and the Caisse de dépôt.

While the relative complementarity of dominant interests in the imperialist space and in the subordinate Quebec space does not seem to cause many problems, such is not the case with the potential rise of Quebec capital to partnership status with Canadian monopolistic capital. Recent interventions by the Quebec and the Canadian governments show the severity of the confrontation. Quebec favours the acquisition of Crédit Foncier by the Banque d'Epargne at the expense of Canadian integration.[30] Ottawa seeks to prevent the provincial integration of Nordair and Québécair through the Caisses d'Entraide économique, preferring their eventual merger with an Eastern-Canadian carrier.[31] Quebec capital cannot develop to the extent and at the rate desired without an economic union with Canada that gives free access to markets in the other provinces. Conversely, when it finds itself cornered, the Canadian bourgeoisie will likely prefer a compromise to a deterioration of the situation.

Conclusion

Thus will conclude the double process of transition in which Quebec society has been involved since the early 1950s: the creation of the Keynesian state in the transition of the monopolistic stage, and the world economic crisis. Thus will have been redefined the place of the Quebec state in the Canadian state and the role of the petty bourgeoisie in the reproduction of social relations. Thus will have been reorganized (for now) the power relations between the fractions of capital in North America through the relative strengthening of the Quebec accumulation base and bourgeoisie. Thus will have been completed the transition of a premonopolistic society with largely precapitalist production relations centred on the local market to the full determinations of monopolistic development. Thus, the national question will remain unresolved. In the same way, independence will not be achieved.

Postscript

Since this article was originally written in late 1978, several significant political events have taken place and these require a brief discussion here. The failure of the May 1980 referendum, the patriation of the Canadian Constitution without Quebec's political consent, and the visible splits within the Parti Québécois following its 1981 reelection cannot be fully understood within the framework of a narrowly nationalistic and single-class analysis; thus, they underscore the accuracy and appropriateness of the problematic developed in this chapter. Of particular importance is the need to consider Quebec only within an analytical context that takes into account the Canadian federal state and the lack of solidarity within the PQ.

For instance, the events that accompanied the patriation of the Constitution revealed the complexity of the Canadian political reality, particularly the domination of the Quebec nation by the Canadian state. Similarly, the latest federal offensive, centred on aboriginal rights, reconfirmed the oppression of the Inuit and native minorities. In the same vein, the distortion by provincial authorities of the federal policy on human rights—henceforth included in the Constitution but rendered virtually ineffectual—illustrates the fact that political problems in Canada cannot be reduced solely to the national question of Quebec, but involve a whole range of regional questions that concern the entire Canadian state. Finally, in light of the last five years of political life, one must bear in mind that the current crisis of federalism, the trend towards centralization, and the resulting national versus regional contradictions cannot be fully understood if they are not—as during the 1930s—put into the context of the global crisis of capitalism.

In the same way, the multiple tensions that have arisen within the Parti Québécois itself show that a narrowly single-class analysis cannot fully explain the political reality of Quebec. The oppression of the PQ membership by its own leaders is a clear indication of the fact that it reflects the many social contradictions and relations of forces that characterize Quebec society as a whole. I have attempted to show that the Parti Québécois is a multiclass party, the formation and development of which is the result of important social and political changes that took place in Quebec between the 1950s and the 1970s. The acceleration of capitalist development and the accompanying transformation of Quebec into a Keynesian state have provoked the emergence on the political scene of a series of new social classes and categories: the bureaucracy, the new petty bourgeoisie, and the working class. These changes have in turn caused an important reorganization of the relations of forces among the different fractions of the bourgeoisie.

If this approach has shed some light on the dynamics and the internal contradictions of the Parti Québécois, it is equally helpful in explaining the present difficulties and limitations of the *Péquiste* alliance. The deepening of the crisis of world capitalism has forced the PQ leadership to revise its economic and social policies and to adopt an anti-crisis strategy identical to those of the advanced capitalist countries. The disengagement of the state is now a priority. Thus, the support given to Quebec's nonmonopoly capital is being progressively adapted to the interests of foreign monopoly capital, state intervention is being reduced, and the public and parapublic sectors are the victims of severe budget cuts. Furthermore, the PQ government is pursuing a policy of salary reductions. This has led to an attack on Quebec's most militant unions, those of the public and parapublic sectors, through the imposition of repressive legislation permitting the reduction of salaries and personnel. This has been accompanied by a general movement towards the lowering of living standards in the private sector as well. Consequently, the PQ government has undermined its own militant base (the bureaucracy and the new petty bourgeoisie) and its largest real and potential political clientele, the working class. Characterized until now by the social and political traits of the Keynesian state, the *Péquiste* alliance is in the process of dissolution; the party leadership's promise to fight the next election on the theme of independence appears to be a sign of despair, or cynicism.

Will the demise of the PQ correspond to that of the Keynesian state? Whatever the answer to this question, it is increasingly obvious that the party will never again be the same, that its chances of survival and success in the future will depend on the capacity of its leadership to form a political alliance that leaves more room for the conservative forces of Quebec society. Although the Parti Québécois will not lead Quebec to its independence, the national question will continue to play a crucial role in the political life of Quebec and Canada.

Notes

1. This article is part of the work of the committee for research on the national question at the Centre de formation populaire. It also takes up—but is not limited to—some of the theses put forward in an introduction to the history of

Quebec which I have coauthored with Anne Légaré, *Le Québec, la question nationale* (Paris: Maspéro, 1979).

2. Jorge Niosi, "La nouvelle bourgeoisie canadienne-française," *Les Cahiers du socialisme* 1 (1978), and "Le gouvernement du Parti Québécois, deux ans après," idem. 2 (1978). The former article appeared in English in *Studies in Political Economy* 1 (1979).
3. Gilles Bourque, "Le Parti Québécois dans les rapports de classes," *Politique Aujourd'hui*, 7-8 (Paris 1978); and Pierre Fournier, "Projet national et affrontement des bourgeoisies québécoise et canadienne," in *La chance au coureur* (Montreal: Nouvelle-Optique, 1978). Pierre Fournier has since corrected his positions. See "Les nouveaux paramètres de la bourgeoisie québécoise," in *Le capitalisme au Québec* (Montreal: Editions Albert Saint-Martin, 1978). See Chapter 12 in this book.
4. Gilles Bourque, "La nouvelle trahison des clercs," *Le Devoir* (Jan. 8-9, 1979), pp. 5-6.
5. René Lévesque, *La passion du Québec* (Montreal: Editions Québec-Amérique, 1978), p. 202.
6. Idem, p. 14.
7. Idem, p. 15.
8. See André Gunder Frank, *Réflexions sur la nouvelle crise économique mondiale* (Paris: Maspéro, 1978), and Arghiri Emmanuel, *Le profit et les crises* (Paris: Maspéro, 1974).
9. See Lizette Jalbert, *Régionalisme et lutte politique* (Doctoral dissertation, Université de Paris VIII, June 1978). See also Chapter 13 in this book.
10. A regional accumulation base does not necessarily imply the existence of a specific parliament. It exists, however, only through a set of regional apparatuses permitting its reproduction: chamber of commerce, a church, trade-union headquarters.
11. I have borrowed the term "hegemonic instrument" (*dispositif hégémonique*) from Renaud Dulong, *Les régions, l'Etat et la société locale* (Paris: PUF, 1978).
12. Pierre Fournier, "Les nouveaux paramètres de la bourgeoisie québécoise," op. cit.
13. Gilles Bourque, "Le Parti Québécois dans les rapports de classes," op. cit.
14. These places are in addition to those already existing at the summit of the state (ministers, deputy ministers, and top-level management of the various branches of the state apparatus) and, like the latter, they determine the class membership of the agents not only in the process of accumulation, but also in the social (capitalist) division of work that the state reproduces in its midst.
15. See Yves Bélanger, "Société d'Etat, bourgeoisie et projet économique du PQ" to be published in *Cahiers du socialisme.* Bélanger's article expresses views similar to my own.
16. See Gilles Bourque, "Question nationale et réforme constitutionnelle," in *La chance au coureur,* op. cit.; "Le Parti Québécois dans les rapports de classes," op. cit.; and Bourque and Légaré, op. cit.
17. Dorval Brunelle, *La désillusion tranquille,* (Montreal: HMH, 1978).
18. Michel Nadeau, "Québécor songe à d'autres acquisitions," *Le Devoir* (Jan. 12, 1979), p. 17.
19. René Lévesque, op. cit., p. 80.

20. See Louis Quéré, *Jeux interdits à la frontière* (Paris: Anthropos, 1978). Quéré analyzes national minority protests in France as phenomena of transitions from societies of notables to capitalist societies dominated by monopolies and technocrats.
21. See A. Negri, *La classe ouvrière contre l'Etat* (Paris: Galilée, 1978); and M. Tronti, *Ouvriers et Capital* (Paris: Bourgeois, 1977). Also see Pierre Desbiens, "Perspective sur l'Etat québécois," in *Le capitalisme au Québec*, op. cit.
22. M. Pelletier and Y. Vaillancourt, *Les politique sociales et les travailleurs*, Cahier IV, *Les années 60*. Also see Michel Van Schendel, "Impérialisme et classe ouvrière au Québec," *Socialisme québécois* 21-22; and Jean-Marc Piotte, "La lutte des travailleurs de l'état," *Les Cahiers du socialisme* 3 (1979).
23. Lévesque, op. cit., p. 187.
24. Idem, p. 13.
25. Idem, p. 13.
26. Jorge Niosi, "Le gouvernement du Parti Québécois, deux ans après," op. cit.
27. See Marie-Agnès Thellier, "Investissement-Québec, Exportation-Québec," *Le Devoir* (Jan. 9, 1979), p. 9.
28. See "Alfred Rouleau élu président de l'Institut de productivité," *Le Devoir* (Jan. 13, 1979), p. 11.
29. See Jean P. Vézina (ed.), *Une politique économique québécoise* (Québec: MIC, 1974).
30. See Claude Picher, "Québec autorise la Banque d'Epargne à prendre le contrôle du Crédit Foncier," *Le Devoir* (Jan. 13, 1979), p. 11.
31. See Michel Nadeau, "Une firme du Lac Saint-Jean acquiert 40% de Québécair," *Le Devoir* (Jan. 12, 1979), p. 1.

Part III/The New Middle Class

The changing nature of class structure in Quebec—in particular the emergence and expansion of a new middle class—has frequently been referred to as playing a central role in Quebec statebuilding. This part addresses some of the main issues related to Quebec *rattrapage* from that perspective.

In the first article, Renaud begins with the hypothesis that the expansion of the state in Quebec occurred in a political and economic context that fundamentally altered the pattern of class relations. Renaud then develops the idea that the new middle class has had a major stake in the development of the state apparatus. Taken to its logical conclusion, independence should be the result.

The next two chapters in this part discuss the nature of the Quebec bourgeoisie. The article by Niosi challenges the traditional perspective on the ethnic composition of the Canadian upper class as being almost exclusively Anglo-Saxon. The author maintains that a new francophone bourgeoisie has emerged in Canada during the postwar period, a development based on the long-term expansion of the Canadian economy since 1945 and the interventionism of the Quebec and federal governments since the 1960s. It is also argued that this francophone bourgeoisie is federalist in its political sympathies and actively opposed to the separation of Quebec from the rest of Canada.

Departing from Niosi's interpretation, Fournier states that one of the key political developments in Quebec since 1960 is the emergence of a relatively autonomous regional bourgeoisie with close ties to the Quebec state. The author argues that this bourgeoisie has been fostered partly in opposition to the Canadian bourgeoisie and that the PQ has systematically favoured its growth and development. It seems, however, that this has not paid dividends in the form of obtaining the support of this regional bourgeoisie for sovereignty-association.

Chapter 10/Quebec New Middle Class in Search of Social Hegemony*

Marc Renaud

Introduction

In the last three decades Quebec has experienced social change to an extent and with a depth perhaps unparalleled in western countries. As a Canadian ambassador to Paris suggested, the recent transformation of Quebec society seems to be "the most rapid industrial, social, educational and religious revolution in the Western world."[1]

An overview of the most often cited indicators will permit an apprecia- tion of the thoroughness of this change.[2] While two-thirds of the Quebec population lived in cities in 1950, more than 80% did in 1971, with the largest increases in the Montreal region, which half the population now inhabits. The Catholic Church was in 1960 the key institution of social control as well as the moral authority and often, indirectly, the political authority. It was also the power holder, if not always the owner, in health, education, and social-welfare organizations. Ten years afterwards, it had been almost totally relegated to its spiritual role, with a sharp decline in the number of people engaging in religious orders, a drastic drop in the level of religious practice, and the state takeover of the health, education, and social-welfare fields. While there were about 2,000 new sacerdotal vocations per year in the late 1940s, only about 100 were recruited in 1970.[3] While roughly 80% of the population practised its religion in 1960, in urban areas only 15% to 35% still do so now. This was paralleled by a substantial and extremely brusque

---

*This article was originally published in *International Review of Community Development* 39-40 (1978), pp. 1-36. The Parti Québécois had not yet begun its reforms of Quebec society and there was no sign of an oncoming economic crisis. Although the PQ's reforms, in its first mandate, reflected the social dynamics described herein, its economic and social policies in the 1980s—after the Referendum and given one of the worst economic crisis of this century—seemed to go in very different, if not opposite, directions. With the economic crisis, a social and cultural crisis seems to have emerged as well: social-mobility patterns have changed—the key positions in the state are occupied by young people, with no openings except for rare job replacements; slowing down, if not reduction, of state support for social-democratic policies. The question that has to be asked is: to what extent will the sort of economic collapse that Quebec recently experienced mean the destruction of its distinctive problem-solving style described in this article? With the new middle class losing its legitimacy in its search for social hegemony, to what extent will its social-democratic ambitions disappear as well? And, to the benefit of whom?

decline in the birth rate, moving from 30 births per 1,000 population to 28 in 1959, to 14 in 1974. During the same period (1950-1974), the divorce rate increased eighteenfold and the suicide rate increased to 4.4 times the 1950 rate!

The organization of the polity also profoundly changed. Provincial government expenditures multiplied by 32 during this period, with the most visible and important increments due to massive state interventions during the Quiet Revolution (1960-65).[4] The traditionally dominant political party, the Union Nationale—which held power from 1936 to 1939 and from 1944 to 1960—gradually lost its importance in the popular vote, to be replaced by the Parti Québécois, which with an entirely different political base took power in November 1976.[5] In the 1960s, public administration was totally reshaped: from parochial and paternalist in style and highly decentralized in its structures, it became centralized, bureaucratic, and typically "modern." A series of events accounts for this change: the growth of the human-service sectors (education, health, and welfare), the government takeover of these sectors, the reorganization of all ministries, the greater involvement of the state in the economy (for example, creation of state enterprises, government involvement in industrial sectors, and the creation of planning agencies), and the creation of a multitude of other government boards and agencies. In 1960 the Quebec provincial public sector employed 36,000 people, while in 1971 almost 350,000 people were employed in its administration, in public enterprises and in health and educational services—that is, an increase from 2% to 15% of the labour force. And this is a gross underestimate of the number of people paid by provincial tax money and by state enterprises. The expenditures of the federal, provincial, and municipal public sectors in Quebec have grown, according to recent estimates, from 33.4% of the Quebec GNP at market prices in 1961 to 45.8% in 1970, with the Quebec public sector accounting for 31.8% of the GNP in 1970 as compared to 17.9% in 1961.[6] The most noticed result of this febrile growth has been a democratization of the access to the previously Church-controlled and highly elitist educational system and a substantial improvement in the access of poorer strata to health services,[7] along with an extremely intense, although not necessarily successful, reshuffling of jobs, personnel, and organizations.

Position of the Question

Except for the brusque character of these changes and the dramatic downfall of the Catholic Church, Ontario, the neighbouring and comparable province, has experienced similar transformations. In particular, contrary to what is often believed, the expansion of the provincial and municipal public sectors of the economy have followed quite similar paths in all provinces and have meant a similar quantitative development of the state. Further, this expansion was in all provinces associated with a change in the ideologically dominant institutions, from religious and rural ones to secular and urban-based political and social ones.

In general, however, in all provinces except Quebec, this expansion did not mean much more than a change in the organization of the economy linked to the worldwide transformation of capitalism into its "post-industrial" or "advanced" stages. The state directly employed many more people, social security policies were much more extensive and progressive, Keynesian economic policies became widespread, the state organizational apparatus was modernized, and the coercive legal and fiscal powers of the governments were increased. But, all things considered, this expansion did not fundamentally alter the basic matrix of interest groups and class relationships within each province. Therefore, it did not look "revolutionary," as it seemingly did in Quebec.

In fact, although the tangible outputs of governmental actions have not markedly differed among provinces, these same actions in Quebec have taken on a colouring that contrast sharply with what has occurred in the anglophone provinces. What is particular to Quebec is not the changes per se, but its style of problem solving. In other words, Quebec has evolved what may be termed as its own distinctive strategy of reform. The growth of the presence of government in Quebec was accompanied by a rhetoric so strongly social democratic, stated objectives of reform so sweeping, and such legislative authoritarianism, that one is forced to recognize the distinctive character of government intervention in Quebec.

In all countries where the structure of the economy is monopolistic, the technocratic point of view that everything needs administrative rationalization is bound to emerge and to confront individualistic, entrepreneurial, or market-oriented points of view. As many have said, the state is bound to grow and to institutionalize more and more aspects of social relations. In Quebec after 1960, not only did the technocratic point of view emerge, but—contrary to elsewhere—it gradually totally dominated and penetrated the state along with social-democratic ideals. Reform after reform, the heralding of fundamental objectives, the systematic recourse to the powers of coercion, and reorganization of the state permitted this point of view to take over the political management of problems and crises, thus determining the emergence of unique political dynamics and of a distinctive political culture.

This strategy of reform boils down to a typical three-act play for government actions.[8] The characteristic initial reaction of the Quebec government to the various social ills or to heavy public pressure has almost always been to arouse seemingly boundless hopes and expectations. Unlike the other Canadian provinces, Quebec has summoned numerous commissions of inquiry and policy-making bodies to elaborate, often in enough detail to be convincing, policies inspired by the desire to rationalize the allocation of resources and by the great social-democratic ideals of our times—equality of opportunity, heritage preservation, collective ownership of natural resources, democratization of education, decisional and consultative participation of citizens and workers, decentralization and regionalization of decision-making, comprehensive medical care, and so on.

The second step in government action, following the policy recommendations and the resulting expectations and cooptations, consists in implementing with lightning speed extremely ambitious plans of total reorganization, restructuring, and reshuffling. This has been done almost solely through the coercive mechanisms of legislation, without extended public debate, pilot projects, or other usual procedures for gradual change. Here again we can see at work a style of political problem solving that is radically different from anything to be found elsewhere in Canada, where the accent is put on pilot projects and other ad hoc or "muddling through" procedures.

According to the scenario, the third act opens a few years later, when it turns out that the reforms have fallen short of their objectives, not only because they bore few solutions to the social problems they were supposed to solve, but also because they were far removed from the many social-democratic ideals they promised to fulfill. The often gaping void separating the ideals from the actual objectives and their operationalization would then become the yeast for the increasingly complex crises to come.

Clearly, this is what happened for the reforms in the education, health, and welfare fields. Whatever the political party in power, the same technocratic and highly ambitious, yet only partially successful, crisis-solving style has by and large pervaded government actions in these fields. The story is different for economic reforms. During the Quiet Revolution, exactly the same scenario was followed. Electric-power companies were nationalized. State financial enterprises were created, along with many public enterprises in the productive sectors. And central and regional planning agencies were set up—all of this in a context of profound economic reform. Afterwards, with the Johnson, Bertrand, and Bourassa administrations (1966-76) these organizations, except for a few, received much less support from government officials. A move away from the development of an indigenous state capitalism seems to have occurred: the overall government strategy shifted back to subsidizing foreign-owned enterprises, as incentives for their investments, thus lending credence to the hypothesis that the political base of these administrations was quite different from the one that supported the Liberal party in the early 1960s and the Parti Québécois in the 1970s.

If this analysis is correct, the important question is the following: how can we explain the distinctive character of Quebec state interventions? How can we understand that, in general, technocratic elites and ideologies have had in Quebec an unparalleled status and legitimacy? How does one explain that, after so many years of passivity and conservatism, the Quebec state suddenly decided with such determination to pursue social-democratic objectives that undoubtedly present a leftist outlook by North American political standards?

There is an emerging consensus among Quebec sociologists to view the Quiet Revolution and later government reforms as the result of two interacting factors. First, there was the deeply felt need in various segments of the population to upgrade Quebec infra- and superstructures to catch up with the rest of North America economically, politically, and culturally. The 1957 economic depression, combined with the political pressures emerging from a structurally rapidly changing population, forced the Quebec government to modernize society to insure economic growth, full employment, and social peace. Second, a newly formed petty bourgeoisie could take advantage of this situation and more or less consciously manoeuvre to replace the Church as the locally dominant hegemonic group.[9] This search for hegemony would be the key feature of class relationships in Quebec in the 1960s and 1970s. Within this new petty bourgeoisie, two segments are often distinguished: one, the neo-capitalist fraction, is linked to private capital and is represented by the Liberal party in the 1970s; the other, the technocratic fraction, is tied to the new managerial roles in a monopolistic economy and can be found in Quebec especially in the top echelons of the public sector. The Party Québécois is its political representative.

The purpose of this paper is to further specify this hypothesis, especially for understanding the distinctive reform strategy of the Quebec government. For reasons of conceptual clarity,[10] I prefer the term "new middle class" to "new petty bourgeoisie." Needless to say, my argument here will be a highly tentative one. As Barrington Moore has stated, "All that the social historian can do is point to a contingent connection among changes in the structure of society." And, given the complexity of the issues to be addressed, their contemporary character and the lack of systematically gathered data, we can only hope to develop a plausible interpretation of the exceptional dominance of technocratic ideologies and elite groups, coloured as they are by social-democratic ideals, in Quebec political arena.

Summary of the Argument

The most plausible and all-embracing hypothesis to explain the distinctive problem-solving style of the Quebec state during the 1960s and 1970s is the emergence of a new middle class with a definite stake in the expansion of the state apparatus and the latter's legitimacy in society. The following summarizes this hypothesis.

Contrary to anglophone provinces, the expansion of the state in Quebec occurred in a political and economic context that radically altered the pattern of class relations. Quebec political economy can be schematically characterized by the following idiosyncratic elements.

First, there have been profound structural changes in Quebec's economy since the end of the Second World War, with the numbers of white-collar workers and skilled manual labourers growing in leaps and bounds compared to the number of unskilled and agricultural jobs. The result has been an impressive surge in the upward mobility of the French-speaking segment of the Quebec population, and an equally impressive increase in the college and university enrolment figures. This trend gathered momentum and, by the mid-1960s, thousands and thousands of young graduates were out looking for jobs.

Second, the private sector of the Quebec economy is less dynamic than in Ontario or British Columbia in terms of productivity, ability to attract new investment, and job-generating power. There is a general agreement among economists[11] to say that the Quebec economy has suffered a relative decline since the Second World War, compared to other Canadian provinces, especially because of its weak manufacturing sector and its heavy reliance on the primary and tertiary sectors for economic growth.

Third, the doors to upper and middle management in the largely English-Canadian and American private corporate world have remained for the most part shut for those who are of French origin, even when they have the same qualifications as their English-speaking colleagues. Several reasons have been suggested for this: the private economy was not expanding quickly enough, many enterprises were absentee owned and controlled, and the institutionalized networks of the business community systematically favoured the recruitment of people speaking the language of the incoming capital.

Unlike most other Canadians, French-speaking Quebeckers have been determined to work in their own province whatever the job situation may be. The politicoeconomic conjuncture in the 1960s and 1970s consequently conferred on the growth of the state apparatus in Quebec dynamics that are distinctive in the Canadian context. Given that the state turned out to be one of the only sources of job openings for the growing proportion of university graduates among the French-speaking population, had the civil service and the public sector not expanded, the gap between English- and French-speaking Quebeckers would have continued to widen, since the already scarce upper- and middle-echelon jobs of the private economy were closed to the francophones. The Quebec state was therefore the only institutional base capable of providing prestigious and well-paid jobs for educated French-speaking Quebeckers. In other words, these people had no choice but to orient themselves toward the state sector of the economy—that is, government, government-owned corporations and autonomous state-managed agencies, and industries or organizations directly or indirectly dependent on the state. In the other Canadian provinces, more and more individuals also became university educated, but, contrary to Quebec, the state was not the almost sole purveyor of jobs for them. They could also work in the private sector of the economy and, if they couldn't find job satisfaction within their native province, they could always go elsewhere in English-speaking North America.

University- or technically-trained francophones can in fact be said to constitute a class in the sense that their academic capital provides them with commonly shared levels of market capacity and with a set of objective common interests in seeing the state evolve, by various means, interesting (i.e.

prestigious, powerful, and well paid) jobs for them. Although this class is by and large composed of the people classified by census statisticians as "professional and technical labour," it is not merely a statistical aggregate. It is not simply the addition of individuals with certain attributes, such as a certain level of education, certain types of occupations, a given level of income, and so on. It is in fact a social collectivity grounded in the material order in a fairly identifiable fashion: specifically, by the similar symbolic skills brought by its members to the labour marketplace. Such a new middle class exists in all Canadian provinces, but in Quebec it has the supplementary cohesiveness-inducing constraints of a relatively closed and declining private economy. That is, contrary to its English-speaking counterpart, it is bound to view and use the Quebec state as its only leverage for survival.

The Quebec new middle class is not a "ruling class" or a "bourgeoisie" in the marxist sense. That is, it is not part of this core group of families who own not only the larger part, but also the socially and culturally most determinant part of the world economy, the monopoly sector. It does not own the means of production in the private economy. The ruling class is for the most part foreign in origin, either English Canadian or American, and its enterprises often are absentee owned and controlled.

The Quebec state with varying intensity throughout its history has had to act in ways that support foreign dominance, either directly (for example, subsidization of multinational enterprises for their investments) or indirectly (socialization of certain costs of production or public works, for example, to compensate for the lack of dynamism of the private economy). State spending has to behave in such a way in order to maintain the growth of the economy and low levels of unemployment.

This reality is undoubtedly harmful for the immediate interests of most of the fractions of the new middle class, but the latter are hard pressed to express their opposition lest they undermine the Quebec state itself. From time to time, when the economic context permits, some of these fractions succeed in manoeuvring themselves into the position of being able to allocate resources in the manufacturing or the financing sectors of the economy, by socializing the purchase price or the investment capital necessary for creating this or that enterprise and nationalizing its profits. Such state actions may have the effect both of providing some new-middle-class elites with the power to allocate resources and of stimulating employment and economic growth to the satisfaction of both the general population and of the capitalist bourgeois class. Generally speaking, however, the new middle class most forcibly seeks to acquire real (if limited) hegemony at the local level in those sectors—especially human services—where the state has the freest hand.

Any action that has the effect of extending the quantitative *and* qualitative influence of the state serves the interests of this class. The new middle class has consequently produced a political culture that favours high-profile wideranging reorganizations that draw on, in the highly politicized context of Quebec, broad social-democratic and nationalist aspirations. Even though state intervention sometimes provokes short-term conflicts among petty-bourgeois fractions (among "technocrats," "professionals," and "neo-capitalists," for instance), there is a common class interest in the self-preservative and self-promoting virtues of increased state initiative, and they spare no pains to impress on the population the idea that the Quebec state is the only collective lever it has. As an ex-Minister of Industry and Commerce said, given the weakness of the private economy and the general leverage of the Quebec state, Quebec would now be on the verge of creating a "socialism by default." This means the appropriation of key economic enterprises by the state and the enactment of thorough bureaucratic reforms aimed at equalizing the distribution of wealth and income in the society.

Against such a backdrop, when technocratic elite groups such as the dominant members of the Parent (education reform) or Castonguay-Nepveu (health and social-welfare reforms) commissions appear for one reason or another on the scene and formulate policies involving highly visible organizational shakeups, premised on larger social-democratic policies for Quebec society, they are automatically greeted with broad social support and open arms in civil service circles. No matter what short-term tensions these elite groups may cause, general class interest dictates that they be provided sweeping power and the legitimacy they need, inasmuch as they contribute to the quantitative *and* qualitative expansion of the state apparatus. This is why these groups have little trouble in obtaining broad cabinet and National Assembly approval for speedy and far-reaching reform, however authoritarian the legislation and regulations enacted may be.

In the very different context of Ontario, for instance, comparable groups have not been legitimized in this way nor received comparable powers. Of course, a new middle class also exists in Ontario, but the state apparatus is not its only means of survival and thus there are no social forces that push for unconditional support to technocratic elites whose aim is to extend state control. To put it another way, it is inconceivable, in a context like that of Ontario, that an elite group like the Castonguay-Nepveu Commission could succeed in completely controlling an entire sector of government activity and imposing its own blueprint for change and its own way of doing things. Again, this is not to say that such groups do not exist in Ontario—quite the contrary. But, given the politicoeconomic conjuncture in this province, their social status could not be as high and their ideologies could not penetrate the state as thoroughly as they have in Quebec.

To clarify the maze of numbers and events that will now be presented in support of this argument, Figure 10-1 diagrams the structure of the argument just summarized: each point in Figure 10-1 will be documented in the alphabetical order presented.

The Evolution of Quebec's Political Economy

This discussion of the evolution of Quebec's economy will use the classification categories developed by James O'Connor in *Fiscal Crisis of the State*.[12] I

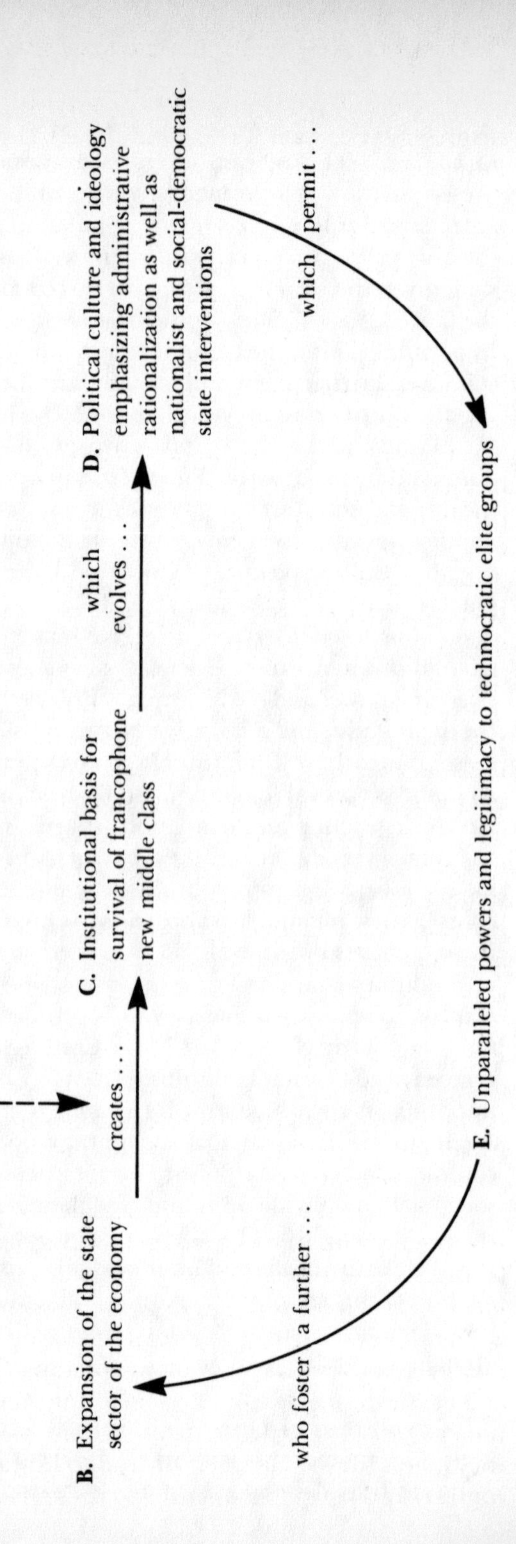

Figure 10-1 The Development of the New Middle Class

will distinguish among the monopolistic sector, the market or competitive sector, and the state sector. The first sector is highly *monopolistic* in concentration of ownership and in economic behaviour (like uses of price fixing). It requires large amounts of fixed capital invested per worker and it is involved in wide-scale markets. Important features of this sector are the high wages and salaries paid, the stable levels of employment, and the tendency toward vertical as well as horizontal integration of production and distribution processes. The market or *competitive* sector was once the largest economic sector, but it is now declining in importance. It is characterized by its lower levels of productivity, smaller-scale production, local or regional markets, lower ratios of capital invested per worker, lower unionization rate, lower wages and salaries, and more unstable levels of employment. Agriculture, construction, retail-trade, and personal-service enterprises are typically part of this sector of the economy. O'Connor also divides up the *state* sector into two categories: production of goods and services organized by the state itself (for instance, mail, education, public health, welfare, and other social services) and production organized by industries owned by the state (state industrial enterprises,) or under contract with the state (such as military equipment and supplies, highway construction).

1920-1945: Competitive Capitalism and the Arrival of Foreign Industry

It was not until the end of the Second World War that fundamental changes in Quebec economy began. After the war, a massive migration took place to the major cities and foreign—especially American—monopoly capital, moved in at an accelerated speed causing the occupational structure to change considerably. Quebec history from about 1900 to the mid-1940s has been thoroughly described elsewhere[13] and there is no need for us to discuss it in other than outline form.

This period was characterized by the fact that most French Canadians were engaged in petty commodity production, mostly in agriculture but also in small-scale industry. Priests, doctors, and lawyers were the local elites, in control of almost all the political, social, and cultural organizations of the community. During this period, foreign capital and its industries began to install themselves in Quebec, but this did not have any impact on the social organization of Quebec.

In fact, till the late 1940s, foreign and local capital largely remained two separate worlds, as they were fulfilling complementary functions. As Guindon has argued,[14] Anglo-Canadian and American industries moved into a society faced with the economic burden of the demographic surplus[15] of French-Canadian rural society. In relieving this acute population surplus, they could accumulate capital by exploiting Quebec's natural-resource base and its cheap labour without encroaching on the traditional social organization of Quebec society or its traditional elites. Furthermore, the foreign group could itself fill the management and technical levels of industry with little conflict, for French Canadians provided only the semi-skilled and unskilled labour.[16] As for French-Canadian society, the absorption of surplus labour by foreign industry permitted its distinctive political and religious elite, its political and social institutions anchored to the rural parish, and its petty commodity-production economy to survive despite the changes in the surrounding material order.[17]

1945-1960: The Growth of the Monopoly Sector and Its Consequences

With more and more francophones working within foreign industry and with the increasing monopolistic characteristics of this industry, the complementarity of functions and the convergence of interests between Quebec traditional elites and foreign entrepreneurs gradually disappeared. By the early 1950s, Quebec economy had changed so much that the traditional social order had stopped being reproduced, despite the length of time it took for this fact to be politically and socially felt.

By the early 1960s, while French Canadians comprised more than 80% of Quebec population and owned 50% of the enterprises, they controlled only 15% of the value added in Quebec industry while some of the 13% of English Canadians and a few Americans controlled 85%.[18] In other words, French-Canadian ownership and control was almost entirely limited to the much less profitable competitive sector of the economy, while English-Canadian and other foreign interests owned and controlled the profitable monopolistic sector.

The ex-President of the Economic Council of Canada, André Raynauld, has done research on industrial enterprises in Quebec in 1961. His results confirm that Quebec economy is characterized by a French-Canadian competitive sector and a foreign monopolistic sector. He writes:

> French-Canadian establishments were at the one extreme in every respect. Foreign establishments were at the other extreme in every respect and Other Canadian establishments were in between. With regard to *size,* Foreign establishments were seven times larger than French Canadian, and four times larger than Other Canadian by *value added.* The *average output* per man was 6500, 8400, and 12000 dollars respectively for French-Canadian, Other Canadian and Foreign establishments. *Wages and salaries* in French-Canadian establishments were 30 percent below those in Foreign, and 12 percent below those in Other Canadian establishments . . .[19]

French-Canadian-owned enterprises, with few exceptions in 1961, were within the competitive or market sector. French-Canadian ownership was concentrated in agriculture, construction, retail trade, and services. According to the Royal Commission on Bilingualism and Biculturalism:

> Francophones are owners and proprietors in large proportions in agriculture and to a lesser degree in the service fields and retail trade. In wholesale they play a still smaller role, while in finance and manufacturing they account for about one-fourth of the total. Moreover, within manufacturing itself, the pattern of ownership is also uneven. In small-scale manufacturing, such as the production of wood products, Francophones predominate;

> but in fields requiring large capital investment and highly advanced technology, such as the manufacture of chemicals and petroleum products, they play virtually no role in ownership or control.[20]

Foreign-owned enterprises constituted Quebec's major enterprises, in terms of value added and outputs. These enterprises can be classified in three main categories. First, from this earlier phase of industrialization, largely created by the National Policy of the federal government in the 1870s, Quebec has inherited secondary industries in labour-intensive sectors (textile, wood, shoes, and other finished products). Second, in the mid-1930s primary industries began to appear exploiting Quebec natural resources (pulp and paper, primary metallic industries). Finally, later on, some large American high-technology enterprises (automobile, electrical equipment) came in, but at an extremely slow pace compared to Ontario.[21] Almost all these enterprises are owned and controlled by American and English-Canadian interests.[22] The second and third categories are largely part of the American monopolistic sector. The first category shows to a lesser extent similar monopolistic features.

Weakness of this Economy

This general structure of the economy in the early 1960s (much of it is still the same) had key economic and social consequences. The economy had two overwhelming characteristics. In the first place, as just seen, the profitable monopolistic sector was almost entirely owned by foreign interests, while the fairly large and unprofitable competitive sector was French-Canadian owned. Second, since the monopolistic sector, with the complicity of Quebec traditional elites, was built on the requirements of foreign interests and their industries, it appeared almost only where high profits could be made. Foreign enterprises therefore exploited Quebec's natural-resource base and cheap labour. In those industrial sectors where labour was abundant and therefore cheap, labour-intensive light consumer-goods industries developed. The dynamism of these enterprises has now considerably declined. Extremely few durable-goods and producer-goods industries have replaced them, even though such enterprises would have been necessary to generate new investments and create new jobs. The combination of a fairly large competitive sector and a partially weak monopolistic sector in light consumer-goods industries means that a relatively large proportion of workers are employed in slow-growth and low-productivity industries.

This situation accounts for the general weaknesses of Quebec economy in contrast to Ontario. Here are a few indices of this relative decline of Quebec's economy. Fewer people worked in the Quebec manufacturing sector in 1971 than in 1961, while this number has increased on the average all over Canada.[23] In fact, as a task force to the Department of Industry and Commerce recently noted, new jobs in Quebec tend to be created in the nonvalue-producing tertiary sector alone, contrary to Ontario:

> About 230,000 jobs have been created between 1966 and 1971, among which 133,000 are in "personal social service- and others" and 22,000 in the public administration. More than 90% of the new jobs are due to the growth of the tertiary sector. During the same period, approximately 50,000 jobs have disappeared in equal parts in construction and in the primary sector, in particular forestry and mining. This means a net creation of 180,000 jobs; that is 36,000 on the average each year in comparison with 85,600 for Ontario (428,000 total for this five-year period).[24]

Further, Quebec consistently had 50% of the bankruptcies in Canada, while its GNP accounts for only 25% of Canada's GNP.[25] Quebec always had a 20% to 50% higher unemployment rate than the Canadian average, usually twice as high as Ontario. Over the last two decades, the personal income per capita in Quebec has been 12% to 15% lower than the Canadian mean, and between 23% to 30% lower than Ontario. The discrepancies between Quebec and English Canada are even clearer if we disaggregate according to ethnicity. André Raynauld has shown that French Canadians were among the most poorly paid workers in Quebec in 1961, ranking 12th in labour income in a list of 14 ethnic groups. He writes:

> The most remarkable fact . . . is that French-Canadian labour income was 12% below the overall average in every province except Quebec, where it was 40% below the overall provincial average. In absolute terms, the gap was about 1000 dollars a year in Canada as a whole, and 2000 dollars in Quebec.[26]

Eliminating the effects of several factors (age, sex composition of labour force, education, occupation, employment status, region, and labour-force participation) on this discrepancy, he found that ethnicity still accounted for more than 50% of the income differential. French Canadians, because they are French Canadians and for no other reason, earn much less than their English-Canadian counterparts in Quebec.

The Closure of the Top Corporate World to French Canadians and the Closed Nature of Quebec Society

Not only was this structure of the economy weak for generating investments and for creating employment, but it also did not provide employment for university- or technically trained francophones. On the one hand, the competitive sector does not possess high-income, high-prestige, and high-power jobs. The competitive sector is largely composed of small enterprises of self-employed individuals and a few workers. On the other hand, the top corporate world was and is closed to francophones. Entries at the top of the occupational hierarchy were and are blocked to French Canadians, whatever their level of education. This has both historical and sociological grounds.

Both because of the "language" of the incoming capital and in view of their earlier higher levels of education, successive English-Canadian generations have always been better placed in the occupational hierarchy. As a consequence, they are still at an advantage over French Canadians for high-income and high-power jobs in the monopolistic sector. English Canadians have systematically preceded French Canadians in their patterns of social mobility, thus blocking the entry of French Canadians in the top jobs of the private economy. Whatever the levels of education now achieved by French Canadians, the institutionalized networks of the big-business community tend to omit French Canadians. Examples of these networks are the well-known links between anglophone universities and enterprises in the monopoly sector. The Royal Commission on Bilingualism and Biculturalism has noted:

> Because of their higher educational level, their position in the occupational structure, and their original position as leaders of Quebec's industrialization, the Anglophones have always been better prepared than the Francophones to enjoy the benefits of the province's economic development. Once socio-economic patterns have been established, they tend to be self-perpetuating; the momentum favouring the Anglophones was never matched in the Francophone community.[27]

As a consequence, very few French Canadians could be considered part of a corporate elite. Porter[28] estimated this group to be 51 persons in 1951 (or 6.7% of the Canadian corporate elite at that time). Milner and Milner[29] and Clement[30] estimate that in 1971, while French Canadians constituted a third of the Canadian population, this group included only 65 persons (or 8.4% of the Canadian corporate elite). In Milner and Milner's words:

> We looked at those Quebec firms controlled by French Canadians, borrowing the results of a study[31] which selected from these firms a sample of the two largest banks, the two largest trust companies, the six largest industries, the three largest insurance companies, and the three largest finance companies. There are 216 positions on the boards of directors of these enterprises held by 163 persons. Of these 163 persons, 65 (40%) hold 118 (54%) of the 216 positions. These men hold among themselves 50% of the directorships of the insurance companies, 68% of the trust companies, 43% of the six industries, and 72% of the banks. These 65 persons thus are a good approximation of the French-Canadian economic elite. . . . Over half of this elite was educated in two schools: Collège Sainte-Marie and Jean de Brébeuf.[32]

It is important to add here that, notwithstanding the enormous fiscal and legal efforts of the Quebec state in the late 1960s to raise the level of education among francophones and to enforce French as the language of work in Quebec, the private economy remained closed to francophones. This runs counter to the popular belief that, with the increased levels of educational attainments of the Quebec population and the corollary rejection of the self-defeating rural and Catholic ideology, French Canadians could be in a position to make significant inroads into the private monopolistic economy.

Wallace Clement has presented convincing evidence to counter this belief. Noticing that the number of French-Canadians in the economic elite had risen only from 51 to 65 from 1951 to 1971, he writes:

> This means a net increase of only 14 more French Canadians or 1.7 per cent more of the elite population over the last 20 years. These have not been uneventful years in French-Anglo relations; quite the contrary, they were supposed to contain the "new awakening" (a loaded phrase which somehow assumes the French have themselves been their own barrier to gaining equality and not their position vis-à-vis the dominant Anglos) and the "quiet revolution" of the 1960s and the not-so-quiet revolution of recent years. In spite of ideological statements to the contrary, the French have not made significant inroads into the economic world.[33]

He then cites the research of Presthus[34] to show that not only have the French not made it to the very top of the corporate world, but they also did not make gains in the middle range and smaller corporations:

> A recent study based on 12,741 names of executives from some 2,400 companies operating in Canada listed in the 1971 *Directory of Directors* found only 9.4% to be French Canadians. This is only about one percent more than are to be found in the economic elite and includes many corporations much smaller than the 113 dominant ones which are the basis of this study.[35]

Further evidence of the restricted mobility of francophones into the private economy is provided by a study of the Institut International d'Economie Quantitative. It shows that, in 1971, 28% of the top management jobs in the private economy earning above $20,000, 28% of the middle management occupations earning between $15,000 and $19,999, and 48% of lower-level management positions earning between $5,000 and $14,999 were held by francophones, while French Canadians constituted 75% of the labour force in 1971.[36] In other words, the proportion of francophones occupying any level of management in the private economy is considerably smaller than the proportion of francophones in the overall labour force. An analysis of the 1971 census has even shown that, at a same level of managerial occupation, French Canadians earn 11% less than their English-Canadian counterparts.[37]

To sum up, university- and technically trained francophones were in the early 1960s and still by the mid-1970s confronted with the following situation: a fairly large competitive economy with practically no appropriate jobs for their training and a monopolistic economy with only a few job outlets, either because enterprises are absentee owned and controlled or because some of them are in such obsolete industrial sectors that they do not expand enough to provide new jobs. When a position does open up, because of the historically determined linkages between the anglophones and the business community, it tends to be given to an anglophone. Almost the only job outlets therefore seem in the state sector of the economy.

One could object that, given this situation, French Canadians have incentives to go to work elsewhere in Canada or North America, as was the case for many French-Canadian unskilled labourers during the 1920s and the Depression years, but the situation was quite different then. In the 1920s and 1930s, the surplus labour of rural Quebec was such that it could not be entirely absorbed by incoming industry. In the 1960s and 1970s, we are talking about a different kind of people, individuals who have over 15 years of formal education and who correctly believe that they have the skills necessary for the top jobs at least as much as their anglophone counterparts. In such cases, cultural barriers impose considerable restrictions on geographic mobility much more than they did in the 1920s or 1930s. The French-Canadian situation is different from that experienced by Canadians in the poorer Atlantic provinces. Maritimers who do not find jobs in their native province will tend to look for jobs anywhere on the North American continent. A corresponding Québécois, unless he accepts the disturbing emotional consequences of becoming an expatriate, is almost glued to Quebec's territory, whatever the job outlets.

Evidence for this phenomenon is overwhelming. For instance, reporting on a study of Quebec engineers, the Royal Commission on Bilingualism and Biculturalism wrote:

> Although 80 per cent of the Francophone engineers in our Montreal sample thought Quebec offered them the best opportunities, only nine per cent of the Anglophones agreed with them; almost half the Anglophone engineers named the United States instead. There are indications that the situation is changing, but the evidence is consistent in showing a lower mobility rate and a lesser willingness to move on the part of Francophone engineers and their wives. If they work for a large corporation, the consequence of this difference is the same as for the managers—a slower rate of promotion. For those who work in small firms of Francophone-owned institutions, this effect, though not as pronounced, is still at work.[38]

Further, if we look at some aggregated migration statistics,[39] the same phenomenon is visible: Quebec loses proportionally fewer inhabitants than any other province and receives the smallest relative proportion of internal migrants. Ontario receives many more internal migrants and few leave the province because of the economic wealth and the immense job opportunities it offers. If these data could be analyzed by ethnic origin, it is probable that even fewer Québécois would appear to be leaving the province.

In this sense, Quebec is a closed society for the Francophone segment of its population. However unfulfilling the job opportunities and whatever one's political opinions, Quebec, in a real sense, is a nation, the borders of which are not easily passed.

The Structural Mobility of French Canadians and the Increased Levels of Education

After the war, the politicoeconomic situation in Quebec changed somewhat. A great number of French Canadians had left the agricultural rural world to become unskilled or semi-skilled labourers in foreign industry. Many of the small commodity producers who in a former era had derived quite a good standard of living from their farms, retail stores, or crafts shops, also joined the ranks of the increasingly urban working class. None of them was educated enough to occupy managerial, professional, or technical positions. During this period, English Canadians occupied the entire top managerial, professional, and technical occupations within industry.

From the 1930s to the early 1960s, two parallel phenomena took place. On the one hand, since francophones increasingly filled the bottom positions of the occupational hierarchy and since more and more anglophones filled the top positions of this hierarchy, French Canadians as an ethnic group were in fact getting proletarianized, in the sense of increasingly having nothing else to sell but their labour power. On the other hand, with the expansion of the monopoly sector and the corollary changes in the occupational structure (technical, clerical, and skilled tasks becoming quantitatively more important than unskilled and primary labour) came a structural mobility of French Canadians. That is, quite independently of their own volition and uniquely because of changes in the structure of the demand for labour, many French Canadians began to perform better paid and somewhat more prestigious tasks. With such a structural mobility, French Canadians began to enjoy better standards of living and began to aspire for better jobs for themselves and their children. More and more people enrolled in school and great pressure was put on the state to facilitate the financial and geographical access to education.

The data that follow are unsatisfying because of the varying definitions of occupational categories used in different research studies and because of the lack of built-in comparability between the studies; however, they are the only published data available. However crude, they provide approximate empirical evidence for the phenomena just described.

The widening of the gap in the occupational hierarchy between anglophones and francophones in Quebec is well illustrated by an analysis performed by John Porter.[40] He compared the percentage of over- or underrepresentation of French and British males in various occupational categories, according to census data in 1931, 1951, and 1961. I have corrected for some slight computational errors in Porter's results and I have computed the same information for 1971. Because census statisticians have redefined certain occupational categories during this period, the results have only an indicative value.[41]

These data show that from 1931 to 1961 Quebeckers of British origin have increasingly been overrepresented at the professional and technical levels, moving from +5% to +7.2%. Conversely, the French have become more and more underrepresented in this group, moving from -0.9% to -1.5%. A similar evolution also seems to have occurred in the category "manager" between 1951 and 1961. For primary and unskilled jobs, although the gap has not been widened as much between 1931 and 1961, French Canadians have been constantly overrepresented, moving from 0.3% to 1.1% in 1961, to 1.3% in 1971. For the other occupational levels, there seems to have been a levelling off of the differences between the two groups, both increasingly tending towards the overall male labour-force distribution.

In other words, between 1931 and 1961, there seems to have been a widening gap between anglophones and francophones. This view is also confirmed by Rocher and de Jocas's analysis[42] of intergenerational mobility of sons in 1954. It showed that the relative proportion of English Canadians was increasing in nonmanual tasks and decreasing in manual jobs. In Rocher and de Jocas's sample, the gap in the top two categories (liberal professions and high management; semi-professionals and middle management) was, in 1954, increasing from 8.5% for the fathers to 15.2% for the sons, in favour of the anglophones, while manual workers were increasingly French in origin, the gap moving from 14.3% to 29.3%.

In the 1971 census, the overall picture changed considerably. For *all* the occupational categories listed, the distribution of anglophones and francophones tended towards the overall labour-force distribution. While the gap for "professionals and technicians" had been widening between 1931 and 1961, it is reduced by more than a half in 1971, the British moving from an overrepresentation of +7.2% in 1961 to only +3.2% in 1971, the French moving from an underrepresentation of -1.5% to -0.8%, for a reduction of the difference from 8.7% in 1961 to 4.0% in 1971. Although this might only be an artifact of the census redefinitions, a similar, yet less drastic, phenomenon seems to have occurred for "managers." The gap between francophones and anglophones in primary and unskilled jobs diminished from 7.0% to 3.6%.

The same phenomenon has been noticed by Jacques Dofny and Muriel Garon-Audy,[43] who studied the intergenerational mobility of sons in 1964, which they compared with the identical study of Rocher and de Jocas for sons in 1954. In 1964, the gap between anglophones and francophones was significantly reduced for all categories except "semi-professionals and middle managers," for "skilled and semi-skilled workers," and for "personal services." They concluded:

> In summary, the reduction of the gaps between French Canadians and English Canadians from the generation of fathers to the generation of sons in contrast to what was observed in 1954 (in 1954, in 6/8 cases the gap was increasing between the two ethnic groups; in 1964, on the contrary, the gap is decreased in 5/8 cases) would underline an acceleration of mobility for French Canadians.[44]

Sociologists call this phenomenon "structural" mobility, as opposed to "individual" mobility. Dofny and Garon-Audy have attempted to quantify its importance. French Canadians have recently experienced an enormous social mobility, much more so than the French Canadians studied in 1954 by Rocher and de Jocas or the English Canadians surveyed in 1964: 75.1% of the

French Canadians studied in 1964 (with 50% upwardly mobile, 15% downwardly mobile, and 10% mobile to approximately equivalent jobs) have been mobile with respect to their father's occupational status, as compared to 64.1% in 1954 (35% upwardly mobile, 20% downwardly mobile, and 10% mobile to equivalent jobs) and to 66.0% of the Anglo-Canadians in 1964. Yet, this recent social mobility of French Canadians is to an important extent solely attributable to changes in the occupational structure—from primary and unskilled labour to skilled and white-collar tasks—that is, the mobility was structural rather than individual. Nearly half (45.0%) of the observed mobility among French Canadians in 1964 is structural, compared to a fourth (27.6%) of the observed mobility in 1954.

The Porter, Rocher-de Jocas, and Dofny-Garon-Audy data underline a key phenomenon. They seem to show that the gap between anglophones and francophones, which had been widening between 1930 and 1960, was transferred during the 1960s to higher levels in the occupational hierarchy because of the structural changes in the economy. The 1971 census data indicate that this gap has perhaps even begun to diminish, with proportionally more French Canadians entering managerial, professional, and technical jobs. In other words, while for a long time it looked as if the whole French-Canadian ethnic group was being increasingly proletarianized, the 1971 census shows, it seems, that an important class cleavage is appearing *within* the francophone community in Quebec. Given the closure of the private monopolistic economy to French Canadians, this can only be attributable to the expansion of the Quebec state sector of the economy. The expansion of the state sector opened up new possibilities for mobility and thus probably did reduce the income, prestige, and power gap between anglophones and francophones.

But before we examine this specific issue, let us consider an important correlate of the structural changes in the economy: the rise of education among French Canadians. This phenomenon explains why proportionally more francophones *could* by the 1960s aspire to professional, managerial, or technical jobs.

The transition of capitalism into its monopolistic advanced stages is associated with increased levels of education in the population. The increasing complexity of industrial tasks, the expanding needs for regulatory jobs, the growth of the human service sector, and so on all demand high levels of formal training. It took Quebec francophones a decade or two longer than anglophones to realize this, partly because their low-level jobs did not require many years in school; partly because it was culturally assumed that academic studies were valuable only to those who wished to become priests, doctors, or lawyers; and partly because of the extremely elitist structure of the Church-controlled educational system. In the 1950s, with the increasingly individually felt changes in the economy, things began to change.

Jacques Brazeau[45] has noted that between 1950 and 1960 the percentage of the population between the ages of five and 24 who attended school rose from 53 to 62; attendance in grades nine to 12 more than doubled and, beyond grade 12, it increased by more than 50%. Yet, the educational sector was incapable of coping with demands for massive school enrolment, as a consequence of the high costs and maldistribution of educational facilities. In 1960, Quebec had the 10th rank among Canadian provinces in secondary schooling (actually, one out of two Quebec adults had less than seven years of schooling), but it had the fourth rank for the proportion of its population holding a university diploma. That this system was ill equipped to fit the needs of children from low-income families is manifested by the fact that the retention rate in Quebec—defined as the enrolment in grade 11 as a percentage of grade two nine years earlier—was the lowest in Canada (33%).[46] The educational reforms of the 1960s resulted from such pressures and the retention rate jumped to 70% in 1967, placing Quebec in the fifth-highest rank among the 10 Canadian provinces. Furthermore, while the Quebec education sector had been oriented for generations towards training in the liberal professions and in the humanities, proportionally more students now enrol in those fields that were not so long ago reserved for anglophones (sciences, engineering, and the like), so that the overall school enrolment picture for francophones increasingly tends to look more like Ontario's.[47]

To sum up, by the early 1960s, quite a few French Canadians had the formal training enabling them to fulfill top managerial, professional, and technical jobs in the economy and, after the educational reforms of the mid-1960s, their number considerably increased. In effect, a new middle class was born—that is, a social collectivity characterized by the fact that only the certified academic capital of its members, as opposed to the classical monetary capital—provides them with bargaining powers on the labour market. This new middle class is, in essence, different from Quebec's old middle class and traditional elites whose power and status derived above all from their position vis-à-vis the religious order.

In the early 1960s, this new middle class was confronted with a private economy quite incapable of generating new job outlets and quite inhospitable to certified French-Canadian skills. The expansion of the state in this context came as a miracle. It provided job outlets to university- and technically trained French Canadians, thus securing the survival of that class within Quebec.

The Expansion of the State Sector of the Economy

As we have seen, all over Canada, the 1950s and the 1960s witnessed an enormous expansion of the state sector of the economy.

This expansion is mainly the expansion of the provincial and local state sectors. Both the provincial and the municipal governments have enormously increased their gross general expenditures[48] in comparison with the federal government: from $101.35 per capita on the average in 1954-55 to $802.54 in 1971-72 for the provinces; from $58.37 in 1952 to $437.64 in 1971 for municipalities; and from $314.99 in 1954-55 to $844.65 in 1971-72 for the federal government.[49] Provincial and municipal expenditures took an increasing share of personal income, while federal expenditures remained fairly constant. In 17 years, the provinces and the municipalities increased their gross general expenditures by 800%, while the federal increased its by less than 300%.

The growth of the provincial level of administration is largely attributable to the expansion of state-controlled social services, which are taking an increasing share (from a half in 1950 to two-thirds in 1970) of an otherwise rapidly increasing total budget. In fact, the administrative responsibility for social-welfare services has shifted almost entirely to provinces. While 34% of consolidated expenditures for health (after elimination of transfer payments between administrations) was assumed by the federal administration in 1947-48, only 2.8% was in 1970-71. The situation is identical for education (2.8% in 1970-71) but differs for welfare expenditures (where 73.4% were federal).[50] Overall, the priorities for provincial expenditures have shifted from roads and agriculture to health and education.

There is, besides governmental administrations, a second important element in the state sector: state enterprises. While the gross general expenditures per capita at the provincial level of government have expanded on the average in Canada by five times during the 1960s, the assets per capita of state enterprises have increased on the average in all Canadian provinces by four times during the same period.[51]

In general, these statistics underestimate the importance and the rate of expansion of the state sector of the economy, for they only partially include the economic activity derived from contracts of various private enterprises with the state. For instance, in Quebec, the economic activity—linked to Expo '67, to the massive construction of schools in the 1960s, hospitals, nursing homes, the Manic and James Bay projects, and the Olympics—is only partially accounted for in the previously presented statistics.

Now, if we compare the evolution of provincial finances, Quebec is strikingly different in three respects. First, because of Quebec's weaker economic structure, the share of provincial and municipal expenditures within personal income is considerably higher than in Ontario and in the other provinces on the average.[52] The consolidated provincial-municipal expenditures represented a relatively equivalent per capita expenditure, but 34.9% of Quebec personal income in 1971, as compared to 27.5% in Ontario and 30.9% across Canada.

Second, the growth of the state sector in Quebec had really only begun in 1960 with the Liberal party administration, while the 1950s had been the takeoff point for Ontario.[53] This is evident in the evolution of provincial and municipal expenditures. It is also evident in the growth of the assets of provincial state enterprises. In the 1960s, there was a sevenfold increase of these assets in Quebec, as compared with a threefold increase in Ontario and a fourfold increase on the average among Canadian provinces, so that these assets represented $6,604,432,000 in 1971 in Quebec (or $1095.63 per capita) and $6,443,001,000 in Ontario (or $836.43 per capita). As a result of this febrile creation and expansion of state enterprises in Quebec, their assets as of 1971, both in absolute terms and per capita, were the highest among all Canadian provinces.

Third, because the growth of the state sector in Quebec gained momentum only in the 1960s, the current public debt in Quebec is much higher than in Ontario. From 1960 to 1968, Quebec's direct debt (the government's) has increased by five times (Ontario, about 1.5 times) and the indirect debt (debt guaranteed to other parts of the state, such as state enterprises) by three times (while in Ontario it remained about the same).[54] In other words, the fiscal efforts were spread out over the 1950s and 1960s in Ontario, but they were condensed into the 1960s for Quebec.

These differences boil down to one sociological observation: the state sector of the economy is qualitatively, if not in strict quantifiable fiscal terms, more important in Quebec than in the other provinces. Since its expansion has been more sudden in its timing, more extensive in its nationalization and creation of enterprises, and more costly to its taxpayers, the state inevitably achieved a much greater presence in people's minds than anywhere else in Canada. This is to say that the state has expanded not only quantitatively, but also qualitatively. This has been well expressed by Claude Morin, a former high state official and Minister of Intergovernmental affairs in the Parti Québécois government:

> In the eyes of French-speaking Quebeckers, Ottawa and Quebec have no authority over each other; each administration is autonomous in its areas of jurisdictions; sometimes their activities are complementary, and if conflicts arise, the Government of Quebec is *a priori* in the right . . . The common denominator of views in the other provinces is that the federal government is the "national" government; neither the Newfoundlander nor British Columbian questions this basic postulate . . . An English-speaking provincial political figure, even a Premier, is considered to have received a promotion if he becomes a federal Cabinet minister. In Quebec, for a politician to move from the Quebec to the federal arena is no longer necessarily a promotion; the two are considered of similar significance.[55]

Because of this, the intensity of the feelings towards the actions of the Quebec government is incomparably higher in Quebec than elsewhere in Canada, as indicated by such things as the virulence of public debates, the much higher amount of press coverage, or the popular imagery surrounding political figures. In this context, given the general ideology surrounding this expansion—which we will describe later—the Quebec state can easily appear as the collective lever for the upward mobility of all the Québécois people, independently of who in fact most tangibly benefits from this expansion of the state.

The Quebec State as the Institutional Basis for the New Middle Class

With more and more French Canadians being university educated but incapable of finding appropriate jobs, the gap between anglophones and francophones would have widened to a historically unparalleled, socially explosive proportion. But the state sector did expand and did provide job outlets for a vast proportion of the new middle class. In so doing, it became the institutional basis for the existence of this class.

The available evidence to support this hypothesis is quite scattered and unsystematic. Yet it describes the issue from so many different angles that it makes a rather convincing case for the assertion that the Quebec state has evolved into being the main locus for the local hegemony of a Quebec francophone new middle class.

A first line of evidence is the following. If we break down the 1971 census category "professional and technical" into occupational specialties, we notice that anglophones are overrepresented in the natural sciences, engineering, architecture, mathematics, and related fields (+18.8%); the francophones, underrepresented (-6.8%). Health and education are, however, significantly overrepresented by francophones (+1.9% and +3.3%, respectively, for French Canadians; -7.6% and -8.4%, respectively, for anglophones).[56] Because census statisticians presented disaggregated data of this sort only in 1971, longitudinal data are unavailable.

This pattern of over- and underrepresentation is not surprising. Health, education, and religion have traditionally been the only institutional sectors where mobility from bottom to top was conceivable for French Canadians. Similarly, because of their earlier association with monopolistic enterprises, anglophones have until recently been more prone to specialize in and to work in hard-science fields.

What is important, however, is that the health and education fields are now almost totally under the jurisdiction of the Quebec state. With the hospitalization insurance plan, the educational reforms, the medical-insurance plan, and the reorganization of welfare services, almost all of the social services have become part of the state sector of the economy. The same has not occurred for the hard-science field. Further, the majority of the new jobs created within Quebec during the 1960s have been in social services. Health, education, and welfare employment has almost doubled, while the absolute number of people employed in manufacturing has slightly diminished. Making the reasonable assumption that the growth of employment in the state-controlled social services occurred for anglophones and francophones in proportion to their relative number in the overall population, this would mean that a large proportion of the Quebec new middle class went to work in these areas and thus in the state sector of the economy. In other words, the emergence of Quebec's new middle class was directly associated with the growth of the state's social-services agencies and departments.

A second line of evidence comes from the comparative examination of the location of work of various professional groupings of both ethnic origins. The Royal Commission on Bilingualism and Biculturalism investigated this question in the mid-1960s. It writes:

> Even among candidates with the educational qualifications suited to careers in industrial management, there appear to be substantial differences between Francophones and Anglophones as to where they actually choose, or are chosen to work. For instance, in 1964, commerce graduates of McGill were employed in industry to a greater extent than graduates of the Ecole des Hautes Etudes Commerciales. . . . The membership list of the Institute of Chartered Accountants of Quebec showed a similar pattern of employment. More than 90 per cent of the chartered accountants employed by the provincial and municipal government were Francophones; in industry and commerce less than 40 per cent were Francophones. Among both commerce graduates and chartered accountants, however, there was a trend among the younger Francophones towards greater participation in the private sector. Even so, Anglophones still outnumbered Francophones to a considerable extent among the younger employees.

The same is true for engineers and scientists:

> The proportion of Francophone engineers working in private industry in 1963 was similarly low; only 25% of Francophone engineers compared with 78% of Anglophone engineers, were employed in this sector. . . . The pattern of employment of science graduates from Francophone universities among industrial sectors has many of the same features as that of Francophone engineers. Among scientists employed by provincial and municipal governments, 85% were Francophones. Their proportion was much lower in teaching (43%), the federal government (39%) and non-salaried professional services (32%). Like the engineers, they had low proportions in the large mining and manufacturing sectors (14%) and in construction, transportation and communication (13%).[57]

The engineers' situation could be looked at from another angle. While one of the biggest electrical power companies employed only 20 francophone engineers out of 175 in 1963 prior to being nationalized, Montreal Quebec Hydro (nationalized in 1944) had 190 Francophone engineers out of 243 at the same date.[58] We can reasonably assume that the nationalization of all electrical power companies has been conducive to the hiring of francophone engineers as opposed to anglophone. The situation in Montreal Quebec Hydro in 1963 has probably gradually been extended to the entire hydro field after nationalization. Again, this would show that the expansion of the state has served Quebec's new middle class.

This observation is strengthened by a third piece of evidence. The Centre de Sondage of the Université de Montréal conducted a study in 1973 on behalf of the Commission d'Enquête sur la situation de la langue française et sur les droits linguistiques au Québec (Gendron Commission). In this study, an inquiry was made into the location of work in a stratified random sample of Quebec university graduates. It showed that, on the aggregate, 25.6% of anglophone university graduates in all fields worked for the Quebec government,[59] while 53.8% of francophones did. In younger cohorts, the proportion is even higher: 65.3% of francophone graduates and 33.8% of anglophones work for the Quebec government. In other words, two-thirds of francophones who graduated from university in the 1960s worked in the Quebec state sector of the economy, while one-third of anglophones did. For those who had graduated from university before the early 1960s, the comparable figures were: about one-half of francophones and one-fifth of anglophones worked for the government.

Finally, not only has the expansion of the state provided, in gigantic proportions, job outlets to university-trained francophones, but it also seems to have provided them with high incomes, perhaps even more so than if they had worked in a comparable job in the private sector of the economy. The relative income position of workers in the state sector considerably increased in the 1960s, while the income status of workers in the private sector either remained stable or decreased. It is remarkable that the entrance of a given occupational category in the state sector (for Quebec, physicians and surgeons in 1970, teachers in 1964, employees of institutions in 1961 for the most part) has meant a considerable amelioration of their relative income status in the following years. While workers in the state sector over the decade increased their declared incomes by at least one and a half times in constant dollars (two and one-third in current dollars), workers in the private sector have only very slightly increased their incomes.[60] Exactly the same phenomenon occurred in Ontario, but, contrary to Quebec, they did not almost exclusively apply to a social collectivity whose survival depended on state expansion.

In short, all the evidence seems to point to the fact that state expansion has provided job outlets to the majority of educated francophones within Quebec. It has created jobs that presumably were much more powerful, prestigious, and well-paid than the jobs the same individuals could have found in the private sector of the economy. To repeat, the expansion of the state and the creation of new job outlets within it are not unique to Quebec. The same phenomenon has occurred in all provinces and quantitatively perhaps to a comparable degree. What is peculiar to Quebec is that this expansion served as the almost sole institutional basis for the francophone new middle class as a whole.

State Interventions and Their Ideology

It would be false to say that state expansion benefited only Quebec's new middle class. For one thing, it helped to modernize considerably the economic infrastructure, to the benefit mainly of the capitalist owning class. The Quiet Revolution can indeed be viewed partially as state interventions aimed at socializing the costs of production of the monopolistic sector, despite the fact that profits were to be privately appropriated in foreign hands. As Milner and Milner write:

> While the reforms of the period were genuine and did transform Quebec society, they operated only at the middle level. The basic pattern of economic control, investment, and development was, except for a few adjustments, basically left untouched. Foreign interests were dominant and indeed many of the reforms were designed to encourage even further foreign takeover by providing the owning class with a modern economic infrastructure. As such there was a definite limit on the changes which the architects of the Quiet Revolution could accomplish, beyond what meant attacking the basic economic system root and branch. For the Liberals, being as always a party supporting and supported by big business, such a possibility was dismissed out of hand.[61]

In fact, never was this Quiet Revolution intended to go to the root economic causes of social inequalities between anglophones and francophones and among the francophone population:

> From our vantage point today, we can make out the significant weaknesses at the base of Quiet Revolution. While it opened up the world of ideas to all possibilities, it limited changes in structure to those which meant catching up with North America. Those spheres of society which had been held back under the older order were permitted to expand and grow. The schools, the media, the arts, all experienced a renaissance and soon became the locus for the spread and discussion of the new ideas. The changes, though fundamental in relation to the older order, did not at any point challenge the underlying economic structure of Quebec. And when some intellectuals and writers were no longer content to rail against Ottawa and devise even more complex constitutional schemata, but instead chose to attack the economic system head on; and when these new ideas began to receive attention and consideration among the students and trade unionists—then the authorities decided that things had simply gone too far. "Law and Order" came back into style.[62]

Furthermore, many state interventions only derived from the imperatives to strengthen the economy and to maintain full employment: the government simply had to do something about the high rates of unemployment, the lack of investment, the comparatively declining growth of Quebec total production, and so on. As many economists have indicated, the Quebec GNP has progressed at a high rate despite a relative decrease in private investments, because of massive public investments:

> Let us remember that, during the period 1961-67, public works such as Manic-Outardes (important dam construction), the construction of the Montreal subway, and the preparation of Expo '67 have sustained growth and carried along the private sector. The construction of schools and hospitals between 1967 and 1970 has permitted to escape catastrophe.

Finally, since 1971, the preparation of the Olympic Games, the prolongation of the Montreal subway, the construction of Mirabel airport, and the James Bay project are above all responsible for economic growth. Consumption has also been largely sustained by governments. Subsidies of all kinds (transfer payments) have increased, over the last 10 years, at the annual rate of 20% and they now represent in Quebec more than 15% of personal income.[63]

In consequence, two journalists were able to write that "every new brick put up in Quebec costs as much to the taxpayer as it costs the private investor."[64] In fact, a task force to the Department of Industry and Commerce estimated that in Quebec over three-quarters of the jobs created between 1966 and 1972 were linked to government actions, while the proportion is much smaller in Ontario.

Yet, despite these imperatives to maintain the growth of the economy, certain government interventions seemed to be more directly aimed at correcting the social makeup of Quebec private economy and at providing top control jobs to members of the new middle class.

James Iain Gow has noted that, while the Duplessis regime in 19 years (1936-40, 1944-1960) had created only five new departments (among which only two remained stable), eight regulatory boards, and one state enterprise:

> ... the 1960s have seen a much more febrile activity as far as the creation of new administrative institutions is concerned. In six years, the Lesage administration has created six departments, three regulatory boards, eight state enterprises and nine consultative councils. The impetus was followed by the Union Nationale Administrations between 1966 and 1970, with the creation of five new departments, seven regulatory boards, five public entreprises and three consultative councils.[65]

Jean-Jacques Simard has likewise tried to compute the quantitative growth of the state apparatus. He writes:

> The Quebec government includes 23 departments among which only one, the Department of Revenue, has not changed vocation since 1960, 55 consultative boards which were nearly all born in the same period, nine judiciary institutions, and 63 organizations aimed at economic management and regulation. Of the 148 para-governmental organizations, 126 date back only 15 years. The growth of the 250 school boards, the CEGEP, universities and schools, the thousand and more municipal councils, the thousand health and social welfare institutions ... brought about in the name of coordination and coherence, was proportional to the increase of the financial, administrative and political dependency of these organizations on the upper echelons of government.[66]

All these councils, departments, boards, and enterprises provided previously unexisting high-prestige and high-power jobs for university-trained francophones. This is indicated, for instance, by the number of people involved in new managerial tasks in the Quebec civil service between

1964 and 1971 (economists, sociologists, social workers, psychologists): it increased by more than 400%, while the traditional professional personnel of the government (like doctors and engineers) increased by only 20%.[67]

A similar job-creating process seems to have occurred through the economic reforms. To sustain production in some declining French-Canadian industries and to encourage an indigenous capitalism, the Société Générale de Financement was created. Electrical power companies were bought up. To create a public fund out of individual savings, the Caisse de Dépôt et de Placement was created. New enterprises were created to venture into value-producing sectors, such as steel, mining, petroleum, forestry, and so on. In all these cases, the costs of maintaining, buying up, or creating enterprises have been socialized, the profits (if any) nationalized, and the high-power control jobs appropriated by members of the new middle class.

Economist Albert Breton suggested in 1964 that the creation of such jobs may well have been their sole purpose:

> The nationalization of private assets is aimed at providing high-income jobs for nationals, rather than at other objectives connected with raising social income, such as control of monopoly, increased investment in industries displaying external economies, or purchases of high-yielding public or social goods. This implication is borne out by the most important act of the new nationalist government of Quebec, namely, the nationalization of eleven private power companies . . . This decision was not a decision about investing in electricity but one about investing in ethnicity. When the decision was made, it was not decided to consider the flow of rewards to society as a whole but only to a group within society . . . the new middle class in Quebec. . . . [The same is true for the Société Générale de Financement where] the resources which could have been invested to increase the social income of the community have been used . . . to keep already existing high-income jobs for the same middle class.[68]

In retrospect, this view is clearly an overstatement. As Carol Jobin has shown, the main impetus behind the nationalization of Quebec private electrical power companies was the inability of these companies to expand in a way that would have been profitable to them.[69] And yet the growth of Quebec economy required such an expansion. That the new middle class benefited from this nationalization is secondary to the economically determined constraints imposed on the government to further expand the hydro field.

The creation of planning agencies and programs has also provided new job openings and a new mystique about the role of the state. During the 1960s, Quebec evolved broad programs and instituted highly advertised supervisory agencies. Their impact seems to have been negligible as far as tangibly developing Quebec economy and reducing regional disparities, but they were important for creating prestigious jobs for francophones. As political scientist Jacques Benjamin has written:

> Everything that has been undertaken in the last twelve years in the field of planning has only an emotive value; Quebec, it seems to me, must first control its economy in one way or the other (directly or indirectly) before creating plans. To first instigate a mystique of the plan and then to control the economy is the same as putting the cart before the horse. For the last twelve years, we have been working backward. We have consciously put the emphasis on the concept of planning while it would have been more fruitful to pay attention to the instruments; the "fever from France" has invaded the offices of the first planners; we wanted to apply the French model integrally to Quebec, while Quebec did not even possess some of the instruments enabling it to operationalize its plans, especially the control of the economy, the coordination between state departments and even political stability in 1968-70.[70]

The reforms of health, education, and welfare displayed gigantic reorganizations but a comparable lack of tangible benefits to the overall population. Although they did considerably facilitate the financial and, to a certain extent, geographical access to medical and educational services, they did not achieve the far-reaching social-democratic ideals that had been put forward. The education reforms were to be conducive to an extensive democratization of education, with new pedagogical relationships, the suppression of class differentials between types of schooling, a decentralization of management to regions, and parents' involvement in decision making. The changes actually implemented have fallen considerably below expectations. The health and social-welfare reforms were to institutionalize a new, more social approach to health and disease, decentralization of decision making to regions and institutions, and worker and consumer participation in the management of these institutions. The reality was again short of what had been promised. The net results of these reforms were huge reorganizations and administrative reshuffling that in a sense did rationalize the allocation of resources. But, above all, these reforms seem either to have maintained or reinforced the powers and privileges of various categories of francophone professionals, or to have created new interesting jobs for university-trained individuals in the state bureaucracy.

The Unparalleled Status and Legitimacy of Technocratic Elite Groups

This overview of the main interventions of the Quebec state during the 1960s and 1970s is rapid and oversimplifies several points. Yet, it underlines a key phenomenon. Because the Quebec state is virtually the sole institutional basis for the new middle class, this class has evolved a unique nationalist and social-democratic political culture. The old all-encompassing rhetoric of bishops in the Church has been superseded by an equally far-reaching rhetoric of elite members of the new middle class in the state, but with a different content. As the religious symbols of the past have helped traditional elites maintain their social status in Quebec traditional society, the nationalist and social-democratic ideals of new-middle-class elites now legitimize and reinforce their recently acquired dominance over an increasingly unionized and politicized population. Nationalism is not new in Quebec politics, but its association with social-democratic ideals is. It is this association between nationalism and a mild form of socialism that characterizes the ideology of Quebec's new middle class. Under different forms and with different emphases, both the Liberal party and the Parti Québécois—at different points in its history for the former and more consistently for the latter—have put forward such an ideology.

Such a political culture camouflages the objective interests of this class while at the same time legitimates intervention into more and more aspects of social life through an administratively rational problem-solving approach, thereby furthering its hegemony as a class.

This is not to say that this class manoeuvres in some conspiratorial manner, as if totally conscious of its interests or unconstrained by larger social, political, and economic forces. This is not to say either that administrative rationalization is useless. Quite the contrary: it is sometimes absolutely imperative. The point is that, because expansion of the state serves its interests, the new middle class will support all actions that will produce huge reorganizing, restructuring, and reshuffling, *independently* of the objective necessity and feasibility of such transformations. This is so because both the quantitative (budget increase, growth of civil service employees and of the assets of state enterprises, and so on) and the qualitative (involvement in the greatest possible number of areas of social life, increase in the prestige and importance of professional expertise in the government, and increase of the visibility of the state) expansion of the state serves its search for jobs and a local hegemony. In this context, technocratic elite groups and ideologies that share the political culture of the new middle class are bound to be endowed with a status, a legitimacy, and political powers unseen in the rest of Canada, thus providing Quebec with a distinctive strategy of social change.

Conclusion

The combination of the objective material interests of a class in seeing the Quebec state sector of the economy expand quantitatively and qualitatively as well as its self-fulfilling ideological emphasis on nationalism and social-democracy, as argued here, is the most plausible explanation for the distinctive character of Quebec state interventions. There has developed in Quebec a systemic logic, so to speak, that has endowed the inevitable expansion of the state with hopes and expectations far beyond what could be delivered in a capitalist economy and under the present system of national government. Yet it did introduce new political dynamics, the results of which one would be hard pressed to predict. It introduced a new "social imagery" that could lead to a further technocratic and professional takeover or—because of the frustrations, inequities, and fiscal problems the reforms have brought on—it may lead to the tangible implementation of the ideals as advertised. Under the guise of deprofessionalizing through consumer and worker participation, of debureaucratizing through decentralization of decision making, and of repatriating the collective heritage and patrimony through nationalization and creation of state enterprises, government actions have in fact led to a further professionalization, bureaucratization, and concentration of powers and privileges. This contradiction may be managed to the advantage of those who benefit from it, but it may also, in the long run, assume a liberating character.

Notes

1. Quoted in Edmond Orban, "Indicateurs, concepts et objectifs," in E. Orban (ed.), *La modernisation politique du Québec* (Québec: Boréal Express, 1976), p. 7.
2. Unless otherwise noted, these indicators are taken from the various essays in E. Orban (ed.), op. cit., and from Gary Caldwell and B. Dan Czarnocki, "Un rattrapage raté: Le changement social dans le Québec d'après-guerre, 1950-1974: une comparaison Québec/Ontario," *Recherches Sociographiques* XVIII: 1 (1977), pp. 9-58.
3. Denis Monière, *Le développement des idéologies au Québec des origines à nos jours* (Montréal: Editions Québec-Amérique, 1977), p. 328.
4. For a discussion of these expenditures consistent with the argument developed in this article, see Daniel Latouche, "La vraie nature ... de la Révolution tranquille," *Revue Canadienne de Sciences Politiques* VII: 3 (Sept. 1974), pp. 525-35.
5. Here is the share of popular vote for the Union Nationale and the Parti Québécois in the last seven elections: 1956 (UN: 51.5%); 1960 (UN: 46.6%); 1962 (UN 42.1%); 1966: (UN: 40.9%); 1970 (UN: 20.0%; PQ: 23.6%); 1973 (UN: 5.0%; PQ: 30.2%); 1976 (UN: 18.2%; PQ: 41.4%). For analyses of these elections, see for instance Vincent Lemieux (ed.), *Quatre élections provinciales* (Québec: Presses de l'Université Laval, 1969); V. Lemieux, M. Gilbert, and A Blais, *Une élection de réalignement* (Montréal: Cahiers de Cité libre, Ed. du Jour, 1970); or Robert Boily, "Genèse et développement des partis politiques au Québec," in E. Orban (ed.), op. cit., pp. 79-100. For a somewhat positive history of the Union Nationale and its leader, Maurice Duplessis, see Conrad Black, *Duplessis* (Montréal: Les Editions de l'Homme, 1977).
6. Given the available data, it is impossible to regionalize the effects of federal spending and to estimate with any precision the total amount of spending by the public sector in a given year in a given province. Therefore, it is difficult to estimate the part of each province's GNP (or more precisely the Gross National Expenditure, which is equivalent) accounted for by government spending. For tentative estimates, see Kemal Wassef, "La situation du gouvernement du Québec dans les affaires économiques de la province" (unpublished manuscript, Confédération des Syndicats Nationaux, October 1971); and B. Roy-Lemoine, "The Growth of the State in Québec," in D. Roussopoulos (ed.), *The Political Economy of the State: Québec/Canada/U.S.A.* (Montreal: Black Rose Books, 1973), pp. 59-87.

7. For the health services, see A.D. McDonald, J.C. McDonald, and P.E. Enterline, "Etudes sur l'assurance-maladie du Québec," and André Billette, "Santé, classes sociales et politiques redistributives," both in *Sociologie et Sociétés: La gestion de la santé* IX: 1 (April 1977), pp. 52-92.
8. I documented this scenario for health reforms in Marc Renaud, "Réforme ou illusion? Une analyse des interventions de l'Etat québécois dans le domaine de la santé," *Sociologie et Sociétés: La gestion de la santé,* IX: 1 (April 1977), pp. 127-52. Further evidence of the omnipresence of this scenario can be found in a variety of publications. See, for instance, *Une certaine révolution tranquille* (Montréal: Ed. La Presse, 1975); Kenneth McRoberts and Dale Posgate, *Québec: Social Change and Political Crisis* (Toronto: McClelland and Stewart Limited, 1976); Pierre Doray, *Une pyramide tronquée: les politiques de sécurité du revenu pour les retraités* (M.Sc. thesis, Département de sociologie, Université de Montréal, 1978); Diane Poliquin-Bourassa, "La réforme de l'éducation: phase II," in Daniel Latouche (ed.), *Premier mandat,* vol. II (Montréal: Editions de l'Aurore, 1977), pp. 15-26; and Michel Pelletier and Yves Vaillancourt, *Les politiques sociales et les travailleurs, Les années 60* (Montréal: available from the authors, 1974).
9. Although present in the literature for a long time (e.g. Hubert Guindon, "Social Unrest, Social Class and Québec's Bureaucratic Revolution," in J.E. Curtis and W.G. Scott (eds.), *Social Stratification in Canada* (Toronto: Prentice-Hall, 1973), this hypothesis has been systematized by Gilles Bourque and Nicole Frenette in "La structure nationale québécoise," *Socialisme québécois* 21: 2 (1970), pp. 109-156. A similar hypothesis has simultaneously been developed in Luc Racine and Roch Denis, "La conjoncture politique depuis 1960," ibid., pp. 17-78. Using different paradigms (in the sense of Robert R. Alford, "Towards a Critical Sociology of Political Power," in Léon Lindberg (ed.), *Stress and Contradictions in Modern Capitalism* [Lexington, 1975] pp. 145-60) a vast series of authors have expanded on a similar hypothesis. See, for instance, Anne Legaré, *Les classes sociales au Québec* (Montréal: Presses de l'Université du Québec, 1977); Pierre Fournier, *The Québec Establishment: The Ruling Class and the State* (Montréal: Black Rose Books, 1976); Marcel Fournier, "La question nationale: les enjeux," *Possibles* 1: 2 (winter 1977), pp. 7-18; Daniel Latouche, op. cit.; Denis Monière, op. cit.
10. For a discussion of these terms, see Anthony Giddens, *The Class Structure of Advanced Societies* (New York: Harper and Row, 1973).
11. See, for instance, Pierre-Paul Proulx (ed.), *Vers une problématique globale du développement de la région de Montréal* (Montréal: CRDE, June 1976); P. Fréchette, R. Jouandet-Bernadat, J.P. Vézina, *L'économie du Québec* (Montréal: Les Editions HRW Ltée, 1975); Ministère de l'Industrie et du Commerce, *Une politique économique québécoise* (Québec, Jan. 1974). This is also confirmed by the study of G. Galdwell and B.D. Czarnocki, op. cit.
12. James O'Connor, *The Fiscal Crisis of the State* (New York: St. Martin's Press, 1973); for further conceptual development, see his *The Corporations and the State: Essays in the Theory of Capitalism and Imperialism* (New York: Harper Colophon Books, Harper and Row, 1975).
13. See, for instance, the essays published in Marcel Rioux and Yves Martin (eds.), *French Canadian Society* (Toronto: McClelland and Stewart, The Carleton

Library no. 18, 1964). See also Denis Monière, op. cit., and Maurice Saint-Germain, *Une économie à libérer: le Québec analysé dans ses structures économiques* (Montréal: Presses de l'Université de Montréal, 1973).

14. Hubert Guindon, "The Social Evolution of Québec Reconsidered", in Rioux and Martin (eds.), op. cit., pp. 137-61; and Social Unrest, Social Class and Québec's Bureaucratic Revolution," op. cit.
15. French Canadians have had one of the highest birth rates in the industrialized world. Now it is among the lowest in Canada. See Jacques Henripin, "From Acceptance of Nature to Control: The Demography of the French Canadians since the Seventeenth Century," in Rioux and Martin (eds.), op. cit., pp. 204-15. See also Bureau de la statistique du Québec, *Tendances passées et perspectives d'évolution de la fécondité au Québec* (Quebec, 1976).
16. Some violent strikes have, however, occurred after the war. For a sociological analysis of these, see Hélène David, "La grève et le bon Dieu: la grève de l'amiante au Québec," *Sociologie et Société* 1:2 (Nov. 1969), pp. 249-76, and "L'état des rapports de classe au Québec de 1945 à 1967," *Sociologie et Sociétés* VII: 2, pp. 33-66. On the beginnings of trade unionism, see Louis Maheu, "Problème social et naissance du syndicalisme catholique," *Sociologie et Société* 1: 1 (May 1969), and Louis-Marie Tremblay, *Le syndicalisme québécois: idéologies de la CSN et de la FTQ 1940-1970* (Montréal: Presses de l'Université de Montréal, 1972).
17. Examples of the convergence of interests between the Church, political leaders, and "foreign" entrepreneurs abound. For instance, the Roman Catholic hierarchy supported simultaneously foreign corporations and French-Canadian workers in the development of trade unions. The actions of political leaders are even clearer as manifest in the proxy battle for the St-Lawrence Corporation, the 99-year leases to Iron Ore and others. For more examples, see the appendices to the manifestoes of the Quebec trade unions (translated in Daniel Drache (ed.), *Québec: Only the Beginning* [Toronto: New Press, 1972], and in *Québec Labour* [Montréal: Black Rose Books, 1972]). On the relations between political leaders and the corporate world, the most systematic study is Pierre Fournier, op. cit. See also Union des Travailleurs du Papier et du Carton Façonnés, *Les Tigres de Carton* (Montreal: Editions Québécoises, undated); Groupe de Recherches Economiques, *Les Compagnies de Finance* (Montréal: Editions Québécoises, undated).
18. André Raynauld, *La propriété des entreprises au Québec* (Montréal: Presses de l'Université de Montréal, 1974), p. 78.
19. André Raynauld, "The Québec Economy: A General Assessment," in Dale C. Thomson (ed.), *Québec Society and Politics: Views from the Inside* (Toronto: McClelland and Stewart, 1973), p. 152, my emphasis.
20. Report of the Royal Commission on Bilingualism and Biculturalism, Book III: *The Work World* (Ottawa: Queen's Printer, September 1969), p. 447.
21. For descriptions of this industrial structure, see Gilles Lebel, *Horizon 1980: une étude sur l'évolution de l'économie du Québec de 1946 à 1968 et sur ses perspectives d'avenir* (Québec: Ministère de l'Industrie et du Commerce, 1970); and P. Fréchette et al., op. cit.
22. For an examination of foreign dominance over the Canadian economy, see Kari Levitt, *Silent Surrender* (Toronto: Macmillan, 1970); R. Laxer (ed.), *Canada Ltd., The Political Economy of Dependency* (Toronto: McClelland and Stewart,

1973); Wallace Clement, *Continental Corporate Power* (Toronto: McClelland and Stewart, 1977); T. Naylor, *The History of Canadian Business* (Toronto: Lorimer, 1975). For an examination of foreign dominance over the Quebec economy, see André Raynauld, op. cit.; Jorge Niosi, "Le gouvernement du PQ, le capital américain et le contrôle canadien" (unpublished paper, Département de sociologie, Université du Québec à Montréal, 1978); and Arnaud Sales, "La différenciation nationale et ethnique de la bourgeoisie industrielle au Québec," and "Le gouvernement du Parti Québécois et les pouvoirs économiques" (unpublished papers, Département de sociologie, Université de Montréal, 1978). As Niosi and Sales have convincingly shown, despite foreign dominance, an identifiable grande bourgeoisie exists among the francophone segment of the Quebec population, but it is comparatively small and concentrated in specific economic sectors.

23. *Canadian Census*, 1961, vol. III, part 2, table 9; *Canadian Census*, 1971, vol. III, part 4, table 10.
24. Ministère de l'Industrie et du Commerce, *Une Politique Economique Québécoise* (mimeographed, 1974), p. 18.
25. Ministère de l'Industrie et du Commerce, op. cit., p. 9.
26. André Raynauld, op. cit., p. 147.
27. Report of the Royal Commission on Bilingualism and Biculturalism, op. cit., p. 81.
28. John Porter, "The Economic Elite and the Social Structure in Canada," in B.R. Blishen, F.E. Jones, K.D. Naegele, J. Porter (eds.), *Canadian Society* (Toronto: Macmillan, 1961), pp. 486-500.
29. Sheilagh Hodgins Milner and Henry Milner, *The Decolonization of Québec: An Analysis of Left-Wing Nationalism* (Toronto: McClelland and Stewart, 1973).
30. Wallace Clement, *The Canadian Corporate Elite: An Analysis of Economic Power* (Toronto: McClelland and Stewart, The Carleton Library no. 89, 1975).
31. André Raynauld, *La Propriété des Entreprises au Québec* (Montréal: Presses de l'Université de Montréal, 1974).
32. Milner and Milner, op. cit., p. 71.
33. Clement, op. cit., p. 233-34.
34. Robert Presthus, *Elite Accommodation in Canadian Politics* (Cambridge: University Press, 1973).
35. Clement, op. cit., p. 234. As Pierre Fournier has argued in "Les tendances nouvelles du pouvoir économique au Québec," *Le Devoir* (June 9 and 10, 1976), there is something intrinsically misleading in this approach. Generally, it tends to underestimate the importance of the French-Canadian bourgeoisie because it computes only the number of persons on corporate boards, a number likely to be substantially increased by legislation forcing French as the language of work in Quebec. Further, since these data are limited to the corporate world, they do not include this segment of the Quebec bourgeoisie linked to the cooperative movement (Mouvement Desjardins, Coopérative Fédérée, Cooperative agricole de Granby) and to state enterprises (like Sidbec, Dosco, and the Société Générale de Financement).
36. Tore Thonstad with C. Fluet and C. Ross, *Simulations de la pénétration des francophones parmi les cadres du secteur privé au Québec, 1971-1986*, Etudes réalisées pour le compte de la Commission d'enquête sur la situation de la

langue française et sur les droits linguistiques au Québec (L'éditeur officiel du Québec, February 1974).
37. Dominique Clift, "French Elite Lags in Salary Scale," *La Presse* (1975).
38. Report of the Royal Commission on Bilingualism and Biculturalism, op. cit., p. 488.
39. M.V. George, *Internal Migration in Canada: Demographic analyses* (Ottawa: Statistics Canada, 1970).
40. John Porter, *The Vertical Mosaic: An Analysis of Social Class and Power in Canada* (Toronto: University of Toronto Press, 1965).
41. For reasons of space, all tables have been dropped from this article. For further detail, see Marc Renaud, *The Political Economy of the Quebec Health-Care Reforms* (Ph.D. thesis, Sociology, University of Wisconsin, Madison, 1976), pp. 411-28.
42. Guy Rocher and Yves de Jocas, "Inter-Generation Occupational Mobility in the Province of Quebec", *The Canadian Journal of Economics and Political Science* 23: 1 (Feb. 1957).
43. Jacques Dofny and Muriel Garon-Audy, "Mobilités Professionnelles au Québec," *Sociologie et Sociétés* 1: 2 (Nov. 1969), pp. 277-302.
44. Ibid., p. 287.
45. Jacques Brazeau, "Québec's Emerging Middle Class," in Rioux and Martin (eds.), op. cit., pp. 296-306.
46. Ian Adams, William Cameron, Brian Hill, and Peter Penz, *The Real Poverty Report* (Edmonton: Hurtig, 1971), p. 219.
47. See Hélène Ostiguy, "Statistiques détaillées relatives à l'enseignement supérieur" (unpublished manuscript, Université de Montréal, Département de Sociologie, September 1971).
48. Gross general expenditures reflect the administrative burden of a given level of government. Net general expenditures reflect the fiscal burden. From an accounting point of view, the difference is constituted by the following items: 1. All revenues of institutions coming under the government; 2. revenues in the form of interests, premiums, and discounts; 3. grants-in-aid and shared-cost contributions; 4. all capital revenue. These revenues are deducted from the corresponding gross expenditures to obtain the net general expenditures.
49. Statistics Canada, *Federal Government Finance, Revenue and Expenditure, Assets and Liabilities* (Catalogue no. 68-211), *Provincial Government Finance, Revenue and Expenditure* (Catalogue no. 68-207), *Local Government Finance, Revenue and Expenditure, Assets and Liabilities* (Catalogue no. 68-204).
50. Research and Statistics Division, Department of National Health and Welfare, *Government Expenditures on Health and Social Welfare—Canada, 1927-1959* (Social Security Series, memorandum no. 16, Ottawa, 1961), p. 45; and Canadian Tax Foundation, *The National Finances 1973-74*, p. 24.
51. Statistics Canada, *Provincial Government Enterprise Finance* (Catalogue no. 61-204); *Federal Government Enterprise Finance* (Catalogue no. 61-203).
52. Statistics Canada, *Consolidated Government Finance—Federal, Provincial and Local Governments, Revenue and Expenditures* (Catalogue no. 68-202).
53. For systematic summaries of the evolution of Ontario, see a series of publications issued by the Ontario Economic Council and entitled *The Evolution of Policy in Contemporary Ontario.*

54. *Annuaire du Québec*, 1971, p. 733.
55. Claude Morin, "The Gospel According to Holy Ottawa," in Dale C. Thomson (ed.), *Quebec Society and Politics: Views from the Inside* (Toronto: McClelland and Stewart, 1973), p. 210.
56. *Canadian Census*, 1971, vol. 3, part III, table 5.
57. Report of the Royal Commission on Bilingualism and Biculturalism, op. cit., pp. 474-75.
58. Pierre-Paul Gagné, "L'Hydro et les Québécois: l'histoire d'amour achève," *La Presse* (June 13, 1975), p. A-8.
59. The Quebec state is here defined as the provincial and municipal governmental bureaucracies as well as the electricity and the relevant parts of the education and health-care fields. It does not include state enterprises other than Hydro-Québec.
60. Department of National Revenue, *Taxation Statistics, Analysing the Returns of Individuals for the 1960, 1965, 1970, 1972, 1974, Taxation Year and Miscellaneous Statistics*, table 9.
61. Milner and Milner, op. cit., p. 169.
62. Ibid., pp. 191-92. A similar observation is expressed in Gérald Bernier, "Le cas québécois et les théories du développement politique et de la dépendance," in E. Orban (ed.), op. cit., pp. 19-54; and in Denis Monière, op. cit., ch. VIII.
63. Translated from Jean-P. Vézina, "Le développement économique: les enjeux en cause," in Daniel Latouche (ed.), *Premier mandat*, op. cit., p. 51.
64. Rhéal Bercier and Robert Pouliot, "Le pénible apprentissage de l'état québécois en matière de croissance: la charrue avant les boeufs . . ." *La Presse* (June 14, 1975), p. A-7.
65. Translated from James Iain Gow, "L'évolution de l'administration publique du Québec 1867-1970" (unpublished paper, Département de Sciences Politiques, Université de Montréal), p. 37. See also his "Modernisation et administration publique," in E. Orban (ed.), op. cit., pp. 157-86.
66. Translated from Jean-Jacques Simard, "La longue marche des technocrates," *Recherches Sociologiques* XVIII: 1 (1977), p. 119.
67. Ibid., p. 122.
68. Albert Breton, "The Economics of Nationalism," *The Journal of Political Economy* (1964), pp. 382, 384, and 385.
69. Carol Jobin, *La nationalisation de l'électricité au Québec en 1962* (M.A. thesis, Université du Québec à Montréal, 1974).
70. Translated from Jacques Benjamin, *Planification et politique au Québec* (Montréal: Les Presses de l'Université de Montréal, 1974), p. 114.

Chapter 11/The Rise of French-Canadian Capitalism*

Jorge Niosi

Traditional perspectives on the ethnic composition of Canadian social and class structures see the upper class as predominantly Anglo-Saxon.[1] This paper challenges this assumption. A new and vigorous francophone bourgeoisie emerged during the postwar period: French-Canadian society became very active in finance, commerce, services, transportation, mass media, and even manufacturing. The economic, political, and social conditions of the emergence of such a group are explored in the first part of this chapter. The second section analyzes the main enterprises and conglomerates under French-Canadian control and presents some aggregate data to support the thesis. The third section examines the political implications of these changes in the Canadian social structure.

How It All Happened: The Determinants of the New Francophone Bourgeoisie

On the eve of the Second World War, Canada's class structure was strongly correlated with its ethnic composition. Almost all the French Canadians were wage earners or farmers. There was a tiny middle class of professionals, bureaucrats, and small-business owners. Large firms were almost exclusively owned and controlled by Anglo-Saxon capitalists. In this context the "ethnic class" view of the francophones was born and developed in both English and French Canada.

But the war and long postwar boom changed this situation. Government orders during the war favoured Canadian companies. Thanks to federal largesse, some small francophone firms such as Bombardier and Simard grew rapidly by selling military vehicles and ships to the Canadian Armed Forces. During the next three decades the postwar boom had an analogous, though more diffuse, effect. Per capita personal income in Quebec grew from $655 in 1946 to $4504 in 1974 (an increase of almost 700%). French Canadians became an increasingly affluent market for financial services of all kinds and turned to the new francophone insurance, banking, trust, and investment companies. Massive urbanization favoured the economic concentration of real estate and commercial activities. As in finance there was no major barrier to the entry of small French-Canadian enterprises to such a dynamic environment: neither minimum capital requirements nor technological barriers

*This chapter develops and updates several of my articles, including "The New French-Canadian Bourgeoisie," *Studies in Political Economy* 1 (spring 1979), and "La multinationalisation des firmes canadiennes françaises," *Recherches Sociographiques* XXIII: 1 (winter 1983).

could help francophone firms from entering and prospering in such "soft" industries.

The rise of literacy and media consumption went along with these changes. French-language newspapers, radio and television stations, and cable-TV companies grew rapidly as new firms and groups under francophone ownership took over these emerging activities. Finally, while the industrial development occurred mostly through foreign and English-Canadian corporations, some French-Canadian companies did participate in older manufacturing such as pulp and paper, food, and printing as well as in more modern industries such as plastics, rubber products, and transportation equipment.

These economic trends have been amplified by the Quebec government since the Quiet Revolution. From 1960 to the present, the Quebec government has established a network of public enterprises that have nurtured the development of a francophone bourgeoisie. Prominent among these public enterprises are the Caisse de dépôt et de placement, the General Investment Corporation (GIC), the Industrial Research Centre, the Société Québécoise d'exploration minière (Soquem), the Société québécoise d'initiatives agro-alimentaires (Soquia) and others. These crown corporations have helped capitalize French-Canadian companies, placed French Canadians on the boards of companies in which they invested, brought new technology to francophone firms, and organized the merger of small- and medium-sized companies.

The Caisse de dépôt et de placement was founded in 1965 by the Liberal government of Premier Jean Lesage, during the first phase of the Quiet Revolution. It is responsible for managing the Quebec pension fund, Medicare plan, and the investment portfolios of several public and semi-public agencies. It invests in bonds (provincial, municipal, Hydro-Québec, and hospital) and in shares of Canadian companies, which make up nearly 15% of its assets. It has published a list of its holdings, showing large blocks of shares in many French-Canadian companies. Table 11-1 summarizes the Caisse's main investments.

The Caisse has also given open support to French-Canadian capitalists in corporate struggles for the control of major Quebec firms. In August 1977, for instance, Provigo, the largest francophone food retailer, was almost taken over by the Sobey Stores group of Nova Scotia. Thanks to the support of the Caisse, the French-Canadian board of directors kept control of the firm in which it had only a minority interest. In June 1979, the Caisse became the main shareholder (24%) of Domtar, one of the largest pulp-and-paper producers in Quebec and in Canada as well as being a supplier of building products and chemicals. The Caisse took over Domtar working in collaboration with the General Investment Corporation and some prominent francophone businessmen.

The General Investment Corporation, founded in 1962 as a mixed enterprise, became a wholly owned government corporation in 1972. In the

Table 11-1 Caisse de dépôt et de placement du Québec
Major Investment in Quebec Companies, to December 31, 1982

Company	% of voting interest
Brascade	30.0%
Vidéotron	30.0%
Provigo	29.9%
Rolland Inc.	27.3%
Prenor Group	27.2%
Domtar	24.2%
Québec-Téléphone	17.5%
Dominion Textile	14.4%
Société d'investissement Desjardins	14.3%
Logistec	13.0%
La Vérendrye	12.1%
Domco Industries	11.6%
Canadian Pacific	9.9%
Trust Général	9.8%
National Bank of Canada	8.7%
Gaz Métropolitain	7.7%
Alcan Aluminium	7.6%
Royal Bank	6.6%
Télé-Métropole	5.3%
Consolidated Bathurst	3.7%

Source: *Annual Report 1982*.

meantime it took an interest in 14 Quebec companies, including Forano, Volcano, Marine Industries, and Donohue. It is involved in three main industries: forest, machinery, and petrochemicals. In the forest industry, its main partner is Normick Perron, a private francophone firm; the GIC and Normick own a modern newsprint plant at Amos, Quebec.

But the Quebec state has also promoted francophone entrepreneurship through the direct nationalization of industrial entreprises. In May 1980, the Quebec government bought the Bell Asbestos Corp., a subsidiary of the British multinational Turner & Newall. The subsidiary owned asbestos mines in Quebec and two manufacturing plants. In November 1981, the government also bought a majority interest in the Asbestos Corp., the second largest asbestos producer in Quebec, from the General Dynamics conglomerate. From then on it has tried to promote the development of a Quebec-based manufacturing industry with both public and private involvement. In a less direct way the provincial government has furthered francophone interests through the development and secularization of the education system, with emphasis on training for professional and technical careers.

Who They Are: The Main Francophone Corporations

The rising French-Canadian bourgeoisie has adopted the corporate organization into which most of North American business has been shaped. It owns and controls large private enterprises that float securities in stock exchanges. Some of these enterprises have also formed conglomerates—that is, companies or groups of companies under unified control that produce goods and services in diverse fields. Table 11-2 summarizes some data on the largest francophone firms.

The first characteristic of the new francophone enterprises is that more than half of them are in finance and insurance. They include the Banque Nationale, the sixth-largest chartered bank in Canada; Great-West Life and the Laurentian Group, the third- and ninth-largest life insurers, respectively; the sixth- and seventh-largest trust companies (Montreal Trust and General Trust); and the only savings bank in Canada (Montreal Savings). Among the 50 largest financial institutions ranked by the *Financial Post* in June 1982, seven (or 14%) were francophones, while five out of the 25 largest Canadian insurance companies (20%) were controlled by French Canadians. In the insurance industry, francophone companies have progressed steadily during the postwar period. In 1945 French-Canadian companies collected 21% of the general-insurance premiums and 30% of the life-insurance premiums in Quebec, but in 1981 the corresponding figures were 34% and 38%.[2]

In the mining and manufacturing industry, the record is much less impressive. Of the 400 largest industrial corporations in Canada (including crown corporations and foreign subsidiaries) only 23 were under francophone control. This latter figure includes many provincial state enterprises. Only 11 corporations were big enough to deserve a place in Table 11-2, and the two largest (Consolidated Bathurst and Domtar) were under anglophone ownership some years ago.

In real estate, only one of the 10 largest developers in Canada was French Canadian in 1981: Campeau Corp. In commerce, only one retailer (Provigo) was francophone among the 10 biggest. Conversely, the two most important engineering firms in Canada (Lavalin and SNC) are Montreal-based francophone companies. Most of the province's mass media, including newspapers, radio, television, and cable-TV are now under French-Canadian control. In all these service industries, new francophone enterprises have been growing rapidly in the postwar period. Most dramatic has been the rise of francophone corporations in food retailing. In 1961 according to census estimates, only 37% of all sales in Quebec were made by French-Canadian firms; 20 years later, more than 80% was done by local chains such as Provigo, Metro-Richelieu, Hudon et Deaudelin, and Cooprix.

Some of the largest corporations are organized into conglomerates. The most prominent one is Power Corporation. Power was a holding company founded in 1925 by the Nesbitt and Thomson families to manage several hydroelectric investments. In 1968, Paul Desmarais took over Power, which was being converted into a general holding corporation, with wide interests in finance, industry, and transportation. Today Power Corporation controls the largest mutual fund in Canada (Investors Group), four daily newspapers in Quebec (with a total daily circulation over 300,000, including *La Presse,* through Gesca Ltd.), the fourth-largest pulp-and-paper company in Canada (Consolidated Bathurst), the third-largest insurance company in Canada (Great-West Life), the sixth-largest trust company (Montreal Trust), and the largest glass producer (Dominion Glass). Other investments include 12% of the voting shares of Canadian Pacific, an 8% interest in the National Bank of Canada, 20% of Pargesa, a Swiss holding company that manages most of the former international network of the Banque de Paris et des Pays Bas nationalized in late 1981 by the French government, and 3% of the Belgian Banque Bruxelles-Lambert. Paul Desmarais's attempt to take over the Canadian Pacific group (the largest Canadian conglomerate) in 1982 with the tacit support of the Caisse de dépôt was stopped by the federal government, by means of Bill S-31, an act forbidding provincial corporations

Table 11-2 The 50 Largest French-Canadian Corporations Assets (in $ millions) and Control in 1981

Corporation	Assets	Control
1. Finance		
National Bank of Canada	19157	Managerial
Mouvement Desjardins	13300	Members
Montreal Savings Bank	4157	Laurentian Group (40%) MBRG Co. (10%) Provigo (10%)
Crédit Foncier	2344	Montreal Savings Bank (100%)
Investors Group	1392	Power Corp. (97%)
Montreal Trust	1375	Power Corp. (50.1%)
Caisse Centrale Desjardins	995	Members
Power Corp.	758	P. Desmarais (69%)
Fiducie du Québec	643	Desjardins Coops (100%)
Laurentide Financial Corp.	229	National Bank (100%)
Savings and Investment Trust	225	Tardif Family (97%)
Innat	200	National Bank (100%)
La Vérendrye Management Corp.	118	Perron Family (43%)
2. Insurance		
Great-West Life	5620	Power Corp. (95%)
Laurentian Group	2800	Mutual
Industrial Life	938	Mutual
Desjardins Life	496	Desjardins Coops (100%)
L'Alliance	425	Mutual
Les Coopérants	378	Mutual
La Sauvegarde	343	Desjardins Coops (100%)
Sodarcan	223	Parizeau Family (+50%)
Commerce Group	200	St Germain Family (65%)
La mutuelle SSQ	173	Mutual
La mutuelle-vie des fonctionnaires	157	Mutual
La Solidarité	96	Mutual
Aeterna-Vie	65	Tardif Family
L'économie mutuelle-vie	61	Mutual
La survivance	44	Mutual

from owning more than 10% of the shares of a federally incorporated transportation company.[3] Whatever the case, Desmarais and three other directors of Power were invited to the CP board early in 1983, showing clearly that Power shares the control of the railway group. Desmarais is also on the board of Pargesa and the Banque Bruxelles-Lambert. Figure 11-1 shows the structure of the Power group in late 1982.

The second-largest conglomerate under private control is the Laurentian Group. A mutual life company, La Laurentienne, is the holding company of the group. A traditional French-Canadian insurance company, La Laurentienne grew rapidly during the 1970s. In 1977 it took over Imperial Life, one of the largest Canadian life insurers, from Power Corporation. Imperial had foreign operations in the United States, Great Britain, and the Bahamas. In 1979 it bought the F-1-C Fund from J.-Louis Lévesque, the

Corporation	Assets	Control
3. Industrials		
Consolidated Bathurst	1433	Power Corp. (40%)
Domtar	1302	Caisse de dépôt (20%) QGIC (22%)
Bombardier	313	Bombardier Family (68%)
Federated Coop.	265	Members
Vidéotron	145	
Agropur	141	Members
Canam-Manac	118	Desjardins Investment Corp. (30%)
Normick Perron		Perron brothers (55%)
Québécor	76	P. Péladeau (69%)
Rolland Inc.	72	L. Rolland (57%) Caisse de dépôt (19%)
Culinar	70	Desjardins Investment Corp. (56%)
Unimédia	50	
Cassidy's	43	Brodeur Family (66%)
4. Services, commerce		
Campeau Corp.	1411	R. Campeau (70%)
Provigo	625	Board of directors (18%) Caisse de dépôt (20%)
Lavalin	200	B. Lamarre et assoc. (100%)
Epiciers Unis/Métro Richelieu	132	
SNC	119	Employees
Québécair	104	J. Hamel (92.5%)
Télé-métropole	103	J.A. deSève Estate (99%)
UAP	74	Préfontaine Family (100%)
Télé-Capital	28	La Vérendrye (75%)

Sources: Financial Post Survey of Industrials (Toronto, 1982): *Rapport du surintendant des assurances du Québec* (Québec, 1982); Statistics Canada (Catalogue no. 61-514, Ottawa, 1981); *Financial Post* (Toronto), *Finance* (Montreal), *Le Journal des Affaires* (Montreal).

Figure 11-1 The Power Corporation Group (November 1982)

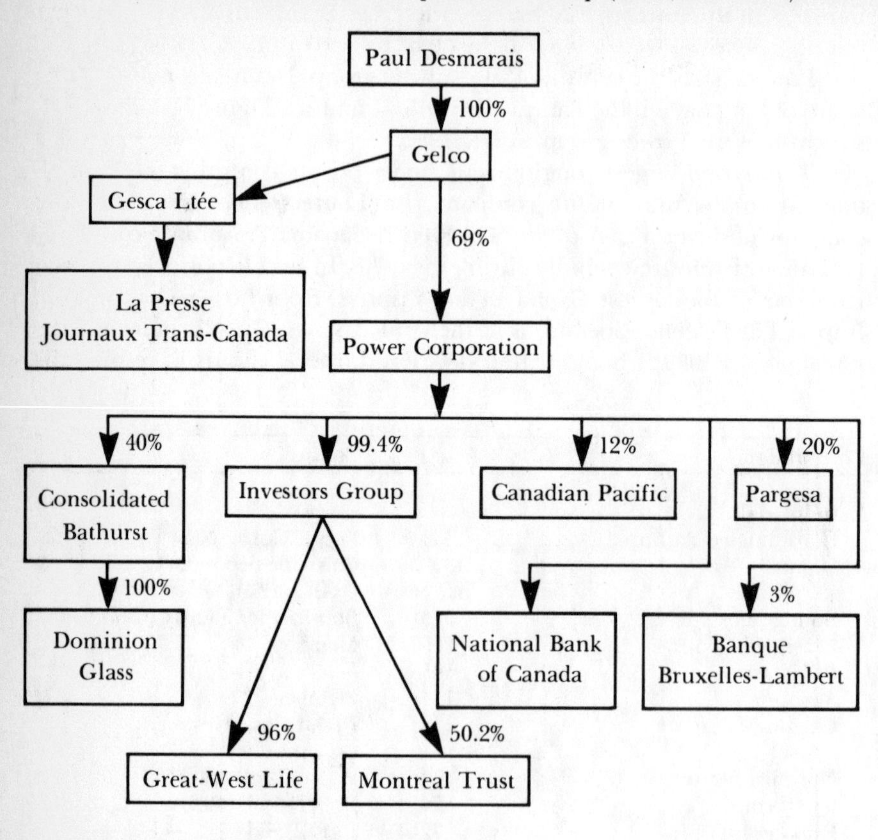

Total assets: $12 billion Canadian.
Sources: *Annual Report*; financial periodicals.

French-Canadian businessman who retired that year. The Fund is a small holding company owning several industrial and commercial firms. In 1980 La Laurentienne took over 40% of the Montreal Savings Bank's voting shares; the Savings Bank had previously absorbed the Crédit Foncier, one of the largest trust companies in Canada, from its French parent. All in all, the Laurentian group controls total assets of more than $10 billion. Its main directors are Jean-Marie Poitras and Claude Castonguay, a former Liberal minister in the Quebec government. Figure 11-2 shows the structure of the conglomerate.

Smaller conglomerates include the Savings and Investment Group and Sodarcan. The Savings and Investment Group was founded in 1928 by Alphonse Tardif under the name Corporation Prêt et Revenu, and control was turned over to Tardif's son, Jean-Paul, in 1947. Diversification began in

Figure 11-2 The Laurentian Group (1982)

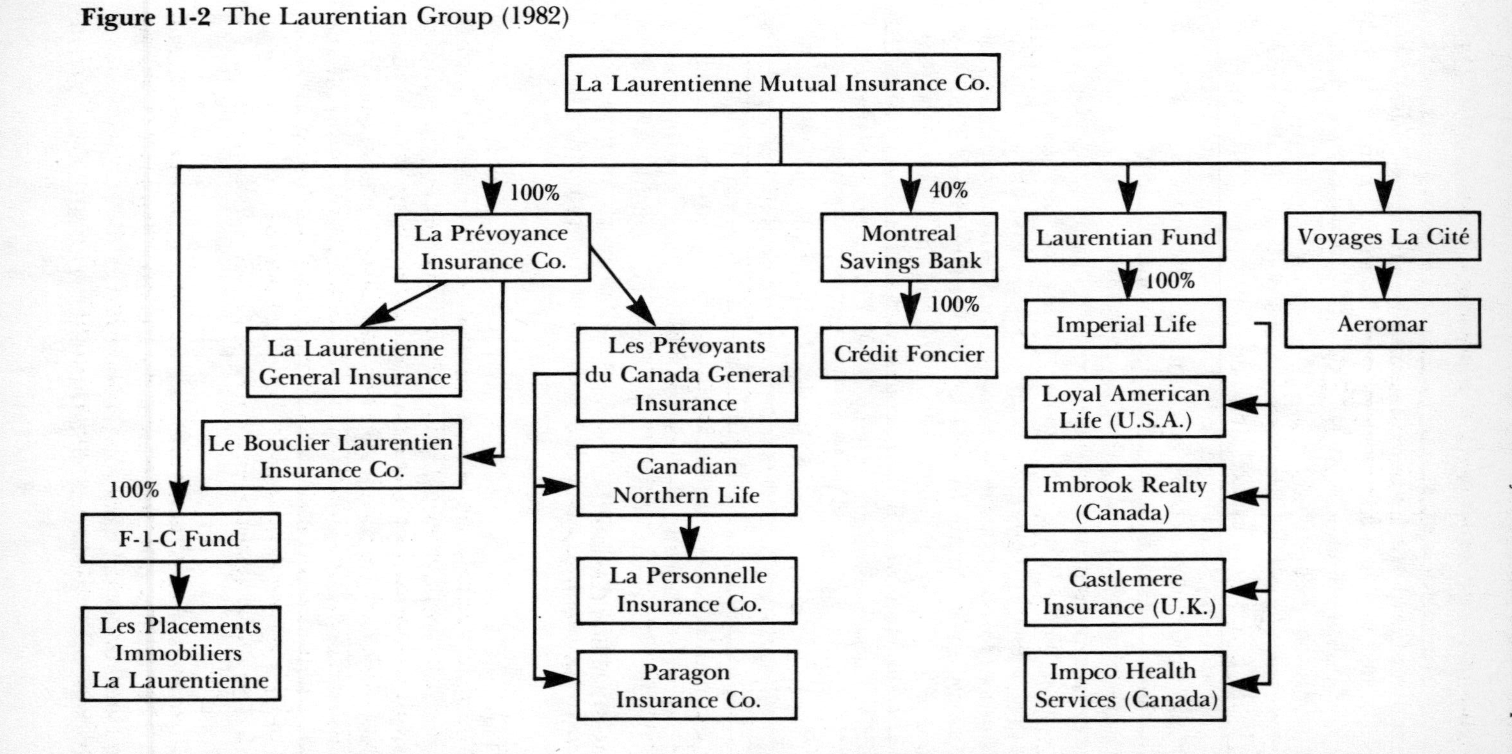

Total assets: $10 billion Canadian.
Source: *Annual Report.*

1953 with the founding of the St-Maurice Life Insurance Company, while in 1957 two new companies were added—Aeterna-Vie Life Insurance and Savings and Investment Mutual Fund. In 1961, the Savings and Investment Trust was founded; new mutual funds were added to the group in 1968, 1972, and 1975. The group, still under tight family control, held total assets of $301 million in 1981. (See Figure 11-3.)

The Sodarcan group comprises 12 companies operating in the fields of reinsurance, insurance, reinsurance brokerage, reinsurance-company management and consulting. (See Figure 11-4.) The holding company, Sodarcan Ltée, was founded in 1972 to centralize control of these firms. A majority of Sodarcan's shares is owned by Robert Parizeau (brother of Jacques Parizeau, Finance Minister in the Parti Québécois government) and their father Gérard Parizeau. The companies in the group were all founded or purchased after the Second World War. La Nationale, Compagnie de réassurance du Canada is the largest company in the conglomerate; it was purchased in 1965 from La Nationale of Paris, of which it was the Canadian subsidiary. In 1980, the Sodarcan group bought the huge Dale Ross Holding Ltd. of Toronto to produce one of the largest firms in brokerage and reinsurance in the country, with a staff of 1200 employees. It also operates in the United States through its reinsurance-brokerage subsidiary, Intermediaries of America. Total assets of the group were $233 million in 1981.

The cooperative movement in Quebec is producing large financial and commercial enterprises. The Fédération de Québec des Caisses populaires Desjardins has total assets of $13.3 billion and controls several important insurance companies (including Desjardins Life, La Sauvegarde, and La Sécurité), one trust company (Fiducie du Québec), and one investment company (Société d'Investissement Desjardins). The Quebec cooperative movement has other components as well, but they are much smaller than the Fédération. In the financial sector they include the Fédération de Montréal

Figure 11-3 The Savings and Investment Group (1981)

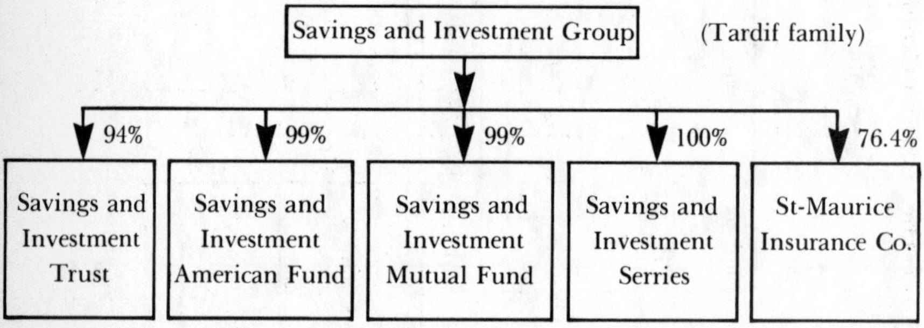

Savings and Investment Group (Tardif family)

94% Savings and Investment Trust

99% Savings and Investment American Fund

99% Savings and Investment Mutual Fund

100% Savings and Investment Serries

76.4% St-Maurice Insurance Co.

Total assets: $301 million Canadian.
Source: Statistics Canada, Catalogue 61-514 (Ottawa, 1981), p. 241.

Figure 11-4 The Sodarcan Group (1981)

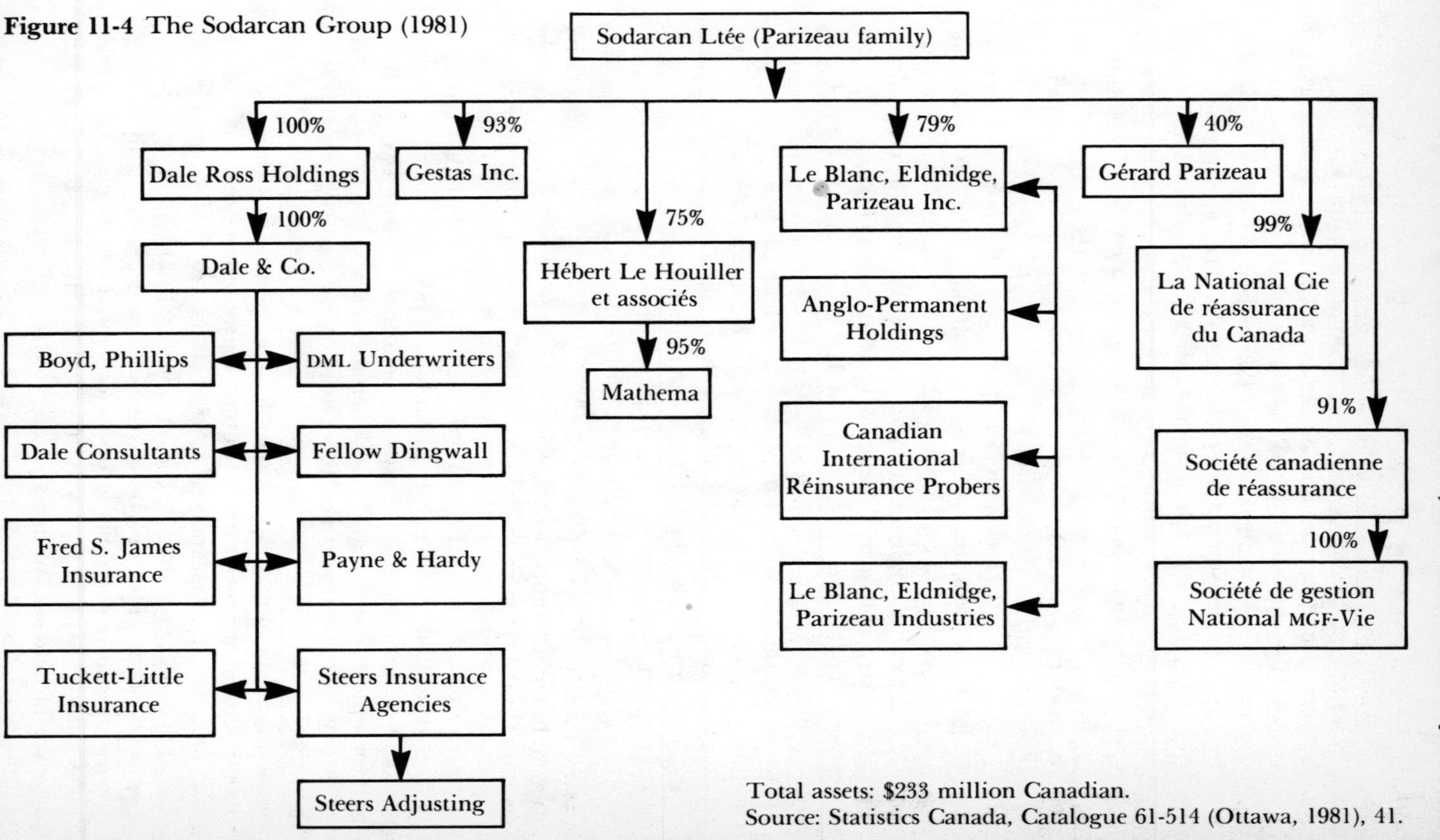

Total assets: $233 million Canadian.
Source: Statistics Canada, Catalogue 61-514 (Ottawa, 1981), 41.

des Caisses Desjardins and the Fédération des Caisses d'économie du Québec. In agriculture the two major firms are Agropur and Federated Cooperatives. In other fields are the Pêcheurs Unis du Québec and Cooprix.

The cooperative movement is managed by the Quebec petty bourgeoisie. They represent the more well-to-do customers of the caisses populaires (lawyers, accountants, doctors, dentists, pharmacists, actuaries, engineers, owners of small business) and they are not the private owners of the movement. Therefore, they cannot use the assets of the institution for their own profit, or finance the political party of their choice. The class that runs the cooperative movement therefore must not be confused with the wealthier French-Canadian bourgeoisie of the private sector. The petty bourgeoisie has neither the economic nor the political power of the group that controls large and medium-sized private enterprises.

Not only large French-Canadian corporations are grouping into conglomerates. Many of them are also becoming multinational firms. Once a big firm gets a dominant position in the Quebec market and a foothold in the close and concentrated English-Canadian market, it chooses foreign expansion as the next step in its growth strategy. The United States is most often the first target of the foreign investments of French-Canadian firms; Great Britain, France, and the Caribbean generally follow.

If we accept the United Nations definition of a multinational corporation as possessing five or more foreign subsidiaries, several French-Canadian firms qualify. They include the Banque Nationale, Lavalin, SNC, and Domtar. Other firms with substantial foreign investments are the Laurentian Group of insurance companies, with operations in the United States, Great Britain, and the Bahamas; Bombardier, with subsidiaries in Austria, the United States and Hong Kong; and Consolidated Bathurst, which owns manufacturing plants in Germany and Great Britain.

The multinational expansion of French-Canadian firms is a recent phenomenon. Apart from several early foreign operations, most francophone firms went abroad in the late 1970s. While the conquest of the Quebec market seems a precondition for foreign expansion, it is evident that francophone corporations choose most often to grow in the United States and Europe than to fight for a piece of the English-Canadian market. The English-Canadian economy may be too concentrated, too sparsely populated, or (probably) not sufficiently receptive to French-Canadian enterprise. Table 11-3 summarizes the most important foreign operations of French-Canadian firms.

French-Canadian present and future multinationals are most often found in the "soft" sectors: finance, services, and commerce. Domtar was a fullfledged transnational firm when it was taken over in 1979 by a coalition of public and private interests in Quebec. Bombardier is the only truly French-Canadian industrial firm with large operations abroad. Bombardier relies on foreign technology to feed its overseas subsidiaries; it manufactures American Motors cars in Ireland (under an AMC license), German streetcar and snowmobile motors in Austria, and French subway cars in the United States. It has also recently landed a $1 billion order to supply New York subway cars and bought Japanese (Kawasaki) technology to build them. Reliance on foreign know-how is a characteristic of all Canadian multinationals and French-Canadian firms are no exception.[4] As for more traditional activities, such as public utilities, mining, and oil and gas, there are no francophone multinationals. Large francophone utilities became mature when the international activities of those firms (such as Brascan) were on the decline. Francophone mining and petroleum companies are simply too small for foreign operations.

Politics and the French-Canadian Bourgeoisie

The political power of the francophone bourgeoisie is necessarily limited. After all, its members are few; its wealth is recent. On the whole it is federalist and overwhelmingly Liberal. The reason for this is simple: as soon as they attain a relatively large scale of production, French-Canadian companies look to the Canadian market as a whole, even if as a secondary market. All the

Table 11-3 Foreign Operations of French-Canadian Firms

Company	Year of foreign investment	Country
National Bank of Canada	1907	France
	1974	U.K.
	1977	United States
	1978	Hong Kong
	1982	South Korea
Domtar	1962	England
	1963	Italy
	1965	United States
	1975	Mexico
La Laurentienne	1977	United States
	1977	U.K.
	1977	Bahamas
Bombardier	1969	Austria
	1979	Ireland
	1981	United States
Montreal Trust	1952	Bahamas
	1971	Bermuda
	1972	New Hebrides
Campeau Corp.	1978	United States
	1982	Hong Kong
Consolidated Bathurst	1967	West Germany
	1982	U.K.
Provigo	1977	United States
Sodarcan	1975	United States
Great-West Life	1906	United States

Source: Annual Reports, *Financial Post*, *Finance*.

companies in the Power Corporation group are Canada-wide. Provigo bought an Ontario subsidiary, M. Loeb & Co., in August 1977. The Laurentian Group took over Imperial Life of Toronto the same year. Bombardier sells snowmobiles and railway cars all over Canada. Campeau Corp. has its head office in Ottawa and does business in Quebec, Ontario, and the west. Cassidy's has subsidiaries in several provinces, while the National Bank owns branches in the francophone districts of New Brunswick, Ontario, and Manitoba. Normick Perron has a factory in Cochrane and Rolland Paper owns a plant in Scarborough, both in Ontario. Sodarcan grows in Ontario through its subsidiary, Dale Ross Holdings. In sum, if Quebec separated, the French-Canadian bourgeoisie's market would be divided. Its companies would have to be reorganized and they would be weakened at both national and international levels.

The French-Canadian bourgeoisie is Liberal. The National Bank of Canada has traditionally been close to the provincial Liberals, while Campeau has largely benefited from the federal largesse.[5] Paul Desmarais is a well-known Liberal backer, while Paul Desruisseaux, former owner of Melcher Distilleries, is a Liberal Senator. Many French-Canadian capitalists are members of the boards of directors of federal crown corporations, including Laurent Beaudoin of Bombardier, Philippe de Gaspé Beaubien of Télémédia, Pierre Côté of Laiterie Laval, and R.B. Casgrain of Casgrain et Cie (Canada Development Corporation), Jean Perron of Normick Perron (Air Canada), Pierre Desmarais II of P. Desmarais Inc. (Canadian National Railways). These are only a few examples of the intimacy between the francophone establishment and the Liberal party.

Since the late 19th century, the Conservative party has been less involved with French-Canadian interests. At one time it supported a centralist variety of federalism that Quebec did not accept. With the possible exception of Brian Mulroney, the Conservatives have not had a French-Canadian leader or strong francophone personnel since shortly after Confederation.

The French-Canadian bourgeoisie is not receptive to the New Democratic party, with its ties to labour and Socialist International. Except for some special cases, it is also not interested by the Parti Québécois. The presence of Jacques Parizeau and Guy Joron in the PQ cabinet did not herald a change in the political allegiance of the francophone bourgeoisie. The Parti Québécois has been and remains a party run by people whose professions involve language: journalists, lawyers, publishers, writers, artists, teachers. These people make a living by manipulating symbols and their interests are most directly threatened by the assimilation of the Quebec nation. Furthermore, the French-Canadian bourgeoisie is haunted by the spectre of separatism, the core policy of the PQ. During the 1980 referendum campaign, all important French-Canadian firms financially supported the federalist committee.

Conclusion

Since the Second World War, a new francophone bourgeoisie has developed primarily, but not exclusively, in Quebec. Its main activities are the provision of financial services, commerce, transportation, real estate and building, and manufacturing. In secondary manufacturing—with the exception of Bombardier—it is concentrated in traditional industries. In sum, it has entered sectors in which technology does not play a major role and where new competitors are not blocked by technological barriers.

The growth of this bourgeoisie has been determined by the rapid increase in the incomes of French Canadians since the war; their entry as consumers into new markets that had previously been inaccessible to them (financial services, insurance, urban real estate, and retailing) have provided indigenous small firms with a steady demand. The late concentration of these activities eluded control by the Anglo-Canadian establishment and permitted the emergence of large francophone corporations.

The creation of provincial state apparatuses in Quebec, willing and able to stimulate the development of French-Canadian entrepreneurship, has helped French-Canadian capitalism in numerous opportunities. This has been the central policy of the Quebec Liberal party, mainly during the Quiet Revolution.

This new bourgeoisie has interests across Canada. It invests money and sells products from coast to coast and profits from federal-government procurements and crown corporations. For that reason it is opposed to the independence of Quebec. The PQ cannot represent the interests of this rising class, which is why I call it a French Canadian, not a Québécois, bourgeoisie.

With no independent capacity for research and development, French-Canadian capitalism cannot compete in dynamic industrial sectors. Like the cooperative movement, it is limited to expansion within the traditional sectors, except for the special occasions in which it takes over more sophisticated industrial corporations from foreign or from English-Canadian capital. Once they consolidate a dominant position in the Quebec market and a secondary position in the rest of Canada, francophone enterprises are ripe for international expansion. Some have become large multinational corporations.

The analysis outlined here directly contradicts all "ethnic class" conceptions of the Quebec nation. It also refutes the analysis of those who see the new French-Canadian bourgeoisie as a developing "national" bourgeoisie. Francophone capitalists are in fact only the French-Canadian section of the Canadian capitalist class.

Notes

1. John Porter, *The Vertical Mosaic* (Toronto: University of Toronto Press, 1965); Marcel Rioux and Yves Martin, *French-Canadian Society* (Toronto: McClelland and Stewart, 1964), pp. 307-18. More recent studies on Quebec often adopt the

same perspective; cf. Sheila Hodgins Milner and Henry Milner, *The Decolonization of Quebec* (Toronto: McClelland and Stewart, 1973), pp. 52-68.

2. *Rapport du Surintendant des Assurances du Québec, 1981*, p. XM.
3. The Bill S-31 died on the order paper a second time in the fall of 1983, however. Several analysts predicted that the bill would be reintroduced when the House of Commons reconvened. See Allan Tupper, *Bill S-31 and the Federalism of State Capitalism*, Discussion Paper no. 17 (Institute of Intergovernmental Relations, Queen's University, fall 1983).
4. For a comparison with English-Canadian multinationals, see J. Niosi, *Les multinationales canadiennes* (Montréal: Boréal-Express, 1982).
5. S. Goldenberg, *Men of Property* (Toronto: Personal Library, 1981), ch.8.

Chapter 12/The New Parameters of the Quebec Bourgeoisie*

Pierre Fournier

For some years now, and especially since the election of a PQ government, much has been written on the Quebec bourgeoisie, its economic power, its cohesiveness, its political intentions. The attempts to define with some precision the contours and parameters of this bourgeoisie remain in an embryonic state, however, and are often contradictory. In my opinion, such studies must be pursued, for they are essential not only to an understanding of the competing forces, including the Parti Québécois, but also to take an enlightened stand on the national question.

This article will essentially involve a refinement and extension of some of my earlier investigation, as well as a certain amount of self-criticism.[1] While some of my observations seem to stand up to analysis, including the definition of the three components of the bourgeoisie and the central role of the state as a cohesive factor, others appear to have been erroneous. I will also criticize, implicitly or explicitly, some other contributions to the analysis of the dominant class in Quebec. There will be, for example, an attempt at a systematic criticism of the ideas of Jorge Niosi.[2]

This study will reject, for example, the concept of a French-Canadian bourgeoisie, an error I also made in 1976, and the hypothesis that this bourgeoisie is simply the francophone wing of the Canadian bourgeoisie.

First, the criteria for the unit of analysis, the Quebec bourgeoisie, will be defined, then in turn the cooperative movement, state corporations, and the private sector will be examined, emphasizing recent developments and emergent tendencies. These three components of the Quebec bourgeoisie will be analyzed not only in terms of their economic power and their internal cohesiveness but also in their relations with the Canadian bourgeoisie and the policies of the Parti Québécois. I will put forward the hypothesis that at several levels the Canadian and Quebec bourgeoisies are in conflict and that the PQ is to a large extent the expression and the reflection of a power struggle between the two fractions. It will also be argued that the Quebec bourgeoisie has grown considerably stronger since 1960, inside and outside the state. Finally, I will show that the Quebec bourgeoisie is much more cohesive and aware of its interests than is generally thought and that it is becoming with the PQ a class not only in itself, but also for itself.

---

*This is an abridged and updated version of "Les nouveaux paramètres de la bourgeoisie québécoise," in Pierre Fournier (ed.), *Le Capitalisme au Québec* (Montréal: Albert St-Martin, 1979), and was originally published in English in *Studies in Political Economy* (spring 1980), pp. 67-92.

The Quebec Bourgeoisie: Definition and Criteria

In his article on the French-Canadian bourgeoisie, Jorge Niosi takes up several arguments and statements that I made in 1976. As I did, he rejects as a criterion for the definition of the economic power of the bourgeoisie, membership on boards of directors and prefers to concentrate on the ownership and control of the largest firms. I also agree with Niosi's assertion that the Quebec francophone bourgeoisie constitutes more than a petty bourgeoisie, whatever fractions may exist, and that certain analysts, such as Gilles Bourque and Nicole Frenette "have underestimated the importance of the big and medium francophone bourgeoisie."[3] His overall conclusion that there exists "a French-Canadian bourgeoisie underrepresented in the major companies under Canadian control, but dynamic and growing quickly,"[4] also agrees with my previous analysis.

There our agreement stops, however. Niosi's fundamental error lies in choosing the French-Canadian rather than the Quebec bourgeoisie as a starting point and category of analysis. Niosi includes in his bourgeoisie all important firms with francophone owners. Throughout this article I shall attempt to demonstrate that Niosi's conception represents a distortion of reality and that the dichotomy between Quebec bourgeoisie and Canadian bourgeoisie provides a much more relevant and realistic basis for analysis. Niosi's other errors, including his perception of the Quebec state and of the cooperative movement as "petty bourgeois," and his hypothesis that the francophone bourgeoisie is a mere wing of the Canadian bourgeoisie stem from his initial postulate.

In adopting exclusively an ethnic criterion for the definition of the French-Canadian bourgeoisie, Niosi eliminates some essential dimensions. He ignores in particular the important superstructural factor and attempts rather to locate class fractions. Thus, Niosi does not seem to consider the possibility that the Quebec state is in fact the main focal point of the bourgeoisie he is attempting to define. As a result, he marginalizes the state and particularly Quebec state corporations as essential pivots and cohesive factors of this new bourgeoisie. By ignoring the Canadian and Quebec states, Niosi does not correctly pinpoint the contradictions that exist and develop between the two bourgeoisies. He also underestimates the strategic cohesiveness and attempts at autonomization that are beginning to develop in the Quebec bourgeoisie.

According to Jorge Niosi, the French-Canadian bourgeoisie is essentially limited to a list of around 50 firms whose owners have French names and whose assets exceed $10 million. By excluding the cooperatives and the state corporations, this list ignores two key components of the Quebec bourgeoisie. On the other hand, Niosi includes firms such as Power Corporation and Rolland which, in my view, are part of the Canadian bourgeoisie.

Even at the empirical level, it is becoming more and more obvious that the subsidiaries of Power Corporation cannot be put into the same category as Provigo, Culinar, or even the Mouvement Desjardins and Hydro-Québec. Even though they belong to francophones, Power and Rolland are intimately connected to the Canadian financial network, which relies on the federal state. Desmarais and Rolland are well and truly represented in the Canadian power structure, for they are part of the Canadian bourgeoisie.

A little investigation reveals that Power and its subsidiaries are in the financial network of the Royal Bank and that Power is to a certain extent the active arm of that bank. It is noteworthy that a large proportion of the expansions and absorptions undertaken by Power have been approved and financed, if not directed, by the largest Canadian bank. This includes the attempt for control over Argus Corporation. It should also be stressed that several Power subsidiaries are located, incorporated, and have an accumulation base outside Quebec. Investors Group, for instance, has a Manitoba charter. In fact, the principal directors of Power and its subsidiaries are anglophone and are linked to the financial and industrial networks of the Canadian bourgeoisie. Paul Desmarais himself is above all a director of Canadian monopolies. Similarly, Lucien Rolland is on the board of such key Canadian firms as Stelco, Canadian Pacific, Bell Canada, and Inco; his company is part of the financial network of the Bank of Montreal. Other empirical evidence is that companies such as Power and Rolland, unlike Quebec bourgeois, employ lawyers, brokers, insurers, consulting actuaries, and auditors from important anglophone offices linked to the Canadian bourgeoisie.

It is also essential, when defining the Quebec bourgeoisie, to avoid another mistake made by Niosi, who considers that Quebec capital that becomes international (Provigo, for instance) is automatically Canadian. In fact, Quebec bourgeois can have pan-Canadian or even international ambitions without losing their Quebec accumulation base and their links with the Quebec superstructure. Would it not be absurd to claim that the Royal Bank is no longer Canadian because its capital has been internationalized over the last 15 years? As Gilles Bourque correctly emphasizes, there is a world of difference between a Quebec firm such as Quebecor, which is attempting to break into the Philadelphia market, and Power Corporation, which is tied to the dominant fraction of the Canadian bourgeoisie and which defends its interests through the federal state.[5]

The Quebec bourgeoisie should also not be seen as totally or essentially under the thumb of large American capital. In my opinion, this bourgeoisie has its own accumulation bases; it is not simply a subcontractor. It is nonetheless greatly dependent on American capital and may even seek to strengthen its ties with American imperialism, either to profit from it directly or to shortcircuit the Canadian bourgeoisie. To a large extent, moreover, one of the objectives of the Parti Québécois and of the Quebec bourgeoisie is to supplant the Canadian bourgeoisie in its role as intermediary between the working class and American capital. Despite this, we believe that Dorval Brunelle, among others, goes too far when he states, "The bourgeoisie at the provincial level is primarily a comprador class."[6]

Finally, the Quebec bourgeoisie can only be adequately defined and delimited on the basis of its conflictual relations with the Canadian bourgeoisie. Over the last 15 years, the Quebec bourgeoisie has attacked head on parts of the Canadian bourgeoisie's foundation—the financial, food, iron and steel, and service sectors—with a great deal of success in several of these medium-technology sectors.

How can the Quebec bourgeoisie be defined, in view of the above indications and criticisms? Recently, Gilles Bourque provided a definition which is, in my opinion, much more accurate than Niosi's, and with which I agree to a large extent. According to Bourque, the Quebec bourgeoisie is:

> ... a class whose accumulation base is primarily Québécois and which relies mainly on the provincial state to defend its interests. This does not exclude the possibility that these Quebec bourgeois own firms elsewhere in Canada, nor even that they take advantage, on occasion, of federal grants, laws, or regulations (nor even that some of them may be anglophone). What is involved is an economic and political anchor point, not isolationism or exclusivism.[7]

Continuing the analysis, Bourque maintains that the Quebec bourgeoisie is essentially a "regional, predominantly nonmonopolistic bourgeoisie," that is not only dispersed and extremely weak economically, but also "splintered without an obvious political and economic cohesiveness."[8] I believe that Bourque underestimates the local bourgeoisie. I will show that, despite numerous contradictions and obvious weaknesses, Quebec capital has demonstrated considerably more cohesiveness over the last few years than he suggests. Once more it becomes apparent that the importance of state corporations as an integral part of the bourgeoisie and as a cohesive factor has not been adequately defined and analyzed.

The notion of "circuit" or "financial network," although requiring theoretical and empirical refinements, seems a good starting point for an analysis of the Quebec bourgeoisie. In financial circuits we could include, for example, ownership and control of a firm, the accumulation base, the suppliers, the market, funding sources, relations with the state (ownership, grants, contracts, market), links with the whole of the network, and relations with other networks.

More specifically, in the case of the Quebec financial network, I make the following hypotheses:

1. Quebec remains the accumulation base and the principal and priority market of the main components of the Quebec bourgeoisie, notably the Banque canadienne nationale, Hydro-Québec, and the Mouvement Desjardins.
2. The firms in the Quebec network may be defined in part on the basis of their superstructural relations, particularly the support they receive from the Quebec state (grants, contracts, financing, legislation).
3. Quebec companies may be defined on the basis of their conflictual

relations with the Canadian bourgeoisie. In the following sections I shall emphasize the effects of the numerous contradictions on the two fractions of the bourgeoisie since the Quiet Revolution.

4. The composition of boards of directors, while it often sheds only partial light on the reality of economic power, may give indications of the cohesiveness of a network and the links between firms may help to identify the often complex relations between the three components of the bourgeoisie.
5. The ownership and real control—including planning and decision making—of Quebec firms are situated in Quebec, either within the firm itself or within the network.
6. Most Quebec firms are financed inside the network.
7. Firms in the Quebec network have a strong tendency to turn to Quebec brokers, lawyers, insurers, actuaries, transfer agents, auditors for services.

On the whole, a dialectical approach must be preferred when attempting to identify a financial network and its firms. Thus, a financial network must be defined on the basis of the firms, but a firm must be described and classified by virtue of the place it occupies inside the network. It should also not be thought that the constituents of the Quebec bourgeoisie will prove to be perfectly homogeneous. It is obvious that, despite their conflicts, the distinction between the Canadian and Quebec bourgeoisies is not watertight. There are numerous points of contact. Moreover, certain firms such as Bombardier-MLW are true borderline cases, in that they seem to fit into both networks and it is not always easy to determine where they belong.

Even if the importance of such a debate may be questioned, I would be tempted to put forward the hypothesis that the Quebec bourgeoisie is now monopolistic rather than nonmonopolistic. The mere statement that the Quebec state is weak or "truncated" (a description requiring qualification in any case) is insufficient evidence for the nonmonopolistic character of the local bourgeoisie. Even if we do not question the domination by American and Canadian capital, the Quebec bourgeoisie, as I define it, orchestrates the exploitation of a large proportion of the Quebec working class, shows a high degree of cohesiveness, and possesses firms with the characteristics generally attributed to monopolies (including total assets, number of employees, degree of integration and concentration, market share).

In the next three sections, I shall examine in turn the three components of the Quebec bourgeoisie: the cooperative movement, the state corporations, and the private sector.

The Cooperative Sector

It is particularly necessary to analyze the cooperative movement separately from the private sector and from the other components of the Quebec bourgeoisie, since several observers persist in seeing the cooperative sector as not capitalist, as economically unimportant, or as involving the petty bourgeoisie rather than the bourgeoisie.

Jorge Niosi, for one, maintains that the Quebec cooperative movement is simply "the unified petty bourgeoisie." He states, moreover, that:

> It would be an error to confuse the petty bourgeoisie that administers the Mouvement Desjardins with the French-Canadian big or medium bourgeoisie of the private sector. This petty bourgeoisie has neither the economic nor the political weight of the bourgeoisie which controls the large and medium-sized noncooperative companies.[9]

Niosi, in fact, sees the cooperatives as organizations formed by the petty bourgeoisie in "its dreams of self-defence against the aggression of big capital."[10]

This view is, in my opinion, pure folklore. The cooperative sector is an integral part of the Quebec bourgeoisie. It is not on the defensive; it is expanding and competing directly with several Canadian firms. In the financial and food-production sectors especially, the large cooperatives show all the characteristics of firms that are not only capitalist, but also monopolistic. At the most they can be seen as constituting an original form of capital accumulation, but they are capitalist all the same. This is confirmed by assets, methods of management, profit objectives, control of a significant part of economic activity in Quebec, and their role in the direct exploitation of Quebec workers.

Niosi's arguments are based in part on an analysis of the boards of directors of the main cooperatives. Finding fewer "capitalists" than "petty bourgeois" (lawyers, notaries, etc.) on these boards, he concludes that they are petty-bourgeois companies. After correctly denouncing the board of directors criterion as a determining factor of economic power and choosing the mark of $10 million in assets as a definition of the important French-Canadian firms, Niosi falls back on the board of directors. Suddenly, the cooperatives' funded assets of several billion dollars are unimportant.

Niosi argues, moreover, that the cooperatives, unlike capitalist firms, are "democratic" because members have the vote at the annual meetings:

> The management of the Mouvement Desjardins set out to be democratic right from the start. The members of the credit unions are the shareholders and, in the annual meetings, each shareholder has one vote. This type of structure has effectively prevented takeover bids by French-Canadian capitalists.[11]

One could maintain that the cooperative movement had democratic pretensions at the beginning and that it was formed by petty bourgeois. But can we seriously say that, in practice, the cooperative movement is controlled by its members? We could just as well maintain that depositors control chartered banks or that Bell Canada is controlled by its million shareholders. After all, even joint stock companies claim to be democratic. The annual meetings of the Mouvement Desjardins and of the other cooperatives amply demonstrate that real control is in the hands of management and that the latter has nothing in common with the petty bourgeois.

Therefore, not only are cooperatives not controlled by the petty bourgeoisie and the farmers, but also they have taken on forms of organization that bear no resemblance to petty-bourgeois associations. We need only consider the virulent denunciations by labour organizations of the "capitalism" of the cooperatives, or the particularly bitter strikes by agricultural cooperative workers in recent years. Agricultural cooperatives are increasingly denounced by farmers. Recently, the president of the Fédération des producteurs de lait du Québec, Marcel Mailloux, condemned the monopoly exercised by the cooperatives and stated:

> Cooperatives seek only profitability and are not concerned with the producers and the consumers . . . and their control over production and marketing is prejudicial to the economy of a good many municipalities and rural regions of the province, as shown by the closing of two dairies in Granby by Québec-Lait.[12]

I will demonstrate that the principal cooperatives are financial empires, which have strengthened their ties with the state and the bourgeoisie, and have not hesitated to absorb private industrial and financial assets, while increasing their political power.

Let us begin with the Mouvement Desjardins, the key element of the cooperative sector, and one of the essential pivots and cohesive factors of the bourgeoisie as a whole. In 1982, the funded assets controlled by the "petty bourgeois" of the Mouvement exceeded $15 billion. With 14,000 employees and 3.5 million members, the caisses populaires surpass all Canadian banks in Quebec. Organized as a holding company, the Mouvement Desjardins directly controls six financial institutions: la Société d'investissement Desjardins, la Fiducie du Québec, la Sécurité, la Société d'assurance des Caisses populaires, l'Assurance-vie Desjardins, and la Sauvegarde. It also has an important interest in Culinar (which controls Vachon Inc.) and the Banque Nationale, which are two companies on Niosi's list! It would be interesting to know by what subtle mechanism the petty bourgeois of the Mouvement Desjardins were able to take over the industrial and financial assets of the bourgeoisie.

A good illustration of the increasing power of the cooperatives in the financial sphere is the insurance sector. According to a study by the Ecole des hautes études commerciales, Quebec companies have made rapid advances in this field, from 15% of the market in 1950 to 33% in 1974. The cooperatives have tripled their share of the market, from 4% to 12%.[13]

In this sector, then, the English-Canadian bourgeoisie has lost ground. As the Quebec bourgeoisie gradually takes over the financial sector (in a restricted sense), a general strengthening of this bourgeoisie can be predicted. Indeed, it has already been proved that non-Quebec companies are responsible for the flight of savings from Quebec and that Quebec companies invest an ever greater share of their assets inside Quebec, in accordance with the internal logic of their financial circuits.

Further evidence that the Mouvement Desjardins is bourgeois and capitalist is that the caisses control their own expansion. They no longer let "a few members start up a caisse populaire with the means at hand." They plan, create, and finance what is already being called "a second generation of caisses populaires." Thus, in 1977, the Mouvement Desjardins, as would a chartered bank, supervised the setting up of a dozen caisses, and did viability studies on numerous other potential branches. According to *Le Devoir*:

> This is a radical change: no doubt one of the most important decisions by the caisses populaires in recent years. The competition with the banks and finance companies may now develop quite differently.[14]

The events surrounding the revision of the Bank Act by the federal government in May 1978 provide the clearest demonstration of the political power of the caisses populaires and of the threat they represent for Canadian banks. In August 1976, the federal government released a white paper on the revisions to the Bank Act, including plans to bring the caisses under federal jurisdiction. They would have been obliged to deposit reserves with the Bank of Canada. In the following months, the caisses attacked the white paper and clearly indicated their desire to remain under provincial jurisdiction.[15] They were strongly supported by both the Liberal and later the new Parti Québécois provincial government.

On May 18, 1978, when the bill was tabled, the federal government had relented, fearing a confrontation with Quebec, and the caisses preserved their autonomy. The press was unanimous in interpreting the bill as a "retreat by Ottawa" and "an important victory for the caissses populaires."[16] It is true that on the other hand the federal government made concessions to Canadian banks, allowing them to reduce their obligatory reserves, and to enter new, profitable fields of activity, such as leasing. While welcoming the new act as a whole, the banks, to quote Rowland Frazee, president of the Royal Bank, were "disappointed that the caisses populaires were given easier conditions than the chartered banks."[17] We see this as further evidence for the increasing economic and political importance of the Mouvement Desjardins and the Quebec bourgeoisie.

With the election of a Parti Québécois government, the cooperative sector was destined to play an even more fundamental economic role, as is clearly shown in the party program. Even closer links have been established with the state. There have been, for instance, the creation of a Société de développement co-opératif, the unconditional support for the caisses in their fight against the Bank Act, numerous grants, the agreement to have automobile licence plates distributed by the caisses, and, at a more symbolic level, the participation of caisses management in miniature economic summit meetings. On this last point, Alfred Rouleau, the president of Mouvement Desjardins, did not hide his satisfaction with "a government which for the first time has recognized the important role of the cooperative movement by inviting us to a meeting of union and business leaders." As I shall show later, it seems that the political and even partisan positions of the caisses are in ever greater agreement with those of the PQ.

The State Corporations

The Quebec state plays two complementary but distinct roles in relation to the Quebec bourgeoisie. On the one hand, it is obvious that the state often gives direct or indirect assistance to some of the local bourgeoisie, notably through the Caisse de dépôt. On the other hand, the state is penetrating more and more the production sphere by directly exploiting the workers: Sidbec and Hydro-Québec, for example. Thus, state corporations are not only "instruments" of the Quebec bourgeoisie, they are themselves part of this bourgeoisie. This does not mean, of course, that there are no contradictions within state corporations, as there are in the private sector as well, but that, globally and by tendency, they are an integral part of the local bourgeoisie, identify with its interests, and participate in its financial circuits.

It is therefore an error to study state corporations with a strictly instrumentalist concept of the state, as I myself have done over the last few years.[18] This point of view, which is related to the theory of state monopoly capitalism, does not correspond to reality. On the one hand, public investment should not be seen as simply aiming to support the development of the private sector. There may be other objectives, such as the desire to support one fraction of the bourgeoisie to the detriment of another. On the other hand, even if state intervention in the production sector may be perceived in part as a reaction to the low profitability of a given sector or as an attempt to improve services and infrastructures for the benefit of private enterprise, the state itself becomes as a consequence the owner of part of the means of production and the exploiter of an increasing share of the labour force.

There can be no doubt about the primordial role of the Quebec state in the provincial economy and its importance as a promoter of the local bourgeoisie. Jorge Niosi himself acknowledges that one of the factors that has contributed to the expansion of the French-Canadian bourgeoisie is the support given French-Canadian capitalists by the Quebec state.[19] He gives the Caisse de dépôt as an example and emphasizes its important role in the promotion of the local bourgeoisie. But there is much more to it than that. The state is not a mere promoter or instrument, as would have become apparent had Niosi studied state corporations in the production sector, such as Sidbec and Hydro-Québec. Moreover, besides his instrumentalist conception of the state, Niosi sees the assistance given the local bourgeoisie by the Caisse and the state corporations as inevitable:

> How could the funds of the Caisse be invested other than in shares and bonds of local firms, in provincial and Hydro-Québec bonds? The Caisse

> cannot but help companies established in Quebec, and particularly those of francophone capitalists.[20]

He also believes that "the apparatus for state economic intervention has already acquired an autonomy that no minister, however reformist, will succeed in modifying."[21]

Besides being contradictory, these two assertions are false. If the Caisse is really so autonomous, why is its investment policy completely different from that of Sun Life, for example? We believe that the Caisse consciously invests its funds to assist the companies and the government of Quebec. As we shall see later, the mandate of the Caisse is quite clear on this point. Moreover, one of my fundamental hypotheses is that the Caisse and most of the other state corporations have greatly changed their praxis over the last 10 years. After rather finicky beginnings and contradictory actions vis-à-vis fractions of the bourgeoisie, the state corporations have been much more consistent in recent years with regard to the Quebec bourgeoisie. The Caisse, for example, has been considerably reducing the proportion of its "Canadian" investments and has come to play a much more active role in the consolidation, integration, and development of Quebec companies. The changes have come about through conscious decisions by the directors of the Caisse, but also, and especially, because of governmental pressures in this direction. Nothing was inevitable, and, with the PQ, the continuation of these changes in all state corporations can be expected.

PQ government policies have since contradicted Niosi's thesis that the state corporations are largely autonomous. In fact, there has been pronounced tightening of control over public companies by the Quebec government. This is happening even if there is now more agreement than before between the ambitions of the state corporations and the objectives of the government. Several projects dear to the state corporations have been or are on the point of being approved. At the level of policy and the type of development proposed, the PQ corresponds much more than previous governments to the aspirations of the management of the state corporations.

Despite this—and even if the state corporations will preserve a relative autonomy—the PQ is profoundly transforming not only each state corporation but also the links between them and the state, with the avowed goal of making the economic objectives of Quebec and the action of the state corporations more compatible. State corporations, including Hydro-Québec, have had their charters modified. The government will have an important role henceforth in appointing management and members of the board. It will have more control over budgets and will rule on the important projects envisaged by the corporations. It is noteworthy that several major changes have occurred in the top management of the corporations since November 1976. Unlike the Liberal party, which tended to pick its protégés from the private sector, the PQ has often chosen high-ranking civil servants to "represent" it within the public companies. Jean-Claude Lebel, for example, who was the president of the l'Office de planification et de développement du Québec (OPDQ), has become the president of the Société générale de financement. Jean Campeau, who was Associate Deputy Minister of Finance, became head of the Caisse de dépôt.

At the government level, the process of reforming relations with state corporations was initiated by a confidential memo sent to the cabinet by Jacques Parizeau and Bernard Landry. This memo, dated January 14, 1977, barely two months after the election of the PQ, demonstrates the great importance given this question by the government and its desire to act in this field: "It is clear that it would be desirable to take action towards a better definition of the content and mode of the relation between the government and the state corporations."[22]

Among the recommendations and the envisaged action are the submission by state corporations of a development plan (every three or five years), the examination of this plan by a group of high-ranking civil servants with appropriate recommendations, and the cabinet's ultimate responsibility to rule on the recommendations and the development plan—all this in order that "the specific objectives [of the corporations] may be further reconciled with general objectives, with a view to greater consistency in government intervention in the Quebec economy."[23]

The Parizeau-Landry memo also mentions the elaboration of performance and efficiency criteria for each corporation, the appointment of a civil servant to the General Secretariat of the Executive Council who would be responsible at the public-service level for relations between the government and the corporations, and the creation of a mechanism in the Public Service:

> ... to monitor, on a comparative basis, the evolution of each state corporation; to prepare, if need be, modifications to their objectives; to participate in the examination of development plans; to contribute to the elaboration and constant revision of performance and efficiency criteria.[24]

The first phase of government action began in the summer of 1977 with the appointment to strategic positions of "strong men, competent administrators in both the public and private domains."[25]

It would be naive to believe that these various measures are empty wishes or that they are insignificant for the state corporations. Indeed, there is evidence that they are causing a stir in several circles. The resignation of Côme Carbonneau, the president of Soquem, is largely due to the tightening of state control. According to Pierre Bellemare of *La Presse*, "In certain state corporations, these measures are seen as less and less amusing and are often interpreted as attacks on administrative autonomy."[26]

It should be noted that the economic role of the Quebec state has developed spectacularly since 1960. Its expenditures rose from 15% of the GNP to over 35% in 1980, compared to an increase of only 2% from 1940 to 1960. In the 1976-80 period, public investment in Quebec stood at close to $3 billion annually, including the James Bay project. The assets of state corporations rose from $10.5 billion in 1975 to $25.8 billion in 1980. Most large and economically stimulating projects, especially in construction, stem from the state. To the Quebec bourgeoise, the "achievements" of the governments since 1960, including Bourassa's, are fundamental. The rapid increase in expenditures, due in part to the battle with Ottawa over tax points, has permitted the Quebec state and bourgeoisie to assume considerable economic power.

Even if the Quebec state is "truncated," in the sense that it lacks several key economic levers, and even if it is federal economic powers that are mainly at stake in the "constitutional crisis," the relative importance of the Quebec government should not be underestimated. At present, Quebec is less affected by federal spending policy than by the provincial budget.[27] I do not agree with those who, like Dorval Brunelle, maintain that Quebec's economic role has decreased since the early 1960s. While it is true, as Brunelle states,[28] that DREE played a key role in the creation of industrial-development strategy in Quebec, it cannot be considered as playing the leading role. Most of the investments by DREE or other federal agencies since 1974 have involved large infrastructure projects, such as the construction of Mirabel Airport, the setting up of a dozen-odd industrial parks, industry studies, and access roads to forest and mining resources. Most of the industrial or directly productive investments by DREE have involved Quebec-controlled projects. The Sidbec expansion and the construction of a pulp-and-paper mill by Donohue St-Félicien, a subsidiary of the SGF, were granted $30 million each. Those have been the two main DREE grants to industrial projects.[29]

I shall now examine in turn the principal state corporations. This study will not be exhaustive, but will concentrate on points illustrating my hypotheses, particularly the role of state corporations vis-à-vis class fractions and, more particularly, the bourgeoisie. It will not involve a global definition of the role of public enterprise or that of the state. I shall argue that the state corporations are an integral part of the Quebec bourgeoisie, they have solidly backed the constitution of Quebec financial networks, and a large part of the action of these corporations is in opposition to and in conflict with the Canadian bourgeoisie. Finally, it is contended that the corporations have become increasingly "nationalist" in recent years and, with a PQ government, they will acquire an even more important role in the development of the Quebec bourgeoisie.

The Caisse de Dépôt

It is well known that the financial system, particularly the banks, is the backbone of the Canadian bourgeoisie. Without their control over financial institutions and connected industrial interests, the Canadian bourgeoisie would be totally under the sway of American imperialism. It has also been demonstrated that a chief obstacle to the development of Quebec (francophone) companies is a lack of access to financing. According to an analysis by the Quebec Ministry of Industry and Commerce, 44.8% of French-Canadian industrialists gave financing as the main obstacle to their expansion, compared to 20.0% of foreigners and 13.7% of English Canadians.[30] It is partly because of this problem that Quebeckers have been trying for some years now to "take into their own hands" the financial sector. In this regard the creation of the Caisse de dépôt in 1965 was without a doubt a major landmark.

With assets of over $11 billion in 1982, the Caisse is one of the pillars of the Quebec financial circuit. The great majority of Quebec's large and medium-sized firms have benefited at one time or another from its financial or technical assistance and, through the action of the Caisse, local productive forces have gained greater monopoly, impact, and cohesiveness.

The Caisse was set up after a difficult fight with the federal government, which wanted to retain control over funds contributed to the universal pension plan. Canadian financial circles, such as Sun Life and Royal Trust, wanted to manage the pension fund themselves, then, as a last resort, exerted pressure to restrict the powers of the Caisse. The Canadian bourgeoisie clearly understood the potential for relative autonomization that the Caisse provided the Quebec bourgeoisie. However, despite the numerous compromises reflected in its charter and the various restrictive clauses that have prevented it from having the impact it might have had, the action of the Caisse has essentially strengthened the Quebec bourgeoisie and state at the expense of the Canadian bourgeoisie.

First, the Caisse has enabled the Quebec government to break much of the hold of the Canadian financial syndicate. In "difficult" political and social circumstances, the Caisse has often come to the assistance of the government through massive purchases of Quebec savings bonds. In 1966, after the election of Daniel Johnson, with his slogan "Equality or Independence," the English-Canadian financial circles were alarmed by Union Nationale nationalism and attempted a squeeze play by boycotting Quebec bonds. The Caisse decided to intervene and made massive bond purchases to support the price.[31] Similarly, during the October Crisis, shares and bonds in the Quebec private and public sectors were having serious difficulties on the market, and the Caisse decided to help stabilize the market through buying securities of the government and of Quebec-based companies. Finally, with the election of the PQ, the Caisse came to the rescue of the new government by buying savings bonds and granting two loans for short-term financing.

It is true, however, that the Canadian bourgeoisie now has few ways to put pressure on the bond market. Quebec bonds have been largely boycotted by Canadian financial institutions for the last 10 years and government securities are now mainly in the hands of francophone Quebec institutions. In 1982, the Caisse made bond purchases worth $875 million from the Quebec government and $150 million from Hydro-Québec.

On the whole, it is no exaggeration to state that the Caisse has given

Quebec considerably greater room to manoeuvre, at the expense of the Canadian bourgeoisie. As Parizeau has noted, "In the 10-year-old struggle in Quebec against the financial syndicate, the foundation of the Caisse was the first breach in the control of the syndicate over the finances of the government of Quebec."[32] The English-Canadian bourgeoisie itself sees the Caisse as a threat. In 1967, when it was having problems with English-Canadian financial circles, the Johnson government was forced by the latter to appoint Charles Neapole, the president of the Montreal Stock Exchange and a former director of the Bank of Montreal, to the board of directors of the Caisse. The English-Canadian bourgeoisie apparently wanted at least to be able to keep an eye on what was happening.

Second, the portfolio of the Caisse clearly indicates the priority given to the purchase of shares and bonds of Quebec companies. It can also be seen that the Caisse has taken its greatest risks with Quebec firms and has made particular efforts to consolidate and reorganize Quebec capital.

The Caisse portfolio was worth $1.4 billion in 1982 and is the single most important portfolio of shares of Canadian companies in Canada. The priority for investment has been, first, Quebec companies, then the "francophone wing" of the Canadian bourgeoisie, and finally Canadian monopolies. This may reflect in part contradictions within Quebec governments, especially Bourassa's, which were to a great extent divided between the interests of the francophone wing and those of the Quebec bourgeoisie. With the PQ, these contradictions have all but disappeared. In fact, the investments of the Caisse clearly favour the Quebec bourgeoisie. Most holdings exceeding 10% of the companies' shares involve large and medium-sized Quebec firms.

The same priority can be observed for bonds. Those issued by the Quebec government (including municipalities, school boards, and hospitals) make up over 60% of the total portfolio. There are also important investments in Quebec firms such as Bombardier, Quebec Poultry, La Vérendrye, Place Dupuis, and Superseal, and in other state corporations such as Sidbec and the Société générale de financement.

According to all indications, the Caisse has matured in recent years and has learned to use its enormous power to promote the Quebec bourgeoisie. The constitution of Provigo, a food monopoly, and its recent takeover of Loeb, an English-Canadian monopoly, stem from a conscious and planned effort to strengthen the Quebec bourgeoisie's position in food distribution. Provigo was formed several years ago from a union of three medium-sized Quebec companies, a merger made possible by substantial input from the Caisse at the managerial and financial level. The next step was the Loeb takeover, which was fiercely opposed by the Loeb family, but which had been carefully and lengthily prepared, through the purchase of 24% of Loeb's shares and the appointment of two Caisse directors to the Loeb board a few years before. The Caisse remains the largest shareholder of the new complex (about 24%) and rejected, in 1977, a very attractive takeover bid from the Canadian monopoly Sobey Stores. More than any other, the Provigo example demonstrates the potential of the Caisse and the trends in its evolution. This potential was clearly seen by Jacques Parizeau in 1972:

> Through combining funds available in the Caisse de dépôt, those that can be provided by savings cooperatives and direct capital outlay by the state and private Quebec shareholders, the repatriation of a great many companies can be immediately secured.[33]

The recent takeovers by the Caisse of two large Canadian companies, Domtar and Gaz Métropolitain, as well as statements from the top managerial ranks of the corporation, indicate that its role as an effective lever for the promotion of Quebec capital will continue to increase, at least as long as the PQ remains in power.

The Société générale de financement

Created in 1962, the SGF constitutes for all practical purposes a state holding company. From 1962 to 1972, the SGF was a "mixed" corporation devoting the bulk of its resources to buying up nearly bankrupt family-run companies in Quebec. This period was financially disastrous and was marked by inconsistency and contradictions in government objectives and action. Sogefor, a management firm in the pulp-and-paper sector, experienced tremendous problems because of the government's refusal to change the system of forest concessions, dominated at that time by CIP and Consolidated Bathurst.

In 1973, the SGF became a state corporation and its orientation was considerably modified. Its role was now to create Quebec industrial complexes and to participate in the management and financing of medium-sized and large Quebec firms. The SGF has thus a small number of important subsidiaries, concentrated particularly in two key economic sectors: pulp and paper (Donohue St-Félicien, Domtar, and Sogefor) and heavy machinery (Marine, Volcano, Forano, and Tanguay).

The St-Félicien project for the construction of an integrated forest complex in the Saguenay-Lac-St-Jean area is of particular significance. First, it involves a considerable investment (approximately $400 million). This was initiated by the SGF, which retains a majority interest of 60%. St-Félicien is indicative of the orientation towards large companies, more capable of withstanding competition and of penetrating markets than small or medium-sized companies. In fact, the new complex competes directly with Canadian monopolies like Consolidated Bathurst.

At another level, the SGF is a financing company, developing already large firms. The best example is probably its important financial participation in Bombardier-MLW. The SGF, in fact, gave indirect financial assistance to the Bombardier complex when it bought, in July 1975, 40% of the shares of MLW for $6.8 million. This action was of considerable help to Bombardier at a time when it sorely needed liquid assets, largely as a result of its takeover of MLW-Worthington in 1974.

As another aspect of its role, the SGF promotes the amalgamation and merger of small and medium-sized firms with growth potential so that they can become financially sound and large enough to be nationally and internationally competitive. As an example, the SGF gave technical and financial assistance for the total integration of three medium-sized furniture companies. The new group, Artopex, markets and sells the production of Bonnex, Artena, and Meubles Opus. With 45% of shares, the SGF is the largest shareholder. Artopex grosses $15 million annually and is the largest such company owned by Quebeckers.

Despite certain problems of profitability, the SGF remains one of the principal Quebec companies, with assets of close to $1 billion in 1982. Its development demonstrates a new political will within the Quebec bourgeoisie.

The Société de développement industriel

Founded in 1971, the SDI is a financial body that subsidizes small and medium-sized Quebec firms in particular. The primary goal of the SDI is to aid "dynamic" small and medium-sized firms to modernize their technology, consolidate or rationalize their activities, and increase their exports. This aid involves providing low-interest loans, taking over part of a loan, or underwriting share capital.

The SDI is perhaps the most "nationalist" of the state corporations. Firms wishing to obtain financial assistance must meet relatively strict conditions established according to the following criteria:

1. Extent of integration into Quebec economic activity, with regard to the percentage of purchases of Quebec-produced raw materials.
2. Percentage of purchases of Quebec-made machinery and equipment.
3. Percentage of budget devoted to research and development.
4. Effects on other sectors of activity in Quebec: engineering and construction, insurance, and so on.
5. Proportion of francophone Quebeckers among upper-level administration personnel and members of board of directors.[34]

These conditions constitute without a doubt an important practical barrier for non-Quebec firms. According to an internal document of the SDI, more than two-thirds of the firms assisted between 1971 and 1976 were Quebec based, 18% were Canadian, and 15% foreign. This same document shows that small and medium-sized companies were preferred: 80% of the companies had under 199 employees; only 9.5% had more than 500. Sidbec and Bombardier-MLW were included in the latter group.[35]

On the whole, the SDI has given important support to small and medium-sized Quebec firms and has certainly been involved in the breakthrough of the local bourgeoisie in metal and chemical products and transportation equipment, sectors where it has concentrated the bulk of its financial intervention.

Hydro-Québec and James Bay

There is no doubt that the 1963 nationalization of Hydro-Québec is of fundamental importance for capital as a whole. The stability and availability of a cheap source of energy have always been essential to economic development—hence the considerable investment to this end by most capitalist governments.

But apart from this, the constitution of Hydro-Québec meant the acquisition by the Quebec bourgeoisie of a vital sector of the economy. Whether or not it is profitable, Hydro-Québec represents considerable economic power. In 1982, the corporation was the largest public utility body in North America, and the most important company in Canada, with assets of over $23 billion and profits of $800 million. Annual investments in the last five years have been close to $2.5 billion, or between 20% and 30% of total new investments in Quebec.

To a large extent, nationalization was an expropriation of English-Canadian capital, which controlled 80% of the sector, and its transfer to the Quebec bourgeoisie. Despite the generous compensation offered, the Canadian bourgeoisie opposed the move. The financial syndicate (the Royal Bank and the Bank of Montreal), at one with Shawinigan Water and Power, one of the finest jewels in the crown of the Canadian bourgeoisie, tried to block the operation by refusing to lend to the Quebec government the $500 million necessary for nationalization. The government was then successful in concluding a financing agreement with Halsey Stewart of New York. Seeing that a profitable transaction was about to escape them completely, the English-Canadian capitalists then decided to accept the government's conditions and formed a consortium with the First Boston Corporation. Thanks to its alliance with American capital, the local bourgeoisie achieved its first major victory over Canadian capital. It was a sign of things to come.

One noteworthy aspect of the role of Hydro-Québec is the promotion of a francophone Quebec economic elite. Francophones make up over 90% of management and employees and French is the working language. This differs from the policy of several companies before nationalization. By the end of 1967, 297 of the 365 top positions at Hydro-Québec were held by French Canadians. In 1962, only 12% of the Shawinigan engineers had been French speaking.

Since 1976, the Quebec government has whittled away at the autonomy of Hydro-Québec, which was largely dependent on the goodwill of the legislators. In May 1978, the government tabled Bill 41, which made changes in the charters of Hydro-Québec and the Société d'énergie de la Baie James. According to Bernard Descoteaux of *Le Devoir*:

> Hydro-Québec will now have to act within the framework of the energy policies of the Quebec government. The government intends to tighten its control by clearly making Hydro its agent as far as energy production is concerned, and by modernizing the company's structure and management.[36]

Henceforth, the management of energy demands will be the responsibility of the government; it will set what percentage of total energy needs is to be made up of electricity. The government may thus oppose the construction of new hydroelectric power stations. Second, the government will appoint the president of the executive committee and the members of the board of directors of Hydro. There is provision for an important number of positions on the board for government representatives, notably from the Ministry of Energy. The terms of the directors will be five years, rather than 10, as had been the case for the five members of the Hydro Commission. Yvan Guay of *La Presse* went so far as to write that "the new law will make Hydro an extension of the state by abolishing a large part of its autonomy."[37] It is indisputable, however, that the government's initiative has reduced the room to manoeuvre enjoyed by its most important state corporation.

Sidbec

Created in 1964, Sidbec was given the mandate to become involved in all stages of steel production: mining, research, processing, distribution, and sale of finished products. As was the case for Hydro-Québec, one of its objectives concerned Quebec capitalists as a whole: the encouragement of the development of metal-processing industries by supplying steel at competitive prices.

In concrete terms, however, the creation of Sidbec had much broader ramifications. On the one hand, the government chose to develop in its midst a veritable industrial giant. In 1982, with sales of $440 million and assets of $851 million, Sidbec was among the major manufacturing firms in Quebec. In July 1977, the PQ government gave a new share capital injection of $126 million; it was estimated that Sidbec had necessitated more than $1 billion worth of government investment. (Sidbec has completed a $600 million project at Fire Lake to exploit an important iron ore deposit and thus to complete its integration.)

On the other hand, the creation of Sidbec was an attempt to break the Canadian bourgeoisie's monopoly on steel. Until recently, despite the abundance of iron ore in the province, companies in Quebec had to pay a much higher price for their steel than those in Ontario. This situation, maintained by the large Ontario steel plants, prevented the Quebec metal industries from developing. Quebec was producing only 8% of Canadian steel, compared to Ontario's 80%. As Parizeau emphasized in 1972, one of Sidbec's objectives was "to break up market structures, established by firms, which were hindering the normal development of a whole industrial sector: the mechanical engineering industries."[38]

Compared to the Ontario giants, Sidbec is still relatively small. It has succeeded, however, in wrestling away part of the Quebec market from the English-Canadian bourgeoisie. The company remains plagued by heavy deficits due to the international situation and its future is uncertain.

The Société québécoise d'exploration minière

Soquem was formed in 1965 and, according to its charter, was to participate in mining exploration and development in Quebec. On the whole, the impact of Soquem on the mining industry has been increasing steadily over the last few years.

Soquem has done a remarkable amount of exploration over the last 10 years. Even more important has been the recent tendency to abandon joint ventures with private enterprise in favour of independent projects. In the field of development, the profitable phase of mining operations, Soquem is growing rapidly.

The Bourassa government refused to increase Soquem's budget.[39] The PQ, however, increased its share capital from $45 to $125 million. Of the $80 million increase, at least $60 million is earmarked for development projects. This demonstrates the political will for Soquem to continue to grow, as well as a major change in its orientation.

Furthermore, the government has considerably tightened its control over Soquem. Its charter was modified in early 1978 (Bill 82), obliging the firm to submit its development plan for approval each year. The Mine Act was also amended (Bill 27) to make Soquem "the exploration arm of the Ministry of Natural Resources." According to *Le Soleil*, "Soquem traditionally owed its autonomy to annual underwriting of its share capital by the Ministry of Finance. With Quebec's decision to combine this with grants, Soquem has just lost its independent status.[40] This immediately brought the resignation of the president, Côme Carbonneau, who refused "to see Soquem become a mere agent of the government."[41]

The Société québécoise d'initiative agro-alimentaire

Soquia is another state corporation destined to play an important role in the food industry. The corporation became "respectable" in 1977 when the PQ decided to increase its share capital from $10 to $40 million. The main Soquia investment to date is its $11 million participation in Culinar (38.6% of shares). This participation was politically motivated. According to Agriculture minister Jean Garon, the government wanted to "prevent a truly Quebec company from being taken over by a firm whose head office is outside Quebec."[42] This is consistent with earlier statements by Garon concerning the "nationalist" vocation of Soquia. He clearly indicated that the principal mandate of the corporation was "to preserve and increase Quebec control over the food industry" and that Soquia would cooperate only with "companies with a majority of Quebec capital."[43]

Finally, there is the nationalization of Asbestos Corporation and the setting up of the Société nationale de l'amiante (SNA). The plans of the PQ represent a major retreat from its electoral program, which promised a majority control over the sector. The "wisdom" of the decision can also be questioned, in view of the outdated plants and the low level of integration with international markets. However, once more the Quebec bourgeoisie is taking over an important mining corporation. And it is now certain that the SNA will be directly involved in the processing of finished products. In May 1978, Natural Resources minister Yves Bérubé announced the construction by the SNA of two processing plants at a cost of $11 million.[44]

The Private Sector

The private sector is the weak link in the chain for the Quebec bourgeoisie. This sector has already been studied extensively by André Raynauld, Jorge Niosi, and the Groupe de recherche sur les élites industrielles. I shall therefore merely emphasize some key points, notably the evolution of the overall position of this sector and its links with the Quebec state.

Most of the principal firms of the Quebec circuit are listed in Niosi's article, "The New French-Canadian Bourgeoisie." As mentioned earlier, however, we should remove firms such as Rolland and Power that are part of the Canadian bourgeoisie. In general, observers agree that the Quebec bourgeoisie of the private sector has improved its relative position since 1960 and not simply in the "traditional" sectors. According to the Groupe de recherches sur les élites industrielles, "French Canadians" in Quebec had by 1975 progressed in several sectors since the Raynauld study (with 1961 figures), including transportation equipment (+29%), metal products (+22%), and chemicals (+15.4%). This trend is accompanied by a decline by the English-Canadian bourgeoisie in several sectors. Niosi's list also reveals that most Quebec firms have been assisted by the Quebec state or are linked to it in one way or another.

The Quebec bourgeoisie has also made substantial progress in the financial sector. In fact, financial institutions, including banks, insurance companies, and trust companies remain the principal source of economic power for the Quebec bourgeoisie in the private sector. Because the Banque Nationale owns almost 50% of Canadian chartered-bank branches in Quebec and the Mouvement Desjardins controls a large share of Quebec savings, it is reasonable to assume that well over 50% of Quebec banking assets are controlled by the Quebec bourgeoisie.

On the surface, the Banque Nationale appears divided between the Quebec and the Canadian bourgeoisies. It maintains links with the latter through, for example, joint ownership with the Royal Bank of Roynat. Closer analysis reveals, however, that most major shareholders are Quebeckers, that the majority of industrial loans are made to small and medium-sized francophone firms, that the board of directors is made up primarily of representatives of the Quebec bourgeoisie,[45] that it is the principal banker for the Quebec government and for the cooperative movement, and that it owns or controls Quebec companies jointly with other members of the circuit.

On the whole, the Quebec financial sector has gained much ground since 1960 at the expense of the English-Canadian bourgeoisie. With the

Mouvement Desjardins and the Caisse de dépôt, along with the "private" financial institutions, the Quebec financial axis (in its restricted sense) is becoming more and more complete and self-centred. It is noteworthy, also, that increasingly closer ties have developed between the various components of the network.

Bombardier-MLW and Provigo are good illustrations of the vigour of the local bourgeoisie, and of the primary role played by the state in the development of this bourgeoisie.

With 5,000 employees and some $400 million in assets, Bombardier-MLW is one of the largest manufacturing firms in Quebec. It is also one of the few which sell over 50% of their production outside Canada. In 1974, Bombardier acquired MLW-Worthington, a large producer of transportation equipment. The Quebec state played a primary role in building and developing Bombardier-MLW. In July 1975, Bombardier had a serious need for liquid assets. The Société générale de financement bought 40% of MLW shares from Bombardier for $6.8 million and 16% of Marine shares for $4 million. This transaction strengthened Bombardier's position and enabled it to make new investments. The Caisse de dépôt and the Société de développement industriel have each invested several million dollars in the company.

With assets of $621 million and sales of $3.7 billion in 1982, Provigo is the largest food retailer in Quebec. At present, its market is 55% in Quebec, 35% in other provinces, and 10% in other countries. The fundamental role of the Caisse de dépôt in financing Provigo's consolidation and expansion has already been outlined. The Caisse, for instance, enabled Provigo to acquire Loeb, despite the opposition of the English-Canadian bourgeoisie, or at least part of it (Loeb-Bronfman).[46] The recent takeover of Dominion Stores also involved financial support from the Caisse. Provigo has an important impact in Quebec and hardly evokes indifference from its competitors. According to Michel Roesler of *La Presse:*

> Provigo annoys its competitors. Very irritating are the share of the Quebec market it is acquiring, its efficiency, its aggressiveness (Provigo is spreading into Ontario), its low vulnerability in price wars, etc. At Steinberg's, it is unsinuated that behind Provigo there is the Caisse de dépôt, and therefore the government of Quebec.[47]

Even if the trend is towards monopolies, the economic weight and the potential of at least certain small and medium-sized companies should not be underestimated. From 1970 to 1980, these companies—which are 60% controlled by Quebec francophones—had a more rapid growth rate than any other category. Although often linked to monopolies through subcontracting, they can be launching pads for future monopolies. The Quebec government, through the Caisse and the SDI and more recently the Centre de recherche industrielle du Québec and the Sociétés de développement de l'entreprise québécoise, devotes a fair amount of energy to their amalgamation, concentration, and increased profitability.

Finally, some essential elements of the private-sector Quebec bourgeoisie are not included in Niosi's list. The best example is engineering firms. The fundamental importance of these firms at the present stage of capitalism has already been demonstrated by Christian Palloix and others. In terms of assets and number of employees, the approximately 400 firms of consulting engineers in Quebec have considerable economic weight.

The Quebec Bourgeoisie and the PQ

It would be naive and inaccurate to state that the PQ is the political vehicle chosen by an aware and united Quebec bourgeoisie for the promotion of its interests. It would be even more ridiculous to claim, as does Jorge Niosi, that the French-Canadian bourgeoisie has no connection with the PQ, which remains a petty-bourgeois party run by "wordsmiths"[48] such as journalists, professors, and lawyers.

Not content with claiming that it is possible for a government of a capitalist country not to be bourgeois, Niosi discovers in the wordsmiths a new social class. Niosi believes that the PQ is not a bourgeois party because of its petty-bourgeois leadership. As Gilles Bourque rightly emphasizes, "We must never confuse the interests defended by a party in the final analysis with the class position of its average political executives, its elected members, or its favourite supporters."[49]

In fact, what is essential is not the class position of the leaders of the PQ, but the objective interests served and defended by its policies. Moreover, the leadership of practically all Canadian political parties, including those in power, is petty bourgeois, but this has never prevented these various parties from pursuing bourgeois policies.

Niosi also examines the political options of the French-Canadian bourgeoisie and concludes that it is federalist and Liberal. In fact, according to Niosi, "the Liberal party, whether federal or provincial, appears to be the most likely channel for the interests of the new francophone bourgeoisie."[50] He then comes back to the fact that the bourgeoisie is not *Péquiste* and that the PQ is therefore not a bourgeois party.

Niosi's view is incorrect for three main reasons. First, as emphasized above, the class position of a party and a government is determined by the policies and not by the partisan options of the various social classes. Second, when he gives a Canadian definition to the francophone bourgeoisie, Niosi amputates two of its principal components and thus arrives at an inaccurate generalization about the political behaviour of the Quebec bourgeoisie. Finally, Niosi's conclusions ignore the empirically verifiable fact that there are very real political and partisan differences between the Canadian and the Quebec bourgeoisies.

It should be remembered that businessmen tend to combine caution and opportunism in politics. An analysis of the political declarations of the leaders of the Quebec bourgeoisie, as defined here, also demonstrates the need for certain qualifications, even if, after all, the political allegiance of the bourgeois is of little importance. The following are a few examples.

Several directors of state corporations have made declarations favourable to the PQ. One is Jean-Paul Gignac, the former president of Sidbec, who stated that his firm was "an important instrument for decolonization" and that "for the first time in Quebec, we have a true statesman at the head of the government, a leader who has more vision than the others, who puts things in the right perspective. And I find that very encouraging."[51] The same tendency can be observed in the leaders of the cooperative movement. Alfred Rouleau, the president of the Mouvement Desjardins, has been showing greater nationalist leanings. In a speech in France on January 12, 1978, he used language characteristic of the PQ and seemed to be inclining towards its constitutional option:

> We have steadfastly resisted, for three centuries, the many open and discreet attacks of the forces of assimilation, and the present is even more serious for the future of Quebeckers as a people. . . . The present situation justifies all the more our demands for adequate decision-making powers for the government of Quebec. . . . I do not see how Quebeckers, in this search for a durable and viable solution to the Canadian crisis, could accept proposals that do not guarantee them the political and fiscal powers necessary for their economic and cultural life.[52]

At the Pépin-Robarts hearings,the Conseil de la coopération du Québec, the official voice of the cooperative movement, took a much-criticized position on the federal government:

> The central power can no longer behave as if Quebec were one of its 10 administrative regions. . . . Under "renewed federalism" or "sovereignty-association," Quebeckers know they can count on the support of the cooperative movement. Our companies are Quebec companies, and we remain calmly confident in the future of Quebec.[53]

Even in the private sector, the Quebec bourgeoisie adopts qualified and rather nationalist positions. The Montreal Chamber of Commerce, comprising mainly small and medium-sized Quebec companies and one of whose goals is "the economic promotion of Quebeckers," complained of "the anglophone domination of centres of economic decision . . . with the result that investments are channelled towards anglophone sectors favouring the creation of firms and of services which belong to members of this linguistic group." This contrasts, of course, with the positions taken by anglophone employers' associations, or the Conseil du patronat. Declarations made, since the election of the PQ, by Germain Perrault, president of the Banque Nationale, and Michel Bélanger, president of the Banque Provinciale, are along the same lines. Both suggest "important changes in the real division of powers in Canada."[54]

An examination of the briefs submitted to the Pépin-Robarts Commission reveals clear differences between "the francophone wing of the Canadian bourgeoisie," notably Power, Rolland, and Canada Steamship Lines—which are strongly anti-separatist—and the Quebec bourgeoisie. Louis

Desmarais, for instance, who gave up the presidency of Canada Steamship Lines, an important Power subsidiary, to become president of the Council for Canadian Unity, has accused the PQ of a "disdain for fundamental individual rights and freedoms since its election." He has also suggested that Quebec should seek greater integration with the rest of Canada.

The Parti Québécois is, in fact, a bourgeois party. As I have shown elsewhere,[55] the essential goal of its program is the expansion of the Quebec bourgeoisie at the expense of the Canadian bourgeoisie. That is, moreover, the only way that the "petty bourgeoisie" of the PQ can itself hope to develop. The aim of the PQ is therefore to a large extent "to make the Quebec bourgeoisie a hegemonic political fraction."[56] It will attempt by all possible means to strengthen the state, the main support for Quebec capital, and to promote the development of the Quebec bourgeoisie in several sectors controlled by the Canadian bourgeoisie and the federal state, including transportation, telecommunications, the financial sector, electrical utilities and equipment. That the PQ program is a threat for the Canadian bourgeoisie can easily be proved by the latter's violent reactions and declarations. The departure of Sun Life and all the other threats of closure are eloquent in this regard.

Whatever may be the outcome of the "constitutional debate," the more crumbs the PQ succeeds in obtaining from Ottawa, the more the local bourgeoisie will profit. The stronger the Quebec state becomes, the more the development of the Quebec bourgeoisie is ensured.

Conclusion

The Quebec bourgeoisie remains very fragile. It is also obvious that its ambitions, with or without sovereignty-association, will be only partially realized. We must not underestimate the counteroffensive by the Canadian bourgeoisie or American hegemony.

However, the Quebec bourgeoisie has become much stronger and more cohesive since 1960. It has also been, for some years now, more aware of itself and its political interests. This is partly confirmed by the PQ itself. Unlike the early 1960s, the material bases for the PQ program are now in place in Quebec. In 1960, an autonomist or independentist government would have been quickly discredited by the financial syndicate and would not have been able, on its own, to effect the bulk of productive investments in Quebec. At present, however, the Quebec bourgeoisie has enough cards in its hand to hope to negotiate either a new division of powers or relative autonomy.

At the strategical level, the project of the Quebec bourgeoisie and the PQ is potentially a tremendous threat to the stability of the Canadian state. In fact, to the extent that the Quebec bourgeoisie succeeds in undermining part of the infrastructural and superstructural bases of the Canadian bourgeoisie, a considerable weakening of the repressive structure of the Canadian state can be expected.

Finally, while this study has concentrated on the nationalism of the bourgeoisie, this does not at all mean that all nationalism is bourgeois. National oppression crosses all social classes. We must therefore take away from the bourgeoisie its monopoly on the national question.

Notes

1. See Pierre Fournier, "Vers une grande bourgeoisie canadienne-française?" paper given at the Congrès des études socialistes (June 1976), *The Quebec Establishment* (Montreal: Black Rose Books, 1976), and several recent articles on state corporations and the Parti Québécois.
2. Jorge Niosi, "The New French-Canadian Bourgeoisie." *Studies in Political Economy* 1 (1979).
3. Ibid., p. 145.
4. Ibid., p. 119.
5. Gilles Bourque, "Le Parti québécois dans les rapports de classe," *Politique Aujourd'hui* 7-8 (1978), p. 87.
6. Dorval Brunelle, "L'intervention de l'Etat dans l'économie et la question du rapport entre le fédéral et les provinces," *Les Cahiers du Socialisme* 1 (1978), p. 79.
7. Bourque, op. cit., p. 87.
8. Ibid., p. 88.
9. Niosi, op. cit., p. 140.
10. Ibid., p. 148.
11. Ibid., p. 140.
12. P. Pouliot, "Les Producteurs laitiers craignent la puissance des grandes coopératives," *La Presse* (Nov. 25, 1976).
13. M. Morin, "Progression très rapide du secteur coopératif dans l'assurance," *Le Soleil* (Dec. 22, 1976). Four Quebec insurance firms—Desjardins, Prenor, Commerce, and La Laurentienne—rank among the top six in the province.
14. L. Cloutier, "L'Union de Montréal assumera sa propre expansion," *Le Devoir* (Nov. 4, 1977).
15. "Importante victoire pour les caisses populaires," *La Presse* (May 19, 1978).
16. Ibid.
17. Ibid.
18. See Pierre Fournier, *The Quebec Establishment* and "Vers une grande bourgeoisie"; *Les Sociétés d'Etat et les objectifs économiques du Québec* (Québec: Editeur officiel du Québec, 1978).
19. Niosi, op. cit., p. 122-23.
20. Niosi, "Le Gouvernement du PQ, le capital américain, et le capital canadien" (unpublished paper, UQÀM, 1978), p. 6.
21. Ibid., p. 6.
22. J. Parizeau et B. Landry, "Les relations entre le gouvernement et les sociétés d'Etat," confidential memo to the Quebec cabinet (Jan. 14, 1977), p. 2.
23. Ibid., p. 2.
24. Ibid., p. 4.
25. P. Bellemare, "Le Ministre Tremblay aura ses cerbères dans plusieurs sociétés d'Etat," *La Presse* (June 9, 1978).

26. Ibid.
27. See L. Salvas-Broussard et al., "Modèle économétrique québécois et optimum macro-économique," *L'Actualité économique* 48: 3 (1973), pp. 349-78.
28. See *Le Capitalisme au Québec*, ch. 3.
29. See "Quebec-potential for development: DREE programs now in second phase," *The Financial Post* (Oct. 15, 1977).
30. Groupe de recherche sur les élites industrielles au Québec, *Les Industriels au Québec et leur rôle dans le développement économique* (Québec: Editeur officiel, Jan. 1976).
31. See J. Parizeau, "Claude Prieur, un grand commis de l'Etat," *Québec-Presse* (April 15, 1973).
32. J. Parizeau, "La Caisse de dépôt, notre grande inconnue," *Québec-Presse* (March 26, 1972).
33. Ibid.
34. Société de développement industriel, *Rapport Annuel 1976* (Montreal, 1977), p. 5.
35. Société de développement industriel, "Dossier de programmes 1977-78: révision des activités de la SDI" (internal document, Aug. 9, 1976).
36. B. Descoteaux, "Québec resserre son contrôle sur l'Hydro," *Le Devoir* (May 26, 1978).
37. Y. Guay, "Le contrôle de l'Hydro," *La Presse* (June 2 1978).
38. J. Parizeau, "Pour apprendre à se servir de l'Etat," *Québec-Presse* (June 25, 1972).
39. J.P. Gagné, "Cournoyer refuse d'augmenter le budget de Soquem," *La Presse* (June 19, 1976).
40. J. Forget, "Le Président Carbonneau remet sa démission," *Le Soleil* (June 6 1977).
41. Ibid.
42. M. Lestage, "Soquia espère réaliser ses propres projets," *Le Soleil* (June 2, 1977).
43. "Soquia collaborera seulement avec des entreprises à capital majoritairement québécois," *Le Soleil* (May 5, 1977).
44. P.P. Gagné, "La Wayagamack servira à la transformation de l'amiante," *La Presse* (May 20, 1978).
45. The Banque Nationale board of directors includes directors of Lévesque-Beaubien, Bombardier-MLW, Omer De Serres, La Laurentienne, and Le Groupe Commerce.
46. See F. Demers, "Faut-il être fier de nos hommes d'affaires?" *Zone Libre* (Oct. 1977), p. 18.
47. M. Roesler, "Provigo tire avantage de la guerre des prix et épuise ses concurrents," *La Presse* (Sept. 9 1976).
48. Niosi, "French-Canadian Bourgeoisie," p. 148.
49. Bourque, op. cit., p. 90.
50. Niosi, op. cit., p. 146.
51. P. Gravel, "Sidbec, un instrument privilégié de décolonisation," *La Presse* (July 30 1977).
52. A. Rouleau, "L'Evolution du Mouvement des caisses populaires Desjardins," *Le Devoir* (Jan. 13 1978).

53. Conseil de la coopération du Québec, brief submitted to the Pépin-Robarts Commission (Montreal, Jan. 18 1978), p. 2.
54. "Le Québec doit apprendre à vivre la croissance lente," *Le Devoir* (Nov. 9 1977).
55. See Pierre Fournier, "Le Parti québécois et les pouvoirs économiques," in J.F. Léonard (ed.), *La Chance du Coureur* (Montreal: Editions Nouvelle-Optique, 1978).
56. Bourque, op. cit., p. 90.

Part IV/The Regional Question

Until recently, the regional question in Quebec has been remote from major political debates, always leaving the foreground to the larger national question. Postwar centralist trends in advanced industrialized states—particularly in Canada—may be pointed to as constituting the precipitating factor in this sublimation of the regional dimension.

Jalbert's contribution is particularly interesting since her article seeks to examine regionalism from a theoretical perspective. It begins by critiquing contemporary approaches to the regional question, then suggests that if the concept of region is to be truly understood it must apply equally to geographic areas as to social movements. Finally, the author discusses regionalism in terms of the larger arena of state authority in Canada and Quebec.

Carey-Bélanger zeroes in on what has become a most cherished case study in Quebec community development: the eastern Quebec area. In this analysis, the regional question is addressed by the state in terms of collective intervention, which in turn is seen as a means to organize, coordinate, and promote participation. Three examples are selected and analyzed in light of their internal dynamic as well as in relation to the forces and constraints in the broader societal context.

In concluding this part, Gagnon differs from traditional emphases that stress the national question and ignore local and regional power structures. This analysis therefore provides a distinctive account of the character of Quebec politics. The author finds the new-middle-class thesis unsatisfactory, since it tends to ignore the role played by other political forces in Quebec provincial politics. The power structure is defined in terms of areas of specific intervention rather than channels between centre and periphery. In this context, it can be argued that, while the political and administrative reforms of the 1960s in Quebec correspond to the establishment of channels between the state and the regions, the rise of popular groups more accurately represents the emergence of new seats of power.

Chapter 13/Regionalism and the Regional Question*

Lizette Jalbert

The trend towards centralization, which is common to all advanced states, has for some time now encountered resistance from movements whose principal aim is the defence of local or regional autonomy. Thus, as the state's role continues to expand, conflict with the regional level increases. As has been the case with many other controversial issues, regional disputes have taken on significant political overtones. They unite those forces opposed to a system of centralized authority designed to promote unity and social interdependence. Regional movements call this function of the state into question, focusing their objections on the mechanisms by which specific differences are either granted or refused recognition. Indeed, they claim that, when the state does take certain differences into account, such recognition is partial and is altered to suit the state's goals of unity and social interdependence. Specific differences are not considered in themselves, but only in a complementary fashion and in a functional relationship to the larger society.

This dichotomy—the simultaneous granting and refusal of formal recognition—that characterizes the state's rhetoric and operation is contradictory only in appearance.[1] It plays a vital role in maintaining a minimum level of consensus without which the social fabric would begin to unravel. It provides the basis for defining or imposing the imaginary collective identity built up around the nation-state. The individual is therefore alone against the state, devoid of any other basis for self-identification. Moreover, the dichotomy legitimizes the liberal state and grants it a role that transcends the individual's role. All citizens are equal before the law. On those occasions when it does recognize the existence of specific differences, the state takes special care to create the illusion that its objectives are nonetheless in the nation's general interest.

By contrast, regionalist movements demand formal recognition of diversity. They point to the existence within the greater society of special social entities whose criteria for inclusion in the system and whose forms of social interdependence fall outside the limits of the political and administra-

---

*This chapter is drawn largely from ideas that I have developed in two other works: "La question régionale comme enjeu politique," *Espace régional et nation* (Montreal: Boréal Express, 1983), and "Régionalisme et crise de l'Etat," *Sociologie et Société* XII: 2 (Oct. 1980). Translated from the French by Roger Ryan (French Department, Concordia University) and Pierre Alvarez (Political Studies Department, Queen's University).

tive categories and structures, which are imposed more or less arbitrarily by the state. In support of their claims, these movements emphasize the unique social, cultural, and historical patterns characteristic of their particular regions. Though they may vary in nature, the demands of such movements are invariably linked to those factors that set their community apart from the rest of society. Movements automatically define their goals in relation to their communities' special traits. This does not imply that the empirical basis to which members turn for self-identification is necessarily identical or permanently fixed once chosen (as it might include any of culture, language, territory, or institutions).

The problem is that regional identities may grow so strong that they may cause a breakdown of the political and social order. The sociological analysis of regionalism has therefore become a matter of current concern. In this chapter I analyze politics in Quebec and the rest of Canada by using the perspective of regionalism and by using regionalism as a main point of reference.

The "Modular Conception" of Regionalism

In Canada, as elsewhere, the discussion of regionalism has long revolved around a few simple arguments, each of which has been presented as sufficient in itself. At different times, regionalism was seen to have emerged from the unequal, though natural, distribution of physical resources, or to have sprung from cultural traditions—language, ethnicity, or religion, for example—or to have been the inevitable consequence of a country's geographic immensity. When regionalism is presented solely in terms of uneven economic development (defined as the unequal distribution of physical resources), when it concentrates exclusively on cultural patterns without taking the slightest account of the supporting institutional and economic material base, or as soon as it becomes solely a function of territorial boundaries—with no thought given to the overriding arbitrariness with which frontiers are set—the discussion loses itself in endless reductionism. Thus, a revitalized approach to the problem should steer clear of both the naturalistic concept of region and the other explanations that tend to reduce it to a single dimension, be it narrowly economic, cultural, or political. Some theories will thus be rejected outright: the "economic theory of comparative advantages," which lends itself to a justification of specialized regional vocations and disparities in development; the "culture-based approach of the regional personality," which explains the opposition of certain regions as a manifestation of a backward mentality opposed to progress; the "empirical arguments" of geographers who maintain that physical factors alone explain not only the origin of regions but the determination of their boundaries as well. In other words, a discussion fails to convey the actual richness and complexity of the problem if that discussion does not take all of the above factors into account. It is therefore necessary to appreciate the linkage of all the structural and conjunctural elements that constitute a region. (In this chapter, *conjunctural* refers to political as well as economic aspects of social reality.)

In addition, to think—or, rather, to rethink—what is meant by *region* supposes that it may no longer be thought of as a natural and functional phenomenon, present once and for all as an immutable and homogeneous constant. It is therefore appropriate to affirm that any theoretical treatment of regionalism emerges from the recognition that it can be defined only with reference to its own process of self-generation in time and space. To put the matter in sociological terms, it is not the region as a fixed entity that is the focal point for analysis, but the dynamics of its actual construction.

The Populist Approach to Intercommunity Conflicts

One approach—the "populist"—has led to a discounting by abstraction of class divisions that have had a substantial impact on the phenomenon of region. This theoretical model has focused more attention on intercommunity conflicts and, by the same token, treated class conflicts as of only secondary importance.[2] Yet it is accepted that class conflicts are constantly operating within the process of communal fragmentation that regionalism embodies. In Canada, as elsewhere, class interests have been active whenever a regional movement has taken form.

Only by taking class struggle into account can be understood fully what appears at first to be a conflict between unevenly developed regions or a conflict of regions against the central authority—and opposition of dominant ethnic and cultural groups to dominated groups. The regional dimension should not be shunted aside, as if class were not a basic structural phenomenon of all contemporary capitalist and socialist societies. This is not an empty exhortation to class struggle. It is in fact possible to demonstrate historically that this problem cuts across all levels of regional and national conflict, while at the same time being coloured by these same conflicts. It is hardly necessary to point out that such a meshing of social phenomena cannot be detected mechanically through the eyes of what might be termed a marxist "purified perception" (in French, "immaculée perception marxiste"). The framework adopted here is not a substitute for a concrete analysis. In fact, the linkage among regionalism, nationalism, and class struggle is never given. The form the linkage takes can vary considerably, depending on the prevailing historical conditions.[3]

Nevertheless, this critique of the populist approach does not seek to reduce the regional question to that of class struggle. That class struggle does not provide all the answers is commonly accepted, just as it is accepted that a society is the product of a multiplicity of contradictions that must be overcome if the society is to continue. Nevertheless, just as it is absurd to label as epiphenomenal any other social division not directly subject to the class-struggle mechanism—which has long been the practice within the orthodox marxist tradition—so we can appreciate the tendency to deny its influence as an idealist movement whose sole reason for existence lies in covert political stances. An approach to the region that does not address itself to class certainly cannot do justice to the entire reality of the regional phenomenon.

By accentuating the homogeneous quality of one subculture vis-à-vis another, this variation of a society fragmented on the basis of cultural communities minimizes the contradictions within each one of them. It cannot do otherwise than remain unaware of both the class struggle at work within every segment of these communities and what their linkage to each other depends on. This highly simplified perspective results in a partially if not totally erroneous picture of the structure of society as a whole.

Moreover, regional demands vis-à-vis the central authority take on a class dimension even if it is not explicitly expressed, since they actually refer to a class-based power structure. Regional opposition, which calls the state's centralized authority into question, is undoubtedly aimed at the power of the dominant classes, who seek to impose a form of social organization to their advantage. Once again the denial of the real causes of social inequalities and rankings legitimizes this position of domination. Thus, resistance from regional movements is a challenge to both the state's management of specific differences and the political domination exercised by those sectors of society that control the instruments of economic development.

Unity or Fragmentation

The regional question has also been the source of conflicting interpretations of the evaluation of the consequences from the internally contradictory process of unification and fragmentation which modern society must deal with. If we reduce these interpretations to their essentials, two approaches emerge whose terms vary according to the point of departure from which an examination of the phenomenon of region proceeds.

A technocratic viewpoint tends to be adopted when the cleavage into regions is viewed from the centre. Society is conceived as a unified rather than diversified whole. More often than not, regional aspects are ignored. Even if their existence is at times acknowledged, their potential for fragmenting the social order is not admitted. The state attempts to deal with the problem of region on its own terms by casting it in a mold of its own choosing, then controlling it by establishing policies reflecting centrally defined objectives. Thus, the state attempts to contain the opposition movement where possible. An administrative apparatus will be designed and made operational with a view to formalizing the relations between the centre and the periphery. The intervention system will be given the task of disorganizing the regional protest groups, rendering them politically neutral and, by the same token, keeping up a façade of unity.

The crises that stem from regionalism will be viewed as short-term problems that can be resolved by appropriate adjustments. Equilibrium is restored if the integration and self-regulation of the social system is exactly—and paradoxically—achieved through one of three mechanisms: "comparative advantages" that each part or region of the country draws from its union with the whole and its relation to the others; the redistributive capacity of the state; or the cultural richness and diversity from which the system can claim to benefit and, in some cases, of which it can boast.[4]

Seen from the point of view of those who support the resistance movement, regionalism takes on a radically different meaning. It is a movement of self-defence to repulse the invasion of control measures dictated from the centre. The movements seem themselves as ramparts against the strategy of the central authority that seeks to erode what remains of local autonomy. Regional movements go so far as to describe their actions as anti-colonial struggles; such is the tenuous sense of identity with the larger society. These movements see society as a mosaic of subsets whose interlinking bands are particularly strained. Thus, regional movements frequently carry with them feelings of being foreigners in the rest of the country. Their approach also leads them to press their assessment of a near-total atomization of society to the limit. When tension is at its peak, the movements choose a view of society in which the latter is in the throes of a never-ending crisis which is tearing it apart.

To some leaders of regional movements, society is so torn by conflict that breakdown seems logically imminent. However, their reading of the future ignores the possibilities for assimilation which encourages the reconciliation of old antagonisms; as well, crises, because of their purging effect on the system, push the unification trend forward, thereby diffusing crises and rendering them manageable.

A sociological approach that seeks to distance itself from these various overly politicized versions of the phenomenon of regionalism should start from the basis that the process of unification/fragmentation at work within modern society must be analyzed as a function of the conjuncture, not as independent trends and countertrends. Such an approach would avoid the pitfall of viewing every crack in the unity of the structures that organize and transmit authority to be dangerous and atypical in themselves. The capitalist state is a system of contradictions; it will not function only towards unity and centrality. This implies that the sociological analysis will focus on the problem of establishing the critical threshold beyond which the unity of the central authority is shattered. This threshold must at all times be evaluated according to the *rapport de force* in the conjuncture, which is by no means determined once and for all: it remains subject to adjustment either upward or downward.

Towards a Definition of Regionalism

Structures of Social Relationships and Social Movements

As stated earlier, it is necessary to view a region as the result of the sum of social, cultural, economic, and political relationships. Through a distinctive combination of these relationships and by adopting a concrete structure, this complex constitutes a region as a specific space of social relationships. The manner in which the region is generated must also be seen as a dynamic process. As it has been defined, the regional space forms a community in continuous flux, subject to never-ending recombinations in response to shifts in the social relationships of which it is formed and tied to the conjuncture. Various forms of resistance and manifestations of consciousness will correspond, more or less exactly, to different periods. Only when seen from such a perspective does the problem of region assume its full sociological meaning. Moreover, it is only then that the region can be defined as a genuine entity within society whose existence carries implications for the ordering of society as a whole.[5]

It should be made clear that, whenever the term *regionalism* is used in its broad sense, it refers to two related aspects of contemporary social reality. On the one hand, regionalism can be understood as a way of structuring space. The definition of a region, insofar as it is a phenomenon that refers to social structures, has implications for the complex of social relationships that delimit a specific space. On the other hand, regionalism also stands for a social movement. As such, it refers to a community's process of self-affirmation as well as an assertion of its interests.[6]

Regionalism embodies the manner in which a community is divided, fragmented, or atomized; regionalism also represents a movement rich in contradictions generated by such a process. It is not a phenomenon strictly derived from economics or geography. However, as history illustrates, regional movements take shape more readily in one sector of the social landscape than in another. Thus, cultural demands will at one time take precedence over economic issues, while at another time political stresses and strains will give expression to the regional question.

The Result of the Linkage/Resistance Process

The process by which a region is defined also necessarily refers to the restrictions imposed by its linkage with the larger complex of which it is a part. Thus, regions exist by virtue of their meshing into the totality constituted by a given society. Generated within this linkage relationship, a region defines its specificity by way of this bond. Whether this specificity is imposed or actively sought, it remains the principal criterion of regional identification with the relationship between an area and the society as a whole. As part of a more complex totality, the regional space will therefore define its linkage to society according to an assimilation/diversification expression of opposition.

More concretely, in order to analyze the process by which a regional entity is generated and transformed, the larger society to which it is bound must be identified. The latter constitutes a unit that both imposes and is subjected to a structure. In western capitalist societies, which is the case discussed here, it is structured historically by social relationships that take shape and tend towards unification, homogenization, and assimilation. It is also a unit that imposes a structure based on uneven development of the accentuation of differences among, domination over, and dependence on its various regions. Thus explained, some light is shed on both the internally contradictory process by which a region is generated and the character of the struggles that arise in the course of this process. Linkage and homogenization will be paired with resistance and the claim to the right to be different. (The difference discussed here is not the disparity generated by the logic of our system, but the difference based on local autonomy, which includes full control over economic, cultural, and political development.) It is therefore preferable to speak of diversification rather than differentiation in order to account for the regional resistance groups' claims to the right to be different.[7] The conclusion to be drawn is that the emergence of regional movements is a phenomenon consistent with the internal contradiction of the linkage-resistance dynamic.

Recasting the Forms of Alliances

The regional question has an impact within the political arena as well. To the extent that it reveals the relationships of dependence, domination, and disparity to which the complex and fragmented societies in which we live are fated, this question carries a considerable potential for splitting the social and political order. Regional movements have for a long time fought centralization on every front. This trend towards a centralized organization of power is becoming more and more pronounced within all advanced states, although its roots go back to the very foundations of these states. Thus, the concentration of power, as much economic as political, was soon perceived as a violation of what were considered fundamental rights. Thus, centralization has become the subject of criticisms which at times have been violent.

In whatever regime they have sprung up, regional resistance movements, by calling into question the relationship of the social unit at the local level with the state, constitute a searching inquiry into the regime's practice, as far as the respect for the right to be different is concerned—in other words, the state's respect for democracy. As François Rangeau has said, "decentralization" and "democracy" are becoming linked in a virtually systematic association. To speak of democracy is also to speak of a belief in the state's ability to ensure equality among its citizens and a measure of redistribution among its regions. From the moment the state gives the appearance that it cannot fulfill the ideals on which the social consensus was built, popular and regional dissatisfaction begins to surface. Then, the bond by which it sought to link itself with its citizens and regions becomes strained to the point of being considered meaningless. Thus, when communication between the regional identity and that of the state breaks down—that is, when the bond between them is severed at the level of an allegiance to a common frame of reference—the problem of region can give rise to a crisis of the legitimacy of the nation-state.[8]

Under our system, the first movements of regional opposition were initiated by groups of people and by classes who placed themselves on the fringes of both the advance of reigning capitalism and the bourgeois institutions and political institutions that were predominantly oriented towards centralization. Are we to say that the resistance initiated by these movements was anti-capitalist in tone? An affirmative answer is by no means inevitable. It was more often the case that the movements represented a rampart of defence for those classes threatened by the monopolistic evolution of capitalism, a development that subjected them to implacable forces tending to erode their time-honoured ways of living and methods of production. Aware that the direction of change was slipping from their grasp and threatening their position within society, the traditional petty bourgeoisie and the peasantry in particular, as well as certain nonmonopolistic elements of the bourgeoisie, were able to unite to form a class alliance imbued with regional concerns.

Within capitalist societies, to which the discussion will be restricted, regional demands have taken another turn within the last few years. The growth of these new movements has been classified as a crisis, symptoms of which could already be detected in the 1960s. At that time, the welfare state was showing signs of failure and was no longer able by means of social-assistance programs to fill in the gaps left by the chaotic development of postwar capitalism. Because the liberal capitalist state could come up with but one solution to the crisis—namely the imposition of a yet higher degree of centralization—a new combination of class alliances centred on the problem of region has materialized.

Regional movements have retained as much social pluralism as ever, but now, rather than being the preferred vehicle of classes and their various strata or segments oriented towards idealized values from the past, they prefer to enlist support from all social groups, be they of longstanding or relative newcomers who have no fear of change in itself. It is nonetheless evident that the nature of this change is being called into question and that a certain type of capitalist development—if not capitalism itself—is being challenged.

This broad analysis of regional movements within a capitalist system in the process of consolidating its position has only touched on some of the main features. As always, the regional question continues to generate various responses and is the exclusive domain of neither the right nor the left. In every case, however, this situation underscores the importance of the regional space as far as the political arena, the balance of powers, and class alliances are concerned. It becomes apparent that both regional underdevelopment and, from a political perspective, the rigidly controlled levers of powers have contributed to an outburst of nonconformist attitudes and practices. Even though the regional movements have not restricted themselves to stable class groupings, they have attracted radical elements who, depending on the stage of development, are sensitive to political conditions. Though their contours are often ill defined and their appeal and support broadly based, regional movements remain nonetheless dominated by a single class or class fraction. Moreover, they have unleashed currents of feeling that it would be wise, for the future of society, not to underestimate.

Regionalism in Canada and Quebec

It is important to note that to reflect on the problem of regionalism in Canada in no way implies that the question of Quebec ought to be reduced to a strictly regional dimension. In spite of everything, this dimension is important for an understanding of Quebec as much as for the rest of Canada. The regional dimension of the Quebec experience has been ignored for too long by the analyses of that province, as if in Canada there exist a national question that concerns Quebec and a regional question that concerns the other provinces or regions. Although analyses of these questions tend to overlap—hence the difficulties in distinguishing their particular consequences—each of them adds to the delineation of Canada's sociopolitical realities.

The approach advocated here grasps the importance of the dual movement at the heart of the regional question in Canada. It can be defined as a constant tension between a trend towards fragmentation and one towards unification. This dual movement has as much of an impact on the preservation of the forms of society as a whole, as it does on the perpetuation of the state and political authority.

The following series of propositions that are intimately linked to each other such that the dual movements, indicated above as essential to the analysis, can be discerned.

1. Because regionalism leads to a relatively uncontrolled unification/fragmentation process operating on the Canadian social makeup, it facilitates the installation of an expanded state structure—10 provincial states and one central state. Over the course of history, this system has been subjected to conflicting pressures which have caused it to swing between the extremes of centralism, on the one hand, and the demands for autonomy of the provincial states on the other. Canada continues to struggle with this question of centralization vs. decentralization without arriving at an acceptable solution to the problem. Many social conflicts are emerging from the wings of this debate, conflicts in which regional dominant classes and popular opposition groups figure prominently.

2. This complex situation, which I term the "dual-state scenario," imposes definite limitations on the functioning of the bourgeois state. These limitations more particularly concern the internal coherence of the state, where the potential cleavage between the federal and provincial branches of the state apparatus is evoked by the existence of several levels of government and administration. These cleavages, or institutional discontinuities, are generally linked to the degree of advancement attained by each of the branches and, hence, by the societies to which they belong. At this level, these cleavages can generate distortions and delays in the framing and implemen-

tation of the state policy. On a more general level, that of the compatibility of separate bureaucratic machineries but still in relation to the specific complexity of the dual state, we can expect the effects of friction between levels to manifest themselves. These are linked more directly to the way in which each bureaucracy, corresponding to these levels, develops its own rules and internal mechanisms or, to put it another way, its own particular interest.[9]

3. Aside from the problem of coherence of state structures, the contradictions which lie at the heart of class power are multiplied by the complexity of the structures of the Canadian state. Thus, at the outset, the problem of the unity of class power is raised precisely to the extent to which the partial autonomy of the provincial state vis-à-vis the central state provides fertile ground in which the growth of local bourgeoisies with potentially conflicting interests is nurtured. What is more, the compromise alliance—itself subject to internal contradictions on which all bourgeois states are built—is complicated in this case. The true limits to the functioning of the Canadian state are encountered at this point. The dual state, by scattering the locations in which the dominant classes organize and represent themselves, heightens the conflicts. It therefore constitutes the source of an eventual weakening that could impede the process of unification of bourgeois power and it tends to maintain a precarious equilibrium. Thus, when the bourgeoisie plunges into the search for a solution to the national-unity dilemma, it is to a large extent searching for a solution to its own problem of unity.

If we insist on the limits imposed by the complexity of the structures of the Canadian state vis-à-vis the unity of class power, it is not due to a static conception of the unitary or centralized state system considered as sole paradigm of capitalist society. Rather, it is in order to indicate that the process of unification must be understood with the help of a grid that deals at the outset with the question of the threshold beyond which the unity of authority throughout the state is shaken.[10]

4. The problem underlying the coherence of state structures and the unity of class power refers to a more fundamental problem, that of class hegemony. This problem has yet to be effectively dealt with. It condenses, at the highest levels of society's mode of functioning, all the contradictions produced by regionalism and the question of national unity. Both generate regions and groups that, when the occasion presents itself, pose threats to the established social order. Whether they were autonomist, nationalist, or regionalist, the opposition's responses to exploitation and oppression constitutes a serious threat to the class seeking to assert itself as the representative of the whole of society.

5. The role of legitimation, among all the roles assumed by the dominant class, has been carried out with the least degree of success.[11] The Canadian bourgeoisie, which is traditionally conservative and rather unimaginative, has always seemed to exercise its control somewhat passively. In these circumstances, it seems astonishing that the system that supports it has succeeded in maintaining itself. Paradoxically, the one factor that seems to account for the relative stability of the situation is regionalism, together with the consequences the various classes have had to suffer. Indeed, if one facet of regionalism has contributed towards weakening the dominant class, the other has, on the contrary, served to counter the negative effects of the first. As a divisive force, regionalism has prevented the development of an autonomous political initiative likely to lead to social transformation. What has contributed to the relative strength of the Canadian bourgeoisie and has helped to maintain its fragile legitimacy has been the weakness of its class adversaries who in turn have had to suffer the divisive effects of regionalism. The control has therefore not needed to be absolute, since the oppressive force of the dominant class has been supported by the difficulty that the subordinate classes have encountered in arriving at an organization and a field of endeavour to deal with all their concerns. The established authority has generally managed to overcome the efforts of these classes to forge, from time to time, an alliance among themselves in response to changing economic conditions. The history of this society and of its dominant class rests, to a certain extent, on this paradox.

6. To explain how the balance of power between classes was struck through the effects of regionalism, it is not sufficient to say that the inability of the Canadian bourgeoisie to impose its legitimacy by way of a coherent program for society was compensated for by the subordinate classes' even more conspicuous lack of unity. To put it more succinctly, this balance rests to a great extent on the institutionalization of a system of relay at the level of the local centres of power. In this way, the leadership of the bourgeoisie has been able to reverse its own weakness relative to the complexity of the apparatus of the Canadian state and turn it to its own advantages. Indeed, as we have seen, the features of this apparatus seemed to present the dominant class with the thorny problem of the distribution of areas of organization and representation. Despite these structural limitations, the dominant class has found a solution to the problem, which has consisted of the implementation at the provincial level of compromise alliances of varied complexity and longevity among the various segments of the bourgeoisie, the petty bourgeoisie, and certain social categories such as the clergy. The leadership of the bourgeoisie, by leaving it up to other classes and segments or social categories to provide for social cohesion and to establish its legitimacy "by proxy," was practising the politics of the possible and unifying bourgeois power under its aegis.[12]

7. What emerges from the preceding is that the provincial states fulfill an important strategic role in the organization and perpetuation of the system of class leadership/domination. They function as linkages within this system not only because they provide the means of internal unification of bourgeois power but also—and especially—because they intervene directly in the reproduction of class divisions by working for the consolidation of the compromise alliances vis-à-vis the subordinate classes. As a result, it is not surprising to note that historically the provincial states have borne the brunt of the pressure from the subordinate classes. As sounding boards for social struggles, they have been able to give warning to soften the first blows of class struggle, before the central state could be hit. The dominant class has thereby been protected to a certain extent by the provincial vanguards.[13]

8. Nevertheless, this mechanism of class leadership through intermediaries does not do away with the contradictions ever present at the core of class power. The danger of a crisis erupting and throwing into question the superstructure of previously established alliances has been pointed out.

On the one hand, the dual state risks that the provincial states, which have considerable resources at their disposal and the appropriate means for legitimating hegemony, may (through the intermediary of "relay classes" or other classes that have remained passive up to that point) act against the claims of the class fraction that had considered its hegemony as firmly established. On the other hand, a risk arises from the difficulty of this class fraction in fulfilling its role directly and on its own as this leads to a very particular dependence vis-à-vis the relay classes. In the absence of revolution, the ultimate risk lies in the fact that the provincial-state segments act as points of resistance for classes, class fractions, or social categories whose interests are secondarily incompatible with the leadership of the dominant class, so as to not only go beyond the phase of bargaining for concessions, which is peculiar to the relays, but even challenge its power to the point of attempting to supplant it.

To this end, these anti-establishment elements will generally rely on regionalist or nationalist demands. Moreover, these elements have already forged (as is frequently the case with relays) or claim to be able to forge links with foreign imperialist capital. If these links are brought into the analysis, they can put the anti-establishment elements into touch with strategies of alliance that they might use in the event of a breakdown in the compromise. Then we can see just how delicate is the situation generated by the complexity of the Canadian state structure and by the stratified organization of power for which it calls.

9. The leadership of the hegemony wishes to be spared the total loss of control it had been threatened with during the 1930s and the Second World War—and during the latest constitutional crisis overlayed onto the international economic crisis. The leadership continues to attempt to strengthen the centralization process at the federal state level. More than ever it seeks to establish the latter as the preferred setting for the organization and reproduction of the power bloc and to turn it into an organization model for the provincial states. To this end, solutions are proposed that are more or less applicable within the political context of Canada: a direct takeover of the provincial state apparatus by the hegemonic fraction or by its representative;

a redeployment of the mechanisms of dialogue which, behind the screen of decentralization, permit the imposition of standards for the policies to be followed; playing one provincial state off against another to isolate recalcitrant opponents. The political crisis, despite the range of solutions available to the central state, is slow to reach a definite conclusion. That is a consequence of the difficulty of implementing and coordinating the appropriate means for a strategy of centralization. Yet the crisis can be expected to work itself out without having to resort to such drastic measures as doing away with the provincial states as points of compromise alliance.

The most immediate danger appears nonetheless to have been avoided. Under the leadership of the Parti Québécois, the opposition from Quebec has failed to produce any dramatic results. The historic bourgeois compromise that it put forward did not generate a response within the dominant class of Canada. Apparently, too many important concessions would have been required, unless the explanation is to be found in the virtual absence of mass mobilization. Indeed, it is possible that the danger most feared by both the federalist and *Péquistes* forces was that the more radical elements would take matters into their own hands. Be that as it may, the federalist-centralizing tendency appears prepared to dominate the Canadian political scene. In the aftermath of the Quebec referendum, it is difficult to envisage how resistance of any importance could organize itself in the near future to counter the current tendency.

Notes

1. I have previously emphasized the importance of this mechanism in Lizette Jalbert, Jean-Guy Lacroix, and Benoit Lévesque, "La question régionale dans le développement du capitalisme au Canada," an address to the Society of Regional Sciences of the Annual Congress of Learned Societies (Montreal, June 6, 1980).
2. From among the many works, see especially F.C. Engelmann and M.A. Schwartz, *Political Parties and the Canadian Social Structure* (Toronto: Prentice-Hall of Canada, 1967).
3. My analysis of third parties in Canada takes issue with the preceding approach and places great importance on social classes; see *Régionalisme et luttes politiques: une analyse des tiers partis au Canada et au Québec* (Montreal: Boréal Express, forthcoming).
4. For an analysis of the concept of crisis, see Nicos Poulantzas, "Les transformations actuelles de l'Etat, la crise politique et la crise de l'Etat," in Nicos Poulantzas (ed.), *La crise de l'Etat* (Paris: PUF, 1976).
5. A similar approach has been developed in France by Renaud Dulong, *Les régions, l'Etat et la société locale* (Paris: PUF, 1978).
6. Regionalism can be defined as a mobilization of the periphery. See François Rangeon, "Le pouvoir régional," in *Le pouvoir régional* (Paris: PUF, 1982), p. 67.

7. The term "differentiation" refers to the remarks of Alain Lipietz, *Le capital et son espace* (Paris: Maspéro, 1977).
8. Yves Mény, "Crises, régions et modernisation de l'Etat," *Pouvoirs* 19 (1981).
9. See especially Joachim Hirsch, "Remarques théoriques sur l'Etat bourgeois et sa crise," in Nicos Poulantzas (ed.), op. cit.
10. Nicos Poulantzas does the best work in defining questions of the unity of class power. See *Pouvoir politique et classes sociales* (Paris: Maspéro, 1968) and *Les classes sociales dans le capitalisme aujourd'hui* (Paris: Seuil, 1974).
11. Leo Panitch, "The Role and Nature of the Canadian State," in Leo Panitch (ed.), *The Canadian State* (Toronto: University of Toronto Press, 1977).
12. Concerning this question of "relay classes," see the above-cited work (note 6) of Renaud Dulong, as well as the volume by Pierre Grémion, *Le pouvoir périphérique* (Paris: Seuil, 1976).
13. In discussing the French case, Jacques Chevalier presents an analysis akin to my own. See Jacques Chevalier, "La réforme régionale," in *Le pouvoir régional* (Paris: PUF, 1982), p. 183.

Chapter 14/Regional Development and Collective Intervention

Elaine Carey-Bélanger

The election of Jean Lesage and the Liberal party in Quebec in 1960 issued in what has become known as the Quiet Revolution. Under the political slogan and electoral promise that the province was to become "master in its own house," the government entered into broad-scale socioeconomic reform and reorganization as well as the search for a new societal model. This socioeconomic and political development was to be promoted within a system of participatory democracy that would take into account individual local and regional needs and aspirations.[1] During this period of profound and accelerated social change, the notion of collective intervention or social animation emerged as a means to organize, coordinate, and promote adhesion to the proposed reforms.

The following is an exploration of the nature and process of this collective intervention in a region that was the scene of intensive development efforts from the early 1960s, the eastern Quebec area. As a result, fundamental and dramatic changes in the mentality and social organization of the region occurred. These changes will be illustrated by three major projects or movements: the BAEQ, Opérations Dignité, and JAL.

In order to encapsulate the experience of eastern Quebec and better understand the cause-effect relationship among the different projects, a typology of different models of community intervention representative of the variety of actions undertaken in eastern Quebec will be proposed. Under the functions of social planning, social action, and community development, the operationalization of the different projects, the interrelation among them, and the way in which the elements of planning, politics, and participation were played out will be discussed.[2]

The analysis will be based on a compilation of data from available studies and will consider specific situational factors giving rise to policy; its nature and scope; the guiding principles of the actors present; organizational resources; and constraints, activities, results, and historical consequences.

As such, the Quebec experience in community intervention was a far from neutral activity.[3] The projected changes necessarily implied redistribution of power and influence among different groups and organizations, conflicts and confrontations among different visions of what society should be and the type of reorganization to be undertaken. Action undertaken must therefore be considered within the general societal context, taking into account economic and sociopolitical factors and the various interests at stake to better understand the coexistence of forces at work which gave rise to paradoxes and tensions in the efforts to harness and control regional development.

The Quebec Context

In the years following the Quiet Revolution, it became clear that the socioeconomic planning and changes envisioned were influenced by the requirements of an economic system that favoured the exploitation of resources through profit-earning enterprises, with emphasis on capital gain, accumulation, and productivity.[4] In addition, in order to realize its objectives, the government was obliged to develop an economic and technological infrastructure in line with the dictates of its advanced capitalist system and the relations of production thus defined.

As a legitimation of this undertaking, the government and its institutions took on a new socioeconomic role and assumed a mandate to explore the differences among the regions, the reasons for existing imbalances, and the need to establish sectorial objectives to bring back to these regions their dynamic force. This was proposed within a framework of rational planning and participation endorsed by technocrats and politicians as the preferred means for all classes to contribute to a collective challenge, but an underlying motivation was the rationalization of government investment to gain maximum profit from each region and thus enrich the national economy.[5]

The contradictions arising from the need to develop resources in line with industrial capitalism, the necessary adaptations for general balance within Quebec's economic system, and the individual and group needs of the different regions—especially those of the rural areas—resulted in confrontations for the redistribution of power and influence among different groups and organizations. Identities were transformed: persons at the periphery of institutional decision making were no longer content to remain there, when socioeconomic planning did not take into account the milieu as such, regional disparities, and the population inhabiting a particular region.

Competing models for the reorganization of the new society or of a particular institutional sector were put forth often in direct conflict with one another[6] and this was accompanied by an overthrow of the traditional alignment of forces within both political and civil society. According to Hamel and Léonard, the debate centred on the question of how to arrive at an equilibrium between those forces that would allow for a new technical and ideological consensus and at the same time take into account economic necessities.[7]

In this context of economic imperatives and political-power realignments, the notion of collective intervention or social animation was introduced. As the impetus for change accelerated, the new forms of community-organization activity were seen as a means to reach underprivileged populations in order to help them find a voice and become conscious that problems in their region were of a structural and functional nature, so they would require collective action for solution. At the same time, the approach was seen as furthering the broader goals of the dominant forces of society and achieving new consensus as to what these goals should be.[8]

Different models of intervention emerged and the following classification can be suggested to understand the forms in which the phenomenon of change took place.

Typology of Community Intervention Model

Social Planning

Social planning is seen as emphasizing a technical process of solving substantive social problems of a broad scope. Basic characteristics of this kind of strategy for change would be fact gathering about problems, followed by decisions on the most rational course of action. The element of elitism is a strong component of this model because of the technical expertise necessary due to the high complexity of problems under study.[9]

In social planning, the planners' most serious decision (or contribution) is what can be called the formulation or description of the planning task. This is done ideally through the constant playing back between the assessment of the relevant aspects of social reality and the preferences of the relevant community and implies that efforts must be made to involve the public and gain their support for the course of action being proposed.[10]

While change is foreseen in this model through consensus or a federation of interests, conflict may also ensue because of the implication of the planners in the power structure and because the government is often the employer or sponsor. When in addition there are competing paradigms for planning among national and global state intervention, decentralization of institutional planning resources, and state as coordinator of the public sector,[11] as in the case of the BAEQ, there is a tendency to confuse or camouflage issues and lose sight of the need for a popular base.

Social Action or Social Movement

A second model generally referred to as social action or social movement aims at making basic changes in major institutions or community practice. This is done through shifting power relationships and resources. It implies the use of political forces in society because of their potential for promoting or resisting projected redistribution and reorganization. Basic change strategy involves crystallization of issues and organization of people to take action against opposition. Characteristic of changes would be conflict confrontation, direct action, and negotiation with the power structure as the external target of action.[12]

Social action is akin to the definition of social movements described by Gagnon as the mobilization of individuals who want to produce fundamental change in society motivated by a sentiment of all persuasive dissatisfaction. These movements may be either political movements aimed at changing the political power structure or protest movements aimed at the more limited goals of changing the decision-making process and redefining the norms that regulate this process. As such, the social movement represents a deliberate and voluntary effort to organize people so that together they act as a pressure group to exercise power or obstruct change.[13]

In order to formulate their aspirations and give a certain coherence to their projects, the persons or group implied will cede the leadership to those who have a coherent insight into the goals of the movement as well as profiting from significant personal contacts. The new leaders are often the "consciousness raisers," animators, catalysers, and guides who are instrumental in the ensuing transformation.[14] Godin adds that these pressure groups are designated as opposition groups, eager to defend the point of view of the "people" and the unorganized. As militants, they play a supervisory role, confronting the structures that work against the public will, as in the second example under discussion (Opérations Dignité I, II, III), and may or may not work towards the creation of new organizational structures.[15]

Community or Locality Development

A third model can be classified as community development and could include what Godin refers to as "*sociétés de gestion.*"[16] Locality development presupposes that community change can be pursued optimally through broad participation of a wide spectrum of people at the local community level in goal determination and action. The basic characteristics of the change process here would be consensus among various community groups and members of the power structure in a common venture and reconciliation of interests.[17]

As it refers to Quebec, the notion of locality development is defined as the formal regrouping of persons who decide to seek the control of territorial resources by the indigenous population. This development takes place within *sociétés de gestion*, which may be of two types—a mixed model that includes collaboration between the government and the local population or through a strictly indigenous administration or a cooperative model of development, as in the third example (JAL). Both locality development and *sociétés de gestion* usually exist as pilot projects when resources are scarce or nonexistent and must depend on government grants for the organization of resources and form local power structures to administer finances and control development.[18]

The Experience of the BAEQ: Government Planning for Territorial Restructuring

The eastern Quebec area (including the regions of the Lower St. Lawrence, Gaspé Peninsula, and Magdalen Islands) was considered one of Canada's most depressed areas. The population, which was historically isolated, had realized particularly since the depression of the 1930s that there was little hope for survival in the region. The choice was between moving to large urban centres or a meagre subsistence from social-welfare benefits.[19] In the postwar years, the artificial prosperity that had been created by the Second World War and the increased demand for foodstuffs and lumber was over. Farming, fishing, and forestry operations were scarce. Industry hardly existed and only large-scale government aid kept the region alive.[20] By 1956, the traditional elites, businessmen, mayors, and a number of local interest groups had formed the Economic Council of the Lower St. Lawrence (COEB), whose task was to promote the economic development and raise the living standard of the whole area.[21]

In February 1961, the Quebec Economic Orientation Council (COEQ)was created and given the mandate to draw up a plan for economic reorganization which would foresee the most complete use possible of human and material resources. The council, composed of 15 bureaucrats and experts from universities and the private sector, proceeded to establish a five-year plan for development. Finally, the Eastern Quebec Planning Bureau (BAEQ), a broad-scale regional-planning effort, came into existence in 1963. Because of the extreme need and because action was already being taken in the region, Quebec designed these three areas as a pilot territory under the aegis of ARDA. Matching legislation was passed and agreements were signed with Ottawa to make funds available for the province; Quebec's first full-scale effort in regional planning was launched. The Eastern Quebec Planning Bureau was constituted and prepared a master plan for the development of the area, with the participation of its people.[22]

The overall project took three years and absorbed a $4 million budget constituting the largest single ARDA project in Canada. Two main divisions—research and social animation—grouped 85 professionals and 65 nonprofessionals.[23] Through the BAEQ, the government proposed a rational reorganization of industrial structures, to insure economic stability and standardize the monopolist exploitation of primary resources.[24] Research groups conducted inquiries into sectorial planning in fishing, forestry, agriculture, and transport as well as social, political, and administrative structures. Social-animation teams were divided into information and media community work, residential leadership training, and area-wide sectorial committees.[25]

Three main concepts were officially involved: government planning, regional development, and self-help. The stated goals were:

1. Modernization of the traditional sectors of the economy (agriculture, fishing, and forestry).
2. The creation of activities to encourage people to stay in the area.
3. Manpower retraining.
4. Raising the consciousness of the area's population to permit identification with overall objectives.

The plan further stated, "One of the fundamental postulates is that putting into effect a process of development in a region consists as much of creating dynamic structures through which the population can acquire a mentality of development and take vital decisions as to investments in vital sectors. . . . This consultative participation would have an influence on the decision makers."[26] Presiding overall was the Plan Council, whose responsibility was to integrate the social research into an economically and politically feasible plan and at the same time take into account the wishes of the population.

At the beginning there seemed to be a real desire to execute the overall development plan with the involvement of the local population, but perhaps with a certain naiveté without fully taking into account the actual lack of flexibility in a process whose broad outlines had already been drawn up subject to economic and political dictates. The plan constituted a decision affecting the general population. It was therefore necessary to support and diffuse this new concept of regional planning, for, if one does not change the social structures and culture at the same time, it would be illusory to count on planning to obtain harmonious development and assure participation. This option for global planning implied an intervention at the level of attitudes, values, and collective consciousness.

The program represented an extensive effort to apply scientific methods through a broad interdisciplinary research program, to assess total resources, and to project plans for their fullest possible development.[27] However, it soon became evident that desirable social change was considered the entry into an industrial, urban, bureaucratic society. As stated by Duval, "The renewal of an underdeveloped region implies a total or partial economic conversion in continuity with the overlying economic reality."[28]

It also gradually became obvious that the rational exploitation of resources would require a certain displacement of the local population toward the urban centres. The dangers of a government social-control perspective loomed on the horizon, as agents of the governing system, economists, political scientists, sociologists, and other experts descended on the region to solve its problems. However, the experts who came to make inventories of the possibilities of "catching up" in this underdeveloped region were quickly confronted by the traditional forces, as the technocratic approach supported by government policy of rationalization and equilibrium met opposition from traditional leaders, business, and commercial interests.[29]

Within the program, participation was seen as having an educational role which would permit the definition of means and objectives by the population through the use of efficient techniques. Thus, although it was only a burgeoning science, social animation was given a large place in the program, for it corresponded to the second objective, that of securing the participation of the population at large:

> This participation was carefully thought out, painstakingly structured, generously staffed and supported; more than one-half of the nearly $4,000,000 utilized by the BAEQ (federal-provincial matching funds) was spent on public information and consultation.[30]

Animation carried out by a staff of recent university graduates was seen as a close relationship between development and decision making, change and leadership and as addressing itself to all interested groups rather than a selective population. The principal animation objective was to encourage a new mentality and a new leadership as an instrument of change. These new leaders would, it was hoped, maintain the structures of participation and thus provide input to the development project. This was attempted in a milieu that had often blocked this kind of participation in favour of traditional structures of influence and decision making. The region had a sparse density of population giving force to local solidarities of a dependent nature. Local associations were highly differentiated and represented particular interests.[31]

This situation created a further dilemma for the animators: where to invest their efforts? Consultations were organized at the regional and local levels, intensive sessions and personal contacts were the accepted strategies, but should the animator neglect the personal contacts for meetings, thus compromising the objective of promotion and leadership formation, or should he neglect committee meetings for personal contacts and thus compromise the objectives of participation? Also, the fundamental problem of the BAEQ was the ambiguity between the formal global structure of the plan with its objectives, theoretical models, and dominant political theory, and the individual and local needs and aspirations.

Social animation in the BAEQ became enmeshed in the practice of the rationalization of governmental processes and power struggles. The politics of the intervention effected in the perspective of state intervention was vulnerable to a form of corporatism through animation.[32]

In reality, the difficulty was in taking a clear position in the midst of the political and economic power struggles, and the weighting of forces that were unequal in nature. Choices among planning and participation, idealism, and reality placed the animation team in a difficult position and became the nemesis of the group and the program itself.

The animator was caught up in the situation in which idealistically he saw himself promoting interaction between actors and systems in a resource exchange of mutual benefit, collaborative and joint planning, and two-way communication. Actually, he was serving as an agent of allocative social planning, inducing innovation acceptance, and trying to maintain citizen commitment. While animation hoped to change the mentality of the population, the population wanted immediate concrete improvement in standard of living without changing habits and without a change of basic traditional values. Few concrete changes having taken place, this led to a major deception.

A like deception was felt by the animators. In the words of Francine Dansereau:

> To transform society is extremely laudable, but it is nevertheless necessary not to confuse vague social ideals with the reality that can be achieved with reasonable probability by the particular action undertaken. Given the partnership relation with the government it is literally impossible to be a force of opposition. In this regard the BAEQ can be mentioned: it was found

impossible to establish, as required by the development plan, programs that conflicted with the vested interests of established institutions and organizations.[33]

By 1966, the BAEQ submitted its master plan for regional development. The plan—made up of 10 well-documented volumes containing technical appendices, maps, and working papers—was presented to the Quebec government. Elaboration of the plan had provided an inventory of the biophysical potential and socioeconomic components of the territory. It included 231 precise recommendations concerning all sectors of activity. Throughout the plan ran the themes of decentralization of industry and decision making by the province, concentration of the population within the region, consolidation of farms and industries of transformation, specialization of urban regions, and subregions and training of the labour force.[34] While some sectorial possibilities such as development of the tourist industry and consolidation of fisheries seemed promising, other sectors—such as municipal regrouping, rationalization, and consolidation—were highly controversial. For the planners, regional development should follow along the coherent lines present in urban centres. Therefore, the restructuring of space, regrouping, and concentration in order to increase the effectiveness and efficiency of public and private investments were recommended as well as the closing of certain areas whose potential for development was considered almost inexistent.[35]

The population had expected a rapid rise in the standard of living and stable employment. In reality, they were faced with the application of recommendations that did not correspond to the hope engendered or provide the solution of problems as promised.[36] The global social-planning approach, despite its important information gathering, leadership training, and rationalization of possible courses of action, was prey to political tension and conflict; in fact, it overruled locally based or self-supporting efforts, thus creating mistrust and resistance. The threatened closing of several parishes presented the last link in a chain of lost illusions.

Reactions to the recommendations brought about a broad-based social-protest movement as the next step in the development of the region.

"Les Opérations Dignité": Social Action, Social Movement

By 1968 a regional development council (CRDEQ) was formed, funded in a large part by the office of Planning and Development of the provincial government. In May 1968 the federal and provincial governments signed a cooperative agreement through which $258 million would be devoted to the development of the 10 counties of the Eastern Quebec area. The CRDEQ was officially recognized as the voice of the local people and responsible for social animation. The Development Office of Eastern Quebec (ODEQ) was also established. This organization was directed by a general representative of the plan with an administrative council made up of coordinators from the ministries concerned. In addition, the federal government was represented by an administrator who, with the general representative, was responsible for the practical direction of the plan. Thus, execution of the plan was dependent on a heavy administrative structure.[37]

The people at first welcomed the signature of the agreement; they hoped that they would profit directly from the $258 million investment. However, disenchantment soon followed. Of the total amount, $114 million would go to manpower retraining and social development, while most of the rest was to be spent on spatial reorganization (roads, urban planning) and resource development.[38] Nothing had been foreseen for the industrialization of the region, although it had been the object of popular demands for a considerable length of time. The desire to encourage mobility of the labour force became evident with a program of resettlement and organization of reception centres in Montreal. The model of regional development did not give the hoped-for result, and scepticism continued to grow. Despite the longtime attitude of resignation characteristic of the population, the three years of BAEQ activity in the region had created expectations that were being frustrated.

Some parts of eastern Quebec were considered economically unproductive and socially unlivable. Forestry and farming were seen as impossible on this land and an organized relocation of the work force was encouraged. The developmental strategy of the BAEQ, above all urban in terms of concentration of population for services and exploitation of natural resources, would have sacrificed certain areas in order to concentrate production for maximum profit. Closing the parishes, argued by the bureaucrats, was the sacrifice that the region must make to attain the level of living of Quebec in general.[39] The plan called for the closing of 85 marginal parishes out of a total of nearly 215.[40] By 1969, a Quebec government decree (no. 2525) called for the closing of 10 parishes and a year later these parishes were effectively closed.[41] When the forced migration was carried out under these regretable circumstances, it was highly unpopular; in fact, it gave rise to the first Opération Dignité.[42]

Between 1968 and 1970, only a small portion of the budget had been spent. The more desired measures of the BAEQ, such as organization of the tourist industry and the creation of a national park, were long in coming, bogged down in administrative red tape and delays. Not only were the people of the region disenchanted with certain provisions of the agreement—especially those concerning relocation—they were also dissatisfied with the difficulty in realizing the more popular measures. A strong protest movement resulted, which was aimed at those responsible for implementing the plan, including politicians and the regional development council. Many local organizations such as the chambers of commerce and county councils left the participatory structures. Some spontaneous protest movements took place for specific issues—such as the people of Cabano, who protested against the processing of the wood from their forests outside of the region, and the citizens of Chandler, who vigorously protested the closing of their unemployment office.[43]

This resistance of the population was expressed in an organized manner within the movements, which became known as Opérations Dignité I, II, and III. Both the movement and the social action undertaken were founded on the high level of resistance to government proposals within the population and represented a desire to consolidate the rural milieu, to reappropriate the economic orientations of the region, and to assume administrative control. Issued from a spontaneous movement of solidarity in reaction to the closing of the parishes, supported and led by both the clergy as moral leaders of the population, and receiving political support from a young federal parliamentarian, Pierre de Bané, the movement gained impetus and became the voice of a new and conscious rural population. Within the framework of Opération Dignité, citizens from more than 65 villages banded together with the common objective of the optimal development and use of natural resources.[44] This objective was founded on the firm belief which became the guiding slogan, "It is possible to live with dignity from the agriculture and timber resources of our region."[45]

While the BAEQ had been led by a group of urban professionals supported by government and financial interests and was of a predominantly urban nature, Opération Dignité was a movement of traditional elites who assumed the protest role. The credibility of the leaders, according to Robert, counted a great deal in the extent of the mobilization. Under the leadership of Charles Banville, curé de Ste-Paule and president of the citizens' committee of the parish, the first effort (Opération Dignité I) came into being. Twenty-three villages and 3,000 citizens attended a general assembly in Ste-Paule. This gathering brought about in October 1970 a manifesto signed by 19 priests. After the people of the region had waited in vain and counted on the government, this movement was a sign of a new determination. In order to achieve their development, the people could count only on themselves to prepare their own plan.[46] The project advocated the development of the forest resources through government financial assistance and claimed the right of the local population to administer through companies which would head up operations. At the end of eight months of briefs and negotiations, the representatives of the 23 municipalities won their cause.[47]

Opération Dignité I's first project aimed to create 160 jobs, prepared a development plan, and establish a structure for self-administration that would allow the people to assume the direction of the plan. It was accepted by the government at a cost of $1.2 million. The Forestry Research Foundation of Laval University (FRUL) was mandated to sign a contract with the government; it was the first time the government recognized an active role for the population in decision making. The members of Opération Dignité I were to be consulted at all phases of conception and execution of the project and to administer resources in cooperation with the Ministry of Forestry.[48]

Tireless, de Bané and Banville extended their efforts to help the neighbouring counties of Rimouski, Rivière-du-Loup, and Témiscouata in the organization of a second project: Opération Dignité II. This second effort regrouped citizens' committees from 27 parishes and municipalities of the region under the leadership of the curé Jean-Marc Gendron of the parish of Esprit-Saint. The mobilization began with a major manifestation in an attempt to attract, once more, the attention of the federal and provincial governments to the problems of the region, and more precisely to obtain government support for further forestry development. Federal and provincial deputies were present at the first meeting.[49]

The collective consciousness of the awakened population continued to evolve, supported by de Bané, who became more and more controversial as the promoter of local autonomy. The movement expanded, despite some opposition, and succeeded when the FRUL agreed to participate in a second project, which would include redevelopment of 500 miles of forest within the three counties.[50] The project eventually would be administered and controlled by the citizens. In order to obtain government participation, the citizens undertook preparation of briefs and negotiation, once again supported by de Bané, who claimed, "The force of the project was in the number of citizens adhering to it and the government would not withstand a united people."[51] The funds were finally obtained and the two Opérations Dignité became a sort of federation of citizens committees who also had the intention of opposing the government projects to close marginal parishes and relocate inhabitants. In the words of curé Banville, "They develop on the one hand and relocate on the other. The government will have to learn to respect the will of the rural population who have decided to live with dignity on their native soil."[52]

The movements won by diverting approximately $200 million to the redevelopment of the forest industry and succeeded in at least halting the forced migration and closing of almost 85 villages, as had been earlier planned.[53]

There was still a prevalent feeling in official circles that it was preferable to have projects initiated by the government which had the necessary tools for planning and measuring feasibility and that the efforts of Opérations Dignité were improvizations of a solution by the local population in the face of government delays.[54] Through broad-based local participation and the use of both political and ecclesiastical force, the movement did succeed in making some basic changes in the original government plans and defied the underlying philosophy of the BAEQ. Through a crystallization of the issue of living with dignity from their natural resources and in the true sense of becoming "masters in their own house," the citizens took action against the government power structure and through structured conflict, confrontation, and negotiation won some early victories. This growing consciousness of the citizens had in fact been facilitated through the years of BAEQ research, in which the population became aware of the overall situation and the continuing regional inequalities. In addition, the leadership formation for the natural leaders enabled them to act as change agents to promote the cause.[55] Faced with a survival issue, they succeeded in creating a common will, a cohesiveness and solidarity which was to characterize future popular action in the region in the years to come.

From an initial position that could be described as "we have nothing to lose; we have nothing,"[56] a formerly passive, downtrodden, but proud people gained hope and, as a result of some success, were determined to take charge of their affairs and define regional development according to fundamental values. The movement forced the government to back off in part from its policy of relocation. However, the seemingly important economic concessions accorded by the government left untouched and unnegotiated the question of the future use of the forest, which was related to the broader question of regional development. On the one hand, the government attempted to recuperate control. On the other hand, efforts for autonomous control became more combative and, although the balance of forces between the government and the movement was unequal, the necessity for negotiation had been legitimized.[57]

"Coopérative de développement Agro-forestier de Témiscouata": JAL—Community Development

By 1971, the original government policy for closing the parishes had been rescinded, although the relocation was to continue on a voluntary and individual basis. Government bonuses were to be given and the Ministry of Agriculture would buy up abandoned land. The temptation to leave despite the movements underway was strengthened,[58] but this was balanced by a rapid realization by the citizens of the localities concerned of the danger brought about by the program. In effect, the departure of a few families could transform the socioeconomic structure of a locality and begin a process of diminishing population which could snowball and further justify relocation and closing.

In the fall of 1971, in the heart of the debate on "territory to develop or population to relocate" and the question of how to use forestry and agricultural resources to provide a harmonious and diversified development, the citizens of three parishes within the territory of Opération Dignité II—St-Juste, Auclair, and Lejeune ("JAL")—began to think of their common interest in regrouping and working together.[59]

The area covered by JAL is situated in the hinterland of the Lower St. Lawrence between Lake Témiscouata and New Brunswick on one side and the villages of Dégelis and Squatteck on the other. With only 2,000 inhabitants in the three localities, they were next on the lists of parishes to be closed. The region had lost 588 inhabitants from 1966 to 1971, including 300 in 1969 and 1970 alone. According to Dionne, it was this emigration that reinforced the desire of the remaining population to stay and resist the provincial regional policy. The movement began from a small nucleus of interested citizens grouped around the curé, kitchen meetings, always discussing pastoral themes, pastoral affairs, and various projects for the region. "Always the mix of tradition and daring, religion and politics."[60] The population was thus sensitized from the start and, while continuing to belong to Opération Dignité II, the three parishes decided to proceed with a more concrete collaboration among themselves. A general reunion was held by the citizens' committee in February 1972.

As a result of these informal sessions and the decision taken by the citizens' committee, a first draft was formulated with the aid of the agronomist of the region.[61] The project was rapidly given government support "in principle," for it fell within the confines of the project outlined by the Agricultural and Forestry research funds of Laval under OD II.

The involvement of the population was insured through a series of community-education courses given in the winter of 1973. The series of 60 hours of courses was divided between the dynamics of working in a group, human relations, and personality and technical instruction in forestry, farming, and craft work; 200 persons attended. This formed a solid nucleus convinced of the capacity of the population to control the administration of its projects. Work groups were then formed to orient and draw up a development plan. At this point the population showed proof of their conviction that something could be done with the region and basic commitment was evident. Both the development of the forest and a self-administered holding company with citizen control were seen as priorities. While the first of these passed without difficulty, the second met with stronger government opposition.

It was clear from the beginning that this project of integral development was opposed by the Quebec government. In the desire to give the project a truly community formula of self-administration, there were risks and problems involved. "The Jalois" had to provoke their own "October Crisis" in 1973 in order for the bureaucrats to respect their offer to collaborate with the popular movement. In the face of government reticence, the government agents were forceably detained until a signed promise was obtained.[62] Finally, in May 1974, after 16 months of pressure through local associations and the local population, the "coopérative de développement agro-forestier du Témiscouata" was legally instituted and recognized by the Quebec government. The cooperative was to be managed by 12 administrators, three from each territorial sector. In addition, there were permanent employees for technical assistance (the manager, secretary, agriculture specialist, and accountant). The actual body of the cooperative was composed of 274 regular and 95 auxiliary members who met regularly.

The major function of this group was to study and carry out suggested projects and to coordinate the various efforts in territorial development. The collaboration and participation of the residents would be required for this study and execution; thus, the major part of the projects came directly from the local citizens regrouped in committees. Members of the cooperative also served as official spokesmen in negotiations with the ministries and government structures. Thus, the cooperative, together with the forestry and manpower centre, made up what was considered the "masterpiece of the JAL territory."[63]

The forest was the most important single undertaking. Making use of the grants of the Ministry of Lands and Forests, the forestry project regrouped the timber of 110 proprietors and rationalized the use of over 10,500 acres through replanting and cutting, thus permitting the employment of more than 65 lumbermen who previously had to expatriate to New Brunswick and Maine.[64] The agricultural committee and the agriculture specialist developed a plan for the commercialization of potato production and, after long and difficult negotiations, succeeded in obtaining a sum of $100,000, which was complemented by local donations of $30,000 to start the enterprise; the project for the extraction of pine essence, in which the contribution of the local population also grew to $100,000, served as another example of the will of the residents to succeed.

In other areas, like a manpower centre, tourist development, housing, and maple sugar production,[65] the residents maintained a broad role not only in defining and implementing development projects, but also in concentrated efforts to ensure appropriate information, formation, and education. Together, these aspects became the key to JAL's eventual success.[66]

While other projects were organized and undertaken, JAL remains unique in its category, the only situation where a population earned the right to be considered as administrator and to intervene on behalf of its members. This was in part due to the capacity of the milieu with the technical aid available to analyze the situation, take inventory of their resources, to construct briefs which were well-documented and difficult to refute, and to develop intervention strategies for rapid action. Recognition was earned through continous confrontation. The notion of authentic participation, as it was lived out in the JAL experience, was extremely demanding. It implied consultation with the milieu, information, heightening the receptivity of the people, group decision making, sharing responsibilities, and putting personal interest in the background. This has not been and is not being accomplished without difficulties, not only from government resistance, but also from the push and pull and varying levels of interest and interest groups. However, the response to the call for unity of action was heard, responded to, and the residents found renewed hope. Where formerly the parishes were emptying and houses falling into disrepair, where lands were being abandoned and returning to forest because no one dared invest in the area, today the population has stabilized.

In less than five years the objectives spelled out in the beginning were achieved as a form of indigenous administration, which has involved one-third of the active population. This community has succeeded in implanting a model along the lines of "small is beautiful," which has eliminated many of the dangers of rural growth. However symbolically, the success of this venture constituted a rupture with the technocratic logic of the state, upsetting the market economy and the consumer society norms.[67]

Despite the fact that this project has maintained local initiative, tracing a global preestablished guiding plan by the community at large and respecting the basic principle of self-determination, it is all too often seen as the exception to the rule. JAL and the numerous other community-development endeavours which have issued from the efforts of the Opérations Dignité, while representing concessions by the state, do not necessarily indicate that the government has rescinded its rational-planning policy.

Conclusion

In 1960, with the election of the Liberal party in Quebec, broad socio-economic and political reform was undertaken within a framework of participatory democracy. This ushered in a period of rapid and accelerated change, confrontation and conflict, as the attempts of the government to rationalize planning were often at odds with local and regional interests. Withing this context, collective intervention emerged as a means to organize, coordinate, and promote participation and later to defend local interests. This collective intervention took various forms, which can be classified as social planning, social action or movement, and community development.

The three examples discussed illustrate these models of community intervention in action, both in the light of their internal dynamic and in relation to the forces and constraints of the general societal context. The first of these, the BAEQ, represented an example of a broad-range social-planning effort under government auspices in an attempt to rationalize the use and productivity of the resources of an underdeveloped region, while at the same time insuring maximum participation of the population.

The state at this time was seen as the major instrument of catching up and national promotion. The intellectuals and specialists long held to silence were strongly engaged in the effort to create a modern society to break regional disparities and inequality of access to resources. When the model of rationalization of resources emerged from this collaboration of government experts and the local population, it was heavily weighted in favour of an urban technological model responding to the dominant economic imperatives rather than one that took into account the basic values and aspirations of the population. A strong negative reaction and protest movement resulted. In Opérations Dignité I, II, and III, the citizens united under the traditional leaders, the clergy, and with political support called for a different societal model more in keeping with the right of the population to live productively on its own territory. From this movement, numerous more specific community-development projects emerged. Of these, JAL is one of the most successful examples of the potential for maximum and efficient participation by the population.

From the examples discussed, the aspirations and expectations of the population have advanced more quickly than the capacity or will of the system to respond, as there are few indications that the government has questioned or revised its regional-development policy.[68]

Practical answers to some concrete situations and the success of some local endeavours have created and maintained a spirit of determination, identification, and cohesion within the popular movements of the region. However, the dilemma of socioeconomic planning will not be solved until there is a commitment not only to factors of economic feasibility, but also to equal weighting of social and quality of life variables throughout the developmental process. The question to be asked is not so much what profit margin can exist, but how can a balance be struck between cost in time and money, and renewed hope and heightened satisfaction of a population. There must be a shared interest and an effective means of continual interaction between the regional population and the government engaging in social planning because, without concrete knowledge, realistic objectives, response to real and perceived needs, and citizen support, such efforts will not succeed.

Today, however, despite the astonishing capacity of resistance and the energy deployed to create alternate structures suited to the needs of the population, the situation remains tentative and the power to undertake an integrated restructuring of resources permanently with local control and adequate budgeting has not yet been realized. With Bill 125 on municipal reorganization, a new wave of government rationalization of structures and planning is in view. It now seems necessary to continue to organize politically on a broader base. As Godin remarks, "If the struggle began with Opération Dignité in 1970, it must continue to find its force in a second wave: Operation Power."[69]

Notes

1. Marcel Rioux, "Aperçu sociologique sur le Québec", *Revue de l'Institut de sociologie* (Bruxelles: Université Libre, 1968), p. 124.
2. This classification is drawn from a wide variety of authors from American and Canadian sources:
   Hugues Dionne et al., *Aménagement intégré des ressources et luttes en milieu rural* (Rimouski: GRIDEQ, Université du Québec à Rimouski, 1983); Gilles Godin, *Développement régional et mouvement populaire: L'exemple de l'Est du Québec* (Quebec: Conseil Régional de Développement de Québec, Jan. 1979) pp. 111-30; Alain G. Gagnon, *Les opérations dignité: naissance d'un mouvement social dans l'Est du Québec* (Montréal: Les Editions Leméac, 1981), pp. 1-17; Alfred Kahn, *Theory and Practice of Social Planning* (New York: Russell Sage, 1969): Jack Rothman, "An Analysis of Goals and Roles in Community Organization Practice," *Social Work* IV: 2 (1964), pp. 24-31.
3. James Draper, "Dilemma of Participation," *Learning* 1:2 (summer 1977), pp. 3-4.
4. Godin, op. cit., p. 113.
5. Pierre Hamel and Jean-François Léonard, "Aménagement du territoire et participation populaire au Québec depuis 1960," in *Aménagement du territoire*

au Québec du rêve au compromis (Montreal: Nouvelle Optique, 1982), pp. 90-115.

6. Raymond Breton, "The Socio-Political Dynamics of the October Events," in Dale C. Thomson (ed.), *Quebec Society and Politics: Views from the Inside* (Toronto: McClelland and Stewart, 1973), pp. 213-19.
7. Hamel and Léonard, op. cit., p. 94.
8. Cap St-Jacques et Maisonneuve, *Dossier Service Social: Le Service Social Instrument d'une classe* (Montreal: Presses du Cirque, 1972), p. 15.
9. Rothman, op. cit., p. 24.
10. Kahn, op. cit., p. 61.
11. Hamel and Léonard, op. cit., pp. 96-97. *National and global state intervention* takes into account both social and economic variables and the role of the private and public sectors. *Decentralization of the institutional planning resources* tends to favour a coordination of central and local apparatuses to produce a dynamic development. The third planning approach restrains the *state coordinator to the public sector* and looks to interdepartmental coordination.
12. Rothman, op. cit., pp. 26-31.
13. Gagnon, op. cit., p. 2.
14. Léon Dion, "Vers une conscience auto-déterminée," *Revue Canadienne de langue française* 1 (1971), p. 9.
15. Godin, op. cit., pp. 111-30.
16. Ibid.
17. Rothman, op. cit., p. 24.
18. Godin, op. cit., pp. 111-30.
19. Hamel and Léonard, op. cit., p. 100.
20. Edward Smith, "Planning for People: The Gaspé Project," in W.E. Mann (ed.), *Social and Cultural Change in Canada*, vol. 2 (Vancouver: Copp Clark, 1970), pp. 170-78.
21. Dionne, op. cit., p. 30.
22. Maurice Croisat, "L'expérience québécoise en matière de régionalisation," *Aménagement du territoire et développement régional*, vol. III (Grenoble: Institut d'Etudes politiques, 1970), pp. 692, 876.
23. Charles E. Hendry, "Investigation and Intervention in Social Development," in James Draper (ed.), *Citizen Participation: Canada* (Toronto: New Press, 1971), p. 432.
24. Hamel and Léonard op. cit., p. 100.
25. Smith, op. cit., pp. 20-21.
26. Bureau d'Aménagement de l'Est du Québec, *Plan de Développement: Région-pilote, Bas St-Laurent, Gaspésie et Iles de la Madeleine*, (Mont-Joli: 1966), pp. 11-12.
27. Hendry, op. cit., p. 432.
28. Louise Duval, *Faits saillants de l'inventaire*, ARDA Report No. 13 (Ottawa: Queen's Printer, June 1968), p. 2.
29. Dionne, op. cit., p. 38.
30. Smith, op. cit., p. 21.
31. Marc A. Morency, *Animation sociale: quelques éléments historiques de l'expérience du BAEQ* (Ottawa: Queen's Printer, 1968).
32. Ibid.
33. Francine Dansereau, in Dimitrios Roussopoulos (ed.), *Quebec and Radical Social Change* (Montreal: Black Rose Books, 1974), pp. 80-81.

34. Smith, op. cit., p. 23.
35. Plan de Développement, Région-pilote Bas-St-Laurent, Gaspésie et Iles de la Madeleine, op. cit.
36. Hamel and Léonard, op. cit., p. 98.
37. Clermont Dugas, "Le développement régional de l'est du Québec de 1963 à 1972," *Cahiers de géographie de Québec* 17:41 (Sept. 1973), p. 286.
38. Dionne, op. cit., p. 50.
39. Jean-Jacques Simard, "Les Opérations Dignité: luttes d'espace et nostalgie," in A.G. Gagnon (ed.), *Les Opérations Dignité: naissance d'un mouvement social dans l'Est du Québec* (Montreal: Editions Leméac, 1981), pp. 91-109.
40. Gagnon, op. cit.
41. Dionne, op. cit., p. 51.
42. Charles Banville, "L'origine et l'impact des Opérations Dignité," in Gagnon, op. cit., p. 109.
43. Dugas, op. cit., p. 287.
44. Lionel Robert, "Les Opérations Dignité à l'origine d'un mouvement populaire," in Gagnon, op. cit., pp. 91-109.
45. *Forest Conservation* (1975), p. 10.
46. Robert, op. cit., p. 93.
47. *Le Devoir* (May 26, 1971).
48. *Le Devoir* (May 27, 1971).
49. *Le Devoir* (Aug. 14, 1971).
50. *Le Devoir* (Aug. 7, 1971).
51. Ibid.
52. Ibid.
53. Robert, op. cit., p. 94.
54. *Le Devoir* (Aug. 14, 1971).
55. Banville, op. cit., p. 109; Gagnon op. cit., p. 166; Robert op. cit., p. 91.
56. Banville, op. cit., p. 115.
57. Robert, op. cit., p. 57.
58. Michel Lambert, "Les villages qui ne voulaient pas mourir," *Actualité* 2:4 (April 1977), pp. 47-50.
59. JAL, *Un espoir pour l'Est du Québec,* Document presented at the Conference, "Community Development at the Crossroads" (Toronto, Feb. 1977).
60. Lamber, op. cit., p. 48.
61. Dionne, op. cit., pp. 84-86.
62. Conseil Régional de Développement de Québec, *Développement Régional et Mouvement Populaire, l'exemple de l'Est du Québec* (Québec: CRD, Jan. 1979).
63. JAL, op. cit., p. 63.
64. CRDQ, op. cit., p. 54.
65. For a more complete discussion, see Dionne, op. cit, pp. 77-153.
66. JAL, p. 12.
67. Hamel and Léonard, op. cit., pp. 102-03. See also Alain G. Gagnon, *Le développement régional, l'Ètat et les groupes populaires* (Ph. D. Dissertation, Carleton University, April 1983), *passim.*
68. Gagnon, op. cit.
69. Godin, op. cit., p. 132.

Chapter 15/The Evolution of Political Forces in Quebec: The Struggle for Supremacy

Alain G. Gagnon

The struggles faced by the regions since the creation of the Bureau d'aménagement de l'Est du Québec (BAEQ) in 1963 are not limited to the fight to ensure the survival of marginal parishes. They reflect considerable realignments of power. Moreover, during the 1960s, "organic intellectuals" (technocrats) appropriated for themselves specific powers to the detriment of "traditional intellectuals" (community leaders, political representatives, priests). The 1970s saw a political will to reverse this trend and reassert the role of parliamentarians. In this campaign, both politicians and technocrats sought to amass the support of local populations (local bourgeoisie and popular groups). In this respect, the organismes de développement communautaire (ODCs), by calling into question certain unpopular governmental policies like relocation, acquired some important support from the rural population. Thus, it is no mystery that politicians and bureaucrats have given these people so much attention in the past few years. Everyone wants them as allies. This is all the more apparent when we realize that the ODCs extend over all the rural area; in fact, they are present in more than 114 of the 200 municipalities of eastern Quebec. It is in this context that the statements made by Harvey draw their full meaning:

> It seems that the different regions other than those of Montreal and Quebec have started to be vocal and define themselves internally—instead of passively accepting to be defined from the outside.
>
> This rise of regional sentiment will bring forth tensions between the Quebec state and the regions with respect to the definition of development policy objectives and their execution. Already, the pressures from the base have permitted the modification of certain policies, notably in the area of forestry.[1]

The ODCs were to constitute a major element of this general rethinking of the government's policies. This clearly became the case, for example, during the negotiations to obtain permits for development—in opposition to the relocation—of rural territories. For its part, the government opted to integrate these groups with its policies: the setting up of the Municipalités régionales de comté (MRC), in which their ascribed territory cuts through that of the ODCs, constitutes an expression of this phenomenon.

I have already shown elsewhere that the active forces of the area (ODCs) occupy a primary role among rural populations,[2] which has limited the ascendancy of a government presence and, in some measure, of politicians. Consequently, power can be defined not just as a function of an actor's capacity to modify the behaviour of others,[3] but also as the possibility of actors "to intervene at points and in areas where others have no access."[4] This last remark contradicts claims made by Crozier, who ascribes extensive powers to high-level administrators. Theoretically, central powers predominate over the peripheries, while in practice high-level administrators often have no other alternatives but to deal with intermediate structures and groups. Also, if we admit this, we can more easily understand the claim made by Grémion that the "central instances" (high-level administrators) "have no possibility of direct intervention with their subordinated groups."[5] This said, it remains that high-level administrators, through the intermediary of governmental structures, are capable of little satisfactory adaptation to regional demands. Should we see here the influence of intermediary agents in the state, those that Dulong designates with the label "frustrés de l'Etat"? Or is it again more of an attempt by political representatives to guarantee for themselves some regional support? In both cases one factor remains: political representatives and bureaucrats have sought to secure subordinates for themselves.

Within the scope of this research, it is important to comprehend the evolution of the position of the actors on the regional scene. In this context, the presentation of the prevailing links between the ODCs and the state remains pertinent and constitutes an important element in the pursuit of this objective.

Elsewhere, I have pointed out the numerous upheavals caused by the decision of popular groups to exercise some pressure to realize an integrated development of resources in the rural areas of eastern Quebec.[6] Tensions created between interests have also been created during the choice of regional capitals (many cities competed with each other), of the designation of agroforestry centres (designated municipalities vs. nondesignated municipalities), and during the creation of the MRCs (the ascendancy of urban municipalities over rural municipalities).

The emergence of these various factors have become occasions for political forces to seek greater and more widespread powers. This search for power has caused some important confrontations during the last decade. Nevertheless, the rivalries born from these governmental policies, while giving a glimpse of the major consequences possible for those political forces existing on the regional scene, also permit us to delimit the underlying dynamics and the regional struggles that flowed therefrom.

The study of the relations between the state and popular groups consequently represents a common area to enable a clearer interpretation of the interests at stake at the regional level. Actually, it is only by starting with an analysis of these relations that an understanding of the political dynamic underlying the manifested power relations is at all possible. It is in this way that we can see the state, through intermediate apparatuses (BAEQ, CAREQ, CRDEQ, ODEQ, OPDQ, and so on), searching to appropriate greater powers for itself. Also, we will see, the local leaders (legislative members or local representatives) frequently represented by the Union des municipalités du Québec (UMQ), the Union des conseils de comté (UCCQ) and, more recently, by the MRCs, trying to strengthen their support bases in the regions. Finally, the "popular" forces of the area (ODC, SAIREQ, unions)[7] took part in the debates by questioning many of the established relations among community leaders, the state, and the population of rural areas. In fact, the crucial debates have arisen among these three protagonists in the last few years.

It is therefore by beginning with an analysis of the relations between the state and popular groups that it is possible to better understand the dynamism underlying the power relations established among community leaders, bureaucrats, and popular forces of the area. (See Figure 15-1.) Three sweeping tendencies characterize the period from the Quiet Revolution to the present. This can be schematized into a first phase typified by the "technocratization" of power, followed by the increasing reestablishment of power for the politicians, to continue in a third phase with the technocracy and the politicians seeking to capitalize on the growth of popular groups in rural areas.

Technocratization of Power

It is commonplace to admit that the expansion of the bureaucratic apparatus in Quebec during the 1960s had as its goal the procurement of power bases for the rising new middle class. The pursuit of this objective had to permit this class (technocrats, professors, members of the liberal professions) entry into the new posts of the expanding state apparatus, while separating the clergy and the community leaders from their traditional positions of authority.[8] Following the usual interpretation, Divay and Léveillée confirm this diagnosis:

> This ascending class became conscious of the fact that the state apparatus of Quebec could be an ideal base on which to seek to liberate itself from its old clerical masters and other forces such as local notables and to consolidate, from a centralized bureaucracy, the hold which it had already started to exercise on Quebec society; this conviction was, from then on, transmitted to larger areas of the public in the form of discourses centered on the urgent collective need to catch up and on the collective capacity to realize, with the help of the state as a tool, a process of reappropriating large parts of the wealth in resources as well as decision-making centres.[9]

For eastern Quebec, the "bureaucratic grid pattern" (Danid Latouche's phrase) developed in three principal stages: creation of the Bureau d'aménagement de l'Est du Québec (BAEQ), the Conseil régional de développement (CRDEQ), and the Office de développement (ODEQ) and, finally, the formation of the Conférence administrative régionale (CAREQ). Each one of these stages constituted an initiative by government to procure for the technocracy those areas of intervention coveted by many. It is important to note in this case that the gains made by the technocracy translated themselves

Figure 15-1 Actors at the Local and Regional Levels

<table>
<tr><th>Actors / Levels</th><th>State technocracy</th><th>Notables (local leaders) mayor, parliamentarians</th><th>Spontaneous forces, popular groups, unions</th></tr>
<tr><td>Local</td><td></td><td>Mayors, municipal representatives</td><td>ODC</td></tr>
<tr><td rowspan="2">Regional</td><td>BAEQ
CRDEQ
ODEQ-OPDQ-CAREQ
DREE</td><td>Federal MPs
UCCQ
MNAs
UMQ</td><td rowspan="2">SAIREQ
UPA
SPB</td></tr>
<tr><td colspan="2">MRC
Regional Council for Intervention</td></tr>
</table>

principally by a loss of power and/or prestige for the community leaders and legislative members.

The case of the BAEQ is revealing in this respect. Seeing their power diminish, legislative and municipal representatives and the chambers of commerce often opposed the presence of directors and planners from the BAEQ. Benjamin confirms in part these claims when he reminds us that "legislative members were ill enthused at the presence of planners in their counties."[10] It was, in fact, very difficult to calm the fears of the traditional forces because all these operations had been done on the fringe of these groups and, in good measure, against them.[11] This situation is all the more bizarre when one considers that the pressures for viable provincial planning frequently originated from this very area. Yet, once situated in the context of collective catching up, an objective sought by the bureaucracy, this effort to marginalize the local leaders is made clearer. A former administrator of the

BAEQ went so far as to describe this experience as the realization of a technocratic project:

> The reports of local and subregional committees were piling up on my desk; we were discussing with the planners how we could analyze these reports. But, already these people had prepared the outline of the plan. All the reports from the base were rejected. It became serious: the technocratic dream was beginning to win.[12]

The process of technocratization would continue throughout the post-BAEQ period. In addition, it was during this time that the CRDEQ, created in 1967 from the fusion of the Conseil d'orientation économique du Bas St.-Laurent and the Conseil régional d'expansion économique de la Gaspésie et des Iles-de-la-Madeleine would be instituted. This organization, given the nature of its mandate, would see itself wedged between the demands from particular areas, which it had to represent to the government, and the government itself. Officially recognized as the privileged speaker on regional development, the CRDEQ would strive to integrate all regional initiatives into the heart of its structure. The rise of the popular movement of eastern Quebec showed a partial failure of this body since, as was affirmed by someone from the area, "If the CRDEQ had fulfilled its role, we would not have needed Opérations Dignité."[13]

In a report recently presented to the administrative council of the CRDEQ, it was emphasized that the organization mostly played the role of forestaller and defuser of tensions in eastern Quebec.[14] The collaboration of the CRDEQ with the established powers (decentralized ministries), especially from 1967 to 1973, would incite numerous regional organizations to retire from this representational structure. Suffice it to note the cases of the county councils, the chambers of commerce,[15] or the refusal by the popular groups to fully participate.[16]

Seeking to change its image, the CRDEQ later reinforced its representation formula. It oversaw the establishment of various specialized councils (culture, leisure, forestry, environment, communications, integrated development and planning, municipalities) and a structure grouping together the unions (UPA, CSN, FTQ, CEQ), employers (CDE), cooperatives (Union régionale des caisses populaires), and community associations (Jeune chambre de commerce, Société nationale de l'est du Québec). Unfortunately, this attempt at sectorial and territorial representation did not, at the outset, give the desired effects.

During the course of its formation period, the task of the CRDEQ would be even more compromised as the parliamentarians, seeing their role diminish at the profit of the ascending technocracy, "wanted to impede the regional development councils from acquiring the least bit of power."[17] Electing himself the spokesman for the local leaders and political representatives, Maurice Tessier, just when he had been nominated Minister responsible for the ODEQ, expressed the desire to give back to the latter the decision-making powers they had previously possessed:

> In the future, as minister responsible for the ODEQ, it will no longer be the CRDEQ which will be my interlocutor, but I will listen instead to all the others, such as the parliamentarians, the municipal councils, and chambers of commerce, who really know the people's needs.[18]

This assertion enables us to ascertain, already at the start of the 1970s, the presence of a malaise in the exercise of power at the local and regional levels. In addition, the government wanted to return power to the traditional elites and, in particular, to the mayors, parliamentarians, and chambers of commerce.[19]

To this it must be added that the arrival of new regional structures like those of the ODEQ and subsequently of the CAREQ would result in the accentuation of tensions between the local leaders and the technocrats: the preeminent place occupied by the former on the regional and local scene diminished considerably with the gains of the technocrats. The establishment of a regional administration signified a weakening of the ability of intervention (others would say of patronage[20]) for the traditional elites. Coulombe has grasped the presence of this dimension in his study on territorial development and planning in Quebec:

> The regionalization of administration is not only exposed to the inertia of the ministries against the reforms demanded, it must also face the awakening of traditional forces and parochialism. It seems that the traditional elites—provincial and federal members of parliament, mayors, and political party organizers—grasped the danger which represents, for them, the presence on their territory of bureaucrats gathered in regional capitals. Indeed, the administrative reassembly could mean, if it is applied completely, the end of the role of liaison agent played by a parliamentarian or anyone who could intercede in Quebec and return to his county or municipality and distribute the favours obtained through the grace of his intervention.[21]

Coulombe's interpretation permits one to take into account the political manoeuvres of traditional elites at the start of a planned development structure in eastern Quebec. At this time, lively polemics were sparked throughout the territory. One of the principal protagonists was the deputy-mayor of Rivière-du-Loup, Rosaire Gendron, who conducted a sustained counterattack against the demands of the BAEQ to create a unitary development and planning council for eastern Quebec. He proposed to subdivide the area into three autonomous subregions in order for his city to retire from the control of the regional capital, Rimouski.[22]

As each decision was made to rationalize the existing infrastructures and to privilege certain centres at the expense of others, the resistances of the traditional forces became stronger. Unable to ignore these forces at the political level, the government often had no choice other than to negotiate with them. As Coulombe reiterates, "These traditional forces have shown their capacity to influence concerned people, which permits them to block the government in its decisions when it does not dare risk a confrontation with those whom it counts on for support during elections."[23]

The prevalent relations between the Office de planification et de développement du Québec (OPDQ) and politicians need also to be mentioned, given that their responsibilities and conceptions of affairs often clashed. Baccigalupo, in a study on public administration in Quebec, distinguishes three important problems with this issue:

> In the regions where it is active, the OPDQ performs tasks the local elected official often considers as under his own particular jurisdiction. In addition, at the regional level the OPDQ contacts and encourages the emergence of new socioeconomic forces (for example, the CRD), out of which can emerge, at some future date, dangerous candidates for the established parliament.
>
> In the third instance, the social animators charged to establish and maintain relations with the populations on matters of planning may often defend and propagate "advanced" ideas not always favourable to the dominant ideology.[24]

We can quite easily understand the apprehension of many politicians and community leaders at the sight of the spread of bureaucratization in the regions. In addition, one should remember that the last structural changes—like the institution of the CRDEQ, the start of the BAEQ, the creation of the ODEQ, or the institution of the CAREQ—did not in the least reassert the role of parliamentarians or local leaders. Within the course of a series of articles on the results and effects after the signing of the Canada-Quebec accord, Damien Gagnon supports these latter points:

> This team of young academics designated as trouble makers by the politicians were badly received by the parliamentarians of the area. The latter saw the BAEQ as a threat to their prestige. They consequently remained distant from the work of the BAEQ.
>
> Still today, the majority of the parliamentarians of the area do not take into account the works of the regional administrative conference and the regional development council of eastern Quebec.[25]

The orientation of the new political forces towards the elaboration of a technocratic society—claimed to be above ideological commitments—represented a major victory for the technocracy over traditional and popular forces. This new direction would nevertheless have important and determining consequences for the development of eastern Quebec. This is what makes Piotte accentuate two principal objectives followed by the BAEQ:

> The solution of the problems of the region resides in the rationalization of socioeconomic relations: the point is not to change the system, but to make

> it operative. This initiative to rationalize the socioeconomic relations of this region had two consequences. On the one hand, the organizers have to initiate the population to this new rationality so that it may accept the plan created by the researchers. On the other hand, the planners have to "rouse" the high-level bureaucrats and ministers to make them functional so that the plan can be accepted and applied by the government.[26]

This raises two important questions concerning the lack of enthusiasm found among the traditional elites for the changes in the existing situation and attempts to modernize the economic structure of the region.[27] The spatial restructuring and the rationalization of economic activities thus underlie the concomitant regional struggles and provide major reference points to better discern the resistance of local interests to planned development.[28]

At another level were the conflicts between parliamentarians affiliated to different political organizations in the area and operating, depending on the case, on the federal or provincial scene. The principal conflicts pitted the provincial Liberals against the Parti Québécois representatives as well as federal Liberal parliamentarians against representatives of the PQ *and* the provincial Liberals. (See Tables 15-1 and 15-2.)

On the provincial side, the Liberal parliamentarians lacked interest when the issue was to take a stand against the changes established since the beginning of the Quiet Revolution. At the same time, the PQ sought to capitalize on the position of the provincial Liberals by proposing, if elected, to put forward reforms seeking greater decentralization and giving more responsibilities to local leaders. On the federal side, in spite of their invisibility at the outset, federal interventions at the regional level (with DREE as intermediary) were to become determinants in the financing and elaboration of the development plan.[29] However, the years following the arrival of the PQ in power would be clearly different from the preceding ones, in that the federal government, like its provincial counterpart, would try to gain the maximum possible benefits from its regional interventions.

The post-BAEQ period marked a particularly interesting conflict—that is, the one between the leader-priests of the rural municipalities and the provincial parliamentarians elected by the same people—during the formation and development period of Opérations Dignité. Exasperated, the representative from Iles-de-la-Madeleine, Louis-Philippe Lacroix, stated, "The priests and the curates be damned. If they want to govern, well then, let them get elected."[30] Subsequently, the publication of the *Manifeste de Matane* in June 1973 incited the Liberal, UN, and Créditiste representatives to brand the organizers of this manifesto as "trouble makers." These organizers were recruited from among mayors, members of municipal councils, and priests of the area and sought nothing more than to sensitize the two principal levels of government to the problems affecting the economy of eastern Quebec.

At this time, only Pierre de Bané was an ally of the priests and local

Table 15-1 Provincial Political Representatives

County	1970		1973		1976		1981	
Bonaventure	G.D. Lévesque Lawyer/Shopkeeper	Lib.	G.D. Lévesque	Lib.	G.D. Lévesque	Lib.	G.D. Lévesque	Lib.
Gaspé Nord	F. Gagnon Bank Official	UN						
			G. Fortier	Lib.	M. Lemoignan Priest	UN	H. Lemay Professor	PQ
Gaspé Sud	G. Fortier Mayor/Doctor	Lib.						
Matane	J. Bienvenue Lawyer	Lib.	M.Y. Côté Professor	Lib.	Y. Bérubé Engineer/Professor	PQ	Y. Bérubé	PQ
Matapédia	B. Arsenault Businessman	Lib.	B. Arsenault	Lib.	L. Marquis Professor	PQ	L. Marquis	PQ
Rimouski	M. Tessier Mayor/lawyer	Lib.	C. St-Hilaire Mayor/engineer	Lib.	A. Marcoux Professor	PQ	A. Marcoux	PQ
Témiscouata	J.M. Simard Mayor/county prefect Businessman	UN	J.M. Pelletier	Lib.	L. Lévesque Churchwarden/Farmer	PQ	L. Lévesque	PQ
Kamouraska	J.M. Pelletier Mayor	Lib.						
Rivière-du-Loup	P. Lafrance Dentist	Lib.	P. Lafrance	Lib.	J. Boucher Bureaucrat	PQ	J. Boucher	PQ
Iles-de-la-Madeleine	L.P. Lacroix Accountant	Lib.	L.P. Lacroix	Lib.	D. Leblanc Professor	PQ	D. Leblanc	PQ

Note: Lib.: Parti libéral du Québec; PQ: Parti québécois; UN: Union nationale.
Source: Gouvernement du Québec, *Répertoire des parlementaires québécois, 1867-1978 (1980).*

Table 15-2 Federal Political Representatives

County	1972		1974		1979		1980	
Bonaventure-Iles-de-la-Madeleine	A. Béchard Notary	Lib.	A. Béchard	Lib.	R. Bujold Lawyer	Lib.	R. Bujold	Lib.
Gaspé	A. Cyr Secretary/Accountant	Lib.	A. Cyr	Lib.	A. Cyr	Lib.	A. Cyr	Lib.
Matane	P. de Bané Lawyer	Lib.	P. de Bané	Lib.	P. de Bané	Lib.	P. de Bané	Lib.
Rimouski	E. Allard Hotel owner	CS	E. Allard	CS	E. Allard	CS	E. Cote Executive Sec'y	Lib.
Kamouraska	C.E. Dionne Lumberjack	CS	C.E. Dionne	CS				
Riviere-du-Loup	R. Gendron Mayor/Accountant	Lib.	R. Gendron	Lib.	R. Gendron	Lib.	R. Gendron	Lib.

Note: Lib.: Liberal party; cs: Créditiste
Source: P.G. Normandin (ed.), *Canadian Parliamentary Guide* (Ottawa).

leaders;[31] in return, he received almost indestructible support from these groups during his electoral campaigns. In other words, de Bané's decision, taken at the beginning of the Opérations Dignité, was extremely beneficial to him. Nonetheless, he defended himself for not being an opportunist:

> I sleep with the citizen councils; he [Parizeau] sleeps with others. That is his business. To each his own business. Everyone here can confirm that it is false to state that I affiliated myself with the citizen councils only when they became successful. I was there at the start, when the risk was greatest. I am not an opportunist.[32]

Many criticized de Bané for seeking political capital. (But is it not the nature of the politician to seek support to assure his election or reelection?) Nevertheless, it is important to note that de Bané's action helped to demystify power. In this respect, his action was considerable: "power, it is only a relation of strength which is organized."[33] However, his interventions alienated many parliamentarians of neighbouring counties, which he canvassed to rally their people to the popular movement. The altercations were as colourful as they were numerous. Suffice it to mention that Tessier, Lacroix, Cyr, and Arsenault were none too enraptured by de Bané's repeated invasions into their respective counties.[34]

The de Bané phenomenon also caused a stir among top officials of the Parti Québécois, especially since he often received the encouragement and support of militant *Péquistes*.[35] The PQ's fears can be explained in part because it did not anticipate that the citizen councils, who usually attract the most activist social forces, would leave their political ranks for this other means to express their dissatisfaction with the established power holders. The PQ wanted, in fact, to mobilize the discontented in order to realize electoral gains. Finally, these ostensibly apolitical groups were restraining the possibilities for the PQ to recruit members among local leaders: whence, from the beginning, there arose a certain coolness towards the popular forces.

Growing Restitution of Power for the Local Forces

Parallel to the technocratization of the governmental apparatus and the growing conflicts between different political formations, the evolution of popular forces and the removal of traditional forces as influential power holders at the local level would become even more striking. The organismes de développement communautaire expressed little interest in engaging in electoral political action. It seems that they preferred to rely on the traditional forces. In this context, the Union des municipalités du Québec (UMQ)[36] and the Union des conseils de comté du Québec (UCCQ)[37] were in the process of increasing their power over the regional scene. Consequently, the meetings with the municipalities were gradually developed by the government party. Also, the provincial Liberals organized the first provincial-municipal conference in May 1971. A second conference was convened in May 1975 when numerous actors on the regional scene were questioning government policies.

The Liberal government of the period wanted to remove the county councils in an effort to integrate them with regional administrations. This reform did not receive the assent of local leaders. It would have assured final approval for the government on decisions on matters of regional planning (through the intermediary of administrative regions), subregional planning (through the intermediary of reassembled municipalities), and local planning.[38] Also, through this reform program, which originated during the UN (Unionist) regime under the auspices of the program Renouveau municipal et urbain:

> The government attacked the whole of the municipal realm, including the rural areas, while the ad-hoc interventions that characterized the Unionist period of 1966 to 1970 mainly addressed themselves to the large urban areas, where the support bases for the party in power were felt less menaced than with the Liberal government after 1970.[39]

The consequences of such an operation were considerable, since the PQ would eventually profit from the malaise generated in many of these areas to solidify its bases of support. (See Table 15-1.)

The political parties, those in power and in opposition, had to ally themselves from this point on with established forces on the regional scene. Two researchers at Institut national de la recherche scientifique-Urbanisation who have specialized in municipal reform in Quebec since the 1960s, describe the principal intermediary bodies in existence at the municipal level, UCCQ and UMQ, as strongly politicized groups. They indicate as well that the preference of each of these two bodies lay in different political tendencies; hence, the importance for them to seek gains with the two municipal organizations:

> The world of the municipalities, represented by the Union des conseils de comté, constantly adapted the strategies and proposals for concertation with the Union des municipalités (urbaines) du Québec, an attitude of suspicion virtually as complete as the one it progressively took with the initiatives proposed by the federal government. Parallel to this cleavage, politicoideological streams and partisan affiliations continued to separate the elected members in the UCCQ and UMQ among Unionists and Liberals and, more recently, between federalists (anti-*Péquiste*) and sovereignists (*Péquiste*).[40]

Thus, we can see the importance for the political formations to simultaneously make inroads at the rural and urban levels. This need to maintain or impose themselves on the regional scene brought the politicians to attenuate their reform proposals in order to assure, beforehand, the support of local leaders. The notions about the amalgamation of the municipalities and the removal of the county councils were banished from the rhetoric; from then on, there was talk of consolidating the rural areas and revitalizing the county councils. One of the first to suffer from such changes was Maurice Tessier, Minister of Municipal Affairs from 1970 to 1973 in

Premier Bourassa's first cabinet, who proclaimed the merits of massive reform at the municipal level; he became part of the first cabinet shuffle. It was no longer possible to alienate the municipal councillors when all other political organizations eagerly sought their support:

> During the electoral campaigns of 1970, 1973, and 1976, the Liberal party and the Parti Québécois were rivals in courting local representatives: the participation of the latter at all partisan manifestations was sought and publicized, while the decision by a rural or urban mayor to be a candidate for one or the other party was presented as a great victory in the increasingly polarized struggle of the 1970s.[41]

The Parti Québécois knew how to profit from the circumstances: it promised to proceed with the decentralization of power at the regional level. This electoral platform seems to have been successful for the party if we rely on the results in eastern Quebec of the 1976 election (see Table 15-1). The inaugural speech of March 1977 confirmed the Lévesque government's intentions to proceed along this road. The enacted reforms of the government party, even if important at the start, did not have scope that was touted.[42] Nonetheless, three reforms elicited special attention: fiscal reform (Bill 57), electoral reform (Bills 44 and 105), and, finally, the reform of agricultural zoning and urban planning (Bills 90 and 125).

The fiscal reform is probably the lynchpin of the framework of the changes and are likely to follow in the municipal sector. Seeking not to alienate the municipal powers, the government party promised them new sources of revenue to meet local needs. Conscious of the local leaders' desires to regain their prestige, the government brought forth the fiscal question during the first provincial-municipal conference in June 1978, entitled "Québec-Municipalités." This reform can essentially be summarized by the transfer of the property tax, collected erstwhile by the school boards, to the municipalities. This is far from demonstrating a decentralization of power; it amounts rather to a reshuffling of power.

In fact, the fiscal reform prepared the way for the collaboration of the traditional forces in maintaining the status quo—that is, the persistence of centralization. Instead of seeing the PQ government meet its promises to decentralize social affairs, education, leisure, and municipal affairs, as promised during its first mandate, local leaders had to content themselves with some decentralization at the planning level. This last responsibility was strongly limited by the ratification of Bill 90 on agricultural zoning:

> Even if the government departed from the responsibility of preparing regional schemes, it retained a considerable role. In accordance with Bill 125, the government, its ministers and representatives, have to indicate to the MRC their orientations in planning as well as in equipment, infrastructural, and development projects. The Minister of State for Development has to oversee the preparation of documents and advice transmitted to the MRC, through the mediation of the Minister of Municipal Affairs, and assure

himself that the documents mirror the preoccupations of the government, especially in matters of regional development, and still respect the functioning of the MRC.[43]

In a sense, they obliterated what was just given to the municipal councillors. Quesnel-Ouellet defends a similar position when she states, "The bill [90] produced at this time an important break in local autonomy. It entrusts the protection of agricultural territory to a provincial commission and forces the municipalities to get their plans for agricultural zoning approved by the government."[44] There was thus little left of the decentralization policy once the PQ began legislating. Only the bill on electoral reform seemed to reestablish local power. In this sense, it proposed the establishment of municipal political parties and obliged them to account for their expenses during electoral campaigns. We know as yet too little of the consequences that could ensue from these changes to categorically pronounce conclusions about these changes.[45]

The PQ government is on the road to realizing a tour de force by making some believe in a major decentralization of state power to the regions. In fact, the decentralization program contains little real change in this direction. As previously emphasized, the MRCs are given some planning responsibilities, but all their decisions come under the scrutiny of the Minister of State for planning and development. In addition, the MRCs have taken over the responsibilities previously held by the county councils—that is, property evaluations, water, and refuse treatment. To cite more, Bill 12, enacted in December 1980, strictly limits the MRCs' powers in these very domains.[46] This situation fits none too well with proposals found in the official platform of the Parti Québécois, which states the recognition of 10 areas of competence for the MRC: planning and development; economic promotion and industrial funds; regional highways; the housing sector, including relocation; the environment; public transportation; the administration of community services and equipment; tourism promotion and development; the administration of regional fisheries; and, finally, the administration of regional police forces.[47]

At this time, the government, far from achieving these objectives, is trying to centralize even more. The establishment of the MRC enables one to predict a greater and significant ascendancy of urban municipalities over rural ones. A passage from Dugas gives credibility to this interpretation:

> We can predict that the obligation for the cities and rural municipalities to plan together will bring serious difficulties in numerous sectors of Quebec. The demographic weight of the cities and their teams of specialized bureaucrats strongly risk swamping any and all attempts by rural localities to affirm themselves. . . . We can state for sure that the rural municipalities will find themselves forced to accept unwanted and unsearched-for development directions. These directions could even spread into peripheral regions to the point of accelerating the destruction of particular localities to the profit of growing city and service centres.[48]

This last incursion by government is strangely reminiscent, under the label of a "decentralizing" bill, of the policies for relocating and concentrating populations put forward at the start of the 1970s. One can easily imagine what it means for the government to permit housing construction only in those areas already equipped with the necessary facilities of aqueducts and drainage systems. The official position seeks to affirm that such measures are to prohibit the scattering of residential centres, as was the case during the 1970s, in order to avoid the excessive costs required from such practices. In reality, the government kills two birds with one stone since it prevents the reappearance of population dispersal throughout Quebec, as well as incites those parishes in decline to direct themselves towards the already equipped urban centres. Dugas, who has written a dissertation on the dispersal problem in eastern Quebec, arrives at analogous claims:

> The bill [125] imposes urbanization plans on all the municipalities which are part of a municipalité régionale de comté. Such a measure is not indispensable in all areas to produce respect for major organizational schema, as in the cases of the agriculture, forestry, and agroforestry areas with a strong demographic decline. The problem with these areas is not to control the expansion of housing and the development of areas, but to avoid the complete emptying of existing residential areas.[49]

The Technocracy in Search of Support from Popular Groups

We can identify two major orientations behind the decisions taken by the PQ government on decentralization. One refers to the government's attempt to remove certain powers from the technocracy and give them to local leaders and parliamentarians; the second concerns the effort to shortcircuit the popular groups. Also, we saw that the PQ government proposed many times to reorganize power in the regions. These reforms have been watered down: the PQ wants to forge links with local forces in the province, while assuring better representation for its politicians at the local level. In fact, this was the reason for the initiative to institute the Regional Intervention Council. The Minister of State for planning and development responsible for this reform, François Gendron, admits in a memorandum presented to the Council of Ministers:

> If the support base for the MRCs is the regional community, there exists at the level of regional administration (eventually adjusted) another level of concentrated efforts for the development of the people of the region. It is important to link this level of dialogue with the prefects of the MRCs and Quebec parliamentarians within one single council. This regional intervention council will have as its task to concentrate the efforts of the area on regional development matters and produce solutions to certain regional problems.[50]

This council, if effectively instituted, will have as its functions to define the orientations and priorities of regional development, to take charge of the

Fonds de développement régional and to inform the government of any progress with provincial programs for local areas.[51]

The arrival of this regional council, uniting regional prefects and parliamentarians, politicized the whole decentralization program and, consequently, all regional development, and will create new dependencies not only, in this case, with respect to regional administrators, but also for local leaders and parliamentarians from the region. The actualization of such a change is questioned by more than one actor. The Conseils régionaux de développement associés du Québec were the first to voice their discontent. Apart from the fact that they risked losing their raison d'être,[52] they saw here an expressly politicized turn of events.

> To begin with, regional interests cannot be discerned solely by politicians and, secondly, in the present form of parliamentarian government, we risk seeing regions administered by a round table of prefects and opposition parliamentarians; it is evident that such possibilities would radically block the development of the regions. . . . In our opinion, the regional intervention council should be formed with representatives from all sectors and be more detached from political power, or else we risk destroying the dynamism of the region and take steps backwards.[53]

This brings us to the second objective of the proposed reform—that is, the desire to destabilize the popular groups and orient the dynamism of the area to contain the choices made by the MRC prefects and parliamentarians. In other words, the whole operation seems detached from the ODCs since it limits itself to giving back the initiative to the traditional forces. By rehabilitating the municipalities, through the MRCs as intermediary, in the decision-making process, the government in effect paralyzes the popular groups.[54] This action is all the more effective since the designated MRCs generally correspond to the territories occupied by the various ODCs. Aware that the municipal representatives have in the past pronounced their majority in favour of the regional elites, which others have designated as the retail and financial bourgeoisie,[55] the institution of the MRCs and of the regional intervention council should produce the same effect, while the popular forces of the region, often absent from municipal administration, will be left out in the cold.

This will to rehabilitate certain powers of the local notables comes forth clearly in an interview given by Gendron, in which the Minister emphasized the basic principles for all future policies of regional development in Quebec.[56] He cited four principles: development must be attuned to the dynamism of the regions, without expecting government intervention; it must include the development of the large centres; the region of origin (MRC) and the administrative region have to share a good part of the responsibilities for development; and, finally, even though development needs the participation and consultation of the population, it is nothing but a political act which recognizes the prerogative of decision-making powers for representatives (mayors, parliamentarians) who are in any event responsible to their constituents through their respective mandates.[57]

Seeing that these reforms would work at its expense, the regional technocracy modified its positions toward popular groups. While it was initially suspicious of regional dynamism, the regional technocracy gradually became favourable to its complete unfolding. No matter if we refer to the conversion of the CRDEQ or the OPDQ-Est, there is little doubt that these organizations clearly reevaluated their initial position. For example, with the CRDEQ, we can see a substantial shift in its positions. It is in this way that the organization retreated from its original demands for the consolidation of different sectors of growth to subsequently make demands for the integrated resource planning of Eastern Quebec's hinterland. Jutras believes that this change of attitude can be directly attributed to the mode of representation which the organization used henceforth to insure the inclusion of all the social and economic sectors of the region.[58] It is also possible to add that, in an effort to conserve the power previously given to it, the CRDEQ, which found few allies among the local leaders, had to search among the popular forces. It was a matter of survival and legitimacy for this body.

The case of the OPDQ-Est is also revealing of an attempt to find support in rural areas. Following the elaboration of a policy to back up regional self-development by encouraging the regions to make use of their own potentials,[59] the OPDQ-Est mainly took a position in favour of the consolidating role of the ODCs in zones with high migration. It was this view which the director of the OPDQ-Est took when he wrote in 1979 that:

> ... these bodies have, in numerous cases, polarized and channelled the efforts to develop the basic resources of the hinterlands formerly slated for closure. They have greatly contributed to the fresh promotion of rural municipalities as well as to the viability, or profitability, of their infrastructures, firms, and services (agricultural production units, forestry processing plants, warehouses, etc.).[60]

Should we see in this *rapprochement* of the regional technocracy to the ODCs an attempt by the former to block the recent initiatives of the government party to give back to the local leaders and politicians the power that had escaped them since the start of the Quiet Revolution? It seems that the new "frustrés de l'Etat" have no other recourse than to ally themselves with popular development struggles, given the fact that both of these formations have been excluded from the promotion of local power.

Admittedly, this about face of the technocracy concerning the ODCs is impressive. It indicates the strong capacity for adaptation which the intermediary agents are capable of, as well as the ability of politicians and local leaders to use various methods to attain their goals. We are thus presented with traditional and new political forces searching for support at the national, regional, and local levels. Each of these actors, intervening ostensibly in the name of the general welfare of the concerned populations, has tried to enhance its decision-making position. In these circumstances, we are confronted by an imposing system of relays, without in the least bit attenuating any of the inherent contradictions of the system.

According to this interpretation, we can understand the interest that local leaders, politicians, and technocrats have had in making themselves the spokesmen for the popular movement. To arrive at their objectives they have proclaimed regional demands and thus have sought support among popular groups to amass credibility for their own actions.

In summary, the exclusion of popular groups from the new directions taken by the PQ government, in the conditions described above, risks weakening even more the technocracy, while giving at the same time a certain importance to local leaders, who were, we must remember, the major losers in the politicoadministrative changes made by government during the 1960s. The seats of power thus alternated according to the utility of certain actors vis-à-vis others. As a consequence, "The 'popular forces' that manifested themselves in the 1960s and found themselves for the most part concentrated, at the regional level, in the regional development councils, have no other option than to become classical elected leaders or to play the 'role of opposition' in the democratic arena defined by the new rules of development and planning."[61]

To the existing tensions between the technocracy and the government, one must add those between the federal and provincial levels. The political struggles are crucial here because they concern the desire of each level for solid support from the municipal world. It is in this spirit that the Quebec government tried to thwart federal initiatives at the regional level. Also, the announcement by de Bané in autumn 1981, to put into effect a federal program specifically addressing the subregions, incited the anxiety of his provincial counterpart. This federal intervention pushed the Minister Gendron to immediately seek an audience before the Council of Ministers:

> The Federal Minister for Regional Economic Expansion is in the process of reviewing his policies. We cannot neglect the possibility of the loss of direct aid to regional bodies. The regional county municipalities, who are starting their development plans and need financing to assure completion, will be very alluring prey. We should also put rapidly in place mechanisms to channel these direct relations.[62]

The tensions elicited from this type of stand reflect, up to a certain point, the nature of the relations between the provinces and the federal government. It appears that the economic recession has accentuated even more the antagonisms between the two governments, since Quebec was betting on the self-financing of the local communities to get out of their economic impasse. But as Quebec invites the municipalities to become self-sufficient for their own financing, Ottawa sees an excellent opportunity to make political gains.[63]

A more detailed study of the popular movements, produced from a review of the development of eastern Quebec, shows that the state is not content merely with regulating social contradictions, but participates in the emergence, the deepening, and the resolving of these contradictions. A prime example is the state's subsidization of popular groups as well as its exclusion of these groups from its promotion of local power.

At the origin of these tensions and contradictions, positions on the real nature of regional power diverge: whether this power constitutes an area of specific intervention or an intermediate relay between the centre and the periphery. The politicoadministrative reforms of the 1960s correspond to the establishment of such channels between the government and the regions, while the rise of popular groups is situated more in the direction of the emergence of new seats of power. In both cases, the old forms of power are questioned. In reaction to this dynamic, local leaders and, especially, the politicians attempt to regain lost territory by directing the demands of popular groups towards strictly political channels. Thus, according to this interpretation, the local leader (like the politician and the technocrat) "defines himself less by his personal attributes than by an action system which is constituted through its close interdependence with the functions assumed by the territorial offices of the administrative apparatus of the state."[64]

The preceding considerations concerning the evolution of political forces in Quebec have demonstrated that the bias which led to a view of Quebec as a homogeneous social entity that transcends social class divisions has fostered an incomplete interpretation. All too often the middle classes have been perceived as the defenders of the Quebec nation, while the role played by other political forces in Quebec provincial politics has been ignored. The discussion presented here gives more credence to popular classes and local leaders as well as addressing the regional question. The central role played by the technocrats during the 1960s and at the beginning of the 1970s has given way to struggle for ascendancy predicated on competition from the local leaders and the popular groups. Recent developments tend to confirm this analysis. However, it remains to be seen to what extent these political forces will be able to place the regional question on the political agenda of the 1980s. In the midst of a reorganization at the regional level, via the establishment of Municipalités régionales de comté, one can predict some serious confrontations ahead, along with further struggles in terms of the larger arena of state power in Canada and Quebec.

Notes

1. Fernand Harvey, "La question régionale au Québec," *La revue d'études canadiennes* 15: 2 (1980), p. 76, my translation.
2. See Alain G. Gagnon, *Le développement régional, l'Etat et le rôle des groupes populaires: le cas de l'est du Québec* (Doctoral dissertation, Carleton University, April 1983).
3. See the study by Robert Dahl, *Qui gouverne?* (Paris: Armand Colin, 1973).

4. Pierre Grémion, *Le pouvoir périphérique: bureaucrates et notables dans le système politique français* (Paris: Seuil, 1976), p. 247, my translation.
5. Ibid., p. 285, my translation.
6. Gagnon, op. cit.
7. The union movement occupies a less than prominent place in the hinterland of eastern Quebec. It is nonetheless important to specify that this movement is not absent from the rural world. It is in this way, for example, that the parish representatives formed the executive committee of OD I. They were mainly members of the Agricultural Producers Union (UPA) and of the Office of Wood Producers which became the Union of Wood Producers (SPB). For more information, see Charles Banville, *Les Opérations Dignité* (Québec: Le fonds de recherches forestières de l'Université Laval, 1977), p. 79.
8. Kenneth McRoberts and Dale Posgate, *Quebec: Social Change and Political Crisis* (Toronto: McClelland and Stewart, 1980), pp. 94-124; Hubert Guindon, "Social Unrest, Social Class and Quebec's Bureaucratic Revolution," *Queen's Quarterly* 71: 2 (1964), pp. 150-62.
9. At the instigation of McRoberts and Posgate, G. Divay and J. Léveillee took this position in *La réforme municipale et l'Etat québécois* (Montréal: INRS-Urbanisation, 1981), p. 29, my translation.
10. Jacques Benjamin, *Planification et politique au Québec* (Montréal: Presses de l'Université de Montréal, 1974), p. 97, my translation.
11. Claude Turcotte, "Le BAEQ, 10 ans après," *La Presse* (Aug. 20, 1973).
12. Roger Guy, "Mon expérience au BAEQ," in Benoît Lévesque (ed.), *Animation sociale, entreprises communautaires et coopératives* (Montréal: Editions co-opératives Albert St-Martin, (1979), p. 61, my translation.
13. Statements grouped together by Charles Banville, *Les Opérations Dignité*, op. cit., p. 82, my translation. For a full study on this movement, one may refer to Alain G. Gagnon, *Les Opérations Dignité: Naissance d'un mouvement social dans l'Est du Québec* (Ottawa: Carleton University, 1981).
14. Robert Carrier and Johanne Jutras, *Quelles orientations pour le CRDEQ: Rapport présenté au conseil d'administration du CRDEQ* (Rimouski: CRDEQ, 1980), p. 11.
15. Clermont Dugas, "Le développement de l'Est du Québec de 1963 à 1972," *Cahiers de géographie de Québec* 17: 41 (1973), p. 287.
16. Charles Banville, op cit., pp. 83-87, discusses the prevalent relations between the Opérations Dignité and the CRDEQ.
17. Jacques Benjamin, op. cit., p. 110, my translation.
18. See the report by Robert Lévesque, "Tessier se dit favorable à la disparition du CRD," *Le Soleil* (Dec. 1, 1970), p. 7, my translation.
19. One can also refer to the analysis by François Demers, "Le livre blanc ne menacera pas les élites locales," *Le Soleil* (Dec. 5, 1970), p. 5.
20. Maurice Croisat, "L'expérience québécoise en matière de régionalisation," in *Aménagement du territoire et développement régional*, vol. III (Grenoble: Institut d'Etudes politiques, 1970), p. 699.
21. Françoise Coulombe, *L'Arda et l'aménagement du territoire au Québec*, (M.A. thesis, Political Science, Université de Montréal, 1968), pp. 189-90, my translation.
22. Many newspaper articles refer to this policy. See, among others, Paul Cliche, "Une réaction conservatrice dans la région et une certaine indifférence 'des

centres de décision' à Québec mettent le projet d'exécution du BAEQ en péril," *Le Devoir* (March 28, 1967), p. 11; Pierre Richard, "Le plan compromis par un manque de volonté politique?" *Le Devoir* (Aug. 16, 1971), pp. 2-3.

23. Françoise Coulombe, op. cit., p. 192, my translation.
24. Alain Baccigalupo, *Les grands rouages de la machine administrative québécoise* (Montréal: Editions Agence d'Arc, 1978), p. 383, my translation.
25. Damien Gagnon, "Huit ans après l'entente," *Le Soleil* (April 5, 1976), my translation.
26. Jean-Marc Piotte, "L'option politique du BAEQ," *Parti Pris* 3: 10 (1966), pp. 47-48, my translation.
27. See Alain G. Gagnon, op. cit., Ch. IV.
28. See the report by Pierre Richard, op. cit., pp. 2-3.
29. Daniel Latouche, *Une société de l'ambiguité: libération et récupération dans le Québec actuel* (Montréal: Boréal Express, 1979), p. 205; Lionel Robert, "L'espace et l'Etat: politiques et mouvements régionaux au Québec," *Critère* 23 (fall 1978), p. 242.
30. Statements reported in *La Voix Gaspésienne* (Jan. 19, 1972), my translation.
31. Banville, op. cit., pp. 67-74.
32. Louis Martin, "Le débat de Bané-Parizeau," *Le Soleil* (Dec. 15, 1971), p. 22, my translation.
33. De Bané's statements reported in *La Voix Gaspésienne* (Aug. 18, 1971), my translation.
34. One can refer here to the study by Banville, *op. cit.*, or consult the press report compiled by Fabrice Jacques. The latter is available in the archives for regional affairs of the Université du Québec à Rimouski.
35. Banville, op. cit., p. 71.
36. The Union des municipalités du Québec represents urban municipalities. These are very well structured at the provincial level.
37. The Union des conseils de comté represents rural municipalities. They encompass more than 70 councils and have exercised more pressure on the political authorities since the return of the provincial Liberals to power in 1970. In addition, the Conférence municipale, one of the specialized bodies of the CDREQ, would be for the most part removed from the decentralization and planning programs. It would later be superseded by the creation of the MRCs.
38. Louise Quesnel-Ouellet, "Aménagement urbain et autonomie," in G. Bergeron and R. Pelletier (eds.), *L'Etat du Québec en devenir* (Montréal: Boréal Express, 1980), pp. 224-31.
39. Ibid., pp. 226-27, my translation.
40. Divay and Léveillée, op. cit., pp. 84-85.
41. Ibid., p. 90, my translation.
42. The study by G. Fortin, J. Léveillée, and L. Parent presented to the colloquium on decentralization organized by the Union des municipalités du Québec merits attention. See *La décentralisation et le pouvoir des municipalités* (Montreal: INRS-Urbanisation, 1982).
43. François Gendron, *Mémoire présenté au Conseil des ministres: Eléments d'une politique de développement des régions et instruments de mise en oeuvre* (Québec: Gouvernement du Québec, Nov. 11, 1981), p. 3, my translation. This document is part of larger reflection, which produced Le choix des régions (1983).

44. Louise Quesnel-Ouellet, op. cit. p. 233, my translation.
45. One can refer, for a more detailed study on the recent modifications brought to municipal electoral proceedings, to Louise Quesnel-Ouellet, op. cit., pp. 234-35, or to Guy Bourassa, "La démocratie municipale: déblocage ou impasse?" *Possibles* 5: 2 (1981), pp. 39-48.
46. Marie-Agnès Thellier, "Un chemin sinueux mène aux municipalités de comté," *Le Devoir* (Feb. 5, 1981), p. 7.
47. *Programme officiel du Parti québécois* (VII Congress, 1980), p. 11.
48. Clermont Dugas, "La loi sur les municipalités régionales de comté: un outil de centralisation," *Le Devoir* (Oct. 7, 1980), p. 17, my translation.
49. Ibid, my translation.
50. Gendron, op. cit., p. 5, my translation.
51. Ibid.
52. Marie-Agnès Thellier, "CRD: ultime lutte pour la survie," *Le Devoir* (Feb. 26, 1981), p. 11; "Québec doit 'dépolitiser' le développement régional," *Le Devoir* (March 13, 1982), p. 13.
53. Conseils régionaux de développement associés du Québec, *Avis au premier ministre du Québec sur le développement régional* (Quebec: CRDAQ, Feb. 19, 1982), p. 7, my translation.
54. Hugues Dionne (ed.), *Aménagement intégré des ressources et luttes en milieu rural* (Rimouski: GRIDEQ-UQAR, 1983), pp. 147-48, 152-55.
55. Harvey, op. cit., p. 86.
56. The major points of this interview are mainly inspired by the memorandum that he presented to the council of Ministers on November 11, 1981, op. cit.
57. Statements reported by Marie-Agnès Thellier, "Québec est prêt à mieux appuyer le développement régional," *Le Devoir* (Jan. 14, 1982), p. 15.
58. Johanne Jutras, *Le conseil régional de développement de l'Est du Québec* (Rimouski: GRIDEQ-UQAR, 1981), p. 120.
59. OPDQ, *Les orientations de développement de l'Est du Québec* (Québec: OPDQ, 1979), pp. 37-40.
60. Jean-Paul Gendron, *Financement des organismes populaires de développement économique* (Est du Québec) (Rimouski: OPDQ-Est, 1979), p. 16, my translation.
61. Divay and Léveillée, op. cit., p. 91, my translation.
62. Gendron, op. cit., pp. 7-8, my translation.
63. Rita Bissonnette-Guénard, "Au coeur d'un nouvel enjeu: les municipalités régionales de comté," *Le Devoir* (March 5, 1982), p. 17.
64. Grémion, op. cit., p. 167, my translation.

Part V/The State and Groups

This part contains studies of relations between the state and groups. Lipsig-Mummé discusses the evolution of Quebec unions while Hudon and Pelletier respectively analyze recent transformations in the Quebec party system. To conclude this section, Archibald and Tanguay examine the government's efforts at consensus building and its attempt to integrate all classes in this process.

For Lipsig-Mummé, all unions in developed capitalist societies are externally dependent institutions. She establishes that conventionally they attempt to reduce their dependence through a choice of different strategies, ranging from pure economism at one extreme, to the subordination of economic objectives, to revolutionary political goals at the other. Central to any union's choice of tactics and strategies are the ways and timing by which the pertinent levels of government intervene in the labour-capital relationship.

Hudon contends that it is the analysis of the polarization over the future of Quebec as a *society*, more than the future of Quebec as a *nation*, that can fundamentally account for the evolution of Quebec politics since the Quiet Revolution. This is especially evident at the level of party politics. Hudon also argues that, since the election of a PQ government in 1976, there has been a trend towards depolarization between political parties. This trend is partly related to the conditions created by the economic crisis and the further transformation of the PQ from party to government.

Pelletier links the development of political parties to the transformations in Quebec society as a whole. Moreover, he considers parties as agents of social transformation. He argues that the perception of problems and the definition of means to resolve them rests on a certain conception of society that can be revealed through an analysis of party programs: parties are to be seen as meeting points between the political and the social.

In his chapter, Archibald maintains that Quebec society has developed some corporatist tendencies. He also argues that a social corporatism, in the shadow of the state apparatus before 1960, was transformed into a political corporatism with the expansion of the state during the Quiet Revolution. Recent PQ programs are said to display neo-corporatist traits.

In the last chapter of this part, Tanguay examines the structure, function, and objectives of the principal instrument of concerted action in Quebec: the socioeconomic conference. By encouraging these periodic consultations between the state and its "social partners," the Parti Québécois government hopes eventually to forge a "new social contract" in the province. According to the terms of the envisaged social compact, the organizations of business and labour will commit themselves to realism and moderation in industrial relations in exchange for an increased voice in determining economic policy.

Chapter 16/The Web of Dependence: Quebec Unions in Politics before 1976*

Carla Lipsig-Mummé

The past decade has not been a propitious one for trade unionism in Quebec and elsewhere in North America. Regardless of ideological hue, trade unions have seen their political influence attenuated, their bargaining power undermined, their membership declining, their acquired rights threatened, their capacity to collect dues crippled, and, occasionally, their legal right to represent their members abolished. For the first time since the 1920s, the unions' long-established role as champion of the underdog has come under attack. In a time of rising unemployment, government spokesmen in the United States, English Canada, and Quebec are manipulating the charged concept of labour aristocracy in order to set the unorganized majority to blaming the unionized minority for the present crisis. Quebec MNA David Payne's statement during the recent conflict in the education industry is typical: "It is truly unacceptable that a group of employees, already privileged in comparison to their private sector counterparts, takes the population as hostage and tries to force the government to pay the ransom."[1]

For the several North American union movements the recent attacks by the state, what David J. Bercuson calls the emergence of "scapegoat politics,"[2] signals the end of a long period of state-structured support for minority trade unionism. Scapegoat politics has emerged as a result of the fiscal crisis of the North American governments, a fiscal crisis triggered by a long-term international reorganization of the division of labour. The North American welfare state is being pressured on the one hand by private capital seeking extended subsidies to shore up unprofitable enterprises, while at the same time it imposes a private-enterprise model of cost effectiveness on the state itself. On the other hand, the state is being pressured by the ranks of the unemployed, swollen both in number and in need. In the face of these zero-sum pressures, North American governments are turning on their union movements, cutting them off from the structural support—the enactment as government policy of threshold conditions which a minority union movement could not hope to win at the bargaining table—that has been the hallmark of labour policy since the New Deal in the United States, since the Second World War in Canada, and since 1960 in Quebec.

Setting the unions adrift goes hand in hand with a piecemeal dismantling of the welfare state. Unions have experienced the dismantling of the welfare state in ways that vary widely from industry to industry and region to

---

*This is a revised and expanded treatment of an argument initially developed in *Studies in Political Economy* 3 (1980).

region. But, overall, the present crisis of North American trade unionism is structural rather than conjunctural. It is a crisis of outmoded union strategies cracking apart to reveal long-rooted self-deceptions, papering over political abdication.

In Quebec, as perhaps nowhere else in North America, the shift in government policy on organized labour is being experienced as a societal rather than a sectorial crisis, partly because it signals the end to the long process of consensual integration by which a modernizing state coopted nationalist unions, partly because it marks the end of the populist phase of the independence movement, and partly because it reveals the confusion and dependence with which the Quebec union movement confronts the problem of state power, even in a time when the class basis of state power stands clearly revealed.

This chapter is a return to source. It is an attempt to provide the background within which the present crisis may be evaluated, by exploring the historic patterns of Quebec labour's perception of politics and its relationship to the state, from the 19th century to 1976. To that end, it is divided into four parts: this, the introduction; a discussion of forms of union political activity; an analysis of the patterns of evolution of that activity in Quebec; and a conclusion, setting out the last century's developments as an explanatory framework for a subsequent analysis of the contemporary crisis of Quebec unionism.

The Political Arena: Forms of Union Intervention

All unions in developed capitalist societies are externally dependent institutions. "What they do," wrote V.L. Allen in 1971, "is always in response to well-established forces such as rising prices, falling prices, unemployment, government action which influences living standards and over which they have little or no control. ... Trade unions are patently not initiators."[3]

Worse, unions are not only dependent on an economic environment over which they have little control, they have also seen their powers progressively coopted by the state. An essential aspect of the external dependence of unions derives from this policy of integration, which developed capitalist states have practised throughout the 20th century. The essence of integration is that the state sets itself between capital and labour and "settles" the problem of class conflict by absorbing piecemeal the powers of one of the conflicting parties. In North America, the state has become omnipresent in the internal affairs of unions, setting narrow limits not only on administrative practices but on ideology and strategy as well. Labour legislation determines when, how, and for whom a union can act, who may hold union office and how a union may use its dues, what issues may be raised during bargaining, at what times and in what ways a union may enter into conflict with management, and how much a union may contribute to electoral politics. Over time, integration by the state (whether it be consensual or coercive) hollows out a union's organizational capacity for autonomous action, a capacity already circumscribed by the power of capital in liberal democracies.

North American unions have historically reacted in two ways to external dependence and integration. On the one hand, in an effort to increase their autonomy, they have chosen to *narrow* the terrain of their intervention in the hopes of *deepening* their margin of manoeuvre in a smaller area. "Narrowing the terrain" refers both to the population the union speaks for and to the issues it pursues in its membership's name: the union narrows its active defence to one craft or the workers in one industry, gives a priority to bread-and-butter issues, eschews organized politics, lobbies only when the bread-and-butter issues of its members necessitates it. (This was the logic by which skilled workers seceded from the Knights of Labor to form the American Federation of Labor in the 1880s; it is equally the logic of an industrial union like the United Steelworkers today.)

On the other hand, unions have sought to *expand* the population they speak for and the social goals they pursue, in an effort to reduce external dependence through a *broadening* of the fronts of conflict and the sources of alliance and the *addition* of political and social methods to the traditional economic ones. "Expanding the population represented" occurs on three levels: an expansion of the umbrella of membership to the multicraft, unskilled, multiindustry groups; an extension of the possibility of tactical alliance to other unionized groups; and extension of the offer of support to exploited groups outside the traditional limits of union membership. (This is the logic by which the United Autoworkers among others supported the civil-rights movement and the unionization of farmworkers in the United States; it is the logic by which the CNTU encourages and facilitates the growth of "groupes populaires" in Quebec today; it is also the logic behind English-Canadian union participation in the NDP.)

Historically, the narrowing or expanding of union objectives for social change has been determined indirectly by the constraints the evolution of capital places on the union's environment. But more directly, or conjuncturally, state policy on unions has influenced the choice of whether, how much, and in what way unions enter politics. Put otherwise, union goals have been more directly affected by capital's action in the economy; methods or strategies have been more directly influenced by state policy. Political action by unions is obviously influenced by a series of structural and conjunctural conditions that vary from society to society. But if we set aside for the moment the task of generalizing about societal preconditions for political action and look to the more descriptive task of defining *types* of union political action, it becomes possible to classify these according to the *goals* the organization articulates and the *methods* it uses to attain these goals. The intersection of these and the various forms of political action they produce are sketched in Figure 16-1.

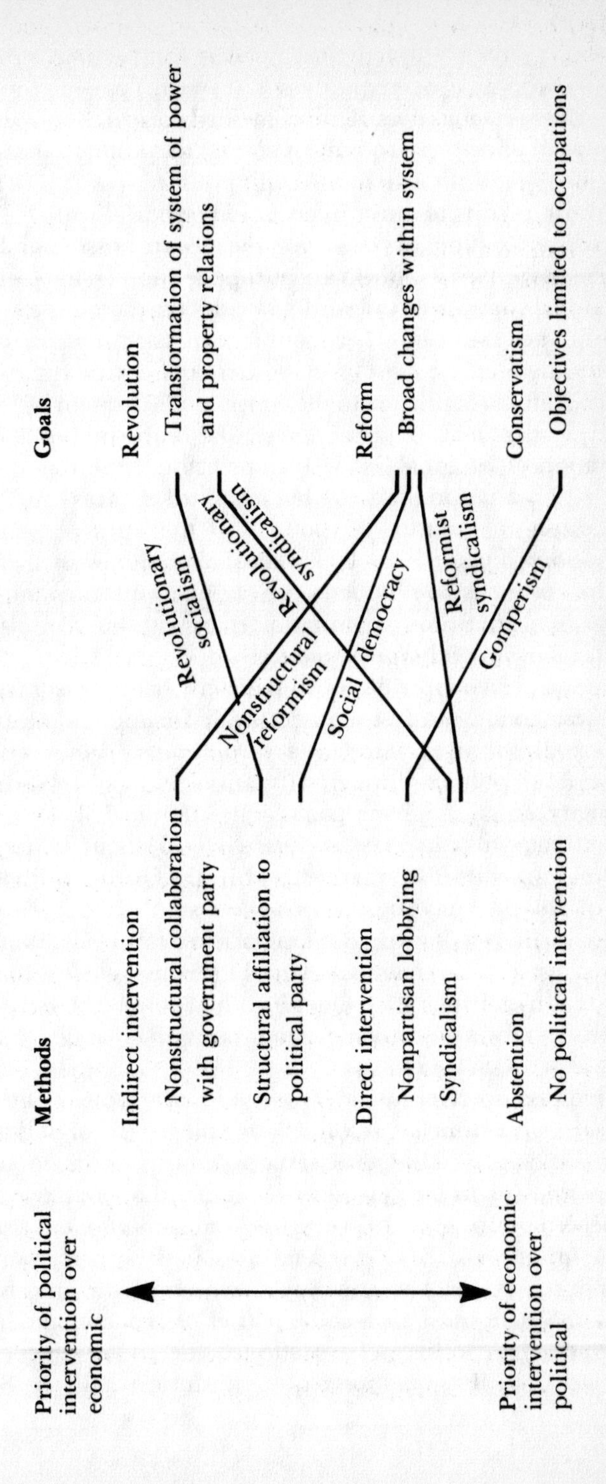

Figure 16-1 Political Action by Labour Unions

Union goals range from the narrowest (occupationally limited, bread-and-butter objectives) through the broadest (transformation of the entire system of power and property in the social system) passing through various types of reformist objectives. Union methods also fall along a spectrum, ranging from abstention (nonintervention in politics) through indirect intervention (political action through political parties), while passing through various sorts of direct intervention (syndicalism).

Many combinations of goals and strategies are possible and unions have experimented with most of them at one time or another. In Quebec, however, only a limited number of political strategies have been used. *Gomperism,* which combines craft-limited economic goals with nonpartisan lobbying, has historically been the most favoured form of political intervention of the Quebec craft unions affiliated to the American Federation of Labor and the Canadian Trades and Labour Congress, and of the unions affiliated to the Confederation of National Trade Unions before 1959. *Reformist syndicalism*—in which a union seeks to obtain limited reforms of the social order through direct intervention in politics in the form of political strikes, demonstrations, and the like—bypasses collaboration with or affiliation to a party. This form has been rather more popular with the rank-and-file and subcentral levels of union organization than with the centrals, and has its roots in the First World War period.

In addition, two types of political activity have occasionally been used and are now coming to figure increasingly in union strategy. These are *reformist indirect intervention* and *revolutionary indirect intervention,* involvement in politics through affiliation with a social-democratic or revolutionary socialist labour party. The Montreal Trades and Labour Council affiliated to or founded several shortlived labour parties from the end of the 19th century through the 1940s, while the Quebec affiliates of the CCL worked towards the founding of a social-democratic labour party in the mid-1950s.[4] Increasingly today, the founding of some form of working-class party is being discussed in the centrals, but until 1980 the vaguely social-democratic platform espoused by the Parti Québécois had both blocked the founding of an independent social-democratic labour party and retarded the founding of a revolutionary socialist one.

In addition to reformist and revolutionary indirect intervention, to gomperism and reformist syndicalism, two other sorts of political intervention were also employed by Quebec unions: *nonstructural affiliation with an existing party,* such as the Quebec Federation of Labour attempted with the Parti Québécois during the 1976 election; and *revolutionary syndicalism,* in which the union took the role of a revolutionary party regrouping a broad coalition of progressive forces under its own leadership and challenged the power of the state through a combination of economic and community confrontations. What forces have affected the choice of one or another strategy over time? The question requires historical analysis. (See Table 16-1.)

Table 16-1 Forms of Intervention

Period	Union	Primary	Secondary	State Posture
I. *1894-1907*	1. Knights of Labor	1. nonstructural affiliation to a party	1. —	Minimal intervention
	2. Trades & Labour Congress (TLC)	2. gomperism	2. abstention	
II. *1907-1944*	1. Confederation of Canadian Catholic Workers (CTCC)	1. gomperism	1. —	Sporadic repressive intervention
	2. TLC	2. gomperism	2. abstention	
III. *1944-1959*	1. CTCC	1. reformist syndicalism	1. nonstructural reformism	Repression and coercive integration
	2. TLC 3. CCL QFL 1957 -	2. gomperism	2. nonstructural reformism	
IV. *1959-1966*	1. CTCC-CNTU	1. nonstructural reformism	1. reformist syndicalism	Incomplete consensual integration
	2. QFL	2. reformist social democracy	2. —	
	3. CEQ	3. nonstructural reformism	3. —	
V. *1966-1972*	1. CNTU	1. reformist syndicalism	1. —	Coercive integration
	2. QFL	2. reformist social democracy	2. —	
	3. CEQ	3. nonstructural reformism	3. revolutionary socialism	
VI. *1972-1976*	1. CNTU	1. revolutionary syndicalism	1. revolutionary socialism	Coercive integration
	2. QFL	2. nonstructural reformism	2. —	
	3. CEQ	3. revolutionary syndicalism	3. revolutionary socialism	
	4. Confédération des Syndicaux Démocratiques	4. abstention	4. gomperism	

Unions in Politics: The Temptation of the State

Union political activity in Quebec may be seen to have passed through a number of stages, distinguished from each other by changes in the nature of intervention and degree of strength manifested by each participant in the industrial-relations system.[5]

The first stage spans the 1800s, trailing off before the First World War. During this long period we see the founding of the first union in Quebec in 1827, the first cross-Canada mobilization of the unionized working class (the Nine Hour Movement, beginning in Toronto in 1872).[6] But it was not until the Knights of Labor established local assemblies in Toronto in 1881 and in Montreal in 1882, that unions began to look seriously towards influencing the state as a means of redressing their economic weakness.[7]

The Knights of Labor gave to the Quebec working class both its earliest style of political action and the first definition of union goals in the political arena. Politically, its objective was to convince the state to shore up labour's perennial weakness vis-à-vis capital. To this end it focused on "educative lobbying" to create within the state both the precedent of and the mechanisms for regulation of child labour, factory safety, the control of the skilled labour market, and the limitation of immigrant workers.[8] It was modestly statist: it saw the state as capable of reestablishing a "natural balance" between labour and capital and it looked to the state to reduce class tensions. At the same time, it recognized the state's hostility to strikes and sought to foster more positive government attitudes towards the working class by developing the state's role in bettering working conditions so that strikes could be (largely) avoided. Capital, not the state, was seen to be the linchpin in the system the Knights worked to transform.

As well as giving certain priority to educative lobbying, the Knights of Labor involved itself electorally. From 1882 onwards it focused on municipal elections and supported working-class candidates for provincial and federal office, whether these were first endorsed by one of the traditional parties or stood as independents. At no time in Quebec did the Knights create a political party or an electoral organization that lasted beyond a particular campaign.

This form of two-pronged pressure-group politics was consonant with the Knights' worldview, with their view of the state, and with state policy itself at the time. The Knights' vision of the just society was nostalgic and preindustrial.[9] While it recognized that the state was no friend of the workingman, that recognition was harnessed ambivalently to a dependence on the state for support in the struggle against capital's excesses. And only because the state had intervened so little could the Knights believe that the election of workingmen might influence the form and content of state policy towards the "working classes." The Knights were militantly reformist and committed, if sporadically, to electoralism; they assumed that the election of a workingman's government would signal the profound and irrevocable transformation of labour's relations with capital.

In the United States the supplanting of the industrially and geographically organized Knights by the nationally linked craft federations of the American Federation of Labor (AFL) was largely completed by 1890. In English Canada the craft-oriented, pro-American tendency within the Trades and Labour Congress (TLC) did not emerge clearly as the stronger until 1894-95, and obtained supremacy only in 1902.[10] In both, the defeat of the Knights spelled the end to effective industrial organizing as well as to its unique form of political action on the municipal and local levels. In Quebec, however, in spite of loss of membership, expulsion from the TLC, and a real decline in importance to working-class organization after 1902, the Knights managed to retain some economic presence until 1921 and to continue its patterns of local political intervention which would, with modification, reemerge as the distinguishing characteristic of union politics in Quebec during the 1960s and 1970s.

The triumph of the AFL tendency within the TLC during the late 1890s assured the ascendance of a strategy of electoral abstention and nonpartisan lobbying. From 1890 onwards, the TLC's Montreal Council refused to endorse or oppose any candidate.[11] It did, however, present various briefs to the federal government. Its rejection of electoral intervention was a luxury based on its assurance that, in the crafts it represented, its ability to maintain a scarcity of skilled labour would allow it to use no more than economic pressure to obtain the conditions it sought. Once "utopian" goals of societal transformation were set aside, the TLC could protect the job-related concerns of its members solely by intervention in the economic domain.

In the first stage of union activity in Quebec, workers also attempted to form working-class parties. In 1894, a Montreal branch of Daniel de Leon's Socialist Labor Party of America (SLPA) was founded; in 1899 and 1904 a Workers' Party (WPA) was established and reestablished.[12] In 1904, the new pan-Canadian central Montreal branches formally affiliated to the Worker's Party and, although it elected a federal MP in Maisonneuve riding in 1906, by 1913 only two of its clubs were still in existence.[13] Neither the SLPA with its revolutionary socialist ideology nor the WPA with its reformist socialism seemed to cast down lasting roots or to set out a tradition on which later unions built.

A final note about the forms of union political action around the turn of the century. Whether reformist or revolutionary syndicalist, pressure-group electoralist or gomperist, Quebec unions focused their major (but not exclusive) energies on influencing the federal, not the provincial, state. However, the narrow and rudimentary forays of the province into regulation of industrial relations seemed to be paralleled for the most part by a sporadic and nonorganizational approach to politics by the unions.

A second stage of union political activity emerged slowly in the years before and after the First World War. While reformist and revolutionary direct action and nonstructural affiliation withered between 1900 and 1914, the TLC's gomperism rooted and spread as the model of political inaction. It imbued, ironically, the emerging Catholic unionism with its philosophy of electoral abstention and came to characterize intervention in politics by the union movement in general until the end of the Second World War. Thus, a period of almost four decades in which American-based craft unions and Quebec-based Catholic unions of both craft and industrial structure, worlds apart in their vision of society and the workers' place therein, shared a gomperist political perspective.

Catholic unionism grew slowly after its debut in Chicoutimi in 1907.[14] Indeed, one commentator asserts that it gained few adherents even outside Montreal before the First World War.[15] By 1921, however, the founding of the Confédération des Travailleurs Catholiques du Canada (CTCC) signalled the implant of a new view of industrial relations based on the principles of the "inequality of social classes, the harmony of capital and labour, and the right to national autonomy."[16] Its central objective was to offer Catholic workers an alternative to the (dangerously) radical, religiously neutral, American international unions affiliated to the TLC. By the 1930s, the CTCC had come to represent 45% of all unionized workers, while the international unions represented 23%.[17]

Gomperism implies electoral abstention combined with legislative lobbying. During the years between the world wars, the TLC affiliates lobbied little—if at all—and played no organized role in elections. Instead, they restricted their activities to the purely economic domain, leading nearly all the strikes that occurred during the period. The economic militancy of the TLC, however relative, thus stood in contrast to its political dormancy.

The CTCC, on the other hand, indulged in energetic gomperism: it lobbied. Although it led only nine of the 507 strikes between 1915 and 1936,[18] it lobbied for and obtained passage of the law incorporating craft unions of white-collar workers and granting legal recognition to their collective agreements in 1923,[19] and of a law to extend collective agreements to cover all workers within an industrial sector in 1934.[20] It was thus moderately statist, appealing to the Taschereau, Duplessis, and Godbout regimes in turn to redress in the political domain the union's extreme weakness in the economic.

The provincial state emerged from the First World War prepared both to extract more powers from the federal in the domain of industrial relations and to use those powers vigorously. During the 1920s and throughout the Depression it intervened both legislatively and judicially in labour-capital relations; it enshrined the rights of capital in hiring, firing, suspensions, and decisions on the organization of production and the allocation of profit. The province also introduced measures defining the legal responsibility of each party to a collective agreement, restricted the rights of unions to intervene in politics, and defined itself as the ultimate arbitrator for an employer with labour problems. The Taschereau and the Duplessis governments saw the TLC as dangerously radical and the striking growth of the CTCC membership during the 1930s was in some measure due to the government's willingness to procure sweetheart deals between the CTCC and employers wishing to avoid unionization by the more militant TLC affiliates.

The late 1920s and 1930s saw as well a return to the use of verbal rather than written collective agreements, a rising proportion of strikes fought and lost over defence of previously acquired rights; and the establishment of a state tactic of playing off one central against the other, a tactic that continued to haunt the unions in the 1970s.[21] The TLC affiliates stayed out of both partisan politics and lobbying because they assumed they could do better through strikes and the threat of strikes. The CTCC eschewed electoralism because it felt politics should be outside the realm of a defensive workers' organization. Throughout the 1930s it too relied on economic means combined with lobbying to attain its modest economic goals. It was not until the Price Company strike during the Second World War (called to force the government to reformulate legislation governing the freedom of workers to choose which union they would affiliate with) that the CTCC began to see the necessity of more direct political action.[22]

To recapitulate, then, between the first decade of the 20th century and the Second World War, unions faced a state which, regardless of which party was in power, interpreted its role as simply the protector of the employers' interests. It acted, in strike after strike, as the deployer of police rather than the conciliator. Yet certain tactics of coercive integration made their first appearance in the 1920s and it was to that combination of repression and embryonic coercive integration that the unions responded. Regardless of the profound differences between the worldviews of the CTCC and the TLC, their methods of political intervention differed in quantity rather than nature. Both eschewed direct electoral action; both concentrated on lobbying. The CTCC simply lobbied more often and more energetically. And in a very real sense the reduction of the unions' economic power during the Depression ran parallel and contributed to retreat in the political arena. Fragmentation of political force between coopting by the Church and abstentionism by the TLC further paralyzed union political action. It was only during the Second World War that the cautious use of economic pressure to obtain greater legal protection suggested to at least some unions that greater influence in the councils of state was essential to the safeguarding of prior economic gains.

A third stage of union political activity in Quebec began with the enactment of the Labour Relations Act of 1944 and ended with the death of Maurice Duplessis in 1959. This 15-year period, which has been called "la grande noirceur," was characterized by an intensification and refinement of the Quebec state's policy towards organized labour, by the introduction of militant social democracy by newly organizing industrial unions affiliated to the Canadian Congress of Labour (and to the American CIO), by the emerging economic militancy of the Catholic unions, by a series of not wholly unsuccessful attempts to create a common front among the centrals, and by the return to direct political activity by the unions.

Of these five characteristics of the industrial relations of this period, one is preeminent and stands in causal relationship to the others. The emergence of the Quebec state as an interventionist and quite partisan force in labour-capital relations transformed modest strikes into major confrontations between organized or organizing workers on one side and the full might of the state allied with national and international employers on the other. The hostility of the state forced the unions back into politics to preserve not only their autonomy but their very existence. The repressive legislation enacted by the Duplessis regime in the late 1940s and the early 1950s not only underscored the necessity for militant opposition to the regime and for collaboration among the competing centrals, but it also set the stage for the state to play off each central against the others. State policy during this period may be characterized as mature coercive integration larded with simple and devastating repression.

The 1944 labour code enacted by the Liberal party transformed the principle of the state's regulative role in industrial relations in operational reality. Based on the American Wagner Act of 1935, La Loi des Relations Ouvrières essentially established the state as the central force in industrial relations, delegating to its judicial, legislative, and executive arms the power to legitimate collective agreements and to control the formation of unions.[23] Under the 1944 Act, unions had to register with the government. The government could revoke the right of the union to represent its members at any time and the provisions of the Act allowed the case of breakdown of collective bargaining. In the same year La Loi des Différends was also enacted, forbidding teachers, firemen, municipal employees, civil servants, and communications workers from striking and submitting them to compulsory arbitration.[24] In other words, the state determined who would represent labour and the condition under which labour and capital confronted each other, legitimated the agreements reached, and limited the degree, type, and timing of sanctions each party could use against the other.

The return of Duplessis to power as the Second World War ended signalled the vigorous application of the new labour code. It should be noted that no break occurred in labour policy during the transition from Liberal to Union Nationale governments. Duplessis extracted from the new labour code the mechanisms to render the unions dependent on the state for their power to bargain and to service, and further refined them during the 1940s and 1950s.[25] Through a series of amendments to the code and "lois d'exception" introduced from 1947 to 1955, he created a repressive apparatus which was controlled directly from the Premier's office and served to supplement the provisions limiting autonomy.[26]

Bill 5—introduced in 1948, withdrawn the following year because of coordinated pressure from the centrals, and reintroduced in fragments throughout the 1950s—ended any participation by unions in industrial-relations decision making.[27] Under Duplessis, the state interposed itself further between unions and their members, forcing unions to obtain the right to service and represent their members from the state rather than from their membership base. The substitution of government-granted recognition for worker-voted recognition, the revocation at will of the union's right to represent its members, the enforcement of compulsory arbitration, and the obligatory registration of union records—all aimed at reducing the unions' attempts at militant and autonomous economic activity. When, following the introduction of Bill 5, the three union representatives on the Conseil Supérieur du Travail resigned in protest, they suggested that a veritable "statification" of the unions was taking place.[28]

The mechanisms of repression became more effective during the 1940s and 1950s. At Asbestos in 1949, Louiseville in 1952, Murdochville, Valleyfield, and Noranda, Duplessis used provincial police to break strikes and judicial intervention to cripple unions.[29] By 1952 it had become clear that the unions could not hope to use economic pressure to neutralize state policies hostile to their interests and that, ultimately, the use of the strike in pursuit of purely economic objectives had been defined by the state as political provocation.

It is within this context that the unions returned to direct political intervention. In 1955, there were three union centrals operating in Quebec. The provincial branches of the Trade and Labour Congress of Canada, affiliated to the American Federation of Labour, remained the largest numerically.[30] They intervene very little on the provincial political scene. During the 1950s they distanced themselves from the other centrals by their refusal to oppose Duplessis openly and benefited to some degree from his differential patronage.[31] The relatively tranquil relationship ended abruptly with the Murdochville strike and the formation of the Quebec Federation of Labour in 1957.[32]

On the other hand, the CTCC underwent a dramatic transformation after the Second World War. The series of violent confrontations that it became embroiled in, as the state moved repeatedly to break its strikes by use of the provincial police, transformed its understanding of the efficacy of political power. From the watershed Asbestos strike of 1948, the CTCC began to fashion two new interpretations of political intervention.

One interpretation, espoused by the central office under Gérard Picard, saw increased political influence as a means of protecting acquired rights rather than as an objective in itself.[33] In order to obtain this influence, the CTCC set out during the early 1950s to demonstrate and lobby against Duplessis' proposed amendments to the labour code. It usually chose to work in common fronts with the CCL affiliates and, more rarely, with the TLC affiliates as well. Vigorous gomperism quite naturally evolved towards a closer relationship with the provincial Liberal party. As the opposition forces to Duplessis crystallized during the middle 1950s, the CTCC moved towards informal collaboration with the Liberal party. The line between gomperism and informal and nonstructural support for a political party is at best blurred and tends to shift erratically over time. Thus, throughout the 1950s the CTCC's official gomperism was supplemented by informal support for the Liberals, on whose behalf it led a campaign of denunciation against Duplessis's Minister of Labour in 1956.[34] By that time, the CTCC's link with the provincial Liberals was just short of formal affiliation.

The second interpretation of political activity might be labelled reformist syndicalism. The deeply rooted syndicalist tradition of the CTCC, increasingly bypassed by the President's office, found new expression at the grass roots level in the regional and interindustrial groupings outside Montreal. Here, local unions moved towards *rapprochement* with locals affiliated to other centrals, concentrated on political education of the rank and file, and involved themselves in community problems of housing, health, and education. It might be said, then, that this philosophy, which defined the union as the logical instrument of all protective action undertaken in the interest of the working class, had its roots in the paternalism of the Church.

The third union organization in Quebec at the time was a relative newcomer, beginning mobilization in Quebec after 1940.[35] The industrial affiliates of the American Congress of Industrial Organization (CIO) and of the Canadian Congress of Labour (CCL) were not so divided over the form and content of political activity. Their strength was drawn from basic industry and from textiles. Through a series of bitter strikes, by the mid-1950s they had established an unparalleled reputation for economic militancy and hostility to the Duplessis regime.[36] By 1954, affiliates of the CCL-CIO were advocating the formation of a social-democratic labour party. In 1955, their Joliette Congress issued a manifesto calling for the founding of such a party in Quebec and for a broad range of economic, political, and social reforms inspired by the CCF's program.[37] The call for an independent labour party was shortlived. During the 1956 elections, some of the CIO and CCL affiliates chose to support Liberal candidates who had incorporated several key planks of the manifesto into the Liberal platform.[38] Particularly in the area of industrial relations reform, the Liberal platform closely resembled the Joliette Manifesto.

The last years of the Duplessis regime, 1956-59, were of particular significance for labour. Following the merger of the AFL and the CIO in the United States in 1955, the TLC and the CCL merged to form the Canadian Labour Congress in 1956 and began talks with the CTCC about the possibility of its inclusion. When these talks broke down, a provincial branch of the new CLC was founded (the QFL), representing 36.8% of the CLC membership in Quebec at its inception.[39] The rest of the CLC's Quebec affiliates joined the QFL gradually over the next decade. The new QFL moved rapidly away from the CLC's implicit support for Duplessis, partly because of the influence of the social-democratic CCL affiliates in its ranks and partly because of the brutality of state intervention in the Murdochville strike of 1957.[40]

At Duplessis' death in 1959, then, organized labour had begun to evolve towards more effective political action. From the gomperism and destructive competition of the 1940s, the unions had moved towards alternative forms of cooperation and had attempted the formation of a reformist labour party. By 1959, the union centrals, led by the CTCC, were assessing how best to extract maximum value from their informal collaboration with the Liberals. We may conclude, then, that the state's insistence on repressive and partisan intervention in collective bargaining after 1944 had forced the unions to move beyond traditional gomperism to experiment with reformist syndicalism and to seek more direct influence in the political arena within which the rules of the workplace are determined.

We come now to the fourth stage of union political intervention: the experience of the Quiet Revolution. Between 1960 and 1966, the coercive integration characteristic of the Duplessis regime gave way to an incomplete consensual integration; the position of both the international and domestic fragments of capital came to be presented to labour through the medium of the neo-nationalist state. To understand the greatly transformed role of the state in industrial relations, however, it is necessary to locate it in relation to the more general changes in the relationship of both the state and the unions to Quebec society.

From 1945 to 1967, Quebec's economy experienced steady and unbroken growth. The GNP rose gradually, from $3 billion in 1946 to $19 billion in 1968.[41] In large measure, American sources had stimulated this growth. In Quebec both the relative and the absolute increase in American investment was made chiefly in the secondary sector, where the external dependence of the key growth industries deepened.[42]

The steady growth during the two postwar decades had two particularly pertinent results. First, the Quebec state was given the financial margin of manoeuvre necessary for modernization. Second, foreign investment, both new and established, remained so central to the primary and secondary sectors that any ideology of modernization would have to first come to terms with its hegemony.

The Liberal party became the vehicle for this pragmatic ideology of modernization; its program was shaped by a new technocratic fraction of the old liberal professional stratum, which had been unable either to find a role for itself in the anachronistic structures of the externally dependent prewar economy or to transform the state into a vehicle for its own aspirations. Its philosophy of industrial relations, which remained largely unchanged during its six years in office, was set out by Jean Lesage in 1959.[43]

Lesage saw a "progressive statism" as the central method of modernization. Focusing on the transformation of the state itself—its takeover of medical and educational services formerly in the hands of the Church, its creation of a social-service network, the professionalization of the civil service, the multiplication of crown corporations—Lesage envisaged an expansion of the superstructure that was meant to modernize the labour force and, in some unspecified way, to "liberate" the economy from foreign domination. To accomplish this it was necessary for capital and labour to organize their members into province-wide organizations which would associate themselves with the state and participate in the elaboration of its strategy. For labour this did not mean unification of the three centrals, but the centralization of negotiating structures within each central at the province-wide level. For capital it meant the creation of a provincial council of business for which not only Lesage as head of government, but also Jean Marchand as head of the CNTU, lobbied repeatedly.[44]

The growth of the state triggered important shifts in the composition of the labour force. Over the long term the primary sector had been shrinking and the tertiary sector growing in terms of numbers employed. Quebec was no different in this regard from other industrialized societies. Thus, between 1947 and 1965, employment in the primary sector shrank from 24.2% to 9.2%, while employment in the tertiary sector rose from 44.5% to 58.1%.[45] In large measure, the growth of the tertiary sector occurred between the late 1950s and 1965, particularly in the public and parapublic sectors and in commerce. Public and parapublic services, between 1961 and 1969, expanded their employment by 65%; commerce, by 35%.[46]

This influx into the labour force of tertiary-sector workers had a massive impact on organized labour. First, the majority of the jobs created were white collar. Second, the large majority of the new workers were in the indirect or direct employ of the state. Third, the majority of those who filled the new state jobs were of blue-collar family origin.

The rapidity with which the public-sector jobs were created was paralleled only by the speed with which the new working class was unionized. Roughly 175,000 new unionists from the public and parapublic sectors entered the ranks of organized labour between 1960 and 1970. State employees now represented over one-third of all organized labour in the province.[47] The new state employees did not spread their affiliation evenly among the centrals. The CNTU benefited most directly from the expansion of state employment. In 1960 its membership was 80,075; in 1968, 199,102; and in 1970, it had risen to 205,783.[48]

The rapid expansion of the CNTU was the result of a complex series of changes both within the organization and in its relationship to Church, state, and the wider society. First, the deconfessionalization of the central, beginning after the Asbestos strike, allowed it to steadily ameliorate the quality of the services it offered to its members, as well as allowing it to embark on more militant collective bargaining. Second, the close collaboration between the CNTU and the Liberal party made use of an instrumental neo-nationalism to identify the modernization program with the nation's destiny, and the CNTU with the natural leadership of the Quebec working class. Regardless of an official ideology which took the state to task from time to time, in the first years of the 1960s the CNTU operated as if it were the trade-union arm of a one-party state. Thus, the remarkable growth of the CNTU during the decade was largely a result of its participation in the Liberal vision. Of the 125,000 new members affiliating with the CNTU during the 1960s, some 106,000 were employed by the state, transforming the CNTU from a central three-quarters of whose members in 1960 were employed in the primary and secondary sectors to a central which, in 1970, represented members over 50% of whom were employees of the state. (However, the bulk of these were in what came to be known as parapublic sectors.)

The Quebec Federation of Labour fared rather less well during the Quiet Revolution. Created in 1957 out of the merger of the AFL and the CIO in the United States and the CCL and the TLC in Canada, it did not, during the first half of the 1960s, have the financial resources, structural freedom, or moral authority to operate as a Québécois central in its own right. It was rather, in Paul Bernard's phrase, a junior government to the senior government of the Canadian Labour Congress.[49]

As the provincial office of a Canadian central over 70% of whose members belonged to branches of American unions, the QFL suffered doubly from the conflicting nationalisms abroad in Quebec during this period. The neo-nationalism of the Lesage government and the affiliation of the QFL with the New Democratic Party combined to make it less than popular with the newly aware Québécois. Further, the close relationship between the CNTU and the government made it difficult for the QFL to compete successfully for representation of the new government employees. In one notable example, the passage of a special law barring unionization of civil servants by any central affiliated to a political party assured the QFL's defeat and the CNTU's success in affiliating some 30,000 provincial civil servants.[50]

Finally, the QFL was itself subject to a series of internal conflicts which reflected the contradictory nature of its membership and status in Quebec. The conflict between Quebec neo-nationalism and American nationalism expressed itself through repeated clashes between the entrenched bureaucracies of affiliated international unions and their members over issues such as francization of services, as well as through secession from pan-Canadian and American unions by Quebec locals.[51] The struggle to gain more organizational power for the QFL in order to operate as a more autonomous union central expressed itself in conflict between the QFL and its affiliated unions over the division of power, between the QFL and the CLC over provincial autonomy, and between the QFL and the CNTU over affiliation of new members.[52] In all, it is not surprising that the QFL's membership did not grow as rapidly during the 1960s. Its share of the new government employees was limited to some hospital workers, employees of school boards and municipalities, and certain categories of Hydro-Québec employees—in the large majority, blue-collar workers from the subcentral levels of government. The QFL remained a blue-collar central whose membership was employed in a large measure by the multinational sectors of private capital.[53]

It was the Teachers' Corporation (CIC-CEQ) that benefited most dramatically from superstructural modernization. The enormous expansion of public education coupled with a government-granted right to the obligatory membership of all teachers in the Catholic school system pushed membership from 12,000 in 1959 to 60,000 in 1968.[54] This 500% leap occasioned a transformation of the power relations within the central as urban, highly trained secular teachers took over positions of power. And the modernization of education triggered within the corporation itself a crisis concerning the relationship between professionalism and trade-union demands—although it would not be until 1967 that professionalism was identified with bourgeois affiliation and set in opposition to working-class consciousness, to alliance with the other centrals, and to confrontation with government.

By 1966, then, the portrait of union representation had changed as dramatically as had that of the state. The infusion of public-sector workers into the movement had forced major changes in affiliation patterns. Further, the modernization programs of the Quiet Revolution made the public-sector unionists potentially the most powerful bloc within the labour movement.

The transformed labour movement operated under a much liberalized labour code.[55] In 1964, after three earlier versions had been modified because of union pressure, a new labour code was enacted.[56] Its provisions, plus the modifications to the Public Service Act passed in 1965, created a veritable revolution of rising expectations. The right to strike was granted to all workers except firemen, police, and prison guards. The onus of compulsory arbitration and binding awards was removed and elaborate safeguards were provided against the coercion and takeover of newly formed unions.[57] In all, the changes in labour legislation during the Lesage era indicated, first, a growing role for the state as legislator in the industrial relations system; second, the crystallization of trade-union expectations concerning the rate at which conditions would be bettered and power shared; and, third, the development of a role for the unions as state agents in the project of societal modernization. In place of the coercive integration of the Duplessis era, the Lesage regime attempted to introduce consensus. How fragile were its provisions would become clear when the economy began to contract. What *was* clear during the heyday of union modernization in the Quiet Revolution, however, was that the unions acquiesced to the strengthening of their dependence on the state.

The acquiescence was rooted in a profound and continuing union paralysis concerning the method of political intervention. From the mid-1950s on, under the impetus of the CCL, some elements in the labour movement had been advocating the creation of a workers' party. Certainly the QFL in 1960 refused support to the Liberals, suggested that its members destroy their ballots, and insisted that the founding of a workers' party was imminent.[58] When the Quebec NDP was founded in 1963, however, the QFL's affiliation took the form of a sort of moral support and passive affiliation rather than an active identification with the new party's future. And even this involvement was clouded by the founding of a rival Parti Socialiste du

Québec (PSQ), attracting important trade-union figures unhappy with the NDP position on federalism.[59]

QFL affliation to the NDP did not, however, stop it from supporting the Liberals on issue after issue during the period.[60] And if nominal affiliation to a workers' party contrasted oddly with conjunctural collaboration with the Liberals, it nonetheless gave form to a quite consistent stance on the part of the QFL vis-à-vis industrial relations. Less involved in the public sector than the CNTU, less enchanted with the nationalist program, and above all less historically committed to state intervention to shore up weak unions, as early as 1959 the QFL suggested that the state's growing role as an employer should push it to set an example for the private sector.[61] Between 1962 and 1966 it repeatedly announced that the state's historic role as third party was anachronistic;[62] its emergence as a major employer made the infusion of politics into collective bargaining inevitable.[63]

The CNTU, on the other hand, manifested an even more dramatic contradiction during the Quiet Revolution. Historically it had practised gomperism, lobbying energetically while refusing electoral commitment. During the Lesage era it ceased to lobby any party but the Liberals. And, while it refused affiliation to the NDP and the PSQ as well as to the Liberals, its executive shared the vision of democratic planning and progressive statism which was the hallmark of state industrial policy.

Yet the CNTU could not avoid recognizing that the expansion of the state necessitated the politicization of its industrial policy. When strike after strike of its public-sector members pitted it against the Liberal government between 1964 and 1966, the CNTU found itself torn between collaboration in the national project and rejection of its implications for labour. The way out during the middle years of the decade seemed to be articulation of an increasingly sophisticated critique of the unchallenged structures of capital, but a critique that chose a cooperative and decentralized alternative, thereby avoiding explicit rejection of the Liberals' nationalism.[64]

In a very real way the national question paralyzed the unions' intervention in politics during the Quiet Revolution. While the state under Duplessis had practised repression and coercive integration, it had been relatively easy for the unions to work together and to recognize the need for a labour party. When a progressive nationalist regime came to power, however, it was able to divide the unions along lines of structural-national affiliation (Québécois vs. international), to set them competing for state favours, and to make the prospect of autonomous union political action not only difficult but somehow disloyal. For each of the three centrals the crystallization of a more militant interpretation of power relations in the economic domain led to an increased political presence, but to relatively little evolution in the method used to articulate new objectives. The tension between the evolving and the stagnant methods—which characterized union political action at the level of the centrals—created a dead space at the heart of the movement which, after 1967, local and regional union groupings felt compelled to fill. In the struggle for concrete political power after 1967, the initiative passed to the rank-and-file and the lower levels of the union organization hierarchy.

The fifth stage of union political activity began during the last months of 1966. The Quiet Revolution's loss of momentum, the slowing down of Quebec's economic growth, and the explosion of expectations concerning union participation in social-policy formation all combined to polarize union hopes and governmental capacity. In this polarization, foreign capital was seen to play a large, but largely undocumented, role. Between 1966 and 1976 the state moved back towards coercive integration and the unions, after almost a decade of collaboration, were incapable of formulating a political defence.

On its return to power in 1966, Daniel Johnson's Union Nationale government began an immediate retreat from the privileged relationship with the unions which had characterized the preceding Liberal regime.[65] Between 1967 and 1972 Johnson, his successor Bertrand, and his Liberal successor Bourassa, refined and expanded the power of the state in industrial relations, expressly to revoke or restrict the gains unions had made in the first part of the decade. The immediate result was an explosion of strikes and lockouts: during 1966-67 alone, more manhours were lost in industrial disputes in Quebec than in Ontario, although the Quebec labour force was some 200,000 smaller. Some 60% of those involved in industrial disputes between 1966 and 1972 were employed by the state.[66]

The emerging state policy was a blend of juridical concern and legislative integration, ranging from the abrogation of collective-bargaining rights and the legislative imposition of contracts to the levying of massive fines on union members as well as unions. The CEQ, for example, lost its power to negotiate with local school boards and its right to secure a contract through free collective bargaining when in 1967 the government legislated a contract.[67] Following seven years of rising expectations concerning an expanded role for unions in educational modernization, Bill 25 first nullified the rights to collective bargaining and then incorporated that right into the state's executive apparatus. Second, the state used its legislative powers to centralize responsibility for contract negotiation and enforcement within each central, reducing the autonomy of affiliated unions and federations and exposing the central to increased legal sanctions. Third, the state used its legislative powers to set the centrals to internecine competition. Legislation enacted during the last years of Bertrand's mandate and the first years of Bourassa's established the principle of the right of the state to rationalize representation within the industrial sectors by allowing no more than one central to bargain for workers within a particular industry, thus setting the centrals to really brutal competition for majority affiliation in those industries where they had traditionally divided the membership. (The construction industry is the most dramatic example.)

In the administrative domain, the government formulated an increasingly effective and standardized wage policy, which it began to enforce for the public sector after 1967. (The government had introduced this policy in 1964, but was not then prepared to push for it during negotiations.) The raises negotiated were popularly believed to derive from guidelines set for the public sector by the major employers in the private sector, and unions in the private sector took the public-sector settlements as an indication of what they could hope to obtain. Finally, the state enforced the principle of massive judicial sanctions against infringement of industrial relations law. Thus, in 1968 teachers affiliated with the SPEQ of the CNTU found a dozen of their leaders jailed after an illegal strike, while the defiance of injunctions issued for the hospital strikers during the celebrated Common Front strike of April and May 1972 resulted in large fines against refractory locals and eventually in the jailing of the presidents of the three union centrals.[68] Undoubtedly, the hardening of the state's position towards the unions, first visible in the late 1960s, began contributing to the very real regression the unions experienced during the 1970s. Several developments, both indications of and contributing factors to that regression, crystallized around 1972.

First among these was the breakdown of the CNTU–Liberal party alliance. When the Liberals returned to power in 1970, they represented the fraction of the petty bourgeoisie who wished to continue the economic growth of Quebec by intensifying the ties with international capital. The fraction who had sought continued modernization through the repatriation of taxes paid to the federal state had left the Liberals in 1967, forming first the Mouvement Souveraineté-Association and then, in 1968, the Parti Québécois. In 1970 and again in 1973, the remaining Liberals under Bourassa pursued the policy of union domestication which had been the hallmark of their Union Nationale predecessor. Thus, between 1968 and 1976 the CNTU, facing a Liberal party shorn of both the personnel and its ideological tendencies most amenable to union aspirations, looked towards the Parti Québécois as a possible political ally. That possibility, however, was approached with little clarity. When, during the 1970 election, the Montreal Council of the CNTU formally endorsed the PQ, it was discreetly reprimanded by the executive of the central.

A second development was the radical weakening of the CNTU. In 1971, 210,000 workers affiliated with the CNTU, the CEQ, and the QFL and employed directly and indirectly by the state, formed a Common Front for negotiations with the government. When these negotiations broke down in the spring of 1972, the Common Front went on strike, ignoring injunctions.[69] The strike having been broken by back-to-work legislation (supported by the Parti Québécois as well as by the more traditional parties) and the eventual jailing of the presidents of all three union centrals for contempt of court, the simmering ideological polarization within the CNTU exploded. During 1972 and 1973 the CNTU suffered the secession of approximately 60,000 of its members. This was an explicit rejection of the political nature of the public-sector strike, of its implications for relations with the Liberal party, and of the marxist interpretation of class relationships that the CNTU central office had been disseminating via working documents and political education sessions since 1971.[70] Some 30,000 of the secessionists, in the most technologically backward sectors, grouped together to form the Confederation of Democratic Trade Unions (CSD), which returned to political collaboration with the Liberal party and to the narrowest of business unionism on the industrial scene.[71]

The additional 30,000 secessionists were members of the Civil Servants Federation (SFPQ); they simply disaffiliated from the CNTU, explaining that they thought they could obtain better material benefits for their members if they were not associated with a radical central.[72] Hard on the heels of this secession, the CNTU became embroiled in a debilitating internal struggle over raising the per capita contributions to the central strike fund. (The need to raise the contributions to the Fonds de défense professionnel arose out of the fines incurred during the Common Front negotiations in the first instance, then, during 1973 and 1974, out of the fines incurred during "illegal" strikes and walkouts held to reopen contract negotiations to take into consideration the steeply rising cost of living.) The debate over contributions, which stretched over several years, pitted the concept of the union as a radical social movement against the image of the union as a limited-issue, self-defence organization and resulted in the suspension of several thousand more members. It also revealed the prohibitive cost of confrontation with the state.

The fragmentation of the CNTU triggered a return to raiding between the QFL and the CNTU. And, while a minimal collaboration on short-term economic issues in the public sector was maintained, middle- and longer-term political coordination all but ceased. Particularly the competition between the two centrals for hegemony of representation in construction skillfully fanned during Bourassa's first mandate so envenomed relations among the centrals that the QFL in 1974 found itself the object of a Royal Commission of Enquiry on Industrial Relations in the Construction Industry, better known as the Cliche Commission. Within the CNTU, no one foresaw the dangerous precedent set by the invoking of such an inquiry until the Commission made its report public. In fact, the CNTU had called on the Bourassa government to intervene in construction locals to protect its minority position. The invitation by one union central to the state to intervene in interunion jurisdictional competition reveals both the depth of the confusions within the CNTU concerning the role of the state in industrial relations and the weakness of the QFL. It is not surprising that after 1973 the QFL began to look increasingly towards affiliation to or collaboration with the PQ as a way out of its seemingly perennial weakness. This allegiance culminated in 1975 with the disaffiliation of the QFL from the NDP and its official endorsement of the PQ.[73]

In this deteriorating situation of rivalry, secession, and an increasing number of hard-fought but unsuccessful strikes in the private sector, the CEQ emerged as the arbiter of the union movement. It remained as an arbiter, however, only so long as it stayed out of jurisdictional disputes with the Canadian Union of Public Employees (QFL) over affiliation of nonteaching staff employees of the school commissions: in other words, until late 1975. Standing between the CNTU and the QFL, the CEQ mediated a truce in construction and their return to cooperation in the public sector. That cooperation began, haltingly, during late 1975, at just the time when the CEQ's own aggressiveness in affiliating nonteaching staff was beginning to place pressure on its relation with the QFL. On the executive level, the CEQ kept itself clear of collaboration with any party, although since the late 1960s it had been informally linked to the NDP.

To summarize, then, the contradictions of the Quebec economy after 1966 coupled with the defeat of the modernizing fraction of the Liberal party under Lesage combined to turn state policy away from the luxuries of rapidly expanding state investment and the dream of union participation in state policy formation. Between 1972 and 1976, the disintegration of the union-Liberal alliance left the unions groping for a new channel of political influence. They faced a state prepared to extract their compliance forcibly, but seemed to have real difficulty seeing the state itself as the adversary. Each central pursued its own inadequate solution, with little collaboration among them. The QFL in this period set about establishing the informal but powerful ties of collaboration with the Parti Québécois, which had characterized the CNTU-Liberal relationship during the Quiet Revolution. Like the CNTU a decade earlier, the QFL eschewed formal affiliation, and certainly the PQ did not encourage it. And, like the CNTU during the 1960s, the QFL was to discover, once the PQ had been elected, that the party entertained no sense of responsibility to the class that had largely accounted for its electoral victory.

The CNTU, on the other hand, manifested an increasingly serious breakdown between ideology and method of political intervention. By 1972, the CNTU could trace the evolution of its perception of class relations in Quebec from social democratic to revolutionary socialist.[74] Marcel Pepin's address to the 1972 CNTU Congress was based on a systematic and sophisticated neo-marxist interpretation of the double colonization of the Quebec working class. (This is possibly the only one of the major orientation papers issued by Pepin that stressed the issue of class domination over that of national domination in the hierarchy of oppression, in clearly marxist terms.) Using André Gunder Frank's metropolis-hinterland formulation, he interpreted Quebec's external economic dependence and the revolutionary responsibilities of unions in ways that could lead to the formation of a radical labour party. However, the CNTU's actual method of political intervention throughout this period continued to reflect the traditional stagnation and confusion as to concrete options. Relations with the post-Quiet Revolution Liberal party having been effectively terminated, the CNTU vacillated between an unstructured collaboration with the PQ, the formation of an independentist workers' party, and the unstable status quo.

In this vacuum of effective action, grassroots mobilization moved to the foreground. On the lower level of worker organization, innovative political solutions were being pursued. Since 1960, the democratization of internal union structures, which had occurred within all three union centrals, had the important result of rekindling a taste for participation in union and provincial politics by the rank and file. "Participation" was defined in terms of opposition: to the union's continued conservatism; to its control by foreign capital and American unions; to the agents of conservatism, capitalism, and colonization: the union leadership. No one group of rank and file focused on all these opponents, and which opponent each focused on determined its ideology. Thus, a determination to participate in union politics to end union control from Washington and the domination of American capital might ignore the problem of entrenched Quebec union leadership and would quite likely lead the adherents of this position to support the PQ. Concern with capitalism only, and with the alliance between the bourgeois provincial state and the collaborationist local union bosses, would lead a rank-and-file militant either to membership in one of the trotskyist and marxist-leninist groups advocating the founding of a revolutionary party, or towards a syndicalist rejection of electoral politics, which by the 1970s had taken on a particularly revolutionary colour.

In the former case, the emphasis on union problems identified with national oppression, most marked in the QFL and the regional councils of the CNTU and the CEQ outside of Montreal, led towards nonstructural affiliation to the PQ for subcentral union structures and the rank-and-file members themselves. Within the QFL in particular, adherence to this position tended to allow rank-and-file militants and the central leadership to make common cause to challenge those American unions they considered most undemocratic, corrupt, and controlled from the United States—in other words, an alliance of the central and local levels of union operation against the intermediary levels of affiliated union leadership, using nationalism to assert central control. In the latter case, emphasis on class issues, with national issues present but secondary, was of greatest significance in some regional councils of the CNTU, in some of its Federation executives, and among rank-and-file teachers and hospital employees. (For a brief time in the mid-1970s, the Federation of Social Affairs of the CNTU was a central rallying point for marxist-leninist positions.) In the CEQ, support for the PQ was geographically based and an urban phenomenon restricted to Montreal and Quebec City.

To say that an emphasis on class issues from some sort of revolutionary perspective was present at various levels of the union movement, however, is not to argue that it was homogeneous. Before 1974, it was possible to distinguish between the impact of revolutionary syndicalism and revolutionary indirect action. Revolutionary syndicalists rejected electoral politics and saw strikes as their most effective political weapon. They concentrated on the occupation of factories, on political education, and on the creation of revolutionary consciousness by numerous methods of "formation." But contained within their orientation was the temptation of electoralism: could elections be entered as an educational device to undermine the credibility and legitimacy of bourgeois politics? Certainly the founding of the Montreal municipal party Front d'Action Politique (FRAP) by unionists and community organizers in 1969 partly reflected that view.[75] Within FRAP and in municipal campaigns elsewhere in the province, the revolutionary-syndicalist perspective before 1974 joined an electoralist nonsectarian socialism in which reformists and revolutionaries made common cause.

By 1974, however, the revolutionary-syndicalist perspective had largely disappeared from the rank-and-file level, fragmented and absorbed by the diverse leftist groups advocating some sort of revolutionary workers' party. Within the CNTU, the role of the revolutionary syndicalists in strikes was increasingly challenged by emergent marxist-leninist extra-central strike-solidarity committees outside the framework of any union central. The most important of these, Le Comité de solidarité aux luttes ouvrières, was founded by *En Lutte*. It went to the aid of striking workers in nonunionized industries, then continued to offer aid to unionized workers involved in long strikes which had begun to embarrass the central. By 1974, the Comité's success and militance had become an example to the centrals and had taken over the work of syndicalists within the centrals.

In local and regional politics, revolutionary-syndicalist intervention had the effect of weakening or destroying local electoral coalitions, so that outside of Montreal, at least, reformist direct action was left to nonsectarian socialists who could make common, if temporary, cause with the PQ. Around 1974, however, the field of rank-and-file and subcentral intervention in politics simplified and polarized. Before then, revolutionary syndicalism competed with reformist direct action and with a still-embryonic revolutionary direct action. After 1974, the emergence of the groups of the revolutionary left—each with its own prescription for the founding of a revolutionary workers' party—absorbed the revolutionary syndicalists and splintered the reformist direct action camp into social-democratic supporters of the PQ and socialists without an organizational base.

Conclusion

By November 1976, after almost 10 years in the political wilderness, the union movement was still painfully divided between those who favoured that kind of collaboration with a governing party which would accelerate the process of integration into the state apparatus and those who, from a variety of perspectives, sought to retard or reverse the process. The lines were drawn between central and central and, within the CNTU and the CEQ, between Montreal and other regions, between some of the regional councils and the executives, between hospital workers and teachers on the one hand and private sector employees on the other. Only the QFL avoided the divisiveness created by the question of the state, as the CNTU had done some 15 years earlier, by denying the existence of the state per se, by focusing on government, and by casting its lot with a party it hoped would be friendly (if not committed) to working class interests once in power. It might be argued that, if the 1960s were the decade in which the CNTU furthered the dependence of the union movement on the state through its relationship with the Liberals, after 1975 the QFL in its relationship with the PQ played a similar role. But regardless of which central occupied the leading position, the process of decreasing union autonomy continued apace, from consensual integration to coercion and back to largely unsuccessful attempts at consensus. Within the unions, the only strategy developed was the abdication of political leadership—the old reformist syndicalism with a vengeance. And its price was high: a hollowing out of the political centre, a polarization of membership, a reduction of the legitimacy of the organs of central union power. In some way between 1966 and 1976, the unions came to be seen as the major institutional opponents to the state, but were incapable of either occupying the role or defending themselves against its consequences. Thus, when a party came to power in 1976 which was the choice of the large majority of the unionized working class, it could present itself as an alternative source of identification to the unions and challenge the unions for the ideological leadership of their own members.

And with the benefit of hindsight from the perspective of 1983, the emerging crisis of the Quebec trade-union movement (more severe than any this generation has known) is itself testimony to the deadly efficiency of integrationist state policy orchestrated by a nationalist political party.

Notes

1. David Payne, "Les limites du pouvoir: Une question de conscience" (Quebec: unpublished, March 21, 1983), p. 1, my translation.
2. David J. Bercuson, "Ottawa Strikes Back," *Saturday Night* (March 1983), p. 48. He is referring to Canadian federal policies only.
3. V.L. Allen, *The Sociology of Industrial Relations* (London: Longman, 1971), p. 47.
4. Roch Denis, *Luttes de classes et question nationale au Québec: 1948-1968* (Montréal: Presses Socialistes Internationales, 1979), pp. 160-67.
5. The *nature of intervention* means the form political activity takes and the worldview which informs that activity. *Degree of strength* is more elusive, but it entails the ability of one institutional participant to influence and/or determine the option(s) of the other(s).
6. Charles Lipton, *The Trade Union Movement in Canada 1827-1959* (Toronto: NC Press, 1973), pp. 1-97.
7. Fernand Harvey, "Les Chevaliers du Travail," in F. Harvey (ed.), *Aspects historiques du mouvement ouvrier au Québec* (Montréal: Boréal Express, 1973), pp. 51, 87-89.
8. Ibid., p. 65.
9. Norman J. Ware, *The Labor Movement in the United States* (New York: Vintage Books, 1964), pp. 320ff.

10. Harvey, op. cit., pp. 69-75.
11. Ibid., p. 107.
12. Alfred Charpentier, "Le mouvement politique ouvrier de Montréal (1883-1929)," in Harvey, op. cit., pp. 151-58.
13. Ibid., p. 159.
14. Louis Maheu, "Problème social et naissance du syndicalisme catholique," in Harvey, op. cit., pp. 119-46.
15. Denis, op. cit., pp. 84-89.
16. Cited in ibid., p. 86, note 7.
17. Drawn from *l'Annuaire du Québec, 1968-69*, p. 399.
18. Black Rose Books Editorial Collective, *Quebec Labour* (Montreal: Black Rose Books, 1972), p. 15; Pierre Vallières, "Les grèves perdues," in Harvey, op. cit., 171-73.
19. Roger Chartier, "La création du Ministère du Travail, l'extension juridique des conventions collectives et les années d'avant-guerre (1931-39)," *Relations Industrielles* 18: 2, p. 215.
20. Ibid., pp. 219-20.
21. Vallières, "Les Grèves", pp. 169-73.
22. Leo Roback, "Les formes historiques de politisation du syndicalisme au Québec," in G. Dion (ed.), *La politisation des relations du travail* (Québec: Les Presses de l'Université Laval, 1973), p. 21.
23. Denis, op. cit., p. 73.
24. Ibid., p. 74.
25. Denis, op. cit., pp. 79-82.
26. Ibid.
27. Roger Chartier, "Contribution à l'histoire de la législation québécoise du travail: 7," *Relations Industrielles* 18: 3, pp. 346-62.
28. Ibid., p. 355.
29. Vallières, op. cit., pp. 169-73; Pierre-Elliott Trudeau (ed.), *La grève de l'amiante* (Montreal: Editions Cité Libre, 1956); Roch Denis, op. cit., pp. 135-39; *En grève* (Montreal: Editions du jour, 1963).
30. Gérard Dion, "Les groupements syndicaux dans la province de Québec" *Relations Industrielles* II: 1, p. 2.
31. Denis, op. cit., pp. 142-44.
32. Ibid., pp. 150-52.
33. Louis-Marie Tremblay, *Le syndicalisme québécois: Idéologies de la CSN et de la FTQ, 1940-1970* (Montréal: Les Presses de l'Université de Montréal, 1972), pp. 165-67.
34. Denis, op. cit., pp. 177ff, discusses the complex relationships which influenced the CTCC's approach to the question of a third party vs. collaboration with the Liberals in the late 1950s.
35. The CCL affiliates did not, however, found a central Quebec organization to regroup its provincial affiliates until 1952.
36. Emile Boudreau, "Murdochville: douze ans d'organisation," *Socialisme* 64: 3-4, pp. 3-30.
37. Michel Grant, *L'Action syndicale et la Fédération des Unions industrielles du Québec* (Master's thesis, Industrial Relations Department, Université de Montréal, 1968), pp. 122-34.
38. Ibid., pp. 140-49.

39. Paul Bernard, *Structures et pouvoirs de la Fédération des travailleurs du Québec* (Ottawa: Queen's Printer, 1969), is the best detailed study of the QFL during the 1950s and 1960s.
40. Boudreau, op. cit., pp. 6-9.
41. Diane Ethier, Jean-Marc Piotte, and Jean Reynolds, *Les travailleurs contre l'Etat bourgeois* (Montréal: L'Aurore, 1975), pp. 17-22.
42. Ibid.
43. Jean Lesage. *Lesage s'engage* (Montréal: Les Editions politiques, 1959). The following discussion is drawn from Denis, op. cit., pp. 232-42.
44. Jean Marchand, "Il est urgent que le patronat s'organise au niveau national," *Le Travail* 39: 2 (Feb. 1963).
45. B. Roy Lemoine, "The Modern Industrial State: Liberator or Exploiter?" *Our Generation* 8: 4, p. 73.
46. Ibid., p. 91.
47. Ethier et al., op. cit., p. 24.
48. Ibid., pp. 22-24.
49. Bernard, op. cit., p. 175.
50. See Jean Boivin, "La négociation collective dans le secteur public québécois, une évaluation des trois premières rondes, 1964-72," *Relations Industrielles* 27: 4, pp. 679-90; J.-R. Cardin, "La création d'un carrefour syndical dans la fonction publique du Québec," *Relations Industrielles* 21: 2, pp. 251-57.
51. Cardin, op. cit., p. 252.
52. Of the 11,261 workers involved in changing union affiliation in 1964-65, some 10,000 passed to the CNTU.
53. For the best summary of union membership before 1970, see Hervé Gauthier, "La syndicalisation au Québec," *Québec Travail* (Quebec: Government Printers, 1972). For more recent summaries see Fernard Harvey, *Le mouvement ouvrier au Québec* (Montréal: Boréal Express, pp. 287-89).
54. Recent work on the CEQ includes a project in progress: James Thwaites, *L'enseignement québécois: 1937-1973* (Université Laval); also *Histoire du mouvement ouvrier du Québec 1825-1976* (Montréal: Coédition CSN/CEQ).
55. *Le Code du Travail I: Des relations du travail*, 8th ed. (Québec: Government Printers, 1964).
56. Louis-Marie Tremblay, "L'évolution du syndicalisme dans la révolution tranquille," *Relations Industrielles* 22: 1, p. 94.
57. Boivin, op. cit., pp. 682-83.
58. Discussed in Denis, op. cit., p. 290.
59. Ibid., pp. 308-52.
60. For example, the nationalization of hydroelectic power.
61. Tremblay, op. cit., p. 317.
62. Ibid., p. 323.
63. Ibid., p. 324.
64. See, for example, Marcel Pépin, "Une société bâtie pour l'homme," *Rapport moral du président général de la CSN* (1966).
65. Ethier et al., op. cit. p. 34, suggests that towards the end of their mandate in 1966 the Liberals were already beginning to harden their line towards the unions, so that Johnson's position in the watershed Bill 25 debate in 1967 was not a rupture with the recent past but a continuation of emerging Liberal policy.

66. Ibid., p. 25.
67. Boivin, op. cit., p. 682.
68. Ethier et al., op. cit., pp. 101-08.
69. The best work on the Common Front is by Ethier et al., op. cit.
70. The best known of these was *Ne Comptons que sur nos propres moyens,* commissioned by the Executive from an outside economist, 100,000 copies of which were distributed during 1971 and 1972.
71. R. Daigneault and M. Rioux, *La Grande Tricherie* (Montréal: CSN, 1973).
72. Jean-Louis Harguindeguy, Intervention during the Plenary of the CNTU Congress at Quebec City (June 1972). For the timing and immediate impact of the secession on the CNTU, see Ethier et al., op. cit., p. 111.
73. *Proceedings,* Congress of the Quebec Federation of Labour (Montreal, Dec. 3-7, 1975).
74. Marcel Pepin, *Pour Vaincre, Rapport moral du président général de la CSN* (Montreal: CSN, 1972).
75. Cf. FRAP's platform, *Les Salariés au Pouvoir* (1970).

Chapter 17/Polarization and Depolarization of Quebec Political Parties*

Raymond Hudon

The 1976 Quebec election revealed no hitherto unsuspected mood or tendency among the voters. In this sense, it was quite different from, for example, the explosion of support for the Créditistes in the federal election of 1962. An increasing polarization between workers and employers has been the most significant development in Quebec over the last few decades, especially since the end of the 1960s. This polarization around the vision of Quebec as a society was accompanied by an outwardly comparable trend articulated around the vision of Quebec as a nation. The way the national or independence question was debated before and after 1976 strongly suggests that this question, and class conflict in Quebec, cannot be analyzed separately. However, it is possible to contend that it is the analysis of the polarization around class confrontations that can fundamentally account for the evolution of Quebec politics since the 1960s.

During the 1970s, this social polarization specifically echoed at the level of political parties through a strained opposition between the Parti Québécois and the Liberals. The major tendencies in the first two-thirds of this decade were:

1. A revulsion against the old-style politics of the Liberals and the Union Nationale.
2. A steady shift (and a *temporary* polarization) on the national question.
3. A more profound (and related) polarization on the basis of class relationships.

Many of those who actively supported the PQ before its coming to power would now consider this presentation inadequate. It has become clear, they would argue, that the PQ government is more and more indistinguishable from a Liberal one, whether one points to its conception of economic development, to its relationships with organized labour, or to its policy on the place and the role of the Quebec state. Such an analysis, though correct, can be completed by referring to the persisting opposition between the PQ and the Liberals on the national question. Moreover, probably because of this opposition, relationships between capital and the PQ are not yet totally close, despite the Lévesque government's many efforts to improve them. Therefore,

---

*This chapter is a substantially revised version of "Political Parties and the Polarization of Quebec Politics," in Hugh Thorburn (ed.), *Party Politics in Canada*, 4th ed. (Toronto: Prentice-Hall of Canada, 1979), pp. 228-42.

despite the deradicalization of the PQ, class politics has not disappeared in Quebec.

This chapter first recalls the process of social and political polarization that took place from the mid-1960s to the second half of the 1970s in Quebec. Second, it briefly describes the trend towards depolarization that now seems to characterize the relative positions of the PQ and the Liberals. Third, some explanations are suggested for the evident reorientation of the PQ—notably the economic crisis and the further institutionalization of the PQ from party to government. Finally, some remarks suggest possible developments of Quebec nationalism in the light of the current political situation.

The Process of Polarization

The reorientation of the Quebec electorate was clear by 1970, when the PQ, in its first campaign, came second in votes. This apparent upsurge was related to longer-term trends apparent in the years after: the electoral decline of the UN from 1956 to 1981 and a comparable decline of the Liberals between 1962 and 1976. In 1966, a significant 43.5% of the Quebec electorate were wishing for the appearance of parties other than the UN and the Liberals.[1] Moreover, in 1966, two independentist parties, the *Rassemblement pour l'indépendance nationale* (RIN) and the *Ralliement national* (RN) received 8.8% of the votes.[2]

The PQ appealed to many Québécois by promising a better government and by offering real participation in the definition of the party's policies. As a new party, it insisted on differentiating itself from the "old parties," the UN and the Liberals. Because of its success in raising funds from the people, it could credibly use such slogans as "la caisse propre" ("clean electoral coffer"). By refusing money from corporations and associations, it could claim that a PQ government would have its hand free and would be able to avoid compromising the interests of the Quebec people. The PQ was thus able to say convincingly that it would be not only the government of the party's friends, but of the people generally.

Over the few years before their electoral defeat in 1976, the Liberals found themselves on the defensive, replying to denunciations by the PQ. The Liberals' continuation of patronage practices—despite their purity claims in 1960, and the apparent worsening of corrupt activities under the Bourassa government—did not help them. The PQ bill on party finance did leave Quebec parties with much less room for manoeuvre. The PQ's statements and actions appeared to have some impact in the short term: following the resignation of Robert Bourassa only a few days after the Liberal defeat on November 15, 1976, the interim Liberal leader defined his mandate as the reform of the Liberal party's structures and fund-raising practices. This was also the platform Claude Ryan promoted in his campaign for the party's leadership in 1978.

Claude Ryan met with failure and resigned in 1982. To balance the negative effect that this could have on the image of the Liberals, the party has repeatedly tried to publicize the PQ government's involvement in more or less well-demonstrated arbitrary patronage practices. Clearly the intent is to convince Quebec voters that, on this point, the PQ can no longer claim to be different from the "older parties."

By stressing the special relationship of the PQ government with unions in the 1979 out of court settlement of the LG2 affair relating to the James Bay Hydro project, the Liberals were reminding people, in spring 1983, that this party (and government) had been close to labour unions in the past. Some days after the election of the PQ in 1976, René Lévesque declared his government's sympathies for the workers. At the same time, the leadership of the Confédération des syndicats nationaux interpreted the victory of the PQ as "a union victory"—"the victory of the Quebec people." This reaction could be explained by the defeat of an anti-union government. Had a minister of the Bourassa government not declared in 1975 that the government's role was to protect employers against too strong unions?[3] Furthermore, did the PQ's official platform not commit it to "establish an economic system which would eliminate every form of exploitation of workers, and which would respond to the real needs of all Québécois, rather than to the demands of a privileged minority"?[4]

From the above, one can appreciate the respective positions in the mid-1970s of the PQ and the Liberals on active social forces in Quebec society. To a great extent, this situation was the result of a process of social polarization that had been developing in the previous 10 years. The "favourable bias" towards workers declared by Lévesque in his first press conference after the 1976 election recalled an invitation made by him in 1960, when he was a minister in the Liberal government: "I urgently ask you to remember that the government is, more than ever, sympathetic to labour."[5] In both cases, 1960 and 1976, the Lesage and the Lévesque governments came to power on the defeat of anti-union governments, those of Duplessis and Bourassa.

At the beginning of the 1960s, the labour movement enthusiastically collaborated with the new government. Social policies, educational reforms, economic orientations of the Lesage reformist government rallied most of the union movement. Moreover, revision of the Labour Code in 1964 appeared a positive move in meeting the interests of organized workers, especially public employees. This last group had expanded significantly following the development and modernization of the Quebec state. But the first round of negotiations with the government as employer after the reform of the Code created disillusionment among union members. As an employer, they came to believe the Lesage government was like any other. Furthermore, the union leadership felt even more strongly that the Lesage Liberals and their successors were to be blamed for the failure to create a more evenly balanced relationship between workers and employers. As Marcel Pepin expressed it in 1970, the state and business were seen as acting together against labour.[6] Consequently, union militants demanded changes in the whole system, rather than mere changes in the governing elites. The problem could no longer be limited to which men occupied which positions in government. The discussion was enlarged to include the role of the state in the capitalist system and its functioning.

The radicalization of the labour movement had direct effects on employers' and businessmen's organizations, which had to clarify their own stands. For instance, an organization like the Chamber of Commerce of the province of Quebec used to claim to represent most sectors of the Quebec population on the basis of its community affiliates at the local and regional levels.[7] Responding to the apparent socialist trend developing among organized workers, the Chamber found itself "obliged" to adhere more unequivocally to liberalism and, above all, to defend private enterprise and capitalism. Since the Quebec labour movement was apparently developing particular analyses and practices, employers felt it necessary to elaborate their responses and to create new organizations to appear more deeply rooted in the modernizing Quebec society. Evidently the Association professionnelle des industriels could not play this role adequately, since its influence was limited by its traditional religious character and its well-known closeness to the UN.[8] Because it was primarily an English-Canadian organization, the Canadian Manufacturers' Association could not speak credibly for Quebec employers and offer appropriate replies to Quebec unions. It was in this context that the *Conseil du patronat du Québec,* which had existed embryonically since the mid-1960s, was founded in 1969.

The effect of these reevaluations and reorientations was an increasing polarization of capital and labour. Other social and political organizations found themselves enmeshed in this process: they had to take a stand for or against. In the late 1960s, the Quebec Liberals made a clear choice. The government elected on April 29, 1970, under the new leadership of Robert Bourassa plainly displayed this evolution through its devotion to free enterprise and economic growth. On their side, corporations and business had actually developed closer links with the state, to organize a better defence against the growing claims of the workers. Admittedly, the Bourassa government, which was so encouraging to investors and businessmen, did not initiate such special relationships. The complacent attitude of the government towards business nonetheless was then pushed to its ultimate.

Under these conditions, the PQ easily obtained the support of many union activists who, from inside the party, made it shift closer to the unions' position. At that time, it was thought that social polarization would bring about political independence, as is illustrated in the following statement of Léon Dion and Micheline de Sève:

> The possibility of independence for Quebec increases to the extent that the social issue takes precedence over the question of nationalism in electoral priorities. It would thus take place as a preliminary step in changing the regime or as a corollary to the assumption of power by the party which

currently carries the progressivist tendencies of the community, while at the same time demanding a new association with Canada.[9]

Such a presentation is contrary to that of those who argued that the central aspect in the evolution of electoral politics since the mid-1960s has been the growing of the nationalist program, specifically in its independentist form. To be sure, the founding of the PQ and its almost unexpected gain in the 1970 election created a "state of emergency"; separatists were no longer a small minority. The action of a very few, whom Pierre Elliott Trudeau tried to present as an "army" in October 1970, provided ammunition for those who wanted to present separatists as dangerous and villainous. Trudeau's argument, describing the independentist movement as a "new treason of the intellectuals," no longer seemed sufficiently strong. In fact, in Trudeau's mind, "modern" Quebec nationalism was inspired similarly to the "old" one. It meant isolation for French Canadians, a kind of retreat from the life of North America. To confine the perception of Quebec nationalism to these primitive forms clearly disregards the transformation of this nationalism from mere survival to a desire for full participation in the economic and social development of Quebec. It is on that basis that the steady shifts in Quebec nationalism since the beginning of the 1960s must be evaluated.

Well before November 15, 1976, the *threat* of separation was used by the Quebec government to force the federal government's hand.[10] The slogan *"Egalité ou indépendance,"* which the UN popularized in 1965-66, led to "negotiations" at a series of constitutional conferences. Even Robert Bourassa's Liberals, who presented themselves as unconditional federalists, began to speak of "cultural sovereignty" and of a "Canadian Common Market" after the refusal of the other provinces at Victoria in 1971 to grant the Quebec government special powers in social matters. Some of these Liberals admitted, for a while, they were revising their position on independence. As expressed in 1982 by an elected member of this party,[11] both parties (the PQ and the Liberals) have the same vision of the Quebec situation and, to a great extent, even of its future. The main point of disagreement between the two parties, he suggested, is the proposed means to correct this situation and to realize this future.

Since the creation of the PQ, it is clear that electoral competition incited the Liberals not to emphasize this steady and general shift in Quebec nationalism since 1960. So the nature of the PQ opposition appeared to polarize Quebec parties around the national question. This perception appeared particularly relevant in the 1973 election, which effectively made voters choose between federalism with the Liberals and independence with the PQ.[12] Misinterpreting the nature and the quality of this polarization, the Liberals assumed that it would work in the 1976 election as it did in 1973: the voters would surely choose the federalist Liberals over the PQ. Clearly, it did not work. In fact, Quebec voters found other issues more important. Moreover, provincial parties other than the PQ had difficulty in clearly articulating their stand. While opposing the PQ's option, they could not accept the constitutional status quo.

Because of these conditions, full polarization of the PQ and the Liberals on the national question could scarcely be seen, but appeared in 1973 and later on, in the 1980 referendum. In any event, the confrontation became so prominent between Trudeau's and Lévesque's parties that it proved difficult for any provincial party other than the PQ to present any intermediate constitutional position that could be clearly perceived. An orthodox federalist position could mean the provincial Liberals' dependence on Trudeau and the federal party. On the other hand, such a preoccupation could inspire legitimation of the PQ's sovereignty-association position. The provincial Liberals were really desperate. Following their electoral defeat in 1976, Bourassa's former ministers called for a debate among Québécois before the referendum and seemed worried about the abilities of the provincial parties to effectively oppose the PQ unless they united behind a leader other than Trudeau. Ironically, it was Trudeau's intervention in the last weeks of the referendum campaign that was the most determinant factor in the federalist victory.

Beyond appearances, the process of polarization that could be observed in party politics did not fundamentally take root in the national debate. Some declarations of business leaders can be reported to provide additional evidence for this statement, if need be. For instance, on a couple of occasions in the mid-1970s, David Rockefeller declared in Montreal that the concept of Quebec independence was not so disturbing. Even Royal Trust, which was directly involved in the famous Brinks truck convoy out of Quebec in the hours before the 1970 election, declared, during the 1976 electoral campaign, that the independence of Quebec was not such a frightening eventuality. Commenting on the speech of Premier Lévesque in New York some months after the election of the PQ government, Dwight Eckerman, President of the Economic Club of New York, said, "I do not blame Québécois for having wanted to affirm their identity. There is an element of patriotism in that. If it is what they want, I am ready to defend them."[13] In spring 1977, a spokesman of the Conseil national du patronat français stated, "This question of an eventual separation of Quebec from the rest of Canada preoccupies us much less than you think."[14] He added that it was the position of the PQ government on foreign investment, the control of resources, and labour relations which would be decisive. The PQ government seems to have taken note of these cool opinions of international capital. Indeed, one must realize that significant reorientations have characterized this government's administration since 1976.

A Trend toward Depolarization

Despite the declared sympathies of the PQ government for workers, important organizations like the Confédération des syndicats nationaux (CSN) and the Centrale de l'enseignement du Québec (CEQ) expressed reservations about the new government. They sought to avoid the mistake they made in 1960 by believing that the defeat of an anti-union government would represent a real change in the relationships between unions and government leaders. In 1976, many labour leaders were inclined to assume that the real solution for the working class would come when a workers' party gained power. Clearly the PQ was not this kind of party. On the other hand, they found it inappropriate to run ahead of their membership by inviting workers to oppose the PQ. After all, only the Liberals could be presented as an alternative. In theoretical terms, there was a feeling that workers should not be pushed to adopt more radical positions until they realized the real nature of their interests.

The PQ government's first budget actually disappointed the labour movement; it was interpreted that the government had chosen first to placate Canadian and foreign investors. Because it looked like a compromise decision compared to initial plans, the government's bill on automobile insurance also was not enthusiastically supported by the labour movement. These policies led a growing number of activists—inside and outside the labour movement—to argue that the PQ had never been, and could not be, a party that workers could count on. In essence, a PQ government was not an ideal solution for the labour movement.

However, other actions of this same government did not please business either. Except for the support of a group of independentist businessmen founded in 1974, the Conseil des hommes d'affaires Québécois that has become the Conseil des gens d'affaires du Québec, the PQ government got a cool reception. The business community was concerned about some of the PQ's social policies, as shown by its reaction to some of the government's decisions: the increase in the minimum wage, the abolition of the Quebec Anti-Inflation Board, the cancellation of more than 7,000 strikers' fines imposed following the Common Front of 1975-76, the important revision of personal income taxes presented in Finance Minister Parizeau's second budget. In addition, during the first year of the government's mandate, a number of declarations of intent were not reassuring. Some time after the election, the Minister of Labour and Immigration promised the enactment of a new "social contract" under which employers would no longer think *only* of making money. A couple of months later, the Minister of Social Development announced the government's intention to impose a series of minimum conditions of work that every employer would have to recognize for all workers, unionized or not. The employers' association, the Conseil du patronat du Québec (CPQ), clearly stated its opposition to any anti-scab law and proposed a one-year moratorium on any change in the Labour Code. The anti-scab law was nonetheless passed.

Apart from some controversial decisions by the new government, it was mainly a question of "climate" that bothered business. Indeed, it was unusual for a minister to denounce blackmail by businessmen and to state that they are not the kind of people she usually looks for.[15] It was also not customary for a minister in a North American government to state that he is suspicious of these people.[16] Businessmen were not prepared for a minister who attacks the myths of North American capitalism and who denounces growth at all costs, while addressing a meeting of businessmen.[17] And it was surprising to hear the parliamentary assistant to the Minister of Labour assert his preference for a politicized union movement over "business unionism."[18] One may suspect that statements of this sort would not make business very happy about a *Péquiste* government.

After the election of the PQ, it was above all the reorientation of the special relationship that used to exist with the Bourassa government which was most disquieting for business. For instance, the President of Montreal Board of Trade affirmed that, for the first time in its history, this organization had to fight openly and publicly: "With previous governments, more discreet negotiations were the rule. Never before did the President of the Board of Trade have to make public declarations."[19] This embarrassment of businessmen was expressed more subtly by other spokesmen.

If the style of the newly elected PQ government shocked businessmen, it was clear that the workers had not come into power. The mere presence of new governing elites is not sufficient to end the tensions within a society or to end the domination of specific interests. Profound transformations of a society require reorientations of the state itself and actions that go beyond declarations of intent. Businessmen did not trust the party because it seemed unable to form a clear consensus within itself on its stand on crucial questions.

From its foundation in 1968 to 1972, the PQ simply espoused a reorientation of capitalist development that would benefit Québécois. With the publication of its manifesto in 1972 and its national conventions since then, it undertook a critique of North American capitalism. Although the dominant group in the government adhered to the first position, businessmen remained concerned about the presence in this party of activists who wanted significant economic and political change. According to a privately expressed opinion by an important member of the milieu, this incited (and incites) enterprises and employers' spokesmen to make theatrical declarations by overemphasizing the "socialist" orientations of the PQ. As he explained, such behaviour was (and is) felt necessary to press the PQ government so that it does not pay too much attention to its more radical wing.

Before 1976, the PQ had to become a credible alternative for those people who were looking for an instrument to throw out the Liberals. Thus, the PQ's program progressively became a typical moderate social-democrat one. As the PQ became a government party, this program was soon revealed to be a serious disadvantage since the reaction of capital was taken into account: capital felt uncomfortable about a party that, though bourgeois, did not seem to be close enough to the bourgeoisie's interests. The PQ government therefore developed a certain ambivalence that produced the rapid disillusionment of the labour movement. It is the question of power, not style, that is important for workers.[20]

The decisions of the labour movement, after contentious debates in the CSN and the CEQ about their relationships with the PQ government, are revealing. After stating their awareness that the government was not a workers' government and was consequently in a vulnerable position in relation to employers, a majority of the union activists in each federation indicated their belief that the new government was nevertheless not hostile to the labour movement. They therefore decided to press for as many reforms as possible in the interest of their organizations and members. Partisans of a further radicalization strongly tried to prevent this "reformism." It is interesting, then, to see where this attempt appeared most successful. The CEQ, the federation that was the most "independentist" oriented, was the least enthusiastic at the leadership level in its support for the PQ government. At the other end, the Fédération des travailleurs du Québec (FTQ), whose membership is much more heavily working class, was the federation that most openly supported the PQ, especially in electoral campaigns.

Obviously, this must be related to a structural factor: the members of the CEQ and the CSN, whose many members are also employed in public and parapublic institutions, have to negotiate more or less directly with the Quebec government as employer. Consequently, these organizations have to remain cautious in their relationships with any government. Another important political factor must be taken into account: since clarity in ideological orientations apparently varies from the CEQ to the CSN to the FTQ, it seems that the more clearly defined the program and the more radical the critique, the more cautious the attitude vis-à-vis the PQ is, and the cooler the PQ's sympathies for the labour movement are.

Those elements clearly intervened in relationships that developed between the PQ government and workers' organizations. Following many attempts to institute dialogue by the means of tripartite meetings after 1977, the PQ government realized that some union leaders were not readily inclined to compromise over fundamental objectives that had been defined during the early 1970s. (See Chapters 19 and 20.) In fact, the union leadership's reluctance could be partly explained by business's corresponding reluctance to compromise significantly on their interests and positions, all the more because they distrusted the PQ government. Some time after the 1976 election, the CPQ, while acknowledging the competence of many members of the PQ government, clearly expressed reservations about its representativeness.[21] To remedy this situation, they suggested that yearly meetings be held to institute dialogue *("concertation")*.[22]

Such meetings were, indeed, held: the PQ had already made it a priority to restore "social peace" in Quebec and had arranged economic summits as a means to achieve that goal. However, it soon appeared to many union leaders—especially those with a majority of members employed in the public service or in public institutions—that compromises were expected by labour more than by capital. From these summits, the results were much less than anticipated. However, "sector-based summits" produced more concrete results, but it is revealing that many were held with employers and workers in declining economic sectors.

A major contentious issue that particularly opposed workers' and employers' spokesmen evolved around the role of the state and its intervention in the economy. From the beginning, the PQ's official stand on the elimination of "every form of exploitation of workers" appeared intolerable for capital. In fact, the PQ's position evolved considerably; the aim gradually became one of protecting less privileged people against more privileged ones. Significantly, the meaning of "privilege" shifted from reference to capitalists to referring to better-paid workers, particularly those employed in public services.

Strong attacks on these employees were explicitly undertaken in a series of laws adopted from 1982 to 1983 by the PQ government. First, in June 1982, Bill 68[23] was passed to reduce the pension benefits of those employed in the public sector. Second, in the same month, Bill 70[24] unilaterally determined the salaries to be paid to employees of the public sector unless an agreement were reached between their union and the government; it was to be understood that such an agreement would have to be true to the "guidelines" originally defined by the government. Understandably, the unions were reluctant to negotiate, although Bill 70 did not settle conditions of work apart from salaries. When it appeared that the December 1982 deadline for agreement established by the political authorities would not be met, the government passed Bill 105.[25] Once again it unilaterally defined conditions of work for public-sector employees until the end of 1985. Moreover, this Bill imposed 20% cutbacks on public-sector salaries for a period of three months at the beginning of 1983, so that increases agreed to in 1979 for the second half of 1982 were mostly taken back. Finally, to end the protest strike of teachers in public schools and CEGEPs, the government voted Bill 111[26] 16 years to the day after the passing of Bill 25[27] by a UN government. Bill 111 was unprecedented in imposing fines and determining the status of unions in the case of the continuation of strikes. Many referred to the Duplessis era.

These actions by the PQ government were strongly denounced by union leaders. But, at the same time, these leaders (except for the President of the CEQ) were participating in secret meetings with representatives of business and employers' associations and with government authorities.[28] One interpretation is that the PQ was realizing its objective of instituting dialogue, at least as far as organized private-sector workers were concerned. However, other decisions were not totally pleasing to employers, as was apparent when the Lévesque government announced, in May 1982, the strengthening of the anti-scab law.

Nevertheless, the PQ government had greatly improved its relationship with employers, particularly by modifying its stand on state intervention in the economy. Although it stated that it was not intended "to call into question the principle of direct state intervention,"[29] the Quebec government made it clear in *Le virage technologique* that the state was no longer so central in the direction of the economy:

> The responsibility for ensuring sufficient and continued development falls first of all on the private sector, because a large majority of companies are found in this sector. The Government of Quebec is primarily concerned with creating and maintaining conditions favourable for the development and the dynamism of private enterprise. It believes that the market economy should generally be preserved as the system most able to ensure the efficient allocation of resources.[30]

From this it could be understood that the PQ has moved closer to the position of a Liberal government, such as the Bourassa government. Six months after the 1976 election, the Liberals published a manifesto that proclaimed a total commitment to free enterprise. During the years Claude Ryan was the party leader, there was some disagreement on this point. The election of Robert Bourassa as Liberal leader in October 1983 should contribute, however, to clarifying once again the Liberal stand on the private sector of the economy.

From the changes that have been observed in the relationship between the PQ and the unions and in the PQ's conception of the role of the state in economic development, one suspects that the PQ's position on the future of Quebec society has become closer to the Liberals' position. To a great extent, this reorientation of the PQ government harmed the Liberals, who could hardly continue to stress the PQ's so-called socialism. In fact, the only course was to relate the economic problems of Quebec to a serious lack of business confidence in the PQ government, mainly because of its attachment to an independent Quebec.

Crisis and Institutionalization

In its preoccupation with making peace with business and employers, the PQ government produced an apparent trend towards depolarization at the level of political parties. It must nevertheless be stressed that this depolarization was possible to a great extent because of an evident "deradicalization" of the labour movement, especially among organized workers of the private sector, since the late 1970s. The economic crisis represents a major factor explaining this process. The unions' memberships became so preoccupied by the increase in unemployment to almost unprecedented levels that long-term political changes were found less and less appealing as solutions to immediate economic problems. To be sure, "reformism" did not become the official program of the unions; they still state that the improvement of the workers' general situation calls for important political changes. Practices, however, were adjusted. Invitations to collaboration sounded better than they had some years before. Some compromises were felt to be urgently necessary to prevent a further deterioration of workers' conditions. The President of the CSN made this clear in April 1983.[31]

To be sure, public-sector employees showed themselves less ready to accept such compromises. First, they generally assumed that the state as an employer did not have to behave like a private entrepreneur. Especially in a time of economic crisis, their leaders argued, the state had an obligation not to exacerbate the social problems created by the economic crisis. Of course, such statements were "unpopular," since most people thought that public-sector employees were much better off regarding job security and working conditions than their counterparts in the private sector. Under these circumstances, the PQ government found itself in an impossible position to press union negotiators for concessions. The union leadership refused to believe that the PQ government would push as far as it formally declared it would; they thought that the initially declared positions at the "national conference" of March 1982 (translated into Bill 68 and Bill 70) were put forward to provide the government with a positive bargaining position in the coming negotiations.

These assumptions by part of the labour movement were rooted, it may be suggested, into the dual analysis that was made of the state in Quebec over the previous 15 or 20 years. On the one hand, the state was repeatedly presented as being at the service of capital and dominant interests; this "real" state had to be converted into an apparatus that would be more focused on the problems of popular classes and of the Quebec people. This "imaginary" state could possibly, it was assumed before 1976, begin to emerge with a PQ government in spite of the limits of its policy on political and social change. This ambivalent vision of the Quebec state, particularly under a PQ government, led union leaders to misinterpret the real determination of the government to reduce the gap between workers of the private and public sectors. As a result, the PQ government found it appropriate to intensify its offensive; it strengthened its position by pointing to the financial situation of the government that a large proportion of the population saw as terrible.

One suspects that the intense attack of the PQ government on the labour movement will inevitably lead to rupture the special relationship between workers' organizations and the party. However, it could also be suggested that the PQ will not necessarily lose much support, since the other political parties do not seem to be benefiting significantly from the disappointment created by the PQ's action. Moreover, workers' organizations have so strongly opposed the Liberals in the recent past that they will likely refuse to support them against the PQ. Furthermore, alternative options on the left have little chance to get significant support in the very near future, principally because their leadership appears either to belong to the "old" political elites, who have oriented Quebec politics since the "Quiet Revolution," or to emerge from social organizations that are no longer (or are not yet) attracting much support. In these conditions, one suspects that the *Péquiste* hegemony over the labour movement is not automatically condemned to become a past reality, although it could possibly be redesigned.

In fact, the PQ has come closer to the Liberals since becoming a government party, just as the Liberals had become more nationalist in the time when they formed the Quebec government from 1970 to 1976. Such shifts are to be related to the transformations that affect any party in power. As long as a party is not a government party, it can and must promote more particularly the interests of those who give its core support. But as soon as this party is a government party, it is responsible for the "management" of the society as a whole. This further step in the general process of political institutionalization means that a party has to take into account the variety of interests present in the society. In a sense, power usually represents a disappointment since, to use Sylvie Biarez's words, "Organization circulates a commitment of which the realization is constantly postponed."[32]

To say that institutionalization often means compromises of programs is not to say that plans are always betrayed. As it became a government party in 1976, the PQ became responsible for the general cohesion of the Quebec society. Consequently, it had to be aware of the many political forces active in this society and the many opinions that these forces were expressing. So those who expected the most felt the most betrayed; this is generally the situation for militants who have waited for a long time before achieving the possibility of realizing their most heart-felt objectives. In the first analysis, it must be remembered that "instability and transformations lead the state and its bureaucracy to look for solutions."[33] To be sure, capital and labour reproached the PQ government for having chosen to favour one side against the other. In fact, this government refused to take sides firmly during its first mandate. Since the 1981 election, however, it has appeared to many that the Lévesque government has been behaving more and more like a bourgeois government, assuming the possibility of accomplishing a better distribution of wealth in society without fundamentally changing the mode of production.

The influence of the process of institutionalization was quite visible in the party functioning in late 1981 and early 1982, as reported by Pierre Fournier:

> In terms of the national question, the progressive wing [of the PQ], which in large majority favours outright independence, suffered a major defeat in the March 1982 party congress. At the December 1981 congress, it had succeeded in dropping the question of "association" from the PQ program. Lévesque then called a referendum within the party, threatened to resign, and succeeded in reversing the decision. After that, several PQ members left the party and rallied behind political movements calling for socialism and independence.[34]

On that basis, it has been argued (or hoped) that the independence option in Quebec would die a natural death. Such a conclusion remains fragile, since it takes a crisis of *Péquisme* for a crisis of nationalism.

Prospects for Quebec Nationalism

In its attempt to unify the Quebec people behind its option, the PQ government has failed. The referendum defeat was seen as a turning point that provided federal authorities with a great advantage:

> After the referendum of May 1980, Prime Minister Trudeau took advantage of the euphoria created by the federalist victory to attack a serious problem of the Canadian economy, one that had lately grown more acute. This was the gradual balkanization of the national economy, mainly under the impact of provincial laws and regulations. The transfer from the British to the Canadian Parliament of authority over the constitution was to be the occasion for a more precise definition of the nature and the extent of the powers of the central government. The leading objective would be to restore the integrity of the Canadian market for goods and services and eliminate all existing obstacles to the free circulation of persons and capital.[35]

It is known that the federal government partly succeeded with the accord of November 5, 1981. But this does not invalidate the necessity of looking at the political evolution of Quebec in the context of capitalist development in Canada. It may be recalled that the economic situation in Quebec has little to do with the concentration of "a minority linguistic group" in the province.[36] Moreover, apart from the independence issue, the economic future of Quebec is not promising,[37] unless energetic government intervention produces radical changes. Quebec, like the New England states, is experiencing the effects of the trend of industrial investment to migrate to the southwest of the North American continent. Ontario investors (which virtually means Canadian investors) did not wait until November 15, 1976, to reduce their investments in Quebec; the trend had been visible since 1970. So, even if separatism has no appeal for investors, neither are they going to "save" Quebec even if it chooses to stay in Confederation. This now appears quite clear. (See Chapter 2.)

The awareness of the nature of capitalist development as the major factor explaining Quebec's economic situation has convinced an increasing number of people of the inadequacy of the independence solution itself. As stated by Gilles Bourque and Anne Legaré, "It is not evident that the working class's organizations have presently to struggle for Canadian centralism, although no support should be given to a pro-imperialist party such as the PQ and no alliance with it should be considered."[38] On the other hand, this suspicion about the PQ and even about independence itself does not discard possible support for independence combined with a larger program of social and political change. One thing at least remains clear: "As long as the Quebec people are dominated, the national question will persist. This is true whatever constitutional solutions are proposed . . ."[39]

If the PQ's sovereignty-association is not completely satisfactory to many, this is largely because it is accompanied by an unsatisfactory policy for the social and political future of Quebec society. However, the 1982

Constitution Act has evidently not resolved the "Quebec problem":

> While it is never easy to predict the future, it would be premature and politically foolish to bury the national question in Quebec, irrespective of the electoral fortunes of the Parti Québécois. The problems and questions which prompted the development of a pro-independence movement in Quebec remain unresolved. While much of the emotion surrounding the national debate has subsided, the new generation and the rising forces of Quebec society continue to support nationalism. The federal government, on the other hand, has moved quickly to fill the vacuum provided by their referendum victory, but may have created the conditions for an even more serious challenge to the federal system.[40]

It is analytically safe to avoid any deterministic view of the future in politics. The same safeguard must be applied to prevent any simple view of politics. The election of a PQ government in 1976 had been almost exclusively interpreted in terms of the politics of nationalism. Consequently, it was thought that the PQ's referendum defeat would lead to the decline of both this party and Quebec nationalism. But the PQ was reelected on April 13, 1981, with increased support. Some promptly pointed to Claude Ryan as the cause of the Liberals' defeat.[41] It must nonetheless be recalled that party politics, far from representing "autonomous" phenomena, are significantly dependent on the level of consciousness that various groups and classes in a society have of their own interests. On that basis, Quebec nationalism has not been discarded once and for all; further realignment of political parties and of their support is not excluded from the future development of Quebec politics.

Notes

1. Vincent Lemieux, Marcel Gilbert, and André Blais, *Une élection de réalignement: L'élection générale du 29 avril 1970* (Montréal: Cahiers de Cité libre, Editions du Jour, 1970), p. 41.
2. Vera Murray, *Le Parti québécois: de la fondation à la prise du pouvoir* (Montreal: Cahiers du Québec, Collection Science politique, Hurtubise/HMH, 1976), p. 19.
3. Minister of Industry and Commerce, Guy Saint-Pierre, as quoted in *Le Jour* (April 10, 1975), p. 10.
4. Parti québécois, *Un gouvernement du Parti québécois s'engage . . .* (Montreal: Les Editions du Parti québécois, 1973), p. 38.
5. Declaration at the Convention of the Quebec Federation of Labour (Dec. 1960).
6. Marcel Pepin, *Un camp de la liberté,* Report of the President to the 1970 Convention of the CSN, p. 25.
7. See Marc Bélanger, *L'association volontaire: le cas des chambres de commerce* (Doctoral dissertation, Sociology, Université Laval, 1968).
8. Jean-Louis Roy, *La marche des Québécois: Le temps des ruptures (1945-1960)* (Ottawa: Leméac, 1976), p. 189.
9. Léon Dion and Micheline de Sève, "Quebec: Interest Groups and the Search for an Alternative Political System," in *The Annals of the American Academy of*

Political and Social Sciences (Interest Groups in International Perspective) 413 (May 1974), pp. 143-44.

10. For one example, see Richard Simeon, *Federal-Provincial Diplomacy: The Making of Recent Policy in Canada* (Toronto: University of Toronto Press, 1972), pp. 43-65.
11. These statements were made in the course of a long conversation with me, only a few days before the resignation of Claude Ryan as the Liberal leader.
12. As a result, the support for the UN sharply dropped to about 5%. The Créditistes, led by Yvon Dupuis, did not achieve the support expected according to a poll taken one year before the 1973 election. See Maurice Pinard, "The Ongoing Political Realignments in Quebec," in Dale C. Thomson (ed.), *Quebec Society and Politics: Views from the Inside* (Toronto: McClelland and Stewart, 1973), pp. 119-38.
13. Quoted in *Le Québec en bref* (a publication of the Ministry of Intergovernmental Affairs, Government of Quebec) 11: 4-5 (April-May 1977), p. 22.
14. *Le Devoir* (May 25, 1977), p. 32.
15. Interview of Minister Lise Payette in *Le Devoir* (April 27, 1977), pp. 1-2.
16. Declaration of Minister Jacques Couture, as quoted in *Le Devoir* (Feb. 11, 1977), p. 20.
17. Speech of Minister Pierre Marois, as reported in *Le Devoir* (Feb. 12, 1977), pp. 1, 6.
18. *Le Devoir* (April 25, 1977), p. 14.
19. *Le Devoir* (May 19, 1977), p. 23.
20. Of course, shocking statements as those reported above do not please owners of capital. On the other hand, it is known that the eradication of capitalism is not really the priority goal of a typical moderate social-democrat government. In this sense, a government of this sort still "manages" a capitalist, or bourgeois, society.
21. Conseil du patronat du Québec, *Certaines questions qui se posent au Québec d'aujourd'hui*, a brief presented to Premier René Lévesque (Jan. 1977), p. 2.
22. Ibid., p. 3.
23. *Loi modifiant diverses dispositions législatives concernant les régimes de retraite* (Quebec National Assembly, 32nd Legislature, 3rd session, assented to on June 23, 1982).
24. *Loi concernant la rémunération dans le secteur public* (Quebec National Assembly, 32nd Legislature, 3rd session, assented to on June 23, 1982).
25. *Loi concernant les conditions de travail dans le secteur public* (Quebec National Assembly, 32nd Legislature, 3rd session, assented to on Dec. 11, 1982).
26. *Loi assurant la reprise des services dans les collèges et les écoles du secteur public* (Quebec National Assembly, 32nd Legislature, 3rd session, assented to on Feb. 17, 1983).
27. *Loi assurant le droit de l'enfant à l'éducation et instituant un nouveau régime de convention collective dans le secteur scolaire* (28th Legislature, 1st session, assented to on Feb. 17, 1967).
28. See "Lévesque a présidé un 'mini-sommet' en secret," in *Le Devoir* (April 6, 1983), p. 3.
29. Government of Quebec (Ministère d'Etat au Développement économique), *Le virage technologique: Bâtir le Québec—Phase 2: Programme d'action économique 1982-1986* (Quebec: Editeur officiel du Québec, 1981), p. 22.

30. Ibid., p. 21.
31. See Pierre Pelchat, "Donatien Corriveau déplore l'absence de concertation," *Le Soleil* (April 16, 1983), p. A4.
32. Sylvie Biarez, *Institutions et groupes sociaux: Hypothèses et problématique* (Paris: Centre d'étude et de recherche sur l'administration et l'aménagement du territoire, 1976), p. 26.
33. Ibid., p. 44.
34. Pierre Fournier, "The Future of Quebec Nationalism," in Keith Banting and Richard Simeon (eds.), *And No One Cheered: Federalism, Democracy, and the Constitution Act* (Toronto: Methuen, 1983), p. 166.
35. Dominique Clift, *Quebec Nationalism in Crisis* (Montreal: McGill-Queen's University Press, 1982), p. 138.
36. Gilles Bourque, *L'Etat capitaliste et la question nationale* (Montréal: Les Presses de l'Université de Montréal, 1977), p. 260.
37. For some views of the possible developments of the Quebec economy, see Pierre-André Julien, Pierre Lamonde, and Daniel Latouche, *Québec 2001: Une société refroidie* (Sillery, Que.: Boréal Express, 1976), ch. 4.
38. Gilles Bourque and Anne Legaré, *Le Québec: La question nationale* (Paris: Maspero, 1979), p. 230.
39. Jean-Marc Piotte, "Un point de vue socialiste: L'espoir péquiste est-il fondé?" *Le Devoir* (Dec. 2, 1976), p. 8.
40. Pierre Fournier, op. cit., pp. 171-72.
41. Dominique Clift, op. cit., p. 148.

Chapter 18/Political Parties and the Quebec State since 1960*

Réjean Pelletier

Trying to analyze the political parties in Quebec during the period 1960-1983, one must inevitably make reference to the transformation of Quebec society, to its problems and its evolution, to new dominant ideologies, and to the transformation of power.[1] To discern this dialectical relationship between parties and society, we can use two complementary roads: analyzing platforms and analyzing policies.

The first mainly situates parties at the societal level or as meeting points between the social and the political, since, in their platform papers, parties identify the problems confronted by society, formulate solutions to resolve these problems and put into concrete form the party's actions, and define objectives that could orient the development of society.[2] In other words, the perception of problems and the definition of means to resolve them rest on a certain conception of society that should normally be exposed by an analysis of the platforms.

The analysis of policies situates parties as meeting points between the political and the social, for parties in power in Quebec since 1960 have usually sought to establish their platforms in such a way as to resolve certain social problems by policies of distribution, regulation, or redistribution.[3] This also conveys a particular view of the state, either as a distributor or redistributor of goods and services, as a creator of structures and instruments for action, or just simply as an organizer of things and people.[4]

The constraints of space here allow only the first road to be explored. This will essentially consist in considering parties as agents of social transformation through an analysis of their programs and some important documents, in order to illustrate in the best possible light both their will to act and their general conception of Quebec society during the period 1960-1983.

The Rupture of 1960[5]

In Quebec, in 1960, urbanization and industrialization were already undeniable facts, and so the opening decade marks, from this perspective, a

---

*This chapter is a revised and updated version of "Les partis politiques et l'Etat," in *L'Etat du Québec en devenir* (Montréal: Boréal Express, 1980), and has been translated by Claude Galipeau, Political Studies Department, Queen's University.

continuity and not a rupture with the preceding period (1945-1960). In fact, the population of Quebec has been mostly urban since 1921—according to the definitions of the Canadian census—and this phenomenon has been amplified regularly in the following decades, if we disregard the major world economic crisis of the 1930s.

At the economic level, we also observe a number of important structural changes. From the Second World War, each of the large sectors of economic activity underwent mutations that affected most of Quebec society in a major way. We find, in effect, a constant and pronounced decline in the participation of the work force in the primary sector, particularly in agriculture. Contrariwise, the secondary sector grew constantly until 1951, then subsequently declined to a percentage of the work force in 1971 less than that of 1941. The decline of these two sectors profited the tertiary sector, which developed considerably during the 1950s, especially in the *private* tertiary sector, and continued to grow during the following decade after the rapid increase of the *public* tertiary sector.

The development of the tertiary sector after the Second World War was linked to the growth of the large cities, particularly to the growth of the metropolitan region of Montreal. In these urban areas, at the same time that the sectors of commerce, finance, insurance, and communications developed, it also became necessary to create institutions of education, health, and welfare which required competent administrators who were chosen more and more, not from the ranks of the clerics short on the necessary skills, but from the recent graduates in the social and administrative sciences. It was in this way that there formed and grew, after important structural changes, a new middle class, which the sociologist Hubert Guindon has described as being "the product of the expansion of bureaucratic organizations."[6]

In this perspective, the rupture of 1960 is situated at the political level rather than at the socioeconomic level, because the relevant structural changes were underway at the end of the Second World War. This rupture was marked by the arrival in power of another political party, but the party received its support mainly from the new middle class or, to be more precise, from a new directing elite born of this class. It is thus through the expediency of the Liberal party that this elite in large part manifested itself and realized its social and economic reforms and affirmed its own neo-nationalism, even if the Liberal party cannot be considered the sole representative of the rupture of 1960.

The new middle class found itself confronted in the 1950s by three "institutions" of resistance that occupied the whole social field: the Catholic Church, which controlled the major parts of social affairs and education; the anglophone bourgeoisie (Canadian and American), which dominated the economic sector; and the federal government, which mainly imposed itself in the political sector following the centralization of powers and resources in

Ottawa and also after the rejection of the Duplessis government by a good part of the new middle class.

To counter the action of these institutions, the new middle class, which rose to power in 1960, used the Quebec state as an instrument for collective action and defined a new ideology, neo-nationalism, to justify the state's actions. This explains the state's intervention simultaneously in the areas of activity traditionally controlled by the Church, in the economy by the creation of public enterprises managed by francophones, and in the political field by opposing the presence of the federal government in some sectors.

This major role given to the state in the areas of the economy, society, and culture essentially defines neo-nationalism, as opposed to the traditional and conservative nationalism, which had a profound distrust of the state. All the other characteristics flow from this: it is *because it is statist* that neo-nationalism was demanding and offensive and no longer defensive, political and not just cultural, more and more sovereignist and not just autonomist, Québécois and no longer French Canadian, attached to technocratic values and no longer religious and rural ones.

This statist neo-nationalism—and here lies my central thesis—inspired some of the programs and general ideology of the political parties in Quebec since the 1960s and permits a separation of each party from the others. In other words, what has characterized the political parties of Quebec during the period 1960-1983 is essentially each party's position on the use and intervention of the state in Quebec society. On this issue, we can separate the period into two, 1968 being a turning point in the history of Quebec and Canadian politics, which is discussed later in this chapter under the heading "The Rupture of 1968."

Political Parties and Statist Intervention (1960-1968)

By interventionism, I mean all measures favouring the growth of the state or the public and parapublic sectors (creation of ministries or boards, nationalizations) or any form of statist control in a sphere of activity. I will qualify as noninterventionist all measures that favour restraining the growth of the state (refusal of intervention or contraction of its sphere of activity) as well as any measure favourable to the private sector's development (and this can take the form of subsidies) or that prompts the private sector to do such or such act.

Statist intervention can take a double orientation: an individualistic orientation, which means individualistic allowances in the form of direct distribution or redistribution of goods and services to individuals, even if these measures have a universal trait (that is, one that touches all individuals); and a collectivist orientation, or favourable measures for the collectivity without direct allowances of goods or services (nationalizations, linguistic policies).[7]

What characterized the political parties of Quebec during the period

1960-1968 and what distinguished each from the others were essentially their relative positions on the axis of intervention. In the main, the Liberal party clearly appeared more interventionist than the Union Nationale, especially until the latter held its congress of orientation in March 1965 and elaborated its electoral platform of 1966. Even in 1966, the Liberals appeared slightly more interventionist than the UN: 57% of the propositions in the Liberal's platform to 54% in the UN's.

An analysis of the electoral platform of the Liberal party from 1960 to 1966 uncovers an accentuation—at least in quantitative terms—of the role of the Quebec state. At the same time, priorities were reoriented since, in the program of 1960, statist action was mainly concentrated in the political and social areas and afterwards in economic and cultural ones. By thus putting an emphasis on politics, this program already announced a Quebec state to be constructed through the creation or reorganization of ministries and boards of all kinds and by the modernization of the public sector. In 1966, the Liberal party's interventionism was concentrated first and foremost in the social and economic sectors, then equally in the cultural and political sectors, even though the cultural sector had the most important growth since 1960.

Thus, the period that opened with the elections of 1966 seemed a little less encouraging for the creation of state mechanisms (except in the economic sector); the actual numbers do not differ much—the Liberals proposed 17 new or reorganized ministries, boards, offices, and commissions in 1960 to 15 in 1966—but the overall effect of those interventions in 1966 was less significant. The Liberal party felt more and more the need to legislate in linguistic areas in order to give a French countenance to Quebec and to assure the priority of the French language in all sectors of social activity. This will to legislate in the linguistic area announced one of the important themes of the following period (1968-1980), which was marked not only by constitutional problems but also by the action of the Quebec state to assure the predominance of the French language.

In summary, if as early as 1960 the Liberal party wished to assure a planned development for Quebec under the aegis of a stronger and more competent public sector and that it gave the state the role of motive force in this growth, by 1966 this situation was not only confirmed but also accentuated, especially in the economic and cultural sectors. From then on, the economic prosperity and cultural blossoming of Quebec seemed to be assured only by the significant action of a state that wished to be more in control and a leader in society.

This statist vision was confirmed in declarations by party leaders. Thus, in June 1961, Jean Lesage was affirming:

> The present conjuncture is forcing us to reconsider our traditional positions. We need powerful means, not only to overcome the inevitable obstacles that we will encounter in the years to come, but also to bring the

> French-Canadian people into the modern world. Now, the only powerful mechanism we have is the Quebec state; it is our state. We can ill afford the luxury of not using it. I do not have the right, as Premier of this state, to tell you that we have to let such a matter reside solely with the efforts of individuals or organized groups.[8]

This conception of the role of the state as a powerful and principal lever of action was reaffirmed with force in the preamble to the 1966 platform paper: "The Liberal party of Quebec believes that the Quebec state is the principal instrument for the emancipation and progress of our people. It is its job to activate and coordinate the indispensable policies of economic and social development."[9]

Even if the platform of 1960 showed some facets of the traditional nationalism, the principal elements of a strongly statist neo-nationalism were already in place. Evidently, the word or the idea of "nationalism" was not used in political discourse because it was still identified with conservative values and anti-statism. But, in its recourse to the Quebec state and its appeal for the modernization of the public sector, the Liberal party had started to define a neo-nationalism that would be recognized as such a few years later. Thus, since the election of 1962, the party clearly showed itself more neo-nationalist by favouring the nationalization of the electrical companies and especially in presenting this nationalization as the primary condition for the economic liberation of Quebec, in order to finally be "masters in our own house." The 1966 platform remained loyal to this orientation, since it placed the Quebec state at the centre of social and economic development and considered this state as an instrument of emancipation and progress.

By comparison, in 1960, the Union Nationale presented itself to the electorate without a real platform; only the electoral publicity can inform us about its orientations. This publicity was based before anything else on the achievements of the party—so much so that, at the beginning of the campaign, Antonio Barrette did not fear to pronounce, "My platform is that of 1944."[10] The Union Nationale committed itself to defend provincial autonomy in the face of the federal government's will to centralize, yet advocated at the same time the open-door policy for foreign investments. This policy of aid and support for the private sector prevailed over the development of social affairs and the education sector, since the UN still considered the best system to be one that relied less on the state. It was a platform of continuity based on the achievements of the party and loyalty to traditional nationalism, which inspired a profound distrust of state action and supported a defensive autonomism against Ottawa. On occasion, allusions were timidly made to the "progressive" measures of Premier Sauvé.

In 1962, the Union Nationale presented a platform where the economic sector occupied the most important place (39% of the propositions). The party tried to adjust to contemporary political events and adopted a more clearly neo-nationalist rhetoric: there was talk of financial independence, of political sovereignty, of the Quebec state and proposals for a greater role for the state in economic development. But, in the same breath, the UN pledged to "surround the competent and dynamic private sector with a climate of confidence and security in order to encourage the industrial expansion of Quebec."[11] Likewise, the Union Nationale defended the conception of the state as a benefactor or redistributor of wealth in the social sector addressing especially the marginalized and the disfavoured, while still upholding respect for the rights of parents and Church in the area of education. All in all, the party was in a period of mutation and adjustment to a new conjuncture created by the coming to power of the Liberal party in 1960. The Union Nationale, in 1962, had not yet renounced its past, but started to distance itself more and more from it.

Not until the orientation congress of March 1965 and especially the platform of 1966 did a "new" Union Nationale emerge. In quantitative terms, this platform gave priority to the political sector (42% of the propositions), followed by the economic, cultural, and social areas. Moreover, the number of interventionist positions increased appreciably (from 31% of the platform in 1962 to 54% in 1966) and a decrease in the number of noninterventionist positions (from 8.5% in 1962 to 5% in 1966).

The interventionism of the Union Nationale manifested itself from this point on as much in the political sector as in the areas of culture and leisure. At the social level, it proceeded at times even further than the Liberal party by offering, to cite but one example, the right to strike even during a period covered by a collective agreement. It was mostly in the economic sector that its policies seemed less interventionist than those of the Liberal party, although it advocated massive state intervention in the forestry industry. Thus, the evolution process begun in 1962 was entrenched in the 1966 platform. The Union Nationale had taken to neo-nationalism in the political, social, and cultural areas. In the economic sector, its platform appeared more as a mixture of conservatism and progressivism.

It appears, then, that what differentiated the Liberal party from the Union Nationale during this period (at least until 1966) were their respective positions on state intervention. In other words, the apparent ideological consensus was broken in 1960 along this line of cleavage between interventionists and noninterventionists, and it was the interventionists of the new middle class who triumphed.

Moreover, if we try to oppose these two parties on an axis of federalism-independentism, we find that the two did not fundamentally question the federalist option, even though they objected to the centralizing designs of Ottawa, reclaimed additional sources of revenue for Quebec, and sought to redefine the constitutional framework. Also, if we oppose these two parties on an axis related to pro-Quebec or pro-Ottawa stands, we can note that both parties were resolutely attached to Quebec, demanding not only the respect for jurisdictions granted to the provinces, but manifesting as well the will to occupy their own jurisdictions.

Thus, when we consider the period 1960-1968 in its totality, the Liberal party can be considered more interventionist than the Union Nationale. Furthermore, even though both parties proposed measures of more individualist than collectivist orientation, the Liberal party appears nonetheless as more collectivist than the Union Nationale during this period, so much so that we can oppose these two parties according to this double polarity. (See Figure 18-1.) On the other hand, the two parties tended more and more to converge toward the end of this period, since the Union Nationale became more interventionist and more collectivist. All in all, we can discern a progressive agreement between these two parties on the form of state organization needed for Quebec society (with certain differences in the economic sector); thus, the victory of the Union Nationale in 1966 does not indicate a break with the preceding situation.

Besides this first polarization, which tended to lessen at the end of this period, what also characterized the party system during these years was the bipartisanism tempered by the arrival of new parties which did not succeed in attracting the electorate. Following from the tendency of the Liberal party and the Union Nationale to converge on the interventionist axis, two new centrifugal tendencies were embodied in two new parties—the Rassemblement pour l'Indépendance Nationale (RIN) and the Ralliement National (RN)—which at the same time presented an essential characteristic of being independentist.

The transformation of the RIN into a political party in March 1963, and especially its presence on the electoral scene in June 1966, did not coincide with important changes in the distribution and composition of the electorate. Thus, the RIN made an appeal to the nationalist supporters of the Union Nationale (with limited success) and especially to the new middle

Figure 18-1 Overall Comparison of Provincial Liberals to Union Nationale on Two Axes, 1960-1968

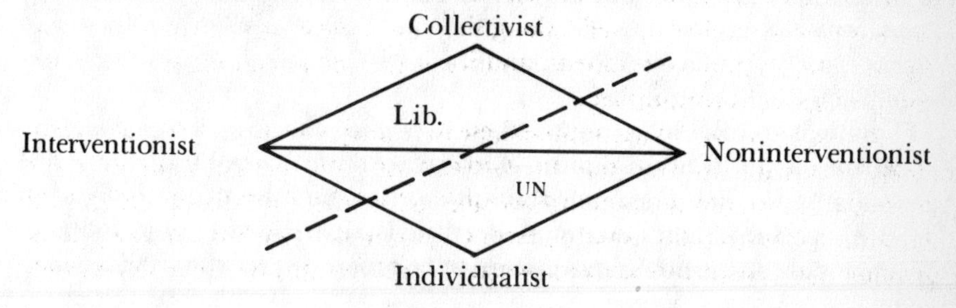

class (already courted by the Liberal party) liable to be attracted by a platform that sought not only political independence for Quebec, but also the planning of the economy and sociocultural affairs under the aegis of the state.

Economic planning, within the RIN's perspective, had to permit the Quebec state to control the factors of production and act with vigour according to the needs of the economy. Also, the state was to be called on to intervene in response to investment and consumption, to exercise its influence on industrial development and manage less developed regions, to put structures into place to integrate foreign investments with a national plan of development and rationalize export activity. Economic planning also had to be complemented by planning in sociocultural affairs, in order to protect citizens from the normal risks of life (accidents, sickness, and the like) and to organize and democratize education, culture, and leisure.[12]

Because the sociological composition and ideological orientation of the RIN were resembling even more those of the Liberal party (excluding, of course, the independentist option) than those of the Union Nationale, its creation and entry on the electoral scene could thus contribute to the victory of the party the furthest away on the ideological continuum—the Union Nationale—to the detriment of the Liberal party, closest to it ideologically.

The Ralliement National, on the other hand, appeared as a party for independence. Its manifesto published in April 1966 demanded a system of associated states. However, it was an independentist party of the Créditiste type—that is, essentially noninterventionist in the economic, cultural, and educational areas, while still at times a little more interventionist in the social sector, especially in its concern for the protection of individual liberties against encroachments from the state. As the manifesto stated, "A just government has to respect and assure the absolute primacy of personal and familial rights."[13]

We can therefore generally determine the position of the major political parties active on the Quebec scene during the period 1960-1968 by ordering them on an axis of interventionism. (See Figure 18-2.) The *rapprochement* between the two dominant parties on this axis from 1965-66 and the arrival of two independentist parties opened the way for a new rupture, which materialized during the pivotal year of 1968.

The Rupture of 1968

Like the one in 1960, the rupture of 1968 was above all a political one. It was essentially translated into a fragmentation within the new middle class between two tendencies, one more clearly federalist, the other more independentist with all the necessary alliances to be progressively established in both

Figure 18-2 Overall Position of Quebec's Political Parties, 1960-1968

The position occupied by the parties refers to their relative position to each other, not their *exact* place on this axis. Moreover, this figure indicates the *dominant* factor that generally distinguishes a party in the *totality* of the period under study. For example, the UN shows itself more interventionist in its 1966 platform, but much less so in 1960 and 1962.

camps. We can even speak of a *sovereignty federalism* and a *sovereignty confederalism*.

On the political scene, the founding of the Parti Québécois in 1968 marked a realignment of forces. Thus, a fraction of the new middle class supported the Liberal party, which advocated a workable federalism, more or less renewed; another fraction supported the Parti Québécois, which advocated political sovereignty for Quebec with an economic association with the rest of Canada. It was thus a question of a predominant political schism within the new middle class that supported, in the main, the same neo-capitalist platform with certain variations, depending on whether the emphasis was placed mainly on private enterprise, as the Liberal party did, or mainly on the state and the cooperative sector, as the Parti Québécois did.[14]

On the other hand, the new middle class—which was split between support for the Liberal party and the Parti Québécois—was confronted during this period, in a very different way, by the three dominant "institutions" cited above. In the areas of education and social affairs, the hold of the Church was much weaker than previously and the state was successfully affirming and imposing itself in these sectors by the creation of CEGEPs in 1967 and the Université du Québec in 1968, which completed the establishment of a public education system covering all levels from kindergarten to university. From this point on, the struggle was to be waged on the excesses or errors of the actualized reforms, especially concerning pedagogical reforms and the centralization and bureaucratization of the Ministry of Education. The same phenomenon applied to the health sector a few years later, since government had to wait for the publication of the Castonguay-Nepveu Report before proceeding to the last reforms. Henceforth, in both these sectors, discussion centred not on growth or expansion, but on the rationalization of expenditures and on budgetary restrictions.

The affirmation of the new middle class against the anglophone bourgeoisie did not really manifest itself during the 1960s, since the institutional division of labour between those two groups precluded any direct confrontation.[15] On the one hand, the new and expanding francophone middle class could easily occupy the places the state created at the heart of the public sector in the social and educational areas, in public and parapublic organizations, as well as posts created in the cooperative sector and in certain francophone private enterprises. On the other hand, the new anglophone middle class, enriched by the advent of skilled immigrants, found itself mainly in private bureaucracies linked to the financial world, in industry and commerce largely dominated by the anglophone bourgeoisie, or in the employment of the federal civil service, which mainly practised a policy of anglophone unilingualism.

The problem would for the most part emerge during the period 1968-1980, when the francophone public and parapublic sectors reached their limit of growth and were unable to respond to anticipations raised by the development of the Quebec state and education sector in the preceding decade. This created a more direct confrontation with the anglophone bourgeoisie, which controlled the private sector of the economy and unwittingly brought forth demands for linguistic policies to satisfy the claims of the new francophone middle class for an official language of work and education (Bills 63, 22, and 101).

Finally, the assertion of the Quebec state against the federal government took on a new sense after 1968. From 1960 to 1968, the task for the Quebec state was mainly to regain jurisdictions that had been taken over by Ottawa or, at least, to occupy fully its own jurisdictions and especially to obtain the necessary fiscal powers to deal with its obligations. After 1968, the situation was to change. With the arrival of Pierre Elliott Trudeau at the helm of the country, the new federal government refused not only to give a special status to Quebec, but also to recognize any distinct character for Quebec. On the contrary, it believed that the aspirations of Quebec could be satisfied with the elaboration of a policy of bilingualism in the public service and a more pronounced presence of francophones in Ottawa, as much in the public sector as in the political sphere. This policy of bilingualism would prove to be both an irritation for a large number of anglophones and inadequate for many francophones.

In Quebec, during this period, the parties realigned on the political scene and adopted more resolutely the federalist option for some (Liberal party, Union Nationale, and even the Ralliement Créditiste) or, on the contrary, opt for a form of independence for Quebec (Parti Québécois). In fact, in 1968, the Liberal party clearly lodged itself in the federalist camp by ignoring the special-status thesis proposed by Paul Gerin-Lajoie after having refused, in the preceding year, René Lévesque's option. This permitted the latter to form the Mouvement Souveraineté-Association in 1967, then to preside over the founding of the Parti Québécois in the following year by merging with the Ralliement National. The RIN dissolved itself two weeks later (October 26 and 27, 1968) at its congress instead of suffering a slow death. Also in 1968, the Union Nationale lost its leader, Daniel Johnson, who had been a firm negotiator with Ottawa and was still seen as the supporter of the "égalité ou indépendance" option;[16] Jean-Jacques Bertrand, who replaced Johnson, preferred compromise to rigidity and was more conciliatory in his negotiations with the federal government.

Thus, after the phase of construction and organization of the Quebec state (1960-1968), which produced at the outset an opposition between parties according to their respective conceptions of the role of the state, a second period began that was dominated by the problem of what place the Quebec state must occupy within the Canadian federation; this issue separated the parties along the federalism-independentism axis. Added to this dominant opposition was a second line of cleavage based on the degree of state intervention in Quebec society.

The Parties and Canadian Federalism, 1968-1981

To discern more clearly the lines of cleavage between the political parties of Quebec, the problem of the place for the Quebec state can be stated according to a double dimension. On the one hand, the place of the Quebec state within the Canadian federation resulted in a crisis of legitimacy of the system with a polarization between federalists and independentists. On the other hand, the place of the Quebec state within Quebec materialized, for example, by the questioning for different reasons of the state's role by both unions and employers, which brought forth a crisis of consensus in the system, with a polarization between interventionists and noninterventionists.

When the Parti Québécois presented itself to the electorate in 1970, it submitted a new option derived from the RIN, but with a heavily watered-down economic plan. This is why the 1970 platform appeared primarily as a political one (even if this area is found at the end of the platform paper), since it was concerned above all else to define the Quebec state, to clearly specify its place on the Canadian scene, before indicating what it would do or how it would do it. The *Péquiste* platform of 1970 was based on one simple postulate: the preliminary necessity of independence or, in the least, a sovereign Quebec with regained powers and taxes, but with a share in economic jurisdictions.

This state, both sovereign and associated, according to the PQ, could assure the development of a "modern and original" society, whether this be in the cultural, economic, or social sectors. The preliminary of political sovereignty was stated as a necessary condition. It was also virtually a sufficient condition for a cultural development conceived and planned by a state that tended to coincide with the nation; for social development based on the workplace, the health sector, the dwelling place and consumer protection; and for economic development made possible mainly by the public sector.

Everywhere in the PQ's platform the state was called on to intervene. Thus, for the social sector, even demanding the active participation of citizens in order to check the excessive bureaucratization of this sector, the platform bluntly affirmed that "we must accept once and for all that the primordial role, which is to elaborate and administer policies, is to be filled by the supreme popular authority, the state."[17] The platform was even more explicit on the central role for the state in the economy, since it recognized that the state was "the main motor of contemporary economies" and that a sovereign Quebec would have "the particular role to increase the scale of our economy" and this, not by multiplying the controls or regulations applicable to private enterprises, but by creating its own instruments for action.[18] Supporting its principles, the Parti Québécois came to this conclusion: "The state has to adopt as a primary form of intervention in the economy a supported extension of the public sector (public or mixed enterprises)."[19]

This central role is reaffirmed in the platforms of 1973, 1976, and even 1981, but the approach was relaxed. The PQ still placed the state and public enterprises at the centre of economic development, but recognized the cooperation of workers and private enterprise for élaborating a plan to modernize and restructure the economy; especially from this time on, it gave a privileged place in the operation of the economy to the cooperative sector and, later, to small and medium-sized companies from Quebec. The party also favoured collective forms of organization to assure the participation of workers in decisions.

This sketch of a Quebec way to social democracy was taken up and completed for social life, based on "an authentic policy of redistribution and social use of resources," in order to arrive at the "establishment of social justice grounded on a just distribution of wealth and the complete elimination of poverty."[20] More than the economic sector, the social sector gave the platform a social-democratic orientation. In other words, the Parti Québécois was more disposed towards the socialization of the mode of distribution of goods than of the mode of production, a tendency also found with the other political parties. But the PQ goes further than the others in its claim to be willing to "subordinate the criteria of economic profitability to the criteria of social profitability."[21]

From this point on, the Parti Québécois was identified with the option of sovereignty-association, even if it added the important stage of the referendum to its 1975 platform,[22] and committed itself more and more to define the type of society to build after independence, which was an attempt to reconcile the "electoralists" and the "participationists" within the party.

This evolution in the platform was, for that matter, confirmed by the data, since the initial importance given to the political sector was lessened in subsequent versions of the platform (1973, 1975, and 1980), where the volume of proposals for the social sector became progressively more important: political propositions dropped from 32% in 1970 to 27% in 1980, while social propositions rose from 24% to 37% of the platform. It is the same for the cultural sector, where the large number of propositions of 1970 constantly diminishes in the later platforms.

In short, the Parti Québécois presented its platform more skillfully. Henceforth, it portrayed a more general and less sector-based vision of the problems faced by society and it especially watered down its initial espousal of a planned economy by searching for coordination and the development of cooperation. But the dominant factor remained the will to use the state in the political, economic, and social sectors, with an accompanied "liberalization" of the platform in the cultural area after 1970. What also characterized the PQ in 1970 was that state intervention had to occur not only for the good of individuals, but also for the good of the collectivity—something that separated it at this level from the Liberal party of the Quiet Revolution, which was a little more individualistic—but individualistic propositions considerably increased between 1970 and 1981. The most striking difference between the Liberal party of the 1960s and the Parti Québécois was found at the political level, where the Parti Québécois advocated a sovereignty option, which linked it to the rupture of 1968.

In fact, the Liberal party clearly chose the federalist option, according to its 1970 platform: "The Liberal Party opts without equivocation for the maintenance of the federal system whose flexibility makes it the most efficient and apt to guarantee the realization of Quebec's fundamental objectives."[23] But this federalism had to take into consideration the particularities of Quebec and consent to a new sharing of jurisdictions and fiscal resources. This profession of faith was repeated in the 1973 election, when the party demanded a decentralized federalism congruent with the cultural sovereignty of Quebec. The Liberals used almost the same theme in 1976, even if at this time the constitutional question introduced the platform instead of being relegated to the last pages. In 1981, the Liberals went for a new federalism and stated that Quebec must again play its prominent role as active and responsible leader for renewing Canadian federalism. The Liberal party's federalism was mainly based on economic arguments and not in the least on any form of Canadian nationalism.

In sum, the provincial Liberals espoused a strong federalism (with modifications) in their platforms and especially opposed separatism that "condemns Quebec to tragic reversals in its development."[24] From this originated the polarization between the clearly federalist option and the option of sovereignty-association and the concomitant difficulty for other parties (the Union Nationale and the Ralliement Créditiste) to find a specific place on this federalism-independentism axis.

If the Liberal party was clearly situated at the federalist pole and vigorously reaffirmed its support for federalism, its conception of the role of the Quebc state evolved more and more towards less interventionism between 1970 and 1981, as though too much of a federalist position would lead to a consequent reduction of the Quebec state's role. In 1970 and 1973, the party favoured state intervention in the development of the social sector and, on occasion, in the cultural sphere, but this interventionism was mainly oriented to benefits and services for individuals. But, in 1976, when it proclaimed itself "as the only real Quebec federalist political party,"[25] it became at the same time less interventionist and even noninterventionist, especially in the economic sector. Generally, the party did not seek to control or direct Quebec's economy, but to orient and rationalize it, clearly recognizing that the state "cannot assume all the responsibilities" and that "*private initiative retain all its importance* in the economic, social, and cultural life of the collectivity."[26] This orientation was all the more significant, since the party traditionally placed prime importance on the economy during this period.

The Liberals' policy resulted in more sharing of tasks between the private sector, which was called on to assure economic development, and the state, which took charge of social welfare and, if need be, the cultural sphere. It was more the benefactor state that dominated and no longer the organizer state of the Quiet Revolution years. The sharing of tasks also occurred at the political level, where the party portrayed itself as the only defender of federalism and left to the Parti Québécois the job of defending the option of political sovereignty.

For its part, the Union Nationale generally advocated a more interventionist policy than did the Liberal party of 1970; the UN committed itself to establish the "instruments for economic conquest," which are the present Société Générale de Financement and the Société de Développement Industriel. The 1970 platform document opened with this article of faith in the Quebec state. For the Québécois:

> The Quebec state is a privileged instrument to control and guide the collectivity's progress. The state becomes an essential tool for the economic and social progress of the nation. Insofar as the state is seen as useful and necessary, Quebec itself, as a national entity, finds itself heightened in the awareness of its citizens.[27]

The role given to the state in the economic and social sectors brought the Union Nationale even closer to the Parti Québécois, while the Liberal party and the Ralliement Créditiste tended to converge with their concept of a state that allowed a great deal of scope for private enterprise, as this position of the Ralliement Créditiste testifies:

> We believe that the production of consumer goods and services, for reasons of efficiency, should be assured by private enterprise. In this area, the role of the state must be limited to the protection of consumers and the monitoring of mechanisms for competition. The state should intervene in the distribution of wealth only in order to assure the welfare of those disadvantaged groups of society.[28]

This conception conforms to the Créditiste philosophy based on the respect of the individual and individual rights and favourable to development of private enterprise, while opposing abuses of the system and, in particular, the creation of monopolies, "which are the negation of economic liberty."[29] The Liberal party's 1970 platform was also favourable to private enterprise and only on occasion depended on state action to assure economic development.

In sum, we can place these four political parties on an interventionist axis, as seen in Figure 18-3. The position of each party is determined by its conception of the state according to its 1970 platform, which in fact closely matches the party's position on the federalism-independentism axis. In other words, the more a party affirmed itself as independentist, the more it wanted to be interventionist; inversely, the more federalist it was, the more it defined itself as noninterventionist, without this indicating that there was a necessary relation of cause and effect between the two (as in the case of the Ralliement Créditiste).

It is in this way that, in 1970, both the Ralliement Créditiste and the Liberal party affirmed their faith in federalism as a political formula, while also demanding constitutional reforms. Moreover, the Ralliement Créditiste strongly opposed the Parti Québécois, which it considered not only as "separatist" but also—and mainly—as "socialist."[30] These two parties, while being the most federalist, were also the least interventionist. On the other side, the Union Nationale above all wanted the Constitution revised to give Quebec "all the powers necessary for its normal and legitimate development,"[31] without making any reference to the benefits of federalism as a political formula: at the same time, the UN was closer to the Parti Québécois in its conception of the state's role.

This first form of realignment of the political parties after 1968 subsequently suffered some modifications. From the beginning, the independentists felt a need to gather favourable forces for the sovereignty of Quebec into a single party that could be viable on the Quebec scene. The

Figure 18-3 Overall Position of Quebec's Political Parties on Two Axes, 1970

merging of the Mouvement Souveraineté-Association and the Ralliement National, then, created the Parti Québécois, which immediately resulted in the disbanding of the Rassemblement pour l'Indépendance Nationale.

The federalist forces were divided mainly between the Union Nationale and the provincial Liberals, since the Ralliement Créditiste preferred to appeal, in the main, to its traditional support which it had acquired on the ideological plane, instead of venturing to become more pragmatic, without clearly defined ideological boundaries. Yvon Dupuis's attempt to appeal to urban voters led to electoral disaster in 1973; even though its percentage of the vote dropped only from 11% in 1970 to 10% in 1973, the Créditistes' support was spread too thinly. In 1976, it maintained its noninterventionist position and watered down its federalist stand by presenting itself as the party of the "third road," the one seeking a special status for Quebec, or as the "party of salvation" (the title of its two 1976 campaign pamphlets), which lodged itself "at the centre, between unconditional federalism and suicidal separatism."[32] The Créditistes' percentage of the vote was cut in half in that election. The party disappeared almost entirely in the 1981 election when the Crédit Social Uni received only 0.04% of the popular vote.

In 1973, the Union Nationale suffered the cost of the existing polarization largely to the profit of both the dominant pro-federalist party, the Liberals, and the only party for independence, the Parti Québécois. In fact, in its 1973 platform paper, the Union Nationale closed in on the Liberals by calling itself less interventionist than before, especially in the economy, while at the same time trying to more clearly detach itself from Liberals on the political level by demanding a new Canadian Constitution that would give more power to the provinces. This option was not sufficient to convince the electorate that it was really being offered a third way between the federalism of the Liberal party and the independentism of the Parti Québécois; as a result, the UN was almost completely eliminated.

In 1976, the Union Nationale tried to give itself a distinct character on the federalist axis to enable it to attract a larger electorate by draining the supporters of the established federalist parties and especially those of the Liberal party. This time, the platform appeared more credible and the Union Nationale was able to contribute to the demise of the dominant federalist party to the gain of the only independentist party. But the polarization of the two dominant parties contributed to the defeat of the UN in 1981, when it received only 4% of the popular vote and no seats.

Thus, the period 1968-1981 was characterized by a polarization of greater and greater force among political parties along the federalist-independentist axis, a polarization that favoured parties with the most "extreme" positions, to the detriment of "third road" parties that sought to remain between these two options. At the same time, there began a sliding of *all* the parties along the interventionist axis as the Parti Québécois abandoned certain forms of collectivist intervention and as all the federalist parties showed themselves to be decreasingly interventionist, when they did not openly opt for nonintervention.

Conclusion

From a *Canadian* perspective, the centrifugal tensions of 1968-1981 are much more important than those of 1960-68, which rested on the interventionist axis, even more so because the distribution of parties on this axis tended towards a convergence near the centre instead of to the extremes. Moreover, the opposition to statist intervention made by these parties did not fundamentally question the prevalent economic system, since, in the neo-capitalist perspective accepted by all the parties, some insisted more on private enterprise to assure economic development and others on the state, to which would later be added the cooperative sector and small and medium-sized companies.

In addition, on the anglophone side, the years of the Quiet Revolution were generally considered as a period of catching up for Quebec, which enabled it to attain politically and economically "the level of development" enjoyed by other provinces, particularly Ontario. The opposition to Quebec's anglophone bourgeoisie did not develop until later when state, parapublic, and private francophone sectors could no longer offer the necessary positions to the increasing members of the new middle class.

Even if this period was to bring a displacement of the Church by the state as the new dominant institution of Quebec, this would not produce a serious confrontation between the two (in spite of Bill 60, for example), nor would it create a Church-state polarization which would have been taken up by the then-current parties or which would have led to a new party system. Rather, the confrontation brought opposition between the partisans for statist intervention and those for nonintervention, even if this type of polarization would inevitably produce in the Quebec of yesteryear an opposition to the Church. It is in a way the social aspect of nationalism that dominated during this period.[33] Contrary to this, the strengthening of the Quebec state had to lead quite rapidly during these years to a confrontation with the federal state, especially over the sources of revenues for Quebec and a new form of sharing powers—as in the conflict over a rent-control board, for example—but without fundamentally questioning the federal system itself or the federal formula.

In summary, the 1960-1968 period did not provoke a crisis of legitimacy or a crisis of the system, which distinguished the following period (1968-1981). Rather, a crisis within the system or a crisis of consensus put an end to the artificial and apparent unanimity of the previous years under a dominant ideological illusion that led to the belief in the tranquil and permanent possession of "the truth." The first step is to situate this period under a Quebec perspective, even if the effects of this rapid mutation were also felt throughout Canada.

The period 1968-1981 had a more important *Canadian* impact, since the national schema of nationalism came to dominate by opposing the parties along the federalist-independentist dimension. From then on, the matter was centred more and more on defining the Quebec state's place in the Canadian federation, especially with the arrival on the political scene of the Parti Québécois, which led to a crisis of legitimacy in the Canadian political system. At the same time, the PQ took up the Liberal party's job of statist intervention, but, contrary to the latter's conception, the Parti Québécois gave the state a more clearly collectivist orientation (especially in the beginning of this period) which was close to the sense of community found in the Quebec of yesteryear, even though this collectivism was tailored to fit new situations and demands.

At the moment when the national question polarized the debate between federalists and independentists and when the parties in fact demoted the social question, social conflicts sprang forth from everywhere and became more and more acute (the October Crisis of 1970; the *La Presse* conflict of 1971; the Front Commun of 1972) to the point where the political parties were unable to adequately respond. It was then that social groups intervened and conflicted according to their respective conception of the state's role (union organizations versus the Conseil du Patronat, for example) and according to the type of development deemed adequate for Quebec society.[34] This background permits a better understanding of the scope and acuteness of social crises under the Bourassa government.

Thus, in each of these periods, the social and national aspects were present and dominated in turn; however, it was mainly the constant dialectic between the social and the national that was at the core of the social and partisan dynamic in Quebec during most of the period 1960-1981. Moreover, if it was really the national schema of nationalism that dominated during the period 1968-1981, then the arrival in power of the Parti Québécois on November 15, 1976, did not mark a break with the preceding period, but a continuity or, more exactly, a normal and logical end for this period. In other words, the national question continued to polarize the political parties of Quebec and to dominate Quebec's political scene at least until the referendum, to the point where the social question became subordinate anew to this more urgent problem, even if both have tended recently to overlap more and more. Thus, neo-nationalism, defined and imposed by the new middle class in power, has become the new unifying ideology in Quebec, especially in its statist formulation, which tries to transcend or to veil the divisions within society, especially class divisions.

But the 1980s have marked a new turn in Quebec political life. In this respect, the referendum of May 1980 and the economic crisis of 1981-1983 can be considered as two important events for Quebec society. On the political scene, the referendum marked the end of a period in which the national question dominated the attention of political parties. It was important—

especially since the rupture of 1968—to delimit the ostensible place of the Quebec state within the Canadian federation. The referendum by the *Péquiste* government on this issue sought to renegotiate this place by giving greater powers to the Quebec state while at the same time maintaining a kind of economic association with the rest of Canada.

After the PQ's setback, the federal government acted to modify the Canadian Constitution with the inclusion of a Charter of Rights and an amendment formula in agreement with the other nine provinces. Certainly, the repatriation of April 1982 did not mark the end of the constitutional debate: Quebec (and other provinces) are still waiting for the reform of federal institutions and a new division of powers. But the failure of the PQ's referendum has fundamentally changed the political situation: opposition to the federal system and the definition of an appropriate place for the Quebec state within this system will probably not dominate the political scene in years to come, even if the Parti Québécois wants to go for "double or nothing" in the next general election with a referendum election.

From now on, the crisis of legitimacy within the Canadian political system will have to concede its place to a crisis of consensus over the role of the state in the daily lives of the people of Quebec. As the state increases its general hold on socioeconomic life, there is a progressive increase of contestation in all sectors of activity. The knowledge and power of the technocracy are questioned, as well as the tendency towards centralization and bureaucratization, the economic inefficiency of the public sector, while the increased participation of citizens is promoted, with calls for local and regional decentralization, and the private sector is strongly valorized. The economic crisis of the 1980s has accentuated this trend.

Political parties in Quebec were progressively adjusting themselves to this situation by becoming, during the past decade, less and less interventionist. Even the Parti Québécois—which has ostensibly always given a primary role to the state—manifested a clear will to increase the role of the private sector when it published its document, *Bâtir le Québec,* in 1979 and since then has sought to "take the technological turn."

Conscious that the economic crisis has produced a fiscal crisis of the state which hampers its capacity to intervene in different sectors of activity, conscious as well that popular dissatisfaction linked to inflation and unemployment lead also to the rejection or questioning of the very nature and role of the state, the *Péquiste* government has shown signs of wanting to reconcile itself with the private sector and is courting private investments regardless of their foreign or indigenous origins. The major objective sought by the government is economic growth; the problem of economic control or the form of property has become secondary.

It is also in this context of an economic crisis that the Parti Québécois government has pursued a policy of confrontation with the public sector—especially the teachers—by the imposition of salary cuts and decrees affecting collective bargaining. This has produced an important social crisis and has put into question the "favourable bias towards the workers" that the Parti Québécois has until recently profited from.

Thus, the situation in the 1980s clearly appears novel compared to the previous two decades. Political, economic, and social crises have combined to create a new and different configuration in Quebec political life. It really seems that, from now on, Quebec will no longer be able to live on the ideals from the Quiet Revolution, so the political parties will have to adjust quickly to this situation.

In this context, the Quebec state will have to redefine its role: instead of imposing and regulating, it is probable that it will search to orient; instead of playing the role of instigator, it will be called to play the role of helper or supporter of the private sector. Statism, planning, and all the technocratic rationality seem to have lost their place to private enterprise, to productivity and the technological boom: these will probably be the principal themes of the next decade in Quebec.

Notes

1. For a general study on parties, see, among others, Jean Charlot, *Les partis politiques* (Paris: A. Colin, "Dossier U," 1971). See also Giovanni Sartoni, *Parties and Party Systems: A Framework for Analysis* (Cambridge: Cambridge University Press, 1976).
2. This definition is borrowed from Daniel Latouche, "Le contenu thématique et l'orientation idéologique des programmes électoraux en 1973," in D. Latouche, G. Lord, and J.G. Vaillancourt (eds.), *Le processus électoral au Québec: les élections provinciales de 1970 et 1973* (Montreal: Hurtubise/HMH, 1976), p. 128.
3. Theodore J. Lowi, "American Business, Public Policy, Case-Studies, and Political Theory," *World Politics* 16: 4 (July 1964), pp. 677-815 and especially pp. 689-91.
4. See Vincent Lemieux, "Quel Etat du Québec?" *Etudes internationales* 13: 2 (June 1977), p. 260.
5. The principal elements of this section have appeared in a more elaborate form in "Nationalisme et étatisme au Québec dans les années 60: une hypothèse de travail pour l'analyse des programmes des partis politiques," *Revue canadienne des études sur le nationalisme* 7: 2 (fall 1980), pp. 329-50.
6. Hubert Guindon, "Social Unrest, Social Class and Quebec's Bureaucratic Revolution," *Queen's Quarterly* 71: 7, (summer 1964), p. 152. See also Kenneth McRoberts and Dale Posgate, *Quebec: Social Change and Political Crisis*, rev. ed. (Toronto: McClelland and Stewart, 1980). But we must also note that the new middle class does not cover the whole of the tertiary sector: it excludes most of rural solicitors and the subordinate workers in the service sector to encompass essentially those people working at a high level in the tertiary sector: high-level bureaucrats in the public service; cadres and directors of the health and educational services, the unions, cooperatives, and information media; and university teachers.
7. It is evident that the propositions of a platform, be they in the form of commitments made by the party or as stated principles, cannot all be classified

along these axes. Thus, to take but one example from the Liberal party's program of 1960, article 40 (the convening by Quebec of an interprovincial conference) is a nonclassifiable proposition on the axes, but counted in the whole of the program; while article 27 (the immediate establishment of a governmental system of health and hospital insurance) is classified as an interventionist proposal (growth of the state) and an individualist one (direct allocation of goods and services to all individuals).

8. Speech given on June 3, 1961, in Ottawa to the Fédération des Sociétés Saint-Jean-Baptiste and cited in part by Jean Lesage in *Un Québec fort dans une nouvelle Confédération* (Québec, 1965), p. 18.
9. Preamble to *Québec en marche: Le programme du Parti Libéral du Québec* (1966), p. 3.
10. Cited by Jean Hamelin and André Garon, "La vie politique au Québec de 1956 à 1966," in Vincent Lemieux (ed.), *Quatre élections provinciales au Québec, 1956-1966* (Québec: PUL, 1969), pp. 12-13.
11. See the Union Nationale's 1962 platform published by Jean-Louis Roy, *Les programmes électoraux du Québec*, vol. II (Montreal: Leméac, 1971), pp. 395-402.
12. See Réjean Pelletier, "L'idéologie du RIN: une idéologie d'affirmation," in Fernand Dumont, Jean Hamelin, and Jean-Paul Montminy (eds.), *Idéologies au Canada français, 1940-1976*, tome III (Québec: PUL, 1981), pp. 213-34.
13. "Manifeste du Ralliement national," *La Nation* (the official organ of the RN) 2: 1 (April 1966), p. 5.
14. See Pierre Fournier, "Les tendances nouvelles du pouvoir économique au Québec," *Le Devoir* (June 9-10, 1976).
15. Hubert Guindon develops this theme in "La modernisation du Québec et la légitimité de l'Etat canadien," *Recherches Sociographiques* 18: 3 (Sept.-Oct. 1977), pp. 337-66; see also McRoberts and Posgate, op. cit.
16. According to the title of his book, *Egalité ou indépendance* (Montreal: Edition Renaissance, 1965).
17. *La solution: Le programme du Parti québécois* (Montréal: Editions du Jour, 1970), p. 51.
18. Ibid., p. 25.
19. Ibid., p. 26.
20. *Le programme, l'action politique, les statuts et règlements* (1973 ed.), p. 17.
21. *Ibid.* (1975 ed.), p. 11.
22. During the 1972 federal electoral campaign, some leaders of the PQ proposed for the first time the idea of consultation with the voters on the question of independence in the eventuality of the party's accession to power. Advertisements by the PQ during the 1973 provincial elections again took up this idea of a referendum on the future of Quebec. Yet it was not until the congress of November 1974 that the official platform contained the proposal to seek recourse through the referendum before unilaterally declaring the independence of Quebec. This recourse was again changed in the 1978 platform, when the Parti Québécois promised to "assure itself, by referendum and at the moment judged to be most propitious, during its first term, of the support of Quebeckers for the sovereignty of Quebec." Finally, the question submitted to the electorate in the referendum of May 1980 announced a second referendum after the first one seeking the permission to negotiate a new deal between Quebec and Canada, based on the option of sovereignty-association.

23. *Québec: Au travail!* (the provincial Liberals' platform, 1970), p. 52.
24. *Un nouveau programme d'action* (1973), p. 75.
25. *Programme 1976*, p. 3.
26. Ibid., p. 7 (underlined in the text).
27. *Objectifs 1970: Programme de l'Union nationale*, préface, p. 3.
28. *Camil Samson et le défi créditiste* (Quebec: Griffon, 1970), p. 125.
29. Ibid., p. 98.
30. Ibid., p. 131.
31. *Objectifs 1970: Programme de l'Union nationale*, p. 65.
32. Camil Samson, Laurent Legault, and J. Noël Gravel, *La planche de salut* (1976), p. 60.
33. Léon Dion makes a distinction between the national form and the social form of nationalism in *Nationalismes et politique au Québec* (Montreal: Hurtubise/HMH, Sciences de l'homme et humanisme, collection, no. 7, 1975), p. 130.
34. See Raymond Hudon, "Les groupes et l'Etat," in G. Bergeron and R. Pelletier (eds.), *L'Etat du Québec en devenir* (Montreal: Boréal Express, 1980), pp. 263-84.

Chapter 19/Corporatist Tendencies in Quebec

Clinton Archibald

While not generally recognized, post-Depression Quebec has developed in a clearly corporatist manner. However, it might be argued that to state that the political behaviour of Quebec government and the ideas of its citizens stem solely from corporatist roots would be going too far.[1] This is supported by the fact that ideas and practices developed elsewhere, mainly in Italy and Portugal, by leaders such as Mussolini and Salazar, have no common denominator with thoughts developed by Quebec's thinkers.[2]

Quebec's political life in the last 50 years may nevertheless be better understood if one looks first at the different corporatist ideologies used by the Catholic Church, whose impact on Quebec's society has been well documented,[3] and second by exposing *l'Action Nationale* and *l'Ecole Sociale Populaire* before 1960 as a quasi-system framework. Until the Quiet Revolution, in fact, a network of *corps intermédiaires* took shape under the aegis of the Church and, influenced by that type of corporatist view of society, Quebec has not evolved as a real political society.

With the discovery of the state apparatus by the Lesage government, however, a new type of corporatism was born. Social groups became involved in trying to influence public decision making rather than attempting to function in isolation. To avoid class conflicts, nationalists and neo-nationalists in Quebec have looked on corporatist schemes as tools for the promotion of social harmony to give the impression that all Quebeckers were united in the pursuit of the same collective goals.[4]

A third period arose with the arrival of Robert Bourassa.[5] At the beginning of the 1970s, the new Liberal leader promised new ways for action that would integrate business, unions, and government to recreate the spirit of reforms of the Quiet Revolution.[6]

With the victory of the Parti Québécois in 1976, some observers have identified a further revival of corporatist ideas, programs, and legislation.[7]

A Definition of Corporatism

The fascist state created by Benito Mussolini in Italy before the Second World War was officially derived from corporatist ideas developed by "Il Duce" himself and syndicalists Michele Bianchi and Edmondo Rossini.[8] It was supposed to incorporate union, business, and state representatives in a system of mutual cooperation. In reality, however, the Italian state became the only viable institution, controlling both the nominations of delegates to the Chamber of Corporations and the day-to-day functioning of each corporatist body.[9]

Corporatist schemes were also elaborated in Spain, Portugal, Germany, and even some countries in Latin America, but all these experiences have more or less suffered from the Italian experience in seeking the predominance of the state.[10] That is not to say that every corporatist proposal has failed, but more to admit that corporatist practices have not followed the original model for a corporatist system. Nigel Harris rightfully points this out when he writes, "Corporatism (in practice) assumes what it is designed to create, and destroys what it seeks to create by pursuing the only practicable means available: coercion. . . ."[11]

But what is the real essence of corporatism? According to Robert Presthus, who believes that the corporatist paradigm is one of the four constitutive elements of our Canadian political culture, it is essentially "a conception of society in which government delegates many of its functions to private groups, which in turn provide guidance regarding the social and economic legislation required in the modern nation-state."[12] Leo Panitch insists on the dichotomy that exists in corporatist practices, since he sees corporatism as "a political structure within advanced capitalism which integrates organized socioeconomic producer groups through a system of representation and cooperative mutual interaction at the leadership level and mobilization and social control at the mass level."[13]

These notions are important, but Philip C. Schmitter is probably more accurate when he writes that corporatism is "a system of interest representation in which the constituent units are organized into a limited number of singular, compulsory, noncompetitive, hierarchically ordered, and functionally differentiated categories, recognized or licensed by the state."[14] Corporatism, therefore, has three components: functional representation of all economic and social sectors in decision-making units of a society; some form of institutionalization of these *intra*governmental structures; and joint decision making in a legislative and executive partnership.[15]

It must be understood that corporatist schemes have clear and definite objectives. All want to diminish (sometimes eliminate) class conflicts in a society by giving labour some appearance of involvement in the political process. They also look for the representation of as many sectors as possible in order to avoid problems related to popular democratic principles based on false representative democracy. Order and efficiency in sociopolitical functions are the favorite slogans. State participation, as opposed to state leadership, is necessary because the state should become a catalyst in the formulation of joint decisions.[16] Finally, some form of institutionalization is necessary if citizens are to feel that they are part of the sectors represented at the apex of power.

With the teachings of the Catholic Church, Quebec's society was a fertile ground for such ideals. In some ways, it might be argued that nationalism and corporatism were inseparable. The idea that French Canadians had to unite in order to defend both their faith and their language evolved because ordinary citizens were led to believe that they could take care of their own affairs without the intervention of the state, which was perceived as an exterior actor.[17]

Social Corporatism: Intermediary Bodies

The notion of developing a network of *corps intermédiaires* was originated in Quebec between 1930 and 1960 and was inspired by Church teachings. Quoting parts of the *Rerum Novarum* encyclical, spokespersons from the Quebec Church maintained that society was nothing more than an immense social corporation headed by the moral authority of the Church.[18] The entire province was perceived as being made of two separate entities, the state and the human corporation—an exact replica of the Church itself, conceived as a "body of bodies," leading to the eternal reward.

In fact, some authors have claimed that before 1960 all social institutions were coloured with a certain degree of Catholicism.[19] Thus, the best way for the Church to act as an intermediary between God and citizens was to supervise the action of most of the social groups in society, to make sure that they were animated by Christian principles (mainly the spiritual wellbeing of all members), and to act as their link with political authorities.

Three important elements in the social life of French Canadians served as catalysts in the establishment of a social-corporatist arrangement of the community. First, the parish was more than a simple ecclesiastical structure. It was, as Jean-Charles Falardeau remarks, the basic social institution of French-Canadian life, replacing in many ways the medieval city and its network of dependent social institutions.[20] With its towering steeple, the local church in rural as well as in small urban settings symbolized the union of all individuals around this larger family, the parish. Everything was organized around it: schools, credit unions, sports, and on and on. Most of the social groups—such as l'Action catholique de la Jeunesse Canadienne, la Jeunesse ouvrière catholique, la Jeunesse Etudiante Catholique—were organized and supervised by parish officials.

The second element was the existence of Catholic unions. Looking for a counterweight to the American influence in the Quebec trade-union movement and animated by the idea of establishing Christian unions, the Quebec church organized, in a relatively short time, more than one-third of the unionized force. As H.A. Logan, one of the most remarkable observers of the trade union movement in Canada, writes of the leaders of that search for church-led unions:

> They are fearful of radicalism because it is opposed to Christian doctrine; they turn away from the internationals because the contact would endanger their French language and traditions; they are not class conscious in a way likely to engender social upheaval; they talk the language of absolutes in all matters of principle, and nothing else will suffice. . . .[21]

Finally, in order to minimize the risk of state intervention in social affairs, perceived as a socialist action, Quebec's bishops publicly argued that they should be the managers of social activities while the state would only be "subsidiary."[22] A joint administration of society was then to be a compact between state and Church officials. According to this view of society, one would say that Church representatives were in an almost authoritarian control of all social activities through a tacit delegation of authority to it from the state.[23]

In return for its delegated control of all social activities, the Church sang the great merit of the nationalist goals of Maurice Duplessis. Abbé Lionel Groulx, father of a conservative nationalist doctrine, was then able to say that French Canadians had a "mission," which essentially meant that they had to show to the rest of the world that a Catholic nation was a living example of the ideal society, at peace with itself and orderly maintained.[24] Nothing endangered that social peace as long as the two worlds were totally isolated. Archbishop Charbonneau, who made some critical comments in favour of strikers in the famous Asbestos strike, had to leave the province because Duplessis and Church officials did not tolerate criticism of the *bonne entente* contract.

Ideas and practices coincided. Abbé Groulx founded *l'Action française* in 1920 and replaced it in 1930 with *l'Action nationale*. In articles written by himself and by Father Arès, *l'Action nationale* developed a complete system of organized social life which was called "un corporatisme éclairé." That meant that Quebec, as the French-Canadian society, would be led by strong leaders who would accept a network of intermediary bodies between the state and society. But these *corps intermédiaires* would not be political, their only link with the state being through Church officials who, in order to preserve this special liaison with the leader of the province, would fight for him and preach a social submission even during difficult economic times.[25] The best social institutions to do just that would be cooperatives inspired by Christian principles, since their members would be supposed to help each other.

As for *l'Ecole Sociale Populaire* directed by Father Joseph Papin Archambault, it insisted on the need for a planned economy, but done by social groups, not the state. This would take the form of a social corporatist organization where owners and workers would sit together at social gatherings and supervise the operation of small units of society and their integration within *l'Action Catholique*. This naturally prevented the development of class consciousness. In fact, what was achieved was the appearance of only one class of Quebeckers, an ethnic class.[26]

Hence, social groups in Quebec before 1960 followed the teachings of the Church. Desjardins's movement, for example, integrated popular credit unions, financial and insurance institutions, consumers' groups, and even some education groups. Added to sports and unions, all organized by parish leaders, one can say that everything appeared to be inspired by corporatist principles. Fernand Harvey summarized it when he wrote, "The answer was found in brotherly love and good fellowship, for ideally the answer lay in corporatism."[27]

The Quiet Revolution and Its Impact on the Church

The Quiet Revolution, says Gérard Bergeron, was a revolution "because suddenly things were happening in Québec, but the pace was quiet, nonviolent."[28] However, relationships between state officials and representatives from social groups changed drastically.

And it was in the administration of the education system that things changed the most. As a result of the recommendations of the Parent Royal Commission, Jean Lesage proposed reform after reform. A Department of Education was established to replace the former Département de l'Instruction publique and 55 regional school boards were formed. This meant that the traditional teaching role of the Church was taken over by a new public body. For Church officials, it was a clear attack on their control of social activities. The state was going to replace the Church in its most important activity. In fact, the new team of reformists was asking individuals and groups to become part of the state. Quebeckers began hearing the words "l'Etat du Québec," which referred to an interventionist body. Hubert Guindon has an explanation for the reformists' behaviour:

> Marginal to traditional culture by training, the new middle class became politically restive by class interest. Because it settled mainly in bureaucracies that did not produce profits, it required outside financial resources, namely state funds, to expand its scope, develop its services, and perform its social role. Functionally indispensable in bringing about the institutional changes required in the urban setting, it became politically aroused and aggressive."[29]

All these changes in attitudes led to the exclusion of Church leaders from important social institutions.[30] The state extended its activities in every field. Federal aid to universities was now accepted, hospitalization was insured by a provincial plan, public unions (for public employees) obtained the right to strike. But these changes were implemented in such a way that the network of *corps intermédiaires* collapsed due to the predominance of the state in all activities.

How did the Church react to these rapid changes? First, a Conseil Supérieur de l'Education was created to advise the government and act as a link between the state and the representatives of social groups. This board was, in many ways, another corporatist body.[31] But this time the intermediary was not under the aegis of the Catholic Church. A new type of corporatism suddenly replaced the old social one. For the first time, social groups were able to directly address the state entities, which had become more important in their lives than the Church. Faced with the establishment of new political relationships, Church delegates tried to influence the preparation of Bill 60, which created the Ministry of Education. Although they were among the only ones who would talk about all the implications of that proposal on an almost equal footing, Premier Lesage claimed that the bill was adopted, in its final form, "almost essentially the same as it was introduced."[32] More important, however, is the fact that other social groups, in trying to act as pressure groups, not only contributed to the end of the *corps intermédiaires* but also neutralized themselves because they were opposed to each other while pursuing their own interests.[33]

A full series of "public agencies" was also created by the Lesage government to help Quebec's economic development as well as to create a substitute to the integrative function formerly performed by Church bodies. For the agents of the Quiet Revolution, it was important to give the impression to the people that they were "part of the action," that they owned the process, and that they were still a collective body. But the immense social corporation was fading away and was being replaced by a giant public entity—a polity.

A good example of this attempt was the nationalization of all hydroelectric companies by Hydro-Québec and the political symbol that subsequently emerged.[34] Hydro-Québec was in many ways the substitute for the Church influence. Nicole Laurin-Frenette writes, "The state and Hydro-Québec become the location of an articulation in new processes that took place inside families, schools, hospitals, sports."[35] Hydro-Québec became the symbol of a new system, a new society, a new Quebec.

But, to be fair, analysts had to point out that ordinary citizens were not part of the entire reformist *projet de société*. The Lesage team—*l'équipe du tonnerre*—was defeated in 1966. The Union Nationale government then tried to incorporate or give the impression that everybody was part of the action. In order to develop an economic plan for the entire province, some efforts were being made at the end of the 1960s for new, concrete, and integrated action. L'Office de planification et de développement du Québec (OPDQ) was created and it tried to include all concerned people in a major program of establishing joint decisions on regional planning.

However, ideas and slogans about a new society, based on an equality of partnership between state and groups' representatives in a new type of corporatism, where individuals could help to make public decisions, were nothing more than a façade. Quebec had become a political society very—if not too—rapidly.[36]

The Failure of Robert Bourassa and the PQ's "Concertation"

When Robert Bourassa, one of the youngest premiers ever, took power in April 1970, the entire population was expecting a change in the provincial economy and a return to social peace. At the end of the 1960s, violent disturbances took place over the future of Quebec in Canada, but also over linguistic questions.

Robert Bourassa had promised more public participation in decision-making structures and a more open and pluralistic society.[37] The new leader was constantly talking about a "new consensus." Quebeckers thought that peaceful and organized relationships were inevitable. They weren't. The October Crisis, the murder of cabinet minister Pierre Laporte, general strikes in the public sector, and the financial difficulties of the Olympics created a climate of social tensions rather than social harmony. Bourassa himself became a recluse in a "bunker" on Grande-Allée boulevard, across from the National Assembly. The regime ended with the PQ's victory.

Forced with the reality of governing on a day-to-day basis while planning for the referendum on sovereignty-association, the Parti Québécois wanted to realize some of its hopes for a social-democratic society, based on the participation of all sectors. Tripartite summits—where leaders of government, unions, and business came to discuss scenarios for development—were organized in many fields. (See Table 19-1.) They were only the extension of elements of the PQ's program. In his book *La solution*, the leader of the party, René Lévesque writes that everyone in Quebec had to be involved in the process of making collective choices.[38]

By inviting all concerned leaders to come and discuss programs, the PQ was doing two things. First, it created a diversion from a discussion that would have taken place between government and representatives from business, opposed to any type of separation. Also, it tried to satisfy the two opposed wings in its elected body, the technocratic one, formed of Members of the National Assembly who would prepare legislation because they had the expertise, and the more participatory side, formed of leftist idealists who believed that the duty of a government was to protect people faced with social problems by asking them to participate in reforms.[39]

These conferences were important. Almost all of the first of PQ's legislation was inspired by speeches made at these summits. In the field of municipal affairs, for example, the province tried to meet the demands of officials for a restructuring of the fiscal and jurisdictional framework. A major plan for an economic solidarity was also created, the Opération Solidarité Economique (OSE). It was supervised by a government Priority Committee under the chairmanship of the Minister of Economic Development. This program was in many ways inspired by neo-corporatist ideals. It meant, if one looks at some official declarations, that the community had to

Table 19-1 Main Socioeconomic Conferences Organized by the PQ Government

Conference	Place	Date
First Economic Summit	Pointe-au-Pic	May 1977
Conference on the shoe industry	Quebec City	September 1977
Conference on fisheries	Gaspé	April 1978
Conference on cultural industries	Quebec City	October 1978
Socioeconomic Summit	Montebello	March 1979
Conference on the dairy industries	Rimouski	March 1980
Conference on Montreal's economy	Montreal	March 1981

be involved in planning new projects. It was assumed that a regional consensus of all socioeconomic partners would help to create a "national" consensus on major activities.[40]

The government outlined its plans for economic development in the report, *Bâtir le Québec*.[41] All major social actors—agricultural, industrial, union representatives—were to act together in decision making. Through various pieces of legislation dealing with such diverse topics as the creation of an Office des consommateurs to a reform of family law, the PQ gave its administration a certain stability. After having lost its important referendum—in part because it had stopped almost a year before to attract and occupy its potential adversaries in the discussions (and preparations) at summit conferences—the party again defeated the Liberals because it succeeded in convincing Quebeckers that, as its slogan said, "it had provided good government."

But the party's attempts at neo-corporatist arrangements have faced major problems.[42] Two of them must be mentioned. First, the PQ is making a mistake if it believes that the socioeconomic partners will go home after the many conferences that they are attending and forget the fight against Quebec's independence. Second, and more important, the party has to govern and cannot at all times carry out the wishes of all participants through legislative action. An example was given during the winter of 1983 when public unions went on strike for a long time, despite the claims by party's officials that they were favourably disposed to workers.[43]

Conclusion

Quebec has always known—in the political thoughts of its leaders at least—some corporatist tendencies. However, in concrete terms, our three variables were not completely met. Joint decision making was not completely attained; nor was the idealistic goal of the institutionalization of a sociopolitical partnership; and, even less, the equal participation by representation of all sectors in decision-making bodies.

But, in politics, appearances are often more important than realities. Corporatist speeches and schemes were used to forge the belief that Quebeckers were different and that together they would be able to develop a different society. In that sense, as noted at the beginning of this chapter, nationalism cannot be explained without reference to the corporative ideals that originated in Catholic teachings. While it is true that the Church does not have the same influence and even power that it once had, the organization of French-Canadian society remains inspired and marked by that weight of the past.

And corporatist ideals were also sung by leaders in order to minimize (not eliminate) class conflicts in the province. As for a constitutional arrangement with the rest of Canada, the unity of views concerning the veto power lost by Quebec (a veto power that was only a tacit agreement with no legal value, according to recent rulings of the Supreme Court) Quebeckers had a certain unity of view concerning their "specificity."

What is the future of corporatist arrangements? It will depend on many elements, the main one being the will of political leaders to adapt political structures to become more open, thus inspiring more joint action and more consensus. Quebec may, like Robert Bourassa, have a second chance at establishing concrete neo-corporatist structures.

Notes

1. Trudeau has argued that democracy was not understood by French Quebeckers who "naturally," blindly followed orders from Catholic Church officials. Trudeau, while admitting that corporatist schemes were developed by some Jesuits, does not go very deeply into this topic. See "Some Obstacles to Democracy in Quebec," *Canadian Journal of Economics and Political Science* 18 (1958).
2. Quebec is not mentioned in comparative studies on corporatism, even in recent books on "new corporatist" structures. F.B. Pike and Thomas Stritch have edited a book on the topic, but Quebec is completely absent from their overview, *The New Corporatism*, (Notre Dame: Notre Dame University Press, 1974).
3. David Kwavnick, "The Roots of French-Canadian Discontent," *Canadian Journal of Economics and Political Science* 31 (1965), gives the essential facts.
4. H.F. Quinn, *The Union Nationale: A Study in Quebec Nationalism*, (Toronto: University of Toronto Press, 1963), has given the best overall picture of this special national question.
5. After an absence of seven years, Robert Bourassa is back in the news. The reader should look at the transcripts of his interview given to Télémédia after his defeat in 1976, because his assessment of Quebec's society since 1960 is important: *Les années Bourassa* (Montreal: Edition Héritage, 1977).
6. For a summary of the latter part of the decade and an overview of the first years of the new era, one can look at Robert Chodos and Nick Auf Der Maur (eds.), *Quebec: A Chronicle: 1968-1972* (Toronto: James, Lewis and Samuel, 1972).
7. Pierre Vallières has seen in the PQ's orientations an old form of corporatism, in *Un Québec impossible* (Montréal: Québec-Amérique, 1977), while Raymond Laliberté believes that the search for new arrangements with labour and business might create a new type of corporatism, but he also has doubts about its success; see his ideas in J.F. Léonard (ed.), *La chance au couleur: bilan de l'action du gouvernement du Parti Québécois* (Montréal: Nouvelle Optique, 1978). With K.Z. Paltiel, I have looked at the difficult avenue developed by the PQ in its search for a "social democrat" organization of society in "L'évolution de l'idée corporatiste au Canada," *Etudes canadiennes* special issue (1979); La vie politique au Canada, proceedings of the colloquium at Mons (April 24-26, 1978).
8. Fascism and corporatism became synonymous because of Mussolini's slogan, "We have created a Fascist state." See William Halperin, *Mussolini and Italian Fascism* (Toronto: Van Nostrand, 1964).
9. "Practically speaking," writes Ernst Nolte in *Three Faces of Fascism; Action française, Italian Fascism, National Socialism* (New York: The New American

Library, 1965) p. 336, "fascist corporatism meant forcing the employees to accept fascist functionaries as their representatives, and welding this representation with the virtually unaltered representation of the industrialists by means of government intervention."

10. James Malloy has even linked authoritarianism and corporatism in the main themes of a colloquium at the University of Pittsburgh in 1976. See the collection subsequently published in J. Malloy (ed.), *Authoritarianism and Corporatism in Latin America* (Pittsburgh: University of Pittsburgh Press, 1977).
11. Nigel Harris, *Competition and the Corporate Society* (London: Methuen, 1972), p. 72.
12. Robert Presthus, *Elite Accommodation in Canadian Politics* (Toronto: Macmillan, 1973), p. 25. The three other elements are deferential patterns of authority, pragmatic evaluation of the government's economic rule, and quasi participation in politics.
13. L.V. Panitch, "The Development of Corporatism in Liberal Democracies," *Comparative Political Studies* 10: 1 (April 1977), p. 66.
14. Philip C. Schmitter, *Corporatism and Public Policy in Authoritarian Portugal* (Beverly Hills: Sage Publications, Contemporary Political Sociology Series, 1975), pp. 8-9.
15. For more details on this definition, see Clinton Archibald, *Un Québec corporatiste?* (Hull: Editions Asticou, 1984).
16. John Kenneth Galbraith has summarized this development: "In notable respects, the mature corporation is an arm of the State. And the State, in important matters, is an instrument of the industrial system." *The New Industrial State* (New York: New American Library, 1971), p. 289.
17. André J. Bélanger sees this perception as being inspired by nothing else than "unpolitical ideologies" in *L'apolitisme des idéologies québécoises: le grand tournant de 1934-36* (Québec: PUL, 1979).
18. See Gilles M. Bélanger, "L'église et les organismes socio-économiques," in *L'Eglise et le Québec* (Montréal: Editions du Jour, 1961).
19. Among them is Nive Voisine. His *Histoire de l'Eglise catholique au Québec (1608-1970)* (Montréal: Fides, 1970) is a clear illustration, with plenty of examples, of that impregnation.
20. Max Weber, *The City* (New York: The Free Press, 1958).
21. H.A. Logan, *Trade Unions in Canada; Their Development and Functioning* (Toronto: Macmillan, 1948), p. 562.
22. F.M. Powicke, "The Christian Life," in Crump and E. Jacob (eds.), *Legacy of the Middle Ages* (Oxford: the Clarendon Press, 1951), writes that the notion of subsidiarity used in *Rerum Novarum* had a medieval colour. It meant that the state would help only if needed and if the social community would ask for that help.
23. Writes André Théry, *Les groupes sociaux: forces vives* (Paris: Editions du Centurion, 1964), p. 208, "Ce que l'Eglise catholique redoute, c'est le vide entre l'Etat et l'individu, car ce vide est nuisible à l'un comme à l'autre; il est générateur de perversion et de sclérose. Ce qu'elle reconnaît par contre comme sain et comme nécessaire, c'est une vie sociale organisée en paliers où chaque sujet, individuel ou collectif, joue un rôle propre en aidant les autres et remplit de ce fait un rôle médiateur."

24. Two of his books can illustrate that thesis: *Directives* (Montreal: Editions du Zodiaque, 1937) and *Notre avenir politique* (Montreal: Editions Albert Lévesque, 1923).
25. It is interesting to note that *l'Action nationale* had among its editors, during the period 1930-1960, Arthur and André Laurendeau, Gérard Filion, Pierre Laporte, and Françoise-Albert Angers.
26. An impossible reality: more than 18% of Quebeckers are not francophones. And even among them, class differences (with education and income indicators) can be perceived. Marcel Rioux, "Conscience ethnique et conscience de classe au Québec," *Recherches sociographiques* 6 (1965), nevertheless believed that the dream of one ethnic class could become a fact.
27. Fernand Harvey, *Aspects historiques du mouvement ouvrier au Québec* (Montréal: Boréal Express, 1973) p. 186.
28. Gérard Bergeron, *Le Canada-Français, après deux siècles de patience* (Paris: Editions du Seuil, 1967), p. 164.
29. Hubert Guindon, "Two Cultures: An Essay on Nationalism, Class and Ethnic Tensions," in R.H. Leach (ed.), *Contemporary Canada* (Durham: Duke University Press, 1968), p. 83.
30. Nive Voisine (op. cit., p. 81) writes, "Clerics were put out of positions of power and, in some cases, practically excluded from subordinate positions."
31. Thomas Sloan, *Une révolution tranquille?* (Montreal: Editions HMH, 1966), p. 68, writes: "Ce conseil pèse d'un poids tel qu'un gouvernement qui l'ignorerait courrait un péril certain. Il distille dans le corps politique québécois *un léger arrière-goût de corporatisme* qui ne met pas en danger la démocratie, bien qu'il faille en surveiller les progrès avec vigilance. Le Conseil offre une excellente illustration de la manière dont le Québec met à contribution ses propres traditions au bénéfice de sa révolution économique et sociale . . ."
32. Léon Dion, *Le bill 60 et la société québécoise* (Montreal: Editions Hurtubise/HMH, 1967), gives a good summary of the "extraordinaire carrière du bill 60."
33. I have analyzed this development elsewhere. See the article coauthored with K.Z. Paltiel, "Du passage des corps intermédiaires aux groupes de pression au Québec: Une illustration par l'exemple du Mouvement Desjardins," *Recherches sociographiques* 18: 1 (1977).
34. Wallace Clement, *The Canadian Corporate Elite* (Toronto: McClelland and Stewart, 1975), p. 236, believes that a new bourgeoisie arose from the new Hydro-Québec to replace the old traditional elite: "A major avenue of mobility for French Canadians into the economic elite has been through connections with the state. . . . Altogether this includes 54% of all the French in the elite. This suggests that the French have been successful in using the state as a means for access to the economic elite and that they have strong relations with the state after gaining access."
35. Nicole Laurin-Frenette, *Productions de l'Etat et formes de la nation* (Montréal: Nouvelle-Optique, 1970), p. 110.
36. Everybody wanted to obtain power, to be the leader. In many ways, the new political corporatism was becoming a political philosophy "of new groups . . . that wanted to secure their advantageous position in the class structure." See H. and S.H. Milner, *The Decolonization of Quebec*, (Toronto: McClelland and Stewart, 1973), p. 175.

37. These were the main themes of his platform published in *Bourassa-Québec: Nous gouvernerons ensemble une société prospère* (Montreal: Les Editions de l'Homme, 1970).
38. *Le programme du Parti Québécois: La solution* (Montréal: Editions du Jour, 1970), p. 51: "On doit favoriser systématiquement la participation active du plus grand nombre possible de citoyens . . . Aussi faut-il susciter auprès de l'administration publique, pour l'éclairer, le stimuler et au besoin la surveiller, des groupements de citoyens à qui l'information la plus complète, et même l'occasion de participer aux décisions, doivent être fournies."
39. This is well explained in Vera Murray's thesis *Le Parti Québécois: de la fondation à la prise du pouvoir* (Montréal: Editions HMH, 1976).
40. See the words of the Hon. Pierre Marois, in *OSE* 2: 2 (Sept. 1979), p. 24.
41. *Bâtir le Québec: énoncé de politique* (Québec: Editeur officiel, 1979).
42. See Clinton Archibald, "Les tendances néo-corporatistes du Parti Québécois," *Perception* 2: 2 (1978).
43. When the public purse had dried up, the PQ's negotiations with the Common Front resembled those of Bourassa's team. For further information, see Chapter 20 in this book.

Chapter 20/Concerted Action in Quebec, 1976-1983: Dialogue of the Deaf*

A. Brian Tanguay

One of the chief preoccupations of the Parti Québécois when it came to power in 1976 was the need to forge a "new social contract" in the province. Confronted with particularly strained industrial relations, a militant labour movement, and a deteriorating economic situation, the PQ hoped to achieve some sort of *rapprochement* between business and labour. If the proper consultative machinery could be established, government leaders reasoned, then harmony and cooperation between the "social partners" would replace the enmity that had characterized their relations during the Bourassa years. It was essentially a matter of reforming the unhealthy attitudes of the province's main economic agents, of instilling in them an enlightened regard for the national interest (a "national consciousness"). The result of this envisioned social partnership, the argument went, would be an attenuation of industrial conflict, a more equitable sharing of economic responsibilities among the social partners, and increased prosperity for all.[1]

The principal instrument of concerted action—the harmonization of class relations carefully nurtured by a (supposedly) neutral state—in Quebec during the PQ's period in office has been the socioeconomic conference. These summit meetings—almost 30 have been held in the past seven years—have united the principal economic decision makers at one table, presumably in the spirit of mutual trust and cooperation. The overriding objective of these highly publicized palavers has been a didactic one: they are designed to educate the social partners and to school them in the rights and responsibilities that pertain to each. The social partners, in the PQ lexicon, are taken to include consumers, cooperatives, business, and labour, but the last two groups are the principal targets of government policy. The government hopes that business and labour, by meeting together in a nonconflictual environment, will eventually come to realize the legitimacy of each other's cause. Once the habits of dialogue and cooperation have been ingrained in the social partners, and perhaps formalized through the creation of a

---

*This chapter is a revised and considerably scaled-down version of my unpublished M.A. thesis, "The Parti Québécois and the Politics of Concerted Action: A New Corporatism?" (Carleton University, October 1980). I should like to thank Professors Reg Whitaker, Leo Panitch, Maureen Molot, and K.Z. Paltiel for their incisive comments on earlier incarnations of this paper. Of course, I alone am responsible for any errors or omissions in this chapter.

tripartite Conseil économique et social, negotiations over a new social contract can begin:

> The long-term prospect for dialogue is to reach an agreement on the sharing of responsibilities for a more productive economy, associated with a better quality of social life, through multipartite actions determined by the different agents directly involved in economic development.[2]

The state's role in this process, and of the enlightened technocrats in its employ, is that of arbiter, remonstrating with the social partners when their blind pursuit of narrow sectional concerns jeopardizes the national interest.

What the PQ is proposing, essentially, is a liberal corporatist strategy of economic development. It is corporatist inasmuch as it is based on state-fostered cooperation between classes. For the organizations of business and labour, the terms of the proposed social contract involve a tradeoff between an increased voice in the determination of economic policy, through their participation in economic summits and a variety of other tripartite consultative bodies, and a commitment on their part to realism and moderation in industrial relations. The industrial peace presumed to be a product of such a social compact will insure that Quebec's economy keeps growing—a precondition to a more equitable distribution of the nation's wealth, as René Lévesque never tires of claiming.[3] This type of economic development strategy—similar in many respects to those pursued for varying lengths of time and with differing degrees of success by governments in Sweden, Austria, the Netherlands and West Germany—involves the devolution of some of parliament's authority over economic matters to institutions not directly accountable to the public. It does not imply the eclipse of parliamentary democracy, however, since parliament and traditional modes of interest representation (interest-group lobbying, for example) retain very important functions in all those countries that might be designated as liberal corporatist.

This chapter provides a critical assessment of the policy of concerted action somewhat haltingly set into motion by the PQ government during the past seven years. It will be divided into three sections: in the first, I shall examine why the PQ's approach to economic development might be deemed a liberal corporatist one. The origins of the concept of corporatism and its recent application to the study of certain features of some advanced capitalist societies will be briefly discussed. As well, I shall explore some of the factors that have contributed to the instability of liberal corporatist structures in most of the western European countries that have adopted this economic-development strategy. In particular, I shall stress the unequal influence exerted by the organizations of business and labour within this structure and the differing benefits that redound to each participant—in short, the class bias inherent in liberal corporatism. At the same time, the state's far from disinterested role in this type of arrangement will be examined. The second section focuses on the structure, function, and results of the socioeconomic conferences held to date in Quebec. The burden of this section of the chapter is that these numerous economic summit meetings have thus far failed to alter the traditional confrontational attitudes of the province's "social partners." Neither business nor labour has yet proved willing to place the national interest, as it has been defined by the government, before its own "parochial" concerns. Moreover, the agreements (or points of convergence, as Premier Lévesque likes to call them) arrived at by the social partners at these conferences have most often been of a banal or innocuous nature. It would seem, then, that the dialogue between the social partners in Quebec has thus far been merely a dialogue of the deaf. In the concluding section of the chapter, I shall briefly assess the prospects for liberal corporatism in Quebec.

Liberal Corporatism in Theory and Practice

In the literature of contemporary social science, the word "corporatism" is quite often understood to be a term of opprobrium. To label a political regime or a party ideology as corporatist is, expressly or implicitly, to link it to the repressive, totalitarian practice of such ostensibly corporatist states as Mussolini's Italy, Portugal under Salazar, and Vichy France. Since the defeat of fascism in 1945, it has often been assumed that corporatism, too, could be relegated to the dustbin of history; its application to the political systems of the advanced capitalist societies of western Europe and North America has been considered by some social scientists to be totally inappropriate. Illustrative of this widespread belief was the reaction of a number of political scientists to a paper read by two of their Canadian colleagues at a recent colloquium on political life in Canada. The authors, whose paper dealt in part with the "neo-corporatist tendencies of the Parti Québécois," were castigated for having associated a democratic and progressive party with naziism and fascism.[4]

In spite of the images of the one-party state still conjured up by the term, more and more social scientists have, in recent years, been attempting to rehabilitate corporatism as an analytical concept. Their objective has been "to strip the concept [of corporatism] of its pejorative tone and implication" and to employ it in the study of certain structural changes that have been occurring in the highly industrialized nations of the west over the past 60 years.[5] According to Samuel Beer, for instance, government's attempts to manage or control the modern capitalist economy from the interwar period on have engendered a form of quasi corporatism in which the three primary economic "interlocutors"—government, organized business, and organized labour—are brought into close and constant contact in a variety of consultative and planning bodies. Through these quasi-corporatist mechanisms, government seeks to secure the *advice*, or expertise, of the large producer groups; their *acquiescence*, or cooperation, in the economic programs pursued by the state; and their *approval* of the overall objectives of state economic policy. This extra-parliamentary process of bargaining and negotiation, Beer argues, tends to displace (in specific policy areas) traditional modes of decision making, and thereby attenuates the authority of Parliament.[6]

The quasi corporatism described by Beer (or *liberal* corporatism, since it emerges in societies that retain all the essential features of liberal democracy—free elections, civil liberties, and parliamentary institutions) represents one possible strategy for coping with the structural difficulties inherent in advanced capitalist economic systems. In particular, three problems confronting western governments during the postwar period have been at the root of the development of liberal corporatist structures in certain western European nations:

1. The increased economic and political strength of the organized working class which accompanied the postwar commitment to policies of full employment.
2. The increased vulnerability of individual nations to shifting patterns of world trade and a rapidly changing technological base.
3. As a corollary of the first two, the need (perceived by the state and the capitalists themselves) to combat an inflationary spiral and to minimize disruptive strikes and lockouts, since inflation and industrial strife undermine a nation's competitive position in the world market.[7]

Faced with this situation, some governments have endeavoured to fashion a *modus vivendi*, or a "new social contract" with the organized producer groups in society. In exchange for giving business and labour representation on economic planning boards or other policy-making bodies, the government expects a commitment to moderation in the formulation of wage demands and the determination of prices. Some form of voluntary incomes policy, national economic planning councils, and other consensus-building mechanisms are thus the key components of a liberal corporatist political structure.

Liberal corporatism has been defined as a "political structure within advanced capitalism which integrates organized socioeconomic producer groups through a system of representation and cooperative mutual interaction at the leadership level and mobilization and social control at the mass level."[8] This definition calls attention to three distinctive features of liberal corporatism which serve to distinguish it from the network of interest group-state relations described in pluralist theory.[9] In the first place, liberal corporatism implies a high degree of collaboration between the organized producer groups in the shaping of economic policy, not merely a one-to-one relationship between the state and various groups, as pluralist theorists have tended to assume. Second, the peak associations of business and labour play a preponderant role in liberal corporatist structures, since the overriding purpose of these institutions is to ensure industrial peace by eliminating conflicts over the distribution of wealth in society. Finally, there is an element of state control over the producer groups, especially labour, in any liberal corporatist arrangement. By collaborating voluntarily with the state in economic policy making, business and labour become responsible for the implementation of these policies. The trade-union federations and business associations are expected to force their members to comply with the decisions made in the various corporatist institutions. Reneging on any of these agreements could bring considerable adverse public opinion to bear against the culprit, leaving it open to the charge of holding the nation up to ransom.

Liberal corporatism is by no means currently the dominant pattern of state-producer group relations in the western democracies, nor has it been at any time in the postwar period. It is a strategy for maintaining profitability, growth, and economic efficiency that recommends itself to government, employers, and trade unions only in certain well-defined situations. Where the peak associations of business and labour are highly centralized and play an active role in collective bargaining; where the social-democratic party has either formed a majority government or participated in a ruling coalition (since the concessions required from organized labour for the operation of a "social contract" are most likely to be secured by a social-democratic government); where ideologies stressing "social partnership" are widespread—in such countries liberal corporatism might be on the political agenda.[10] Thus, Sweden, the Netherlands, and Austria are the most commonly cited examples of liberal corporatism in practice, and these three countries meet most or all of the above conditions. Denmark, West Germany (with its *Konzertierte Aktion*, 1967-1977), and Great Britain (with its National Economic Development Council, set up in 1962, and the Callaghan government's "social contract") have all tried to institute some form of corporatist strategy, but with only limited success. Italy and France, with large segments of their labour movements allied to powerful Communist countries, have proven impervious to corporatist developments.[11]

Even in Sweden and the Netherlands, liberal corporatist structures, once implanted, have proved to be singularly unstable. The principal causes of this instability are the bias inherent in this structure and the contradictory position in which it places the trade-union leadership. Despite the voluntary nature of the social contract—each participant is nominally free to enter into or leave the corporatist arrangement—this type of entente is hardly an exchange between equals. There is a more or less tacit alliance between the representatives of government and those of business: it is mainly management's expertise and information that the state seeks, not those of organized labour. Union participation in tripartism is sought primarily to give credence to the myth of partnership and because union cooperation is essential if voluntary wage restraint is to be secured. Labour is expected to speak the same *language* as management, one which defines in advance a hierarchy of problems facing the modern economy and the range of acceptable solutions to them.

Thus, the burden of restraint entailed in the social contract falls principally on organized labour. The trade-union leadership may find it increasingly difficult to convince the rank and file of the validity of such an arrangement when wage restraint is not offset by controls on other forms of income, or by any effort to alter the distribution of wealth. Rank-and-file discontent may eventually erupt into wildcat strikes and other forms of industrial strife, leading to the temporary or permanent collapse of the social contract—as it did in the Netherlands in the late 1950s and early 1960s, and in Sweden in the early 1970s. Often the breakdown of liberal corporatism will elicit a coercive response from government, whether in the form of statutory incomes policy, restrictions on the right to strike, or measures to strengthen the union federations (to enable them to discipline their affiliates).[12] Alternatively, government may be forced to grant further concessions to organized labour—profit-sharing, participation in investment planning, or some form of codetermination, for example—in order to secure labour's continued commitment to the social contract.

The Lévesque government was the first in Canada, at either the provincial or federal level, to make a determined effort to extract from the organized producer groups a commitment to social peace in exchange for an increased voice in economic policy making. Trading on its image as a progressive, "social democratic" party, the PQ sought to overcome Quebec labour's antipathy to the state (particularly evident during the Bourassa years) and secure its participation in a Swedish-style social partnership. (The PQ leaders seemed unaware of the travails of liberal corporatism in that country.) As I argue in the remainder of the chapter, however, neither the attitudes of the social partners nor the nature of the province's economic and political institutions augured well for the success of the PQ's enterprise.

The Parti Québécois in Search of a Social Contract

In 1976, the newly installed Parti Québécois government was faced with a number of intractable economic problems: in the month preceding the November election, a chronic unemployment problem had worsened to the point where over 10% of the labour force was out of work; this at a time when the annual rate of inflation approached 7%. Industrial relations in the province, especially in the parapublic and construction sectors, had been severely strained in 1976; during that year almost 6.5 million mandays were lost due to strikes or lockouts, a figure that rivalled that of Italy (taking account of the differences in the sizes of the work force).[13] To the PQ leadership, this dismal economic performance was due in no small measure to the Bourassa government's desultory approach to economic development and to its "big stick" labour-relations policy. Rather than rely on the disjointed efforts of numerous economic actors, as the Liberals had done, the

PQ would coordinate and rationalize the activities of the major industrial partners and elaborate an overall economic plan. The planning process, the PQ was careful to point out, would not take place without consultations between the government and its partners. This dialogue, it was felt, would gradually instill in the social partners a new attitude of mutual trust and cooperation. Thus, the call went out to business and labour to join the government in an "economic summit conference" to be held in the spring of 1977.

Several ideological factors, in addition to the structural ones cited above, predisposed the Parti Québécois to adopt a liberal corporatist strategy of economic development. In the first place, there is a genuine corporatist strand in the PQ's ideology, as at least one observer has pointed out.[14] Perhaps the frankest expression of this liberal corporatist vision of society was uttered by Camille Laurin, then Minister of State for Cultural Development in the PQ government, at the "mini-summit" (which I discuss in greater detail below) on tourism held in 1978. Asked why his government seemed to assign such great importance to these gatherings of the social partners, Laurin replied:

> It is because the government wants to be modern. It realizes that the goods produced by our firms or our services are the result of the combined efforts of several agents . . . just as the health of an individual is the product of the silent but harmonious action of various organs and limbs. . . . In our society we must first get the partners to know one another and to work together in a harmonious and unitary fashion if we want the final product to correspond to the goals we have set for ourselves.[15]

Though it might be more indicative of his professional background than of any latent corporatist tendencies, Laurin's use of the medical analogy (society = body) in the above quotation is at the very least suggestive of the affinity between corporatist thought and certain strands of *Péquiste* ideology. It should be noted that this corporatist vision of a grand reconciliation of classes within a planned, efficient economy (what might be called corporatism *à la suédoise*) is most clearly articulated by the *technocratic* faction of the PQ—that group of moderately reformist liberals and social democrats associated with René Lévesque.[16] Theirs is an essentially *liberal* corporatism: it is a far remove from the romantic version of corporatism (often tinctured with authoritarianism) espoused by various contributors to *l'Action nationale* in the 1930s.

As well as being an expression of the PQ's (or at least of the dominant faction within it) fundamental vision of the proper role of the state in a modern society, the government's efforts at consensus building in the early part of its first mandate were obviously related to its need to rally a majority of Québécois—from all social classes—to the cause of sovereignty-association. With its emphasis on consensus, harmony, and class collaboration, the PQ's policy of concerted action was expected to assist in the cultivation of a favourable climate for the passage of the referendum on Quebec's constitutional future. The PQ hoped to appease labour and capital simultaneously—a characteristic of all liberal corporatist arrangements—and thus "attenuate the differing perceptions of different social classes which would otherwise be diametrically opposed. The PQ hopes in this fashion to develop a national consciousness."[17]

On the one hand, the PQ was seeking to illustrate its alleged "favourable bias" towards the working class and to demonstrate that it was indeed a progressive administration in social and economic matters. (After all, what government aside from theirs had even bothered to consult the trade unions on a broad range of policy issues?) On the other hand, the PQ wanted to assuage business's fears and show that it contemplated no radical changes in the existing structure of authority in capitalist society. Thus, at the second "grand summit" held at Montebello in 1979, Premier Lévesque assured the business contingent that his government recognized the necessity and legitimacy of profit, and agreed that the key role in Quebec's economic development would have to be played by the private sector.[18] Whatever hopes the PQ might have had of parlaying its consensus-building activities into some sort of "national consciousness" (and the term is used in *Bâtir le Québec*) have obviously been dashed—not only by the outcome of the 1980 referendum, but also by the failure of the numerous economic summits since 1976 to produce anything remotely resembling a consensus on the nation's economic priorities.

The PQ's failure to forge a new social contract in Quebec has certainly not been for want of trying. Twenty socioeconomic conferences were convened by the government between May 1977 and April 1982. Of these, three were "grand summits" which addressed themselves to global economic trends and national concerns. These three grand summits were held at Pointe-au-Pic (May 1977), Montebello (March 1979), and Quebec City (April 1982)—the last two occurring, interestingly enough, just as the government was preparing to enter into negotiations with the public-sector unions represented by the Common Front. (I discuss this happy coincidence below.) The remaining 17 conferences were mini-summits which dealt with the problems specific to one sector of the economy. Four of these examined the "soft sectors" of the provincial economy (textiles, clothing, footwear, and furniture); six dealt with various aspects of the agricultural and food industries; four focused on the fishing, cooperative, tourism, and cultural industries in the province; the remainder dealt respectively with municipal government, the economic future of Montreal, and handicapped people. In 1982-83, several *regional* conferences were held, each dealing with the various concerns of a specific region (the national capital, la Mauricie, and so on) and bringing together local political, business, and labour groups.

All of the socioeconomic conferences in Quebec operate according to the principles of the round table: one participant advances his or her own analysis of the problem under discussion, the next responds to these views and in turn puts forward his or her own proposals, and so on. A certain amount of bargaining and moderating of initial positions is supposed to take place, with the ultimate objective being the attainment of some sort of consensus on the province's social and economic priorities for an unspecified period of time. It is customary for the government, represented either by the Prime Minister or by a top-level cabinet minister, to lead off the discussions and to sum up the conference's activities. The only difference between the structures of grand and mini-summits consists in the latter's reliance on workshops (*travaux en ateliers*) for the discussion of certain topics; at the grand summits, all deliberations take place at a plenary session. No joint communiqué is issued by the conference's participants, but the government representative, in his closing remarks, usually calls attention to the various "points of convergence"—no matter how banal—reached by the social partners. A report of the proceedings, along with the background documents presented to the conference, is then published by the Secrétariat permanent des conférences socio-économiques.

The Secrétariat, created by order-in-council on November 23, 1977, is charged with providing the leadership and expertise necessary for the smooth functioning of concerted action in Quebec. Attached to the Executive Council, the Secrétariat acts as chief coordinator and propagandizer of the periodic economic summit meetings in the province. It can draw on the resources and personnel of other departments in the bureaucracy in order to edit and distribute background documents for the summits. It draws up the agenda for each conference and decides on its major themes (after consultations with the social partners). It determines the criteria for selecting the delegates to each conference—total number invited, the number of representatives from each social partner, the organizations within each interest area that will be invited—and until recently the Secrétariat actually chose the participants after consulting the organization in question. (The social partners now choose their own representatives, subject to the guidelines laid down by the Secrétariat.) Finally, it provides the necessary logistical support for the summits (lodgings, catering, transportation), publishes the reports of the conference proceedings, and disseminates the reports to the media and the public.[19]

This brief summary of the responsibilities assigned to the Secrétariat underscores two features of concerted action in Quebec which distinguish it from the practice of liberal corporatism in most of the western European countries that have adopted this approach to economic planning: its comparatively informal nature and the prominent role played by government in this arrangement. A third characteristic of concerted action in Quebec—namely the broad range and great number of social and economic interests represented at the intermittent summits—is considered below. Regarding the first of these features, concerted action in the province can be said to have a very low degree of institutionalization. In contrast to the situation in Sweden or Austria, where more or less autonomous tripartite institutions such as the Joint Commission on Prices and Wages or the National Labour Market Board play a well-defined role in economic policy making, the economic summits in Quebec have no life of their own. Rather, they are called into existence when the government deems the moment propitious. No binding decisions are made at the conferences, nor are the participants—with the occasional exception of the government—formally committed to a future course of action.

The government has at several times mentioned the possibility—and, indeed, the desirability—of moving to a statutory, permanent form of concerted action in the province. In *Bâtir le Québec,* for example, the government proposed to create, after consultations with its partners, a Conseil économique et social, though it did not specify the powers that this body would have or the criteria by which its members would be chosen. As well, one of the "points of convergence" culled by Premier Lévesque from the debate at the most recent grand summit in Quebec City was the need to create a Conseil économique et social, again of unspecified form. This consensus would seem to be tenuous at best, however: business on the whole favours such a proposal, whereas organized labour's response ranges from wholehearted endorsement to outright hostility. Representatives of the Fédération des travailleurs du Québec (FTQ), the Confédération des syndicats nationaux (CSN), and the Centrale de l'enseignement du Québec (CEQ) all noted that the "objective conditions" for such an institution—especially increased access to unionization—were not yet in place in Quebec. The CEQ, for its part, went so far as to state that it rejected the very notion of concerted action. Only the tiny Centrale des syndicats démocratiques (CSD), whose members are drawn primarily from the private sector, unequivocally endorsed the proposal.[20] This split between public- and private-sector unions has characterized concerted action in Quebec from its inception, with the CSD and FTQ (predominantly private sector) favouring increased collaboration with the government, and the CSN (its affiliate unions are divided about equally between the public and private sectors) and CEQ (overwhelmingly public sector) being much more skeptical of the government's corporatist intentions.

A second characteristic of concerted action in Quebec is the preponderant role played by the government at the economic summits. As Gilles Châtillon, Director-General of the Secrétariat permanent des conférences socio-économiques, has pointed out:

> The government is the driving force; it convenes, prepares, and organizes the conferences. It is not the sort of concerted action in which the government is only one partner like the others but rather a consultative, decision-making procedure in which the government is the host and the principal actor.[21]

As befits its technocratic orientation, the PQ has made certain that the government and its corps of experts retain ultimate control over every phase of the consultative process, from the selection of the participants to the determination of the topics for discussion.

The responsibilities assigned to the Secrétariat tend to place the other participants at the summits in a reactive, defensive posture. In the first place, the Secrétariat, with the vast research facilities of the government and the academic world at its disposal, produces exhaustively documented background papers which are the focus of all discussions at the conference. The social partners, especially the trade-union representatives, are compelled to react to the proposals contained in the government documents and have little opportunity to put forward their own detailed analyses—if such exist—of the problems under discussion, or to deflect the talks to other areas of concern. The Secrétariat, of course, claims that the agenda for each conference is drawn up only after consultations between the government and its partners, so that the government is aware of the social partners' concerns and demands—and presumably incorporates them into its discussion papers. But this preliminary consultation is far removed from actually allowing the labour organizations or business associations (though the latter need not often be worried by this) to participate in drafting the conference's agenda. As Norbert Rodrigue, then President of the CSN, remarked at Pointe-au-Pic:

> We could not help but notice that we were not asked to help organize this conference, that we were consulted neither on the topics that will be discussed nor even on all the regulations that will be in force throughout the proceedings. ... Economic summit meetings in social-democratic regimes share one characteristic: they are jointly prepared by the governing social-democratic parties and the trade-union organizations from which these parties spring. ... That is a model of government and of economic summits far removed from your own.[22]

Although there has undoubtedly been greater consultation between the government and its interlocutors prior to subsequent summits (the Secrétariat did not exist at the time of the Pointe-au-Pic conference), the trade unions have often expressed dissatisfaction with the government's choice of topics for discussion. The three major themes of the Montebello conference, for example—access to markets, investments, and human resources—were generally considered to ignore the real concerns of Quebec's workers. The background documents and the conference agenda, it was felt, were drawn up from a "managerialist" perspective. To the consternation of the union federations, the government chose not to allow any discussion of the issue of worker health and safety at Montebello, on the grounds that a bill dealing with this matter was in parliamentary committee (a line of reasoning the CSN dismissed as an unconvincing pretext). Similarly, the major themes drawn up by the Secrétariat for the conference on Montreal's economic future (which the CSN chose not to attend)—airports, port facilities, traditional industry, the tertiary sector, and tourism—were thought to ignore pressing social and economic problems of concern to all Québécois. According to Paul-Emile Dalpé, then President of the CSD, the unions would have liked to discuss such questions as public transit and housing, but these were left off the agenda for "political reasons." The government, with a provincial election in the offing, presumably did not want to risk a confrontation between the social partners at the Montreal summit.[23]

To date, then, the effectiveness of concerted action in Quebec has been hampered by the unwillingness of sections of the province's labour movement to participate in a more formal tripartite institution with wideranging powers, and by the suspicion among some trade-union leaders that labour is something less than an equal partner with the government and business. The CSN and the CEQ, in particular, have rejected the government's posture of neutrality and have detected an obvious congruence between management's objectives and those of the state. The public-sector unions suspect that the government and business view labour as a "partner" only when there is a need to increase labour productivity, dampen wage claims, or adopt other forms of belt tightening. These unions have therefore been most unwilling partners in the PQ's search for a social contract.

A third factor militates against the success of concerted action in Quebec: the sheer number of participants at the economic summits makes them a rather unwieldy planning mechanism. Almost 100 representatives of government, business, labour, consumers, the cooperative movement, and the academic world took part in each of the three grand summits—and this figure excludes those who attended as advisers or observers without the right to speak. More important than this is the fact that each social partner is represented by a variety of organizations, some of which have conflicting aims and priorities. Business, for instance, has been represented by:

1. Le Conseil du Patronat du Québec (CPQ), a federation of some 125 business associations and 275 individual companies. The CPQ is represented on many governmental advisory boards and is generally regarded as the most "effective spokesman for management vis-à-vis the Quebec government and Quebec society as a whole."[24]
2. La Chambre de Commerce de la Province du Québec.
3. La Chambre of Commerce du District de Montréal and the Montreal Board of Trade.
4. Le Centre des dirigeants d'entreprise (CDE), an association of approximately 1000 businessmen, representing 400 firms (mostly small and medium-sized industry). Created in 1943 and originally animated by the Social Catholic doctrine, the CDE has been one of the most vocal advocates of concerted action in Quebec.
5. The Canadian Manufacturers' Association (Quebec Division).
6. Le Conseil des gens d'affaires du Québec; created in 1973, this association of 600 independentist businessmen has as its primary objective the

promotion of Quebec's political sovereignty and the defense of the French language.

Obviously, then, it would be inaccurate to speak of "business" as though it were a cohesive social partner with a unified voice. What may be good for the CPQ and its members, for example, might seem inimical to the interests of the small and medium-sized firms in the province. Labour, riven as it is by the conflict (not always open, admittedly) between public- and private-sector unions, has presented even less of a unified front at the summits than business. These conflicts within organized business and labour, potential and actual, make it extremely difficult for the major social partners to arrive at a common analysis of the most pressing problems facing Quebec's economy, let alone agree to any future course of action.

Other social groups—consumers, women's groups, cooperatives, and the Union des producteurs agricoles (UPA, an association of farm owners)—have of course been invited to the economic summits, but with the exception of the cooperatives (especially the Mouvement Desjardins), their contributions to the debates have been relatively insignificant. Many of the consumers' and women's groups simply lack the resources necessary to contribute substantially to the discussions at the summit meetings. It would not be unreasonable to assert that the government's chief purpose in inviting these two social groups has been to give the conferences an artificially pluralist image and thus to block the possible charge of corporatism (or tripartism). Certainly the topics for discussion at the grand summits have largely ignored the concerns of consumers and feminists, which prompted Christiane Bérubé Gagné, President of the Association féminine d'éducation et d'action sociale, to remark at the Quebec summit:

> From the beginning of the conference, whenever anyone has mentioned the "social partners," I've often had the impression (and I don't think that I'm suffering from a complex) that it's the government, the employers, and the unions that one has in mind, and that consumers, and especially women, are curiously left out of all this.[25]

The cooperatives and the UPA have played a more prominent role at the socioeconomic conferences than have either the consumers' or women's groups, but this ought not to detract from the fact that the economic summits, in terms of their overriding purpose (to secure social peace), are tripartite institutions.

The principal concern manifested by the Secrétariat in its choice of participants has been to bring to the conference table the major "decision makers" ("*les décideurs*") from the key sectors of the economy. Thus, the government is always represented by a cabinet minister, in order that he or she might hear firsthand the concerns and demands of the state's interlocutors and formulate policy accordingly. Other organizations are represented by elected officials (in the case of the trade unions, business associations, and other interest groups) or presidents (in the case of individual corporations). The reasoning behind this choice of participants is quite simple: if the economic conferences are to be something more than an exercise in public relations, if there is to be an actual sharing of responsibilities for Quebec's future development, then the government must meet with representatives who can effectively speak for their members and commit them to a specific course of action.

Although the Secrétariat's choice of participants might, on the face of it, appear to give the conferences some chance of being effective policy-making bodies, the structure of trade-union federations and business associations in Quebec, and the absence of any federal-government representation at the summits, tend to make them little more than media extravaganzas. As noted earlier, countries that have managed to check wage militancy and to diminish industrial conflict (at least temporarily) by means of tripartite national planning boards and voluntary incomes policies have been characterized by strongly centralized trade-union federations and employers' associations and by a system of national- or industry-level bargaining. Unfortunately for the PQ's corporatist designs, neither of these conditions is present in Quebec. None of the trade-union federations in the province is highly centralized; the idea that the FTQ, the CSN, or even the CEQ could force their affiliates to comply with decisions taken at the summits is laughable. As well, the labour federations, for the most part, do not play an important role in collective bargaining. Quebec in this regard follows the North American and British tradition of plant-level bargaining; none of the union centrals plays more than an advisory role in this process, supplying the locals with economic data and undertaking studies related to the negotiations. There are exceptions to this rule, the result of special laws passed by successive governments in Quebec. Bill 290 (1968), for example, instituted a type of industry-wide bargaining in the construction sector in Quebec and gave to the union federations a preponderant role in this process. Bill 25 (1967) made the CEQ the sole bargaining agent for the teachers' unions in the province, and the PQ's own Bill 55 (1978)—regulating collective bargaining in the educational sector, the social services (primarily hospitals), and government organizations—confirmed the trend towards centralized negotiations in Quebec's public and parapublic sectors.[26] For the most part, however, collective agreements in Quebec, as in the rest of Canada, are negotiated between the union local and the individual employer, a situation that makes the institutionalization of concerted action in the province highly improbable, inasmuch as the trade-union federations lack the power to extract from their affiliates the responsibility and moderation in collective bargaining that such a policy is designed to obtain.

Business organization in Quebec poses another problem for the PQ's search for a social contract. Those employers' associations that do exist in the province are primarily lobbying groups whose chief purposes are to keep government apprised of the concerns and demands of the business world and to urge legislators to adopt policies that are compatibile with a healthy business climate. Individual employers, especially those in the small and medium-sized industries, have been extremely reluctant to delegate any decision-making authority to employers' associations. Thus, concerted action as it is presently constituted in Quebec lacks a powerful business federation to influence and control its members; certainly the CMA, the CDE, and the Chambre de Commerce do not wield this sort of authority. As for the CPQ, which is clearly the most influential business organization in the province, it has no control whatsoever over the bargaining strategies or the pricing policies of its member firms. This contrasts with the situation in Sweden, for example, where the employers' federation, the SAF, is "represented in all key negotiations" and where every "labour contract must have SAF's approval, and members are liable to penalties if they ignore this rule or break the employer front in an open conflict by making a separate agreement contrary to the SAF line."[27]

Finally, the absence of one very important social partner—the federal government—from the economic summits limits the effectiveness of these conferences. Since jurisdiction over economic matters is shared between the federal and provincial governments, it would seem to make sense to have federal ministers and top-ranking civil servants present at the summits to bargain with the other economic agents. Few specific policies could be decided on at the mini-summits on the "soft sectors" (clothing, textiles, footwear, and furniture), for instance, since the setting of tariffs and quotas on imports of these commodities is a federal concern. The "points of convergence" reached by the social partners at these four mini-summits amounted to asking the provincial government to pressure Ottawa to maintain tariff barriers at existing levels and to set quotas on imports of clothing, footwear, and textiles at 1975 levels for a five-year period. Such pressure may have been more effective had it been exerted directly on the federal government at a highly publicized economic summit. (In late 1978 and early 1979, the federal government did indeed impose quotas on these products, though not at the levels desired by the Quebec government.) Similarly, the conference on Montreal's economic future might have benefited from the presence of federal politicians to discuss such questions as the role of Montreal's airports and the renovation of its port facilities. Nonetheless, the Quebec government has doggedly refused to invite Ottawa to its economic summits, other than as observers. According to Bernard Landry:

> Concerted action is part of a Québécois model based on a type of equilibrium among participants all in search of a consensus. There is already too much contention between the two levels of government for us to risk destroying this fragile equilibrium.[28]

In this case, a possible increase in the effectiveness of the economic summits has been sacrificed to the ongoing constitutional jousting between Ottawa and Quebec.

It would be inaccurate to say that concerted action in Quebec has had absolutely no impact on the attitudes of the social partners, or that it has yielded virtually no substantive policy innovations. The socioeconomic conferences, especially the mini-summits, have produced some concrete results, but on the whole these have been of a rather pedestrian nature. For instance, the conference on agriculture and the food industries committed the partners to a development strategy that would rely on Quebec's comparative advantages and called for the creation of an export agency to promote the sale of Quebec's products. The maritime-fisheries summit called for the establishment of a multipartite (comprising fishermen, cooperatives, business, labour, consumers, and government) fisheries advisory board to oversee the development of this industry in Quebec. Such a board, composed of 12 members, was created by order-in-council in August 1978. The conference on Quebec's municipalities (which was strictly a government affair—neither business nor labour was invited to participate) was the occasion for the government's unveiling of its plans for administrative decentralization. The tourism summit led to an agreement on the necessity of rationalizing road signs and signals in the province in order to attract foreign visitors, while the conference on the cultural industries announced the creation of a new crown corporation, La Société de développement des industries culturelles, which would invest in a variety of cultural endeavours in the province (theatre, recording industry, publishing) in an attempt to safeguard and promote Quebec's unique culture.

The four mini-summits on the "soft sectors," as noted above, resulted in a commitment to pressure Ottawa to maintain tariffs and quotas on textiles, clothing, and footwear, and in the provincial government's promise to increase financial and technical assistance to these troubled industries, primarily by relaxing the terms on which the Société de développement industriel (SDI) can extend credit to industries in the province. The "soft sectors" did experience a mild upturn in 1978, but to suggest, as Bernard Landry had done, that this improved performance had anything to do with the holding of the mini-summits would require a complete suspension of disbelief.[29] The stabilization or growth of employment and the increases in production and retail sales experienced by these four industries in 1978 were almost certainly attributable to a number of factors entirely unrelated to "dialogue" among the social partners. Chief among these were the devaluation of the Canadian dollar, the selective removal on April 13, 1978, of the provincial sales tax on clothing, textiles, footwear, and furniture, and the implementation of the federal quotas. The last two measures, though briefly discussed at the sectorial conferences, were government initiatives. There is no evidence to suggest that the mini-summits hastened their adoption. Indeed, in the case of the abolition of the provincial sales tax on certain items, Finance Minister Parizeau may have been more concerned with upstaging his federal counterpart than he was with fulfilling the government's obligations to its social partners.[30]

The grand summits have perhaps been less effective than the mini-summits, given their highly publicized nature and the inevitable tendency for the social partners to posture for the sake of the media. Nonetheless, some specific commitments have been reached at these conferences: at Pointe-au-Pic, the government pledged to adopt a "Buy Quebec" plan for state-owned corporations in order to stimulate the local manufacturing sector and proposed to study the possibility of creating a national productivity institute. (It was established in June 1978.) The government also promised to set up an information bureau within the Ministry of Labour to gather statistics on labour relations and disseminate them to the social partners. (This, too, was set up in late 1978). At the Montebello conference, the government pledged, among other things, to extend greater financial and technical assistance to industry in order to boost Quebec's exports. It also undertook to *study*—a typical response to controversial proposals advanced by the trade unions—labour's demands for an employment stabilization fund (financed by contributions from all employers in the province) which would compensate those workers involved in mass layoffs and for a form of sectorial collective bargaining (of which more below). Perhaps the most important outcome of the Quebec City conference was the decision to set up an emergency housing-construction program, along the lines suggested by the FTQ's representatives at the summit. This eventually materialized in the form of Corvée Habitation, a mortgage-assistance scheme intended to create approximately 50,000 jobs in the construction sector.

On the whole, business and the private-sector unions (represented by the FTQ and the CSD) have been quite satisfied with the functioning of concerted action in Quebec: business, because of the increased amount and variety of state largesse promised to it at the various summits; the private-sector unions, because of the specific "concessions" they have secured from the government. Among these concessions the FTQ and CSD would undoubtedly number Corvée Habitation, the anti-scab provisions in the Labour Code, and (to the FTQ at any rate) the government's support for the Fonds de solidarité, an investment fund financed by worker contributions to provide venture capital for Quebec industries. Thus, both business and the FTQ would probably be happy to continue concerted action in its present form. The FTQ, significantly, has warned the PQ not to expect too much from its policy of concerted action:

> The very structure and tradition of our movement prevent us from thinking that this type of dialogue will evolve into the negotiation of some sort of social contract. Our entire history is marked by a profound attachment to the autonomy of the local section.[31]

Nor is business willing to alter its traditional suspicion of the labour movement and accept it as an equal partner. Far from being an accepted interlocutor, the trade unions are often viewed by the business community as an intemperate and dangerous pressure group whose demands, if met, would shake the social order to its foundations.

It is in the industrial relations of the public sector that the PQ's policy of concerted action has most obviously failed. For, in spite of the government's rhetoric about labour's new-found status as an industrial partner, it has not hesitated to resort to the "big stick" (back-to-work laws and injunctions brandished so frequently by the Bourassa regime) once its appeals to labour's "common sense," "civic responsibility," and "awareness of the common good" have proven ineffectual. A telling example of the PQ's substitution of state coercion for a consensual approach to industrial relations occurred during the Common Front negotiations of 1979 and 1982-83. In each case, a grand summit (those at Montebello and Quebec City) preceded the round of negotiations and was obviously intended to set the tone for the bargaining—even though the topic of public-sector negotiations was formally excluded from the summit's agenda. Prior to the Quebec conference, for example, Gilles Châtillon of the Secrétariat expressed the hope that the summit would result in the "social compromise" that Quebec so badly needed: "The unions would agree to negotiate a deal, to accept certain social clauses (such as unionization) in exchange for the money the government does not have."[32]

In neither case, however, did the government's appeals have the desired effect. In 1979, the government was forced to pass Bill 62 in order to avert a general strike of hospital workers and teachers. In 1982-83, the government was forced to pass Bills 70 and 105, rolling back wage increases in the public and parapublic sectors by 20%, and determining working conditions and remuneration in these sectors for a period of three years, to 1986. This action was taken after the Common Front unions had refused to accept the Lévesque government's offer of a "social compromise." In particular, the unions had refused to help the government cover its $700 million budgetary "hole"—which Lévesque and his ministers had insisted at the Quebec summit could be offset only by voluntary wage restraint in the public sector. In February 1983, Bill 111, probably the harshest piece of back-to-work legislation in Quebec's history, brought an end to an illegal teachers' strike.

With each piece of emergency legislation, the PQ's self-proclaimed "favourable prejudice towards the workers" has become more and more derisory—especially in the eyes of the public-sector unions. At the same time, the government's hopes for a social contract in the province have been rendered chimerical: the PQ, like so many other would-be corporatist regimes before it, has found that state coercion is sometimes necessary to achieve the "harmony" and social peace that are supposed to be the products of concerted action.[33]

Conclusions: The Prospects for Concerted Action in Quebec

It would appear that some essential ingredients are missing from the PQ government's recipe for social harmony and economic progress based on functional representation in the decision-making structures of the economy.

In the first place, two of the three largest trade-union federations (the CEQ and the CSN) reject the ideology of social partnership articulated by the PQ. Second, business in Quebec is reluctant to accept organized labour as even a junior partner; it wants concerted action, but at no cost to itself. Up till now, business has appeared unwilling to grant the minimal concessions to labour that would make the latter's cooperation in concerted action more likely. In particular, the various business associations in the province have unequivocally rejected labour's call for sectorial bargaining in Quebec, a system of collective bargaining that, by replacing plant-level with industry-wide negotiations, would greatly increase the power of the trade-union federations vis-à-vis the rank and file. It would, at the same time, greatly increase the level of unionization in the province, another precondition of a reasonably meaningful policy of concerted action. At present, with only 36-37% of the work force unionized (a figure which drops to 21% in the private sector[34]), the trade-union federations can hardly be said to "represent" all workers in the province. Despite its social-democratic pretensions, however, the PQ government has not hastened to implement such a measure, preferring instead to enact reforms that help to protect Quebec's unorganized workers without at the same time requiring them to join a union. The government's legislation on labour norms (1979), for example, actually hinders the efforts of the federations to organize those sectors of the economy that have traditionally resisted unionization—restaurants, hotels, wholesale and retail trade, financial institutions, and small manufacturing, for instance.[35]

The PQ government's apparent unwillingness to revise the Labour Code and give to the labour federations a more prominent role in collective bargaining raises some fundamental doubts about the viability of concerted action in Quebec. The PQ would like to integrate the trade-union leadership into the state's decision-making structures in order to attenuate class conflict, yet it paradoxically fears and mistrusts this same union leadership, as was evident in the public debate accompanying the passage of Bills 62, 70, 105, and 111. Thus, the government has shied away from any measures—such as sectorial bargaining—which would strengthen this leadership's role for the rank and file and thus increase the chances (no matter how slim) for a "rational" tripartite approach to economic planning in Quebec. So it is that the immediate prospects for the PQ's version of liberal corporatism are not at all good.

Notes

1. These themes are apparent in several government documents and the speeches of government leaders from this period. See, in particular, René Lévesque, "Speech to the Economic Club in New York," *Globe and Mail* (January 26, 1977); Bernard Landry, cited in Pierre Fournier, "The Parti Québécois and the Power of Business," *Our Generation* 12: 3 (spring 1979), p. 6. See also Gouvernement du Québec, *Bâtir le Québec* (Québec, 1979), pp. 72-73, 77-89, my translation.
2. Gouvernement du Québec, *Le Bilan des conférences socio-économiques du Québec* (Québec, 1979), p. 93, my translation.

3. René Lévesque, *La Passion du Québec* (Montréal: Editions Québec-Amérique, 1978), p. 78: "We must have a pie that is getting bigger so we can divide it up more equally." My translation.
4. K.Z. Paltiel and Clinton Archibald, "L'évolution de l'idée corporatiste au Canada," *Etudes canadiennes* special issue (1979), La vie politique au Canada, proceedings of the colloquium at Mons (April 24-26, 1978), p. 83.
5. Philippe Schmitter, "Still the Century of Corporatism?" *The Review of Politics* 36: 1 (Jan. 1974), p. 86.
6. Samuel Beer, *British Politics in the Collectivist Age* (New York: Knopf, 1967), chs. 3, 12, and pp. 389-90.
7. These three factors which facilitate the growth of liberal corporatism are mentioned by Leo Panitch, "The Development of Corporatism in Liberal Democracies," *Comparative Political Studies* 10: 1 (April 1977), p. 76; and Andrew Shonfield, *Modern Capitalism* (London: Oxford University Press, 1965), pp. 230-33.
8. Panitch, op. cit., p. 66.
9. For an effective contrast between pluralist and corporatist theories of interest representation, see the useful collection of essays in Suzanne Berger (ed.), *Organizing Interests in Western Europe* (Cambridge: Cambridge University Press, 1981).
10. This list of the prerequisites of a stable liberal corporatism draws from a number of sources; among them are Gerhard Lehmbruch, "Liberal Corporatism and Party Government," *Comparative Politial Studies* 10: 1 (April 1977), pp. 111, 119; Bruce Headey, "Trade Unions and National Wages Policies," *The Journal of Politics* 32: 2 (May 1970), pp. 407-39; Panitch, op. cit., pp. 72, 79-80.
11. For information on individual countries, see Jack Barbash, *Trade Unions and National Economic Policy* (Baltimore: Johns Hopkins Press, 1972); and Gerhard Lehmbruch, "Introduction: Neo-Corporatism in Comparative Perspective," in Lehmbruch and Philippe Schmitter (eds.), *Patterns of Corporatist Policy-Making* (Beverley Hills: Sage, 1982) pp. 1-28.
12. These points are made by Panitch, op. cit., pp. 81-84. See also Michael Watson, "A Comparative Evaluation of Planning Practice in the Liberal Democratic State," in J. Hayward and M. Watson (eds.), *Planning, Politics and Public Policy* (London: Cambridge University Press, 1975), pp. 449, 458-59, 468-70.
13. Gouvernement du Québec, *L'Etat de la situation socio-économique* (Document prepared for Montebello Summit Meeting, 14-16 March 1979), Tables 1, 27 (pp. 8, 90).
14. Clinton Archibald, "Les tendances néo-corporatistes du Parti québécois," *Perception* 2: 2 (Nov.-Dec. 1978), pp. 14-18.
15. Gouvernement du Québec, *Le tourisme, perspectives de relance, Rapport* (Sherbrooke, Oct. 30–Nov. 1, 1978), p. 4, my translation.
16. For an excellent discussion of some of the different tendencies within the PQ, see Vera Murray, *Le Parti québécois: de la fondation à la prise du pouvoir* (Montréal: Hurtubise/HMH, 1976).
17. Archibald, op. cit., p. 17, my translation.
18. Gouvernement du Québec, *Conférence au sommet de Montebello, Rapport* (March 1979), p. 214.
19. On the role of the Secrétariat, see Gouvernement du Québec, *Le Bilan des conférences socio-économiques* (1979), pp. 8-12.

20. Gouvernement du Québec, *La conférence au sommet Québec 1982, Rapport* (Québec, 1982), pp. 261-69.
21. Michelle La Santé, "Les sommets et les conditions du dialogue entre les agents socio-économiques du Québec," *OSE* 1: 5 (Jan. 1979), pp. 6-7, my translation.
22. Gouvernement du Québec, *Rapport, le sommet économique* (Pointe-au-Pic, May 1977), p. 27.
23. See CSN, *Positions de la CSN au sommet économique de Montebello* (March 14-15, 1979), pp. 20-22; Michel Morin, "La qualité de vie, au premier plan pour les syndicats," *Le Devoir* (Feb. 28, 1981).
24. Pierre Fournier, *The Quebec Establishment*, 2nd ed. (Montreal: Black Rose Books, 1978), p. 63.
25. Gouvernement du Québec, *Conférence au sommet Québec 1982*, op. cit., p. 263, my translation.
26. See Gérard Hébert, "Pouvoir et 'pouvoirs' dans les syndicats," in *Pouvoir et 'pouvoirs' dans les relations de travail*, 25e congrès de relations industrielles de l'Université Laval (Québec, 1970), pp. 94-95, 100.
27. Barbash, op cit., p. 25.
28. Quoted in Michel Morin, "Une demi-douzaine de projets majeurs devraient débloquer," *Le Devoir* (Feb. 26, 1981), my translation.
29. See Gouvernement du Québec. *Montebello, Rapport*, p. 55.
30. See Orland French, "Was Parizeau Right on Sales Tax?" *The Ottawa Citizen* (Oct. 6, 1978).
31. FTQ, *Un programme pour maintenant* (15th biennial congress, Nov. 28-Dec. 2, 1977), p. 20, my translation.
32. Paule des Rivières, "Sommet de trocs en avril?" *Le Devoir* (Feb. 18, 1982), my translation.
33. Nigel Harris, *Competition and the Corporate Society* (London: Methuen, 1972), p. 72.
34. Gouvernement du Québec, *L'Etat de la situation socio-économique* (Québec, April 1982), pp. 59-60.
35. Léo Roback, *La syndicalisation sectorielle* (Montreal: Institut de recherche appliquée sur le travail, Bulletin no. 10, 1977).

Part VI/Language Policies and Educational Reforms

The last two contributions in this book attempt to come to grips with the evolution of language policies and the various educational reforms that have taken place in recent Quebec history.

In his chapter, William Coleman examines in a historical perspective the development of the issue of language reform in the period following the Second World War. He focuses on demands for legislation to regulate language practices in the private corporate sector and in the educational system. To this end he closely examines the provisions of Bills 22 and 101 in these areas. For Coleman, language policies must be situated in the historical conjuncture of the postwar period, when Quebec's economy came even more under the domination of monopoly capital. Viewed in this light, an important aspect of language reforms is their ability to legitimate the dominance of these corporations.

Milner addresses some particularly contentious issues, since his essay deals with the most recent changes proposed for Quebec educational reforms. The main purpose of his study is to establish whether Law 40 (Quebec's diluted plan to reform its school system) is a victory of sorts over a powerful coalition of conservative forces. This reform is particularly significant since it has pitted the Quebec state against the most significant group within this coalition, the anglophone educational establishment.

Chapter 21/The Class Bases of Language Policy in Quebec, 1949-1983*

William D. Coleman

It is generally accepted that the key to understanding political change in Quebec after the Second World War is the character of the Quiet Revolution. The latter sometimes refers to the period that ranges from the death of Maurice Duplessis in 1959 until early 1965. The interpretation given to this period varies significantly among competing characterizations of change in the province. The most common view places great importance on the accession to power of the provincial Liberals in June 1960. This change in governments is seen to be the watershed for a series of critical changes, the most important of which being a change from ascriptive, religious values to achievement-oriented, secular values. The arrival of the Lesage Liberals marked, it is felt, the ascent of the *Etat québécois* to a dominant position in society, thereby displacing the ancient guardian, the Roman Catholic Church. This assertion of the political instance was followed by a series of institutional changes that set the society on the road to political "modernization," hence toward *rattrapage* in relation to the rest of North America. On the social plane, the key precipitating force is usually seen to be a new middle class of white-collar workers, technicians, and public servants. This class is said to have rejected the traditional myths of agriculturalism and corporatism for industrialization and liberal democracy. It is said to be the primary beneficiary of the reforms of the period.

This view of the Quiet Revolution, however simplified in its presentation here, has entered the realm of the symbolic and mythological and is invoked often in political discourse in Quebec. At the same time, studies by a series of social scientists in the past decade have called into question important components of this characterization. Jean-Louis Roy has shown that major reflection and critiques of social, labour, and educational policies were already well developed in the 1950s.[1] Further, this thinking drew on a rapidly growing social-science community. Even in the economic sphere, the expanding cooperative movement was educating many Québécois on economic issues. Hence, Léon Dion notes that the election in 1960 simply capped changes that had already occurred and was not the "total social phenomenon" described by Marcel Rioux.[2] Rocher writes that, if there was a "revolution" in the usual sense of the word, it was in the realm of ideology and culture.[3] Nevitte and Gingras say that even such changes were rather limited in scope.[4] (See Chapter 1.) They show that religion and its

---

*This chapter is a revised and updated version of an article that appeared in *Studies in Political Economy* 3 (spring 1980).

accompanying values hardly made the speedy exit from the world of the Québécois that is often assumed.

Finally, recent works by Brunelle, Coleman, and Fournier, among others, have called into question the hypothesized central role of the new middle class.[5] Here the analysis begins with the perception that the Quebec economy was being increasingly dominated by a relatively small number of large corporations in oligopoly situations, a process that generates severe financial constraints for smaller enterprises. Francophone employers, it is well known, fall overwhelmingly into this latter group. According to Brunelle, then, the problem that occupied more and more of the authorities' attention in the postwar period was the role and place that should be occupied by the francophone bourgeoisie—not the new middle class—in the Quebec economy. It is argued further that many of the economic reforms of the 1959-1965 period emerged from the Conseil d'orientation économique du Québec (COEQ), a body specifically created by the Lesage government to articulate the demands of the francophone bourgeoisie.[6] The new middle class increased in size as a result of these reforms, perhaps even benefited to an extent, but was certainly not the prime instigator nor the main beneficiary.

This chapter extends these revisions of accepted wisdom by examining the evolution of language policy in Quebec in the postwar period up to and including Bill 101, the Charter of the French Language of 1977. The analysis of language will obviously be an important one for this debate because of the central place it has come to occupy in the nationalist ideology. René Lévesque, the most obvious political leader of the nationalist movement, has written of the personality of the Québécois: "At the core of this personality is the fact that we speak French. Everything else depends on this one essential element and follows from it or leads us infallibly back to it."[7] Language is not only a concern of the ideologue but has also become a field of social and political struggle in Quebec. It is a primary mode in which a culture is lived and, hence, has to be defended in everyday contexts. Further, it is a mode of symbolization, a means for identifying the boundaries of social community. In singling out and defining particular phenomena—that is, by signifying inclusion or exclusion—language becomes a means for legitimation. Both of these dimensions of language, the medium of daily life and the defence of boundaries, enter fully into the political arena in the postwar period.

First, then, in terms of daily existence, the strengthening in position of large, mainly English-Canadian or American corporations raised questions about the language of work for not only the French-speaking bourgeoisie but the other classes as well. The impact of these economic changes extended to the language used by the provincial administration and by the school system. The debates over these questions polarized regularly along fairly clear class lines. In this chapter, I shall show that government policies responded more to the concerns of the francophone employer class than those of the new petty bourgeoisie.[8] At the same time, the policies were of such a form as to strengthen the position of the capitalist class in general in Quebec. Further, it will be demonstrated that the language debate served as a catalyst to cooperation among the various fractions of the bourgeoisie and did *not* lead to any coalition between the francophone employer class and the new petty bourgeoisie. On the other hand, the debate did serve to promote a coalition among the new petty bourgeoisie, the traditional petty bourgeoisie, the leadership of organized labour, and elements of the working class.

Second, language as definer of boundaries has related to issues concerning the legitimacy of both economic and political institutions. Various theorists have argued that in the system of advanced capitalism, implementation of political decisions, and—one should add—economic decisions rests on what Easton has called diffuse support. In the advanced capitalist system, political activity becomes both complex and more direct in sustaining capital accumulation. It is then grounded in the mobilization of diffuse support—that is, "a reservoir of favourable attitudes or good will that helps members to accept or tolerate outputs to which they are opposed or the effect of which they see as damaging of their wants."[9] Habermas writes of a need for "an input of mass loyalty that is as diffuse as possible."[10] The consequence is that decisions come to be accepted in a "nearly motive free and matter of fact way."[11] It will be argued below that various components of the language policy that emerged in the 1960s and early 1970s laid the foundation for the maintenance of diffuse support for capitalist economic institutions and for the political regime.

The arguments will be traced by examining, in turn, the articulation of demands and formulation of policies in three spheres: the economic enterprise, the provincial regime, and the education system.

Language and the Economic System

In the economic sphere in Quebec, language draws its significance from the fact that the dominant fractions of the capitalist class are nonfrancophone. Accordingly, such fractions are identified in linguistic terms. Language becomes a lightning rod for the critique of the capitalist class per se. Such a rod becomes more prominent the more the Quebec economy approximates the advanced capitalist model. This tendency is marked by increased predominance of a large multinational corporate sector. This more evident presence of "foreign" institutions occurs in conjunction with a rise in direct political involvement in support of those institutions. Language policy related to economic institutions, then, is designed to integrate them more solidly into Quebec society and to deflect attention from increased political support of those institutions. The first form of this policy, francization, is designed to give corporations and other businesses a French "face" (*"visage français"*).

Members of the traditional petty bourgeoisie—the liberal professions, shopkeepers, clerics, farmers—had long criticized the presence of an English-speaking capitalism in Quebec. Given their position largely outside these capitalist institutions, the focal point of their critique remained the external face of those same institutions. Members of this class had erected and relied on a series of organizations such as the Société du bon parler français and the Comité permanent de la survivance française (later the Conseil de la vie française [CVF]) to promote pride in the use of French language. Longstanding nationalist societies such as the Société Saint-Jean-Baptiste and the Ligue d'Action Nationale (a successor to the Ligue des droits du français) were also controlled by members of this class and joined the former organizations in mass campaigns to make the external face of business more French.[12] Usually they demanded that businesses at a minimum have bilingual names, label products in French, and write notices and signs in French.[13] In the postwar period, at least until 1957, such campaigns remained common. A typical example was the struggle in the mid-1950s over the naming of the new Canadian National Railways hotel being built in Montreal. The CNR had proposed to name it "The Queen Elizabeth," a move opposed by the nationalists, who preferred the name "Le Château Maisonneuve," a name they felt was consistent with CNR practice in Quebec City and Ottawa. The Ligue d'Action nationale organized an intense media campaign on the issue, collecting a petition with over 200,000 signatures, all to no avail. In the same vein, a more general campaign to francize business names was waged in 1956 and 1957 by these same organizations, presumably on the instigation of the secret nationalist order, the Ordre de Jacques Cartier.[14]

After 1957, mass campaigns on the face of business disappeared, but the demands persisted in the yearly resolutions of the nationalist societies and gradually penetrated political platforms and French business organizations such as the Chambre de Commerce du District de Montréal (CCDM) and the Chambre de Commerce de la Province du Québec (CCPQ).[15] These organizations were the more prominent spokesmen for the francophone business class and combined demands of the traditional petty bourgeoisie and small-factory owners. The additional weight of these organizations helped to prompt a response by authorities after half a century of campaigns. The first step in this response came in 1967.

The language policy took its inspiration from a general position that French should be the language "with priority" in Quebec. This notion was articulated first by Pierre Laporte, then Minister of Cultural Affairs, in an unpublished white paper written in 1965.[16] It became a plank in the official platform of the provincial Liberals in the 1966 election. It was later to be promoted by the Société Saint-Jean-Baptiste de Québec (SSJBQ) and the CVF, heralding a split in the nationalist ranks.[17] The terms of reference of the Commission of Inquiry on the Position of the French Language and on Language Rights in Quebec (Gendron Commission) were phrased to express this position.[18] Accordingly, the concept of "priority" obtained its fullest elaboration in the report of this commission. "Priority" implied that French should be a means of communication employed in all spheres of social existence, particularly the economy. At the same time, the rights of anglophones in the province should be respected and to a degree guaranteed. Given that protection of the right to use English is often synonymous with protection of the prerogatives of employers in Quebec's economic context, the philosophy of "French priority" was one that pointed to avenues to legitimation of large nonfrancophone-controlled businesses without seriously compromising their economic capacity. Giving business a *visage français* is a means to deflect criticism of the "foreign" character of corporations, and perhaps indirectly of capitalism itself.

The concept was first implemented in March 1967 in an order-in-council regulating food. Speaking of the markings for food products, the order states:

> The use of French is obligatory in all inscriptions, and inscriptions in another language must not take precedence over those in French. This regulation does not apply to a document accompanying the sale and drawn up in the language of the buyer.[19]

A similar order was drawn up for the regulation of dairy products in 1970.[20] In the Official Languages Act of 1974, this kind of rule was generalized to cover most forms of external symbolism of enterprises.[21]

When the Parti Québécois came to power in 1976, it brought to the government the concerns of what we shall call the nationalist coalition—an organized grouping of the labour centrals, the new and the traditional petty bourgeoisie. Its task as the governing party was one of balancing the electoral commitments it made to this coalition and the constraints placed on it as part of the state with responsibilities for insuring the continuation of the process of capital accumulation. I have argued elsewhere that a party in such a situation will respond by acceding to the bourgeoisie on issues that most clearly affect the accumulation process and by rewarding its constituency on issues more distant from this same process.[22] The external image of the enterprise is not as central to its making profits as the language it uses for internal operations or the linguistic capacities of its personnel. Hence, one might expect the PQ to be more attentive to its constituency on the former issue. Bill 101 reflected this by toughening Bill 22. Firms were compelled to use only French for much of their external image. The French-priority approach was abandoned.

The concern with the external presentation of enterprises in Quebec became supplemented with a relatively novel set of demands beginning in the early 1960s. These demands related more to the internal dynamics of the operations of industry and originated with a class closely involved in those dynamics, the working class. A basis for workers' discontent was centred on the problem of language of work. A survey conducted by the CNTU in 1965 showed that French was often relegated to a second-class position in the workplace.[23] In enterprises owned by nonfrancophones, only 50% of the workers used French in speaking with their bosses. While company regulations were usually published in French, only 70% of the workers were able to bargain collectively in French and only 52.4% had a collective agreement drawn up solely in French. In 61.4% of the cases, English was the official language of the collective agreement. Another survey conducted by the Quebec Division of the CMA found that only 54% of supervisory positions could be filled by workers who knew no English.[24] Conditions were better in enterprises owned by francophones, but these also were smaller and less significant economically.[25]

Extensive studies by the Gendron Commission substantiated these early surveys. On the shop floor, French was the language used 95% of the time.[26] However, the use of French dropped sharply as the activity became more characteristic of management: French was used in only 37% of reading activity.[27] Francophone administrators could use French only in communicating orally with anglophone superiors 22% of the time.[28] In contrast, anglophones used English orally with French administrators 83% of the time.[29] The Commission concluded:

> We have defined a socio-linguistic structure which proves beyond question that the domain of the French language is particularly characterized by inferior duties, small enterprises, low incomes and low levels of education. The domain of the English language is the exact opposite, that of superior duties involving initiative and command, and large enterprises, and high levels of education and income.[30]

The Fédération des travailleurs du Québec (FTQ) took aim at this situation as early as 1960 when it passed a resolution at its convention demanding that francophones who did not know English no longer be discriminated against in hiring and promotions.[31] As the decade progressed, the FTQ was joined by the CNTU and together the labour centrals expanded on this issue. They regretted that workers in Quebec were not able in many cases to bargain collectively in French and to communicate with superiors in French. These various issues were eventually subsumed under a blanket demand—that all workers in Quebec have the right to work in French.[32] Organized labour was joined early on in this quest by the traditional petty bourgeoisie through the nationalist societies and eventually by the Centrale de l'enseignement du Québec (CEQ) and the more radical Association québécoise des professeurs du français (AQPF). Even the Royal Commission on Bilingualism and Biculturalism (with the significant exception of Commissioner F.R. Scott) made recommendations along these lines.[33]

The entry of organized labour into the language debate and the increased salience of practices within the enterprise—practices which bore directly on the efficacy of the enterprise—resulted in the mobilization of employers' representatives. The challenge being mounted on the linguistic front by labour complemented other critiques emanating from a rapidly radicalizing movement and helped precipitate more concerted action by the capitalist class. Long-existing proposals from the Association professionnelle des industriels (later the Centre des dirigeants d'entreprise [CDE]) for an overarching employers' association were suddenly acted on with the creation of the Conseil du Patronat du Québec (CPQ).[34] The most powerful industrialists in the province also formed a General Council of Industry, which was given privileged access to the provincial cabinet through regular private meetings.[35]

Specifically, employers' representatives became more active in the language debate. The response to the demand for the use of French in collective bargaining was uniformly positive, provided that the rights of anglophone workers were not ignored. On the other hand, the issue of internal communications brought more qualified replies. There was little disagreement with the proposal that employers communicate in writing in French with their workers, but at the same time reluctance to guarantee all communications would be in French or that knowledge of English would not be considered in promotions.[36] These feelings were manifested in responses by employers to the demand that workers have the right to work in French. These responses took two forms, depending on the ethnicity and by implication the size of the enterprise involved.

French-Canadian business organizations, the representatives of small employers in the main, recognized the principle of such a right and demanded that it be implemented voluntarily by the enterprises involved.[37] They strongly resisted the idea that the state be involved and further expressed a desire to limit the application of pressure to enterprises where the majority of workers were francophones. This position, of course, is consistent with the notion put forth by Brunelle that this fraction was seeking to insure its integration into corporate capitalism in this period. The new petty bourgeoisie tended to side more with labour and demanded that French be made the language of work directly and not through persuasive means as recommended by the francophone employers' associations. On the other hand, representatives of anglophone business organizations such as the Montreal Board of Trade and the CMA as well as several prominent firms (Imperial Oil, Dominion Glass) refused even to recognize the right.[38] They were supported in this position by the Fantus Report, a report on the state of Quebec industry carried out at the request of the provincial government by a Chicago consulting firm. The report concluded that such a policy could severely inhibit Quebec's ability to attract new industry.[39] All of these groups noted that it would precipitate the departure of head offices from Montreal.

The response of the political authorities to these competing demands was carefully selective, in that they sought to dilute the English character of business operations, thereby deflecting a possibly sustained, more general critique of capitalism. Again the "French priority" rule was applied.[40] Section 24 of the Official Language Act stipulated that written communications from employers to workers were to be in French with accompanying

English versions if desired. Section 25 declared French the language of labour relations, while leaving it possible to use English as well.

The PQ, attentive to its labour support, considerably expanded the scope for the use of French on the shop floor. It gave workers an explicit right to work in French. It insured that all aspects of the industrial-relations system would function in French. Finally, it sought to provide guarantees that workers would not be discriminated against in hirings and promotions if they knew only French.

However, when it came to the language used at higher levels of the firm, matters became more complex. The French-language business groups had suggested to the Liberals in the early 1970s that the government use moral persuasion to encourage the expansion of the use of French at these levels. Any action beyond that would involve the state in the internal affairs of the enterprise. On the other side, the nationalist coalition argued for direct coercive measures to force the expansion of French at these levels.

The Liberals produced a compromise mechanism that went a little beyond persuasion but still left the enterprise with a fair amount of discretion. Section 27 of Bill 22 gave the government the power to require firms to adopt a program of francization. Section 28 added to this by requiring all firms doing business with the government to obtain such a certificate. Awarding a permanent certificate was to be based on the firm's implementing a plan to expand the use of French, which was to be jointly developed with an agency called the Régie de la langue française.

In the end, Bill 101 used basically the same approach and diverged from the Liberal law in only two major respects. First, it required all firms of over 50 employees to obtain a francization certificate, not just those doing business with the government. Second, it made it possible for head offices and research institutes to get exemptions from the requirement. In this respect, Bill 101 was more accommodating to business concerns than was Bill 22.[41]

The question of the legitimacy of capitalist enterprises in Quebec was not to be resolved for both the francophone bourgeoisie and the new petty bourgeoisie only by changing the face and the language of operations of enterprises. Rather, positions at senior executive levels in the large corporations had to be made available to francophones as well. The demand for francization was a demand to be part of the system. The story here is well known and need not be retold. Francophones have been virtually absent from the top echelons of industry in Quebec, as studies by Hughes and McDonald, Vézina, Raynauld, and Sales have shown.[42] Nationalists from the traditional petty bourgeoisie, of course, had remarked on this in the past.[43] Nonetheless, a renewed volley in this debate began in the mid-1950s, when the CCDM registered concern over this issue.[44] Clearly, members of the French-Canadian employer class would feel this exclusion in their dealings with their larger corporate counterparts. One might expect as well that their sons and daughters would be more likely to try to penetrate this realm.

Explicit recognition of the problem was given in the platform of the

Liberals in the 1960 election campaign.[45] The concerns were reiterated in the preamble creating the Ministry of Natural Resources in 1961, by the Ministry of Industry and Commerce in a special brief to the Royal Commission on Education in 1962, and in many policies proposed by the COEQ.[46] No direct action was taken, however. Accordingly, these appeared to be initial political attempts to defuse the issue by indicating concern only. The demands continued to be pressed by the CCDM and with especial vigour by the Parti Québécois after its formation in 1968. Hence, in 1973, the CPQ conceded that francophones should be represented at a rate closer to their strength in the population.[47] Again, however, the means proposed in realizing francization differed for the new petty bourgeoisie compared to the francophone bourgeoisie. The former wanted francization imposed directly by law, while the latter preferred governmental "encouragement" and "persuasion." It is also important to note that the francophone bourgeoisie generally received support from the large corporations on this issue.

The political response to these demands followed the "indirect approach" described above where interference with the accumulation process was minimized and accordingly was more consistent with the proposals elaborated by the francophone bourgeoisie than those of the new middle class. Under the terms of Bill 22, an additional factor to be taken into account for francization certificates was the "degree of francophone presence in management." The CCDM immediately claimed the provision was too vague, in that it failed to specify that francophones should be represented at the highest echelons of industry.[48] On the other hand, the Chambre also found the provision offensive because it was coercive rather than persuasive.[49] The PQ law retained this approach by legislating that francization programs should involve an increase in the number of persons "having a good knowledge of the French language" at all levels of the enterprise. Like the Liberals, the PQ refrained from direct coercion in this matter.

This strategy of the authorities to promote francization while minimizing interference with production itself was also evident in the treatment given to professionals. In its brief to the Gendron Commission, the Corporation des ingénieurs du Québec had demanded that all practising engineers being licensed be required to have a working knowledge of French.[50] The Gendron Commission generalized this suggestion to include all professional corporations.[51] Both Bill 22 and Bill 101 followed this lead and bound such corporations to issue work permits only to those who had a working knowledge of French. Such a move would promote increased francization because more professionals would be able to work in French. At the same time, both laws exempted from this provision those professionals who worked in jobs with no direct contact with the public.

In short, language policy in the economic sphere may be seen as facilitating the integration of capitalist institutions into Quebec society. This process was accomplished by constraining enterprises to communicate with both consumers and workers in French. It also involved a series of indirect pressures on enterprises to absorb more French speakers in professional and managerial capacities. At the same time, the policy was designed to intervene minimally in the operations of the enterprise, thus reflecting more the desires of employers than their opponents. The explanation for these developments would appear to involve several factors.

One hypothesis is that this movement in language policy is related to other changes in the relationship between the state and society. Theories of capitalist society emphasize several kinds of changes that take place in this relationship in the advanced stages. First, the economic system becomes increasingly unable to provide the inputs for capital accumulation both because of dislocations precipitated by the presence of a large oligopolistic sector and the inability of the employer class to forge a unified perspective.[52] The state is called on to provide various material and capital inputs needed to sustain economic growth.

Many of the economic policies sponsored by the provincial government in Quebec after 1960 follow these lines. The private electrical companies were nationalized and merged into a rationalized, less costly system of power distribution. Agencies were created to support smaller companies (Société générale de Financement) and to facilitate resource exploration (SOQUEM and SOQUIP). A flurry of legislation was passed in the late 1960s that was supportive of the private sector and especially the most technologically advanced firms—the Quebec Industrial Credit Bureau Act, the Regional Industrial Development Act, key amendments to the Corporation Tax Act, the Quebec Industrial Assistance Act, and the Quebec Industrial Development Corporation Act. The Department of Industry and Commerce also set up a Financial Assistance Program for Certain Industrial Sectors and a Financial Assistance Program for High Technology Industries.[53] New trade offices were opened in Boston, Chicago, Dallas, Los Angeles, and Düsseldorf. A Centre de recherches industrielles and a Centre de recherches minérales were created to serve the private sector. In short, the provincial regime made an explicit commitment to the support and subsidization of the leading companies of the industrial sector.

A second characteristic of advanced capitalist society is the increase in the size of the pool of surplus labour because of the introduction of labour-saving machinery and the pressure on small independent producers and merchants that arises from the expansion and penetration of the large corporations. This surplus force is more and more absorbed into service industries, both public and private. Other components are supported by a variety of social-welfare programs. In short, there is a significant expansion of the social-welfare institutions administered by the political authorities. In Quebec, such an expansion was marked by the integration of institutions formerly controlled by the Church's educational bodies and social institutions such as hospitals into the public sector. This process of integration was accompanied by comprehensive attempts to "modernize" these institutions. At the same time, there was a need to substantially increase wages, which had been very low due to the Church's presence. Inevitably, confrontations developed between the workers in this sector, with their raised expectations, and the authorities. In response, the labour movement radicalized and formally adopted socialism in the early 1970s.[54] With this radicalization, of course, came sharp attacks on the capitalist class and capitalist economic system. (See Chapter 16.)

Accordingly, the provincial regime had embarked on a policy of collaboration and support of the corporate sector at the same time as it was being faced with a hostile and socialist labour leadership. The various language policies, then, may be seen as attempts by the regime to increase the legitimacy of institutions more and more under attack. At the same time, increased interaction with those institutions was also possibly blurred in the minds of the petty bourgeoisie in particular by the authorities' attempts to gain them positions in those institutions and to render the behaviour of those institutions less foreign to their experience. As Offe has postulated, therefore, an expansion in the state's involvement in accumulation is accompanied by an expansion in legitimation activity and the cultivation of diffuse support.[55]

Language and Education

The increased predominance of large, often multinational corporations in Quebec's economy and the more systematic support for those corporations tendered by the provincial government was bound to have an impact on the education system as well. To the extent that the education system was to provide cadres for these institutions—and this was largely the orientation given to those institutions in the reforms of the 1960s—the issue of the knowledge of English was certain to arise. As is well known, the disputes over language of instruction were the most visible of all involving language, occasioning massive demonstrations, scattered violence, and much bitterness and recrimination. Even by 1983, the issues that had given rise to disputes in the late 1960s were not finally resolved. The PQ had had the good sense to rid the province of the odious testing procedures of Bill 22, but then had gone on to restrict access to English-language education, thereby upsetting corporate concerns. The federal government had entered the fray on the side of the latter with its new Charter of Rights and Freedoms. The one question that then naturally arises is: why have the disputes over language of instruction been so intense and so difficult to resolve over the past 15 years?

The language-of-instruction issue was bound to be an essential one for the petty bourgeoisie. The large influx of immigrants to Quebec between 1950 and 1965, when coupled with a birth rate that would fall even below that of Ontario by 1973, placed this class in a less tenable position economically and politically. Economically, the children of immigrants were seen to be competing with francophones for the expanding positions in the private corporate bureaucracies. In a situation where language of work was not regulated, those possessing knowledge of English would be advantaged. In 1969, figures revealed in Volume III of the Report of the Royal Commission on Bilingualism and Biculturalism showed that most ethnic groups in Quebec already had leaped ahead of francophones in income. These figures became public knowledge virtually at the same time Henripin, Legaré, and Charbonneau published their demographic articles in *Le Devoir* and forecast a significant weakening of the francophone majority in Quebec and in Montreal.[56] It follows that the education system was seen to be giving immigrants a head start and studies showed that immigrants were to become a larger and larger part of Quebec society.

Second, the attractiveness of and desire for careers in the private sector lured francophones themselves toward more intensive study of English. Figures available indicate, for example, an increase in the tendency for French speakers to enrol in the English-language school systems. From 1969 to 1973, the percentage of French students in English schools rose from 1.6% to 1.8%, an increase of 13%.[57] By 1973, then, French-speaking students constituted 12.4% of all students in English schools.[58] The concomitant fear that some of *les nôtres* would be lost to assimilation is not one emphasized very often but one that may be even stronger than fear of the immigrants. It is essential here to recall that starting in 1964 the education system in Quebec was no longer under Church control and had been moving rapidly toward a more "relevant" stance vis-à-vis the labour market. Formerly, the education system had been a primary socializing agent into the mores of French-Canadian cultures, particularly for political elites. The new system showed no tendency to continue in that role, despite the recommendations of the Parent Commission. With the education system no longer able to exercise the same influence, the chances were increased that there would be greater crossover to the anglophone system and, with the crossover, a fracturing of the petty bourgeoisie into a less viable political force. At this juncture, it should also be emphasized that education occupies a special place in the ideologies of the petty bourgeoisie, both new and traditional. Poulantzas describes an aspect of these ideologies that focuses on the myth of social promotion and mobility and the desire to realize change this way rather than with revolutionary means.[59] A key institution for the realization of this promotion is the education system. It is believed that changing one's condition can best be realized through a relevant and democratized educational system. In Quebec, however, the bifurcation of the education system along linguistic lines prohibited actualization of that belief because students in the English system enjoyed an additional advantage in the process of social promotion. In short, the education system, structure, and orientation are matters that generate intense feelings among the members of the petty bourgeoisie.

These hypotheses about the important place of the educational struggle in the political action of this class are substantiated somewhat when its particular demands at this time are analyzed. First, it was suggested that

French-language schools begin instruction in English as a second language only at the secondary level. Otherwise, it was argued, the development of the full French personality of the students and the roots of the mother tongue would be seriously compromised. At the time this demand was first made (the early 1960s by the traditional nationalist societies), instruction in English began in grade five at a pace of two hours per week. The traditional nationalists who were joined in this quest by the CEQ, AQPF, and elements of the PQ thought that grade five was too soon.[60] On the other hand, representatives of the French-Canadian employers and of the large anglophone corporations tended to think the existing system provided too little too late.[61] In its brief to the Gendron Commission, the CDE justified this position by referring to Quebec's position in anglophone North America, its reliance on international trade, the need for mobile manpower, and so on.[62] For the former group, instruction in English was essential if francophones were to become integrated into the dominant corporations. It is interesting that those who sometimes speak for the new petty bourgeoisie, such as the PQ, maintain a certain diffidence to instruction in English. This fact illustrates the different roads to *rattrapage* proposed by the francophone bourgeois fraction and the new petty bourgeoisie: the former advocates collaboration with the large corporations, while the latter advocates an expanded (presumably francophone) public sector. Organized labour has also tended to depart from the petty bourgeoisie here. As late as its 1969 Convention, the FTQ demanded that English be taught earlier rather than later in French-language schools.[63]

The response by the authorities was essentially to stand pat. The grade-five starting point was not altered. In 1969, a program entitled *Les Oraliens* was introduced into the French system to strengthen the oral performance of young francophones. The Minister of Education presented a grand plan for language of instruction in April 1973, which was designed in part to strengthen the teaching of English as a second language. The initial version of the Official Language Act made no provision for instruction in English as a second language. After some intercessions, the final version contained a provision that the Minister of Education should insure instruction in English as a second language.[64] This provision was later dropped by the PQ from Bill 101.

The second major demand by the petty bourgeoisie was that the English-language schools be reserved for those whose mother tongue was English. Such a policy would redirect immigrant children to French schools and prevent the crossover of French children to English schools. This demand was supported by a broad coalition of nationalist organizations—the PQ, the FTQ, CEQ, to a degree the CNTU,[65] and student associations. It was gradually elaborated and refined. For example, the PQ initially proposed that quotas be imposed on English schools, but in 1975 modified this position by saying that English schools should be reserved for Quebeckers of English descent. Accompanying the expression of this demand was often a statement of concern over the loss of potential students. The CEQ suggested in 1974 that all francophones and immigrants in English schools should be repatriated to the French system.[66]

On the other hand, the usual coalition of representation of anglophone corporations and French-Canadian businessmen demanded that parents have the right to choose their children's language of instruction. Again the concern here for the francophone employers was retaining the opportunity to educate their children sufficiently in English to facilitate their social mobility. This usually meant enrolling them in English schools for two or three years as a supplement to instruction in English as a second language. They were supported in this position by both the Union Nationale and the Liberals as well as by the representatives of the immigrant community and the English-language educational system. The authorities—first through Bill 85 in 1968, which was withdrawn under nationalist pressure, and then Bill 63 in 1969—sought to consecrate this right of freedom of choice. The bills had been preceded by a series of bitter conflicts in the Montreal suburb of St-Léonard, where the nationalist-backed Mouvement pour l'intégration scolaire had sought to direct immigrant children to French schools.

Bill 63 itself was the focal point of a massive political debate. On the initiative of François-Albert Angers, then President of the SSJBM, the informal coalition of the new and traditional petty bourgeoisie, students, and organized labour was given institutional form with the creation of the Front du Québec français (FQF).[67] The FQF conducted an intense campaign against Bill 63 but lost. Nonetheless, the FQF and its successor, the Mouvement Québec français (MQF) continued the battle against the bill. The authorities made a third attempt to resolve the issue in the Official Language Act. Under its provisions, entrants to the English system needed to demonstrate possession of a "sufficient knowledge" of English first of all. If this "sufficient knowledge" could not be demonstrated, the student was automatically directed to the French system. In addition, the act empowered the authorities to draw up tests for determining whether "sufficient knowledge" existed and, in the event of too many "successes," to set quotas for the total number of registrants in the English system. These provisions were emphatically rejected by both sides. The nationalist-labour front argued that they gave recognition to a new right for anglophones, the right to instruction in English. Further, the way was still open for francophones to attend English schools, which led to a court challenge.[68] On the other hand, the employers' representatives felt that the bill dangerously compromised the right to freedom of choice and to an education in English.[69] Finally, the dissatisfaction with the Official Language Act (and Bill 63 before it) led to limited support for an old proposal of the SSJBM—namely that the English system gradually be phased out altogether and supplanted by a single French-language system.[70] Such tendencies led the CPQ, the Montreal Board of Trade, and the CCPQ, among others, to call for even more explicit guarantees for the right of the English-language system to exist.[71]

In short, when the PQ came to power late in 1976, the education system was still very much in turmoil. Bill 101 sought to end the disputes by making English-language education available only to those children one of whose parents had been educated in Quebec.[72] It added the option of allowing those who were moving to Quebec temporarily to apply for a three-year exemption (renewable for an additional three years) from this article. This policy had the virtue of being clear and unambiguous. It also created difficulties for companies interested in bringing personnel from other parts of Canada or the United States to work in Quebec. Unless these individuals could be designated as being only temporarily in Quebec, they were compelled to send their children to French schools. Such individuals became reluctant to move to Quebec. Section 23 of the new federal Charter of Rights and Freedoms makes English-language education available to any Canadian educated in elementary school in English. The first court case testing the Charter against Bill 101 on this matter was decided in favour of the federal law. It is likely that the Supreme Court of Canada will reach a similar decision in the next several years.

Referring to the questions introducing the education debate in this chapter, then, the issue of language has had such an impact because a confluence of disturbing demographic and economic information brought into question the capacity of the French-language education system to assure social mobility. Such a belief in the efficacy of education is central to the petty bourgeois and, hence, served as an impetus for political mobilization. The various employers' associations responded in a diametrically opposed fashion. The ensuing class-based struggle fostered in turn an increased emphasis on the anti-capitalist component of the petty-bourgeoisie ideology.[73] Hence, the provincial government found itself in a contradictory position. It was evident that it needed to defuse this conflict; thus, some concessions had to be made to the nationalist coalition. On the other hand, any dismantling of the English-language system promised to weaken support from the employer interests possibly to the point that some would withdraw operations from the province. Such a withdrawal would imply that the government's own resource base would be weakened and perhaps with it its capacity to guarantee the conditions for accumulation. The positions were so diametrically opposed that compromise was ineffectual. Furthermore, the strength of the nationalist coalition on the education issue was superior by far to that mustered on the unilingualism and language-of-work issues, particularly once the PQ came to power. A failure to accede to the demands of this group promised a major decline in that party's electoral fortunes. In short, the authorities were placed in a position where two of the functions of political activity—the cultivation of support and fostering the capitalist economy—implied contradictory responses.

Conclusions

Several conclusions arise from this analysis, some of which relevant to Quebec specifically and others related to the theory of the state in advanced capitalism. First, if one can take the empirically expressed demands of the various representative associations examined above as being an expression of class interest, the political response to these demands tended to favour the bourgeoisie in the areas most directly related to capital accumulation. The programs designed to francize the operations of the firm in Bill 101 closely followed the approach endorsed by the capitalist groups in Bill 22. Head offices and research institutes were dealt with flexibly and exempted from the basic francization schemes. In areas of less direct concern to the bourgeoisie—the public service and the linguistic image of the firm—the francophone petty bourgeoisie had more success. The language-of-education issue remains a continuing terrain of struggle; the balance has now shifted back toward the bourgeoisie because of the enactment of the Charter of Rights and Freedoms.

The big, largely foreign, bourgeoisie was hardly a loser as a result of these policies. The various language policies helped to better integrate major capitalist institutions into Quebec society. Efforts to francize theoretically increase their acceptance among members of the francophone bourgeois fraction and the new petty bourgeoisie. The aspects of their operations most likely to generate resentment—communications with workers and the linguistic image presented to society—were francized. The increased interchange between the corporations and the provincial administration was regulated to solidify the use of French in the public sector. This helped avoid placing undue bilingualism pressure on public servants and hence generating further legitimacy problems. One major cloud on the horizon—the restricted availability of a parallel English-language school system—has been pushed aside a little by the new Charter of Rights and Freedoms. In all instances of the language policy, the authorities took pains to insure that the operations essential to profit making were not interfered with.

In reviewing these various policies, it is important to note that in most cases, except for the language-of-work issue, the francophone bourgeoisie was close to the position of the dominant bourgeois fractions and not to that of the petty bourgeoisie. The frustration generated among members of the latter class often led to the entry of terms such as "traitor," "*vendus*," and the like into political discourse. The issues related to language helped foster a political unity among fractions of the bourgeoisie that belied the divisions usually found between the monopoly and competitive sectors, divisions not irrelevant to politics in Quebec in other areas. The explanation for this cohesion must lie in the fact that language was most significant for the legitimation of capitalism and less relevant to capital accumulation.

The interpretation of aspects of language policy as instruments for the cultivation of legitimacy merges well with some hypotheses by Claus Offe on the nature of the capitalist state.[74] Offe has postulated that an expansion of legitimation activity accompanies an expansion by the political system of its administration of capital accumulation. Further, the motives and justifications that accompany the legitimation activity will differ in content from the changes in activity in support of accumulation. Hence, the legitimation activity tends to draw attention away from or even to hide the character of the expansion of support for accumulation. In this chapter, it has been shown first that the implementation of a language policy paralleled an expansion by the provincial government of its programs and institutions supporting the private sector, particularly the leading industrial companies. Further, the language policy was developed in tandem with a radicalization of the labour movement and a hardening of the provincial authorities toward that movement. The various language policies were each presented as attempts to build a French Quebec, to reinforce francophones' control of their own daily lives. Hence, they countered what was in effect an increase in the dependency of the society on dominant corporations engineered in part by the state. They added to the acceptability of these corporations in Quebec society.

In the case of the education dispute, moreover, it appeared that the system bordered on a crisis, in that the prerequisites for developing diffuse support (language policy) were in contradiction with the conditions that needed to be maintained to sustain the production process. This crisis is not dissimilar to one described by Offe as characteristic of the capitalist state. He postulates that the nonidentity between the motives for legitimation (language policy) and those for economic expansion may provide the basis for a collision where satisfying legitimation demands is possible only by obstructing the state's capacity to provide the basis for capital accumulation and vice versa.

An additional point that may be drawn from this analysis relates to the definition of a social class. Poulantzas has written that classes are defined principally but not exclusively by their place in the production process. Przeworski has radicalized this position even further by arguing that class formation takes place entirely in the field of (mainly political) struggle.[75] The link with production is retained by saying that the struggle is determined by the totality of economic, political, and ideological relations. What is clear from the analysis above is that political struggle plays an obvious role in giving shape to—if not in forming—a class. The several struggles over language forced some articulation of positions by the various fractions of the bourgeoisie. Traditionally, the ethnic barrier had reinforced the divisions among the fractions of this class. The various interest associations had certainly followed separate paths. In the debates over language, it was immediately evident to those involved that there were interests in common and certainly opponents in common. Institutionally this recognition was reflected in the cooperation behind the establishment of the CPQ, in the unsuccessful yet surprising talks of merger between the Montreal Board of Trade and the CCDM, and in the collaboration in bodies such as the Canada Committee (and later the Positive Action Committee). On the other hand, the language debates helped forge an anti-capitalist coalition among the new and traditional bourgeoisie, the labour elite, and limited sectors of the working class. They helped give the working class a political shape by drawing them into political action. Finally, the debates were a significant factor in the political organization of the petty bourgeoisie, particularly in the energy they fostered that led to the formation of the PQ.

Notes

1. Jean-Louis Roy, *La Marche des Québécois: le temps des ruptures (1945-1960)* (Montreal: Leméac, 1976).
2. Léon Dion, *Quebec: The Unfinished Revolution,* Therese Rohmer (trans.) (Montreal: McGill-Queen's University Press, 1976), p. 130; Marcel Rioux, *Quebec in Question,* James Boake (trans.) (Toronto: James, Lewis and Samuel, 1971), p. 74.
3. Guy Rocher, *Le Québec en mutation* (Montréal: Hurtubise/HMH, 1973), pp. 13-32.
4. Neil Nevitte and François-Pierre Gingras, "The Religious Factor in Quebec Politics Reconsidered," Paper presented to the Annual Meeting of the Canadian Political Science Association (London, Ontario, 1978).
5. Dorval Brunelle, *La désillusion tranquille* (Montréal: Hurtubise/HMH, 1978); Pierre Fournier, series of articles on "la souveraineté-association" in *Le Devoir* (March 1979); William D. Coleman, *The Formation of the Indépendantiste Coalition in Quebec: 1945-1980* (Toronto: University of Toronto Press, forthcoming).
6. For a discussion of the COEQ, see Brunelle, op. cit., Ch. 2.
7. René Lévesque, *An Option for Quebec* (Toronto: McClelland and Stewart, 1968), p. 14.
8. Simply to speak here of a new petty bourgeoisie or even of the working class plunges one into the midst of a serious debate about how class is defined or determined. In this chapter, I will follow the road suggested by Poulantzas and see social classes as groupings defined principally *but not exclusively* by their place in the production process. Hence, Poulantzas adds that classes are defined in practice or in opposition. For him, there is no class in itself.

   The new petty bourgeoisie, then, refers to those who do not belong to the capitalist class because they neither own nor possess means of production. On the other hand, they do not engage in productive labour; rather, they perform services whose products and activities are consumed directly as use values. They help redistribute profits among components of the capitalist class. The case of civil servants and teachers, also members of this class, is more complex than service workers. The traditional petty-bourgeoisie class refers to independent commodity producers, owners of small establishments, and some members of liberal professions.

   See Nicos Poulantzas, *Classes in Contemporary Capitalism,* David Fernbach (trans.) (London: Verso, 1978).
9. David Easton, *A Systems Analysis of Political Life* (New York: Wiley, 1965), p. 273.
10. Jürgen Habermas, *Legitimation Crisis,* Thomas McCarthy (trans.) (Boston: Beacon Press, 1975), p. 46.
11. Niklas Luhmann, "Sociology of Political Systems," *German Political Studies* I (1974), pp. 3-29.

12. The Ligue des droits du français was founded in 1913. It became the Ligue d'Action française in 1917 and the Ligue d'Action nationale in the thirties.
13. For examples of such demands, see Jean-Marc Léger, "La langue française menacée au Québec," *L'Action nationale* XLV: 1 (1955), pp. 43-58. The Confédération des travailleurs catholiques du Canada (CTCC) at its 1954 convention called on cigarette manufacturers to provide bilingual packages. In 1951, the Pulp and Paper Federation of the CTCC produced a resolution for the francization of highway signs in the province. Significantly, the convention rejected the resolution, arguing that bilingual signs already existed. The Comité de refrancisation of the Société Saint-Jean-Baptiste de Québec made similar suggestions in a letter to tourist houses. See *Relations* 113 (1950).
14. See Roger Cyr, *La Patente* (Montreal: Editions du Jour, 1964), and the joint statement of the Société Saint-Jean-Baptiste de Montréal, the Conseil de la vie française, and the Fédération des Sociétés Saint-Jean-Baptiste du Québec, reported in *Le Bulletin de la SSJBM VI*: 5 (1957), p. 7.
15. See, for example, CCPQ, *Politiques d'Action 1963* (Montreal: CCPQ, 1963), p. 58. The Chambre suggested that this be done using financial incentives and not in a direct fashion, a position that often distinguishes francophone business groups from the nationalists.
16. The unpublished white paper was later published in Jean-Paul L'Allier, Ministre des Affaires culturelles, *Pour l'évolution de la politique culturelle: Document de travail* (Québec: Editeur officiel, 1976).
17. The position of the CVF is best elaborated in its brief to the Gendron Commission entitled *Un Québec français* (Quebec: Editions Ferland, 1969). For the SSJBQ, see the statement by its president, M. Emile Jacob, reported in *Québec Presse* (Oct. 19, 1969), p. 5.
18. The Commission was asked to recommend measures to guarantee (1) the linguistic rights of the majority as well as the protection of the rights of the minority and (2) the full expansion and diffusion of the French language in Quebec in all fields of activity. O.C. 3958 (Dec. 9, 1968), *Gazette officielle du Québec*.
19. O.C. 683, Food Regulations, ibid. (March 15, 1967). A regulation a year earlier was more in a bilingual vein. It read, "The aforesaid information shall appear without abbreviation, in French or in French and English, readily discernible letters . . ." O.C. 623, Regulation on Fresh Fruit and Vegetables (April 5, 1966), *ibid.*
20. O.C. 658, Regulations concerning standards of composition and the use of vitamins in dairy products, ibid. (Feb. 18, 1970).
21. Official Language Act, section 34, *Lois du Québec*, Ch. 6.
22. W.D. Coleman, "A Comparative Study of Language Policy in Quebec: A Political Economy Approach," in M.M. Atkinson and M.A. Chandler (eds.), *The Politics of Canadian Public Policy* (Toronto: University of Toronto Press, 1983), pp. 21-42.
23. The survey was conducted for the CNTU in 1965. The figures reported here were gleaned by the author from computer output held in the offices of the CNTU. The actual results have never been published.
24. The results of the survey are reported in the business publication *Les Affaires* (Montreal, March 29, 1971), pp. 13-14.

25. Figures to support this contention can be found in still another survey, this time by the Centre des dirigeants d'entreprise (CDE). A report on the survey is contained in the brief of the CDE to the Gendron Commission.
26. Commission of Inquiry on the Position of the French Language and on Language Rights in Quebec, *Report*, vol. I, (Quebec: Editeur officiel, 1972), p. 37.
27. Ibid., p. 44.
28. Ibid., p. 91.
29. Ibid.
30. Ibid., p. 77.
31. Questions arise, of course, on why the FTQ made the demand and why at this particular time. The FTQ had unionized more of the firms controlled by anglophones than had the CNTU. The reason for the time is less readily speculated on. One might hypothesize that some frustration was being voiced by the base over discrimination and the new political climate in 1960 helped facilitate its articulation.
32. Such a demand was made as early as 1963 by the FSSJBQ. For the CEQ and AQPF, see their respective briefs to the Gendron Commission.
33. The Commission had called for the creation of French Language Units at middle and upper levels of enterprises in Quebec. Scott argued against this proposal, stating that it meant acceptance of the notion that the majority language should be the official language of a given territory. He felt that it would lead to a unilingual Quebec. See Royal Commission on Bilingualism and Biculturalism, *Report*, Vol. III (Ottawa: Queen's Printer, 1969), pp. 525, 565-67.
34. The CPQ was first constituted in 1966 but only became active when a permanent secretariat was established in January 1969. It is essentially a federation of employers' associations. Its leadership is usually francophone, although its financial backing is from the anglophone establishment. For example, C-I-L, the Royal Bank, and Canada Cement Lafarge were among those involved with it in its formative stages. It has representatives on government bodies and has an annual meeting with the Premier and Minister of Finance over the budget. It later modified its structure to allow direct corporate membership. The two most important francophone employers' associations, the CCPQ and the CCDM, are not members.
35. The Council was created on February 26, 1969, and was made up of 60 senior level industrialists and financiers including the heads of the Bank of Montreal, the Royal Bank, Canadian Pacific, Power Corporation, Iron Ore of Canada, Texaco, Alcan, Steinberg's, Price Brothers, etc. See Pierre Fournier, *The Quebec Establishment* (Montreal: Black Rose Books, 1975), p. 167.
36. See, for example, CPQ, *Détruire le système actuel? C'est à y penser* (Montreal: Publication les Affaires, 1973).
37. This is evident in the briefs of the CDE and the CCDM to the Gendron Commission. See also the position of the CCPQ reported in *Faits et Tendances* (Oct. 1970), p. 11.
38. See Montreal Board of Trade, *Annual Report 1970-71*, p. 3; Canadian Manufacturers' Association (Quebec Division), *An Industrial Policy for Quebec: A Submission to Mr. Guy St-Pierre, Ministry of Industry and Commerce* (Montreal: CMA, 1972), Appendix F, p. 1. The position of Imperial Oil is

reported in *Le Soleil* (March 13, 1970) and that of Dominion Glass in *Le Devoir* (Dec. 11, 1969).

39. This is noted in Fournier, op. cit., p. 121.
40. The following references are all to the Official Language Act.
41. This argument is elaborated on in W.D. Coleman, "From Bill 22 to Bill 101: The Politics of Language under the Parti Québécois," *Canadian Journal of Political Science* 14 (1981).
42. Everett C. Hughes and Margaret L. McDonald, "French and English in the Economic Structure of Montreal," *Canadian Journal of Economics and Political Science* VIII: 4 (1941), pp. 493-505; Roger Vézina, "La Position des Canadiens-français dans l'industrie et le commerce," *Culture* XV: 3 (1954), pp. 291-99; André Raynauld, *La propriété des entreprises au Québec* (Montréal: Les Presses de l'Université de Montréal, 1974); Arnaud Sales, *La bourgeoisie industrielle au Québec* (Montréal: Les Presses de l'Université de Montréal, 1979).
43. For example, see the brief of the LAN to the Royal Commission of Inquiry on Constitutional Problems (Tremblay Commission).
44. CCDM, "Editorial," *Commerce Montreal* (June 26, 1956).
45. Parti Libéral du Québec, "Programme—1960," in Jean-Louis Roy, *Les programmes électoraux du Québec*, vol. II (Montreal: Leméac, 1971), p. 379.
46. Brief presented to the Royal Commission on Education (Parent Commission) (May 31, 1962), p. 20.
47. CPQ, op. cit., p. 46.
48. CCDM, Submission to the Parliamentary Commission on Bill 22 (June 1974), p. 11.
49. Ibid., p. 2.
50. CIQ, Brief to the Gendron Commission (July 1971), p. 2.
51. Gendron Commission, *Report*, Vol. I, p. 172.
52. Claus Offe, "The Theory of the Capitalist State and the Problem of Policy Formation," in Leon Lindberg et al. (eds.), *Stress and Contradiction in Modern Capitalism: Public Policy and the Theory of the State* (Lexington, Mass.: Lexington Books, 1975), pp. 129-33.
53. For a description of these programs, see Department of Industry and Commerce, *Annual Report, 1969-70* (Quebec: Editeur officiel, 1970).
54. This radicalization may be traced ideologically in the moral reports of Marcel Pepin given to successive conventions of the CNTU: *Une société bâtie pour l'homme* (1966), *Le Deuxième Front* (1968), *Un camp de la liberté* (1970); the culminating documents were *Ne comptons que sur nos propres moyens* (CNTU) and *L'Etat, "Rouage" de notre exploitation* (FTQ).
55. Claus Offe, "Class Rule and the Political System: On the Selectiveness of Political Institutions," *German Political Studies* I (1974), pp. 49-50.
56. Hubert Charbonneau, Jacques Henripin, and Jacques Legaré, "La situation démographique des francophones au Québec et à Montréal," *Le Devoir* (Nov. 4, 1969).
57. See Gary G. Caldwell, "Assimilation and the Demographic Future of Quebec," in John R. Mallea (ed.), *Quebec's Language Policies: Background and Response*, Publications of the International Centre for Research on Bilingualism (Quebec: Les Presses de l'Université Laval, 1977), p. 61.
58. Ibid.

59. Poulantzas, op. cit., pp. 289ff.
60. The nationalist ranks were less divided on this issue. Hence, the CVF subscribed to this position. At the Etats généraux du Canada français held in November 1967, of the 100 Quebec delegates who voted on this issue, 94 voted for a later start. See the report on the proceedings in *L'Action nationale* special issue (1968).
61. See for example the briefs of the CMA(Q) and the CCDM to the Gendron Commission.
62. CDE, Brief to the Gendron Commission, p. 16.
63. The FTQ felt that students would still learn English, but in the private system. Hence, the bulk of the working class would be further disadvantaged. See FTQ, *Resolutions*, 1969 Convention (Montreal: FTQ, 1970).
64. The intercessions came from the Canada Committee and the Conseil des fédérations ethniques to the Parliamentary Commission studying Bill 22. See their respective briefs.
65. The CNTU at first opposed this principle but then shifted during the course of the Bill 63 dispute.
66. See the submission of the CEQ to the Parliamentary Commission studying Bill 22, p. 9.
67. Leaders of the FQF included Angers, Raymond Lemieux (Ligue pour l'intégration scolaire), Gaston Miron, Lise Coupal (CNTU), André Lamy, Emile Bessette (AQPF), Vincent Harvey (*Maintenant*), and a representative of the CEQ.
68. The challenge came from a group of parents in Ste-Foy. Chief Justice Jules Deschênes of the Quebec Superior Court heard the case eventually and ruled against the parents. See *Le Devoir* (Dec. 30, 1975).
69. The exception to this statement was the CDE, which argued that nonanglophone immigrants entering Quebec after the Official Language Act was proclaimed should receive no financial support unless their children entered French schools. See their submission to the Parliamentary Commission studying Bill 22, p. 5.
70. As early as 1962, the SSJBM proposed that all English-language schools be converted into bilingual schools. The RIN in 1964, the FSSJBQ in 1966, and the SSJBM in 1967 changed the status from bilingual to French only. By 1974, these nationalist organizations had the support of the CEQ and AQPF as well.
71. See their respective submissions to the Parliamentary Commission studying Bill 22.
72. For elaboration upon the educational provisions of Bill 101, see Coleman, "From Bill 22," op. cit.
73. Poulantzas, op. cit., p. 289.
74. Offe, "Class Rule," op. cit., pp. 49-50.
75. Adam Przeworski, "Proletariat into a Class: The Process of Class Formation from Karl Kautsky's *The Class Struggle* to Recent Controversies," *Politics and Society* VII: 4 (1977), pp. 343-401.

Chapter 22/Quebec Educational Reform and the Protestant School Establishment

Henry Milner

Two events took place on June 20, 1983; a third, a week earlier. Together, they symbolize the temporary culmination of a major chapter in the 20-year effort to reform Quebec's public school system. The first was the Montreal Island school-board elections of June 13. At that election, the 104 members of the six Catholic and two Protestant boards that govern schools on the Island of Montreal were elected. The average turnout—in the contested seats—was 16%.

On June 20, the Parti Québécois lost three byelections, all seats that it had won in 1981 when it was returned to power. While the party was used to losing byelections, the losses testified to the weak position of the government, a direct consequence of the economic crisis and the battles with its unionized employees in the previous ten months.

That same day, education minister Camille Laurin tabled Bill 40, his much-modified plan to reform the Quebec school structure. The new bill, while faithful to the goals of the white paper of the previous June, so diluted many of the basic measures outlined in it that it would appear to have become another victim of the government's political weakness at the time. Yet, in light of the 20-year history of aborted reforms, the bill—which has yet to be passed—may be characterized as a victory of sorts over the powerful coalition of conservative forces (propped up by section 93 of the BNA Act) that defend the status quo in Quebec education. The most powerful group in this coalition is the anglophone educational establishment.

The Quebec Education System before 1960

The Acts of 1841, 1845, and 1846 shaped the basic legislative contours of Quebec's unique system of education. These laws constituted a working compromise between the clergy who wanted Church-controlled schools and those who sought common public schools.[1] For Montreal and Quebec, there would be two kinds of schools, both officially "common" or public, one run by a Catholic and the other by a Protestant council, composed of six members named by the municipal authorities. Elsewhere there was to be only one set of common schools run by elected school boards, but in each township the minority denomination (usually the Protestants) could set up separate "dissentient" schools for their children. In addition, a certain level of supervision was to be provided by a superintendent of instruction who reported to the government.

The 30 years following 1867 consolidated the victory of the highly conservative ultramontane Catholicism in Quebec. And nowhere were the consequences of this victory as evident and significant as in education.

Ironically, it was (and, as we shall see, still is) the English-speaking Protestants who had always favoured common public schools along American lines, who helped consolidate the Church's position in Quebec education. The leading Protestant politician, Alexander Galt of Sherbrooke, maintained that the only way to keep the schools of his community free of French-Catholic influence was to have separate systems for each denomination outside the control of the Quebec government. As one of Canada's delegates to London, Galt succeeded at enshrining the confessional nature of the schools and school system in section 93 of the BNA Act.

Subsection 1 of Section 93 denied the provinces the right to make laws that "prejudicially affect any Right or Privilege with respect to denominational schools," and subsection 3 gave the Protestant and Roman Catholic minorities the right to appeal any possible infringements of these rights to the "Governor General in Council," the federal government.

In 1869, the structure of the Council of Public Instruction that had been set up in the 1850s was altered. The Council was now divided into two separate entities, one Catholic with 14 members and one Protestant with seven. Members of the clergy were to sit ex-officio on each.

It was the law of 1875 abolishing the Ministry of Public Instruction that definitively established the principle of clerical domination. The Council stopped meeting as one body. Instead, its work was done by the Catholic and Protestant committees that had been formed. The superintendant of education now reported to them. The bishops were given half the seats on the Catholic Committee of the Council of Public Education. In effect, they had a working majority at meetings, since only they could name substitutes in cases of absence.

One indication of this triumph of Church over state in education may be found in the following figures. The proportion of Quebec government expenditures on education and culture was actually declining, and quite considerably—from 23.5% in 1867-68 to under 10% by 1875-76—and remained that low for many years.[2] While in 1910-11 6.4% of Quebec civil servants were employed in education, that percentage dropped to 1.9% in 1930-31.[3]

By the turn of the century the level of Church control went far beyond the guarantees enshrined in the constitution, even if some schools were officially "common," since their curriculum was prepared and their teachers certified by—and only by—the Catholic or Protestant Committee. In addition, most private education was provided in ecclesiastical institutions such as the *collèges classiques* and Laval University.

The history of Protestant education in Quebec followed quite a different course. Even at the outset, and more so as the system evolved, Protestant schools were denominational in structure rather than in content.[4] There being no single Protestant denomination analogous to the Roman Catholics, the Protestant view of religion in the schools tended to be pluralistic and nondoctrinaire. Religious teaching was generally confined to the universal human values associated with Christian morality and to fostering the exploration of different religious beliefs. Furthermore, the Protestant system was blessed with greater resources. Due to the greater tax base at its disposal and smaller average family size, between one and one-half and two times as much was spent on each Protestant as compared to Catholic student in Montreal.[5]

Another source of innovation in the Protestant system was the increasing diversity of the student body. Beginning with the Jews, non-Catholic (and even some nominally Catholic) immigrant groups found their way into the Protestant rather than Catholic system, though both were legally common.

The francophone Catholics were quite content to let the non-Catholics find their way into the Protestant system. The logic was the same as what fostered the creation of an autonomous English-Catholic sector to serve not only the Irish but, later, a good many children of other Catholic nonfrancophone origins who might otherwise have attended French schools. This attitude was closely tied to the ultramontane views espoused by the elites of the early 20th century. The French-Canadian nation's survival, its essence, lay in its language and religion and the institutions that maintained them. What mattered, thus, was the strength and security of its families, schools, and parishes. A vital mainstay of the world it sought was the local French-Catholic school, to be kept as free as possible of any and all outside influences.

Attempts at Reforming the Education System

Paul Gérin-Lajoie, Minister of Youth when the Liberals took office under Jean Lesage in 1960, initiated a series of reforms that came to be called the "Magna Carta" of Quebec education. The emphasis of the early legislation was on secondary education: resources were made available to improve teacher training and upgrade instructional materials; school districts were consolidated. Gérin-Lajoie's efforts culminated in 1964 when he was appointed Quebec's first Minister of Education since 1875.

In May 1961, Gérin-Lajoie appointed the Royal Commission of Inquiry on Education in the Province of Quebec under Monsignor Alphonse-Marie Parent, Vice-Rector of Laval University. Two years later, the first volume of its report came out. Its starting point was the democratic principle that everyone be guaranteed an education consistent with his or her interests and needs. The main recommendations of the Parent Report's first volume dealt with the overall structure of the educational system. When, soon afterwards, they were presented to the legislature as Bill 60, a major year-long public debate ensued, in which every important segment of Quebec society participated.

Though modified to suit the bishops, it was nonetheless a largely intact Bill 60 that became the law of the land. As of May 1964, the Council of Public Instruction was replaced by a 24-member advisory body, the Conseil supérieur de l'éducation (CSE). The Catholic and Protestant Committees were to oversee religious and moral instruction and religious services in all schools and, from the standpoint of the denomination's religious values, to approve curricula and texts for all confessional schools.

Even as the Bill 60 debate continued, the Parent Commission continued its deliberations; in 1964, it made public the second and third volumes of its report. The report reviewed and revamped every level of education: kindergarten-level instruction was to be extended throughout Quebec, general curriculum standards were to be established for primary and secondary schools, a network of postsecondary general and vocational community colleges (later known as CEGEPs) was proposed, and teacher training was to be taken over by the universities. In 1965, Regulation 1 was issued, the first and most significant of several orders-in-council that translated into practice many of the detailed proposals.

The final two volumes of the Parent Commission Report were a bombshell dropped on the new Johnson government in 1966. The commissioners had addressed the confessional nature of the school boards. The Commission's position was straightforward. While it wished to maintain Catholic and Protestant schools, as well as establish neutral ones where required, its view was that religious status, like language, should be determined by the parents and the school community. It was contradictory for the school boards, whose mandate was to administer pedagogical services, to be confessional in nature: all that was needed to meet the schools' requirements for religious instruction and services was available through the confessional committees of the CSE.

The controversy centred on two of the commission's proposals. Recommendation 55 called for unified school commissions to serve all schools, Catholic, Protestant, and neutral, French and English, in a given territory. Recommendation 56 proposed seven unified commissions to replace the existing 24 Catholic and 15 Protestant boards on the Island of Montreal.

The commissioners cited the nondenominational pluralist nature of the Protestant system as a model for the development they sought.[6] Ironically, the (English) Protestants most objected to the proposals. Their representatives on the CSE and its confessional committees, to whom the new government had first turned for guidance, dissented from the majority's generally favourable response.

Further delay was gained through the creation of the Council for School Reorganization on the Island of Montreal, mandated to investigate the controversial plan for Montreal. In its final form, the council had 18 members, appointed by the school commissions, teachers' unions, and parents' associations. It was carefully balanced along religious and linguistic lines and was chaired by Montreal school commissioner Joseph Pagé.

The highly representative nature of the council virtually assured that it would be unable to reach consensus. The chairperson in the end abandoned the mixed linguistic-confessional model he had initially advanced in favour of unified boards. In this, he was supported by the English-speaking Catholic members. The largest number preferred a linguistic scheme of nine French and four English boards. But the Protestants demurred. They wanted a constitutionally embedded confessional structure, not merely a legislated linguistic one. Thus, unable to provide any clear-cut guidelines, the council's final report was effectively politically irrelevant by the time it was submitted in October 1968.

The Pagé report was overshadowed by the St-Léonard School crisis.[7] The battle over the language of education that was to become the main educational issue of the next decade first broke out in this northeastern Montreal suburb late in 1968. The local Catholic school board sought to phase out English elementary schools, against the wishes of the primarily italophone population served by them. The board was supported by the resurging nationalist movement.

Jean-Jacques Bertrand, who became Premier after Daniel Johnson's death in 1968, responded with a package deal designed by education minister Jean-Guy Cardinal: Bill 63 was to guarantee access for all to English-language schooling, while Bill 62 was to placate the nationalists by replacing the existing boards with eleven unified school boards on the Island of Montreal, as Pagé had recommended.

The legislative outcome of these two bills is highly instructive. A moderate nationalist government, with no electoral support to speak of from the English community, weathered intensive opposition and unprecedented public protest from the francophone community to see Bill 63 adopted.[8] However, Bill 62 was referred to the Education Committee of the National Assembly for further study.

Hearings on Bill 62 began only in early 1970. The majority of presentations were from anglophone groups. All were hostile. But anglophone opposition was not limited to these activities. Almost alone in English-speaking Quebec, the *Montreal Star* supported the bill and denounced as "insidious" and "unbecoming" certain statements made by leading anglophone opponents from the Protestant school boards and the Board of Trade. It singled out McGill's principal, H.R. Robertson, who had protested that passage of the bill would lead to the eventual "disappearance" of the English culture, and its Vice-Principal, Stanley Frost, who had claimed that the bill would "do away with all English-language schools."[9] To the usual cultural defence of the existing educational system, the Montreal Board of Trade added an economic argument that was to be heard again and again in the various rounds of the linguistic and national debate. Bill 62 was harmful, it warned, because it would discourage investment by English companies and thus damage the economy.[10]

There was evidently a general feeling of relief in the English-speaking community when Bill 62 died on the order paper as Premier Bertrand called an early election for June 1970. On the other hand, the outcome was a disappointment to most francophone opinion leaders, including the majority of editorialists and school commissioners. The confessional system, however, was not without its staunch defenders among francophones, notably in the Association des parents catholiques (APCQ) and its ally, the new Archbishop of Montreal, Paul Grégoire.

Yet the APCQ's apprehensions failed to strike a responsive chord among francophones. At this point there existed a consensus among opinion leaders and politicians of all stripes that the Parent Commission had resolved the religious question. But it was not secularization that worried the English-speaking Protestant leadership; what they feared was unification and the consequent sharing of authority and resources.

In 1970, anglophones voted massively for the victorious Liberals under Robert Bourassa. The new education minister, Guy St-Pierre, chose to move slowly and carefully. A man with close connections in the business community, he was keen to win English support for reform. It took more than a year for legislation affecting Montreal school-board structures to find its way back to the Assembly. In fact, as it has since been discovered, Protestant School Board of Greater Montreal (PSBGM) leaders were given copies of Bill 28 in advance of its presentation to the Assembly, a courtesy not extended to Montreal Catholic School Commission (CECM) members.[11]

When finally presented, Bill 28 was coupled with Bill 27, which replaced existing school boards outside Montreal with some 200 boards divided into two separate networks: one for Catholics, the other for Protestants. Bill 28 retained the eleven unified boards for Montreal.

Led by the PSBGM, the opposition campaign was again mounted by the same groups and individuals. This time, recourse to a constitutional challenge—if the legislative battle were lost—was invoked. Testimony at another series of hearings before the Education Committee revealed that anglophone Protestants were the only sector of the population who opposed the reform principle as such.

Bill 28 was lost in the increasing social polarization over language. Articulating the general fear that Bill 63 served to guarantee that all newcomers to Quebec would adopt English, Claude Charron of the PQ moved an amendment to Bill 28 that would in effect abolish Bill 63. He mounted a filibuster, supported notably by *Le Devoir*'s Claude Ryan. Caught in the middle, St-Pierre retreated and withdrew the bill.

In July 1972, the new education minister, François Cloutier, officially announced the demise of Bill 28. Instead, Montreal's 33 school commissions were replaced by 8 elected boards, 6 for Catholics and 2 for Protestants. Cloutier's solution to the confessionality problem was to relegate it to the newly created representative Island School Council. It was only at the end of 1974 that the Council's School Board Reorganization Committee began its deliberations.

The only group entirely dissatisfied with Bill 71 was the English-speaking Catholics, who saw their position effectively weakened under the system since they had no guaranteed representation on any of the boards. The Protestant leaders and the APCQ had what they wanted: separate confessional structures throughout Quebec.

As might have been expected, the Island Council did not alter the situation. The lengthy deliberations of its subcommittee on school-board reorganization—which resulted in the postponement for a year of the second round of elections for the eight school boards—ended inconclusively. The councillors' work thus served to perpetuate the status quo under Bill 71.

And so the matter ended. The newly elected Parti Québécois government, although programmatically favouring deconfessionalized structures, was not in much of a hurry to rock this particular boat at that point. It was already embarked on the Bill 101 battle, in which eligibility to English schooling was the most controversial element.

Just as the Pagé report was lost in the clamour over St-Léonard which led, ultimately, to Bill 63, so the work of the Island Council's School Board Reorganization Committee was caught in the throes of the next two rounds of the language battle, first over the Liberal's ill-fated Bill 22, then over Bill 101. Confessionality became increasingly linked to the emotionally explosive issue of language.

The Fear of Assimilation

The significantly declining birth rate presented a serious danger to the francophone position. So did the fact that the latest wave of immigrants, it was apparent, was selecting English rather than French schools for its children in even larger proportions than before. And figures from the federally appointed Royal Commission on Bilingualism and Biculturalism (RCBB) revealed in graphic detail what had long been perceived. Francophones (in 1961) earned on average only 60% as much as anglophones in Quebec; as a group, unilingual anglophones were the best paid, better even than bilingual anglophones.[12] No wonder so many parents—even some francophones—chose to send their children to English schools.

Post-Quiet Revolution Quebeckers looked to the state to attend to their collective interests. The federal government had missed its chance. It had oriented the recommendations of the RCBB, which had well diagnosed important aspects of the problem, away from territorially based language policies under which Quebec would be French as other provinces are English. Redress had to come from Quebec and the French-speaking population was getting impatient.

The impatience had been revealed in the unprecedented public protest that greeted Bill 63 in 1969. While the issue was temporarily shelved during the early 1970s in anticipation of the Gendron Commission's report, it was far from resolved.

When it finally did come out in 1973 after several delays, the Gendron Commission's report provided no real guidance to the government. Its figures, as expected, were devastating. It demonstrated that, when the two cultures came into contact in the workplace, the burden of bilingualism in Quebec fell almost entirely on the French-speaking majority. Bill 22 was adopted in 1974. The fundamental issue it raised for nonfrancophones concerned its educational provisions: only anglophone children would be allowed access to English schools. And to determine such eligibility in situations of doubt, the law provided for special language tests for children entering school.

The image of tense five year olds being subjected to an examination, the outcome of which they believed could determine their future, destroyed whatever possible credibility Bill 22 had. It was viciously attacked by both sides.[13] On the English side, the opposition was of unprecedented vigour, with petitions, radio campaigns, and demonstrations. English-speaking members of the government were bitterly denounced as collaborators.[14] The concordat had been broken by the Quebec Liberal party, the party that nonfrancophones had loyally supported for decades.

The Bill 22 crisis finished off a government already beset with scandal and dissension.[15] In the subsequent election, a sufficient number of nonfrancophone voters bolted—voting for the temporarily resuscitated Union Nationale—with the result that the Parti Québécois was able to register an unexpectedly crushing victory. The result was even more abhorrent to the English-speaking minority: the election of a "separatist" government. Yet, at least at the outset, the reaction to the new government's tougher language law, Bill 101, was less emotional. This was due to the fact that Bill 101 was clearer than Bill 22 and replaced the testing of children by parental language of schooling as the criterion for determining a child's eligibility to attend English schools.

The principle underlying Bill 101, the Charter of the French language, was straightforward. English schooling was guaranteed and limited to children and descendants and those who constituted the English-speaking Quebec community up to the time the law went into effect. All children permanently residing in Quebec were required to attend public or publicly supported French elementary and secondary schools with the following exceptions, who were eligible for English schooling: children residing in Quebec on August 26th, 1977, one of whose parents had received his or her primary education in English; children, one of whose parents had received primary education in English in Quebec; and children having an older sibling already in an English school in Quebec. These provisions were modified by section 23 of the Constitution of 1982 which, in effect, replaced Quebec by Canada in the second and third of these clauses.

It was only a matter of a few years before the changed formal and informal position of the two linguistic communities came to be reflected in enrolment and population trends and figures. In 1975-76, the proportion of students being educated in English in primary and secondary public schools reached its peak, attaining 16.8%. By the end of the decade, it had declined to 14.8%.[16] Still, 14.8 was well above the 10.9% of Quebeckers whom the 1981 census revealed to be of English mother tongue.

Education Reforms

While the great controversy raged over which students (distinguished by language) could go to which kind of school (also distinguished by language), the educational system remained structured along confessional and not linguistic lines. Obviously, something did not fit. In a secular society, a confessionally based educational system struck a discordant note. The impact of the new law on language of education added an immediate and conspicuous disconcerting element. The inappropriateness of the whole system was not lost on the many families personally caught up in it. These families were concentrated in the Montreal area, where the nonfrancophone population is largest and where the decline in Catholic religious conviction among francophones is most pronounced.

Typically, the family sends its children to a French school as required by law or voluntarily. The home is not a Catholic one. The local French public school is Catholic and operated by a Catholic board. The child is educated in an environment that, at least to some extent, reflects an alien religious doctrine.

In many parts of the Montreal area, one other option exists. The child can be sent to a French Protestant school, though in most cases this requires busing well outside his or her neighbourhood. The distances involved and the resulting separation from neighbourhood friends are not the only problems raised by this option. Such de facto neutral schools resolve the religion problem but create another: namely that of integration. For, while the language of instruction is French, the most common language of the children is English. Indeed, many of these French schools are merely a series of French classes within English schools. It is hardly consistent with the principles underlying the French Language Charter to give over the integration of nonfrancophones to Protestant school boards run by anglophones for anglophones.

Yet solutions exist. While the language laws made the problem of marginalization in the confessional system more acute, it also removed a politically explosive element from the issue of appropriate school-board structures. In the 1960s, placing anglophone schools under unified school boards was seen as a method of limiting the power of the minority to integrate the neo-Québécois. Bill 101 had taken care of that problem. The Parent Commission had proposed a system of neutral schools for the children of nonpractising francophone Catholics, thereby also serving the purposes of non-Catholic nonfrancophones' sending their children to French schools.

The establishment of such a third system was conceivable when Quebec was building schools for the baby-boom generation. But shrinking enrolments have ruled out this possibility.

Though the linguistic dimension of education preoccupied government in the 1970s, the confessional issue did not disappear. The battleground shifted from the legislature to the local communities most affected, grand reform schemes gave way to conflicts over specific schools, and the election campaigns of the commissioners who administer them. The most famous was Notre-Dame-des-Neiges elementary school in Montreal.

A typical Catholic school until the 1970s, the parents at NDN decided that the future of their school lay in reflecting the changed reality of their community, now characterized by a varied population including many immigrant groups and University of Montreal professors. NDN's open policies vis-à-vis religious instruction conflicted with the school's confessional status. The parents' committee thus sought to gain legal sanction for their pluralist neighbourhood school. Religious instruction for their children would be assured, while children of parents with differing religious inclinations could also feel at home in the school. Teachers and administrators readily gave their consent. Parents were polled: 80% endorsed the pluralist concept.

A few months later, the Catholic Committee of the CSE granted NDN its pluralist status. But, on April 17, 1980, Superior Court Judge Jules Deschesnes held that, since the CECM was the direct descendant of the Catholic board of the City of Montreal as it existed prior to 1867, its privileges at that time were guaranteed by section 93 of the BNA Act and could not be diminished. Since it administered only Catholic elementary schools in 1867, it could not be obliged today to administer other schools: Notre-Dame-des-Neiges could not be pluralist and still be Notre-Dame-des-Neiges. The Deschesnes ruling left the Quebec authorities in a rather sticky situation. If Deschesnes's interpretation stood, reform within existing structures would be difficult indeed.

And so the matter stood when, in 1981, the newly reelected Parti Québécois government first leaked its intentions to reform the school structures, a reform that envisaged "two, three, many . . ." NDNs.

Near the end of the first mandate, René Lévesque appointed Camille Laurin, the determined and controversial father of Law 101, Minister of Education, thus serving notice that change was in the offing. Laurin's plan, published in June 1982 as a white paper entitled *The Quebec School: A Responsible Force in the Community*, aimed at replacing a public-education system based on confessional school boards to one based on parent-teacher-run school councils. Laurin's white paper presented a lucid diagnosis of the deficiencies in Quebec's system of elementary and secondary education and a systematic program for its reorganization. According to the white paper, the fundamental failing of the school system was its basis on structures not reflecting Quebec reality. These structures discourage rather than encourage parent and teacher participation in education.

At the centre of the envisaged new structures was the school: not only a dispenser of learning, but also a vital building block of the neighbourhood or village. The school was to become a corporate entity under the authority of a council composed of elected parent representatives, as well as delegates from the teaching and nonteaching staff, representatives of the community, and senior students in the secondary schools.

Each school council was to name a representative to the school commission for its region. These commissioners were to be joined by others chosen by the municipalities. The mandate of these commissions would be to serve the schools, not to run them. The commissioners from the English-language schools in the approximately 100 regions would form subcommissions to coordinate English-language instruction. On the Island of Montreal, where 60% of the anglophones reside, the linguistic structures were to be parallel and entirely autonomous.

The school council's first duty was to elaborate the school's education program. Within the framework of Quebec-wide standards, the project would spell out the objectives to guide the school's curricular and extracurricular activities. On the basis of its education program, the school council would select the principal from qualified applicants, deploy its staff (respecting seniority and other guarantees in the provincially negotiated collective agreement), and recruit students. Operating within an envelope set according to province-wide norms, the schools would administer their own budget with the aid of the administrative apparatus of the new commissions.

Unlike previous reform plans, this one went further in not only restructuring the boards along nonconfessional lines, but also in altering the power relationships between school and school board. Hence, it threatened the interests of powerful groups—most important among which were the school boards and their administrative apparatus. Yet there were elements of compromise as well. To gain the support of the bishops, Laurin agreed to allow individual schools—the majority of whose parents so desired—the right to a confessional status as long as its exercise did not violate the Quebec Charter of Rights. And he compromised on linguistic boards, agreeing to them for Montreal and leaving the door open to extending the principle elsewhere in Quebec. Still, the most ferocious opponents of the reform were the English Protestant organizations, true to their longstanding traditions.

The real political weight in the anti-reform coalition of traditionalist Catholics and the English-Protestant education establishment lies with the latter. Centred on the Montreal business community, anglophone elites in Quebec have usually spoken with one voice. In education, that voice has generally been that of the Protestant School Board of Greater Montreal (PSBGM) at the centre of a network linking the Quebec Association of Protestant School Boards, the Quebec Home and School Association, the

Association of Protestant School Administrators, and, usually, the Provincial Association of Protestant Teachers.

The fundamental aims of the PSBGM and its network of allies have changed very little. In all its interventions, its primary and often exclusive concern has been to protect its own autonomous system of English education. From this perspective, every general change in Quebec education has eroded that autonomy. Hence, the Protestant educational leaders opposed each major educational reform since the Quiet Revolution—including Bill 63. This bill, which in effect extended the right to English schooling to English Catholics, was vociferously opposed by the PSBGM as an infringement of its autonomy, since it required all English schools to have their students attain some competence in French.[17]

Like its traditionalist Catholic allies, the English-Protestant bloc has mobilized its supporters and waged media campaigns. But such tactics were often unnecessary since, under the Liberals and the UN, it was able to take advantage of the direct access to political decision makers provided by its business connections. The same was true of court action. With the coming to power of the Parti Québécois in 1976, and their resultant isolation from political power, the Protestant boards launched constitutional appeals as a matter of course.

The various bills and regulations affecting language of education provoked constitutional challenges. The first was a vain effort to petition the federal government to disallow Bill 63.[18] In 1969, the PSBGM's lawyers had concluded that a case existed for interpreting the denominational protections in section 93 as applying to language. The board's subsequent public position and strategy were based on the presumption that all provincial legislation limiting access to English education was illegal. As expected, when the test came with Bill 22, the PSBGM's argument was flatly rejected by both the courts and the federal government.[19]

In the face of this setback, the Protestant bloc's constitutional strategy was revised. The PSBGM has sought to weaken the powers of the province over education and to take every possible advantage of the confessional guarantees in the constitution. Hence, they have been unwilling even to consider a compromise based on linguistic structures in their response to the Laurin plan. Moreover, as part of this new overall strategy, the Protestant boards have moved to test the constitutionality of various directives from the Quebec government. In January 1983, the PSBGM and three other boards announced a Superior Court challenge to the adoption of the new curricular "régime pédagogique" being implemented throughout the school system. Fighting this long-awaited product of years of work by teachers and specialists in every discipline of study was the outcome of a philosophy in which autonomy was the overriding concern.[20]

The anglophone leaders' decision to defend the confessional structure to insure their control over the English "Protestant" schools has isolated the

English Catholics, who have no such protections. And it has also angered many francophone observers, especially opponents of confessionality. The latter find it unacceptable for a neutral anglophone system to use its constitutional rights to, in effect, impose confessional Catholic structures on francophones.

In fighting the Laurin plan, the Protestant establishment was by no means alone. The reform directly threatened the interests of all the school boards. A well-coordinated opposition was mounted in fall 1982 by the Catholic and Protestant board federations and supported by the Liberal party. Still, on the francophone side, opposition was by no means universal, since the associations representing parents and school principals tended to be favourable, and a year-long dialogue on the reform ensued.

On the English side, there was very little disposition to debate the issue. Public unanimity had been achieved against Bill 101; that sentiment extended to the reform even before it was presented. The task for the boards was to mobilize rather than to persuade. This was the primary purpose of the public meetings organized by the Protestant boards and the letters addressed to parents through their children, like that signed by PSBGM Chairman Allan Butler, dated September 10, inviting them to attend gatherings concerning the "threat to democracy, the development of good schools, and the survival of English-language education."

Dr. Laurin's courageous forays into English-language territory during his fall tour to promote his plan—braving bomb threats on at least one occasion, in south-shore Laprairie on November 22—served mainly as occasions for the venting of resentment. The large and noisy demonstrations organized by anglophone groups outside the first public meeting on Laurin's tour in Laval on September 16 set the tone, a tone reproduced on his visit to the Quebec Home and School Association in Pointe Claire a month later. Outside, hundreds of angry anglophones jeered as he entered with the aid of a police escort and cheered spokespersons, including Liberal MNA and former PSBGM chairperson Joan Dougherty, as they denounced the plan.[21] Inside, after listening politely to his careful presentation, the delegates went up to the microphones to tell him that his "totalitarian" reform was an attack on their rights that they would not tolerate. Before them were documents prepared by their leaders in association with the Protestant boards outlining a strategy to fight the plan which, after Laurin's departure, was discussed and adopted.

The events between June 1982 and early spring 1983 made it clear that the opposition to the reform would have to be taken into account. Even under more propitious circumstances, backtracking on the reform would have been in order: in its actual form, the white paper simply would not stand. The government's weakness after its confrontation with the teachers and other unionized employees made it imperative.

Bill 40 includes three main changes from the white paper, each incorporating a major opposition criticism. The first amendment is the abandonment of corporate status for the school, though the school would exist as an institution with the powers and responsibilities of its council defined by law. This change signifies that the schools will still be subject to a certain level of control from the boards and that the relationship would vary significantly from school to school and board to board, depending on the circumstances. The second amendment is the reintroduction of direct universal suffrage. All electors identifying with a particular school would elect the member of their school board from their community. The final amendment provided for the creation of linguistic commissions throughout Quebec.

These three amendments brought the reform into general accord with a proposal that had been made a year earlier. A coalition of the English-Protestant and English-Catholic teachers (PAPT and PACT), the Associations representing Protestant and Catholic school administrators (QASA and QACSA), and school principals (ADGPSBQ and ADES), and the McGill Faculty of Education advocated a linguistically oriented plan, this time calling for nine English school boards, three of which would be on the Island of Montreal.

For the first time, the English-speaking leadership was divided. Not only the English-Catholic but also the English-Protestant educators sought to replace confessional structures with linguistic ones. The Protestant boards, however, would not hear of it and they were supported by the Protestant Committee of the CSE.

As PSBGM Chairperson Butler put it in his letter, linguistic structures were "a cleverly devised trap [to give up] our constitutional right to keep control of our education system." For John Simms, QAPSB president, there was no question of compromise; the plan had to be withdrawn: "we are not about to arrange the deck chairs on the Titanic."[22] And the Protestant Committee of the CSE questioned the desirability of uniting English-Protestant and English-Catholic children in the same school-board system, ruling out any reform that did not leave the Protestant school system in place. The proposal was a threat to the very existence of Protestant schools, it asserted, in that these would be slowly taken over by Catholic pupils. The committee felt no reassurance in the creation of a system of linguistic boards, given that the minister behind the plan was the author of Bill 101.[23] But was language or religion at issue? As *Le Devoir*'s Jean-Pierre Proulx noted, "It was hardly possible at yesterday's press conference to get any precise answers to the question of the nature of 'the Protestant identity.' But it was clear that . . . Quebec Protestanism could accommodate Judaism and Greek Orthodoxy but feels threatened by Catholicism."[24]

For those who saw in the white paper an exciting development toward a more decentralized and participatory society, the compromises in Bill 40 constitute an unfortunate setback. But for most who take the long view and look at it as a modest but still necessary and long-awaited restructuring, its adoption will hardly be without significance. For one thing, after suitable last-minute adjustments, the white paper should achieve the necessary consensus to isolate the Protestant establishment—which is preparing to fight it in court based on BNA section 93—from just about everyone else.

Notes

1. See Jacques Monet, *The Last Cannon Shot: A Study of French-Canadian Nationalism 1837-1850* (Toronto: University of Toronto Press, 1969), pp. 242-43. Useful information on the Church's attitudes during this formative stage of Quebec education may also be found in Bernard Lefebvre, *L'école sous la mitre* (Sherbrooke: Editions Paulines, 1980). For a definitive early history of Quebec education, see Louis-Philippe Audet, *Le système scolaire de la Province de Québec* (Québec: Presses universitaires Laval, 1956).
2. James Ian Gow, "L'administration québécoise de 1867 à 1900: un état en formation," *Canadian Journal of Political Science* (Sept. 1979), p. 559.
3. James Ian Gow, "Situation, organisation et fonctionnement de l'administration québécoise, 1897-1936" (unpublished manuscript, Département des sciences politiques, Université de Montréal, 1982), p. 44.
4. A fine study of Protestant education in Quebec was completed by Nathan H. Mair, *Quest for Quality in the Protestant Public Schools of Quebec* (Quebec: Gouvernement du Québec, Conseil supérieur de l'éducation, Comité protestant, 1980).
5. Roger Magnusen, *A History of Quebec Education: 1640 to Parti Québécois* (Montreal: Harvest House, 1980), p. 79.
6. *Rapport de la Commission royale d'enquête sur l'enseignement dans la province de Québec* (Parent Commission), vol. 4, (Montréal: Editeur Officiel, 1966), p. 196.
7. See Paul Cappon, *Conflit entre les néo-Canadiens et les francophones de Montréal* (Québec: Presses universitaires Laval, 1974), for insight into the tensions underlying this conflict.
8. For a description of the polarization over language during this period, see H. Milner and S. Hodgins Milner, *The Decolonization of Quebec* (Toronto: McClelland and Stewart, 1973), pp. 195-99.
9. See Pierre Fournier, "A Political Analysis of School Reorganization in Montreal" (M.A. thesis, McGill University, 1971), pp. 95, 100.
10. Quoted in ibid., p. 97.
11. Ibid., pp. 106-07.
12. See Milner and Hodgins Milner, op. cit., pp. 55-65.
13. See W.D. Coleman, "The Class Bases of Language Policy in Quebec, 1949-1983" (Chapter 21 in this book), for, on the whole, a useful description of the origins and content of and reaction to Bill 22.
14. The situation is described by William Tetley, a member of the Bourassa cabinet, in G. Caldwell and E. Waddell (eds.), *The English of Quebec: From Majority to Minority Status* (Quebec: Institut québécois de recherche sur la culture, 1982).
15. See H. Milner, *Politics in the New Quebec* (Toronto: McClelland and Stewart, 1978), pp. 137-50.
16. Based on figures compiled in Claude St-Germain, *La situation linguistique dans les commissions scolaires du Québec de 1976-77 à 1979-80* (Québec: Conseil de la langue française, 1981), p. 7.

17. See William Tetley, "The English and Language Legislation: A Personal History," in C. Caldwell and E. Waddell (eds.), op. cit.
18. See Ibid.
19. Ibid.
20. See Angèle Dagenais, "Les anglophones: la communauté réclame le droit au développement pédagogique," as well as others in the series of articles on the new "Régime pédagogique," *Le Devoir* (Jan. 20, 1983).
21. Paul Delean, "Laurin ignores noisy protest at school," *The Gazette* (Oct. 18, 1982).
22. "Meeting slams Laurin school reform package," *Sunday Express* (Nov. 21, 1982).
23. Jean-Pierre Proulx, "Le comité protestant repousse avec vigueur le nouveau projet Laurin," *Le Devoir* (April 19, 1983).
24. Ibid.

Chapter 23/The Political Economy of Quebec: A Selective Annotated Bibliography*

Jean-Guy Vaillancourt

The following bibliography has been compiled in order to furnish up-to-date information to English Canadians concerning books recently published in French by Québécois authors on the political economy of Quebec. Only books or book-length publications that have appeared between 1979 and 1982 have been included. The books are categorized under eight general topics and are presented in each of the eight categories, in alphabetical order of names of authors for each of these four years of publication. There is an intentional bias in the bibliography in favour of authors and books that are both progressive and scholarly, although one might possibly find some exceptions to that rule. Most references are annotated in order to give the reader some idea of the content of the book.

In the last few years, there has been a tremendous outpouring of high-quality books concerning Quebec, many of which do not get much publicity. I have chosen not to include any books published before 1979, nor any English translations of books by Québécois authors, because the bibliography is already quite long and because such books are easier to find in English Canada than the more recent, original works listed here.

I hope that the list will be useful for teachers, scholars, and activists who are interested in what is going on in Quebec.

1. Socioeconomic and Political History of Quebec

Confédération des syndicats nationaux/Centrale des enseignants du Québec. *Histoire du mouvement ouvrier au Québec (1825-1976): cent cinquante ans de luttes*. Québec: CSN/CEQ, 1979.

This book was written by a team of eight specialists on the history of the Quebec working class, who are also well-known left-wing intellectuals.

Marcel Fournier. *Communisme et anti-communisme au Québec (1920-1950)*. Montréal: Editions coopératives Albert St-Martin, 1979.

This is a history of the Communist party in Quebec by a sociologist from the Université de Montréal.

Paul-André Linteau, René Durocher, and Jean-Claude Robert. *Histoire du Québec contemporain: De la confédération à la crise*. Montréal: Boréal Express, 1979.

A comprehensive history of contemporary Quebec, from Confederation to the Depression, based on recent research and with a focus on the workers'

*This bibliography was originally published in *Socialist Studies* 1 (1983), pp. 275-98.

movement, agriculture, the situation of women, religious institutions, living conditions, and cultural reproduction.

Jacques Rouillard. *Les syndicats nationaux au Québec de 1900 à 1930.* Québec: Les Presses de l'Université Laval, 1979.

A history of trade unions in Quebec between 1900 and 1930 by a specialist on the history of the Quebec working class who teaches at the Université de Montréal.

Gérard Boismenu, Laurent Mailhot, and Jacques Rouillard. *Le Québec en textes, 1940-1980*. Montreal: Boréal Express, 1980.

A social history of Quebec since the Second World War presented through a variety of writings. The themes touched on are: the war, economic development and urbanization, Duplessis and his opponents, the Quiet Revolution and the development of the state, work and the economy, Montreal, the national question, and class struggles.

Robert Comeau and Bernard Dionne. *Les communistes au Québec, 1936-1956*. Montreal: Les Presses de l'Unité, 1980.

A brief history of the Communist party of Canada, its ideology, crises, and activities in Quebec from 1936 to the revelations of the XXth Congress in 1956.

Fernand Harvey. *Le mouvement ouvrier au Québec*. Montreal: Boréal Express, 1980.

On the basis of recent writings on the subject, the author reconstitutes a thematic history of the workers' movement in Quebec from the middle of the 19th century to the 1970s.

Gérard Boismenu. *Le Duplessisme, politique économique et rapports de force 1944-1960*. Montreal: Les Presses de l'Université de Montréal, 1981.

Duplessis's reign is analyzed from a marxist perspective as "a form of government that represents a particular combination of ruling interests."

François Cyr and Rémi Roy. *Eléments d'histoire de la FTQ*. Montreal: Albert Saint-Martin, 1981.

A brief history of one of Quebec's major trade-union federation, the Quebec Federation of Labour.

Pierre Godin. *La lutte pour l'information: Histoire de la presse écrite au Québec*. Montreal: Editions du Jour, 1981.

A history of the written press in Quebec, from the point of view of a radical journalist who has participated in many of the struggles for the people's right to be well informed.

Jean Hamelin and Jean Provencher. *Brève histoire du Québec*. Montreal: Boréal Express, 1981.

This is a panoramic view of the political and socioeconomic history of Quebec, from the period of New France to our day. The focus is on politics.

Jacques Rouillard. *Histoire de la CSN, 1921-1981*. Montreal: Boréal Express et CSN, 1981.

The history of Quebec's most powerful trade-union federation, the Confederation of National Trade Unions, from its founding in 1921, to 1981. The book was copublished by the CNTU.

J. Bélanger, M. Desjardins, and Y. Frenette, *Histoire de la Gaspésie*, Montréal: Boréal Express, 1982.

This book narrates the history of the Gaspé region, from the prehistoric period to the present. It was prepared in collaboration with the Gaspé Historical Society, and the Quebec Institute for Research on Culture.

Paul-André Comeau. *Le bloc populaire, 1942-1948*. Montreal: Editions Québec-Amérique, 1982.

Paul-André Comeau, a political scientist turned journalist, brilliantly describes the brief history of a very important Quebec political party born in opposition to conscription and to the war effort.

Jean Gérin-Lajoie. *Les Métallos (1936-1981)*. Montreal: Boréal Express, 1982.

The history of the Metalworkers Union, a 45,000 member affiliate of the QFL, by one of its past presidents who has been a key figure of the Quebec nationalist left since the early 1960s.

2. The Economy, Social Classes, and Work

Pierre Fournier. *Le patronat québécois au pouvoir: 1970-1976*. Montreal: Hurtubise/HMH, 1979.

This book was originally published in English under the title *The Quebec Establishment* by Black Rose Press in 1976. It is a study of the influence of big business over the Bourassa government.

Fernand Harvey and Gilles Houle. *Les classes sociales au Canada et au Québec: bibliographie annotée*. Quebec: Institut Supérieur des Sciences Humaines, Université Laval, 1979.

An annotated bibliography on social classes in Quebec and Canada by a historian and a sociologist.

Jorge Niosi. *La bourgeoisie canadienne: La formation et le développement d'une classe dominante*. Montreal: Boréal Express, 1980.

This is the second of Niosi's major studies on the Canadian bourgeoisie. In five major essays, the author explores the internal composition and the economic anatomy of this class, showing how it controls major private and public corporations.

François Moreau. *Le capital financier québécois*. Montréal: CEQ et Editions Albert St-Martin, 1981.

Moreau studies the financial institutions controlled by Québécois interests and indicates that their political power is increasing. He sides with Pierre Fournier and Jean-Guy Loranger over Jorge Niosi in the debates over the relationship between the Quebec bourgeoisie and the Quebec state, and over financial capitalism.

Colette Bernier et al. *Travailler au Québec: actes du colloque de l'ACSALF: 1980*. Montreal: Editions Albert St-Martin, 1981.

This book contains the papers presented at the 1980 annual meeting of the Canadian Association of French-speaking sociologists and anthropologists on the themes of work organization and the division of labour in Quebec.

Hélène David and Colette Bernier. *A l'ouvrage: L'organisation du travail au Québec*. Montreal: IRAT, 1981.

This book on problems of work organization in Quebec was prepared by two sociologists employed as researchers at the Institute for Applied Research on Work, an organization under the joint sponsorship of Quebec trade unions and universities.

Diane Bellemare and Lise Poulin-Simon. *Le plein emploi: pourquoi?* Montreal: Les Presses de l'Université du Québec et l'Institut de recherche appliquée sur le travail, 1982.

The authors analyze the exorbitant economic and social costs of unemployment in Quebec and show that the real challenge of full employment is political rather than technical.

Jacques Cousineau. *L'Eglise d'ici et le social, 1940-1960: La Commission sacerdotale d'études sociales*. Montreal: Editions Bellarmin, 1982.

A participant's view of the history of the activities of an influential clerical group in social issues during the Duplessis era.

Jacques Dofny and Camille Legendre. *Catastrophe dans une mine d'or: Etude sur le milieu minier québécois*. Québec: Gouvernement du Québec, Conseil Exécutif, 1982.

This book presents the results of research done for the Beaudry Commission on the tragedy of the Belmoral mine and on security conditions in underground mines.

Gilles, Dostaler. *La crise économique et sa gestion*. Montreal: Editions Québec-Amérique, 1982.

These are the papers presented at an important international symposium organized by the Quebec Association of Political Economists on the theme of the economic crisis.

Yvan Lamonde, Lucia Ferretti, and Daniel Leblanc. *La culture ouvrière à Montréal (1880-1920): Bilan historiographique*. Montreal: Institut québécois de recherche sur la culture, 1982.

A histographical study of working class culture in Montreal between 1880 and 1920, by an interdisciplinary team of social scientists.

Jorge Niosi. *Les multinationales canadiennes*. Montreal: Boréal Express, 1982.

This third book by Niosi looks at direct Canadian investments in other countries through a study of 15 Canadian multinationals.

3. Power, Politics, and the State

Robert Dion. *Les crimes de la police montée*. Montreal: Editions Albert St-Martin, 1979.

A detailed description of the techniques used by the RCMP to sabotage the Agence de Presse libre du Québec and to steal the Parti Québécois's list of members.

Pierre Fournier. *Les sociétés d'Etat et les objectifs économiques du Québec: une évaluation préliminaire*. Québec: Editeur officiel du Québec, 1979.

A preliminary evaluation of Quebec's state enterprises by the chairman of the Political Science department at UQAM.

C. Montmarquette et al. *Economie du Québec et choix politiques*. Montreal: Les Presses de l'Université du Québec, 1979.

Jean-Jacques Simard. *La longue marche des technocrates*. Montréal: Editions Albert St-Martin, 1979.

A study of the role of technocrats in the Quiet Revolution.

Nadia Assimopoulos et al. *La transformation du pouvoir au Québec: Actes du colloque de l'ACSALF: 1979*. Montreal: Editions Albert St-Martin, 1980.

The question of the transformation of power since 1960 is studied in the areas of health, technology, minorities, politics, etc.

Gérard Bergeron and Réjean Pelletier, eds. *L'Etat du Québec en devenir*. Montreal: Boréal Express, 1980.

A collective book on the development of the state apparatus in Quebec since 1960.

Pierre Fournier, ed. *Capitalisme et politique au Québec*. Montreal: Editions Albert St-Martin, 1981.

This book presents a critical analysis of the major economic and social programs implemented by the Parti Québécois during its first term.

Pierre Hamel and Jean-François Léonard. *Les organisations populaires: L'Etat et la démocratie*. Montreal: Nouvelle Optique, 1981.

The authors show how popular groups in Quebec challenge the state's social control and invent new forms of social organization.

Frédéric Lesemann. *Du pain et des services: la réforme de la santé et des services sociaux au Québec*. Montreal: Editions Albert St-Martin, 1981.

Lesemann analyzes the way health and social services were transformed in contemporary Quebec.

Dorval Brunelle. *L'Etat solide. Sociologie du fédéralisme au Canada et au Québec*. Boucherville: Editions métropolitaines, 1982.

A study of Canadian federalism by a UQAM sociologist.

Louis Larochelle. *En flagrant délit de pouvoir*. Montréal: Boréal Express, 1982.

A journalist's chronicle of political events in Quebec from the death of Duplessis to the 1980 referendum.

Vincent Lemieux, ed. *Personnel et partis politiques au Québec*. Montreal: Boréal Express, 1982.

A collection of essays on political personnel and parties, from the *Patriotes* to the *Péquistes*.

Michel Pelletier. *De la sécurité sociale à la sécurité du revenu: essais sur la politique économique et sociale contemporaine*. Montréal, 1982 (à compte d'auteur).

A collection of essays on social and economic policy issues by the coauthor of a multivolume history of social policies and workers in Quebec.

4. Nationalist Groups and Ideologies, the National Question, and Quebec Culture

Paul Bernard et al. *L'évolution de la situation socio-économique des francophones et des non-francophones au Québec (1971-1978)*. Québec: Editeur officiel du Québec, 1979.

A research report on the socioeconomic situation of Quebeckers.

Roch Denis. *Luttes de classe et question nationale au Québec 1948-1968*. Montréal: Presses socialistes internationales, 1979.

A study of the relationship between the national question and the workers' movement in postwar Quebec.

Jacques Mascotto and Pierre-Yves Soucy. *Sociologie politique de la question nationale*. Montréal: Editions Albert St-Martin, 1979.

An analysis of social development in Quebec in the light of the cultural division of work and of the populist forms of integration.

Jean-Marc Piotte. *Un parti pris politique*. Montreal: VLB éditeur, 1979.
Collection of essays written between 1963 and 1979 on the national question and class struggle.

Robert Sévigny. *Le Québec en héritage: la vie de trois familles montréalaises*. Montreal: Editions Albert St-Martin, 1979.
The author studies the social and cultural values of families from three different neighbourhoods in Montreal.

Léon Dion. *Le Québec et le Canada: Les voies de l'avenir*. Montreal: Québécor, 1980.
Dion's discussion of the constitutional debate and his view of the future of Quebec and Canada.

Marcel Rioux and Susan Crean. *Deux pays pour vivre: un plaidoyer*. Montréal: Editions Albert St-Martin, 1980.
Two sociologists reflect on their national identity vis-à-vis cultural imperialism.

Fernand Dumont, Jean Hamelin, and Jean-Paul Montminy, eds. *Idéologies au Canada français (1940-1976)*. Québec: Les Presses de l'Université Laval, 1981.
This is the fourth book of a series published by these authors on ideologies in French Canada.

Nicole Laurin-Frenette and Jean-François Léonard. *L'impasse: Enjeux et perspectives de l'après-référendum*. Montreal: Nouvelle Optique, 1981.
A collection of essays on the postreferendum perspectives in Quebec.

Pierre Bourgault. *Ecrits polémiques 1960-1981. 1. La politique*. Montreal: VLB éditeur, 1982.
An anthology of Bourgault's best writings produced over the past 20 years.

Louis Fournier. *FLQ: Histoire d'un mouvement clandestin*. Montreal: Editions Québec-Amérique, 1982.
The best book on the history of the Quebec Liberation Front.

L. Mailhot and L. Gauvin. *Guide culturel du Québec*. Montreal: Boréal Express, 1982.
A guide to the major sectors of Quebec culture.

Francis Simard. *Pour en finir avec octobre*. Montreal: Stanké, 1982.
One of the members of the Chenier cell of the FLQ writes on the October 1970 events and Pierre Laporte's death.

5. Women and Feminism

E. J. Lacelle, ed. *La femme et la religion au Canada français: un fait socio-culturel, perspectives et prospectives*. Montreal: Editions Bellarmin, 1979.

Francine Descarries-Bélanger. *L'école rose ... et les cols roses*. Montreal: Editions Albert St-Martin, 1980.

An analysis of the role of schools on the sexual division of labour.

Geneviève Auger and Raymonde Lamothe. *De la poêle à frire à la ligne de feu: la vie quotidienne des Québécoises pendant la Deuxième Guerre Mondiale*. Montréal: Boréal Express, 1981.

A picture book which reveals the sexist ideology of the federal government and of big business in Canada during the Second World War.

Yolande Cohen, ed. *Femmes et politique*. Montreal: Le Jour, 1981.

A collection of essays by some women psychologists, historians, and sociologists on the limited access of women to political roles.

Centre de Formation Populaire. *Le mouvement des femmes au Québec*. Montreal: CFP, 1981.

A history of women's struggles in Quebec, from 1893 to the present.

Nicole Laurin-Frenette, ed. *Les femmes dans la sociologie*. Special issue of *Sociologie et Sociétés* 13: 2 (1981).

A special issue by women sociologists on the place of women in sociology.

Renée Cloutier et al. *Femmes et culture au Québec*. Québec: Institut québécois de recherche sur la culture, 1982.

Collectif Clio. *L'histoire des femmes au Québec depuis quatre siècles*. Montreal: Editions Quinze, 1982.

A global study of the place of women in the history of Quebec, written by four feminist historians.

Denise Lemieux and Lucie Mercier. *La recherche sur les femmes au Québec: bilan et bibliographie*. Quebec: Institut québécois de recherche sur la culture, 1982.

Simone Monet Chartrand. *Ma vie comme une rivière*, tome 2, récit autobiographique 1939-1949. Montreal: Editions du Remue-Ménage, 1982.

The second part of Simone Chartrand's autobiography, covering 10 important years of the history of Quebec.

Véronique O'Leary and Louise Toupin. *Québécoise deboutte*, tome 1. Montreal: Editions du Remue-Ménage, 1982.

This book retraces the recent history of the Quebec feminist movement through a study of two groups, the Women's Liberation Front and the Women's Centre.

Lise Payette. *Le pouvoir? Connais pas?* Montreal: Editions Québec-Amérique, 1982.

This book narrates the political experiences of Ms. Payette from a feminist perspective.

Evelyne Tardy. *La politique: un monde d'hommes. Une étude sur les mairesses au Québec.* Montreal: Hurtubise/HMH, 1982.

Alain Vinet. *La condition féminine en milieu ouvrier: une enquête.* Québec: Institut québécois de recherche sur la culture, 1982.

A study of the changing work, family, and leisure behaviour of women workers from five factories in the Quebec City area.

6. Ecology and Health

Denis Gravel. *Fin du monde? Fin d'un monde.* Montreal: Editions La Presse, 1979.

A hard-hitting book on the environmental crisis in Quebec.

Hélène Lajambe. *L'autonomie énergétique du Québec dans une perspective écologique.* St-Bruno: Hélio-Québec, 1979.

A solid analysis of the possibility of autonomy of Quebec in the area of energy.

Québec-Science. *Face au nucléaire.* Montreal: Les Presses de l'Université du Québec, 1979.

The pros and especially the cons of nuclear energy, debated by some well-qualified scientific journalists.

Solanges Vincent. *La fiction nucléaire.* Montréal: Editions Québec-Amérique, 1979.

A fact-filled book on energy, especially nuclear energy, in Quebec.

Luciano Bozzini et al. *Médecine et société: les années 1980.* Montreal: Editions Albert St-Martin, 1981.

A reader with essays that study contemporary medicine as an apparatus of social control with limited therapeutic usefulness.

Thérèse Dumesnil. *Pierre Dansereau. L'écologiste aux pieds nus.* Montreal: Nouvelle Optique, 1981.

A biography of Quebec's leading ecologist.

Michel Jurdant. *Les insolences d'un écologiste.* Montreal: Boréal Express, 1981.

A militant ecologist's call for a society where the environment will be respected.

Serge Mongeau. *Vivre en santé.* Montreal: Editions Québec-Amérique, 1981.

Jean-Pierre Rogel. *Le paradis de la pollution.* Québec: Editions Québec-Science, 1981.

A scientific journalist's description of various kinds of pollution found in Quebec.

Jean-Guy Vaillancourt. *Ecologie sociale et mouvements écologistes.* Special issue of *Sociologie et Sociétés* 13: 1 (1981).

A special issue on social ecology and on various aspects of the ecological movement.

Louise Guyon, Roxanne Simard, and Louise Nadeau. *Va te faire soigner, t'es malade*. Montreal: Stanké, 1982.

Two psychiatrists and an anthropologist write on women's dependence on male doctors, and the need to change that situation.

Serge Mongeau. *Adieu médecine, bonjour santé*. Montréal: Editions Québec-Amérique, 1982.

An ex-practising doctor's attack against official medicine.

Serge Mongeau. *Survivre aux soins médicaux*. Montreal: Editions Québec-Amérique, 1982.

Collette Provost. *Dissiper le brouillard*. Montréal: Presses métropolitaines, 1982.

A militant ecologist writes on various ecological problems and gives a list of groups doing something about them.

Jean-Guy Vaillancourt. *Mouvement écologiste, énergie et environnement: essais d'écologie*. Montreal: Editions Albert St-Martin, 1982.

A group of 25 essays written between 1972 and 1983 by the author on the ecological movement, energy, and the environment.

7. Popular Groups, the Urban Question, and Regional Development

Conseil régional de développement du Québec. *Développement régional et mouvement populaire: l'exemple de l'est du Québec*. Québec: CRDQ, 1979.

Gérard Divay and Jacques Godbout. *La décentralisation en pratique. Quelques expériences montréalaises, 1970-1977*. Montreal: INRS-Urbanisation, 1979.

Marc Choko. *La crise du logement à Montréal (1860-1939)*. Montreal: Editions Albert St-Martin, 1980.

A historical analysis of the housing question in the Montreal area.

EZOP-Québec. *Une ville à vendre*. Montreal: Editions Albert St-Martin, 1981.

A critical examination of the impact of capitalism on the development of Quebec City.

Paul-André Linteau. *Maisonneuve. Comment des promoteurs fabriquent une ville*. Montreal: Boréal Express, 1981.

This book narrates the story of the role of promoters in the creation of the city of Maisonneuve, which has since been incorporated into Montreal.

Caroline Andrew, Serge Bordeleau, and Alain Guimont. *L'urbanisation: une affaire, l'appropriation du sol et l'Etat local: le cas de l'Outaouais québécois*. Ottawa: Editions de l'Université d'Ottawa, 1982.

The authors show how urbanization is the product of the interplay of various actors.

Maurice Drapeau and Jean-Guy Gagnon. *Défaire la défaite! Histoire des luttes des paroisses du Bas du Fleuve*. Rimouski: Société d'aménagement intégré des ressources, 1982.

The authors describe how the people in some small towns of eastern Quebec struggled to survive.

Jean-Pierre Dupuis, Andrée Fortin, Gabriel Gagnon, Robert Laplante, and Marcel Rioux. *Les pratiques émancipatoires en milieu populaire*. Quebec: Institut québécois de recherche sur la culture, 1982.

Pierre Hamel, Jean-François Léonard, and Robert Mayer. *Les mobilisations populaires urbaines au Québec (1960-1980)*. Montreal: Nouvelle Optique, 1983.

Jacques Léveillée, ed. *L'aménagement du territoire au Québec: Du rêve au compromis*. Montréal: Nouvelle Optique, 1982.

The authors analyze the December 1979 Quebec law on planning and urbanism.

8. Cooperatives, Self-Management, and Socialism

Benoit Lévesque, ed. *Animation sociale, entreprises communautaires et coopératives*. Montreal: Editions Albert St-Martin, 1979.

Gilles Bourque and Gilles Dostaler. *Socialisme et indépendance*. Montreal: Boréal Express, 1980.

A series of essays on social and national movements written over the past few years by two UQAM professors who are also active socialists and independentists.

G. Deschênes. *Le mouvement coopératif québécois: guide bibliographique*. Montreal: Editions du Jour et Revue du CIRIEC, 1980.

Marielle Désy et al. *La conjoncture au Québec au début des années '80: les enjeux pour le mouvement ouvrier et populaire*. Rimouski: Librairie socialiste de l'Est du Québec, 1980.

An important statement on the current economic crisis and on ways out of it by some of the founding members of the Regroupement pour le socialisme.

Comité des Cent. *Pour un Québec socialiste. Manifeste du Mouvement pour un Québec socialiste, indépendant, démocratique et pour l'égalité entre les hommes et les femmes*. Montreal: Mouvement socialiste, 1981.

The Socialist Movement's Manifesto, written by the Committee of One Hundred.

Pierre Drouilly and Robert Barberis. *Les illusions du pouvoir. Les erreurs stratégiques du gouvernement Lévesque.* Montréal: Editions Select, 1981.

A collection of essays by two radical independentists. The book also contains electoral and referendum statistics.

Jules Duchastel. *Marcel Rioux, entre l'utopie et la raison.* Montreal: Nouvelle Optique, 1981.

A biography of one of Quebec's leading sociologists, by one of his ex-students.

Marc Ferland and Yves Vaillancourt. *Socialisme et indépendance au Québec: pistes pour le mouvement ouvrier et populaire.* Montreal: Editions Albert St-Martin, 1981.

An important statement on the questions of socialism and independence since the 1981 referendum by two of the founders of the Regroupement pour le socialisme.

Micheline Renaud-Mayer and Alberte Le Doyen, eds. *L'intervention sociale: actes du colloque annuel de l'ACSALF: 1981.* Montreal: Editions Albert St-Martin, 1982.

Paul-André Boucher, in collaboration with Jean-Louis Martel and le Centre de gestion des coopératives des HEC, *Tricofil tel que vécu.* Montréal: Editions CIRIEC, 1982.

The story of the Tricofil adventure told by one of the key participants.

Serge Proulx and Pierre Vallières, eds. *Changer de société.* Montreal: Editions Québec-Amérique, 1982.

A series of essays written from countercultural and ecological perspectives.